KU-528-150

UNITED NATIONS, DIVIDED WORLD

THE UN'S ROLES IN INTERNATIONAL RELATIONS

EDITED BY

Adam Roberts
and
Benedict Kingsbury

SECOND EDITION

CLARENDON PRESS · OXFORD

Oxford University Press, Walton Street, Oxford OX2 6DP
Oxford New York
Athens Auckland Bangkok Bombay
Calcutta Cape Town Dar es Salaam Delhi
Florence Hong Kong Istanbul Karachi
Kuala Lumpur Madras Madrid Melbourne
Mexico City Nairobi Paris Singapore
Taipei Tokyo Toronto
and associated companies in
Berlin Ibadan

Oxford is a trade mark of Oxford University Press

Published in the United States
by Oxford University Press Inc., New York

© Adam Roberts, Benedict Kingsbury, and the several contributors 1993

First edition published 1988 (hardback) 1989 (paperback)
Second edition published in hardback and paperback 1993
Reprinted 1993 (twice) 1994
(with minor corrections) 1994

All rights reserved. No part of this publication may be reproduced,
stored in a retrieval system, or transmitted, in any form or by any means,
without the prior permission in writing of Oxford University Press.
Within the UK, exceptions are allowed in respect of any fair dealing for the
purpose of research or private study, or criticism or review, as permitted
under the Copyright, Designs and Patents Act, 1988, or in the case of
reprographic reproduction in accordance with the terms of the licences
issued by the Copyright Licensing Agency. Enquiries concerning
reproduction outside these terms and in other countries should be
sent to the Rights Department, Oxford University Press,
at the address above

The paperback edition of this book is sold subject to the condition that it shall not, by way
of trade or otherwise, be lent, re-sold, hired out or otherwise circulated
without the publisher's prior consent in any form of binding or cover
other than that in which it is published and without a similar condition
including this condition being imposed on the subsequent purchaser

British Library Cataloguing in Publication Data
Data available

Library of Congress Cataloging in Publication Data
United Nations, Divided World: the UN's roles in international relations/
edited by Adam Roberts and Benedict Kingsbury.—2nd ed.
Includes bibliographical references and index.
1. United Nations.   2. International relations.
I. Roberts, Adam.   II. Kingsbury, Benedict.
JX1977.U42587   1993   341.23—dc20   93–2566
ISBN 0–19–827906–X.
ISBN 0–19–827926–4 (pbk).

Printed in Great Britain
on acid-free paper by
Biddles Ltd, Guildford and King's Lynn

NOTE ON SECOND EDITION

THIS is an extensively revised, updated, and expanded edition of *United Nations, Divided World: The UN's Roles in International Relations* (287 pp.), which was first published in 1988 and went into several printings in its original form.

The revision takes into account a wide range of developments: the rapid expansion of UN peacekeeping and election-monitoring activities; the consequences of the collapse of communist rule in eastern Europe and the Soviet Union; the 1990–1 Gulf conflict and its aftermath; attempts at settlement of many regional conflicts; UN involvements in fractured societies, including Cambodia, Somalia, and former Yugoslavia; and the increased focus on the political and resource limits of the UN's capabilities. This edition also takes full account of new sources, writings, and debates.

There are four completely new chapters: those by Patricia Birnie, Sally Morphet, Brian Urquhart, and Peter Wilenski. In addition, Secretary-General Boutros-Ghali has kindly agreed to the inclusion of his 1992 report *An Agenda for Peace*, to which he has added an introduction for this book.

All the chapters in the original edition have been completely revised and updated by their authors, in two cases with new co-authors. The only exceptions are the chapters by Javier Pérez de Cuéllar, which is the definitive text of his Oxford lecture; by Nagendra Singh, who died in December 1988, to which we have simply added the minimum necessary updatings; and by Evan Luard, who died in February 1991, whose chapter we did not think it proper to revise ourselves, but which we felt ought not to be reproduced in this edition because it was essentially part of a debate in the late 1980s about the role of the UN which has now been overtaken by events.

Despite the ending of a fundamental division in post-1945 international politics—that based on the confrontation between the Soviet-led group of states and the West—we have deliberately not changed the book's title. As we wrote on pp. 9–10 of the Introduction to the first edition, the title referred, not just to the East–West divide, but also to the many other deep divisions within and between states which have caused so much conflict and cost so many lives; and to all the other consequences of the division of the world into separate sovereign states. In these senses, even in a new decade in which the UN's role has become more central, the world remains very much divided.

The appendices and index have been revised for this edition.

In preparing this edition, we would like to thank particularly Colin Jones, Gerhard Jandl, and Lt.-Col. Marcel Duval for help in obtaining materials; Sudhir Hazareesingh for helpful comments on Chapter 1; Frank Pert for the Index; and Marga Lyall at the Centre for International Studies in Oxford for typing many of the drafts, and for her unfailing good humour.

A.R.
B.K.

Oxford
July 1993

WITHDRAWN

LIVERPOOL
JOHN MOORES UNIVERSITY
TRUEMAN STREET LIBRARY
TEL 051 231 4022/4023

UNITED NATIONS, DIVIDED WORLD

Books are to be returned on or before
the last date below.

7-DAY

FINE PER DAY

17
LIVERPOOL JMU LIBRARY

3 1111 00623 0237

WITHDRAWN

CONTENTS

Appendices

NOTES ON CONTRIBUTORS

MAURICE BERTRAND is a former Senior Counsellor at the Cour des Comptes, France. Member of the UN Joint Inspection Unit, 1968–85; Member of the Group of High-level Intergovernmental Experts to Review the Efficiency of the Administrative and Financial Functioning of the UN, 1986. His publications include *Refaire l'ONU: Un programme pour la paix* (Geneva, 1986).

PATRICIA BIRNIE was Director of the IMO International Maritime Law Institute in Malta, 1989–92. She was previously Lecturer in Public International Law at the University of Edinburgh, and Senior Lecturer at the London School of Economics, specializing in the law of the sea and international environmental law. Her publications include (with Alan Boyle) *International Law and the Environment* (Oxford, 1992).

BOUTROS BOUTROS-GHALI has been Secretary-General of the United Nations since 1 January 1992. He was previously Professor of International Law and International Relations at Cairo University, 1949–77; and Minister of State for Foreign Affairs, Egypt, 1977–91. His publications include *Contribution à l'étude des ententes régionales* (Paris, 1949).

KENNETH DADZIE has been Secretary-General of UNCTAD since 1986 and is currently on an additional assignment as Special Adviser and Delegate of the Secretary-General on the reform of the economic and social sectors of the UN. He has held numerous posts in the UN Secretariat and in the Ghana Foreign Service, including that of High Commissioner of Ghana in London, 1982–6. He has also served as a member of Ghanaian teams for negotiations with the IMF, World Bank, and other international institutions.

TOM J. FARER is Professor of Law and Director of the Joint-Degree Program in Law and International Relations at The American University, Washington DC. He was previously Special Assistant to the Assistant-Secretary of State for Inter-American Affairs, 1975; Member and President of the Inter-American Commission on Human Rights of the OAS, 1976–83; President of the University of New Mexico, 1985–6; and Distinguished Professor of Law, Rutgers University, 1971–85. His publications include *The Grand Strategy of the United States in Latin America* (New Brunswick, NJ, 1987).

THOMAS M. FRANCK is Murry and Ida Becker Professor of Law at New York University, Director of its Center for International Studies, and Editor-in-Chief of the *American Journal of International Law*. Director of Research, UN Institute for Training and Research, 1981–3. His publications include *Nation against Nation: What Happened to the UN Dream and What the US Can Do about It* (New York, 1985).

FELICE D. GAER is Director, Jacob Blaustein Institute for Human Rights, American Jewish Committee, New York. She was previously Executive Director, International League for Human Rights; and Executive Director, European Programs, United Nations Association of the USA. She has written numerous reports and articles on human rights issues, and given expert testimony to committees of the US Congress.

SIR MICHAEL HOWARD, D.Litt., FBA, was Lovett Professor of Military and Naval History, Yale University, 1989–93. He was previously Professor of War Studies, King's College, London, 1963–8; Chichele Professor of the History of War, Oxford University, 1977–80; and Regius Professor of Modern History, Oxford University, 1980–9. His publications include *War in European History* (Oxford, 1976) and *War and the Liberal Conscience* (London, 1978).

BENEDICT KINGSBURY is Professor of Law, Duke University School of Law, North Carolina. He was previously University Lecturer in Law at Oxford University and a Fellow of Exeter College, 1990–3. He specializes in international law and human rights, and is completing a book on Indigenous Peoples in International Law. A New Zealand citizen, his books include (ed. with Hedley Bull and Adam Roberts) *Hugo Grotius and International Relations* (Oxford, 1990) and (ed. with Andrew Hurrell) *The International Politics of the Environment* (Oxford, 1992).

SALLY MORPHET has worked in the Research and Analysis Department of the Foreign and Commonwealth Office since 1966. She specialized first on South and South-East Asia, and from 1974 on general international and UN questions. She has published material on the non-aligned, the Security Council, and human rights.

GEORG NOLTE, Dr. Jur., is Research Fellow at the Max Planck Institute for Comparative Public Law and International Law,

Heidelberg. During the spring semester 1992 he was Senior 1992 he was Senior Fellow at the Center for International Studies at New York University School of Law. His publications include *Beleidigungsschutz in der freiheitlichen Demokratie* (Berlin/Heidelberg/ New York, 1992).

SIR ANTHONY PARSONS was UK Permanent Representative to the UN, 1979–82, and Adviser on Foreign Affairs to the Prime Minister, 1982–3. He was previously Counsellor, UK Mission to UN, 1969–71, and Ambassador to Iran, 1974–9. His publications include *The Pride and the Fall* (London, 1984).

JAVIER PÉREZ DE CUÉLLAR was Secretary-General of the UN from 1 January 1982 to 31 December 1991. Between 1944 and 1981 he held numerous posts in the Peruvian foreign service and in the UN, including Ambassador of Peru to the Soviet Union, Poland, Switzerland, and Venezuela; Permanent Representative of Peru to the UN, 1971–5; Special Representative of the UN Secretary-General in Cyprus, 1975–7; and Under-Secretary-General for Special Political Affairs, 1979–81. His publications include *Manual de derecho diplomático* (1964).

ADAM ROBERTS, FBA, is Montague Burton Professor of International Relations, University of Oxford, and a Fellow of Balliol College. He was previously Lecturer in International Relations, London School of Economics and Political Science, 1968–81. His publications include *Nations in Arms: The Theory and Practice of Territorial Defence* (2nd edn., London, 1986); and (with Richard Guelff) *Documents on the Laws of War* (2nd edn., Oxford, 1989).

NAGENDRA SINGH, who died in December 1988, had been a Member of the International Court of Justice since 1973, and President, 1985–8. He was previously a member of the Constituent Assembly of India, 1947–8, and Secretary to the Indian Ministries of Defence and Transport, and to the President of India. He was a corresponding member of the British Academy. His publications include *Nuclear Weapons and International Law* (London, 1959).

SIR BRIAN URQUHART is Scholar-in-Residence in the International Affairs Program of the Ford Foundation, New York. He was a member of the UN Secretariat, 1945–86, and Under-Secretary-General for Special Political Affairs, 1974–86. His publications include *Hammarskjöld* (New York, 1972) and *A Life in Peace and War* (London, 1987).

PETER WILENSKI is Secretary of the Australian Department of Foreign Affairs and Trade. He was Australian Ambassador to the UN, New York, 1989–92. He was previously head of a number of other departments and intergovernmental bodies, a Professor of Management and of Political Science, and a consultant to the OECD, UNESCO, and the World Bank. His publications include *Public Power and Public Administration* (Sydney, 1986).

ABBREVIATIONS

THESE are the principal abbreviations used in this book; all sixteen of the specialized agencies of the UN (marked by an asterisk *); and UN peacekeeping or observer forces (marked by a dagger †). For more information on the latter see Appendix E. Many other acronyms can be found in the index.

ACABQ	Advisory Committee on Administrative and Budgetary Questions
ACC	Administrative Committee on Co-ordination
CSD	Commission on Sustainable Development
DOEM	Designated Officials for Environmental Matters
†DOMREP	Mission of the Representative of the Secretary-General in the Dominican Republic
ECOSOC	Economic and Social Council (of the UN)
*FAO	Food and Agriculture Organization of the United Nations
GA	General Assembly
GATT	General Agreement on Tariffs and Trade
IAEA	International Atomic Energy Agency
*IBRD	International Bank for Reconstruction and Development (the World Bank)
*ICAO	International Civil Aviation Organization
ICJ	International Court of Justice
*IDA	International Development Association (the soft-loan arm of the World Bank)
*IFAD	International Fund for Agricultural Development
*IFC	International Finance Corporation (part of the World Bank group)
*ILO	International Labour Organization
*IMF	International Monetary Fund
*IMO	International Maritime Organization (formerly IMCO)
INSTRAW	International Research and Training Institute for the Advancement of Women
*ITU	International Telecommunication Union
JIU	Joint Inspection Unit
†MINURSO	United Nations Mission for the Referendum in Western Sahara

†ONUC	United Nations Operation in the Congo
†ONUCA	United Nations Observer Group in Central America
†ONUMOZ	United Nations Operation in Mozambique
†ONUSAL	United Nations Observer Mission in El Salvador
OPEC	Organization of Petroleum Exporting Countries
SC	Security Council
SOLAS	International Convention for the Safety of Life at Sea
†UNAMIC	United Nations Advance Mission in Cambodia
†UNAVEM	United Nations Angola Verification Mission
†UNAVEM II	United Nations Angola Verification Mission II
UNCED	United Nations Conference on Environment and Development (Rio, 1992)
UNCHE	United Nations Conference on the Human Environment (Stockholm, 1972)
UNCLOS III	Third United Nations Conference on the Law of the Sea (1973–82)
UNCTAD	United Nations Conference on Trade and Development
†UNDOF	United Nations Disengagement Observer Force
UNDP	United Nations Development Programme
UNDRO	United Nations Disaster Relief Office
†UNEF I	United Nations Emergency Force (1956–67)
†UNEF II	United Nations Emergency Force II (1973–9)
UNEP	United Nations Environment Programme
*UNESCO	United Nations Educational, Scientific and Cultural Organization
†UNFICYP	United Nations Peacekeeping Force in Cyprus
†UNGOMAP	United Nations Good Offices Mission in Afghanistan and Pakistan
UNHCR	Office of the United Nations High Commissioner for Refugees
UNICEF	United Nations Children's Fund
*UNIDO	United Nations Industrial Development Organization
†UNIFIL	United Nations Interim Force in Lebanon
†UNIIMOG	United Nations Iran–Iraq Military Observer Group
†UNIKOM	United Nations Iraq–Kuwait Observation Mission

†UNIPOM	United Nations India–Pakistan Observation Mission
UNITAF	Unified Task Force (Somalia, 1992–3)
UNITAR	United Nations Institute for Training and Research
†UNMOGIP	United Nations Military Observer Group in India and Pakistan
†UNOGIL	United Nations Observation Group in Lebanon
†UNOMUR	United Nations Observer Mission Uganda–Rwanda
†UNOSOM	United Nations Operation in Somalia
†UNOSOM II	United Nations Operation in Somalia II
†UNPROFOR	United Nations Protection Force (Croatia; Bosnia and Herzegovina; and Macedonia)
UNRWA	United Nations Relief and Works Agency for Palestine Refugees in the Near East
UNSCOB	United Nations Special Committee on the Balkans
†UNSF	United Nations Security Force in West New Guinea
†UNTAC	United Nations Transitional Authority in Cambodia
†UNTAG	United Nations Transition Assistance Group (Namibia)
†UNTSO	United Nations Truce Supervision Organization (Middle East)
†UNYOM	United Nations Yemen Observation Mission
*UPU	Universal Postal Union
*WHO	World Health Organization
*WIPO	World Intellectual Property Organization
*WMO	World Meteorological Organization

Introduction: The UN's Roles in International Society since 1945

ADAM ROBERTS AND BENEDICT KINGSBURY

IN the half century since its foundation in 1945, the United Nations has been a central institution in the conduct of international relations. This book is an assessment of the UN's many roles in a world which has remained obstinately divided: roles which have changed over time, and have been the subject of different interpretations, fears, and hopes. It is a study of how, in the era of the UN, international society has been modified, but not totally transformed. It examines the UN's opportunities and difficulties in the new and confused circumstances of the post-Cold War era. Behind all these issues lurks the fear that the UN has by no means overcome the range of problems which have in the past bedevilled efforts at collective security and global organization.

The international system over which the UN in some sense presides is historically unique. For the first time in human history, the world has come to consist of nominally equal sovereign states; almost all of them are members of one world organization and subscribe to a single set of principles—those of the UN Charter; there is a functioning global organization which has the capacity to take important decisions, especially in the sphere of security—as was done in the Gulf crisis of 1990–1. Yet despite these elements of uniqueness which distinguish the UN era from earlier times, international society remains 'anarchical' in the sense that, even though there is order of a kind and a wide range of international institutions, there is no central authority having the character of a government.[1]

The UN era has also been notable for the continuing—and in many respects burgeoning—role in international society of actors other than states. The UN itself has provided a political space for non-governmental organizations, especially in such fields as human rights and environmental protection, and it provides fora in which all manner of non-state groups can articulate demands and pursue their interests. More generally, some have argued that a transnational civil society is beginning to emerge, constructed upon the growing density and ease of cross-border interactions, and characterized by the diffusion or contagion of multi-party democracy, market liberalism, and related political and social values.[2] In this view, power is shifting from increasingly enmeshed states to cross-state groupings or to international institutions; territoriality is declining as a central principle of organization; and state sovereignty is being recast to accommodate human rights, economic aspirations, and internal and external conceptions of legitimacy.[3] Perceptions of national interest are broadening, and normative convergence at the domestic, transnational, and international levels is gathering pace to the extent that these levels are themselves beginning to merge. The European Community has been a popular model for proponents of the thesis that state sovereignty is gradually being transcended and

[1] The concept of a global international society is examined in Hedley Bull, *The Anarchical Society* (London, 1977); and Hedley Bull and Adam Watson (eds.), *The Expansion of International Society* (Oxford, 1984).

[2] See generally James N. Rosenau and Ernst-Otto Czempiel (eds.), *Governance Without Government: Order and Change in World Politics* (Cambridge, 1992); M. J. Peterson, 'Transnational Activity, International Society and World Politics', *Millennium*, 21 (1992), pp. 371–88; and Anne-Marie Slaughter Burley, 'International Law and International Relations Theory: A Dual Agenda', *American Journal of International Law*, 87 (1993), pp. 205–39.

[3] On sovereignty see R. B. J. Walker, *Inside/Outside: International Relations as Political Theory* (Cambridge, 1993). On territoriality and sovereignty, see John Gerard Ruggie, 'Territoriality and Beyond', *International Organization*, 47 (1993), pp. 139–74. A wide-ranging presentation of these perspectives is Ronnie D. Lipschutz and Ken Conca (eds.), *The State and Social Power in Global Environmental Politics* (New York, 1993). Cf. Immanuel Wallerstein, *Geopolitics and Geoculture: Essays on the Changing World System* (Cambridge, 1991).

that international civil society is being established by progressive enlargement from a liberal heartland.

International society is indeed changing, as are the issues and forms of its politics. Particular states or societies cannot easily remain outside the core institutions of economic, social, and political interaction. There are changes in the nature, forms, and uses of power, some of which result from interdependence or from the asymmetries which frequently accompany interdependence.[4] There are shared norms and values, which the UN both reflects and projects. Not all states work well, and the state is perhaps not quite sacrosanct as the building block of international society in the way it was thought to be at other times during the twentieth century. Nevertheless the state remains the principal institution for achieving domestic order, and the inter-state system continues to provide the skeletal ordering framework for international society. The UN as an organization created and maintained by states is built upon an inter-governmental framework which some find unrealistic or unsatisfactory. Proposals for reshaping the framework, for instance by establishing a nationally-elected parliamentary assembly alongside the General Assembly, may attract greater interest in the future. But for the time being the structures and activities of the UN, while in some tension with the changing circumstances and needs of international society, necessarily continue to reflect the essential role of states and the difficulties of the contemporary states system.

In the post-Cold War era the international system is beset by a bewildering multitude of problems, many of which derive from ancient and enduring features of international politics. Although the East–West divide of the Cold War period has largely disappeared, the world is still divided into separate sovereign states, with their own interests, types of government, and differing world-views. There are other fundamental divisions: North v. South; regional animosities; and communal cleavages which in

---

[4] See e.g. Carl Kaysen, 'Is War Obsolete?', *International Security*, 14 (1990), pp. 42–64.

many cases cut through states and across frontiers, raising challenges for the existing domestic and international order. Power still counts, whether in the decision-making processes of the UN or in the wider and messier realities beyond. The spectre of war, both civil and international, has not been banished. Many urgent crises which crowd the UN's agenda today derive from these divisions.

Global international organizations which proclaim as their goal the radical restructuring of the unsatisfactory condition of international relations inevitably attract high hopes—and subsequent disappointment.[5] This has been true of the various communist internationals since the First International was founded in 1864, and of the League of Nations founded in 1919–20. The UN has had its fair share of such disappointed hopes, and will do so again. Yet it has achieved a utility, an institutional durability, even a degree of permanence, that eluded its predecessors.

In the immediate aftermath of the Cold War, an attractively teleological view of the UN's place in the international order gained some currency. In this view, the UN, for over four decades in which the world had been divided between East and West, had been unable to act effectively; indeed, in matters relating to war and peace it had been almost completely powerless due to frequent threat or use of the veto in the Security Council. Then, with the end of the Cold War in the late 1980s, it was at last in a position to act more or less as its founders had intended, taking a decisive role in many crises, including in the Gulf in 1991. It now had an opportunity to advance, if not to world government, at least towards a centrally regulated and well ordered international system.[6]

This view was always open to challenge. First, the UN's performance in the long decades of the Cold War was much more impressive than the picture of a stymied

[5] The pattern of vision and disillusion in the history of proposals for international organizations to maintain peace is traced in F. H. Hinsley, *Power and the Pursuit of Peace* (Cambridge, 1963). See also J. Ter Meulen, *Der Gedanke der internationalen Organisation in seiner Entwicklung*, 2 vols. (The Hague, 1917, 1929).

[6] Elements of such a view are evident in Secretary-General Boutros Boutros-Ghali's report, *An Agenda for Peace*, June 1992. Text in Appendix A below.

organization suggests. It was in the years of East–West hostility that the UN became the world's first truly universal organization of states; helped to develop international standards on a wide range of matters, including human rights; and built up peacekeeping and diplomatic services which proved useful in addressing several conflicts. Secondly, since the end of the Cold War, the UN has faced some problems of a kind which have since time immemorial defeated the best efforts of the international community, and can be expected to do so again.

Many of the divisions within and between states have become more serious in the UN era than before—not least because the UN, somewhat paradoxically, has presided over a further phase in the triumphant advance of the idea of the 'sovereign state'. In the wake of European decolonization and the collapse of the Soviet Union, the total number of such states has more than tripled. Many conflicts of our time have their origins in partitions and disputes following upon the end of empires, and the attendant uncertainties about the legitimacy of new postcolonial states, regimes, institutions, and frontiers. Such problems have been especially marked following the disintegration of the USSR and Yugoslavia: indeed, the newly emerging regimes and frontiers were called into question more quickly there than in most former European colonies. The world is, and is likely to remain, divided into separate sovereign states, which have a capacity for making war, and many of which are conscious of their internal fragility and external vulnerability. Processes of integration and disintegration, cooperation and competition, liberation and domination, understanding and incomprehension, which have always characterized the system of states, will continue even if in new forms.

(a) Short Factual Description of the UN System[7]

The origins of the term 'United Nations' are to be found in the events surrounding the Washington

---

[7] The term 'UN system' refers not just to the United Nations itself, as outlined in the Charter, but also to the various subsidiary bodies and specialized agencies which operate under its auspices.

Declaration of 1 January 1942, in which twenty-six Allied countries, which came to be called the 'United Nations', pledged themselves to employ their full resources against Germany, Italy, and Japan; and the Moscow Four-Nation Declaration of 30 October 1943, which frequently called the Allies 'the United Nations'. (These declarations are mentioned in Articles 3 and 106 of the UN Charter.)[8] The term 'United Nations' thus emerged in an atmosphere of wartime hyperbole; and it was partly to distinguish itself from the wartime alliance out of which it had grown that, in its early years, the UN was very widely known as the United Nations *Organization* (UNO). This formulation is now seldom used, except occasionally for the limited purpose of distinguishing the UN proper (often just called 'the organization') from the specialized agencies. Not only has the wartime alliance receded into the distant past, but when it is remembered, its members are usually called 'the Allies'. The term 'the United Nations' has long since been effectively appropriated by the international organization created in 1945.

The first blueprints for the UN were drafted by the USA, the UK, the USSR, and their allies during World War II, reflecting their conceptions of the post-war international order. The Charter was finally adopted by fifty states meeting at San Francisco in June 1945. Although the nature and work of the UN has evolved considerably, the Charter has remained virtually unchanged.[9] The UN was formally established on 24 October 1945, when its basic constitutive instrument, the UN Charter, entered into force.

In the years since 1945 the number of member states of the UN has steadily increased, due mainly to the effects of successive waves of decolonization and disintegration of states. In 1945 the UN had fifty-one original members; by

---

[8] The Washington Declaration, the Moscow Declaration, and other instruments of the wartime United Nations are conveniently reprinted in Royal Institute of International Affairs, *United Nations Documents 1941–1945* (London, 1946); and in Louise W. Holborn, *War and Peace Aims of the United Nations*, 2 vols. (Boston, 1943, 1948).

[9] The text of the UN Charter, with all amendments, is in Appendix B below.

the end of 1960, one hundred; by the end of 1984, one hundred and fifty-nine; and by July 1993, one hundred and eighty-four. Throughout its history, the UN has had as members the great majority of states. Despite trends towards regional integration, there have only exceptionally been enduring cases of UN member states unifying to form a single larger state: Tanzania (1964), Yemen (1990), and Germany (1990).

The most conspicuous case of non-membership was the People's Republic of China from the revolution in 1949 until 1971, during which period China was represented by the regime in Taiwan. Since 1971 the UN's claims to near-universalism have had real substance. Its members include virtually all the states of the contemporary world.[10] No member state has ever left the UN. However, during 1950 the USSR refused to participate in the Security Council in protest against the UN's refusal to accept the government of the People's Republic of China as representative of China; and in 1965–6 Indonesia temporarily withdrew from the UN. In some cases the credentials of particular authorities to represent their state have not been accepted; and the Federal Republic of Yugoslavia (Serbia and Montenegro) was advised in 1992 by the Security Council and by the General Assembly that it could not continue the membership of the former Socialist Federal Republic of Yugoslavia, although it was able to continue participation in some UN bodies.

Six 'principal organs' of the UN were established by the Charter: the General Assembly, the Security Council, the Secretariat, the International Court of Justice (ICJ),

---

[10] A list of the 184 member states (as at 31 July 1993) is in Appendix C. Non-members of the UN include Switzerland (which has never applied for UN membership), Taiwan (which does not claim to be a state distinct from China, and was expelled from China's seat in the UN in 1971), a number of microstates, and dependent or non-self-governing territories. Many of these non-members are nevertheless involved in various aspects of the UN system, and some are members of specialized agencies. Other entities not members of the UN include Northern Cyprus (which is not regarded as a state except by itself and Turkey), and Western Sahara and Palestine (which do not have effective governmental control of their respective territories, but have received a certain degree of recognition by parts of the international community).

the Trusteeship Council, and the Economic and Social Council (ECOSOC).

The *General Assembly* as the plenary body controls much of the work of the UN. It meets in regular session for approximately the last quarter of every year (with sessions spilling over well into the new year), and occasionally holds special or emergency sessions to consider specific issues. The General Assembly approves the budget, adopts priorities, calls international conferences, superintends the operations of the Secretariat and of numerous committees and subsidiary organs, and debates and adopts resolutions on diverse issues. It played a major role in supervising European decolonization, and has also become involved in human rights supervision and election-monitoring in independent countries. The many subsidiary bodies created by the General Assembly include the United Nations Children's Fund (UNICEF), the Office of the United Nations High Commissioner for Refugees (UNHCR), the United Nations Conference on Trade and Development (UNCTAD), the United Nations Development Programme (UNDP), and the United Nations Environment Programme (UNEP). Much of the work of the General Assembly is done in permanent or *ad hoc* committees responsible for particular fields of UN activity or deliberation. The General Assembly's agenda also includes many areas of activity in which states prefer rhetoric to real action.[11]

The fifteen-member *Security Council* is dominated by its five Permanent Members (China, France, Russia, the UK, and the USA), each of which has power to veto any draft resolution on substantive matters. The ten non-permanent members (six until a Charter amendment came into force in 1965) are elected for two-year periods by the General Assembly. The Security Council has primary responsibility for the maintenance of international peace and security, and unlike the General Assembly is able to take decisions which are supposed to be binding on all members of the

---

[11] The importance of symbolic resolutions to coalition maintenance within the UN is demonstrated by M. J. Peterson, *The General Assembly in World Politics* (Boston, 1986), pp. 187 ff.

UN. It meets almost continuously throughout the year, mainly to consider armed conflicts and other situations or disputes where international peace and security are threatened. It is empowered to order mandatory sanctions, call for cease-fires, and even to authorize military action on behalf of the UN.

The Security Council has also had a central role in the development of the institution of UN peacekeeping forces, which were not envisaged at all in the Charter. The blue berets or helmets worn by members of national military units working in the service of the UN have become a well-known symbol. UN peacekeeping forces, ranging from small observer units to larger forces for purposes of interposition, policing, and humanitarian assistance, have been established by the Security Council in numerous countries. On a few occasions, it has been the General Assembly rather than the Security Council which has initiated the use of such forces: the General Assembly created the UN Emergency Force in the aftermath of the Suez crisis in 1956 when the Security Council was prevented by veto from acting, and it also in similar circumstances issued recommendations concerning UN forces in Korea (1950–3) and the Congo (1960–4). However, control of peacekeeping has now returned firmly to the Security Council.[12]

The Security Council has played an important role in easing or containing numerous crises, and it provides a high-level forum for diplomatic contact and negotiation. The Security Council also has a role, with the General Assembly, in the admission of new members to the UN, the appointment of the Secretary-General, and the election of judges to the ICJ.

The Charter provision that the Council must operate on the basis of unanimity of its Permanent Members was not the product of impractical idealism: the memoirs of some of those who helped frame the Charter confirm that they knew what they were doing in this as in many other

---

[12] For details of UN peacekeeping, see Sally Morphet's chapter below; and Appendices A and E.

respects.[13] The provision, which has been interpreted in practice to mean that any one of the Permanent Members has to vote against a resolution in order to veto it, reflects a highly realistic belief that UN action will not be possible if one of the great powers seriously dissents from it.[14]

Both the actual use of the veto, and the constant possibility of its use, have been central features of the functioning of the Security Council throughout the UN's history. In the period from 1945 to the end of 1992 the following vetoes were cast: Soviet Union 114; United States 69; United Kingdom 30; France 18; China 3. The changing pattern of use of the veto by the five Permanent Members is indicated by the following figures:

1946–55 China 1, France 2, UK 0, USA 0, USSR 75;
1956–65 China 0, France 2, UK 3, USA 0, USSR 26;
1966–75 China 2, France 2, UK 8, USA 12, USSR 7;
1976–85 China 0, France 9, UK 11, USA 34, USSR 6;
1986–92 China 0, France 3, UK 8, USA 23, USSR 0.[15]

These figures reflect the fact that a Permanent Member of the Security Council can avoid having to make direct use of the veto power if it is sure that the proposal in question will not in any event obtain the requisite two-thirds majority. The Western states, in particular, were frequently able to use this tactic in the early years of the UN, the Soviet Union in the 1970s and 1980s. To some

[13] The UN Charter provision for unanimity among the Permanent Members of the Security Council (the veto) was the result of extensive discussion, including at Dumbarton Oaks (Aug.–Oct. 1944) and Yalta (Feb. 1945). The evidence is that the UK, USA, USSR, and France all favoured the principle of unanimity, and that they were motivated in this by a hard-headed concern to protect their own sovereign rights and national interest. See e.g. Winston S. Churchill, *The Second World War*, vol. 6: *Triumph and Tragedy* (London, 1954), pp. 181–2 and 308–13; Harry S. Truman, *Year of Decisions: 1945* (London, 1955), pp. 194–5, 201, and 206–7; Charles de Gaulle, *War Memoirs: Salvation 1944–1946—Documents*, tr. Murchie and Erskine (London, 1960), pp. 94–5. Truman, who became President of the USA in Apr. 1945, went so far as to write in his memoirs: 'All our experts, civil and military, favoured it, and without such a veto no arrangement would have passed the Senate' (p. 207).

[14] For discussion of the question of possible changes in the Security Council's composition and in the veto, see below, p. 39 ff.

[15] Foreign and Commonwealth Office, Research and Analysis Department Memorandum, 'Table of Vetoed Draft Resolutions in the United Nations Security Council 1946–1991', London, Jan. 1992.

extent the use of the veto has reflected a degree of diplomatic isolation of the vetoing state(s) on the particular issue. Forcing such resolutions to a vote has been a diplomatic strategy to demonstrate the isolation of particular states. The period from 31 May 1990 (when the USA vetoed a resolution on the Israeli-occupied territories) to 11 May 1993 (when Russia vetoed a resolution on the financing of the peacekeeping force in Cyprus) was notable as the longest without use of the veto in the history of the UN.

Because of the veto, the Security Council could contribute little to the amelioration of armed conflicts in which its Permanent Members were directly involved—as, for example, in Suez (1956), Hungary (1956), Vietnam (1946–75), and the Sino-Vietnamese war (1979). Since the mid-1980s the Security Council has had a more central role in international security, discussed on pp. 29–39.

The *UN Secretariat*, which is headed by the Secretary-General, comprises some 14,000 people at UN Headquarters in New York and at other UN offices (the largest of which is Geneva). The UN Charter requires that merit is to be the paramount consideration in their employment, but the UN has not always been able to adhere unswervingly to this principle. While the nature and quality of the UN's work depends greatly on the comparatively 'faceless' Secretariat, the Secretary-General is also a significant figure in international diplomacy.[16]

The role of the Secretary-General has developed very significantly since 1945. The chapters by Javier Pérez de Cuéllar, and by Thomas Franck and Georg Nolte, show how the Secretary-General has taken on—or has had forced upon him—a wide range of functions: fact-finding, mediating in disputes between states, and responding to rapidly moving crises in which other UN bodies, because of disagreement among members or the sheer pace of events, have only limited possibilities of doing anything.

The *International Court of Justice* (ICJ) is the successor to the Permanent Court of International Justice, which had

---

[16] The Secretaries-General of the UN since 1945 are listed in Appendix D.

been established at The Hague in 1922. The ICJ's Statute was adopted in 1945 at the same time as the UN Charter, and all UN member states are parties, as are certain other states. The ICJ is empowered to issue binding decisions in cases between states which have in some way consented to its jurisdiction. It also provides advisory opinions when requested to do so by competent international organizations. A list of its judgments and opinions is in Appendix F.

The *Trusteeship Council* superintended the transition of trust territories to self-government. However, within the UN system the main pressure for European decolonization in the 1960s and 1970s came from other quarters—the Special Committee on Decolonization, dominated by 'Third World' states; and from the General Assembly's Fourth Committee. It does not at present have an active role beyond its remaining duties concerning Palau.

The *Economic and Social Council* comprises fifty-four states elected by the General Assembly. Many non-governmental organizations also participate in its proceedings. It supervises the work of numerous commissions, committees, and expert bodies in the economic and social fields, and endeavours, so far with only limited success, to coordinate the efforts of the many UN specialized agencies in this area.

The UN system extends beyond the six UN organs created by the Charter, and the various subsidiary bodies established subsequently by the UN, to include also a host of specialized agencies with their own separate constitutions, memberships, and budgets. These agencies constitute a distinct part of the UN system. In the words of Article 57 of the UN Charter they are 'established by intergovernmental agreement' and have 'wide international responsibilities, as defined in their basic instruments, in economic, social, cultural, educational, health, and related fields'. There are sixteen such specialized agencies associated with the UN: apart from the financial agencies—the main ones being the International Monetary Fund (IMF) and the World Bank (IBRD)—the 'big four' are the International Labour Organization (ILO); the Food and Agriculture Organization (FAO); the United Nations Educational, Scientific and Cultural Organization

(UNESCO); and the World Health Organization (WHO).[17] Other intergovernmental organizations closely associated with the UN include the International Atomic Energy Agency (IAEA) and the General Agreement on Tariffs and Trade (GATT).

In 1992 the budget for the UN and its affiliated programmes (but excluding the specialized agencies) was over $US 5.2 billion. There are three major modes of financing from member states: compulsory assessed contributions to the regular UN budget ($1.2 billion in 1992); compulsory assessed contributions towards peace-keeping operations ($1.3 billion in 1992); and voluntary contributions ($2.7 billion in 1992). Thus more than half of the UN budget is financed by voluntary contributions, with most of the remainder contributed by member states in accordance with binding assessments based mainly on gross and per capita national incomes. Some costs, particularly some of those for peacekeeping, are absorbed directly by member states. The maximum share of assess-ments for the regular budget is 25 per cent (paid by the USA), and the minimum is 0.01 per cent (paid by numerous member states). For peacekeeping greater contributions are levied on the permanent five: the USA is assessed at 30.8 per cent, and the minimum is 0.001 per cent. The UN has been in financial difficulties arising from non-payment of assessed contributions since the early 1960s, and the deficit increased sharply in the 1980s. At the end of 1992 member states owed $500 million in past arrears to the regular budget, and $765 million in past and current peacekeeping arrears. Despite attempts to improve this situation, reserves are inadequate, and the UN continues to face serious cash-flow problems, making management and planning unnecessarily difficult.[18]

[17] For a list which includes all sixteen specialized agencies, see Abbreviations. See further David Pitt and Thomas G. Weiss (eds.), *The Nature of United Nations Bureaucracies* (London, 1986); and Douglas Williams, *The Specialized Agencies and the United Nations: The System in Crisis* (London, 1987).

[18] Figures from *Financing an Effective United Nations: A Report of the Independent Advisory Group on U.N. Financing* (Ford Foundation, New York, 1993), pp. 8 and 30. The UN's perennial financial crisis is discussed in the chapters by Javier Pérez de Cuéllar, Maurice Bertrand, and Peter Wilenski. Percentage figures for each member state's assessed contribution to the UN regular budget are in Appendix C below.

(b) Problems of Evaluating the UN

International organizations present peculiarly difficult problems of evaluation. In view of the fundamental importance of many international issues, and the limited powers of states to deal satisfactorily with them, the needs potentially filled by an international organization of general competence such as the UN are almost limitless. Different states and groups see these needs differently: they have formed their own expectations, and evaluate the UN by different standards.

The UN is too often evaluated by standards unrelated to its actual capacities. Some have judged the UN against the standard of a prototype world government; or at least as a means of eliminating completely one of the plagues of international life, namely war.[19] Such expectations were built up at the time of the UN's foundation. Even now, many see the organization in idealistic terms (sometimes reflecting the language of the Charter) as standing on a higher moral plane than the states of which it is composed, especially because of its advocacy of such principles as human rights, non-use of force, and disarmament. Others have used the non-fulfillment of these highly idealistic expectations as a starting-point for bitter criticism. The UN is all talk and no action; it is an arena in which governments hypocritically proclaim one set of values while themselves practising another; it is a vehicle for the pursuit of power politics in disguise, not for their replacement. In the late 1970s and early 1980s these critical views became more prevalent and more influential, especially in that country where idealism about the UN had once been particularly strong—the USA.[20] Such views, idealistic or dismissive, evaluated the UN in simple terms, assumed that the UN must be judged by the aspirational standards set for

[19] See e.g. Clyde Eagleton, *International Government* (3rd rev. edn., New York, 1957).
[20] See e.g. Daniel Patrick Moynihan, *A Dangerous Place* (London, 1979); and Burton Yale Pines (ed.), *A World without a UN: What Would Happen if the UN Shut Down?* (Heritage Foundation, Washington DC, 1984).

it in the Charter, and made few distinctions between the UN's numerous different roles.[21]

This book seeks to examine the UN's performance against a modest yardstick rather than an impossible ideal; to see how the UN has changed since its foundation in 1945, and might change further; to describe its successes, not the least of which is the mere fact of enduring for half a century; to account for its equally notable failures; and to consider how it might address some of its current problems. Above all, it is an exploration of how to think about the UN, whose place in international relations has proved different from that envisaged both by its advocates and by its critics.

A general inter-governmental organization, be it regional or global, cannot be evaluated in quite the same terms as governments:[22] its decision-making and implementation powers are limited, it lacks the boundaries which define and distinguish a territorial entity, and it is always operating concurrently with governments and other entities which it does not control. Such results as are achieved are often difficult to attribute to any single body.

One long-established method of assessing the UN consists of compiling 'balance sheets' of achievements. Fixation with such assessments, to which the UN has been subject to an extent almost unparalleled in any political system, seems as immutable as the Charter.[23] In fact, the UN's achievements cannot be neatly entered into profit and loss columns: the attempt to do so involves crude reductionism and a misguided search for single attributions, causes, and characterizations. The difficulty of

---

[21] The relationship between these two approaches in the US debate is cogently analysed by Thomas M. Franck, *Nation against Nation: What Happened to the UN Dream and What the US Can Do about It* (New York, 1985).

[22] On the problems of false analogies between the principles which sustain order within states and those of international society, see Hidemi Suganami, *The Domestic Analogy and World Order Proposals* (Cambridge, 1989).

[23] Examples of the balance-sheet approach include G. Niemeyer, 'The Balance-Sheet of the League Experiment', *International Organization*, 6 (1952), pp. 537–58; Sir Alexander Cadogan, 'The United Nations: A Balance Sheet', *Year Book of World Affairs*, 5 (1951), pp. 1–11; and Juliana G. Pilon, *The United States and the United Nations: A Balance Sheet* (Heritage Foundation, Washington DC, 1982).

agreeing substantive standards for judging the UN's effectiveness has heightened the tendency to focus on comforting quantitative measures such as value for money. Problems of waste, inefficiency, and corruption, important as they are, have been the subject of such magnified scrutiny as to divert attention from more fundamental evaluations of the organization.

It is not easy to evaluate the performance of the UN separately from that of the member states. The UN is, as former US Secretary of State Dean Rusk observed, a political institution whose members 'are pursuing their national interests as they see them'.[24] It was created by governments, and it can do little without the assent of at least the majority of them. This view is a necessary antidote to the widespread misapprehension that the UN is in the course of superseding the states system, and that the UN can and ought to take strong action on its own initiative irrespective of the views of states. But the UN cannot be adequately understood as simply the sum of its parts. Like all institutions, whatever their origins and power base, it has developed a life and an ethos of its own. The UN framework influences states' perceptions of their interests, the ordering of their priorities and preferences, and the possibilities they see of best advancing their interests.[25] The UN has also come to embody a limited sense of a collective interest, distinct in specific cases

[24] Cited in *Harvard International Law Journal*, 17 (1976), p. 606.
[25] The most substantial and methodologically rigorous work on the impact of international institutions on state behaviour has come from regime theory and related work on international cooperation. The category of 'regimes' is broader than formal international institutions, encompassing 'sets of implicit or explicit principles, norms, rules, and decision-making procedures around which actors' expectations converge'. Partly because much of this work has focused on particular issue areas, the performance of the UN itself has received surprisingly little attention. For a penetrating statement of the neo-liberal institutionalist perspective, see Robert O. Keohane, *International Institutions and State Power: Essays in International Relations Theory* (Boulder, Colo., 1989). Work on international cooperation has begun to pay more attention to issues of compliance and enforcement: see e.g. Oran Young, 'On The Effectiveness of International Institutions', in Rosenau and Czempiel (eds.), *Governance Without Government* (1992). For a wider perspective on international institutions in a multilateral system, see John Gerard Ruggie *et al.*, 'Symposium: Multilateralism', *International Organization*, 46 (Summer 1992).

from the particular interests of individual states. In these respects the UN has specific functions or roles against which its performance may be evaluated, even while responsibility for the quality of this performance may lie in great part with member states as well as with individual functionaries or with features of institutional design.

A practical problem of evaluation is that the formidable quantities of documentation produced by the UN, including records of debates and reports on a wide range of topics both internal and external, in some cases shed surprisingly little light on factors influencing decisions or on the wider context in which they are taken. Official records often give limited information, e.g. about personal considerations, informal discussions which frequently precede formal meetings, and underlying reasons why a particular actor took a particular line. Strategic and tactical considerations, trade-offs, compromises, misunderstandings, chance occurrences, and personal agendas are seldom officially documented, and it can be especially difficult to ascertain from the documents why little or no action was taken on a particular issue.[26]

(c) The UN's Different Roles

A general international organization has many quite distinct roles at any given time, and even in respect of the same conflict or issue-area; its roles can change from one period to the next; and can even vary significantly from those set forth in its original constitutive instrument.

The League of Nations (established in 1920, and only formally wound up in April 1946) is generally evaluated on the basis of its primary role 'to achieve international

---

[26] In addition to material in UN archives, several other archives have been established to supplement the official records and published memoirs in these respects, including through memoranda, diaries, letters, and interviews with people concerned with episodes of UN history. Examples are the collection of the Yale Institution for Social and Policy Studies; the UN Career Records Project, established in the Western Manuscripts Department of the Bodleian Library, Oxford, in 1992; and the project set up in Copenhagen in 1992 by the Nordic Association of Former International Civil Servants.

peace and security' and to avoid war.[27] In this matter it conspicuously failed. Yet the League did have some useful roles apart from the unintended one of providing an object lesson in how *not* to prevent war. The League and associated bodies were effective in some specialized areas such as labour and health. As to the League's many shortcomings, whether in the narrowness of its membership or in the inadequacies of its arrangements for keeping the peace, some of the lessons of its failure were learned. This experience helps to explain why the UN Charter provided a better framework than the League Covenant, both in its general statements of principles, and in the procedures it laid down for reaching and implementing decisions in the field of international security.

When the United Nations was established in the immediate aftermath of the Second World War, it was viewed similarly as being concerned above all with the maintenance of peace. However, in the years of East–West rivalry its role in this area sometimes seemed marginal. In the field of international security, while some major developments took place wholly or partly within a UN framework, many did not. For example, many fundamental issues between the USA and USSR, and also between countries of eastern and western Europe, were addressed outside UN institutions. The same is true of most security issues involving the People's Republic of China; and of many elements of the Arab–Israeli conflict. In such cases, more private bilateral or multilateral frameworks were preferred from which unwelcome states could be excluded, and in which there was less pressure to follow some established UN principles and practices. However, the UN did maintain an effective involvement in many security issues, including in regional conflicts in southern Africa and the Indian sub-continent. The UN involvement in regional security issues has increased dramatically since the late 1980s. Even in this period of heightened activity,

---

[27] For a useful assessment see F. P. Walters, *A History of the League of Nations* (Oxford, 1960).

the UN remains only part of the wider international framework for addressing security concerns.

Against this background, it is not surprising that the UN's contribution came to be seen by many as being less in the field of peace between the major powers than in other areas: defusing certain regional conflicts, advocating self-determination, assisting decolonization, codifying international law, protecting human rights, and providing a possible framework for social and economic improvement, even for redistribution of wealth on a global scale.

(d) Disjunctions between Myth and Reality

Any serious assessment of the UN's successes and failures cannot neglect the importance of myth, symbol, and drama in the UN. Nor can it neglect the contrast between the high principles espoused at the UN and the more mundane realities and controversies which have characterized much of its history.

There is a complex relation between the UN's attempts to fulfil the terms of its innumerable express mandates and its more abstract role as a symbol of both the constraints and the possibilities of international society. The UN should be judged, not just by what it does in particular fields of activity, or in particular crises, but also by the way in which, through its very existence, through the influence of its Charter, through the questions it addresses, and through its diplomatic rituals, it proclaims certain values and sets the terms of international debates.

If the UN proclaims high principles, it also reflects the faults and frailties of both individuals and states. If it is an institution for taking decisions, it is also one for postponing them. If it has a far clearer decision-making machinery than most international organizations, it also sees much putting up of proposals in order to have them defeated. If it is an institution for punishing transgressing states, it is also one for finding face-saving solutions. Actions and statements at, and by, the UN should not always be taken at face value.

The very term 'United Nations' is a misnomer with a strong element of myth about it, and has been so ever since the foundation of the UN in 1945. One potentially misleading element in the term is the implied claim that there is unity both within and between states. While the very existence of the UN attests to a general unity of acceptance of an international society with certain agreed institutions, it is division, not unity, which has been the more conspicuous feature of the world since 1945, as indeed it was of the world before that date.[28] A related misleading element in the term 'United Nations' has to do with the word 'nation'. Indeed, 'Divided States' might be a brutally accurate if uninspiring characterization. There is a dimension of political mythology in the 'nations' part of the title 'United Nations'. If the term 'nation', properly used, refers to a people holding in common such attributes as ethnicity, history, culture, religion, language, and having a common perception of who their enemies are, then there are few 'nations' indeed among the member states of the United Nations. Many of these states are engaged in the difficult business of 'nation-building', and may indeed over time generate a sense of nationhood. Meanwhile there will continue to be deep divisions within states as well as between them—divisions of region, race, nationality, tribe, religion, and class. 'Nations' and 'states' are far from co-terminous; witness the phenomena of divided nations, of multi-national states, and of states with irredentist claims. Indeed, many major wars of this century, including the two world wars, originated partly in problems arising from the crucial disjunction between 'nation' and 'state'.[29] Yet

---

[28] President de Gaulle of France, as committed to country as he was dismissive of international organizations, spoke of the UN as 'les nations dites unies'—the said-to-be united nations.

[29] On the difference between 'nation' and 'state' see Hugh Seton-Watson, *Nations and States* (London, 1977). See also Benedict Anderson, *Imagined Communities: Reflections on the Origin and Spread of Nationalism* (London, 1983); José de Obieta Chalbaud, *El derecho humano de la autodeterminación de los pueblos* (Madrid, 1985); Anthony D. Smith, *The Ethnic Origins of Nations* (Oxford, 1986); and Daniel Patrick Moynihan, *Pandaemonium: Ethnicity in International Politics* (Oxford, 1993).

the use of the term 'nation' as supposedly synonymous with 'state' or 'country' is deeply ingrained in contemporary idiom, not just in the title of the UN itself, but in the very word 'international'. At all events, such uses of the terms 'nations' and 'United Nations' should not cloud judgement by conveying an excessively simple image of those complex entities, sovereign states.

The UN has always been a theatre for standard-setting and myth-making—for appealing to higher standards than those which commonly prevail in international relations, and for holding out the promise of a better-ordered world. In *The United Nations: Sacred Drama*, which remains one of the most challenging books on the subject, Conor Cruise O'Brien suggested that the function of the UN was to act—not in the sense of taking executive action, but rather in the sense of acting in a theatre. He suggested that the UN Charter, and much UN activity, reflected

the feeling that the thing feared may be averted, and the thing hoped for be won, by the solemn and collective use of appropriate words. This prayer still converges on the United Nations—as on a holy place—at times when, as in the Cuban missile crisis in 1962, or the Middle Eastern crisis of the summer of 1967, the scourge of war seems once more to be about to descend. It is the prayer that makes the drama sacred.[30]

O'Brien saw the UN's espousal of certain ideas and principles—peace, decolonization, multiracialism among them—as its most important contribution to international life. He conceded, however, that the UN drama swings from tragedy to farce and back again, with neither bathos nor buffoonery alien to it.

The UN has indeed always been beset by some controversy, not all of an edifying kind. The first two Secretaries-General both ended their service on almost intolerably bad terms with the Soviet Union.[31] From 1986 on, there were accusations that Kurt Waldheim, UN Secretary-General

---

[30] Conor Cruise O'Brien, *The United Nations: Sacred Drama* (London, 1968), p. 11. The theatrical metaphor was also used by Hernane Tavares de Sá, *The Play within a Play: The Inside Story of the UN* (New York, 1966).

[31] On Lie's and Hammarskjöld's difficulties with the USSR, see Brian Urquhart, *Hammarskjöld* (New York, 1972), pp. 456–72; and Urquhart, *Ralph Bunche: An American Life* (New York, 1993), pp. 335–7.

1972–81, had concealed vital facts about his past role with German occupation forces in Greece and Yugoslavia during World War II, and might even have had some involvement in war crimes;[32] but there was no clear evidence that any of the decision-makers involved in Waldheim's elections knew anything of this. McCarthyism and accusations of espionage had both cast a shadow over the Secretariat by 1950;[33] and accusations of espionage by members of the UN staff recurred periodically. The UN's perennial financial crisis began in the 1950s and early 1960s, with UNEF and ONUC; and carried through into the 1980s and 1990s with a failure by many states, most notably the USA and Russia, to pay their dues to the organization. Secretaries-General have had prominent disagreements with respected senior staff about policy questions, such as that which led to the departure in 1982 of the Director of the UN Human Rights Centre, Theo van Boven. The specialized agencies have attracted particular controversy. The USSR and other states withdrew their cooperation from WHO in the early 1950s. The USA threatened permanent withdrawal from the ILO in the late 1970s; and the USA, UK, and Singapore withdrew from UNESCO in 1984–5. From the 1980s onwards there were sharp criticisms, overwhelmingly Western, of the performance of the heads of several specialized agencies, including Amadou Mahtar M'Bow (Director-General of UNESCO 1974–87), Edouard Saouma (Director-General of FAO from 1976), and Hiroshi Nakajima (Director-General of WHO from 1988).

(e) Doctrines on Use of Force by States and Liberation Movements

The maintenance of limits on the use of force by states has been a central preoccupation of the UN throughout its existence. While the non-use of force has remained a core

---

[32] See Seymour M. Finger and Arnold A. Saltzman, *Bending with the Winds: Kurt Waldheim and the United Nations* (New York, 1990).

[33] See generally Shirley Hazzard, *Defeat of an Ideal: A Study of the Self-Destruction of the United Nations* (Boston, 1973).

principle, the UN has had to confront many difficult problems concerning its scope, and also concerning its application to non-state bodies. (The question of use of force under UN auspices is considered in the next section.)

Articles 2(4) and 51 of the UN Charter largely restrict the right of states to use force to one circumstance: individual or collective self-defence. In the past, this has usually been interpreted to mean that states have the right to use force when there is an attack on a member state's territory—and presumably only then. All this is derived from the idea, which is perhaps too simple, that readily discernible 'aggression' is the main cause of war, and that stopping aggression will stop all war. But reality has proved more complex. The UN era has seen uses of force by states in a wide range of circumstances, with Article 51 being almost routinely cited by the perpetrator in justification. These have included uses of force in pursuit of territorial claims; in anticipation of a possible attack or future threat; in support of self-determination; to stop unwanted political developments within a so-called 'sphere of influence'; by way of reprisal; to protect nationals abroad; in response to alleged terrorist acts; and to rescue victims of hijackings. In such cases, the practice of states has been modified by the words of the Charter only to a limited extent.[34]

Despite marked divergences in the interpretation of specific provisions and indeed of its whole ethos, the UN Charter does affect the behaviour of states. It has reinforced the idea that there is a strong presumption in most cases against the legitimacy of the uninvited use of force by a state outside its accepted international frontiers.[35] For example, the fact that in the years

[34] See M. Virally on Art. 2(4), and A. Cassese on Art. 51, in J.-P. Cot and A. Pellet (eds.), *La Charte des Nations Unies* (2nd edn., Paris, 1991), pp. 115–28 and 771–95. The relationship between rhetoric and practice is also examined in Hedley Bull (ed.), *Intervention in World Politics* (Oxford, 1984), pp. 186–95.

[35] UN practice also evinces doubt about the legitimacy of large-scale uses of force, especially against internal rebellion, even where an invitation has been issued by the government concerned. See Louise Doswald-Beck, 'The Legal Validity of Military Intervention by Invitation of the Government', *British Year Book of International Law 1985*, pp. 198–252.

after 1973 there was no attempt by Western European countries, Japan, or the USA to seize oil resources on which they were heavily dependent, the price of which had increased phenomenally, is evidence not just of the possible adverse physical consequences which would have ensued, but also of the strength of the principle of non-intervention. It is certainly hard to answer positively the hypothetical question: In what previous era would such a situation not have resulted in interventions by some of these states?[36]

The tendency of UN resolutions has been to condemn most invasions and occupations, irrespective of their motives or results, except when broadly under UN auspices. There have inevitably been accusations of political partiality regarding such resolutions, as when in 1962 the General Assembly failed to condemn India's invasion of Goa, and when in the 1970s it repeatedly condemned armed actions by Israel and South Africa. However, from 1979 onwards the General Assembly did repeatedly demand the withdrawal of Vietnamese forces following their December 1978 intervention in Cambodia, and of Soviet forces following their December 1979 intervention in Afghanistan.[37] It later condemned the US-led invasions of Grenada in 1983, and of Panama in 1989.[38] Such condemnations reflected a view widely held in the international community that force should be avoided wherever possible, and the UN should not rush to applaud even beneficent consequences of the use of force. This idea, that there should be a taboo on the use

[36] Although the so-called Kissinger doctrine did foreshadow the possibility of intervention to protect supplies vital to Western security, no such intervention ensued, at least until the exceptional naval involvements in the Gulf in 1987, and then the UN-authorized coalition action in 1991–2. These latter actions occurred in much-changed circumstances.

[37] See e.g. GA Res. 34/22 of 14 Nov. 1979, on Cambodia; and GA Res. 2(ES-VI) of 14 Jan. 1980, on Afghanistan. On the relative impartiality of General Assembly criticism of users of force see Franck, *Nation against Nation*, pp. 224–31.

[38] The armed intervention in Grenada was deplored as 'a flagrant violation of international law' in GA Res. 38/7 of 2 Nov. 1983; the invasion of Panama was similarly deplored in GA Res. 44/240 of 29 Dec. 1989.

of force, or at least on its first use, is thoroughly understandable in a world which is grossly over-armed.

Although the UN has tended to deplore most uses of force by states, it has not thereby avoided getting caught up in many of the complexities which surround the whole question of the use of force in international relations. For example, the UN may condemn what is seen by a majority as a first or illegitimate use of force; but this very condemnation may, consciously or otherwise, give some encouragement to the use of counter-force. Thus the UN's criticisms of military incursions—for example, the Israeli occupation of Arab territories since 1967, the Soviet intervention in Afghanistan in 1979, the Argentine invasion of the Falkland Islands in 1982, and the Iraqi invasion of Kuwait in 1990—have all in their way had the effect of lending some legitimacy to the subsequent armed struggles to reverse these interventions. Furthermore, the implicit endorsement by the UN of such principles of justice as the retrocession of colonial enclaves may have encouraged certain decisions to resort to force. Thus preoccupation with principles by no means leads inevitably to a reduction in the use of force. On the contrary, it may (whether rightly or wrongly) help justify certain uses of force: and part of the concern about developments in the UN in the 1970s and 1980s was due to a fear that this was indeed proving to be so.

Another example of the difficulties for the UN in developing and espousing coherent principles has been in connection with an age-old question of international law and relations: In what circumstances are people entitled to engage in armed struggle against an existing state? And in what circumstances may other states assist such rebels? There are no neat general answers to these questions, which are reflections of the enduring tension between the principle of non-intervention and other fundamental priorities of states. Traditionally, states have been careful (though far from consistently so) in guarding their mono-poly of the right to use force, and have resisted general

acceptance of any right of non-state groups to use force.[39]
However, states do often provide assistance to certain
rebel groups in other countries, whether to destabilize an
adversary regime, or out of kinship or sympathy with
the plight or objectives of the rebels. Such assistance,
associated with many different types of political system
and doctrine, and generally justified more in political
than in legal terms, was a notable and often destructive
characteristic of East–West relations in the Cold War
period, especially in the Third World.[40] It did not
disappear in the post-Cold War period: conflicts in the
former Yugoslavia and former Soviet Union were among
the many attestations to the enduring difficulty of bringing
international rules to bear on such uses of force, especially
in cases where ethnic or other special ties link combatants
and their external supporters.

The UN has faced the problem of the legitimacy of
support for rebel groups in several different contexts. The
major attempt to address it, in the 1970s, was and remains
controversial. Due largely to the advent of new Third World
members—particularly critical of Israel, South Africa,
Rhodesia, and of continued European colonial rule in Africa
and elsewhere—the UN went a long way in the 1970s
towards recognizing the legitimacy of the use of force by
a particular category of non-state bodies, namely 'national
liberation movements'. Thus in 1970 the General Assembly
approved in Resolution 2625 (XXV) the 'Declaration on
Principles of International Law Concerning Friendly
Relations and Cooperation Among States in Accordance

---

[39] Questions related to the use of force by non-state groups are discussed in
John Norton Moore (ed.), *Law and Civil War in the Modern World* (Baltimore,
1974); Michael Bothe, Karl Partsch, and Waldemar Solf, *New Rules for Victims of
Armed Conflicts: Commentary on the Two 1977 Protocols Additional to the Geneva
Conventions of 1949* (The Hague, 1982), pp. 36–52 and 232–58; and Michel
Veuthey, *Guérilla et droit humanitaire* (2nd edn., Geneva, 1983).

[40] For an account of Soviet doctrines and activities see Neil MacFarlane,
Superpower Rivalry and Third World Radicalism: The Idea of National Liberation
(Baltimore, 1985). For one of the final expositions of the 'Reagan doctrine',
which affirmed the legitimacy of US support for an insurgency against a
dictatorial government that depends on external support, see Constantine C.
Menges, *The Twilight Struggle: The Soviet Union v. the United States Today*
(Washington DC, 1990).

with the Charter of the UN', which contained the remarkable proposition:

Every State has the duty to refrain from any forcible action which deprives peoples . . . of their right to self-determination and freedom and independence. In their actions against, and resistance to, such forcible action in pursuit of the exercise of their right to self-determination, such peoples are entitled to seek and to receive support in accordance with the purposes and principles of the Charter.

This formulation, in common with other General Assembly resolutions on the topic of self-determination, failed to establish effective criteria for determining which peoples are appropriate candidates for self-determination, and which groups representing them are entitled to international support. Moreover, it was in completely unresolved conflict with another proposition asserted with equal firmness in the same Declaration:

Every State has the duty to refrain from organizing, instigating, assisting or participating in acts of civil strife or terrorist acts in another State or acquiescing in organized activities within its territory directed towards the commission of such acts, when the acts referred to in the present paragraph involve a threat or use of force.

The enunciation of apparently contradictory principles with respect to the legality of support for national liberation movements was not confined to this 1970 document. Fundamental differences of view on this matter were also manifest in the 1974 Definition of Aggression.[41]

At the diplomatic level, the UN accorded observer status in the General Assembly to the Palestine Liberation Organization in 1974,[42] as well as varying degrees of participation in UN conferences and committees to certain other national liberation movements.

[41] Annexed to GA Res. 3314 (XXIX) of 14 Dec. 1974. See esp. Arts. 3(g) and 7. A parallel tension regarding self-determination is evident in the Declaration of the 1993 World Conference on Human Rights in Vienna.

[42] GA Res. 3237 (XXIX) of 22 Nov. 1974. Already on 13 Nov. 1974 the PLO Chairman, Mr Yasser Arafat, had addressed the UN General Assembly: with the exception of Pope Paul in 1965, he was the first such person not representing the government of a UN member state to do so. See also below, p. 56.

The UN's general support for self-determination struggles won it respect in the post-colonial world, and successfully identified the UN with the emergence to independence of many such states, including Zimbabwe and Namibia. However, aspects of its approach, particularly its support for some national liberation movements, came to be seen in the USA and elsewhere, especially from the mid-1970s to the late 1980s, as casting serious doubt on the independence and impartiality of the organization.[43] The 1975 General Assembly resolution equating Zionism with 'racism and racial discrimination' was a particular focus of criticism: its revocation in 1991 was a notable symbol of a new balance between consensus and confrontation in the politics of the General Assembly.[44]

A particular problem with the resolutions actively supporting self-determination was that they said little about the question whether any restraints should govern the methods used in self-determination struggles. Almost nothing was said about the applicability of the laws of war to combat by national liberation movements or other insurgents—a matter tackled separately, and with limited practical effect, in the 1977 Geneva Protocols I and II negotiated under the auspices of the International Committee of the Red Cross. Tactics regarded (especially in the West) as terrorism, and which were used by some national liberation movements and certain other groups, were addressed only slowly and in piecemeal fashion by UN bodies. A near-consensus did gradually emerge.[45]

---

[43] See e.g. Moynihan, *A Dangerous Place*, n. 20 above, pp. 181–205.

[44] GA Res. 3379 (XXX) of 10 Nov. 1975. Revoked by GA Res. 46/86 of 16 Dec. 1991.

[45] UN efforts to achieve consensus on aspects of terrorism include GA Res. 3166 (XXVIII) of 14 Dec. 1973, adopting the text of the 1973 Convention on the Protection and Punishment of Crimes against Internationally Protected Persons, including Diplomatic Agents (which entered into force on 20 Feb. 1977); GA Res. 34/146 of 17 Dec. 1979, approving the text of the 1979 International Convention Against the Taking of Hostages (which entered into force on 3 June 1983); and GA Res. 40/61 of 9 Dec. 1985, which 'condemns as criminal all acts, methods and practices of terrorism wherever and by whomever committed'.

One aspect of terrorism posing special problems, including for the UN, has been state support of terrorist groups and activities. The UN Charter system is primarily geared to dealing with organized large-scale uses of force by states externally. Terrorism, on the other hand, has largely been conceived as an outlaw or non-state activity, against which all states would act within their sphere of jurisdiction. Problems have arisen where states employ terrorist methods externally, through the use of more or less deniable groups, or simply provide shelter to terrorists. One response has been the use of force by states against some (but by no means all) allegedly terrorist states:[46] however effective, this interpretation of the right of self-defence is open to abuse, weakens the general prohibition on the use of force, and remains contentious. Another response has been non-forcible attempts, in some cases under UN auspices, to compel allegedly terrorist states to act.

(f) Coercion and Peacekeeping under UN Auspices

The UN Charter, principally in Chapter VII, envisaged that the UN itself would have more means of exercising pressure and coercion at its disposal, and better means of decision-making in crises, than did the League of Nations. In order to enable the UN to deal with threats to the peace, the Security Council was seen as having responsibility for the use of sanctions of various types, and for use of military forces. The overall approach of the Charter is, on the one hand to establish a system of collective security, and on the other to preserve the right of states

---

[46] In April 1986, when US aircraft bombed targets in Libya in response to terrorist attacks on US citizens overseas, it was claimed that the USA was acting in self-defence in conformity with Article 51 of the UN Charter. Speech by Vernon Walters, US Ambassador to the UN, on 15 Apr. 1986 during a debate in the UN Security Council. On 21 Apr. 1986 France, the UK, and the USA vetoed a draft resolution which would have condemned the armed attack on Libya by the USA. *UN Chronicle* (New York), 23, no. 4 (Aug. 1986), pp. 46–7. See also Abraham D. Sofaer, Legal Adviser to the US State Department, 'Terrorism and the Law', *Foreign Affairs*, 64 (1986), pp. 921–2. Other states questioned the USA's interpretation of both the facts and the law. In June 1993, the US employed similar justifications for an attack on Baghdad following alleged Iraqi government involvement in a plot to assassinate ex-President Bush in Kuwait in April. Again, responses of other states varied.

to individual or collective self-defence, at least until the Security Council has taken necessary measures.

The term 'collective security' normally refers to a system in which each state in the system accepts that the security of one is the concern of all, and agrees to join in a collective response to aggression. In this sense it is distinct from systems of alliance security, in which groups of states ally with each other, principally against possible external threats.

The idea of 'collective security' has a history almost as long as systems of states, and was aired for instance at the negotiations which led to the 1648 Peace of Westphalia.[47] This attractive central idea, with its many variants, frequently proves to have fundamental flaws when tested in practice against some basic questions.[48] Among the problems are:.defining which territories and land boundaries are included within the system; reaching agreement on whether the system covers effectively certain types of threat (e.g. acts of terrorism, environmental despoliation, genocide within a state); assuring participating states that the system protects them all equally; coping with severe power imbalances within the system, especially the presence of superpowers; defining the role of alliances; ensuring that the system effectively deters rather than simply responds after the fact; developing a decision-making procedure to reach effective and consistent determinations that a threat to or breach of the peace requiring a response has occurred, and to decide what action is necessary; agreeing an effective system of force-maintenance, command and control; deciding whether all participating states must maintain standing forces and provide them upon request for extra-territorial enforcement

---

[47] On the recurrence of collective security practices and proposals over the centuries see Martin Wight, *Systems of States* (Leicester, 1977), pp. 62 and 149–50; and F. H. Hinsley, *Power and the Pursuit of Peace*.

[48] For an excellent enumeration of questions relating to collective security systems see Andrew Hurrell, 'Collective Security and International Order Revisited', *International Relations* (London), 11, no. 1 (Apr. 1992), pp. 37–55. See also Leon Gordenker and Thomas G. Weiss, 'The Collective Security Idea and Changing World Politics', in Weiss (ed.), *Collective Security in a Changing World* (Boulder, Colo., 1993), pp. 3–18.

actions; maintaining some space for established practices of neutrality in peace and war; working out an effective system of finance, compensation, and burden-sharing; ensuring that states do not abuse the protection of the system, or their indispensable role within it, to pursue unnecessarily confrontational policies towards other states; and determining how far collective security depends upon an effective system of disarmament and arms control, especially as regards weapons of mass destruction.

After 1945, the ambitious scheme for collective security in Chapter VII of the UN Charter was not implemented. The most obvious reason was the inability of the Permanent Members of the Security Council to reach agreement across the Cold War divide. Article 43 agreements, necessary to place national forces at the disposal of the UN, were never concluded. The immediate problem was ideological mistrust, but there has also been a continuing underlying reluctance on the part of states to see their forces committed to participate in distant, controversial, and risky military operations without their express consent and command.

Such actual international security arrangements as did emerge were centred less on the UN than on bilateral and regional alliances—the latter including the Rio Treaty, NATO, and the Warsaw Pact. Although Chapter VIII of the UN Charter had envisaged regional security arrangements, it had also provided for the Security Council to exercise a general supervisory role in respect of enforcement action by such bodies: this did not materialize in practice for most of the Cold War period.

The UN has nevertheless developed useful methods for responding to many situations of international and internal conflict. To a large extent these methods were not provided for in the Charter scheme, although the Charter allocation of primary responsibility to the Security Council has been respected at least since the 1960s. The UN has developed a sophisticated system of peacekeeping forces; it has adopted non-forcible sanctions under Article 41 of the Charter and made some innovative provision for their implementation and enforcement; it has authorized member states to use force in response to specific security problems; and in the period following the Cold War the Security Council has begun in a limited and incremental way to expand the scope of UN action. This latter development has been associated with a further blurring of the traditional lines between the various categories of UN action. Many hybrid forms are emerging, involving various combinations of peacekeeping, sanctions, enforcement, good offices, humanitarian assistance, political support, election-monitoring, and coordinated action by other states and international organizations.

Peacekeeping forces generally consist of separate national contingents carrying out, in the name of the UN, a wide variety of tasks such as the monitoring and enforcement of cease-fires, observation of frontier lines, interposition between belligerents, election-monitoring, protection and delivery of humanitarian aid, and the maintenance of government and public order. During the Cold War they had no role in central areas of direct East–West rivalry—for example, in Hungary in 1956, in Czechoslovakia in 1968, and in Indo-China from 1946 to 1991. As Sally Morphet's chapter shows, such forces have been used both in international conflicts (as between Israel and its neighbours), and in internal conflicts with international aspects (as in the Congo, Cyprus, Angola, Yugoslavia, Cambodia, Somalia, and Mozambique).

UN peacekeeping has in several cases failed to prevent war and unilateral intervention. In 1967, Secretary-General U Thant felt obliged to accede to the Egyptian government's request for the withdrawal of UNEF, even though it was widely understood that this action was a prologue to the war between Israel and Egypt in June of that year. In Lebanon, the presence of UN forces failed to prevent either the country's slide into anarchy and communal warfare, or the Israeli invasion in 1982. In Cyprus, the UN forces which existed to keep the peace between the Greek and Turkish communities could not prevent external involvement in that communal conflict, culminating in the 1974 Turkish invasion of northern Cyprus. In Angola in 1992, UN-monitored elections were followed by a new outbreak of the long-standing civil war.

Despite these limitations, the UN's peacekeeping activities remain one of the most significant innovations of the organization. In many matters to do with security, success is by definition almost unnoticed. The involvement of the UN has helped to isolate certain conflicts from great power rivalry. In many cases the presence of peacekeeping forces stabilized conflicts, but paradoxically in so doing may have reduced pressure for long-term solutions.

Sanctions are another important tool available to the Security Council in responding to conflicts and threats to international peace under Chapter VII of the Charter. The UN's use of sanctions, fairly rare until 1990, has had general support, but there has also been concern about their exact purposes, their effects and effectiveness.[49] General economic sanctions were applied to Rhodesia (1966–79); Iraq following its invasion of Kuwait (1990–); and Serbia and Montenegro (1992–). An air traffic embargo was imposed on Libya (1992–). There were also embargoes on the supply of arms to South Africa (1977–); former Yugoslavia (1991–); Somalia (1992–); and Liberia (1992–). Arms and petroleum sanctions were imposed on Haiti in June 1993. As many of these cases demonstrate, sanctions have symbolic functions, and are often used as a form of communication of international values. They can be a means of warning an adversary of the seriousness with which a particular matter is viewed, and of the prospect of more forceful action. They may also be used with the rather different purpose of assuaging domestic opinion in states taking part in the sanctions, often with the intention of avoiding military action or other unpalatable options. There can in some cases be serious questions about their compatibility with the human

---

[49] See generally Margaret Doxey, *International Sanctions in Contemporary Perspective* (London, 1987); David Leyton-Brown (ed.), *The Utility of Economic Sanctions* (New York, 1987); David A. Baldwin, *Economic Statecraft* (Princeton, NJ, 1985); Barry E. Carter, *International Economic Sanctions: Improving the Haphazard US Legal Regime* (Cambridge, 1988); Gary Hufbauer *et al.*, *Economic Sanctions Reconsidered* (Institute for International Economics, Washington DC, 1990); and Patrick Clawson, 'Sanctions as Punishment, Enforcement, and Prelude to Further Action', *Ethics and International Affairs* (New York), 7 (1993), pp. 17–37.

rights of the target state population, particularly where the instrumentalist calculation is that if there is enough domestic suffering the people will rise up against their government.

When confronted by situations requiring the large-scale use of force, the Security Council has not been able, in the years since 1945, to itself command substantial military action in the way envisaged in Chapter VII. Its primary method for dealing with this problem has been to authorize the use of force by member states. As mentioned in Brian Urquhart's chapter, the Security Council has authorized the use of armed forces by US-led coalitions, rather than under the command of the UN as such, in the cases of Korea (1950), Iraq–Kuwait (1990), and Somalia (1992). UN authorization of limited use of force by states has also become a common method for enforcing sanctions, air exclusion zones, and other restrictions on particular states and activities.

There are advantages in an arrangement whereby forces are authorized by the Security Council but remain national in command. It reflects the reality that not all states feel equally involved in every enforcement action. Moreover, military action requires an extremely close relation between intelligence-gathering and operations, a smoothly functioning decision-making machine, and forces with some experience of working together to perform dangerous and complex tasks. These things are more likely to be achieved through existing national armed forces, alliances, and military relationships than they are within the structure of a UN command. As habits of cooperation between armed forces develop, and as the UN itself grows, the scope for action under direct UN command may increase: but it must be a slow process.

For the UN there may be risks in too-direct involvement in the management of military force: when terrible mistakes occur, as they inevitably do in military operations, they reflect badly on the organization, and could threaten its universal character.

In the wake of the Cold War, the Security Council came to have a more active role in the employment—or at least authorization—of methods of pressure and force. A possibility of greater East–West cooperation within the UN system had already been indicated by the consensus of the five Permanent Members of the Security Council in agreeing resolution 598 of 20 July 1987 demanding a cease-fire in the Iran–Iraq war; and a cease-fire was achieved in 1988. In November 1990 it authorized the use of force to reverse Iraq's invasion and purported annexation of Kuwait. In December 1992 it authorized the use of force in Somalia 'to establish as soon as possible a secure environment for humanitarian relief operations'.

In some of its new involvements, the Security Council collectively, and its Western Permanent Members individually, were seen by many to be taking some hesitant steps towards a new doctrine and practice of humanitarian intervention—that is, military intervention in a state, without the approval of its authorities, and with the purpose of preventing widespread suffering or death among the inhabitants.[50] The UN Security Council expressly attached great importance to the delivery of humanitarian aid and to other humanitarian concerns in several crises, including those over the Kurds in northern Iraq from 1991, over Somalia and Yugoslavia from 1992, and over Azerbaijan from 1993. In respect of Iraq, the Security Council did say in resolution 688 of 5 April 1991 (which received only ten affirmative votes) that it 'insists that Iraq allow immediate access by international humanitarian organizations to all those in need of assistance in all parts of Iraq'; but such legal justification as could be furnished for the US-led Operation Provide Comfort, which followed, lay in a view of customary law or in a very broad interpretation of the mandate in resolution 678 of November 1990 'to restore international peace and

---

[50] For general discussion of problems concerning the legitimacy of humanitarian intervention see R. Lillich (ed.), *Humanitarian Intervention and the United Nations* (London, 1973); Thomas Franck and Nigel Rodley, 'After Bangladesh: The Law of Humanitarian Intervention by Military Force', *American Journal of International Law*, 67 (1973), p. 275; Michael Akehurst, 'Humanitarian Intervention', in Bull (ed.), *Intervention in World Politics*, pp. 95–118; and Nigel Rodley (ed.), *To Loose the Bands of Wickedness: International Intervention in Defence of Human Rights* (London, 1992).

security in the area'. The operation has to be seen partly in the special context of post-war actions by victors in the territory of defeated adversaries. Further, there were elements of Iraqi consent in the subsequent presence of UN guards in northern Iraq. In Somalia, there was no government to give or refuse consent, so the UN-authorized intervention by UNITAF in December 1992, and its continuation by UNOSOM II in May 1993, can hardly be seen as a classic case of humanitarian intervention. There seems little prospect of the majority of states formally agreeing to any new general doctrine of humanitarian intervention. Indeed, there remains a very strong commitment among many states to the principle of non-intervention. What has occurred is a subtly developing practice in special circumstances, and in which some degree of authority from the Security Council has a significant part.

As UN-controlled forces get involved in more complex missions, in which neat distinctions between humanitarian missions, peacekeeping and enforcement get eroded, the adequacy of the UN's existing machinery for controlling operations is increasingly called into question. In late 1992, leading figures connected with UN peacekeeping activities in both Somalia and Bosnia-Herzegovina had significant disagreements with UN Headquarters in New York. The UN Special Representative for Somalia, Mohammed Sahnoun, resigned on 26 October 1992; and the former head of UN forces in Sarajevo, Major-General Lewis MacKenzie, made a forceful complaint about UN management of operations.[51] That there were problems of supply, command, and control, and a need to strengthen both the staff in New York and headquarters in the field, was readily acknowledged in the Secretariat: the eventual responses included the creation in 1993 of a 'war room' in UN Headquarters to keep it linked with all peacekeeping operations.[52] Nevertheless the capacity of the UN itself to

---

[51] Simon Jones, 'General MacKenzie Slams UN's Nine-to-Fivers', report in *Independent* (London), 31 Jan. 1993.
[52] See Marrack Goulding, Under-Secretary-General for Political Affairs, in his Cyril Foster Lecture at Oxford University, 4 Mar. 1993, 'The Evolution of United Nations Peacekeeping', *International Affairs* (London), 69, no. 3 (July 1993), pp. 460 and 463; and Paul Lewis, 'UN is Developing Control Centre to Coordinate Growing Peacekeeping Role', *New York Times*, 28 Mar. 1993, p. 10.

conduct certain forms of large-scale operations, especially where a stable peace does not exist on the ground, remains limited; and UN forces are not immune from ill-discipline, blunders, and accusations of partisanship and neo-colonialism.

The increasing scope of UN activity in the post-Cold War era has raised the issue of the resuscitation of the extensive Chapter VII provisions for the Security Council itself to have armed forces on call, and to make plans for their use through its Military Staff Committee. *An Agenda for Peace* advances the idea that the UN Security Council might have forces available on a permanent basis, in accord with Article 43, as one means of increasing its credibility and its power to deter.[53] However, this report offers no serious discussion of the reasons why states have traditionally been nervous about proposals for making forces permanently available to the UN. States may well prefer that the provision of military force for UN activities is managed in an *ad hoc* manner, giving them greater control over events. States still guard their power jealously, including their power to decide the exact circumstances in which their armed forces will or will not be used.

Permanent large-scale transfer of forces to the UN in advance of any crisis remains improbable. However, there has been progress on the earmarking, preparation, and training of national military units for possible UN use. This development is roughly in conformity with the modest proposal advanced by Boutros-Ghali in 1993 that national force structures could be broken down into standard 'building blocks' of operational capability, available to the UN on a stand-by basis.[54]

There has been extensive discussion of breathing some life into the UN Military Staff Committee, established under Article 47 of the UN Charter and comprising military representatives of the five Permanent Members.

[53] Boutros-Ghali, *Agenda for Peace*, June 1992, para. 43.
[54] Boutros-Ghali, statement at New York University, 22 Jan. 1993, p. 3; and speech in Washington DC on 25 Mar. 1993. Such an approach was also stressed by Under-Secretary-General Goulding, 'Evolution of UN Peacekeeping', p. 460. These proposals are more modest than the ambitious suggestions in *Agenda for Peace*, esp. para. 43.

Although this committee has met regularly, it has been notoriously ineffective. This was often seen as a consequence of the Cold War, but continued into the 1990s despite the improvements in relations among the Permanent Members: the Western members in particular have remained sceptical of command of enforcement, or even peacekeeping, operations by such a disparate committee. There is little prospect at present of realizing the Charter vision of unified UN command of major military operations. However, the committee has been used for informal exchanges, as in the 1990–1 Gulf crisis. It could conceivably address such matters as the development of rules of engagement and the harmonization of rules of war as they affect multilateral forces, and even tender military advice on general issues.

Although the UN has been much more actively involved in military and other action to maintain the peace than many feared after the rapid disintegration of the World War II alliance, its principal activities have been markedly different from those foreshadowed in the Charter. Boutros-Ghali's *An Agenda for Peace* presents a vision of the UN playing a central role in international security matters, including peacekeeping, but otherwise close to the scheme of the Charter. While many of the ideas he presents in it—including increased peacekeeping activities, and preventive deployments of forces to stop threatened invasions—have already been given some effect in UN operations, the realities are likely to remain more difficult and complex than this vision allows. Differences of perceptions and interests among states, prominent in the Cold War period, continue to be pronounced, making united action on security issues uncertain and difficult. Peacekeeping works well only when there is some peace to keep. In some situations the cost of trying to impose peace is too high. In civil conflicts in particular, peacekeeping and enforcement action may be close to impossible: especially where communal hatreds have become deep-seated, there are no viable geographical lines separating combatants, and the types of weapons used are easily available and difficult to control.

The Charter scheme does not deal specifically with the

question of breakdown of order within states and the outbreak of communal war. Since very early in the UN's history, states have seen the UN as a convenient repository for many such difficult problems. In some such cases, including El Salvador from 1991 onwards, the UN has contributed to the achievement of political solutions. However, the complexity of these problems makes UN involvement risky in each case, and repeatedly forces unsatisfactory choices about whether and how to get involved.

The record of actions under UN auspices, while too significant to deserve a pejorative label of 'selective security', has been too patchy to constitute a reliable system of collective security. In some cases the UN has not acted at all, and indeed in some it has not even been asked to act. When it has acted, many of the means employed have been problematic, both because of the difficulty of the issues, and because of the reluctance of states to commit themselves deeply or take great risks. Despite important exceptions, there has been a tendency to prefer methods of remote control (economic sanctions, air exclusion zones, arms embargoes, attempts to broker cease-fires) or limited involvement with the consent of the parties (peacekeeping, observer, and humanitarian activities). A further problem associated with UN-controlled operations is the rigidity of their mandates and rules of engagement. The fact that the mission of UN forces has to be the subject of advance international agreement can seriously reduce their flexibility in fast-changing situations, leading to criticism from within and from outside.

(g) Possible Changes in the Security Council's Composition and Powers

The UN Charter provisions regarding the composition, procedures, and powers of the Security Council have long been the subject of criticism. It is especially natural that these matters should be debated when, as in the post-Cold War era, the Security Council actually wields considerable power. Many chapters in this volume, especially that by

Peter Wilenski, discuss the tangled problem of Security Council membership and powers. A key difficulty is identifying and agreeing reforms that would not undermine, or might even enhance, the Council's capacity to take effective decisions.

The criticisms of the composition of the Security Council involve several elements: doubt about preserving unaltered, half a century later, the special position of those countries which were allies in World War II; concern that three of those powers—France, the UK, and the USA—make most of the running in the Security Council; irritation, especially on the part of Germany and Japan, about 'taxation without representation'; and frustration that the views of the non-permanent members of the Security Council, and indeed of the great majority of the General Assembly, count for little. These criticisms could become much more serious if perceptions mount of the Security Council having pursued unacceptable or ill-advised policies on central issues.

It is natural that over time, as circumstances change, there should be pressures for reform of the arrangements regarding the composition of the main decision-making body of an international organization. Whether such reforms will lead to a better decision-making process is, inevitably, uncertain. One unpromising precedent is that between 1922 and 1936 the number of non-permanent members of the League of Nations Council was successively increased from four to eleven—a reform which was of marginal relevance to the larger question of the League's capacity to act effectively.

Change of the UN Security Council's composition is by no means impossible: in 1965, through amendment to Article 23 of the Charter, the number of non-permanent members was increased from six to ten. Now there are various widely canvassed proposals for further expansion. Japan and Germany have often been named as possible Permanent Members of the Security Council, especially in American statements.[55] However, there is bound to be

[55] Bill Clinton said while campaigning for the presidency: 'Japan and Germany should be made permanent members of the UN Security Council'

resistance to increasing the number of vetoes, and to any proposal which would give two conspicuously 'Northern' states the same status as the five, while leaving out Brazil, Egypt, India, Indonesia, Nigeria, and others. More acceptable proposals for Charter amendment might involve a new category of Permanent Member without veto; or, perhaps most likely if there is any change, an expansion of the number of non-permanent members.

The veto system privileges a group of five states in a way that is bound to be contentious; and it is widely perceived as having held the UN back from fulfilling its functions in the Cold War years. Yet the veto has merits as well as faults: it helped to get and keep the major powers within a UN framework when they would otherwise have either not joined it in the first place or else deserted it; it may have saved the UN from damaging conflicts with its major members, and from involvement in divisive or impossible missions; it has contributed to a sense of responsibility and a habit of careful consultation among the permanent five; and it reduces the risk of acute discrepancies between power politics and the law of the UN Charter. In short, the veto can be viewed as one of several factors which have made for the superiority of the UN's decision-making procedures over those of its predecessor the League of Nations, and over many regional organizations.

Modification or abandonment of the veto would be problematic. The procedures governing the matter of Charter amendment make any change affecting this power particularly difficult, as the consent of the countries concerned would be required. Article 108 stipulates that all Charter amendments must be adopted by two thirds of the members of the General Assembly; and be ratified, in accord with their respective constitutional processes, by two-thirds of members of the UN, including all the Permanent Members of the Security Council.

(address to Foreign Policy Association, 1 Apr. 1992). In June 1993, pursuant to GA Res. 47/62 of 11 Dec. 1992, the US informed the Secretary-General that it 'supports permanent membership for Japan and Germany'; that it was 'also prepared to consider carefully how the Council might be further expanded to include a modest number of additional seats'; and that other means of involving non-members of the Council should be explored.

Membership in the permanent five entails heavy costs as well as privilege. In problematic UN undertakings it brings the risk of direct association with failure. Membership also involves assuming a larger share of costs of peacekeeping forces;[56] and in some cases pressure to follow up votes in the Security Council with the commitment of forces in crisis-torn areas. That power has its rewards is indicated by the tenacity with which Britain and France hang on to their position as members of the permanent five. Yet the overextension of Britain's and France's capabilities, so familiar in the nineteenth century, may be re-emerging in UN colours.

Meanwhile, other states have vetoes of a kind on enforcement actions. First, there is the so-called 'sixth veto' on the Security Council—the capacity of the Security Council members to defeat a resolution by denying it the nine affirmative votes needed to pass. Secondly, despite the words of the Charter, states do not have to take part in enforcement or peacekeeping operations if they do not so wish. In the matter of use of their forces, they are more than mere pawns of the UN.

In the history of the United Nations, much has been achieved by changes in practice rather than Charter revision.[57] Further changes could include strengthening existing arrangements so that the selection of non-permanent members more closely reflects contributions to the UN's work as well as equitable geographical distribution; and developing more regular Security Council consultation with major states and interested parties. Such changes, though hard to implement when UN decision-making procedures are so overloaded, might go at least some way toward meeting the strong

[56] Developed countries are levied at the same rate for peacekeeping as for the regular budget; less-developed countries at 20% of their regular rate; least-developed countries at 10%. The Permanent Members are assessed the remainder: USA 30.38 % of peacekeeping costs, France 7.29%, UK 6.1%, China 0.94%. Reallocation of the USSR's 11.44% has caused difficulties.

[57] The succession of Russia to the USSR seat in the Security Council in Dec. 1991/Jan. 1992 was a remarkably smooth example: Art. 23 was not amended.

concerns of certain states about being left out of decisions that affect them vitally.[58]

Just as the power of national governments needs to be subject to constraints both internal and external, so the UN itself, even the Security Council, is far from infallible. The UN faces the familiar constitutional problem of maintaining and enhancing the effectiveness of the Security Council while simultaneously ensuring that it is subject to adequate controls. The Council is constrained by the general prudence of member-states, and the factual limitations of what is actually possible. Other long-established controls—many of which have also limited the Council's effectiveness—include the composition and voting rules of the Council, the inability of the Council to commit forces without the express consent of the troop-contributing states, limitations on the effective enforcement of sanctions, and budgetary constraints through the General Assembly. There remain difficulties in devising controls on contentious actions by the Security Council in several situations: where the Council takes an exceptionally wide view of what constitutes a threat to or breach of the peace, thus investing itself with the extensive powers of Chapter VII; where the Council confers a very wide power, as in resolution 678 of 29 November 1990 authorizing the use of force against Iraq to 'restore international peace and security in the area'; or where the Council purports by resolution to determine certain fundamental legal rights and duties. The question of judicial review of Security Council actions has arisen tangentially in cases brought in the International Court of Justice by Libya in 1992 and Bosnia-Herzegovina in 1993, but the Court has not ventured far in this area.[59]

[58] A twenty-strong 'Chapter VII Consultation Committee' of the General Assembly, to keep an open line between the Security Council and the General Assembly, is proposed by W. Michael Reisman, 'The Constitutional Crisis in the United Nations', *American Journal of International Law*, 87 (1993), p. 98.

[59] *Questions of Interpretation and Application of the 1971 Montreal Convention arising from the Aerial Incident at Lockerbie*, (*Libya* v. *USA* and *Libya* v. *UK*), Provisional Measures (Orders of 14 Apr. 1992), *ICJ Reports*, 1992, pp. 3 and 114; *Case Concerning Application of the Convention on the Prevention and Punishment of the Crime of Genocide (Bosnia and Herzegovina* v. *Federal Republic of Yugoslavia (Serbia and Montenegro))*, Order Indicating Provisional Measures of Protection, 8 Apr. 1993, *ICJ Reports*, 1993.

(h) Equality and Dominance in the UN

The UN Charter enshrines the principle of the sovereign equality of states. The commitment of international organizations in the UN period to the global application of this principle is historically unparalleled. Almost all earlier systems of states contained strong elements of suzerainty and other types of formal or informal relationships of dominance.[60] Many such elements have in fact remained features of international relations in the UN era. Nevertheless the strength of the commitment to sovereign equality has added legitimacy to attacks on inequality and dominance, and has shaped the structure of these relations.

Perceptions of dominance are the stuff of rhetoric, and require careful analysis. The complexity of the problem is illustrated by the fact that two states can each perceive the other as dominant; by the phenomenon that some states accused of domination see themselves as essentially anti-imperialistic; and by the way in which accusations of domination can themselves be used by governments as justifications for exerting pressure on other states.

Arguments that the UN system itself is improperly used as an instrument of domination have had continuous currency throughout the history of the organization. In the early years there were repeated accusations, mainly from the USSR and its allies, that the organization as a whole, and the General Assembly in particular, were controlled by the USA. The rise of the Third World majority in the UN General Assembly in the 1960s, and the frequent Soviet support of Third World positions, led to a completely different perception, especially in the USA, of an organization biased against the West. Then, once regular cooperation became established in the Security Council from about 1987, a new perception began to emerge of an activist Security Council dominated by the USA and its allies. Some Third World states

[60] See esp. Adam Watson, *The Evolution of International Society: A Comparative Historical Analysis* (London, 1992).

expressed the fear that the UN might be becoming a cloak for a new form of imperialism. In general, perceptions of the UN as a whole being dominated by particular states involve gross oversimplifications.

Each of these perceptions was accompanied by accusations of 'double standards', that the UN would act in support of dominant interests but neglect other cases of equal or greater merit. Such accusations were already rife by the time of the Suez crisis.[61] They have persisted ever since, and are an almost unavoidable feature of politics. In an organization which has to take decisions in matters involving both general principles and harsh realities, substantive consistency is extraordinarily difficult to achieve, even where procedural standards are applied evenly.

Perceptions that the UN is dominated by particular states can have serious consequences. They have led to refusals to make contributions to various parts of the UN budget; to disregard of General Assembly resolutions; and to mixed support for Security Council enforcement initiatives.

The Charter does make some accommodation with hierarchies of power, most notably in the provisions regarding the Permanent Five in the Security Council, and also regarding trusteeship. Inequality, if not hegemony, is a fundamental feature of international life, and it would be remarkable if it were not reflected in the practice of the UN. While past UN practice has not always been premissed on the substantive equality of states, it has generally accepted the core idea of equal sovereignty for independent states. In response to the problems of massive human rights violations, endemic civil wars, and failing states, the Security Council has begun to countenance deeper inroads into traditional state prerogatives. The possibility of new forms of dominance emerging

---

[61] One illustration is L. C. Green, 'The Double Standard of the United Nations', *Year Book of World Affairs*, 11 (1957), pp. 104–37. The author was principally concerned to indict the USA and India for embracing double standards in their criticisms of the British role in the 1956 Suez crisis.

under UN auspices is a source of concern to governments in potential target areas.

(i) Peaceful Change

A central issue in evaluating the UN has to be its contribution, or otherwise, to the achievement of peaceful change. It was well recognized at the time of the UN's foundation, as it had been during the League of Nations period, that to attempt simply to maintain peace, without providing mechanisms for peaceful change, would be a recipe for immobilism and eventual failure. Bearing in mind the scope of changes in the world since 1945—the process of European decolonization, the decline of old powers and the emergence or re-emergence of new ones, shifts in the sources and nature of economic power, the rapid development of military technology, the collapse of regimes in eastern Europe and the Soviet Union in 1989–91—it is striking how many developments which could easily have occasioned major wars did not do so. While by no means all change has been peaceful, a great deal of peaceful change has been achieved. The UN does not deserve all the credit for this, but it does deserve some.

The general structure of international order embodied by the UN, and some of the principles and rhetoric associated with it, may have played some part in providing a relatively benign framework for changes in ideologies and political systems. Such changes have deep causes, unconnected with the UN. However, during the Gorbachev era the framework of cooperative international order made it easier for Soviet leaders to down-play the centrality of ideological division as a governing feature of international relations. There was a corresponding emphasis in Gorbachev's foreign policy on a much increased role for the UN, initiated in his sweeping proposals of September 1987.[62] This emphasis was pursued in some respects by

---

[62] Mikhail Gorbachev, 'Reality and the Guarantees of a Secure World', *Pravda* (Moscow), 17 Sept. 1987. In this long article the Soviet leader suggested *inter alia* setting up 'under the aegis of the UN a mechanism for extensive international verification of compliance with agreements to lessen international

the successor Russian leadership even after the demise of the Gorbachev regime and the USSR in December 1991.[63]

Although there has been peaceful change, it is also true that much important change has not been achieved: most notably in fields of international justice between advantaged and disadvantaged, included and marginalized, North and South. The UN has done much to fuel the revolution of rising expectations which has given voice and strength to diverse and sometimes inconsistent demands for global justice. These demands were themselves translated by their proponents into higher standards against which to measure and criticize the UN's performance, especially during the heyday of arguments for a New International Economic Order in the 1970s. Fundamental differences within the international community about these demands (and about the legitimacy of some of them) were not resolved within or outside the UN. The UN has in some limited respects been seen as an obstacle to their realization, but the principal obstacles to peaceful change in this area are so great as to be largely beyond the UN's resources. This point has been increasingly accepted by many political leaders in South and North, and there has been a gradual and limited convergence of views about what the UN can and should do, reflected for example in the 1992 Cartagena agreement about the future direction of the UN Conference on Trade and Development (UNCTAD). Other demands for justice, including on gender equality and religious freedom, expose sharp differences. The UN is constantly implicated in compromises between values of order and justice, but the system remains weighted toward maintaining order.

tension, limit arms and monitor the military situation in areas of conflict'. He also proposed wider use of 'UN military observers and UN peacekeeping forces in disengaging the troops of warring sides and monitoring cease-fire and armistice agreements': this did presage an increased use of such forces in subsequent years. See too his speech at the UN General Assembly, on 7 Dec. 1988.

[63] e.g. Pres. Yeltsin's speech at the Security Council summit, 31 Jan. 1992. Facing economic difficulties, and pressure on it to address conflicts in neighbouring states, Russia later became more concerned at the mounting bills for UN peacekeeping, and more sceptical generally about UN capacities.

(j) Role in Proclaiming International Priorities and Principles

Despite all its failings, the UN has by no means lost its importance as a proclaimer of international standards. This is a complex role, which is central both to the maintenance of a viable international order and to the communication, consolidation and development of shared values within international society.

The centre-piece of the UN's proclamation of international principles and standards remains even today the Charter of 1945. The Charter, or at least the Charter order, proclaims such principles as sovereign equality; territorial integrity and political independence of states; equal rights and self-determination of peoples; non-intervention in internal affairs except under Chapter VII; peaceful settlement of disputes; abstention from threats or uses of force; fulfillment in good faith of international obligations; international cooperation; and respect for and promotion of human rights and fundamental freedoms without discrimination.[64] Inevitably there are differences in interpretation of terse statements of principle drawn up by a limited group of states in a somewhat different world. Nevertheless the dominant diplomatic view, expressed by the late Judge Nagendra Singh in his chapter below, has been that the Charter principles are an exemplary basis for the conduct of international relations, and that the need is not to rethink any of them but to focus, as the UN has done, on elaborating them and developing new principles where necessary. There are, however, fundamental tensions between some of the principles, as between territorial integrity and self-determination, or non-intervention and human rights.[65] Where revisionist pressures have become

[64] On the declaratory tradition, represented *par excellence* by the UN, as a form of international ethical discourse, see Dorothy V. Jones, 'The Declaratory Tradition in Modern International Law', in Terry Nardin and David R. Mapel (eds.), *Traditions of International Ethics* (Cambridge, 1992), pp. 42–61.

[65] Contrast e.g. H. Lauterpacht, *International Law and Human Rights* (London, 1950), with J. S. Watson, 'Autointerpretation, Competence, and the Continuing Validity of Article 2(7) of the UN Charter', *American Journal of International Law*, 71 (1977), p. 60. See also the Declaration on the Inadmissibility of Intervention in the Domestic Affairs of States and the Protection of their Independence and Sovereignty—GA Res. 2131 (XX) of 21 Dec. 1965.

very strong there has been controversy about relations between values of order and of justice, expressed for instance in debates about the relations of the principles of peaceful settlement and non-use of force on the one hand and human rights and self-determination on the other. There has also been criticism of the state-centric nature of the set of Charter principles, occasionally because of fundamental dissatisfaction with the Charter scheme as a foundation for global order, but more often with a view to adding further principles directed towards re-distributing wealth or power, to empowering non-state groups (especially 'peoples'), or to reorienting priorities toward, for example, developmental or ecological concerns.[66]

Another view of the Charter principles is that they are incorrigibly idealistic. In many ways, however, the Charter is a distinctly hard-headed document.[67] For example, it is extremely cautious in what it says about disarmament; and it refers not to the long-asserted but highly problematic principle of 'national self-determination', but to the much vaguer formulation 'equal rights and self-determination of peoples', which was less haunted by ghosts from Europe's history between the two world wars.[68] To some extent the Charter anticipated the growth of concern with economic and social matters and with human rights, the advent of regional security organizations, and the process of decolonization.

In addition to these different interpretations of the Charter's actual provisions, there are different views of its whole ethos. Some, particularly those steeped in constitutionalist domestic polities such as the USA, are inclined to find the solution to questions of all sorts in

[66] For one such perspective, see Richard A. Falk, Samuel S. Kim, and Saul H. Mendlovitz (eds.), *The United Nations and a Just World Order* (Boulder, Colo., 1991).

[67] Note the remarks of Ian Brownlie, 'The United Nations as a Form of World Government', *Harvard International Law Journal*, 13 (1972), p. 421.

[68] On the development of thought and practice about self-determination in the UN framework, see A. Rigo Sureda, *The Evolution of the Right to Self-Determination* (Leiden, 1973); and Michla Pomerance, *Self-Determination in Law and Practice: The New Doctrine in the United Nations* (London, 1982).

the interpretation and reinterpretation of the Charter provisions. This tendency has often coincided with organic views of an expanding and diversifying UN, founded on an ethos of continuous progress, and sustained by teleological interpretations of the original Charter language. The Charter embodies the architecture of a dynamic organization, but it is not a complete constitution for international society. The Charter's foundational principles do not contain prescriptions for all problems of international public order, let alone for all issues of international justice. The UN has thus been concerned both to elaborate existing principles and to formulate new standards, a task it has shared with many other international institutions.

The UN serves an important function in shaping the international agenda, and in both facilitating and conditioning the articulation of new political demands. It has contributed to global awareness of numerous issues, including racial discrimination, torture and disappearances, rights of children, illiteracy, international dimensions of poverty, problems relating to refugees, and protection of cultural heritage. It has got deeply involved in a wide range of environmental issues: Patricia Birnie's chapter points both to the UN's contribution and to the problems of simultaneous and sometimes uncoordinated action in areas of environmental policy by a multitude of UN subsidiary bodies and specialized agencies. The UN has roles in areas such as the control of the production, trade, and consumption of narcotics, where international coordination of national policies and actions is more effective if accompanied by collective legitimation of otherwise controversial measures.[69] More generally, UN endorsement lends legitimacy to doctrines and ideas, as with those concerning development assistance, the 'common heritage of mankind' in the deep sea-bed and outer space, and the unacceptability of colonialism. UN endorsement may also legitimize compromise solutions

[69] See e.g. Ethan A. Nadelmann, 'Global Prohibition Regimes: The Evolution of Norms in International Society', *International Organization*, 44 (1990), pp. 479–526.

reached in particular international disputes and crises—a point developed in Anthony Parsons' chapter.

UN and regional standard-setting instruments, and the bodies charged with their implementation, have prompted a convergence of the public pronouncements of states in a common international rhetoric of human rights. To a much smaller extent this convergence is mirrored in domestic practice. It remains the case that, despite the existence of many purportedly definitive agreements on the subject, different societies have and will continue to have very different conceptions of the nature, content, and importance of human rights.[70] Nevertheless, the growth in importance attached to human rights in most states is in significant measure a product of the extensive activity stimulated by the UN: international standards and institutions have provided a basis for domestic human rights activism and resistance to governmental oppression as well as for international pressure.

There are signs, albeit limited, that the UN may be becoming more closely associated with the promotion of multi-party democracy. Since the late 1980s it has been involved in election-monitoring activities in many independent countries, including Nicaragua, Haiti, El Salvador, Angola, Cambodia, and Mozambique. While several of these operations have related to international peace and security and been undertaken under the auspices of the Security Council, there is also noticeably less opposition in the General Assembly to such activities than in earlier periods. Boutros-Ghali has put great emphasis on democracy and its significance both for economic development and for international peace.[71] However, many states continue to emphasize the principle

---

[70] See generally Aldeeb Abu-Sahlieh *et al.* (eds.), *Universalité des droits de l'homme et diversité des cultures* (Fribourg, 1984); John Humphrey, *Human Rights and the United Nations: A Great Adventure* (Dobbs Ferry, NY, 1984); Jack Donnelly, *The Concept of Human Rights* (London, 1985); R. J. Vincent, *Human Rights and International Relations* (Cambridge, 1986). Sharply differenct views as to the nature and place of human rights were pressed at the 1993 World Conference on Human Rights in Vienna, discussed by Farer and Gaer, p. 295 below.

[71] Boutros-Ghali, *Agenda for Peace*, paras. 9, 81–2. He also discussed this in speeches in Boston on 16 Mar. 1993 and Washington DC on 25 Mar. 1993.

of non-interference in internal affairs, and there is no
consensus on the universal desirability of particular democratic models. Moreover, the vast problems of transition
from authoritarian to democratic systems, and of establishing democratic structures in the face of severe communal division, involve much more than the UN and
other international agencies can realistically provide, as
developments in some successor states of the former
Yugoslavia and the former Soviet Union make clear.
Nevertheless, the legitimizing effect of pro-democratic
incantations and international observation, and such
practical contributions as electoral aid and voter education, may well be important for emerging democracies and
for vulnerable existing democracies.[72]

UN standard-setting, while often useful, can be deeply
flawed. The necessities of coalition maintenance may lead
to incoherent compromises, or to the agglomeration of
demands in such grand abstractions as the 'New World
Information and Communication Order'.[73] The UN has
sometimes been involved in the advocacy of principles
which are undefined, contradictory, or essentially and
fiercely contested. One of many possible examples is that
relating to the principles which were recognized in
the charter and judgment of the International Military
Tribunal at Nuremberg in 1945–6, at which German war
criminals were convicted. On 11 December 1946 the UN
General Assembly unanimously adopted a brief resolution
affirming these Nuremberg principles. Subsequent attempts
by the International Law Commission and other bodies to
codify these principles did not gain general acceptance by
states, partly because of the resistance of some states to
recognizing the legitimacy of disobeying superior orders.
However, the Statute of the International Tribunal on war
crimes in former Yugoslavia, adopted unanimously by the
Security Council in May 1993, did contain provisions on
superior orders and other key principles.[74]

---

[72] See generally Larry Diamond, Juan Linz, and Seymour Martin Lipset (eds),
Democracy in Developing Countries, 4 vols. (Boulder, Colo., 1989–92).

[73] See generally Peterson, *The General Assembly in World Politics*.

[74] The affirmation of the principles of international law recognized at

In many cases the rhetorical declamation of sweeping principles by the UN has clouded judgement. In this respect there are some highly simplistic elements in the ethos of the organization which need to be questioned from within as well as without. To take just one example, the UN increasingly committed itself over the years to the goal of general and complete disarmament, and the General Assembly held Special Sessions on disarmament in 1978, 1982 and 1988. However, there was little analysis under UN auspices of why ambitious calls for disarmament, which have been a persistent feature of international life since at least 1899, have invariably failed. In particular, the possibility that the idea of general and complete disarmament as commonly proposed may contain some inbuilt defects (rather than merely face external 'obstacles') seldom got a hearing. General and complete disarmament had the character of a myth to which the UN subscribed, rather than an issue which it rigorously analysed. This disarmament approach, about which Michael Howard is notably sceptical in his chapter, has several possible costs. First, it can contribute to verbal hostility between states, as they blame each other for the failure to achieve disarmament. Second, by presenting a mythological alternative to armaments it may distract attention from other possibly more fruitful approaches to the urgent problem of controlling and limiting military force—including many approaches in arms control and laws of war matters which the UN has pursued. And third, it risks having the same effect as did the League of Nations' commitment to disarmament in the 1920s and 1930s—namely, not just that it will fail to produce results, but that in so doing it will weaken the international organization which had committed itself so deeply to this

Nuremberg is in GA Res. 95 (I) of 11 Dec. 1946. The International Law Commission's formulation of the Nuremberg principles is in *Yearbook of the International Law Commission* (1950), vol. 2, pp. 374–8. The General Assembly's non-committal response to this formulation is in GA Res. 488 (V) of 12 Dec. 1950. On the subsequent history of this issue see also *Yearbook of the International Law Commission* (1954), vol. 2, pp. 150–2; and GA Res. 897 (IX) of 4 Dec. 1954. The International Tribunal on Yugoslavia was provided for in SC Res. 827 of 25 May 1993, approving the Statute in UN doc. S/25704 of 3 May 1993.

approach.[75] In the post-Cold War era there are signs that the UN, including its Office of Disarmament Affairs, is taking a less propagandistic view of disarmament, but it is not yet clear that a coherent vision of the place of arms limitation in international politics has emerged.[76]

Other principles espoused by the UN have also proved problematical in practice. In the post-Cold War era, crises arising from the distintegration of federal states have raised questions about the appropriateness of asserting the instant and undifferentiated applicability of certain vital principles derived from the somewhat different context of inter-state relations. The principle that the changing of frontiers by force can never be accepted is fundamental in contemporary international relations, and was immediately invoked by the international community in connection with the Yugoslav crisis.[77] It was held to be applicable both because of the characterization of the crisis as a conflict between states, and because dangerous precedents could be set by successful grabs for territory on largely ethnic grounds. Yet there must be a question as to whether it was wise to express this legal principle so forcefully in the special context of the disintegration of federal states where, as in this case, some of the existing 'frontiers' have no physical existence and lack both logic and legitimacy, where there are such deep-seated ethnic problems, and where almost any imaginable outcome short of massive conflagration involves some *de facto* success for those who have sought to change frontiers by force.

[75] For critical examinations of the idea of 'general and complete disarmament' see Hedley Bull, *The Control of the Arms Race* (London, 1961); and John W. Spanier and Joseph L. Nogee, *The Politics of Disarmament* (New York, 1962). See also R. B. Byers and Stanley Ing (eds.), *Arms Limitation and the United Nations* (Toronto, 1982).

[76] See esp. Boutros-Ghali, 'New Dimensions of Arms Regulation and Disarmament in the Post-Cold War Era: Report of the Secretary-General on the Occasion of Disarmament Week, 27 October 1992', UN doc. A/C.1/47/7, issued by UN Dept. for Public Information, Oct. 1992.

[77] See e.g. the Declaration of 3 Sept. 1991 of the CSCE states; SC Res. 713 of 25 Sept. 1991, and numerous subsequent Security Council resolutions; the Statement on the Situation in Yugoslavia, issued by the North Atlantic Council meeting in Rome, 7–8 Nov. 1991, para. 2; and the Statement of Principles adopted on 26 Aug. 1992 by the London Conference on the Former Socialist Federal Republic of Yugoslavia, para. ii.

The experience of the UN era has shown that there are problems, not only in the unequal application of principles in comparable cases, but also in attempts to apply the same principles to very different situations, regions, and countries. It is in the nature of a global organization to seek to develop and apply common standards. The universalizing tendency is continuously confronted with differences, whether between high technology and low technology countries in ability to control toxic emissions, or secular democracies and non-democratic theocracies in governmental and social attitudes to the position of women, or maritime and landlocked countries in ability to exploit freedom of high seas fishing. The UN has developed numerous exceptions allowing differential application of general principles for developing countries, or specially affected states, or states with special needs, and many principles themselves are carefully contextualized.

The UN has had particular difficulty in enunciating effective principles for tackling perhaps the most basic and fundamental division of international life—the division between the largely affluent societies of the North and the largely poor societies of the South.[78] Conscious of a link between economic disruption and war, those who framed the UN Charter placed much emphasis on economic and social progress;[79] after a long period of virtual silence on the subject, the Security Council began to return rhetorically to the theme of the connection between development and international peace in the early 1990s, although with little in the way of immediate results. The UN General Assembly began to proclaim an ideology of development, couched increasingly in terms of rights or entitlements, from the mid-1960s. However, in this area more than in many others there has been a huge gulf between the UN rhetoric and the progress actually achieved in large parts of the South. As Kenneth Dadzie's

[78] For a useful political history of UN debates see Peter Marshall, 'The North–South Dialogue: Britain at Odds', in Erik Jensen and Thomas Fisher (eds.), *The United Kingdom—The United Nations* (London, 1990), pp. 159–208.
[79] See esp. UN Charter, preamble and Chaps. IX and X.

chapter shows, expectations that the UN could play a central role in development issues have had to yield to a more cautious and nuanced view of its actual and potential role, and indeed of the nature of the development process itself. The rhetorical and programmatic UN commitment to development has nevertheless continued, although it has proved increasingly difficult to integrate this commitment to other UN priorities. A long-running debate on the real relations between human rights against the state and state-supervised development has never been effectively resolved beyond superficial agreement on the formula that they are mutually interdependent. The debate on relations between environment and development has similarly produced a verbal commitment to 'sustainable development', but without an underlying reconciliation of the very different agendas. The backdrop of the general unwillingness of the North to make the sacrifices necessary to finance the development urged by the South has not changed greatly throughout the UN period, but the UN has contributed to improved understanding of the issues.

Although it has been embroiled in controversy on matters to do with the principles it espouses, as well as in other areas of its activities, the UN has by no means lost its legitimacy. Nor has it lost its important capacity to confer legitimacy.[80] Participation in UN activities has helped confer legitimacy on new states which might otherwise be uncertain of their status; on particular regimes within states; and on certain non-state entities, such as the Palestine Liberation Organization and the South West Africa People's Organization.[81]

---

[80] An early study of the importance of the UN's role in conferring legitimacy is Inis Claude, 'Collective Legitimization as a Political Function of the United Nations', *International Organization*, 20 (1966), p. 367.

[81] National liberation movements recognized by the Organization of African Unity or the League of Arab States were granted observer status in the UN Conference on the Representation of States in Their Relations with International Organizations by the General Assembly 'in accordance with the practice of the United Nations'—GA Res. 3247 (XXIX) of 29 Nov. 1974. Numerous other resolutions and administrative decisions also confer status on such groups: the African National Congress (ANC), the PLO, the Pan-Africanist

The UN has an important role in the matter of recognition of states and governments. Its record is far from perfect—witness the exclusion of communist China from the UN from 1949 to 1971. However, the considerable (though by no means total) agreement about what states exist, and what governments represent those states, is due in part to the role of the UN as an intergovernmental body which admits (or refuses to admit) states as members, and examines the credentials of the representatives of those states. When the UN admits member states, it is not only conferring recognition on them, but also implicitly giving them a kind of guarantee against external attack. However, in their practice during the collapse of the Soviet Union and Yugoslavia in 1991–2 UN members appeared to pay little attention to traditional criteria for recognition of new states, which include consideration as to whether a state really exists and coheres as a political and social entity.[82] While there may exceptionally be a case for hasty acts of recognition, they are in principle undesirable, and in some circumstances risk dragging the UN even further into costly ethnic and territorial conflicts.

The UN's functions in proclaiming principles and conferring legitimacy remain central to the effective maintenance of international society. If international society is to develop further, however, a much greater emphasis on effective implementation of standards must be the highest priority.[83] As Frank Berman puts it:

It seems to many that the problem is not to discover what the law is, or how to apply it to the particular case, or even whether the existing rule is 'satisfactory' or not, but rather how to secure or compel compliance with the law at all. It may be that we have

Congress of Azania (PAC), and the South West Africa People's Organization (SWAPO) were permitted, for instance, to sign the Final Act of the Third UN Conference on the Law of the Sea in 1982, though not to sign the Convention accompanying it.

[82] For materials on these issues in respect of the emergence of states from Yugoslavia, see Daniel Bethlehem and Marc Weller (eds.), *The 'Yugoslav' Crisis in International Law* (Cambridge, 1993, forthcoming).

[83] For an example of useful work on implementation in the human rights field, see Philip Alston (ed.), *The United Nations and Human Rights: A Critical Appraisal* (Oxford, 1992).

now passed from a great phase of new law-making to a period where the focus is not on new substantive law but on how to make existing law more effective.[84]

(k) Problems of Rhetoric and Reform

While the UN has considerable achievements to its credit, it also has ingrained faults—not least in its institutional ethos and its organizational structure. Some of these have adversely affected its performance: indeed, the UN can at times exacerbate the problems it is intended to ameliorate.

The faults of the institutional ethos have been of several kinds. The long-established diplomatic practice of using verbal formulas to conceal real differences has flourished to excess in the UN framework. The equally ancient habit of resorting to rhetorical approaches to complex problems has also had a prominent place in the General Assembly and in many other parts of the system. Such styles of discourse can cloud analysis and hamper effective decision-making. There has been a tendency to sententious proclamation which exaggerates the importance of resolutions and texts at the expense of serious consideration of the substantive realities which underlie them. Especially in the Security Council, but also elsewhere, there has been occasional evidence of escalating isolation from reality: participants have sometimes appeared to assume that what is solemnly resolved in New York will be capable of being, and will actually be, transformed into effective action.

Within the UN system there has not been a tradition of reflective debate about the organization's overall place in international relations; and the contribution of the academic community to major UN debates has been relatively limited. There has often been a simplified view of the past, reinforcing tendencies toward temporal parochialism. The UN system has also been characterized by a parochial form of internationalism, employing

---

[84] Frank Berman (Legal Adviser to the UK Foreign and Commonwealth Office), Preface to Hazel Fox and Michael Meyer (eds.), *Effecting Compliance* (London, 1993), p. xii.

rhetoric which suggests that all peoples and countries think alike, that they share the same concerns and the same interests, when the practical experience of the organization itself has frequently testified to the contrary. Similarly there has often been blithe disregard in face of well-founded or politically damning criticism.

As to its organizational structure and formal procedures, the urgency of reform is now widely acknowledged, and there remain pressing needs for streamlining and rationalization within and beyond the UN system. The UN has a successful if unexciting history of evolution, and will certainly need to change further to meet its wide range of responsibilities. The need to reform or strengthen the UN has been argued with passion since its inception.[85] In this book, Maurice Bertrand outlines the history of efforts at reform, based on a frank assessment of the organization's failures; and Peter Wilenski gives a very full account of the problems of UN reform as they have emerged in the post-Cold War era. These and other chapters illustrate the point that adaptation and change in organizational structures, in procedures, and in practices is an organic process. It involves responding pragmatically, with elements of precedent and common law, to problems for which old frameworks or approaches are inadequate. Many such changes have not come under the crusading banner of 'reform'.

(l) Conclusion

The roles of the UN must not be seen in isolation from other aspects of international relations. Part of the genius of the Charter order is precisely the integration of the UN into the wider structure of the international system.[86]

---

[85] e.g. Commission to Study the Organization of Peace, *Strengthening the United Nations* (New York, 1957).

[86] In *International Law is a Divided World* (Oxford, 1986), Antonio Cassese identifies a traditional 'Westphalia model' and a new 'UN Charter model' of international law (pp. 396–407), but finds that at present 'international law possesses "two souls", and the second seems incapable of supplanting the first' (p. 4).

The ancient institutions of diplomacy and balance of power, operating only slightly differently in the UN era, remain fundamental features of the international system. Over centuries, states have devised numerous means of harmonizing their interests, mitigating their conflicts, or at least preventing disputes from leading to total war. True, these means have been far from perfect—witness the outbreak of two world wars in this century. But many of the functions which the UN performs can be—and sometimes are—performed also by other entities. If the UN has mediated in some disputes, it is also true that in other conflicts other mediators or arbitrators have been used: for example, in 1979–84 it was papal mediation which settled the long-standing Beagle Channel dispute between Argentina and Chile.[87] If UN peacekeeping forces have been used in some conflicts, non-UN forces have helped settle other long-standing problems: for example, the Commonwealth forces which monitored the elections and transfer of power in Zimbabwe in 1980 following the Lancaster House agreement of the previous year. If the UN has contributed notably to the development of international law, it is also true that this body of law is very much older than the UN, is well rooted in the overlapping interests of states, develops outside as well as within UN auspices, and would continue to exist even if the UN were to disappear tomorrow.[88] If states have on occasion paid a high political price for ignoring UN principles and procedures, in other cases the political restraints on state behaviour have operated quite independently of the UN.

[87] For a succinct summary of the papal mediation between Argentina and Chile see *Keesing's Contemporary Archives* (1984), p. 32781; and (1985), p. 33517. See also E. Lauterpacht in *Mélanges Virally* (Paris, 1991), pp. 359–71.

[88] Evidence of the vitality of legal development outside the UN framework may be gleaned, for instance, by reference to the fact that the four Geneva Conventions on the protection of victims of war, concluded by states under the auspices of the International Committee of the Red Cross rather than the UN, had 181 parties on 16 June 1993—not counting two ex-Soviet states which are bound through succession, but had not yet formally indicated this. The work of The Hague Conference on Private International Law, of the Commonwealth, and of regional intergovernmental organizations may also be cited in this context.

Many states and groups of states have achieved a degree of stability in their international relations by means which do not depend on the UN, but which are compatible with (and even foreseen by) the UN system. Many governments rely on their individual or collective possession of military power, rather than on any benign UN framework.

The UN era has been characterized also by the development of a remarkable variety of regional and sub-regional organizations whether of a political, economic, or military character. Chapter VIII of the UN Charter envisaged a significant place for such organizations, but in fact their roles have been disparate. Reasons for using regional organizations in handling disputes include participation by local powers, burden-sharing, relief of UN overload, and avoidance of controversial involvement of extra-regional powers. Possible drawbacks include local hegemony, lack of regional cooperation and resources, proximity creating vulnerability, and multiplicity of possible organizations in a single region with consequent problems of choice, rivalry, and confusion. Regional organizations may well take on greater roles, as Boutros-Ghali has urged, but in most cases there is little prospect that they will supplant the role of the UN.[89]

The UN has become, over the course of its first half century, an established part of the firmament of international relations. It is involved in a huge range of activities, many of them central to the functioning of international society. The UN is best seen, not as a vehicle for completely restructuring or replacing the system of sovereign states, so much as ameliorating the problems spawned by its imperfections, and managing processes of rapid change in many distinct fields. The UN finds roles for itself in those areas of activity which are most appropriately tackled either on a truly multilateral basis, or by individuals representing, not a particular state, but the collectivity of states. To the extent that the UN is involved in the transformation of international society, it is not by creating a new and conceptually simple supra-national

---

[89] *Agenda for Peace*, paras. 60–5.

structure, but by participating in a more general process whereby management of different problems is allocated to different, albeit overlapping and fluctuating, levels.

'The tents have been struck, and the great caravan of humanity is once more on the march.' So said Jan Christian Smuts in 1918, at the time of the planning of the League of Nations.[90] It is tempting to dismiss such views as merely part of the inflated rhetoric which international organizations seem so often to attract. But in our still divided world, there remains a need for an institution which can in some way, however imperfectly, articulate the twin ideas of a universal society of states and the cosmopolitan universality of humankind.

[90] Jan Christian Smuts, *The League of Nations: A Practical Suggestion* (London, 1918), p. 71.

The Historical Development of the UN's Role in International Security

MICHAEL HOWARD

T HE concept of 'international security' implies a common interest in security transcending the particular interests of sovereign states. The recognition of that common interest carries with it the aspiration to create a communal framework to replace the need for unilateral national security measures. That aspiration had led the victorious powers, under the determined leadership of President Wilson, to create in 1919 a League of Nations whose collective action would provide for the security of each of its several members. The failure of the League to achieve that goal was taken by Anglo-Saxon leaders in World War II as a reason, not to abandon the concept, but to try again.

(a) The System of the UN Charter

From the very outset the establishment of a new framework for international security was seen as the United Nations' primary task. President Roosevelt in particular welcomed the creation of the United Nations as the beginning of a new international order: 'It spells—and it ought to spell—the end of the system of unilateral action, exclusive alliances, and spheres of influence, and balances of power, and all the other expedients which have been tried for centuries and have always failed.'[1]

That was certainly the intention of its founders. As early as November 1943 the representatives of Britain, the

[1] Quoted in Brian Urquhart, 'The Role of the UN in Maintaining and Improving International Security' (Alastair Buchan Memorial Lecture), *Survival*, 28, no. 5 (Sept.–Oct. 1986), p. 388.

USA, the Soviet Union, and China promulgated a Declaration on General Security in which they recognized 'the necessity of establishing at the earliest practicable date a general international organization . . . for the maintenance of international peace and security'.[2] When the Charter came to be drafted, the Preamble committed the signatories to unite their 'strength to maintain international peace and security, and to ensure . . . that armed force shall not be used, save in the common interest'. And Article 1 of the Charter defines the primary purpose of the UN as being:

To maintain international peace and security, and to that end: to take effective collective measures for the prevention and removal of threats to the peace, and for the suppression of acts of aggression or other breaches of the peace, and to bring about by peaceful means, and in conformity with the principles of justice and international law, adjustment or settlement of international disputes or situations which might lead to a breach of the peace.

Only later in Article 1 does the Charter speak of 'international cooperation in solving international problems of an economic, social, cultural, or humanitarian character, and in promoting and encouraging respect for human rights'. The term 'collective security' was not used: it smelled of the failures of the 1930s. But the same intention was expressed in the phrase 'to unite our strength to maintain international peace and security.'

The assumptions underlying this declaration of intent deserve examination. In the first place, there was no hint of supranationalism. The sovereign state was still the building block of the international order. The functioning of the system depended upon the goodwill of its members. Secondly, a basic cultural and ideological compatibility was assumed to exist among those states, sufficient at least to make it possible to proceed by consensus. Thirdly there was assumed a willingness on the part of the signatories, however powerful they might be and however circumstances

[2] US Department of State, *Towards the Peace Documents* (Publication 2298, 1945), p. 6.

might alter, never unilaterally to use force to defend their own interests. Finally, and most important, a general and equal interest was assumed in the preservation of the *status quo post bellum*. Change would be possible, but only by general consent. The post-war world was conceived, in fact, in somewhat static terms.

The settlement resembled that in 1814 in that it visualized a continuing coalition of the victorious powers to maintain the settlement created by their victory. It resembled that of 1918 to the extent that it recognized that new states might come into being and that they should be made members of the club when they did. But executive power was firmly entrusted to those with the capacity to use it. The Security Council was basically a condominium of the victorious major Allies, who would jointly keep the rest in order. The General Assembly might hold discussion and make recommendations and call matters to the attention of the Security Council, but it had no power of decision for action. It was a *parlement*, rather than a parliament. Article 39 of the Charter placed responsibility for action firmly on the Security Council: 'The Security Council shall determine the existence of any threat to the peace, breach of the peace, or act of aggression and shall make recommendations, or decide what measures shall be taken . . . to maintain or restore international peace and security.'

The core of the Charter lay in Chapter VII: 'Action with Respect to Threats to the Peace, Breaches of the Peace, and Acts of Aggression'—the 'teeth' which the League of Nations was thought to have lacked. The Security Council was empowered, if it thought fit, to call upon the members of the UN to apply sanctions short of war; and if these failed, to 'take such action by air, sea or land forces as may be necessary to maintain or restore international peace and security'. Members undertook to make available such forces or facilities as were required, and to 'hold immediately available national air-force contingents for combined international enforcement action'. (Bombing was evidently foreseen as the most effective means of deterring or punishing aggressors.) A Military Staff

Committee, consisting of the Chiefs of Staff of the Permanent Members of the Security Council, stood ready to advise and assist.

(b) Changes in UN Practice and Assumptions

The system collapsed almost before it was put to the test. The Military Staff Committee, unable to agree what kind of force was required and whether each member should provide the same size of contingent, rapidly became a nonentity. In 1950 the procedure described in the Charter was put into effect to deal with the invasion of South Korea by North Korea; but this was feasible only because the Soviet Union was at the time boycotting the Security Council for its refusal to seat a representative from the People's Republic of China in place of the sitting member representing Chiang Kai-shek. When the Russians resumed their place they effectively prevented any further action. Their veto was circumvented on 3 November 1950 when the Western powers, by securing the passage of the 'Uniting for Peace' resolution in the General Assembly, created a new role for a General Assembly in which they commanded, and believed that they would continue to command, a majority supporting their views. This 'Uniting for Peace' resolution stated:

If the Security Council, because of lack of unanimity of the permanent members, fails to exercise its primary responsibility for the maintenance of international peace and security in any case where there appears to be a threat to peace, breach of the peace, or act of aggression, the General Assembly shall consider the matter immediately with a view to making appropriate recommendations to Members for collective measures, including in the case of a breach of the peace or acts of aggression the use of armed force when necessary, to maintain or restore international peace and security. If not in session at the time the General Assembly may meet in emergency special session within twenty four hours of the request therefor. Such emergency special session may be called if requested by the Security Council on the vote of any seven members, or by a majority of the members of the United Nations.

All members of the General Assembly were asked to hold armed forces ready for action, available even if not formally called upon by the Security Council.[3]

This expedient, which was never accepted as legitimate by the Soviet Union, implicitly acknowledged that the original concept expressed in the Charter, of international security being maintained by consensus among the Great Powers, was unworkable, as indeed it had proved after 1815; and replaced it by the use of a majority of votes the next time it was used to overrule a dissident minority. But ironically the next time it was used—and the occasion of its most spectacular success—was when, six years later, it was employed against two of its original sponsors, Britain and France, after they had vetoed any action by the Security Council over their attack on Egypt in 1956. The General Assembly then called for an immediate cease-fire, and the withdrawal of forces from the Suez Canal. Britain, followed by France, acquiesced; less out of any respect for or fear of the united stength of the United Nations than because of the effective economic muscle of the United States. But a similar and nearly simultaneous resolution by the General Assembly calling upon the Soviet Union to withdraw its forces from Hungary was ignored, and no action followed. This was not simply because France and Britain were 'persuadable' in a way that the Soviet Union was not. It was because in the case of the Soviet Union the UN did not dare to do more than try to persuade, and the Russians knew it.

The lessons of 1956 were clear. First, the UN could take action against 'aggression' only if the two great powers were agreed, or if one of them was indifferent; second, there were only two powers who counted. So, for many years, it remained. Whatever resolutions might be passed in the General Assembly, the UN was no more likely to take action against the Soviet Union over, say, Afghanistan than it was against the United States over Nicaragua. Whatever measures of collective security might be created,

---

[3] GA Res. 377 (V) of 3 Nov. 1950. See also H. G. Nicholas, *The United Nations as a Political Institution* (3rd edn., Oxford, 1967), p. 53.

the superpowers could effectively defy them, and any state enjoying the vigorous support of either could probably do the same.

Within a few years a further and even more significant development was to occur. The assembly became at least as ready to 'unite for peace' against the United States as it was against the Soviet Union, if not more so. Whereas in the first ten years of its existence the General Assembly had a built-in majority hostile to the Soviet Union, the great influx of new members from the 'Third World' produced a majority at least potentially hostile to the United States. The USA could no longer expect the Assembly automatically to endorse its policies; but though the Soviet Union might build up or exploit declaratory majorities against the USA, there could be no outcome from resolutions passed against the most powerful country in the world. The result was to reduce the General Assembly to eloquent impotence, the more impotent among its members tending to be the most eloquent. With the General Assembly powerless and the Security Council deadlocked, a disproportionate weight of responsibility fell on the shoulders of the third element in the structure, the Secretariat, and in particular the Secretary-General, who became the scapegoat for the shortcomings of the organization as a whole.

But of more fundamental importance than changes in the balance and structure of the UN was the change in assumptions about the nature of international society. We have seen how the founding fathers of the UN visualized an essentially static world system: one incrementally deve-loping through peaceful change but in which 'peace and security' implied the maintenance of a status quo which only 'aggressors' (criminals whose motivation was irrelevant) would disturb. Korea (1950) fitted neatly into this pattern. Suez and Hungary (1956) did not. Both the latter were unilateral actions by major powers to preserve the status quo threatened by a disruptive and apparently irreversible change. The Soviet Union succeeded in re-establishing the status quo; Britain and France failed. But in the world that was taking shape in the 1950s, the colonial structure of the late 1940s was the last thing that the majority of states wanted to preserve. For the newly created nations—and even more, those still aspiring to nationhood—the world was dynamic rather than static. Peace was to be sought not in the maintenance of order, but in the securing of justice. It was something to be achieved, if necessary fought for, rather than preserved.

The problem of reconciling this view with the world picture implicit in the Charter can be seen in the Declaration in the Final Document which emerged from the first special session of the General Assembly on Disarmament in June 1978. This reiterated the obligations of the Charter with respect to 'refraining from the threat or use of force against the sovereignty, territorial integrity or political independence of any state', but added *or against peoples under colonial or foreign domination, seeking to exercise their right to self-determination and to achieve independence'* (emphasis added).[4]

Here we have, simultaneously, an adjuration against the use of force, and a restatement of the principles of the Just War. Attempts forcibly to prevent 'justifiable' changes in the status quo are equated with attempts, on another level, to disturb the status quo—two conflicting concepts of the nature of peace which are inherently almost impossible to reconcile.

(c) The Requirements of International Peace and Security

In such a world, what can 'international peace and security' really mean, and what part can the UN play in maintaining it? There are, surely, two minimal requirements: first, the prevention of armed conflict and the peaceful resolution of disputes between major powers; and second, the containment, failing reconciliation, of regional and civil conflicts, to prevent them from escalating to the point where they might affect global stability. Let us examine each of these in turn.

[4] Quoted in *The United Nations and Disarmament 1945–1985* (UN Department of Disarmament Affairs, New York, 1985), p. 6.

1. Great power relations and arms regulation

Relations between the major powers must inevitably be a matter of direct intercourse between them, however much others may oil the wheels by provision of mediation and general good offices. The creation of the UN in 1945 has not prevented the great powers from continuing to deal directly with one another on matters of primary importance to themselves. Nor, when those negotiations became soured by mutual suspicion, did it prevent them from seeking security in all the old expedients of alliances, armaments, and balance of power which the UN had been intended to replace. Such measures were indeed legitimized under Article 51 of the Charter, which specified 'the inherent right of individual or collective self-defence if an armed attack occurs against a Member of the United Nations'; but this was seen as a purely interim expedient 'until the Security Council has taken measures necessary to maintain international peace and security'. However, the interim nature of those measures was quickly lost to sight, and states have continued to make such provision for their own security as lies in their power.

It is true, however, that the security arrangements of the post-1945 world have been made compatible with the principles of the UN, especially in their emphasis on collective defence, and on the principle that defence is the only legitimate basis for the use of force. This is evident in the 1949 North Atlantic Treaty and the 1955 Warsaw Treaty, which referred in almost identical terms to the UN Charter provisions. Both treaties began with an acceptance of the principles of peaceful settlement of disputes and non-use of force contained in Articles 2(3) and 2(4) of the UN Charter. Both treaties also echoed the provisions of Article 51 and 52 on self-defence and regional arrangements. For example, Article 5 of the North Atlantic Treaty (which was closely mirrored in Article 4 of the Warsaw Treaty) stated:

The Parties agree that an armed attack against one or more of them in Europe or North America shall be considered an attack against them all, and consequently they agree that, if such an armed attack occurs, each of them, in exercise of the right of individual or collective self-defence recognized in Article 51 of the Charter of the United Nations, will assist the Party or Parties so attacked by taking forthwith, individually, and in concert with the other Parties, such action as it deems necessary, including the use of armed force, to restore and maintain the security of the North Atlantic area.

Any such armed attack and all measures taken as a result thereof shall immediately be reported to the Security Council. Such measures shall be terminated when the Security Council has taken the measures necessary to restore and maintain international peace and security.[5]

Regional security arrangements and UN Charter language generally have also been invoked in many collective military interventions, including those in the Dominican Republic in 1965 and in Czechoslovakia in 1968. All this may have been no more than lip-service, but it is evidence that UN Charter principles were still seen as having some pertinence to the affairs of the real world.

One important element in the preservation of peaceful relations between major powers has been—or so it is generally believed—the regulation of their armaments. It has been a truism in discourse about international politics, albeit one seldom critically examined, that the lower the level of their armaments, the better the relations between states is likely to be. But when the UN was established, disarmament as such was not seen as being in itself necessarily desirable. The lessons of the 1930s were too fresh in every mind. 'Uniting of strength' implied that there would be strength to unite. The Four Nations' Declaration of 1943 had agreed only on cooperation 'to bring about a practicable general agreement with respect to the regulation of armaments in the post-war period'.[6]

By Article 26 of the Charter, the Security Council was made responsible 'for formulating . . . plans to be submitted to the Members of the United Nations for the

---

[5] The text of the 1949 North Atlantic Treaty is in *United Nations Treaty Series*, vol. 34, p. 243. The text of the 1955 Warsaw Treaty is in ibid., vol. 219, p. 3. Texts of both may also be found in T. B. Millar (ed.), *Current International Treaties* (London, 1984), pp. 440 and 464. The Warsaw Treaty was annulled on 1 Apr. 1991. [6] See n. 2 above.

establishment of a system for the regulation of arma-ments'. At the same time, by Article 11, the General Assembly was empowered to 'consider the general principles of cooperation in the maintenance of inter-national peace and security, including the principles governing disarmament and the regulation of armaments, and may make recommendations with regard to such principles to the Members or to the Security Council or to both'.

It may be wondered how the UN progressed, or regres-sed, from these cautious and realistic guide-lines to the grandiose resolutions in favour of 'General and Complete Disarmament under effective international control' which the General Assembly, with the support of both super-powers, passed in 1959, and which have remained a substantial part of the UN agenda ever since. It was in fact in consequence of two events unanticipated at the time that the Charter was drafted: the explosion of the first nuclear weapons, and the onset of the Cold War.

The control of nuclear weapons was at once seen as a problem of a different order of magnitude from the regulation of what became known as 'conventional' armaments; a problem both more important and, given the novelty of nuclear weapons and the monopoly initially enjoyed by the USA, more practicable. The first resolution of the General Assembly, when it met in January 1946, created an Atomic Energy Commission with broad responsibilities. It was to provide, among other things, for control of atomic energy to the extent necessary to ensure its use only for peaceful purposes; for the elimina-tion from national armaments of atomic 'and all other major weapons adaptable to mass destruction'; and 'for effective safeguards by way of inspection and other means to protect complying states against the hazards of violations and evasions': all matters which have remained on the international agenda ever since.[7]

In response to this challenge the USA produced

---

[7] US Department of State, *The International Control of Atomic Energy: Growth of a Policy* (Publication 2702, 1946), p. 127.

the Baruch Plan, which was certainly imaginative and apparently generous. This provided for an international authority—indeed, since it would be veto-free, a supra-national authority—to control the entire process of the production of nuclear weapons, from the uranium mines and the laboratories to the bombs themselves; an authority possessing total powers of inspection and enforcement throughout the world. The United States, however, refused to give up their own weapons until the new authority was established and in working order. The Soviet Union saw this as a blatant device for the perpetuation of a US-controlled monopoly, and countered with their own proposals. All states, these demanded, should bind themselves not to use, produce, or store nuclear weapons, and to destroy all existing stocks. International inspection should be limited to those stocks which the host government declared to exist. This the Americans saw as an equally blatant attempt to disarm them, with no assurance that the Russians were not building up stocks of their own.[8]

As the Cold War deepened, each side entrenched itself more firmly. The United States used its majority in the General Assembly to make the UN adopt the Baruch Plan. The Soviet Union turned to extramural propaganda and mounted a massive Peace Offensive (dove designed by Picasso) demanding the complete prohibition of nuclear weapons and a one-third cut of conventional forces across the board. Since they made this proposal in September 1948 at the time of the Berlin blockade, when the Western powers were at their wits' end to find sufficient armed forces to balance the Soviet conventional superiority, this could be regarded only as a propaganda ploy. The 'Peace Offensive' reached its climax with the Stockholm Peace Appeal of March 1950, with its demand for 'the absolute banning of the atom weapon, arms of terror and mass extermination of populations'.[9] Like Trotsky at Brest-Litovsk in 1918, the Soviet Union was shouting over the

---

[8] Bernhard G. Bechhoefer, *Postwar Negotiations for Arms Control* (Washington DC, 1961), pp. 41 ff. [9] Ibid., pp. 155–62.

heads of government to the peoples they represented. Disarmament had become a matter not for serious negotiation but for competitive propaganda.

In the 1950s the situation improved slightly. The acquisition of their own nuclear weapons put the Soviet Union in a more favourable frame of mind for realistic discussions, and after Stalin's death a leadership came into power concerned to restore a more reasonable relationship with the West. More important, the development by both sides of thermonuclear weapons made the prospect of nuclear war a thousandfold more terrible; yet at the same time, since more destruction could be achieved with a smaller amount of fissile material, it made the problem of international inspection very much more difficult. So although serious discussions were resumed between the superpowers, they came to focus less on the ultimate goal of abolition and more on such preliminary and partial measures as the monitoring or suspension of nuclear tests, the cut-off of the production of fissile material, the non-proliferation of nuclear weapons, and the prevention of surprise attack.

These questions were initially discussed under the auspices of the UN in a Disarmament Commission which had been set up in 1952 to deal with both nuclear and conventional disarmament; matters which had hitherto been considered separately. The Commission was instructed to draft

proposals to be embodied in a draft treaty (or treaties) for the regulation, limitation and balanced reduction of all armed forces and all armaments, for the elimination of all major weapons adaptable to mass destruction and for the effective control of atomic energy to ensure the prohibition of atomic weapons and the use of atomic energy for peaceful purposes only.[10]

But as the questions involved became increasingly technical and the discussions increasingly serious, so the negotiations shifted away from the Commission to bilateral dialogue between the superpowers, and such

[10] Ibid., p. 166.

significant negotiations as the Surprise Attack Conference in 1958 took place outside the UN framework altogether. This development was not welcomed by a General Assembly increasingly consisting of non-aligned states who resented being left out of the discussions. In November 1958 it passed a resolution sponsored by India and Yugoslavia which enlarged the Disarmament Commission to include all members of the General Assembly; which of course made effective negotiation impossible.[11]

So in 1959 a pattern was established which continued for the next three decades. A General Assembly dominated by Third World states, resentful of their exclusion from effective power, seized on the disarmament issue as a stick with which to beat the superpowers. In that year it placed on the agenda at the behest of the Soviet Union the item 'General and Complete Disarmament under effective international control'. Ten years later it designated the 1970s as 'the First Disarmament Decade'. In 1976 it convened a Special Session on Disarmament 'intended to set a new course in international affairs and turn states away from the nuclear and conventional arms race by means of a global strategy for the future course of disarmament'. This was held from 23 May to 30 June 1978. In 1979 the General Assembly designated the 1980s as 'the Second Disarmament Decade'. In June–July 1982 it had a second Special Session on Disarmament. In this, according to the official UN handbook, 140 states took part and expressed their views, together with 3,000 representatives from 450 non-governmental organizations, while representatives of fifty-three non-governmental organizations and twenty-two research institutes made statements. 'In addition, thousands of communications, petitions and appeals with many millions of signatories were received by the UN from organizations, groups, and individuals all over the world.' Regrettably the Assembly 'was unable to reach consensus on any specific course of action' except the launching of a World Disarmament Campaign. It did however agree to convene another

---

[11] Ibid., p. 461.

Special Session, which duly met, equally inconclusively, in 1988.[12]

To plough through the huge body of literature engendered by all this well-meant activity is a deeply depressing experience. How far any of it had any bearing on the actual course of relations between the superpowers, which were increasingly conducted bilaterally outside the framework of the UN, or to the various agreements they succeeded in reaching, through for example the Strategic Arms Limitation Talks, is hard to judge. It would probably, however, be fair to say that the activities of the UN maintained an atmosphere in which it was difficult for the superpowers and their allies altogether to abandon the search for arms agreements.

This search did ultimately produce results. The United States and the Soviet Union signed bilateral agreements on the establishment of Nuclear Risk Reduction Centres in September 1987; on the Elimination of Intermediate Range Missiles in December 1987; on Verification of the Threshold Test Ban Treaty and Peaceful Nuclear Explosions, and on Chemical Weapons Destruction in June 1990; and the Strategic Arms Reduction Treaty itself in July 1991. Simultaneously, sweeping measures of confidence-building and arms control were enacted in the Final Document of the CSCE Stockholm Security Conference in September 1986, and the Treaty on Conventional Armed Forces in Europe in November 1990. It would be fairer, however, to attribute these agreements to the astonishing reversal of Soviet policy carried out by Mikhail Gorbachev and Eduard Shevardnadze than to any pressure from the UN General Assembly.

On the other hand, the atmosphere engendered at the UN provided a constant temptation for both sides to substitute grandiose and unrealistic declaratory policies for careful and unspectacular incremental agreements. It was also one in which a totally disproportionate importance became attached to negotiations between

---

[12] *The United Nations and Disarmament 1945–1985*, pp. 5–8; and *The United Nations Disarmament Yearbook 1988*, pp. 37–105.

the superpowers about arms control, at the expense of discussions about more immediate and potentially explosive areas of conflict such as Central America, southern Africa, and the Middle East; conflicts discussed elsewhere in this volume. While the UN General Assembly spent countless hours of time and reams of paper discussing grandiose projects for disarmament, no action was taken over such overt instances of inter-state aggression as Iraq's assault on Iran in 1980, Israel's invasion of Lebanon in 1982, or Indonesia's annexation of East Timor in 1975. Only in 1990, confronted with the blatant aggression of Iraq against Kuwait, did the UN take any action, and the circumstances then were exceptional. The interests of all major Western powers were involved; the Soviet Union and the People's Republic of China were virtual pensioners of the United States; the great majority of Middle Eastern states were alarmed at the prospect of Saddam Hussein so suddenly and brutally extending his power. For the first time the UN acted as its founders had intended. It is an encouraging precedent, but we would be deceiving ourselves if we thought that such an exceptional combination of circumstances was likely often to recur.

2. Containment of local conflicts

The other role of the UN is one about which little is said in the Charter, and which was inherited not so much from the League of Nations as from the Concert of Powers which kept order in Europe before 1914: the containment of local conflicts through peacekeeping, reconciliation, and good offices. This is discussed elsewhere in this volume, but a brief word seems appropriate here.

UN peacekeeping forces, in the form in which they have emerged, were not even envisaged in the UN Charter. As observer, interposition, or buffer forces, they simply grew in response to numerous crises within and between states: in Israel and neighbouring states (since 1948), in India and Pakistan (since 1949), in West Irian (1962–3), in the Congo (1960–4), in Yemen (1963–4), and in Cyprus (since

1964).[13] It is noteworthy that these peacekeeping operations were all in post-colonial areas, where there were great uncertainties about the legitimacy of regimes and/or boundaries, and where the great powers were able, if not to agree on action, at least not to disagree so strongly as fatally to undermine the UN effort.

Peacekeeping, reconciliation, and good offices are of course activities of the highest importance. In the Middle East in particular, the intervention of the UN has repeatedly made possible the defusing of critical situations which threatened to erupt into major conflict. But the effect of this activity was limited in the UN's first four decades. Sir Brian Urquhart, who had forty years' experience of peacekeeping in the UN Secretariat and was personally responsible for much of it, explained why in the 1986 Alastair Buchan Memorial Lecture in London. At best, he explained, UN intervention could freeze or contain conflicts. Seldom, if ever, could it resolve them. The reason for this was that the Security Council, because of its dissensions, had failed to create 'a benevolent international framework to assist combatants to resolve their differences and to provide the necessary protective apparatus. . . . Without such an international framework it is often impossible for the parties to a situation that is violent, deep-rooted and complex to make progress on their own and in the open.'[14]

Considerable efforts have been made since the mid-1980s to establish such a framework. These efforts are documented in this volume in Boutros-Ghali's *An Agenda for Peace*, and in the chapters by Brian Urquhart and Sally Morphet. Although peacekeeping operations have expanded in number and objectives, there continue to be serious obstacles and limitations to such efforts. No situation that has confronted the UN has been more violent, deep-seated, and complex than that which arose from the civil war in Yugoslavia in 1991. It resembled that

[13] On UN peacekeeping forces see the four volumes by Rosalyn Higgins on *United Nations Peacekeeping* (Oxford, 1969–81). See also the chapter by Sally Morphet below, and (for a list of such forces) Appendix E below.

[14] Urquhart, 'Role of the UN', p. 393.

in Lebanon in that it resulted from the disintegration of a multi-cultural state; but it far transcended that conflict in its sheer scale and in the bitterness of the ethnic hatreds it unleashed. Only briefly and in limited regions did a peace emerge that could be 'kept', or was intervention possible to provide a limited degree of humanitarian relief. 'Peace-making' would have involved the kind of 'pacification' indistinguishable from military conquest, with the consequent and open-ended obligation to maintain order thereafter. No member of the UN at the time of writing shows any real desire to undertake such a responsibility.

(d) Conclusion: Obstacles to the Creation of an Effective Global Structure

To sum up: because of the dissensions among its leading members the UN failed, or rather the nations composing it failed, to create the framework of international security intended by its founders. And it was that failure, as Urquhart pointed out, which rendered nugatory all the rhetoric and exhortation about disarmament. 'It is now seldom recalled that the original Charter idea was that *the collective security system of the UN would provide the sense of security and mutual confidence* which would allow disarmament and arms control to proceed under the auspices of the Security Council' (emphasis added).[15] It is indeed clear that, unless such a sense of security could be established, the demands and proposals sponsored by the General Assembly would continue to be totally ineffective—however numerous, repetitive, and well meant.

The UN has achieved much, and those achievements are discussed elsewhere in this volume. It preserved those elements of international cooperation—the World Health Organization, the International Labour Organization, and the International Court of Justice—which already existed, and added to them many more. It eased the transformation of the world from a Eurocentric to a truly global

---

[15] Ibid.

system, and can take much of the credit for the remarkably orderly and comparatively amicable fashion in which this took place. It provided, and continues to provide, a focus for world politics which enables the smallest and least considerable of its members to feel themselves part of a world community. But it has not succeeded in its primary task. It has not created a new world order in which every state derives its security from the collective strength of the whole. It has been able only to reflect the disorders, fears, and rivalries of the world, and do what it could to mitigate them.

It remains to be seen whether the end of the Cold War will eventually restore the capacity of the UN to fulfil the role set out in its Charter; or whether, as seems more likely, the disappearance of superpower confrontation will only reveal deeper systemic obstacles to the creation of an effective global structure of international security.

The UN and International Security
after the Cold War

BRIAN URQUHART

BY 1990 it seemed that the United Nations, and particularly the Security Council, were beginning to function more or less as the UN's founders had intended. The five Permanent Members had begun to work regularly together for the solution of major problems, and the results were fairly impressive. The Iran–Iraq war came to an end in August 1988 on the basis of a Security Council resolution devised by the five Permanent Members;[1] Soviet forces withdrew from Afghanistan in 1988–9 under a plan negotiated by the Secretary-General; Namibian independence was finally achieved in March 1990, on the basis of a 1978 UN resolution;[2] Cuban forces began a staged withdrawal from Angola in 1989; and UN peace-keeping and good offices were employed with growing effect in Central America.

Two major developments subsequently raised questions about whether the UN was really working as intended. The first of these was the swallowing of Kuwait by Iraq in 1990, and the measures subsequently taken by, and through, the Security Council to reverse Iraq's aggression and restore peace in the region. The second was the increasing incidence of massive violence within the borders of states or former states, usually on ethnic lines: the UN's authority and capacity to take effective action in such cases is now being put to the test in former Yugoslavia, Somalia, and soon, probably, in a number of other places as well.

These two developments raise some basic issues about

---

[1] SC Res. 598 of 20 July 1987.   [2] SC Res. 435 of 29 Sept. 1978.

the nature and roles of the UN which are explored in this chapter. The first—the Gulf crisis of 1990–1—posed the question of the workability of the course of action set out in Chapter VII of the Charter (Action with Respect to Threats to the Peace, Breaches of the Peace and Acts of Aggression). The second—the problem of essentially internal violence—raises a wider question of the UN's role in matters of peace and security: whether the organization's basic function is to deter aggression and stop conflict between states, or whether it now also includes dealing with massive episodes of violence and abuse of human rights *within* the borders of states—in other words a broad commitment to justice, law, and order.

The credibility of the UN is being tested and found wanting in former Yugoslavia, as it was in Angola after the 1992 election. It may be seriously damaged in Cambodia and Somalia. Many of the Security Council's decisions on conflict resolution at present lack either the legal and political strength to make them respected, or the means to implement them in an effective way. After a brief post-Cold War honeymoon, the UN is once again suffering from the inability to enforce its decisions in critical situations, this time without the excuse of the obstacles created by the Cold War. If this trend is not reversed, both the credibility and relevance of the world organization as the agent for maintaining peace and security will be in more and more doubt.

(a) Action against Aggression

When Saddam Hussein invaded Kuwait on 2 August 1990 the Security Council reacted with unusual speed and decisiveness. Between 2 August and 29 November it adopted, under Chapter VII of the Charter, twelve resolutions on different aspects of the Kuwait crisis.[3] It imposed

---

[3] The first was SC Res. 660 of 2 Aug. 1990 condemning the Iraqi invasion of Kuwait which had taken place earlier the same day.

sanctions;[4] a naval embargo;[5] and then, on 29 November, it finally authorized the use of force if Iraq did not comply with its resolutions by 15 January 1991.[6]

While the Council's unprecedented sense of urgency and determination in dealing with aggression were widely praised, it was not acting precisely according to Chapter VII of the Charter. Articles 46 and 47 clearly imply that enforcement measures under Chapter VII will be under the control of the Security Council and its Military Staff Committee. Thus, already on 25 August, when it asked the states with maritime forces in the Gulf area to monitor shipping, the Council had begun to depart from the precise terms of Chapter VII of the Charter. On 29 November, in resolution 678, the Council diverged still further from the terms of Chapter VII when it authorized 'Member States co-operating with the Government of Kuwait . . . to use all necessary means' (i.e. the use of force) if Iraq had not withdrawn by 15 January 1991. A comparable departure from the course envisaged in Chapter VII had also occurred in the Korean war (1950–3), in which there was also US control of military operations.[7]

The tendency to diverge from the Charter was inherent from the beginning of the 1990–1 Gulf crisis, and for a very good reason. In the forty years of the Cold War the Security Council had made none of the preparations necessary to meet a crisis of this kind in the way suggested in the Charter. The Military Staff Committee had held no substantive meetings since 1948, and had done no preparatory staff work or contingency planning. No agreements with member states to make forces available to the Council had been concluded under Article 43. Thus, when the Council denounced Iraq's aggression in August 1990, it was not in a position to assure the security of other states in the region—most notably Saudi Arabia—against a possible attack by Iraq.

Instead, a parallel operation was mounted under US leadership to protect Saudi Arabia. This was justified

[4] SC Res. 661 of 6 Aug. 1990.
[5] SC Res. 665 of 25 Aug. 1990.
[6] SC Res. 678 of 29 Nov. 1990.
[7] SC Res. 84 of 7 July 1950.

primarily under Article 51 of the Charter, which provides for the inherent right of individual or collective self-defence. When this operation, involving a massive deployment of forces, began, its name, Desert Shield, gave the impression that it was defensive, and that UN sanctions and embargoes were to be the means of eventually forcing Iraq to withdraw from Kuwait. Later on, however, when the US build-up became so large as to have offensive capacity, and sanctions seemed to be having little effect on Saddam Hussein's determination to hold on to Kuwait, the choice of the main instrument to reverse Iraq's aggression shifted from sanctions to the use of force.

The wisdom of the change from sanctions to force was a matter of much debate at the time, more particularly since the enforcement operation would be under the command of the USA rather than of a command structure designated by the Security Council. Moreover, the goal of Chapter VII is action short of force if possible. Article 42 states: 'Should the Security Council consider that measures provided for in Article 41 [sanctions] would be inadequate or have proved to be inadequate, it may take such action by air, sea, or land forces as may be necessary to maintain or restore international peace and security.'

No formal determination as to the inadequacy of sanctions was ever made by the Security Council before Operation Desert Storm was launched. In retrospect it seems that sanctions, even when rigorously applied, are unlikely, in the short run at any rate, to force a dictatorial and unscrupulous leader to reverse his course. Saddam Hussein may well also have believed that the Security Council's threat of force was a bluff which would never become a reality. When he had invaded Iran in 1980, the Security Council had sat on its hands, neither demanding withdrawal nor imposing sanctions. His assessment of the determination of the Security Council to reverse aggression was certainly influenced by this experience.

The USA and its coalition partners commenced the major military operation on the night of 16–17 January 1991 with Operation Desert Storm, an air offensive against Iraqi targets in Iraq and Kuwait. The main coalition land offensive began on 24 February. A suspension of coalition offensive combat operations came into effect on 28 February after coalition forces had taken over all of Kuwait and part of southern Iraq.

After the end of this war, Saddam Hussein was required to carry out the terms of a monumental cease-fire resolution.[8] This requires, among other things, the destruction or removal of all weapons of mass destruction, including chemical and nuclear weapons, as well as missiles with a range greater than 150 kilometres. It also requires reparations and the return of all Kuwaiti property, and maintains the sanctions on Iraq until these and other provisions are fulfilled. Sanctions also provide the background for international efforts to protect the Kurdish population of northern Iraq and the Shiites of the south from the tender mercies of the central government. 'Safe heavens', 'no-fly zones', a UN guard force, and massive relief operations are all part of the complex aftermath of Desert Storm. Iraq resisted many of the conditions imposed on it by the UN and by some of the coalition powers, who responded with air attacks on targets in Iraq on 14 and 18 January 1993.

The forceful reaction in January–February 1991 to Saddam Hussein's Kuwait adventure may well prove something of a deterrent to future aggressors. However, such a clear case of aggression in a strategically sensitive region is unlikely to recur in the foreseeable future; and the long-term impact of that reaction was inevitably weakened by the fact that Saddam Hussein remained firmly in power in Iraq. At all events, the episode shed much light on the capacity of the UN as an instrument of collective security.

In the existing state of international leadership and military preparedness, an operation of the size and strength of Desert Storm could not be undertaken without the leadership and military commitment of the USA. That fact has already contributed to negative interpretations, in

---

[8] SC Res. 687 of 3 Apr. 1991, 'the mother of all resolutions'. This had been preceded by Res. 686 of 2 Mar. 1991, outlining necessary measures by Iraq which would permit a definitive end to the hostilities.

some quarters, of the Security Council's conduct over Kuwait. It has also, partly due to the unfortunate use of the phrase 'new world order', created much speculation as to the US government's conception of the future role of the USA, the sole surviving superpower, *vis-à-vis* the rest of the world.

As far as the Security Council is concerned, there seems little or no will to make a literal reality of the articles of Chapter VII of the Charter. There is no inclination at the present time to resuscitate the Military Staff Committee even in a contingency-planning role. Nor is there any sign of a governmental response to Secretary-General Boutros-Ghali's urging that governments conclude agreements under Article 43 to make forces available to the Security Council.[9]

On the other hand, Chapter VII, the enforcement chapter—used partially, and only on rare occasions, to impose sanctions during the Cold War—is far more freely invoked in the post-Cold War era. This tendency is causing considerable concern in the developing world as a harbinger of a new great power hegemony. For this, among other reasons, the vexed questions of the structure of the Security Council and the anachronistic present arrangement of Permanent Members are becoming pressing political issues.

In spite of the recommendations in Boutros-Ghali's *Agenda for Peace*, there seems little concern at present to put the UN and the Security Council in a better position to respond in full accordance with the terms of Chapter VII of the Charter to a new and serious act of aggression— nor indeed to give the organization the capacity to deal with more limited challenges. The deterrent to major acts of aggression—and to disastrous disruptions of civil order—thus remains largely the military power of the USA and one or two of its allies, and the determining factor in responding to future emergencies will be the interest and concern of the USA and its allies in a given

---

[9] Boutros Boutros-Ghali, *An Agenda for Peace*, June 1992, para. 43. (Below, Appendix A.)

situation. There is no guarantee that forceful action can, or will, be taken against acts of aggression wherever they may occur. However, there is still a practical possibility of the UN taking less extreme steps, such as interruption of diplomatic relations and communications, and sanctions. In May 1992, for example, although there was little support for major military intervention in former Yugoslavia, the Security Council adopted stringent sanctions against Serbia and Montenegro; these were toughened further in 1993.[10]

₁(b) Ethnic and Intra-state Conflicts

At the present time the question of dealing with acts of aggression is of less immediate concern to governments, and especially to members of the Security Council, than the almost daily dilemma of how to react to situations of massive violence, humanitarian emergencies, breakdowns of authority, and gross abuses of human rights within the borders of states or former states. Since the end of the Cold War, with the exception of Iraq and Kuwait, waves of killing and destruction have tended to be more within national borders, sometimes on ethnic lines, than between sovereign states. This raises fundamental questions concerning the balance between national sovereignty and international responsibility, and about the nature of the UN's basic mission. Member states, many of which have ethnic skeletons in their own cupboards, are understandably reluctant to face such issues in general terms, or to create new legal criteria and precedents for international intervention. Recent outbreaks of ethnic violence and civil war have therefore been dealt with on a largely *ad hoc* basis.

1. The Kurds of northern Iraq

The case of Iraq, in this as in other matters, is something of an exception. After the end of Desert Storm, the plight of the Iraqi Kurds evoked resolution 688, which ostensibly

[10] SC Res. 757 of 30 May 1992; SC Res. 820 of 17 Apr. 1993.

set new standards for UN intervention within the
boundaries of a state. The resolution:

> *Requests* the Secretary-General ... pursue his humanitarian
> efforts in Iraq and to report forthwith ... on the plight of
> the Iraqi civilian population, and in particular the Kurdish
> population, suffering from the repression in all its forms
> inflicted by the Iraqi authorities;
> *Requests* further the Secretary-General to use all the resources
> at his disposal, including those of the relevant United Nations
> agencies, to address urgently the critical needs of the refugees
> and displaced Iraqi population;
> *Demands* that Iraq cooperate with the Secretary-General to
> these ends.[11]

With the withdrawal of the coalition forces from northern
Iraq, a new international mechanism, unarmed UN
'guards', was devised to provide a visible international
presence and to reassure the suffering Kurds. After initial
scepticism, this device has proved reasonably successful as
a half-way house between a military UN presence and
purely humanitarian activity. It operated, however, in an
unusual context, in a country still under UN sanctions and
a series of mandatory resolutions under Chapter VII
of the Charter, and with very powerful US Air Force
elements only a few minutes' flight away in Turkey.
The perennial problem of open-ended commitments also
haunts UN efforts to help the Kurds of Iraq. How long
should such an effort continue after the original crisis has
subsided?

2. *Yugoslavia and Somalia*

There is no basis for such an arrangement in Yugoslavia
and Somalia, the maelstroms of violence which deeply
preoccupied the UN from 1992. Both of these situations
defied the normal process by which international organizations were supposed to be instrumental in defusing
cycles of violence. In both, the relevant regional organizations failed to get a grip on the problem and referred the
matter to the UN Security Council. In both, despite

---

[11] SC Res. 688 of 5 Apr. 1991.

intensive efforts, UN representatives failed over many
months to get the fighting parties to stick to cease-fire
arrangements, let alone to participate constructively in the
conciliation process. In both, traditional peacekeeping
forces were not able to control a chaotic situation. And
in both, humanitarian efforts of all kinds have been
threatened, harassed, and rendered ineffective by the
continuing violence.

In Yugoslavia, after much debate and some bickering
about the cost, a UN peacekeeping force was finally
dispatched in early 1992 to operate mainly in Croatia,
although its headquarters was stationed, before Bosnia's
statehood, in Bosnia at Sarajevo.[12] The arrival of the
UN peacekeeping force coincided with the European
diplomatic recognition of Bosnia-Herzegovina and the
anticipated eruption of ethnic conflict in the newly
recognized republic. A UN peacekeeping force is unsuited
to deal with such a situation. The Secretary-General
so informed the Security Council. The killing and
destruction continued, and was slowed neither by the
Security Council's imposition of sanctions on Serbia at the
end of May, nor by the numerous efforts under EC and
UN auspices to get a negotiated settlement. Further
forces, from NATO countries, arrived from the second
half of 1992 to protect the humanitarian relief operations.
More forceful measures were discussed in 1992 and 1993,
but only limited agreement was reached.

On Somalia the Security Council was originally less
forthcoming. Only after many months did the Council
decide, in April 1992, on a very small peacekeeping
operation.[13] At the same time representatives of the

---

[12] UNPROFOR was established under SC Res. 743 of 21 Feb. 1992.
Subsequently, under SC Res. 758 of 8 June 1992, its mandate was expanded to
cover the delivery of humanitarian supplies to Bosnia and Herzegovina.

[13] SC Res. 751 of 24 Apr. 1992 decided to establish a UN operation in
Somalia (UNOSOM), authorized the sending of fifty UN observers to monitor
a cease-fire in Mogadishu, and agreed in principle to establish a UN security
force in Somalia to provide protection for humanitarian assistance. Subsequent
resolutions (SC Res. 767 of 27 July and 775 of 28 Aug.) outlined aspects of
UNOSOM's mission and authorized an increase in its strength. The first
observers only arrived in Somalia in July, and the first group of security
personnel on 14 Sept. 1992.

Secretary-General attempted, in cooperation with the Organization of African Unity, to further a process of national reconciliation. The small peacekeeping force took three months to arrive, humanitarian relief efforts were increasingly debilitated by the activities of armed gangs, and conciliation efforts languished. Chaos and famine, vividly reported on the world's television screens, finally evoked a more active response.

In December 1992, after the US presidential election and in response to an appeal from Boutros-Ghali, the USA volunteered a military expedition into Somalia, in which others were invited to participate. The Security Council 'authorized' this action, which was taken under Chapter VII of the Charter and was intended to 'promote the process of relief distribution, reconciliation and political settlement in Somalia'.[14] Operation Restore Hope, which was under US command and involved forces from several countries beside the USA, began its intervention in Somalia on 9 December 1992. This operation had the right to use its weapons, if necessary. It was the prototype of an armed police action, a form of intervention which may well be needed frequently in the future. In early May 1993 the US commander formally handed over responsibility to the UN commander of UNOSOM II.

✱ (c) Questions for the Future

The tragedies of Yugoslavia and Somalia raise important questions regarding the functioning of the international system. The questions addressed here are particularly difficult because regional organizations, even supposedly strong European ones, have proved incapable, in both cases, of effective and timely intervention or even of agreed policies and courses of action. The conflicting policies of their members have reduced both their credibility and their impartiality in the eyes of important parties to the conflicts. At present they apparently lack the expertise and operational capacity to mount either

---

[14] SC Res. 794 of 3 Dec. 1992.

preventive measures or effective peacekeeping or peace-enforcement operations. The responsibility for trying to stem the tide of destruction and disaster has thus mainly devolved on the UN.

1. A new pattern of UN involvement

With Article 2(7) of its Charter restraining it from intervention in matters within the domestic jurisdiction of a state, the UN has traditionally been reluctant to be involved in what are ostensibly internal or domestic affairs, and its efforts have been belated and hesitant. This hesitancy is compounded by the organization's financial situation, and the reluctance of its largest contributors to incur increasing costs for its operations as well as escalating involvement for themselves. With the UN's burgeoning commitments, the bill for peacekeeping operations is much higher than ever before, and is more than the regular budget of the UN.[15]

Quite apart from immediate questions of effectiveness and cost, current developments raise basic issues about the nature of UN responsibility, the organization's right—and its obligation—to intervene, and its capacity to do so. There is no convenient legal model to provide comprehensive answers to such questions. It is likely therefore that the world organization will have to proceed by an *ad hoc* process of trial and error, distilling from its actions, where possible, precedents and legal norms which may be useful in constructing a more effective international system in the future. Such a system should be comprehensive and impartial; and should have the support and participation of all its members according to their capacity.

The predominant mechanism now used by the UN for conflict control is peacekeeping. Peacekeeping, not mentioned in the UN Charter, was originally developed

---

[15] The so-called 'annualized' cost of peacekeeping operations, i.e. the cost of twelve-months for each of the operations in their different budgetary cycles, was estimated as \$US 3 bn.—more than four times the previous highest annual figure—in the Secretary-General's 1992 annual report, UN doc. A/47/1 of 11 Sept. 1992, para. 18.

during the post-war decolonization period as a means of filling the power vacuums caused by decolonization, and of reducing the friction and temperature, so that an effort could be made to negotiate a permanent settlement of post-colonial conflict situations, in Palestine, Kashmir, the Congo, Cyprus, and elsewhere. Later on, especially in the Middle East, peacekeeping proved a useful method of disengaging the combatants after a conflict and establishing a neutral buffer zone between them. It was most controversial when it dealt with conflicts within the borders of states (the Congo, Cyprus) and in situations where there was no governmental authority and most of the fighting was done by irregulars who were not bound by agreements or UN decisions (south Lebanon, Bosnia-Herzegovina).

Since the end of the Cold War both the demand for, and the scope of, peacekeeping operations have steadily increased. More peacekeeping operations were initiated in the six years from 1987 than in the previous forty. Their scope now includes the disarming of factions, the return of refugees, temporary administration (as in Cambodia), assisting humanitarian relief, and the organization and supervision of elections. Since the end of the Cold War these new operations have had one incomparable advantage over their predecessors—the unanimous support of *all* the members of the Security Council.

The very success of peacekeeping, however, raises new questions. Is there a limit of the capacity of the UN to undertake new tasks? And is there, as recent evidence suggests, a limit to the financial support available for new operations? These major problems have to be addressed seriously. Apart from the financial question, it should be possible to devise a system which, by drawing on the resources of all member states and on a small part of their defence budgets and installations, would provide the UN with the capacity to act effectively in any part of the world if the situation demanded it. If the organization is to command the respect and confidence of *all* its members, it must be seen to be able to act *universally* and not be perceived to act only *selectively* when the interests of its most powerful members are involved. It may be added that the cost of peacekeeping is often exaggerated. The peacekeeping bill for 1992, although higher than ever before, was less than the cost of one US Stealth bomber.

It has been suggested that regional organizations might take on more of these tasks. The original intention of the Charter was certainly that regional organizations should, if possible, deal with conflicts in their region. Various difficulties have emerged. In some regions there is no comprehensively constituted or accepted regional organization. Existing regional organizations tend to be perceived as partial to one side or another in many regional conflicts. Regional organizations do not at present have the capacity, expertise, or resources to mount large peacekeeping operations. The remedy for at least some of these shortcomings would be better and more systematic contact and more joint ventures with the UN, such as are now taking place in Central America, Europe, and Africa.

Traditional peacekeeping, with its ban on the use of force except in self-defence and its reliance on prior agreements for a cease-fire and cooperation with the conflicting parties, has not proved to be a suitable technique for breaking the cycle of violence in such places as Yugoslavia or Somalia. In both of these situations much of the trouble is with irregular forces which are not parties to agreements and do not respect the cooperative, non-forceful nature of traditional UN peacekeeping.

The situation in Somalia, and the belated US intervention, pointed to the need for a third category of UN military operation, somewhere between peacekeeping and large-scale enforcement. The purpose of such operations would be to put an end to random and uncontrolled violence and to provide a reasonable degree of peace and order so that humanitarian relief work would go forward, and a conciliation and settlement process be undertaken. Such armed police actions would use highly trained but relatively small numbers of troops and would not have military objectives as such. Unlike peacekeeping forces they would be required to take certain combat risks and if necessary to use a limited degree of force. Such contingencies would be greatly reduced by the capacity to give an impressive show of disciplined strength.

The need for a UN capacity to mount such operations is increasingly indicated by the present trend in violence world-wide. Important political, legal, and practical questions are involved. New criteria for intervention and rules of engagement would have to be devised and generally agreed on, initially, at any rate, case by case. Staff, training, planning, and command structures would have to be developed. Highly trained and well-led military contingents from countries throughout the world would have to be available for immediate service. Governments should be encouraged to conclude agreements under Article 43 and to have such contingents on stand-by for UN service where the cycle of violence cannot be broken except by firm intervention. At a time when the old forms of military service are less in demand, this kind of skilled international duty could provide an inspiring new dimension for national military service. Given the requisite leadership and political will, there is no reason why such a capacity, relatively limited in scope and expense, cannot be developed by the UN. Boutros-Ghali has broached this matter in his suggestion of 'peace-enforcement units'.[16] The response of governments has so far been muted.

2. A system for peace and security

If collective security, peacekeeping, and peace-enforcement are to function more effectively in future, a far more consistent pattern of activity needs to be established. Hitherto the reactions of the UN, and especially the Security Council, to threats to international peace and security have been haphazard and selective. Each case has been dealt with *ad hoc*, with measures improvised from scratch, usually after the main disaster had already occurred. In the past there may have been good political and other reasons for this very unsystematic and inconsistent performance. Most of these no longer exist.

[16] *Agenda for Peace*, paras. 44 and 45.

The question is whether, in the new international, post-Cold War climate, the countries of the world are capable of the effort, and expenditure, to create and maintain in the UN a *system* for international peace, security, and stability based on vigilance, consensus, common interest, generally accepted principles, collective action, and international law. The basic function of such a system would be to keep a permanent watch on the state of peace, security, and stability around the world, seek peaceful solutions, mediate disputes, pre-empt or prevent conflict, assure the protection of the weak, and deal authoritatively with aggressors or would-be aggressors. Admittedly this is a tall order, but we should also recognize that, unless the level of international peace and security is greatly improved, it will be very difficult, if not impossible, to mobilize the necessary effort and resources required to deal with the so-called global problems which will determine the general state, if not the fate, of the human race in the next century.

It seems likely that we are entering a period of great instability in the world. The thaw of the Cold War has brought many long-standing but submerged rivalries and feuds to the surface. National sovereignty and national boundaries are unravelling in many places. There is an increasing demand for international intervention in humanitarian emergencies, massacres, and human rights violations. Widespread poverty and deep economic inequities are dramatized by instant world-wide communication. Population pressures, vast economic migrations, natural and ecological disasters, and imminent scarcities of vital natural resources all contribute to the likelihood of an unstable future. In such a situation, a system of international peace and security will serve little more than a cosmetic function unless it is accompanied by a determined effort to create the long-term conditions for peace and security and to remove the basic causes of conflict.

A reliable international system of security and stability—such as we have come to depend on and expect in a well-run country—involves more than reacting, however forcefully, to a crisis that has already happened. It requires both the creation of conditions in which peace and stability can be maintained and the capacity to anticipate and to prevent conflict and disruption.

The creation of conditions of peace and stability is the basic function of most of the organizations of the UN system as well as of the UN itself. This function is in urgent need of being reformulated, focused, and rationalized. A few examples of the necessary measures must suffice.

(i) *Arms control.* One of the most obvious conditions for future peace and stability is the control and reduction of the flow of arms. It is no small irony that the five Permanent Members of the Security Council, whose new-found cordiality is now supposed to be the best hope for peace, are also the world's five largest arms exporters. The immense sums of money involved in the arms trade, and the almost universal addiction to arms, make the arms flow, like the drug trade, particularly hard to control or reduce. But if the flow of arms is not reduced, a basic element of violence and conflict will remain.

There are a few small steps in the right direction. In 1991, the General Assembly decided that a register of conventional arms should be established.[17] It is only slowly coming into existence, and only a few governments have so far agreed to provide information. The register covers 'conventional arms, to include data on international arms transfers', and, as a voluntary option, information on military holdings and procurement through national production. There is also considerable interest in making foreign aid conditional on limiting arms purchases. The problems of conversion from military to civilian economy are beginning to be studied. There are, however, as yet no great governmental initiatives, nor a massive groundswell of public opinion, to support significant moves for arms control, disarmament, and the demilitarization of human society.

[17] GA Res. 46/36 L of 9 Dec. 1991. See also the follow-up decisions in GA Res. 47/521 L of 15 Dec. 1992.

The problems involved in inspecting and dismantling Iraq's weapons of mass destruction under Security Council resolution 687 vividly demonstrate the complexity of even a relatively small international arms control effort.

(ii) *Economic, social, and environmental issues.* A world divided into a rich minority and a desperately poor majority can never, especially in the age of communications and explosive population growth, be stable. Quite apart from moral questions, massive despair and deprivation manipulated by skilled demagogues in the name of ideology or militant religion, and with the vast possibilities which modern technology provides for the imaginative terrorist, can well become a formidable challenge to the comfortable industrialized world. Although migration from poor to rich countries is a growing phenomenon, large international and bilateral programmes to fight poverty or achieve sustainable development have lost much of their impetus since the end of the Cold War. If any reasonable degree of stability is to be achieved for the next century, much more attention and effort must be given to the most pressing economic, social, and environmental problems.

The connection between the absence of democracy, gross human rights abuses, and the propensity for aggression and other forms of international irresponsibility was clearly established even before Iraq's attack on Kuwait. The spread of democracy, and respect for human rights, are indispensable elements of a more stable, less violent human society, and are, as such, a legitimate—indeed an indispensable—international concern.

These are only some of the most obvious items on the 'hidden agenda' of international peace and security. A serious effort to tackle them is the vital underpinning of any future international system for maintaining the peace.

3. Can the elements be combined into a coherent whole?

Many of the elements of a system of international peace and security already exist. Hitherto, however, they have not been used consistently as part of a single system. There are the Charter provisions for the peaceful settlement of disputes and for dealing with threats to the peace, breaches of the peace, and acts of aggression. There are the Security Council and the Secretary-General, whose responsibility and activity in this field have vastly increased since 1945. There are regional organizations of varying scope and effectiveness. There are alliances and *ad hoc* groups for particular purposes. There are various military techniques, including some, like UN military observers or peacekeeping, which are not in the Charter at all.

With the Cold War over, the UN machinery unblocked (at least temporarily), and with a whole new generation of problems and challenges, the question is whether governments are capable of the effort, the vision, and the relatively modest expenditure to combine these elements into a consistent and reliable system of international peace and security.

The steps and phases of such a system are obvious. The precise mechanisms to be used and the development of new criteria and rules—for international intervention, for example—will, quite naturally, be the subject of lively debate and will take time and effort to develop. The important thing is that the debate and the effort should start and should produce results. The parallel task of dealing with actual crises as they occur should be helpful in providing experience, incentives, and new ideas.

The first essential of any security system is vigilance, information, and evaluation. A constant watch on the world situation and on possible threats to international peace and security has always been maintained by the Secretary-General and the Secretariat. The trouble hitherto has been a lack of resources, a lack of means to acquire first-hand information, and—most serious of all—a marked unwillingness of governments, even in the Security Council, to heed warnings and to take preventive action. The conditions are now present for a great improvement in this situation.

The Security Council has never been so active as in the period since 1990, and the relationship between the Council and the Secretary-General is far closer and more cooperative than in the Cold War period. With

Boutros-Ghali's reorganization of the Secretariat in 1992 the gathering and evaluation of information has taken its rightful place in the political department. Better collection of information from both governmental and non-governmental sources should allow the Secretary-General to be in a position both to take preliminary measures—fact-finding, good offices, etc.—and to alert the Security Council to potential conflicts. Two factors are crucial to the success of these arrangements: the capacity to evaluate information and developments perceptively and objectively (the Iraq–Kuwait experience provides an object lesson in how *not* to do this), and the responsiveness of the Security Council (including its willingness to take preventive measures *before* a disaster occurs). The conditions for improved alertness and for more effective preventive measures are better than ever before. Only time will tell whether the Secretary-General and the Security Council will take full advantage of them.

There is now more emphasis than ever before on the merits of preventive action. The newly cooperative international atmosphere could certainly make such action—diplomatic, economic, political, or even military—more effective. Much will depend on the way in which the different strands of preventive action can be coordinated to further a single policy. As the case of Yugoslavia has amply demonstrated, even in the post-Cold War period this is not so easy as it sounds. It may well be that the Security Council, and even the General Assembly, could play a useful role in initiating and coordinating preventive measures to head off a conflict or to de-escalate a crisis. Much closer cooperation with regional organizations would be an indispensable part of such an effort. Greater use of the International Court of Justice on the justiciable aspects of international disputes can also provide a useful preventive instrument. The Secretary-General's good offices role, which operated effectively even during the Cold War years, is a valuable preventive mechanism. In the present circumstances the Secretary-General will be less circumscribed in such efforts, and, it is to be hoped, better supported. Far more thought will have to be given to means of de-escalating and resolving the ethnic and minority problems which seem likely to be a main source of violence and tragedy in the coming years.

There is also now a greater possibility of using peace-keeping techniques as a preventive measure *before* a conflict has broken out. Stationing of military observers or a small peacekeeping force in areas of tension, even on one side if necessary, could provide a warning, a symbol of international concern, and a source of accurate, up-to-the-minute information. (A preventive peacekeeping group was deployed in Macedonia in December 1992.) The idea of peacekeeping as a trip-wire is superficially attractive, but it needs a great deal of serious thought. Understandably, it is not particularly popular with the military. A peacekeeping force serving as a trip-wire could only be justified if there was a firm guarantee—and the necessary preparation—for instant and effective enforcement action in the event that the trip-wire was crossed.

Preventive measures will carry far more weight if they are part of a systematic course of international action, a progression of measures. If it is known that certain acts will have certain inevitable international consequences— economic pressures or sanctions, for example—and that the Security Council has taken such actions in the past and is capable of taking them in the future, the impact of international preventive action will be greatly enhanced.

Preventive peace-making (in the UN sense) and peace-keeping measures are likely to continue as the mainstays of the action of the Security Council and the Secretary-General. If, however, they prove ineffective, their failure should be systematically linked to a different sort of action through the transition from Chapter VI of the Charter (Pacific Settlement of Disputes) to Chapter VII (Action with Respect to Threats to the Peace, Breaches of the Peace, and Acts of Aggression). The knowledge of this systematic link, which was notably lacking during the Cold War period, should greatly strengthen the hand of the Council, and the Secretary-General, in the pacific settlement of disputes. The increased willingness of the Council in recent years to consider action under Chapter VII begins to move the UN away from the era of unenforceable and disrespected decisions which eroded the Security Council's stature and effectiveness.

To be effective this systematic approach will require much effort, including effective evaluation of information, staff work, contingency planning, the ready availability of forces, resources and logistics, and a sound programme of training. Much attention has been given to these matters in relation to peacekeeping. Little, if any, attention is as yet being given to preparing for measures under Chapter VII—embargoes, sanctions, peace-enforcement, and deterrent and enforcement action. The knowledge that such measures can readily be mobilized and used might well prove in many cases to be the deterrent that would make their actual use a rare necessity.

The question of economic sanctions needs attention. Sanctions seem useful as a rallying point for the international system: but their effectiveness in changing behaviour is more in doubt. They can cause pain without necessarily changing the behaviour of the target government. Perhaps, even if sanctions do not work against megalomaniac dictators, they remain a necessary step in the escalation to the actual use of force. The history of sanctions needs much careful study, including the highly sensitive question of their humanitarian implications.

The lack of any UN system or resources for enforcement action dictated the need for the US-led alliance to achieve the goals of the Security Council in the Gulf, and later on in Somalia. Does this mean that the Security Council is never to have some capacity to realize the most important provisions of Chapter VII of the Charter? The obvious point at which to start building such a capacity would be the Military Staff Committee, suitably supplemented to represent the changes in military and economic power since 1945: but there appears at present to be no interest whatsoever among the five Permanent Members in using the Military Staff Committee (one of the greatest innovations of the Charter in 1945) to provide the Security

Council with at least some capacity for staff work and contingency planning under Chapter VII. Since Article 43, which provides for agreements whereby governments will make forces available to the Security Council, also remains unawakened from its Cold War sleep, the UN continues to lack a capacity of its own to mount an armed police action.

Recent UN experiences provide a good argument for at least considering the establishment of an immediately available élite UN force directly recruited from volunteers worldwide.[18] Hitherto the Security Council has lacked the capacity to deploy a convincing military presence at the outset of a crisis before the situation has disintegrated and become uncontrollable. In fact, the first Secretary-General, Trygve Lie, suggested such a force for precisely this purpose in 1948, in the early stages of the first Arab–Israeli war.

There are numerous possible objections to such a force. However, there is one overwhelming argument for it. It might give the Security Council (and the Secretary-General) the capacity to display strength and determination at a point where larger disasters could be avoided. If the Security Council is to retain its credibility and relevance in the kind of low-level conflicts in which it is now widely involved, it urgently needs a capacity for immediate 'peace-enforcement' action.

The differences of perception and interest between the industrialized and the developing world—the so-called 'North–South' problem—have become intensified in the post-Cold War period. During and after the Gulf crisis, the dominant role of the five Permanent Members, and especially the USA, caused considerable criticism and resentment in the developing world. The fact that the veto power prevents any collective action which in any way goes against the interests of any one of the five Permanent Members of the Security Council still leaves a very large hole in the concept of a universal system of collective security. Any restructuring of the Security Council should

---

[18] See Brian Urquhart, 'For a UN Volunteer Military Force', *New York Review of Books*, 10 June 1993, pp. 3–4, and comments in subsequent issues.

aim to alleviate rather than exacerbate this problem. The new trend for intervention in some internal situations and in humanitarian or human rights situations makes a serious and sensitive handling of the North–South question more necessary than ever. A better system of international security must take account of this problem if it is to succeed.

All member states should be required to participate in international actions according to their ability. The UN should have the will and the capacity to deal with situations, especially those involving the defence of the weak, regardless of whether they are of major concern to the industrialized powers. The UN must remain a universal organization and must avoid becoming what is perceived by a large part of its membership as élitist.

4. The need for a radical improvement of international institutions

These are but a few of the questions which need to be addressed in the effort to build a more reliable and effective system of international peace and security. The UN is now confronted with a series of urgent global problems, and a confused and unstable situation in many parts of the world. Its ability to deal with the global problems may well be a determining factor in the desirability of life on this planet in a hundred years or so. A disorderly end to the human experiment cannot, unfortunately, be ruled out. That is the main incentive for working for a radical improvement of international institutions. Such an improvement will require international cooperation and understanding, resources, performance, and leadership of an order unknown in the past. Both governments and the private sector will have to raise their sights from short-term interests to long-term concerns. It is unlikely that this will happen if the world is preoccupied with, and its resources are tied up in, uncertainties about peace and security. That is why a consistent and reliable system for maintaining international peace and security is quite literally vital for the future.

The UN and the National Interests of States

ANTHONY PARSONS

UNLIKE its predecessor, the League of Nations, which suffered almost as many withdrawals as it gained accessions in its short life, the United Nations quickly became an established feature of the international landscape. It became virtually automatic for newly independent states to seek membership; and the older members continued to value their membership of the UN.[1] Even when decolonization altered the parliamentary situation to the disadvantage of the West, and some governments privately questioned the practical value of the UN in terms of immediate national interest, public rhetoric remained supportive of the organization in principle if critical of some of its practices. No government, even the South African during the long period of its pariah status, has yet taken the view that withdrawal would serve its interests better than remaining within. In an attempt to shock extravagant and incompetent specialized agencies into mending their ways, there have been defectors at the periphery—the USA from the ILO in the 1970s, the USA and Britain from UNESCO in the 1980s—but there has been no sign of structural erosion of the UN itself. The UN has been through several periods of crisis, probably the most acute of which was in the mid-1980s, but in each case states have ultimately taken the view that the continuance—and indeed the strengthening—of the UN best serves their national interests.

---

[1] A useful survey of the importance of the UN to British interests can be found in Erik Jensen and Thomas Fisher (eds.), *The United Kingdom, the United Nations* (London, 1990).

(a) Positive Achievements in the Cold War Era

Even during the UN's first four decades, experience on a number of occasions showed that it could act as an effective instrument to ameliorate disputes, to defuse crises, and to act as a catalytic agent to persuade parties to come together and negotiate. The UN could only act successfully when the conditions were right: it is a truism that the actual solution of disputes must be a matter for the parties themselves in direct negotiation. It is no use expecting outside bodies, including the UN, to draw up detailed blueprints and to impose them on unwilling parties. This simply does not work.

The UN possessed effective machinery, if properly used, to address disputes and crises. First there was the *public diplomacy* of the Security Council and, to a lesser extent, the General Assembly. Through these forums, the UN could draw up guide-lines for the settlement of disputes. It could create the necessary atmosphere for peaceful negotiations by deploying its peacekeeping capability (not foreseen in the Charter, which envisages military action only in terms of enforcement) with the consent of parties, namely the blue helmets and blue berets with which the world had become familiar: this had proved to be one of the UN's most important functions.[2]

Then, over the years, the *private diplomacy* of the UN evolved in the form of the 'good offices' of the Secretary-General, unique in their confidentiality, impartiality, and in commanding the confidence of even the most suspicious member states.[3]

Third, and perhaps most important of all, the UN functioned on many occasions as an *escape-route* or ladder down which states could climb when their national policies had led them into dangerously high and exposed positions.

Over the first forty-odd years of the UN's existence, these different functions of the UN proved invaluable to the interests of Britain, of many other countries, and

---

[2] See the chapter by Sally Morphet below.
[3] See the chapter by Thomas M. Franck and Georg Nolte below.

in certain cases to the interests of global peace. Some examples follow.

1. The Suez crisis of 1956

Shortly after the Anglo-French forces had landed in the Suez Canal Zone on 5 November 1956, it must have become clear to the governments in London and Paris that the operation would have to be called off. Virtually the whole world was opposed to it, including even our closest ally, the USA. Britain and France had succeeded in achieving the almost impossible, namely uniting the two superpowers at a time when one of them was actively repressing a small European country, Hungary. But how could Britain and France withdraw without unacceptable humiliation in the eyes of their own peoples? Public opinion in Britain was already showing signs of deep division, and a major domestic crisis was looming. To have pulled out the British units, and for them to have been replaced by Egyptian forces, would clearly have been politically intolerable. This was where the UN came in.

With the Security Council blocked by Anglo-French vetoes, the General Assembly authorized a UN Emergency Force (UNEF I). This was the first-ever UN peacekeeping force of the kind that has since become familiar in many parts of the world. It replaced the British and French, and eventually the Israeli, forces which were at the time occupying Sinai. To accept replacement by international forces from the organization of which Britain and France were themselves founder-members was politically tolerable, and withdrawal could take place with some honour and dignity. The UN had provided an escape-route for two major powers which had taken up an untenable position, and an even more serious crisis had been averted.

2. The Cuban missile crisis of 1962

During this crisis in October 1962, it quickly became clear to the Soviet Union that the US government would not tolerate the deployment of Russian ground-to-ground missiles only seventy miles from the continental United

States. The Soviet Union faced the choice of war with the United States or climbing down unilaterally. It has become public knowledge that the Americans would have delivered a pin-point conventional bombing attack on the missile sites if the Soviet merchant ships carrying more missiles and related equipment had not agreed to stop while still some distance from Cuba. Had the American attack been delivered, there were many who believed that the Soviet Union would have retaliated with a similar attack on the American Jupiter missile sites in Turkey. The next rung in the ladder of escalation could have brought close a nuclear exchange.

Khrushchev's problem was how to climb down without unacceptable loss of face *vis-à-vis* the Third World, to which the symbolic importance of the missile deployment was to demonstrate that the Soviet Union was prepared to underwrite any friendly state threatened by 'Yankee imperialism'. He was helped out of his dilemma by the Secretary-General of the UN, U Thant.[4] Identical letters and responses from and to the Secretary-General were drafted, agreed, and exchanged with the parties. Khrushchev felt able to be seen deferring to a plea from the highest official of the international community to take action to defuse what had become a crisis immediately endangering world peace. The UN escape-route had worked.

3. Southern Rhodesia 1965–1979

When Ian Smith declared unilateral independence in November 1965, the British government was faced with two equally unacceptable choices: to use force to crush the rebellion, or to acquiesce in the new situation. The first was rejected for a whole series of reasons, the second because of the catastrophic effect it would have had on Britain's international relations. But there was a third choice—recourse to the UN Security Council—which enabled the government to escape from the trap. UN

---

[4] See Ramses Nassif, *U Thant in New York, 1961–1971* (London, 1988), pp. 25–48.

involvement culminated in May 1968 in the unanimous adoption by the Security Council of comprehensive mandatory sanctions against the illegal regime. I am not arguing that these sanctions were effective in bringing an end to the rebellion.[5] They were not. But the searchlight of the Security Council, trained as it was for nearly fifteen years on Southern Rhodesia, not only enabled successive British governments to side-step the other unacceptable choices, but also discouraged creeping international recognition of the Smith regime until the time came when vigorous diplomacy, conducted bilaterally and through the Commonwealth, was at last in the autumn of 1979 able to bring all parties round the same negotiating table, the essential prerequisite for the peaceful settlement of any dispute.

4. *The Iranian claim to Bahrain 1968–1970*

When, at the beginning of 1968, the British government announced that British protection of the Arab states of the Lower Gulf would be terminated at the end of 1971, the most critical unsolved problem in the area was the Iranian claim to the Bahrain Islands. Historically Iran regarded Bahrain as an integral part of its territory and it was referred to as the fourteenth province: two seats in the Iranian parliament were reserved for Bahraini deputies. The emotional attitude in Iran towards Bahrain was analogous to the Argentine attitude towards the Malvinas. However, for nearly 200 years Bahrain had been ruled as an independent Arab state under an Arab dynasty, the Al Khalifah. During the century and a half of British protection, successive shahs of Iran had been able to excuse themselves in the eyes of their people from forcibly restoring Bahrain to Iranian sovereignty by the presence there of a powerful European state—Britain.

When the anouncement of the imminent withdrawal of British protection was made, the Shah faced two unacceptable choices. He could either prosecute his claim

---

[5] A useful discussion of the effectiveness of sanctions is Robin Renwick, *Economic Sanctions* (Cambridge, Mass., 1981).

by force, thus precipitating a general war between Iran and the Arab world, or he could unilaterally drop the claim, thus attracting major criticism within Iran. The good offices of the UN Secretary-General provided a third course. The Shah made clear that, although he had no doubt that Bahrain was part of Iran, he would be prepared to accept that the people of Bahrain might have changed over the centuries; he would be ready to acquiesce in their wishes as to their future, provided that they were properly and impartially ascertained and confirmed by the international community. In short, Iran, as a founder-member in good standing in the organization, felt able to accept the verdict of the UN.

Complex and, above all, confidential negotiations followed, culminating, in early 1970, in an ascertainment of Bahrain opinion carried out by a senior UN official, Sr. Winspeare Guicciardi, representing the Secretary-General. His report, the conclusion of which was that the people of Bahrain overwhelmingly wished to be citizens of an independent Arab state, was submitted to the Security Council and unanimously adopted in May 1970.[6] The 200-year-old claim had been laid to rest, the threat to peace and the obstacle to Bahraini development had been removed, and Britain's task of winding up her long-standing relationship with Bahrain had been greatly eased.

This was a classic case of the UN providing the vehicle on which parties to a dispute could reach a settlement. The UN was crucial, but so was the willingness and statesmanship of the parties. The settlement has survived the Iranian revolution, and the fact that it was concluded is a testimonial to the wisdom of the late Shah, who has been so severely criticized in recent years.

5. The October war of 1973[7]

In the closing stages of the war in the Middle East in October 1973, Israeli forces in the southern sector had

---

[6] The report of the Secretary-General's Representative is contained in UN doc. S/9772 of 30 Apr. 1970. Endorsed in SC Res. 278 of 11 May 1970.

[7] For a discussion of the Oct. 1973 war and the UN see Brian Urquhart, *A Life in Peace and War* (London, 1987), pp. 235–53.

crossed the Suez Canal in a westerly direction and were bottling up an Egyptian formation of about 20,000 men— the Third Army— in the area of Suez town. A Security Council cease-fire had broken down.[8] A real danger developed of the two superpowers flying airborne forces into the battle zone. The world was unquestionably closer to a superpower confrontation than at any time since the Cuban missile crisis. What happened? After some backstage consultation, the non-aligned members of the Security Council tabled a resolution designed to bring about a cease-fire and the deployment of UN peacekeeping forces to separate the combatants and to create the peaceful conditions in which negotiations could be resumed. The superpowers had been provided with the ladder down which to climb from their dangerously exposed positions, and the crisis passed. It is awe-inspiring to contemplate what the outcome might have been if the superpowers had not had the UN alternative to bilateral action, or if they had not been in the mood to make use of the UN machinery when the chips were down.

6. The Falklands crisis of April–June 1982

This was a notable occasion on which the British national interest was well served by the UN. From 1 April 1982, the day before the Argentine surprise attack on the islands, the British government was able to use the Security Council as the focal point for mobilizing international support for the proposition that, regardless of the views of the majority of the membership on the question of sovereignty, the use of force to settle a political dispute was unacceptable. As a consequence, non-aligned backing was forthcoming for the British-sponsored Security Council resolution demanding Argentine withdrawal.[9] Moreover, through the negotiations conducted under the aegis of the present Secretary-General, the British government was seen by the world to have exerted all efforts to achieve Argentine withdrawal peacefully.[10] This

[8] The cease-fire was called for in SC Res. 338 of 22 Oct. 1973.
[9] SC Res. 502 of 3 Apr. 1982.
[10] A full account is contained in my article in *International Affairs*, 59, no. 2 (Spring 1983).

made it easier for Britain's friends and allies to provide moral and material support when she was left with the only alternative to redeem the aggression—military action. Had Britain failed to secure and to sustain this international support, matters might well have turned out very differently.

(b) The UN in the Mid-1980s

The above examples of the various ways in which the UN played a key role in the interests of member states in political disputes or conflict situations were all drawn from that long period in which the organization was supposedly 'paralysed' by the Cold War. Nevertheless, by 1986 the UN was in deep trouble, perhaps at the lowest ebb in its history. It had experienced previous downward spirals, but the situation in the mid-1980s was more serious than on earlier such occasions: a financial crisis precipitated by the reluctance of the United States and the Soviet Union to pay their full contributions was a dangerous extra symptom of the prevailing malaise. The UN had reached the bottom after a long fall from the pinnacle of exaggerated expectations which had characterized its creation. It had been conceived as an instrument of world-wide collective security, armed with non-military (sanctions) and military instruments of enforcement, a projection into peacetime of the wartime alliance of great powers, buttressed by the (narrowly based) like-mindedness of the whole membership who had qualified to join at the creation by declaring war on the Axis powers. The wartime alliance had collapsed into the sterility of the Cold War, the like-mindedness had dissipated with decolonization and the exponential increase in the membership. The coercive powers of the UN became to all intents and purposes a dead letter. The world had fallen back for its collective security on the historical pattern of regional alliances—most notably NATO and the Warsaw Pact. The UN had become an instrument of *persuasion* only and, with the rapid decolonization of the European empires, an instrument of persuasion preoccupied with the problems of the newly independent majority, namely the dangerous disputes in the so-called Third World, principally in Asia and Africa, and the chasm of economic disparity between rich North and poor, newly decolonized South. With the direct superpower confrontation being conducted outside the UN, it was to be expected that the majority should set the agenda. But this was not the UN anticipated by the founding fathers, especially in Washington, Moscow, and London: and the negative attitude of the sceptics intensified as the organization drifted ever further from its original aspirations. This scepticism also blinded governments and peoples to the real achievements of the UN in terms of the national interests of its members, even in the most unpropitious international climate.

In the early 1980s the UN had experienced few successes and many failures in issues of peace and war, and in other fields. It had done nothing to prevent war from breaking out between Iraq and Iran in September 1980, or Israel from invading Lebanon in June 1982. For all the efforts of Secretary-General Javier Pérez de Cuéllar, the Security Council had failed to bring about a peaceful Argentine withdrawal from the Falkland Islands in spring and early summer 1982. In spite of the con-demnation. of the General Assembly majority, over 100,000 Soviet troops appeared to be permanently en-trenched in Afghanistan. The Secretary-General's 'good offices' had failed to extract any flexibility from the opposing parties in the Cyprus dispute. The North–South economic dialogue had collapsed in a bad-tempered welter of frustration. Certain major Western powers, particularly the USA, were taking a more negative attitude towards the UN than at any time in the past, and there was a growing tendency to conduct foreign policies bilaterally and regionally outside the UN framework. In the mid-1980s different states and groups of states held different views as to whether the UN ought to be taken seriously by national policy-makers in its role as guardian of inter-national peace and security or as promoter of economic well-being.

The Soviet Union, its foreign policy yet to be downgraded

from the global ambitions of the Brezhnev era, did find the UN useful to its national interest, albeit for an unedifying reason. The Soviet Union had for many years found the UN a valuable forum in which to bid for the hearts and minds of the non-aligned majority by vigorously espousing their causes, by posing as a champion of national liberation, and by putting the West, in particular the USA and the ex-imperial European powers, at a corresponding disadvantage. Soviet policy-makers would have stated with complacency that they had been able to pursue these diplomatic objectives at minimal cost. By pretending to a fundamentalist purity towards the Charter, they had been able to avoid paying their share of the expenses involved in UN peacekeeping operations, and by inventing the notion that North–South economic disparity was the result of 'Western imperialism' which should therefore pay the price of redressing the imbalance, they had got away with paying only derisory sums towards the UN's economic and humanitarian activities.

However, by the mid-1980s the Soviet Union's complacency was beginning to yield to anxiety. For nearly three decades Soviet leaders had been confident that the General Assembly majority would always give them the benefit of the doubt while denying it to the West—the famous 'double standard'. The massive non-aligned condemnation of the 1979 invasion of Afghanistan, repeated with increased vote in successive General Assemblies, had worried Moscow and was a factor not only in persuading the Soviet Union to cooperate with the UN-sponsored initiative to bring about withdrawal of troops and a peaceful settlement of the Afghan problem, but also in restraining Moscow in its reaction to the rise of the Solidarity Movement in Poland in 1981—there was to be no repetition of the military extinction of the Prague Spring of 1968. In a nutshell, even before the Gorbachev era the UN had become the focal point for demonstrating to the Kremlin that military adventurism had its political cost to Soviet interests.

The smaller states took the perfectly justified view that the UN was the only forum in the world where they could make their voices heard; the UN was and is important to them as a confirmation of international recognition of statehood, indeed a kind of guarantee of integrity. Until the Iraqi invasion of Kuwait in 1990 no member state had attempted forcibly to annex another. With the exception of Switzerland, all states which felt able to assume the minimal financial and diplomatic obligations of membership had joined the UN and only one, Indonesia, had left it in a huff for any length of time.

The larger non-aligned states had long tended to regard the UN as a useful place in which to mobilize and trade support for causes to which they attached importance individually or collectively—especially in relation to the Arab–Israeli dispute, Rhodesia, and South Africa. The non-aligned states regarded as routine the accumulation year by year of growing majorities in the Security Council and General Assembly for propositions such as economic sanctions against South Africa over apartheid and Namibia, the need for total Israeli withdrawal from the Arab territories occupied by Israel in 1967, the establishment of an independent Palestinian state, and so on. The trap was the tendency to equate increased voting support with genuinely increased pressure on the states to which the resolutions were addressed. In practice, the regular reiteration of the same or similar demands had hardened the attitudes of those states, particularly the USA, which found themselves on the receiving end of hostile rhetoric and condemnatory resolutions.

Against this background the USA became increasingly doubtful as to the extent of the UN's usefulness to US interests. In the Reagan administration's critical climate regarding the UN, the attitude and writings of right-wing ideologues, 'American firsters', and devoted supporters of Israel revealed a mounting temperature of angry contempt. Some Americans regretted the deterioration from the 'good old days' in the UN when like-minded states, led by the USA, were in an effortless majority—a parliamentary situation which had gone, seemingly never to return. American opinion increasingly regarded the UN as a quarry for the mining of virulently anti-American rhetoric, particularly in the Arab–Israeli context; a place where problems were complicated rather than simplified; a propaganda tool of the Kremlin; and, at best, an ineffective body to be avoided by serious negotiators. Moreover, the USA was expected to pay 25 per cent of the cost of the privilege of being a whipping-boy, and could not prevent the adoption of fresh (and often undesirable) programmes for which again they had to pay the lion's share: not surprisingly, this galled a substantial body of American opinion, especially in the Congress.

Western European states generally maintained more positive views of the UN's usefulness, albeit each for different reasons. The spectrum ranged from the high idealism of Scandinavia through the more hard-headed realism of the larger members of the European Community to the southern European attitude, which was closer to that of the non-aligned movement. But all generally agreed that, although the performance of the UN had fallen far below the impossible aspirations of its rhetoric, it had no equal as a diplomatic forum (Guatemala and Britain for example had been able to meet and discuss their problems in the UN for many years in spite of having no diplomatic relations) and that it had great value as a place in which to develop multilateral coalitions in pursuit of common aims—European Community coordination across virtually the whole spectrum of the UN agenda being a striking case in point.

(c) The UN in the 'New World'

The constraints (far short of 'paralysis' as I hope I have demonstrated) arising out of the East–West confrontation began to loosen in 1987. In that year the new Soviet foreign policy, directed by Messrs Gorbachev and Shevardnadze, began to manifest itself in the UN arena. For the first time ever, the five Permanent Members of the Security Council *jointly* drafted a mandatory resolution.[11]

---

[11] SC Res. 598 of 20 July 1987.

This helped a year later to bring to an end one of the bloodiest inter-state conflicts of the post-1945 period, the Iran–Iraq war. The combatants did not immediately comply with the resolution but, when mutual exhaustion set in a year later, it provided them with the ladder down which to climb to a cease-fire. From that time the two superpowers began to withdraw their support from opposing sides in a number of apparently intractable regional disputes, thus facilitating effective UN mediatory action in, for example, Afghanistan, Namibia, Cambodia, and El Salvador.

In September 1987 President Gorbachev unveiled a fresh Soviet approach towards the UN which altered previous policy through 180 degrees.[12] He called for strengthening of the Security Council as the organ which, rather than great power arrangements made outside the framework of the UN, should be the principal guardian of international security; he pledged Soviet support for UN peacekeeping operations (hitherto regarded as *ultra vires*) and undertook to pay the past contributions which the Soviet Union had previously refused; he also expressed support for a stronger role for the Secretary-General (previously an object of suspicion); and, in effect, he challenged the USA to follow this lead.

On 2 August 1990, with the invasion of Kuwait by Iraq, the newly born cooperation amongst the five Permanent Members of the Security Council faced its first dramatic test. The Council moved swiftly and decisively into Chapter VII of the Charter, demanding the unconditional restoration of the *status quo ante*;[13] and, when Iraq ignored this demand, imposing comprehensive sanctions, a naval blockade, air sanctions, and finally authorizing member states to use force to liberate Kuwait.[14] After the war it imposed the most stringent and intrusive cease-fire provisions imposed on any state since the Treaty of Versailles.[15] In the months of the Gulf crisis of 1990–1,

[12] Mikhail Gorbachev, 'Reality and the Guarantees of a Secure World', *Pravda* (Moscow), 17 Sept. 1987.   [13] SC Res. 660 of 2 Aug. 1990.
[14] SC Res. 678 of 29 Nov. 1990.   [15] SC Res. 687 of 3 Apr. 1991.

the Council adopted almost as many mandatory resolutions as in the whole of its previous history.

In 1991 and 1992 the UN was required to address a series of exceptionally difficult problems, including in former Yugoslavia (complementing the peace-making efforts of the European Community) and in Cambodia (as part of the comprehensive UN-sponsored peace plan). The way in which states turned to the UN over such issues was encouraging, suggesting that the UN was seen as central; and worrying, as the problems in Yugoslavia and Cambodia were so intractable.

When the Security Council met at the level of heads of government in January 1992, all speakers expressed confidence regarding the peace-making and peacekeeping capability of the organization in the post-Cold War climate, and many undertook to strengthen its capacity to act pre-emptively before disputes degenerated into conflict. There was no hint from any delegation that the UN was anything but a major asset in terms of national interest, let alone global peace—a far cry from the equivocations of the mid-1980s. However, much of this optimism subsequently evaporated as the UN struggled unsuccessfully with the complex problems of Angola and Bosnia.

(d) Conclusions

1. *Observations*

Since 1990 the UN has been functioning in conditions close to what the founders would have regarded as ideal— the five Permanent Members cooperating rather than competing, the old parliamentary arithmetic of East versus West bidding for the non-aligned majority a thing of the past, with an overall desire on the part of all geographical groupings to make the organization work in its primary function of preserving international peace and security. Certain important lessons have emerged:

1. The 1990–1 Gulf crisis demonstrated that the Security Council can act quickly and decisively in a

declaratory and in a legislative sense but that, even in the most propitious circumstances, it cannot itself conduct a dynamic military campaign as originally envisaged in the so-called military articles of the Charter—especially Articles 46 and 47(3), which delegate to the Council and the Military Staff Committee the responsibility for planning the use of armed force and for its strategic direction. In this regard the Council, roughly as it did over forty years ago in the case of Korea, can only authorize member states to take the necessary action. It is too cumbersome, too diversified, and too insecure to play the part exercised by for example the US Central Command in planning and executing Operation Desert Storm. This view was reinforced by the decision to authorize rather than command the intervention force sent to Somalia in 1992–3.[16]

2. The UN, without formal Charter amendment, is flexible enough to reinterpret the restriction in Article 2(7) on intervening in the domestic affairs of states. Generally with the consent, and indeed in some cases with the preference, of the parties, it has become actively involved in internal problems in El Salvador, Haiti, Croatia, Bosnia-Herzegovina, Cambodia, Mozambique, Angola, northern Iraq, and Somalia. Such involvement is going to spread and to constitute the principal preoccupation of the UN in the field of peace, security, and humanitarian considerations.[17] Inter-state conflict is becoming rare while civil wars are proliferating, arising out of ethnic and religious rivalries released by the culmination of the process of decolonization. In the years to come Article 2(7) may well be seen as a dead letter similar to the military articles. However, the UN is already experiencing the toils of involvement in such crises, compared to which inter-state quarrels are relatively simple.

3. Given the boost to the prestige of the UN emanating from its performance over the Gulf crisis, states have learnt that it is a more valuable forum than they had

[16] SC Res. 794 of 3 Dec. 1992.
[17] See Nigel Rodley (ed.), *To Loose the Bands of Wickedness: International Intervention in Defence of Human Rights* (London, 1992).

previously thought for the conduct of business normally carried on bilaterally or in small groups. A striking example is disarmament and arms control. The evidence of the massive transfer of weaponry and military techno-logy from the industrialized countries of Iraq (and many other Middle Eastern states) shocked the world. The five Permanent Members (themselves responsible for 85 per cent of global arms exports) have drawn up guide-lines to restrain the transfer of arms to conflict areas, and the General Assembly adopted in December 1991 a resolution calling for the establishment of a register of arms transfers.[18] The UN is engaged in the monitoring and destruction of Iraqi weapons of mass destruction, and consideration is being given to tightening up the non-proliferation machinery of the International Atomic Energy Agency.

It can thus be asserted that, in ideal circumstances, the UN can perform more effectively than in the 'bad old days', but that there has been no qualitative change in its capability. It is still principally an instrument of persuasion, acting with the consent of parties. Its coercive powers are not proven to be effective: it can impose mandatory sanctions, but the Gulf crisis and its aftermath, and the crisis in Yugoslavia, confirm the scepticism of previous doubters regarding the effectiveness of this instrument. The Security Council can authorize states to use force to redress aggression, but it cannot itself direct the operation as was intended when the Charter was formulated. Furthermore, states are proving reluctant to commit forces to enforcement action in civil war situations when significant casualties and protracted involvement may result.

There is no change in the essentials of the UN's public and private diplomacy, including the 'good offices' of the Secretary-General, only in the increased willingness of the membership to make use of these facilities.

In today's world, no member state, except perhaps

---

[18] GA Res. 46/36 of 9 Dec. 1991, on 'Transparency in Armaments'. See also GA Res. 46/336H of 6 Dec. 1991.

those against which mandatory action has been taken or authorized, would deny that the UN is an asset to national foreign policy. Indeed, in recent years the organization has received more encouragement from great powers than at any time since the creation. By the same token, the impotence of regional organizations as demonstrated in Bosnia-Herzegovina and Somalia is stimulating an increased tendency on the part of small and threatened states to have recourse to the UN. So far from the world order merging into larger geopolitical units, the reverse is the case as existing states fragment and the new entities rush to shelter within the United Nations, the constituted guardian of the state system and of the doctrine of national sovereignty.

2. *Recommendations*

In a world of rapid communications in which many issues transcend national boundaries, it is generally accepted that a universal organization with a permanent secretariat is essential in the search for consensus over such questions as the environment, population, the war against drugs, human rights, world food, and health; as well as more narrowly functional questions such as civil aviation and telecommunications. The list now covers all fields of human endeavour: were a central organization not in existence, the need to create one would long ago have been felt. However, in this essay I have concerned myself mainly with the heart of the matter, international peace and security, and the following recommendations are directed to that area although some are of general application:

1. The UN only functions to full capacity when *all* members believe that it is working in their national interest. This was not so in the first ten years when the Americans could use their majority to force Soviet vetoes and to isolate the Soviet Union almost at will. The Soviet Union and its associates were disillusioned by this experience and were disposed to conduct serious foreign policy business outside a forum in which they could count on being wrong-footed. By the same token, the UN

was partially crippled over the next thirty years when decolonization produced a new majority to which Moscow and its baggage train of supporters attached themselves, thus consigning the USA and the West to a regular voting minority—a reversal of the original tables.

In today's circumstances the USA and its junior partners must guard against a return to the notion that what is good for Washington is necessarily good for all, and that they are justified in using their present ascendancy to isolate and pillory those states which do not regard the 'New World' in this light. In particular, too intrusive a policy towards the domestic jurisdiction of states which do not measure up to Western criteria will make such states— China being a leading example—doubt whether the UN is serving their interests: fresh divisions will open and the backlash will reduce the effectiveness of the whole organization. Western power in the UN must be used with discretion and sensitivity; there is already a mounting neurosis that the organization is being 'hijacked' by the USA (as it was in practice hijacked by the non-aligned movement for so many years). This anxiety was demonstrated in the Security Council in the context of the authorization of a US-led coalition in December 1992 to use military force if necessary to distribute humanitarian supplies in Somalia. The majority in the Council insisted that the unqualified *carte blanche* of resolution 678 should not be given, and that mechanisms should be established by the Secretary-General to keep the Council informed of the progress of the operation. The US administration appears to have taken the point, as indicated by the agreed transfer of control of the Somali operation to the UN itself in 1993.

2. By the same token care must be taken to avoid a fresh North–South polarization from emerging in the economic context. With the global move towards market economics and bilateralism over aid, the old dialogue between rich and poor at the UN, inconclusive and bitter though it periodically was, has increasingly been replaced by the subjection of poorer states to stringent reconstruction programmes dictated by the IMF and World Bank. There

is a danger that these institutions will come to be regarded (and rejected) as outposts of the foreign and economic policies of the affluent North, in particular the USA, thus enhancing the suspicion that the 'UN family' as a whole is an instrument of Western, not world-wide, interests.

3. Some of these tensions would relax if the UN could solve its perennial financial crisis, which is due mainly to the late payment or default on payment of the assessed contributions of the major donors. The most debilitating factor is the disproportion between the contribution of the USA (25 per cent) and that of the remainder of the membership—the next largest contributor being Japan (12 per cent), with the great majority paying the minimum contribution of 0.01 per cent. This disproportion creates fear of US domination within the membership, as well as a combination of resentment and conviction in US governmental and congressional circles that the piper should be able to call the tune. A possible alternative would be to alter the equation on which contributions are assessed, introduce the ingredient of GNP *per head*, and fix a maximum ceiling of 4 per cent per state. This would mean that no state would, in present circumstances, pay more than about $US 40 million a year to the regular budget (roughly the present UK contribution), while the contributions of small, rich states (also in many cases the most vulnerable and most in need of UN protection) would rise to that ceiling—Kuwait, Qatar, the UAE, Saudi Arabia, Singapore, Brunei, Malaysia, and South Korea come to mind. A system on these lines would remove the gross inequalities of the present system, and there would be no excuse for late payment or withholding of such relatively small sums.

4. Given that the UN's non-military coercive measures (sanctions) are of dubious effectiveness and that the 'military articles' are as unworkable in the favourable circumstances of the 1990s as they were in the 'bad old days', i.e. that the Security Council itself cannot conduct a dynamic military campaign, the logical conclusion is that the UN must strengthen its deterrent, pre-emptive

capability so that potential breaches of the peace or acts of aggression can be defused before they explode into conflicts which have to be dealt with by powerful member states acting either unilaterally or with the authority of the Council.

The need for preventive action, either by invoking the public diplomacy of the Security Council to focus a searchlight on a potential aggressor, or by firm diplomatic action by the five Permanent Members acting in concert, or by combining these actions with the dispatch of a deterrent force to the presumed victim's side of a frontier, mandated and armed to fight if attacked, has been evident for decades. It has been pointed out by several commentators, including myself, that such action could almost certainly have prevented Iraq's invasion of Iran in 1980, Israel's invasion of the Lebanon in 1982, Iraq's invasion of Kuwait in 1990, and possibly the outbreak of war in Yugoslavia in 1991.

It is encouraging that the participants in the Security Council summit of 31 January 1992 grasped this point, and that all major states as well as the Secretary-General have since been speaking in terms of closer collaboration within the Security Council and between the Council and regional organizations in the interests of preventing breaches of the peace. This and other points are fully covered in the Secretary-General's report, presented in response to the request made at the Security Council summit, *An Agenda for Peace*.[19] It is vital that the whole report should be carefully studied by the membership and as many as practicable of its recommendations adopted. The danger of its burial under a shower of eulogy must be avoided. However, a warning note must be struck. The Bosnian experience and to some extent the Cambodian evolution have shown that the new-found cooperation amongst the Permanent Members cannot be wholly relied on. These and other cases, including Liberia and Sudan,

---

[19] Boutros Boutros-Ghali, *An Agenda for Peace*, June 1992. See full text at Appendix A.

have demonstrated that the membership as a whole is reluctant to move to enforcement action unless it is virtually risk-free. These factors point to the strong likelihood of dilution of some of the more robust recommendations in *An Agenda for Peace*.

The Role of the UN Secretary-General

JAVIER PÉREZ DE CUÉLLAR

I HAVE been asked to discuss a very contemporary subject. I am, of course, deeply involved in it personally. At first I thought it too limited for this occasion. But my reluctance was overcome by two considerations. First, my distinguished predecessor, the late Dag Hammarskjöld, spoke here in Oxford on a rather similar subject a quarter of a century ago.[1] His exposition was, of course, influenced by the difficult situation he faced at that time. But some of what he said seems to me to be worth re-saying in the perspectives of today. Second, the subject is relevant in many ways to a much larger theme. To understand correctly the role of the Secretary-General is to appreciate the whole mission of the United Nations. And that, in turn, is central to the way international life is organized.

In keeping with the spirit of Oxford University and the rigorously objective manner appropriate thereto, I shall try to discuss the role of the Secretary-General regardless of who may be Secretary-General at any point in time. Men come and go, but institutions remain.

The Charter of the United Nations contains a chapter (Chapter XV) devoted to the Secretariat. It consists of Articles 97 to 101. It assigns two different functions to the Secretary-General: one political and the other administrative. The political function, though much studied and

This is the text of the Cyril Foster Lecture delivered in the Sheldonian Theatre, Oxford, 13 May 1986. Footnotes added later by the Secretary-General's office.

[1] Dag Hammarskjöld, *The International Civil Servant in Law and in Fact* (Clarendon Press, Oxford, 1961). Lecture delivered in the Sheldonian Theatre, Oxford, on 30 May 1961. Also published as UN DPI Press Release SG/1035 of 29 May 1961.

discussed, has never been very precisely defined. The way it is used depends on the state of international relations at the time and also on the political character of the Secretary-General—on his (or, one day, perhaps, her) courage, prudence, and fidelity to the aims of the Charter. This elasticity, if I may call it that, is not peculiar to this office: in varying degrees, it occurs in any institution which has to respond to the complexity of human affairs.

(a) The Secretary-General's Political Functions

Anyone who has the honour to be cast as Secretary-General has to avoid two extremes in playing his, or her, role. On one side is the Scylla of trying to inflate the role through too liberal a reading of the text: of succumbing, that is, to vanity and wishful thinking. On the other is the Charybdis of trying to limit the role to only those responsibilities which are explicitly conferred by the Charter and are impossible to escape: that is, succumbing to modesty, to the instinct of self-effacement, and to the desire to avoid controversy. There are, thus, temptations on both sides. Both are equally damaging to the vitality of the institution. I submit that no Secretary-General should give way to either of them.

The first, the temptation to aggrandizement, can discredit the institution of Secretary-General, and thus the organization as a whole, because it can lead the Secretary-General into courses of action which are not realistically sustainable. When, because of lack of support from the Security Council or the General Assembly, these courses of action have to be abandoned or reversed, the prestige of the organization is bound to suffer. The second, the temptation to extreme caution, can be equally discrediting because situations can, and do, arise when the Secretary-General has to exercise his powers to the full, as the bearer of a sacred trust, and as the guardian of the principles of the Charter. Moreover, in choosing the safer course, he risks causing, through disuse, paralysis of the peace-making and other functions which the Charter vests in him.

The political functions of the Secretary-General are defined in Articles 98 and 99.[2] These authorize him, respectively, to make an annual report to the General Assembly on the work of the organization, and to bring to the attention of the Security Council any matter which, in his opinion, may threaten the maintenance of international peace and security. These functions cannot be fully understood unless we first identify how the Secretary-General fits into the scheme envisaged in the Charter.

Article 7 designates the Secretariat as one of what the founding fathers chose to call the principal organs of the UN. The Secretariat, in turn, is described in Article 97 as comprising a Secretary-General *and* such staff as the organization might require. However, it is the Secretary-General who appoints the staff and it is he alone who is accountable to the member states for the work of the Secretariat. This means that he is co-responsible with the other organs (the General Assembly, the Security Council, and so on) for achieving the organization's aims and purposes. He has thus a dual capacity: in addition to acting as chief administrative officer in the meetings of the General Assembly, the Security Council, the Economic and Social Council, and the Trusteeship Council, he has the independent responsibilities of 'a principal organ'. This may seem a rather fine constitutional point, but failure to understand it can have an adverse effect on attitudes and policies towards the UN.

Misunderstanding can arise from the associations of the word 'secretary' as used in such expressions as the secretary of a committee. Many of the founders of the UN wanted to give a different designation to the occupant of this office. Franklin Roosevelt wished to call him the

---

[2] Art. 98 of the Charter provides: 'The Secretary-General shall act in that capacity in all meetings of the General Assembly, of the Security Council, of the Economic and Social Council, and of the Trusteeship Council, and shall perform such other functions as are entrusted to him by these organs. The Secretary-General shall make an annual report to the General Assembly on the work of the Organization.' Art. 99 of the Charter provides: 'The Secretary-General may bring to the attention of the Security Council any matter which in his opinion may threaten the maintenance of international peace and security.'

World's Moderator;[3] some others proposed having a President and a Director-General for the UN.[4] This gives rise to a question: in choosing the less high-sounding and more conventional term 'Secretary-General', and in entrusting to one person the leadership of the political, administrative, and constitutional functions of the Secretariat, did the framers of the Charter wish to limit the Secretary-General's rights and duties to those given to his predecessor in the League of Nations? I am sure that the answer is no. For they departed radically from the Covenant of the League by including Article 99 and part of Article 98, and thereby giving the Secretary-General the authority to take the initiative in apprising the Security Council of potential threats to international peace and security, and to make an annual report to the General Assembly.

This was not a fortuitous development. On the contrary, it was dictated by the experience of the League of Nations. The League's Covenant, and its practice, were based on a purely administrative conception of the post of Secretary-General. The calamitous events which led to the Second World War revealed that this had been a mistake. A dangerous void had existed: in a situation of dissent and disarray among the European powers, there was no one who could speak for the wider international interest, an

[3] As one history of the UN Charter puts it: 'The President [Roosevelt] . . . brought up a suggestion that he wanted to see worked into the plan of organization, namely, provision for a head of the entire institution . . . [He] seems to have used the term "moderator" in describing his idea of this official.' Ruth B. Russell and Jeanette E. Muther, *A History of the United Nations Charter* (Washington DC, 1958), p. 373. Secretary-General U Thant later said: 'President Roosevelt suggested that the chief officer of the United Nations should be called "moderator" and I know of no better single word to describe my own idea of the office.' U Thant, *The Role of the Secretary-General*, address delivered at the Dag Hammarskjöld Memorial Scholarship Fund of the UN Correspondents' Association, 16 Sept. 1971.

[4] Under one proposed 'Possible Plan for a General International Organization': 'There would be two permanent international officials, the President and the Director-General. The latter would confine himself to administrative functions. The President, "a person of widely recognized eminence", would preside over the executive council, and perform such other duties of a "general political character" as were entrusted to him by the general assembly or by the executive council.' S. M. Schwebel, 'The Origins and Development of Article 99 of the Charter', *British Year Book of International Law 1951*, pp. 373–4.

interest greater than the sum of the interests of the member states. There was no one in a position to initiate timely intervention by the League to avert the collapse of the international system. The framers of the Charter were most anxious not to let such a void occur again. This explains the difference between Article 6 of the League Covenant and Articles 97 to 101 of the UN Charter. Sir Eric Drummond, the first Secretary-General of the League, is said to have remarked that if Article 99 of the Charter had been at his disposal, the position of his office—and, by implication, the influence of the League on events—would have developed differently.

Let me now return to Articles 98 and 99 of the Charter. Article 98 is the constitutional basis on which the Secretary-General makes an annual report to the General Assembly on the work of the organization. This is not meant to be, and should never become, a mere rapporteur's job: 'the work of the organization' is a broad term. It includes, but is not confined to, whatever the organization has done, or had failed to do, or is required to do. Its submission is one of the ways in which the Secretary-General can act as an initiator and can galvanize the efforts of the other parts of the UN. I myself have sought to give a thematic focus to the annual reports submitted during my mandate;[5] I am grateful for the reception they have met, but most of the steps I have suggested are, in 1986, yet to be taken.

As for Article 99 of the Charter, this, as I have said, authorizes the Secretary-General to bring to the attention of the Security Council any matter which in his opinion may threaten the maintenance of international peace and security. This authority contains the three elements of right, responsibility, and discretion. The Secretary-General's right is apparent from the wording and has never been the subject of dispute. However, the other two elements—responsibility and discretion—are interrelated.

---

[5] Annual Reports by the present Secretary-General have the following DPI reference numbers: DPI/721-40992 (Sept. 1982); DPI/785-41191 (Sept. 1983); DPI/829-41364 (Sept. 1984); DPI/862-41361 (Sept. 1985); DPI/897-41114 (Sept. 1986).

In considering them, it is worth bearing in mind that, when the Charter was being drafted, a proposal to amend the Article so as to make its invocation a *duty* of the Secretary-General had to be withdrawn.[6]

Before invoking the Article, the Secretary-General has to consider carefully how his initiative will fare, given the agreement or lack thereof among the Permanent Members and also the positions of the Non-permanent Members. A situation may in certain cases be aggravated and not eased if the Secretary-General draws attention, under Article 99, and the Security Council then does nothing. Situations that threaten the peace are usually highly complicated and require a flexible and finely tuned response from the Secretary-General. Hence the discretion allowed him by Article 99. Two situations with equally dangerous potential may have to be dealt with in two different ways, depending on how far they can be insulated from great power rivalries, how far the parties are susceptible to moral suasion, and, in some cases, whether one or both of them is reluctant to face exposure in the Security Council. It is worth adding that the possibility that invocation of Article 99 might displease a member state, whether or not a party to the dispute, most certainly ought *not* to be a consideration inhibiting the Secretary-General.

I have said earlier that the chastening failure of the League of Nations was much in the mind of the drafters of the UN Charter. Article 99 makes it clear that they envisage the Secretary-General, in addition to his other functions, as someone with the power to anticipate and prevent crises. The words 'in his opinion' and 'may threaten' clearly signify, first, that the right vested in him can be exercised in relation not only to actual but also to potential causes of conflict; and, second, that he is expected to evaluate constantly and independently all matters which have a bearing on peace and security. It is also noteworthy that the Article uses the much broader

---

[6] United Nations Conference on International Organization, San Francisco, 1945, *Documents*, vol. 7 (London, 1945), pp. 392 and 556.

term 'matter' and not 'situation or dispute'. The term covers all developments which (to quote the words of the Preparatory Commission of the United Nations) 'could have serious political implications remediable only by political action'.

The Secretary-General is thus given a reservoir of authority, a wide margin of discretion, which requires the most careful political judgement and is limited only by prudence. The ways in which this authority would be exercised and this discretion used could not have been anticipated at the time the Charter was framed. Nor did the drafters of the Charter foresee the circumstances in which Article 99 would be invoked. They had relied on a scheme of collective security predicated on agreement among the Permanent Members of the Security Council. When this basic assumption of great power unanimity broke down, indecision or inaction in the Council was often the result. Over the years, therefore, the practice grew for the Secretary-General himself to help to moderate conflicts or negotiate solutions, without, of course, detracting in any way from the Council's primary role. This kind of action by the Secretary-General does not necessarily require a formal invocation of Article 99. In my own experience, it has usually had to be discharged without such invocation. A topical instance is the reported use of chemical weapons in the Iran–Iraq war.[7]

Article 99 is concerned with action by the Secretary-General *vis-à-vis* the Security Council. He is given comparable powers *vis-à-vis* the General Assembly by the rule which accords him the right to place on the Assembly's provisional agenda all items which he deems necessary.[8] In both these cases, this function of the Secretary-General is not merely an attribute of his office but also one of the essential ways in which the UN can respond to the demands of the international situation. In the present state of international affairs, the Security Council is often

[7] See the following Reports of the Secretary-General: S/16433 (26 Mar. 1984); S/17127 (17 Apr. 1985); S/17911 (12 Mar. 1986).

[8] Rule 13(G) of the General Assembly Rules of Procedure (UN publication sales no. E.85.I.13).

unable to adopt a resolution because of division among its Permanent Members. Equally often, it makes a recommendation which is rejected by one of the parties, or it adopts a resolution which is not supported, or is perceived as not being supported, by some important states directly or indirectly involved. In all such cases, the Secretary-General has to act as the main intermediary between the parties, and to help pave the way, if he can, for an eventual accommodation or agreement between them. In 1986, the Secretary-General remains the only channel of communication between the parties involved in questions relating to Afghanistan, the Iran–Iraq war, Cyprus, and south Lebanon. In such efforts, the Secretary-General has to improvise, and may sometimes feel compelled to suggest means other than those which had been envisaged by the Security Council in its original discussions of the matter. The same is true with the General Assembly. Controversy often persists after the Assembly adopts a resolution. Here again, it becomes the duty of the Secretary-General to ensure, as far as he can, that the parties remain open to dialogue.

A caveat, however, must be entered here. It is of great importance that trust should be placed in the Secretary-General by the Security Council, by the General Assembly, and by governments, but delegation of responsibility to him should not be a way for member states to escape the responsibilities placed on them by the Charter. We must cling to the Charter concept of collective action for peace and security, and we must do nothing to weaken the chances of eventually putting it into practice. It cannot be repeated too often that it is the Security Council which bears the primary responsibility for such action. Disharmony between the different organs does not help the effective development of the UN. Moreover, it would gravely harm the interests of peace if the Secretary-General were ever to become a façade, behind which there was only deadlock and disagreement. He must not become an alibi for inaction. No authority delegated to the Secretary-General, and no exercise by him of this authority, can fill the existing vacuum in collective security. This vacuum is due to dissension among the Permanent Members of the Security Council, to the failure of member states to resort to the Charter's mechanisms for the settlement of disputes, and to their lack of respect for the decisions of the Security Council.

When the Secretary-General exercises his good offices, under the specific mandates given him, and within the general purview of Article 33 of the Charter, which requires the parties to a dispute to seek a solution by peaceful means, the UN is using quiet diplomacy, the diplomacy of reconciliation. There does not seem to be enough appreciation of the advantages of the UN in this respect. This is indicated by the many instances today where the UN is bypassed.

Multilateral diplomacy of the kind in which the Secretary-General is frequently engaged differs from traditional diplomacy in several ways. As it is conducted in accordance with the principles of the Charter, it does not place the weaker party in an unfavourable position. It seeks an objective and lasting settlement of a dispute and not merely one which responds to the expediencies of the day. In a multilateral approach, all the member states of the UN have a direct or indirect influence: this can assure, as much as anything can, that the vital interests of all parties are taken into account. Such an approach can spot points of potential agreement which may not be obvious at first sight or in the context of power-political interests. The aim of traditional diplomacy was often limited to a stable balance of power: whether the balance conformed to justice was a lesser concern. But peace as envisaged by the UN Charter is a just peace: take that moral dimension away and we are back to the disorder and the injustice of power politics.

If quiet diplomacy is to succeed, it needs the confidence of all parties. And that means that the Secretary-General must not only be impartial but must be perceived to be so. He must not allow his independence of judgement to be impaired or distorted by pressures from governments. He should have no part in any diplomatic deal or undertaking which ignores the principles of the Charter or the relevant pronouncements of the competent organs of the UN.

However, moral concern must not become moral hubris. The Secretary-General must not allow himself to be influenced by his own judgement of the moral worth of either party's position or, for that matter, by what the leaders or media of one country glibly say about the position of the other. Subjective attitudes must not be allowed to hinder progress towards mutual understanding between the parties.

This is perhaps the severest demand the job makes on the Secretary-General. It is hard to suppress one's sympathies and preferences and harder still to endure the frustrations and discouragements which quiet diplomacy entails. But the Secretary-General does not have the option of being partial or of being discouraged. In saying that, however, I do not claim that the Secretary-General has at his disposal moral resources greater than his fellow men. What I do assert is that he cannot shoulder the burden of his office without unlimited patience, and an unfailing sense of justice and humanity.

When states are in conflict, the Secretary-General has to try to understand the roots of insecurity, the fears and resentments and the legitimate aspirations which inspire a people or a state to take the positions they do. International conflicts often occur when one party and its supporters ignore the fears of the other. If a third party is to succeed in resolving the conflict, he has to address the fears of each with empathy and imagination.

This process is not equally helpful in all cases, and should not be endless in any case. Sometimes the leadership of a state takes a stubborn stand and seems immune to rational persuasion. In such a case, the Secretary-General should go on as far as the point at which further exercise of his good offices can only disguise the reality: he should then state the facts plainly, without denunciation but without hiding the facts.

Apart from the exercise of good offices, the Secretary-General is often entrusted with other functions by the main organs of the UN. Often a report is requested from him. I strongly believe that such requests should not be made as a matter of routine or to cover up the failure of the body concerned to agree on effective action. Another common occurrence is for the Secretary-General to be asked to secure compliance with a resolution. Difficulties can then arise if there is disagreement amongst the member states about how the resolution is to be interpreted. There are very few absolutes in international affairs. The principles of the Charter no doubt command everyone's assent. But, because of different perceptions and values, there is often controversy about how they should be applied in a complicated situation. In such a case, the powers delegated to the Secretary-General do not always provide the answer. All he can do is to interpret as faithfully as he can the directives of the competent bodies, and the rights and obligations of the UN under international law.

Impartiality is thus the heart and soul of the office of the Secretary General. His impartiality must remain untainted by any feeling of indebtedness to governments which may have supported his appointment. I attach the greatest importance to this point and I therefore suggest that we should re-establish the healthy convention that no person should ever be a candidate, declared or undeclared, for this office. It is a post that should come *unsought* to a qualified person. However impeccable a person's integrity may be, he cannot in fact retain the necessary independence if he proclaims his candidacy and conducts a kind of election campaign, overt or covert. Some promises are bound to be made during his canvassing. But the only promise a future Secretary-General can properly make is to fulfil his duties under the Charter. There is no reason to fear that the convention I propose would make it more difficult for the member states to select a Secretary-General. Governments will always have a list of persons whom they consider qualified for the office. If it was a firm rule that such persons and their governments should go no further than answering enquiries about their availability, this would, I am sure, reinforce the moral authority which any Secretary-General must have.

In today's world, neither the functions of the Secretary-General nor multilateral diplomacy should be limited to good offices or negotiation. One of the UN's duties in a crisis is to be alert to all the nuances, and to use its contacts with governments to try to allay the underlying fears and suspicions. If it is successful in this, it may elicit concessions which the adversaries, left to themselves, would never consider. However, this requires a conscious decision on the part of the member states to strengthen the role of the Secretary-General and to provide him with better means to keep a watch over actual and potential points of conflict. At present, the UN lacks independent sources of information: its means of obtaining up-to-date information are primitive by comparison with those of member states—and indeed of most transnational corporations. To judge whether a matter may threaten international peace and security, the Secretary-General needs more than news reports and analyses made by outside experts: he needs full and impartial data, and he needs to be able to monitor developments world-wide. To enable the Secretariat to do this would in no way alter the distribution of functions and powers between the principal organs of the UN. Strengthening the institutional basis of preventive diplomacy would not diminish the role of the Security Council: on the contrary, it would enhance its effectiveness. The Secretary-General is, after all, a collaborator of the Security Council and not its competitor.

(b) The Secretary-General's Administrative Role

I have so far concentrated on the political role of the Secretary-General, as this is the part of his responsibilities which attracts the most interest. But equally important is his administrative function under Article 97 of the Charter which designates him as the chief administrative officer of the organization.

The responsibilities of the UN are now so widespread in the political, economic, social, and humanitarian fields that the Secretariat requires a staff highly qualified in most of the modern scientific and cultural disciplines. Articles 100 and 101 of the Charter saw the Secretariat as a genuinely international civil service, responsible only to the organization, and gave the Secretary-General the exclusive power of appointing the staff, bearing in mind the need for the highest standards of efficiency, competence, and integrity.

It is ironic and unfortunate that, while there has been a dramatic rise in the Secretary-General's political responsibilities, his powers in the administrative field have been steadily eroded over the years. First of all, governments profess their dedication to the principle of an independent international civil service, but few refrain from trying to bring pressure to bear in favour of their own particular interests, especially on the personnel side. Second, the distribution of functions between the legislature and the executive, so essential to sound management, tends to be blurred when increasingly detailed directives about management policy are issued by the General Assembly. All this raises serious questions of organizational responsibility. The member states cannot ignore these if they want an efficient apparatus at their disposal to fulfil the purposes of the Charter. The problem has been aggravated by the financial crisis caused by the withholding of part of their contributions by a number of member states. The morale of the staff, the efficient execution of programmes, and the orderly management of the organization—all are jeopardized by the member states' failure to agree on a budgetary process and a scale of contributions acceptable to all.

The General Assembly reconvened its fortieth session on 28 April 1986 at my request to address this question urgently, for it threatens the viability and the very existence of the organization.[9] I proposed to the Assembly a

---

[9] Para. 13 of the Report of the Secretary-General on the Current Financial Crisis of the United Nations submitted to the General Assembly on 12 Apr. 1986 (UN doc. A/40/1102) summarized the situation as follows:

A. Arrears as at 1 Jan. 1986	$242.4 m.
B. Amount of 1986 assessments	$735.6 m.
C. Total payments due (A + B)	$978 m.
D. *Less* expected payments in 1986	$715 to $703 m.
E. Arrears projected at 31 Dec. 1986 (C − D)	$263 to $275 m.
F. *Less* estimated reserves projected to 31 Dec. 1986	$199.2 m.
G. Resulting shortfall projected to 31 Dec. 1986 (E − F)	$63.8 to $75.8 m.

package of measures to deal with this emergency and to preserve the operational effectiveness of the UN. At the same time, I made it clear that the Assembly was faced with questions about the future—the future of a UN sound in structure and enjoying the wide confidence and support which it must have to accomplish its great tasks. I am happy to say that the Assembly broadly endorsed my proposals; but the long-term problem remains.[10]

The international civil service is facing perhaps its most serious challenge ever. It would best be strengthened if member states would accept that the Secretary-General should carry out his functions as chief administrative officer without undue interference or political pressure. It must be recognized that it is the responsibility of the Secretary-General to ensure that the organization has at its disposal the staff necessary to perform all the functions given to it by the legislative bodies. It would be a refreshing change if the General Assembly and individual member states were to exercise more forbearance and give the Secretary-General the flexibility he needs to ensure the smooth and efficient functioning of the Secretariat.

(c) Priority Areas of International Concern

Over and above the adminstrative and political functions I have described, the Secretary-General's concerns must embrace the situation of the human community in general. Four areas at present demand priority.

---

[10] On 9 May 1986 the General Assembly accepted budgetary proposals along the lines proposed by the Secretary-General.

On 19 Dec. 1986 the General Assembly decided that the recommendations of the Group of High-Level Intergovernmental Experts to Review the Efficiency of the Adminstrative and Financial Functioning of the UN (*GAOR*, supplement no. 49 (UN doc. A/41/49)) should be implemented by the Secretary-General taking into account a number of complementary points made by the Assembly (GA Res. 41/213). In the same resolution, the Assembly defined a revised procedure for determining the biennial budget and the longer-range medium-term plan.

On 11 Dec. 1986 the General Assembly had approved the continuation in 1987, with judicious adjustment, of the economy measures introduced in 1986 (GA Res. 41/204). This action was based on the Secretary-General's projection of possible further withholdings in 1987 and a resultant cash shortfall of $US 85 m.

The first is that of disarmament, particularly nuclear disarmament. The Secretary-General has the duty to stress the profound and incalculable danger that lies in the arms race. He has to avoid untimely interventions on specific issues, but he cannot remain a silent witness to a process by which a responsibility that belongs to all nations is monopolized by a few—the responsibility of assuring the survival of humanity and of organized society on this earth.

The second area of urgent concern is human rights. Frequent and sometimes massive violations of human rights are taking place in various parts of the world. Cruel penalties are inflicted on an untold number of people for no reason other than that they assert their basic rights. Human dignity is being denied and human lives and talent mutilated. Faced with these tragic realities, the Secretary-General must consider it one of his principal duties to help bring relief, whenever and wherever he can, to the victims of oppression. This is one of my daily preoccupations and a major anxiety. But in this area, too, great caution is needed: given the susceptibilities of governments, an indiscreet intervention, though morally satisfying, can have the opposite of the desired effect and serve only to aggravate the suffering of the persecuted. The main criterion must be the achievement of concrete results, whether or not a statement or report or silence by the Secretary-General serves the political interest of one side or another.

The third area is the shaming disparity of living standards between those who live in the developed world—the North—and their less fortunate brethren in the developing world—the South. This all-pervading problem touches on many of the Secretary-General's other concerns. For such disparities of wealth are unjust in themselves: and, in the world, as in individual countries, they provoke envy and strife, which, in turn, cause political conflict, with all the misery that flows from it. It has become a truism that a fraction of the resources spent on armaments could produce a radical improvement in the living standards of the developing world. These are questions that take up much of the General Assembly's time. Again, the Secretary-General's role is to do all he can to foster agreement between the North and the South on economic relations between them.

The fourth area of special concern is how the world should respond to natural or man-made disasters. The Secretary-General serves as a rallying point for its response. He should be the one who summons help on a systematic and organized basis. Recent and current action to relieve the plight of Africa demonstrates his role in this respect. I was inspired by the proof it gave of a sense of human solidarity. I hope that a response in the same spirit will be made to the dire situation now existing in Bolivia[11] and Haiti,[12] not only to relieve suffering, but also to encourage political and social progress.

(d) The Special Position of the Secretary-General

All this goes to show that the Secretary-General has a constituency unlike any other. It is a two-tier constituency. On the one hand, he is elected by the governments of 159 sovereign states, and it is to them that he is answerable for the way he discharges his mandate. But every one of those

[11] The Secretary-General's actions in the case of Bolivia arose from a personal request in Dec. 1982 by the President of the newly installed democratic government of Bolivia. The President requested that the Secretary-General use his good offices to mobilize financial support from the international community to assist the Bolivian government in its efforts to resolve the severe economic and social difficulties which it inherited on assuming office and which, if unresolved, were of sufficient gravity to undermine the democratic process so recently restored. To this end, the Secretary-General immediately appointed a Special Representative for Bolivia, and subsequently convened numerous special meetings of representatives of UN member states and of international financial institutions. His most recent initiative has been to assist in the establishment of a social emergency fund destined for specific programmes in support of economic reactivation and improved living conditions to offset the inevitable social impact of the 1985 economic stabilization programme.

[12] The former President of Haiti, Jean-Claude Duvalier, left the country on 7 Feb. 1986. A new government was then constituted under General Henri Namphy. The Secretary-General paid an official visit to Haiti later in 1986. His actions in the case of Haiti took place against the economic and social background described in the *Programme interimaire de développement 1986–88*, published by the Commissariat à la Promotion Régional et à l'Administration Publique, Port au Prince, Oct. 1986: in particular, chap. 1.

governments is attached to its own perceptions of its national interests, which means that the Secretary-General could not perform his duties under the Charter if he did not sometimes act above and beyond national positions.

Of course the Secretary-General is supposed to represent the member states' common interest in implementation of the principles laid down in the Charter. But the problem is that common interest does not always exist—or, rather, is not always perceived to exist. As I said earlier, when there are conflicting interpretations of these principles in a particular situation, the Secretary-General can be pulled in opposite directions by the member states. When agreement does not exist among governments, the first-tier constituency—the governments which elected him—can offer the Secretary-General little strength and support. It is then that he sometimes has to think of his second-tier constituency, namely the peoples for whom those governments act—all the peoples of the world who together form a single constituency for peace.

It is, therefore, not only the right but also the duty of the Secretary-General to maintain contact as best he can with the adherents of the principles of the UN Charter who exist in every society in the world. Time and the meagre resources at his disposal limit him severely in this respect. He must, nevertheless, do all he can to expound the principles of the United Nations, and what he is doing to implement them, to the parliaments, the media, and the universities of different countries. In doing so, he does not seek to incite criticism of their governments' policies; his aim is to encourage a clearer and fairer view of matters affecting other countries, and sometimes the whole world. I have been assured by many governments that, far from creating difficulties for them, such action by the Secretary-General helps them to counteract the parochialism of their domestic opinion.

I should like to end on a personal note. The Secretary-General is constantly subjected to many and diverse pressures. But in the last analysis, his office is a lonely one. He cannot stand idle. Yet helplessness is often his lot. The idealism and hope of which the Charter is a luminous expression have to confront the narrow dictates of national policies. The Secretary-General's efforts must be based on reason but, behind many a government's allegedly logical position, there are myths and silent fears. The voice of the Charter is often drowned by clashes and conflicts between states. If the Secretary-General is to ride above these contradictions in international life, two qualities are essential.

One is faith that humanity can move—and indeed is moving—towards a less irrational, less violent, more compassionate, and more generous international order. However grim the past and present may seem, the Secretary-General has to remain firm in his belief that, although people are swayed by short-term interests and local preoccupations, the movement towards good has an enduring appeal, and that good will triumph in the end.

The other essential quality is to feel that he is a citizen of the world. This sounds a cliché, but the Secretary-General would not deserve his mandate if he did not develop a sense of belonging to every nation or culture, reaching out as best he can to the impulse for peace and good that exists in all of them. He is a world citizen because all world problems are *his* problems; the Charter is his home and his ideology, and its principles are his moral creed.

6

The Good Offices Function of the UN Secretary-General

THOMAS M. FRANCK and GEORG NOLTE

THE immediate aftermath of the Cold War witnessed a remarkable blossoming of the United Nations. This was reflected in the growth of peacekeeping operations,[1] and in the stream of mandatory resolutions from the Security Council. Concurrently, the political role of the Secretary-General, including the 'good offices' function, also appeared to be expanding.

This was recognized on the occasion of the first-ever summit meeting of the leaders of the states members of the Security Council: they invited the Secretary-General to prepare recommendations on, *inter alia*, 'how greater use might be made of his good offices'.[2] They were thereby mainly referring to the comparatively independent political role which the Secretary-General plays in the prevention or resolution of conflicts of international concern.[3]

Thanks are expressed to the Filomen D'Agostino and Max E. Greenberg Research Fund of New York University School of Law for financial assistance supporting Prof. Franck's research. This is a version of part of Professor Franck's 1993 General Course in Public International Law at the Hague Academy of International Law.

[1] Listed below in Appendix E. See also Sally Morphet's chapter below.

[2] UN doc. S/23500 of 31 Jan. 1992, p. 4.

[3] The traditional meaning of the term 'good offices' is more restricted. In UN parlance and practice, however, it has come to cover not only 'mediation' (see Handbook on the Peaceful Settlement of Disputes betwen States, in: 'Report of the Special Committee on the Charter of the UN and on the Strengthening of the Role of the Organization', *GAOR*, supplement no. 33 (A/46/33), p. 61), but also fact-finding missions (see e.g. UN Press Release SG/SM/4727/ Rev. 1, 10 Apr. 1992, p. 6; and GA Res. 46/59 of 17 Jan. 1992). The word is even used in connection with an operation to oversee a troop withdrawal, such

Although this activity is rarely visible to the public, it constitutes one of the most important functions of the UN. As former Secretary-General Pérez de Cuéllar put it: 'No one will ever know how many conflicts have been prevented or limited through contacts which have taken place in the famous glass mansion which can become fairly opaque when necessary'.[4] But the good offices function is not only noteworthy for its practical importance. Its exercise has also always been the most crucial indicator of the Secretary-General's evolving constitutional role within the UN system.

(a) Historical Perspective: Earlier Cases

As early as September 1946, when the Security Council was considering whether to send a commission of inquiry to investigate alleged infiltration across Greece's northern frontier, Secretary-General Trygve Lie announced that his office claimed an independent power of investigation separate from that of the Council. He said:

I hope the Council will understand that the Secretary-General must reserve his rights to make such enquiries or investigations as he may think necessary, in order to determine whether or not he should consider bringing any aspect of this matter up to the attention of the Council under the provisions of the Charter.[5]

In October 1948 he again stepped forward with his own detailed solutions to the Berlin crisis:[6] these proposals were not accepted.[7] Undaunted, two years later he sought to negotiate with China's emissary to start talks on a settlement of the Korean war.[8]

---

as the UN Good Offices Mission to Afghanistan and Pakistan (UNGOMAP): see SC Res. 622 of 31 Oct. 1988, para. 1. The Secretary-General has stressed that this 'is a very flexible term as it may mean very little or very much'. Handbook, cited above, p. 62.

[4] UN Press Release SG/SM/4124, 20 Apr. 1988, pp. 7–8.

[5] SCOR, 1st year, 70th mtg., 20 Sept. 1946, p. 404.

[6] Arthur W. Rovine, The First Fifty Years: The Secretary-General in World Politics 1920–1970 (Leiden, 1970), p. 227; Evan Luard, A History of the United Nations, vol. 1 (New York, 1982), p. 347.

[7] Rovine, The First Fifty Years, pp. 227–8.   [8] Ibid., pp. 244–5.

Much more successful and celebrated was Hammar-skjöld's initiative in obtaining the release in 1955 of American aircrew imprisoned by Beijing. Although his initiative was specifically authorized by the General Assembly,[9] Hammarskjöld, inventing what became known as the 'Peking Formula', dissociated himself from that resolution, in part because it was too judgemental, and in part because he wished to assert clearly his independent powers of intervention, untethered to prescriptions devised by one of the political organs.[10] In 1956, after Nasser's nationalization of the Suez Canal, Hammarskjöld, on his own authority, initiated private negotiations between the foreign ministers of Egypt, Britain, and France. Two years later, during the landing of the American Marines in Lebanon, Hammarskjöld acted on his own authority in the face of a deadlocked Security Council to augment the UN Observer Group in Lebanon (UNOGIL) in order to make it strong enough to replace the American presence. 'Were you to disapprove,' he said to the Security Council, 'I would of course accept the consequences of your judgement'.[11] In so formulating the limits of his authority, the Secretary-General indicated his belief that he could act in the interest of world peace when the political organs had fallen into desuetude, at least until such time as the political organs acted to rescind his claimed authority.

In the autumn of 1959, during the Laotian civil war, Hammarskjöld accepted an invitation from the government of that kingdom to go to investigate in order to give himself the 'opportunity to get, at first hand, as complete a picture as possible of conditions and developments in Laos of relevance from the point of view of the general responsibilities of the Secretary-General'.[12] This he justified on the basis of his 'general responsibilities ... regarding

[9] GA Res. 906 (IX) of 10 Dec. 1954.
[10] UN doc. A/2888 of 17 Dec. 1954; Report SG A/2954 of 9 Sept. 1955; Brian Urquhart, *Hammarskjöld* (New York, 1972), p. 101.
[11] *SCOR*, 13th year, 837th mtg., 22 July 1958, p. 4.
[12] Urquhart, *Hammarskjöld*, p. 352 (quoting letter from Hammarskjöld to each member of the Security Council).

developments which may threaten peace and security' and his administrative authority under the Charter.[13] The mission neither sought, nor received, approval from the deadlocked Security Council. When Thailand and Cambodia proposed taking the dispute to the Security Council, he quietly urged them to accept, instead, mediation of his Personal Representative, Yohan Beck-Friis of Sweden. 'You can see how much more effective and smooth working such a technique is than the regular one,' he wrote, 'which involves all the meetings and debates and so on.'[14]

In July 1961, during the French occupation of the city of Bizerta, Hammarskjöld flew to Tunisia at the request of the Tunisian government.[15] Two years later, the new Secretary-General, U Thant, took the initiative in working out an agreement between the parties to the Yemeni civil war. It called for UN observers to be posted along the demilitarized zone at the Yemeni–Saudi border to prevent infiltration.[16] Without seeking authorization, U Thant sent a team of 114 Yugoslavs borrowed from the UN Emergency Force in the Middle East, augmenting it with fifty personnel borrowed from the Royal Canadian Air Force. Although that initiative had the approval of the parties to the conflict, the Security Council did not meet to authorize the force until several days after it had been in place.[17] In October 1962, U Thant also took a series of personal initiatives in regard to the Cuban missile crisis, none of which had been authorized by other organs or by the parties.[18] When fighting erupted between India and Pakistan in August 1965, he took the lead in setting up a new observer group, the UN India–Pakistan Observer Mission (UNIPOM), to monitor the truce he had helped to negotiate. The funding for UNIPOM was drawn from

[13] Ibid.
[14] Wilder Foote (ed.), *Dag Hammarskjöld—Servant of Peace: A Selection of his Speeches and Statements* (New York, 1962), p. 264.
[15] Urquhart, *Hammarskjöld*, p. 533.
[16] UN doc. S/5298 of 29 Apr. 1963, pp. 1–3.
[17] SC Res. 179 of 11 June 1963.
[18] See UN Press Release SG/1357, 26 Oct. 1962, p. 1; UN Press Release SG/1358, 26 Oct. 1962, p. 2.

an account for unforeseen peacekeeping contingencies, and $US 2 million were expended without prior budgetary authorization.

In 1970, U Thant agreed to mediate the dispute over the future of Bahrain, on which Britain was about to bestow independence, but which was claimed by Iran. The actual negotiations were undertaken for him by Ralph Bunche and eventually led to an agreement which averted a crisis. Ambassador Vittorio Winspeare Guicciardi was sent to conduct a field inquiry which reported that the people of that territory desired independence rather than union with Iran, a finding accepted by both adversaries and ultimately endorsed by the Security Council.[19]

Perhaps most remarkable, if not successful, was U Thant's determined search for a negotiated peace in Vietnam during 1964–5, even though that conflict had never been brought before any UN organ, and despite considerable lack of enthusiasm for his efforts first by the United States[20] and later by North Vietnam.[21]

When Kurt Waldheim, on Christmas Eve 1977, brought about the release of eight French hostages being held by the Saharawi liberation movement (Polisario) and personally flew them from Algiers to Paris, he, too, neither requested nor received authorization from the Security Council or the General Assembly.[22] On a much larger scale, he took personal initiatives in convening a sixty-five-country meeting on Vietnamese refugees and displaced persons in July 1979, at which he secured a doubling of the number of resettlement places (to 260,000) and elicited $US 190 million in new funds for resettlement centres. He also negotiated an agreement with Hanoi that resulted in the introduction of orderly departure

---

[19] SC Res. 278 of 11 May 1970. See also Anthony Parsons' discussion of the Bahrain issue, pp. 108–9 above.   [20] *New York Times*, 7 Aug. 1964, p. 1.

[21] Ibid., 12 Apr. 1965, p. 1.

[22] Kurt Waldheim, *The Challenge of Peace* (New York, 1980), pp. 1–2; see *New York Times*, 13 Nov. 1977, p. A3; 16 Dec. 1977, p. A7; *The Times* (London), 21 Dec. 1977, p. 5; *New York Times*, 24 Dec. 1977, p. 2; UN Press Release SG/SM/2521/Rev. 1, 14 Dec. 1977, p. 1.

procedures.[23] This was followed by a highly successful pledging conference on behalf of Kampuchean refugees, a step taken entirely on the Secretary-General's own authority.[24]

By the time Javier Pérez de Cuéllar assumed the office of Secretary-General, his predecessors had created for themselves a dispute-settlement role separate and often different from the expressed policy of some, or even most, members. Secretaries-General had felt justified, at times, in acting on their own to safeguard what they perceived to be minimum standards of world order; and they had been completely successful in drawing a line between their role and the role played by the political organs at the behest of member states. By the mid-1980s there could be little doubt that the only important winner in the intra-institutional power struggle had been the Secretary-General.[25] The General Assembly could make more noise, and the Security Council could act more decisively, if there ever was unanimity among the Permanent Members. But to the limited extent that the UN was having any salutary effect on the real world beyond its own compound, it was primarily because of the functions being performed by the Secretary-General.[26]

---

[23] T. T. B. Koh, 'The United Nations: Perception and Reality', speech to a meeting of Asian mass media, sponsored by the UN Department of Public Information, Manila, 12–14 May 1983, p. 14 (mimeo); and *New York Times*, 22 July 1979, p. 1. See also Memorandum of Understanding, 30 May 1979, between the government of the Socialist Republic of Vietnam and the UN High Commissioner for Refugees (UNHCR) concerning the departure of persons from the Socialist Republic of Vietnam. (UN doc. A/C.3/34/7 of 2 Nov. 1979, annexe.) The announcement on the moratorium on expulsions—two-thirds of which were ethnic Chinese—by sea was made by Waldheim in a press conference at the end of the Geneva meeting. (UN Press Release SG/REF/8, 23 July 1979, p. 1). In a dissonant note, officials of the UNHCR were quoted as dissociating themselves from the agreement and expressing distaste for its provisions limiting the rights of Vietnamese to flee their country (UN Press Release SG/REF/8, p. 1).   [24] See Koh, 'The United Nations', p. 1.

[25] Pérez de Cuéllar emphasized this development in his important 1986 lecture at Oxford University. See above, pp. 131–2.

[26] Some more instances of the 'good offices' role of the Secretary-General until 1985 are collected in Handbook on the Peaceful Settlement of Disputes between States, *GAOR*, supplement no. 33 (A/46/33), pp. 64–6.

(b) Recent Examples of the 'Good Offices' Role

That was the situation up to the end of the conflict between the superpowers. More recently, things have begun to change. Despite the fact that the Secretary-General, together with the rest of the UN system, has gained in stature since the easing of the Cold War tensions, the impact of the new era on his office's capacity for taking independent initiatives is ambiguous.

1. Afghanistan

The first of the recent series of major successes in the exercise of the Secretary-General's good offices function was the conclusion of the Geneva accords of April 1988 which provided, *inter alia*, for the withdrawal of the Soviet troops from Afghanistan.[27] This was the culmination of a lengthy and often frustrating effort. The General Assembly had first called for the exercise of his good offices in 1980,[28] whereupon the Secretary-General had approached the parties to induce them to enter into negotiations. But since the General Assembly, at the same time, had also called for an immediate troop withdrawal, the Afghan and Soviet governments initially found the resolution to be an unsatisfactory basis for the Secretary-General's mandate. Thus, when Afghanistan did enter into negotiations with Pakistan under the auspices of the Secretary-General, in June 1982, it did so on the tacit understanding, deliberately encouraged by the Secretary-General, that a state may reject Assembly resolutions and yet enter into negotiations with him:[29] a variation of the 'Peking Formula'.

The negotiations themselves are an instructive example of the good offices process. At first, the Special Representative of the Secretary-General, Diego Cordovez, using the UN Palais des Nations in Geneva, received the two delegations at different times. Two years later, as the talks advanced, he shuttled between the parties, who were

---

[27] UN doc. S/19835 of 26 Apr. 1988, p. 3; UN Press Release S/1860, 14 Apr. 1988.   [28] GA Res. ES–6/2 of 14 Jan. 1980.
[29] See UN Press Release SG/SM/4124, 20 Apr. 1988, p. 8.

located in different parts of the UN building ('proximity talks'). At the same time, he initiated consultations in the capitals of the states concerned. Progress in the procedures for consultation was matched by movement towards progress on matters of substance. In 1985, the parties agreed to a package of linked accords with the United States and the Soviet Union to act as their co-guarantors.[30] It was not until early 1988 that the two sides reached consensus on a time-frame for troop withdrawal and the establishment of a supervisory mechanism. A year later, the UN Good Offices Mission in Afghanistan and Pakistan (UNGOMAP) was able to report the timely completion of the withdrawal.[31]

The Geneva accords on Afghanistan had only led to a withdrawal of Soviet forces, but left the Afghan civil war unresolved. Such an internal conflict poses quite different and more complex problems for a Secretary-General than does a crisis in relations between states. Pérez de Cuéllar himself acknowledged this inhibition of his office: the UN, he said, is an 'organisation of governments'. It would be 'against our philosophy to be in touch with the enemies of governments'.[32] A year later, however, this position began to evolve, as Soviet objection to a UN role in this 'domestic' matter began to soften. The Secretary-General now thought that it was an appropriate task for the UN to help to set up a broad-based government in Afghanistan.[33] A few months later, this view was confirmed by a General Assembly resolution requesting him to 'facilitate . . . a comprehensive political agreement'.[34] To carry out this new good offices function, the Secretary-General redeployed personnel from UNGOMAP, whose mandate was, in any event, about to expire.[35]

The new phase of Afghani good offices was assigned to the Secretary-General's Personal Representative, Benon

---

[30] UN Press Release SG/1859, 13 Apr. 1988, pp. 1 and 2.
[31] UN doc. S/20465 of 15 Feb. 1989, p. 1.
[32] UN Press Release SG/SM/4127, 27 Apr. 1988, p. 6.
[33] UN Press Release SG/SM/4263, 16 Feb. 1989, p. 1.
[34] GA Res. 44/15 of 1 Nov. 1989, para. 10; GA Res. 45/12 of 7 Nov. 1990, para. 9.   [35] UN doc. S/21188 of 12 Mar. 1990.

Sevan. He at once emphasized the important change of parameters which marked the shift from the intergovernmental first phase of the negotiations to the new stage that would 'be a strictly Afghan process'.[36] Intensive consultations ensued, during which the Representative engaged the principal parties in separate discussions, seeking a formula for beginning substantive negotiations. By early 1992 Sevan's five-point plan[37] had received sufficient support to allow the Secretary-General to announce an agreement to form a pre-transitional Governing Council and to convene a formal peace conference in the immediate future.[38] The military collapse of the Najibullah regime, however, almost at once overtook this plan.

2. Cambodia

The Secretary-General also made a major contribution to the 1991 Paris agreement on the Cambodian question. As with Afghanistan, his role as a neutral good officer was affected by a history of resolutions passed by the political organs. The invasion of Cambodia by Vietnam had been condemned by successive General Assembly resolutions which had called for an immediate troop withdrawal.[39] Thus, once more, the Secretary-General asserted his independent authority in order to qualify as an acceptable intermediary,[40] even as he based his initiative on those parts of the resolutions which had called on him to exercise his good offices.[41]

In 1985, after a round of consultations with ASEAN states, the Secretary-General outlined 'a number of elements which seemed to be generally acceptable as a basis' for an overall solution.[42] In June 1988 he formulated more 'concrete ideas' and submitted them informally to

---

[36] Report SG A/46/577-S/23146 of 17 Oct. 1991, p. 10.   [37] Ibid.

[38] UN Press Release SG/SM/4727/Rev. 1, 10 Apr. 1992, p. 1.

[39] GA Res. 44/22 of 16 Nov. 1989, paras. 1 and 2; GA Res. 34/22 of 14 Nov. 1979, para. 9.

[40] UN Press Release SG/SM/4011/Rev. 1, 19 June 1987, pp. 7–8; UN Press Release (ST)DPI/1091, p. 1.

[41] See e.g. Report SG A/41/707 of 14 Oct. 1986, p. 1; GA Res. 34/22 of 14 Nov. 1979, para. 11.   [42] Report SG A/40/759 of 17 Oct. 1985, p. 3.

the parties involved.[43] The momentum for a comprehensive political settlement began to gather. In this situation, France and Indonesia took the initiative to invite the Cambodian factions and a number of states to a Peace Conference which opened in Paris in July–August 1989. The Secretary-General participated, although limiting his role primarily to the submission of proposals concerning the possible implementation of the envisaged accord.[44] After a negotiating hiatus of more than a year, in which period the Secretary-General played a key negotiating role, the Peace Conference reached an Agreement signed in Paris on 23 October 1991.[45] This provided for an unprecedentedly comprehensive supervisory and administrative role for the UN Transitional Authority in Cambodia (UNTAC).[46]

3. Central America

The Secretary-General's role in the Central American peace process consisted of three separate and different interventions, in crises in Nicaragua, El Salvador, and Guatemala. These had been treated as one conflict by the Contadora states and the Esquipulas II-Agreement of 1987.[47]

In late 1986, when, in the view of the Secretary-General, the negotiations within the Contadora framework seemed to lose steam, the Secretaries-General of the OAS and the UN informally agreed on a joint initiative whereby the heads of the two organizations would lend their good offices.[48] As a result of this initiative, the countries concerned joined in a framework agreement, Esquipulas II,

---

[43] UN Press Release SG/SM/4315, 31 July 1989, p. 2; Report SG A/43/730 of 21 Oct. 1988, p. 2.   [44] See SC Res. 668 of 20 Sept. 1990, para. 10.

[45] Text of the Paris Agreement on a Comprehensive Political Settlement of the Cambodia Conflict is in UN doc. A/46/608-S/23177 of 30 Oct. 1991. On the role of the Secretary-General see no. 8 of the Final Act of the Paris Conference, ibid., p. 5.

[46] On UNTAC see also SC Res. 745 of 28 Feb. 1992; Report SG S/23613 of 19 Feb. 1992; and Sally Morphet's chapter below, pp. 223–4.

[47] Esquipulas II-Agreement, published in Report SG A/42/521–S/19085 of 31 Aug. 1987, p. 8. On Central America, see also Morphet's chapter, pp. 216–19.

[48] Report SG A/42/127–S/18686 of 12 Feb. 1987, pp. 1–2.

which envisaged that the UN would assist in the verification of any commitments entered into through the
process.[49]

Nicaragua's civil war was the first of the Central
American crises to yield to negotiations, although here
the UN Secretary-General's political role was limited to
negotiations leading to the agreement on the steps to
demobilize the guerrillas.[50] At the next stage in 1989,
however, the Secretary-General assumed an important
role through the establishment of the UN Observer
Mission to verify the electoral process in Nicaragua
(ONUVEN) and the UN Observer Group in Central
America (ONUCA), among whose tasks was overseeing
the Contra guerrillas' demobilization.

In El Salvador, by contrast, the Secretary-General came
to play an increasingly active role in mediating between
the parties to achieve an agreed solution to the civil war.
In December 1989 he was specifically requested by the
presidents of the five Central American countries to help
to bring about a resumption of the dialogue between the
government of El Salvador and the FMLN guerrillas.[51]
Four months later the Secretary-General was able to
announce a remarkably detailed agreement on the
objectives and the format of the talks. In this 'Geneva'
Agreement the parties committed themselves to a
'continuous and uninterrupted' negotiating process with
a view to achieving a comprehensive political settlement.[52]
The Secretary-General was to participate actively as an
intermediary in the negotiations, have the exclusive right
to provide public information about progress made, and
was permitted, at his discretion, to maintain confidential
contacts for purposes of consultations with any state

---

[49] The countries concerned, in this instance, were the five Central American republics.

[50] Reports SG A/44/344–S/20699 of 9 Oct. 1989, p. 3; A/44/886–S/21029 of 21 Dec. 1989, pp. 2–3; A/45/706–S/21931 of 8 Nov. 1990, pp. 2–6.

[51] Declaration of San Isidro, Report SG A/44/872–S/21019 of 12 Dec. 1989, p. 2.

[52] UN doc. A/46/551–S/23128 of 9 Oct. 1991; this is a rare instance of publication of the 'terms of reference' of a good offices mission.

outside the negotiations and also with individual Salvadoreans.

These arrangements began to bear fruit. In July 1990, the San José Human Rights Accord was concluded. In it, the government of El Salvador agreed to have its compliance monitored by a UN mission.[53] On several occasions, in an effort to promote further progress, the Personal Representative of the Secretary-General, Alvaro de Soto, successfully proposed initiatives in the negotiations. For example, the parties, in agreement with the Representative, decided that the San José Agreement, which had been intended to come into effect as part of an overall peace settlement, could, instead, be implemented at once, before such a comprehensive settlement or even a cease-fire had been agreed.[54] To verify the parties' compliance with human rights obligations under the San José Agreement, the Security Council established the UN Observer Mission in El Salvador (ONUSAL) with the intent that it became part of an integrated mechanism to verify all the agreements to be reached by the parties in future.[55] The Secretary-General's representative was also helpful in breaking another deadlock between the parties by persuading them that negotiations on outstanding issues, including the future of the armed forces, police and guerrillas in an overall political settlement, should be tackled in 'compressed negotiations', that is, together with the negotiation of a cease-fire, rather than subsequent thereto.[56]

The Peace Agreement, signed on 16 January 1992, provides not only for demobilization of the guerrillas and their reintegration into Salvadorean society, but also for extensive changes in the constitutional and institutional framework of the country, not least a complete restructuring of the armed forces.[57] The Peace Agreement also provides for supervision of its implementation, in part, by

[53] UN doc. A/44/971–S/21541 of 16 Aug. 1990, annexe.
[54] Report SG S/22494 of 16 Apr. 1991.
[55] SC Res. 693 of 20 May 1991, para. 3.
[56] UN doc. A/46/502/Add. 1–S/23082/Add. 1 of 7 Oct. 1991, p. 2.
[57] UN doc. A/46/864–S/23501 of 30 Jan. 1992.

a civilian 'Peace Commission' (COPAZ) and partly by a greatly expanded ONUSAL mission. The Secretary-General rightly called the outcome a 'revolution achieved by negotiation'.[58]

Negotiations were also begun in Guatemala, in 1990, between the government and the insurgents.[59] In these, a representative of the Secretary-General has been invited to participate. Although his role is designated as that of observer,[60] in practice he plays a more active part.[61]

4. Cyprus

The case of Cyprus is both the longest-running good offices effort of the Secretary-General and the one which best illustrates the potential and the limits of this function. Ever since the stationing of UN peacekeeping forces on the island in 1964, the Secretary-General has been involved in the process of resolving the island's communal constitutional crisis through agreement on a confederal structure of government.[62] The Security Council has renewed his good offices mandate semiannually.[63]

In the years following the Turkish invasion of Cyprus in 1974, numerous mediating efforts were made by the Secretary-General. To date, he has had only modest successes. These came in the form of two agreements, in 1977 and 1979, which established a framework for negotiation but did not lead to any substantive agreement.[64] On three occasions substantive agreement did seem within reach. In 1986 the Secretary-General presented a new set of proposals to the leaders of both communities envisaging fairly precise parameters for a bi-communal federal structure. Although at first accepted in principle by both

---

[58] UN Press Release SG/SM/4685, 16 Jan. 1992, p. 2.

[59] Report SG A/46/713–S/23256 of 2 Dec. 1991, pp. 5–7.

[60] See Mexico Agreement of 26 Apr. 1991, UN doc. A/45/1007–S/22563 of 2 May 1991, p. 3.   [61] UN doc. E/CN.4/1992/5 of 21 Jan. 1992, p. 7.

[62] SC Res. 186 of 4 Mar. 1964, para. 7 ('mediator'); SC Res. 244 of 22 Dec. 1967, para. 3 ('good offices'). On peacekeeping in Cyprus, see Morphet's chapter below, pp. 195–6, 205, and 214.

[63] SC Res. 723 of 12 Dec. 1991, para. 2; SC Res. 367 of 12 Mar. 1975, para. 6.

[64] Reports SG S/12323 of 30 Apr. 1977, pp. 2–3; S/13369 of 31 May 1979, p. 13.

parties, these were later repudiated by the Greek Cypriots.[65] In 1988–9 the Secretary-General tried again. This time, instead of putting forward substantive proposals, he invited both leaders to negotiate in person, in his presence, at UN Headquarters in New York.

While such a deliberate pressure tactic—convening the negotiators at the highest level in an effort to raise public expectations—may work at times, it did not do so on this occasion.[66] In 1991 fresh hopes were raised once again when US President George Bush, after meeting with the Greek and Turkish prime ministers, gave strong public support to a renewed effort by the Secretary-General. However, hopes were dashed again when the Turkish Cypriot leaders adamantly reiterated their demand for a constitutional right to secession in any future constitutional arrangement.[67] Under these circumstances the new Secretary-General Boutros-Ghali publicly considered 'an alternate course of action'.[68] By this he acknowledged that critics now view the UN's role in Cyprus as contributing as much to the problem as to its solution by inadvertently encouraging the parties to remain safely intransigent behind the UN-policed truce line.

Nevertheless, the effort has persisted. In an April 1992 resolution, the Security Council specifically endorsed a 'set of ideas' drafted by the Secretary-General which outlined 'guiding principles for a settlement' and was sufficiently detailed about allocation of 'powers and functions' as to be almost a draft constitution.[69] After his representatives had conducted further discussions in Cyprus during May, a new round of negotiations was initiated by the Secretary-General at Headquarters from June to August. These meetings were adjourned 'for reflection' until October 1992. In a toughly-phrased text, the Secretary-General said that 'it was long past time for the parties to take the important political decisions necessary for an agreed,

---

[65] Report SG S/18102/Add. 1 of 11 June 1986, pp. 3–5.
[66] Report SG S/21183 of 8 Mar. 1990.
[67] Report SG S/23121 of 8 Oct. 1991, p. 4.
[68] Report SG S/23780 of 3 Apr. 1992, p. 9; see also SC Res. 750 of 10 Apr. 1992.   [69] UN doc. S/24472 of 21 Aug. 1992, annexe, p. 9.

compromise solution and that the continuation of the status quo was not a viable option'.[70] To that end, he produced a map, in July, which proposed a specific new border between the Turkish and Greek communal federated states:[71] a calculatedly risky initiative for the good officer.

The risk was acceptable because the patience of UN members with the recalcitrant parties to this dispute had worn out. It had already been urged that, absent the political will to compromise, the cost of UNFICYP be shifted from the international community to the taxpayers of the two Cypriot communities.

Whatever the outcome of the Secretary-General's Cypriot good offices, they clearly served a necessary function. On the one hand, by providing a visible forum for diplomacy, they augmented the role of UNFICYP in generating a climate in which Cypriot Turks and Greeks were less likely to resume their fratricidal war. On the other hand, they also helped prevent the UNFICYP-patrolled cease-fire from becoming a *de facto* partition of Cyprus by keeping highly visible on the international agenda the need to secure a form of constitutional unity for Cyprus and the rectification of communal boundaries.

5. East Timor

The Secretary-General's involvement in the dispute over East Timor is another example of his usefulness, even when the basic positions of the antagonists appear irreconcilable. Ever since its invasion and annexation by Indonesia in 1975, East Timor has been the object of UN concern, stimulated by Portugal, the former colonial power. The Security Council and the General Assembly initially called for the East Timorese people to be allowed to exercise their right of self-determination.[72] In 1982 the Assembly requested the Secretary-General to initiate consultations with all parties directly concerned.[73]

---

[70] Ibid., p. 3.
[71] Ibid., pp. 4–5.
[72] SC Res. 384 of 22 Dec. 1975; GA Res. 3485 (XXX) of 12 Dec. 1975.
[73] GA Res. 37/30 of 23 Nov. 1982.

LIVERPOOL
JOHN MOORES UNIVERSITY
TRUEMAN STREET LIBRARY
TEL. 051 231 4022/4023

Although international opinion seems to have relegated the East Timor issue to the 'back burner'—the Assembly has not reiterated its call for self-determination since 1982—the Secretary-General nevertheless continues to pursue his mission of good offices, issuing annual 'progress reports' to the General Assembly. This, at a minimum, keeps the item alive and helps keep it on the agenda.[74]

On the other hand, it is debatable whether the entrusting of such a good offices mission to the Secretary-General really advances the cause of peace or has a benevolent effect on the office of the Chief Executive. Some believe that it represents a way for members of the UN to create the illusion, without the reality, of action and, moreover, that this shifts responsibility for failure from the UN's political organs to the Secretary-General, who is thereby made to appear ineffective.

There is a good case to be made, however, that, even in assuming such tasks with a low probability of success, the Secretary-General can make a modest contribution which must be judged solely against the alternative of a gradual acceptance of the illegal status quo.

6. *Falkland Islands/Malvinas*

On two occasions the Secretary-General has been involved in the conflict between the United Kingdom and Argentina over the Falkland Islands/Malvinas. In 1982 he had sought to arrange an Argentine withdrawal just before the British counter-attack.[75] When the war was over, successive General Assembly resolutions asked him to resume his good offices.[76] Although the United Kingdom formally refused, citing its objections to various General Assembly resolutions that appeared to prejudge the outcome in Argentina's favour,[77] it nevertheless agreed to discuss the dispute informally with the Secretary-General.[78] Since

---

[74] GA Dec. 46/402 of 20 Sept. 1991.

[75] See the Statement of the Secretary-General before the Security Council, UN doc. S/PV.2360 of 21 May 1982, pp. 3–12.

[76] GA Res. 43/25 of 17 Nov. 1988.

[77] UN Press Release SG/SM/4011/Rev. 1, 19 June 1987, p. 3; SG/SM/3956, 13 Jan. 1987, p. 11.   [78] UN Press Release SG/SM/4124, 20 Apr. 1988, p. 8.

then, the parties have resumed diplomatic relations and concluded several confidence-building agreements,[79] whereupon the Secretary-General felt able to suspend his efforts even though the item remains inactively on the General Assembly's agenda.[80]

7. *Guyana–Venezuela*

The Secretary-General has focused his good offices not only on highly political disputes but also on some which have been of a basically legal nature. A recent example is the agreement between Guyana and Venezuela to use his good offices to resolve their long-simmering border dispute.[81]

8. *Hostages held in Lebanon*

In 1991, after a number of other intermediaries had failed, the Secretary-General—without seeking formal authorization from either Assembly or Council—launched a 'humanitarian'[82] effort to secure the release of Western hostages in Lebanon. Dispatching special envoy Giandomenico Picco to negotiate with the hostage-takers and the governments concerned, he came up with a plan which led to the release of almost all Western hostages by the end of the year.[83] While it is hard to assess the exact impact of the Secretary-General's efforts to bring about the hostages' release, it seems clear that the trust that different sides had in him and his envoy was an important ingredient in securing a favourable outcome.[84]

9. *Iran–Iraq*

The war between Iran and Iraq further demonstrates how the Secretary-General can effectively exercise his good offices, in combination with other means at his disposal, to bring relevant pressure to bear on parties to a grave conflict.

---

[79] See UN doc. A/46/596–S/23164 of 24 Oct. 1991; UN doc. A/45/136–S/21159 of 21 Feb. 1990.   [80] GA Dec. 46/406 of 13 Nov. 1991.
[81] UN Press Release SG/A/430, 1 Feb. 1990; UN Press Release SG/SM/4556, 5 Apr. 1991.   [82] UN Press Release SG/SM/4668, 9 Dec. 1991.
[83] *New York Times*, 19 Jan. 1992, p. 1.   [84] Ibid.

In November 1983, Iran alleged that Iraq was using chemical weapons. In his role as finder of fact and acting on his own authority, the Secretary-General dispatched several missions to examine evidence on the ground. These studies, undertaken from March 1984 onwards, confirmed that such weapons had been used.[85] Despite the fact that this may have damaged his impartiality in Iraqi eyes, both parties to the conflict continued to accept him as a good mediator and he continued to advance proposals to both sides.[86] Indeed, he also sent a mission at the request of Iraq to examine the condition of prisoners of war in both countries.

Not only did the Secretary-General publicly urge the parties to end their hostilities,[87] but he was instrumental in promoting the Security Council's passage of resolution 598 on 20 July 1987, which mandated an immediate cease-fire between the combatants utilizing the authority of the Charter's Chapter VII. It took a year for Iran to accept.[88] During this interval, the Secretary-General's good offices mission, technically transformed into a mission charged to secure the implementation of resolution 598, continued to search for the key to a cease-fire[89] while issuing public appeals for military restraint.[90] At the same time he sent further missions to investigate more allegations of chemical warfare.[91] When Iran did accept resolution 598 it was the Secretary-General who set the actual date for the cease-fire to enter into force (8 August 1988).[92] Taken as a whole, the Iran–Iraq conflict demonstrates that, under favourable conditions, the Secretary-General can integrate several different roles: as impartial intermediary, investigator, and voice of world conscience.

[85] See UN doc. S/20060 of 20 July 1988, which also contains references to all previous reports.
[86] UN Press Release SG/SM/3956, 13 Jan. 1987, p. 4.
[87] UN Press Release SG/SM/4011/Rev. 1, 19 June 1987, p. 5.
[88] UN Press Release SG/SM/4166, 18 July 1988.
[89] See UN Press Release SG/T/1452, 15 Sept. 1987.
[90] UN Press Release SG/SM/4090, 1 Mar. 1988.
[91] UN Press Release SG/SM/4127, 27 Apr. 1988, pp. 4 and 9; SG/SM/4154, 28 June 1988; and SG/SM/4176, 11 Aug. 1988.
[92] UN doc. S/20095 of 8 Aug. 1988. The immediate crisis thus having been resolved, the Secretary-General did not lapse into inactivity. An additional mediation mission was authorized by the Council to help 'to achieve . . . a settlement . . . of all outstanding issues', SC Res. 598 of 20 July 1987, para. 4.

10. Iraq–Kuwait

The Secretary-General had been the driving force behind the 1988 Iran–Iraq cease-fire. When a second Gulf conflict erupted with the Iraqi invasion of Kuwait on 2 August 1990, major changes had taken place in the global power structure which also affected the Secretary-General's role and options. The end of the Cold War had unleashed the previously stymied Security Council: it was the Council, not the Secretary-General, which now took the initiative.

This change of circumstance was not immediately apparent to the naked eye. Shortly after the Iraqi invasion, the Council authorized the Secretary-General to undertake a highly visible mission to Amman in an effort to persuade Foreign Minister Tariq Aziz to comply with the demands for Iraqi withdrawal. On 29 October the Council again specifically asked the Secretary-General to undertake a mission to Baghdad in one more effort to head off war.[93] The terms of this resolution appeared to give him great latitude. He was to make his good offices available 'as he considers appropriate', and seemed to have virtual *carte blanche* to 'undertake diplomatic efforts to reach a peaceful solution'.

In practice, however, this is not how the Council's authorization appeared to the Secretary-General. The Council had invoked Chapter VII to order Iraq out of Kuwait, and underscored its order by imposing mandatory sanctions. Inevitably, the Secretary-General felt constrained to limit his negotiations to securing Iraqi compliance.[94] No 'Peking Formula' could be asserted in these circumstances to justify an independent mediating role. If the Charter had left him in any doubt on that score, it was resolved by unambiguous private communications from Permanent Members of the Council. According

---

[93] SC Res. 674 of 29 Oct. 1990, para. 12: 'Reposes its trust in the Secretary-General to make available his good offices and, as he considers appropriate, to pursue them and to undertake diplomatic efforts in order to reach a peaceful solution'; see also SC Res. 664 of 18 Aug. 1990 and SC Res. 670 of 25 Sept. 1990.

[94] UN Press Release SG/T/1624, 30 Aug. 1990; SG/SM/4487, 4 Sept. 1990; UN Press Release SG/T/1640 and 1643, 14 Jan. 1991.

to several of his staff, the Secretary-General was also actively discouraged from going to Baghdad until after the failure of US Secretary of State James Baker's own mission, by which time it was far too late.

11. Libya

Perhaps the most extreme example so far of a post-Cold War good offices mission in which the Secretary-General had little room for independent manœuvre is his role in the 1992 crisis concerning the British–French–American demands on Libya for the extradition of suspected terrorists involved in two airline bombings.[95] Acting on the basis of a request of the Security Council 'to seek the cooperation of the Libyan government to provide a full and effective response' to the requests by Britain, France, and the United States to extradite the suspects of the terrorist attacks on two passenger planes,[96] the Secretary-General sent Under-Secretary-General Vasily Safronchuk to Tripoli, where, however, he felt obliged to state that his mission was not one of mediation, but, merely, to 'take note' of Libya's 'preliminary response'.[97] After this first visit of his emissary, the Secretary-General declined an invitation of the Libyan government to negotiate a 'mechanism' to implement the resolution, emphasizing that his own authority under the Council's terms was too limited to permit such an initiative.[98] This could be an unfortunate shrinkage of role. Perhaps the Secretary-General could have interpreted the Libyan offer as a positive response, one leading to informal consultations on modalities of Libyan compliance with the Council's mandate. That he did not choose to avail himself of that opportunity may indicate his assessment, probably prompted by consultation with key members of the Council, that the Libyan offer was not a bona fide one; or it may reflect his sense of his office's diminished room for manœuvre in the new era of Council activism. A second visit to Tripoli by Safronchuk, and two further visits by

---

[95] UN Press Release SG/SM/4727/Rev. 1, 10 Apr. 1992, p. 5.
[96] SC Res. 731 of 21 Jan. 1992, para. 4.
[97] Report SG S/23574 of 11 Feb. 1992, p. 1.   [98] Ibid., p. 2.

Under-Secretary-General Vladimir Petrovsky, appeared to confirm this impression, with the Secretary's emissary relegated essentially to effectuating an exchange of messages. In the event, the content of the message relayed was formulated less by the Secretary-General than by Britain, France, and the USA.[99]

This gives cause for reflection. When the Secretary-General, in the face of a newly resurgent and activist Security Council, is relegated to what some have dubbed a 'letter-carrier function', then certain questions arise which are likely to be of increasing importance in the post-Cold War circumstances of the UN system. Among these is whether the good offices function—still a necessary part of the UN's repertory—suffers when the Secretary-General is reduced to so constrained a role.

12. Middle East

The Secretary-General has been authorized to engage in good offices between Israel and its neighbours since the adoption of Security Council resolution 242 of 1967. This sets the parameters for a peaceful settlement and requests the Secretary-General to assist in promoting it 'in accordance with the provisions and principles in this resolution'.[100] Gunnar Jarring served as the Secretary-General's Special Representative for twenty-four years, to be succeeded in 1991 by Edouard Brunner of Switzerland.

Their efforts have not met with much success. Israel has chosen to regard various General Assembly resolutions outlining the conditions for a settlement as constituting an unacceptable mandate for the conduct of fruitful good offices by the Special Representative.[101] The General Assembly's call, moreover, for an 'international peace conference under the auspices of the United Nations with the participation of all parties to the conflict, including the Palestine Liberation Organisation'[102] has constituted

---

[99] Report SG S/23672 of 3 Mar. 1992.

[100] SC Res. 242 of 22 Nov. 1967, para. 3; UN Press Release SG/A/453, 21 Mar. 1991.   [101] See report SG S/10929 of 18 May 1973, p. 37.

[102] GA Res. 46/75 of 11 Dec. 1991, para. 2, is a mellowed version of the previous formulation in GA Res. 45/68 of 6 Dec. 1990, para. 2.

another so far insurmountable obstacle. Conversely, the Secretary-General has not been prepared to accept an invitation to participate at the current Russian–US-sponsored Peace Conference on the Middle East expressly because he was invited solely as an observer in a largely ceremonial capacity, and not as a full participant.[103] Nevertheless, he helped get the process under way by quietly urging sceptical UN members to consider the Russian–US approach as a promising alternative to that preferred by the Assembly's majority.[104]

13. Namibia

The good offices function of the Secretary-General is sometimes carried out under another rubric. His role in resolving the prolonged Namibia crisis is a good example, being designated as 'implementation' but, in fact, involving him in protracted, delicate, and, ultimately, important negotiations.

In 1978 the Security Council established the UN Transition Assistance Group (UNTAG)[105] by a resolution outlining the parameters for Namibia's transition from illegal South African control to independence. The South African government, however, did not accede until after almost a decade of delicate negotiations about the modalities for implementing the Council's resolution. These negotiations were pursued concurrently by the Secretary-General and a five-nation 'Contact Group' which exerted considerable political leverage on South Africa.[106]

Only in 1985 did the Secretary-General succeed in obtaining South African agreement to the terms for holding UN supervised elections as a final step to Namibian independence.[107] This agreement facilitated South Africa's conversion to the peaceful transition envisaged by the Council. When, in August 1988, Angola agreed to the

[103] UN Press Release SG/SM/4718, 19 Mar. 1992, p. 6; SG/SM/4621, 20 Sept. 1991, p. 10.
[104] See Report SG A/46/623–S/23204 of 8 Nov. 1991, p. 5; UN Press Release SG/SM/4752, 18 May 1992, p. 9.   [105] SC Res. 435 of 2 Sept. 1978, para. 3.
[106] Report SG S/15776 of 19 May 1983, pp. 1–2.
[107] Report SG S/18767 of 31 Mar. 1987, p. 2; Agreement finalized on 10 Mar. 1989, Report SG S/20412/Add. 1 of 16 Mar. 1989.

withdrawal of Cuban troops,[108] the last South African obstacle was removed and the path cleared for the UN to carry out what was to become one of the organization's largest and most successful operations.[109]

14. The Rainbow Warrior dispute

Another facet of the 'good offices' function is demonstrated by the role of the Secretary-General, in the summer of 1986, in resolving the Rainbow Warrior dispute between New Zealand and France. That conflict was occasioned by the role of French agents in the death of a Dutch citizen aboard the Rainbow Warrior and the demolition of that vessel as it was intending to make itself hostage to French Pacific nuclear tests in Muroroa Atoll. Two French agents were captured by New Zealand authorities and sentenced to ten-year prison terms. So acrimonious had the dispute become that it threatened to thwart European Community operations because of French retaliation against New Zealand agricultural products.

On 19 June 1986, at the suggestion of the Dutch government, the parties asked the Secretary-General to arbitrate the differences between them. Simple procedures were employed. The parties made a written submission in which they outlined the problem, the elements of a solution they had already negotiated, and indicated remaining aspects of the dispute which they had been unable to resolve. They also agreed, in advance, to treat the Secretary-General's decisions as binding. The Secretary-General then addressed written enquiries to the parties, and produced a written proposal which the parties implemented as agreed.[110] It involved a formal apology by France to New Zealand, the payment of $US 7 million in compensation, and the release of the two French agents to French custody on the understanding that they would serve three years 'on assignment' at a totally isolated post

[108] Report SG S/20412 of 23 Jan. 1989, pp. 3–4 and 21.

[109] See Statement of Secretary-General at Namibia's independence celebration, UN Press Release SG/SM/4422, 20 Mar. 1990.

[110] The text of the UN Secretary-General's ruling of 6 July 1986 on the Rainbow Warrior affair is published in American Journal of International Law, 81 (1987), p. 325.

on the French island of Hao in Polynesia. France also undertook not to try to restrict New Zealand butter, mutton, and goat trade with the European Community.

This solution is not without critics in both countries and there is reason to question the bona fides of its execution by France. However, the lesson to be derived from this small instance of good offices is that the settlement proved much more acceptable—precisely because of its unimpeachable source—than would have been the same, or any other, solution arrived at solely by the parties themselves. Neither government, at the time, could be accused by its internal critics of having yielded to the other. Thus, both arbitration and legitimization entered into the Secretary-General's role.[111]

15. Somalia

At times, and perhaps increasingly in the post-Cold War era, the Secretary-General may have reason to prefer to work in tandem with a regional organization. An important example of such cooperation occurred in the Somali civil war crisis.

In early 1992 the Security Council asked the Secretary-General 'to assist in the process of a political settlement of the conflict' in that country.[112] The resolution asks him to join for this purpose with the Secretaries-General of the Organization of African Unity (OAU) and of the Arab League.

The joint good offices of the Secretaries-General of the three organizations began with the two main rival factions being invited to meet with them in New York. In the face of an inflamed civil war and intense personal rivalries among the factional leadership, the representatives of the three Secretaries-General managed to secure an agreement to a cease-fire.[113] In an effort to make this

---

[111] For another instance of a quasi-arbitral function of the Secretary-General see the 'New York Act', an agreement which was concluded in the context of the El Salvador talks, by which the parties undertook to accept as binding proposals submitted by the Secretary-General if they were unable to agree among themselves within a certain time-limit. UN doc. A/46/863–S/23504 of 30 Jan. 1992, p. 2.   [112] SC Res. 733 of 23 Jan. 1992, para. 3.
[113] Report SG S/23693 of 11 Mar. 1992, pp. 6–7.

fragile cease-fire take effective hold, the Secretary-General next sent his Representative to join a delegation of officials of the UN, Organization of African Unity, League of Arab States, and Islamic Conference for an on-site visit to Somalia's capital Mogadishu, to investigate the situation and explore the prospects for political settlement.

In his extensive report to the Security Council in March 1992, the Secretary-General described the situation and the efforts of the joint delegation in remarkably candid terms. Noting that the prevailing conditions did not yet permit even the distribution of humanitarian aid, let alone the deployment of a UN peacekeeping force, he nevertheless stressed that the collaboration with the regional organizations 'had proved to be very effective and set a useful precedent for future cooperation'.[114]

The Secretary-General continued joint efforts with the regional organizations to convene a conference of national reconciliation. Recognizing, however, the scale of the human tragedy which threatened in Somalia while these efforts proceeded, he was also instrumental in the Security Council's creation of the UN Operation in Somalia (UNOSOM), its subsequent authorization of the US-led Unified Task Force (UNITAF), and the eventual replacement of UNITAF by UNOSOM II in May 1993.[115]

16. Western Sahara

In 1975, echoing an advisory opinion of the ICJ,[116] the Assembly passed a resolution reaffirming the right of self-determination of the people of the former Spanish Western Sahara.[117] Concurrently, in a brokered political compromise, the Assembly passed another resolution implicitly recognizing the territory's occupation by Morocco and Mauritania.[118] In the first of these resolutions, further compounding the confusion, the Assembly requested the Secretary-General 'to make the necessary

---

[114] Ibid., pp. 16–18.
[115] SC Res. 751 of 24 Apr. 1992; SC Res. 794 of 3 Dec. 1992; and SC Res. 814 of 26 Mar. 1993.   [116] *ICJ Reports*, 1975, pp. 12–176.
[117] GA Res. 3458A (XXX) of 10 Dec. 1975.
[118] GA Res. 3458B (XXX) of 10 Dec. 1975.

arrangements for the supervision of the act of self-determination'. After a futile and rather perfunctory effort, the Secretary-General publicly rejected the assignment as hopeless.[119]

After 1986, however, the global context, as well as local conditions, had begun to change. Thus, the General Assembly,[120] followed by the Security Council,[121] seized the opportunity again to authorize the Secretary-General to bring about self-determination. By this time Morocco had absorbed the Mauritanian-occupied part of the territory, so the Secretary-General began his good offices function in the summer of 1986 with a visit to King Hassan II of Morocco. There ensued a period of intensive shuttle diplomacy in an effort to reach an agreement between Morocco and the Polisario liberation movement over the terms of a popular referendum.[122]

In August 1988 the two parties agreed 'in principle' to a set of proposals put forward by the Secretary-General.[123] Thereupon the Security Council invited the Secretary-General[124] first to 'clarify specific matters',[125] and later to take 'sole and exclusive responsibility' for the organization of the long-sought referendum.[126] After almost three more years of negotiations the Secretary-General at last was able to recommend that the Security Council establish a UN Mission for the Referendum in Western Sahara (MINURSO).[127]

Despite these favourable auguries, the referendum did not take place in January 1992 as intended.[128] Morocco and Polisario were (and are) still quarrelling over the criteria for determining the eligibility of voters.[129] This

---

[119] For a fuller account see Thomas M. Franck, 'The Stealing of the Sahara', *American Journal of International Law*, 70 (1976), p. 70.

[120] GA Res. 46/67 of 11 Dec. 1991; GA Res. 40/50 of 2 Dec. 1985.

[121] SC Res. 725 of 31 Dec. 1991; SC Res. 690 of 29 Apr. 1991; SC Res. 621 of 20 Sept. 1988.

[122] Report SG A/41/673 of 3 Oct. 1986, p. 3; A/42/601 of 1 Oct. 1987.

[123] Report SG S/21360 of 18 June 1990, p. 4.

[124] SC Res. 621 of 20 Sept. 1988.

[125] Report SG A/44/634 of 12 Oct. 1989, p. 6.

[126] Report SG S/22646 of 19 Apr. 1991, p. 4.

[127] Report SG S/22532 of 24 Apr. 1991, p. 2; SC Res. 690 of 29 Apr. 1991.

[128] Report SG S/23464 of 19 Apr. 1991, p. 12.

[129] Report SG S/23662 of 28 Mar. 1992, p. 6.

has caused some criticism of the Secretary-General's *modus operandi*. The question of voters' rolls, these critics allege, had not been resolved with sufficient precision in the 1988 'Agreement in Principle'.[130] Controversy arose over the Secretary-General's 'instructions' to MINURSO's Identification Commission, which was charged with the crucial task of deciding who was entitled to vote in the referendum.[131] According to Polisario, the Instructions Relating to the Tasks of the Identification Commission[132] misinterpreted the 'Agreement in Principle' and exceeded the discretion the parties had agreed to give the Secretary-General.

While there has been much criticism—not only from Polisario—both of the vagueness of the 'Agreement in Principle' and of the Secretary-General's belated effort to be more specific, it is not clear that an unambiguous agreement could have been reached in the negotiations. It is undoubtedly sometimes the case that important points of disagreement are deliberately left open, to be resolved at the implementing, rather than the negotiating, stage. This strategy has proven its utility in other crises. Once agreement in principle has been achieved, the Secretary-General has reasoned, the resulting momentum, augmented by raised public expectations, may carry the parties to closure in what had previously been an intractable issue. This is a reasonable negotiating theory: however, it must not be expected always to succeed.

The good offices efforts of the Secretary-General did at least lead to a cease-fire:[133] no mean accomplishment against the background of nearly a decade of fighting. On the other hand, there are those who feel that a cease-fire, in such circumstances of armed resistance to a status quo, rather heavily favours the occupying power.

17. Yugoslavia

The Secretary-General's part in addressing the crisis precipitated by the disintegration of Yugoslavia provides

---

[130] See Report SG S/22646 of 19 Apr. 1991, p. 6.
[131] Report SG S/23299 of 19 Dec. 1991, p. 5; see also UN Press Release SG/SM/4727/Rev. 1, 10 Apr. 1992, p. 6.
[132] Report SG S/23299 of 19 Dec. 1991, annexe.
[133] Report S/23299 of 19 Dec. 1991, p. 2.

an example of how the good offices role can be combined with other functions of the UN and with those of a regional organization.

Following a request by the European Community and its member states,[134] the Security Council invited the Secretary-General 'to offer his assistance' to the parties in the Croatian aspect of the conflict.[135] As his Personal Envoy, the Secretary-General appointed former US Secretary of State Cyrus Vance. Between October 1991 and January 1992 Vance undertook five missions to the area. In mid-February the Secretary-General was finally able, on the basis of his representatives' on-the-ground assessments and negotiations with the parties to the conflict, to recommend the establishment of a UN Protection Force (UNPROFOR) to be deployed in some of those parts of Croatia which had been occupied by the remnants of the Yugoslav National Army and by Serbian irregulars.[136]

The stated purpose of the Vance missions had been to investigate whether there existed conditions for the deployment of a UN peacekeeping force.[137] In practice, however, the activity of the Special Representative went much further. At the time of his visits, European governments were still in disagreement as to whether recognition of breakaway republics of the former Yugoslavia would advance or retard the cause of peace.[138] In this dispute, Vance openly sided with those who argued that recognition, especially of Bosnia–Herzegovina, would exacerbate the fighting. Moreover, Vance successfully urged that, whatever the outcome of the debate on recognition, a UN presence was necessary to create the cease-fire that must precede, or at least accompany, efforts of the European Community to arrange an agreed political solution.

---

[134] UN doc. S/23060 of 23 Sept. 1991, p. 3.

[135] SC Res. 713 of 25 Sept. 1991, para. 3.

[136] Report SG S/23592 of 15 Feb. 1992, pp. 6–7; SC Res. 743 of 21 Feb. 1992, para. 2; and SC Res. 749 of 7 Apr. 1992, para. 2.

[137] Report SG S/23169 of 25 Oct. 1991, p. 3; SC Res. 721 of 11 Dec. 1991, para. 1; Report SG S/23363 of 5 Jan. 1992, p. 1.

[138] See Report SG S/23280 of 11 Dec. 1991, p. 21.

Vance's personal prestige put pressure on the Yugoslav parties—at least in Croatia—to respect a cease-fire agreement, justifying the Secretary-General's decision to depute a senior world statesman, rather than a Secretariat professional, to perform the good offices function.

The Croatian segment of the Yugoslav crisis also demonstrates the uses of collaborative efforts in the conduct of good offices. First, it is apparent that Vance's personal leverage and his authority as the Secretary-General's Representative was further augmented by the fact that the Security Council had delegated to the Secretary-General the power to decide precisely when conditions on the ground would warrant the dispatch of a peacekeeping force. By refusing to make that recommendation prematurely, Vance was able to push all sides to make the necessary concessions.[139] Second, the role played by Vance was significantly abetted, but also complicated, by a division of labour between the UN on the one hand and, on the other, the member states of the European Community and the Commission headed by Lord Carrington, charged with negotiating a political solution to the secessionist developments. This allocation of functions allowed the Secretary-General to focus his negotiations on the securing of a viable cease-fire and its implementation as well as on humanitarian relief efforts.[140] At the same time, it exposed him to uninformed but widespread criticism for not having tackled forcefully the solution of the political problems of the region. The press, in particular, but also governments and public opinion have difficulty in grasping that it is sometimes useful to pursue an approach which assigns different roles to different actors to fulfil the distinct functions of peacekeeping and peace-making.

Such problems arose in even sharper form in connection with the Bosnian aspect of the Yugoslav crisis. In 1992–3 Cyrus Vance (the UN Special Envoy) and Lord Owen (the European Community Special Envoy) were part of a

---

[139] Report SG S/23280 of 11 Dec. 1991, p. 5; see also Report SG S/23363 of 5 Jan. 1992, pp. 3–4.
[140] See UN Press release SG/SM/4718, 19 Mar. 1992, pp. 1 and 4.

process of bringing international pressure to bear on the parties, both to stop the brutal fighting and to move towards a settlement. All this took place against a background of grave war crimes, including 'ethnic cleansing', mass murder and mass rape; and of hesitation in the international community to commit major ground forces with the purpose of stopping this bitter and complex war.

The limits of good offices were evidenced by the long, frustrating and widely if unfairly criticized Vance–Owen efforts as brokers for a Bosnian peace plan. It is not a flaw in the good offices function that some parties to a conflict prefer to spill blood rather than negotiate in good faith. What the experience of the Vance–Owen mission did illustrate was the extreme difficulty of halting such a conflict, of establishing an effective peacekeeping presence, and of preserving intact a deeply divided Bosnia-Herzegovina. It also illustrated the complexity of the interaction between good offices and collective use of force. Paradoxically, some states, as also some individuals, lack the patience or commitment necessary to achieve a negotiated solution until everyone else has lost patience with them and is prepared to bring them to their senses by force. This subtle interplay between the uses of force and reason is not, however, unique to the domain of the Secretary-General and his good offices.

(c) Differences in Style and Content

As the foregoing examples show, the various exercises of the Secretary-General's 'good offices' function differ significantly in style and content. Indeed, since the 'good offices' function is not expressly mentioned in the UN Charter, but grew from context and necessity, its precise outlines are hard to draw.[141]

1. Sources and limitations of the Secretary-General's authority
The Secretary-General's good offices functions may derive from at least four different kinds of authorization: from

---

[141] The legal basis for the 'good offices' function is usually inferred from Arts. 33 and 99 of the Charter: see Vratislav Pechota, *The Quiet Approach* (UNITAR, New York, 1972), pp. 8–10. See also the explanation of 'good offices' above, n. 3.

resolutions of the Security Council or General Assembly, or as an emanation of his inherent powers, or by agreement of disputatious parties. These sources of his authority subtly affect its discharge. Even more subtle is the effect on the Secretary-General's authority of certain institutional factors which may limit, in practice, authority which he appears to have in theory.

The Secretary-General's good offices role in Cyprus,[142] East Timor,[143] Libya,[144] the Middle East,[145] Namibia,[146] and Yugoslavia[147] originated in mandates extended by resolutions of the Security Council. His activities in connection with the disputes over Afghanistan and the Western Sahara, by contrast, were authorized by resolutions of the General Assembly.[148]

These last two instances, however, also demonstrate the difficulty in drawing bright lines regarding authorization. Prior to both Assembly resolutions, the Secretary-General had already begun to exercise his good offices on his own authority.[149] Similarly, in Cambodia,[150] the Falkland Islands, Iran–Iraq,[151] Iraq–Kuwait, and Somalia[152] he became active at the same time that the political organs, taking jurisdiction, gave his efforts formal approval. In still other instances, the Secretary-General has acted entirely on his own. His Central American initiative was only

[142] SC Res. 367 of 12 Mar. 1975, para. 6.
[143] SC Res. 384 of 22 Dec. 1975, para. 5.
[144] SC Res. 731 of 21 Jan. 1992, para. 4.
[145] SC Res. 242 of 22 Nov. 1967, para. 3.
[146] SC Res. 435 of 2 Sept. 1978, para. 3.
[147] SC Res. 713 of 25 Sept. 1991, para. 3.
[148] GA Res. ES–6/2 of 14 Jan. 1980, para. 7; GA Res. 36/34 of 18 Nov. 1981, para. 6 (Afghanistan); GA Res. 40/50 of 2 Dec. 1985, para. 4 (Western Sahara). The General Assembly, by its Commission on Human Rights, also confers mandates on independent experts who are to review the human rights situation in a particular country and thereby provide 'advisory service' to the government. Such missions are also a form of 'good offices'. See e.g. 'Report by the independent expert, Mr Christian Tomuschat, on the situation of human rights in Guatemala', UN doc. E/CN.4/1992/5 of 21 Jan. 1992.
[149] See e.g. Report SG A/36/653–S/14745 of 6 Nov. 1981, p. 1 (Afghanistan); Report SG A/40/692 of 30 Sept. 1985, pp. 3–4 (Western Sahara).
[150] Report SG A/35/501 of 30 Sept. 1980, pp. 1–2; GA Res. 34/22 of 14 Nov. 1979, para. 11.
[151] SC Dec. S/14190 of 23 Sept. 1980; SC Res. 479 of 28 Sept. 1980, para. 4.
[152] SC Res. 733 of 23 Jan. 1992, para. 3.

approved many months after its inception.[153] His efforts to resolve the Lebanon hostage crisis occurred without any involvement of the political organs.

When parties acting outside the UN framework agree to invoke the Secretary-General's good offices function, he acts on his own authority although not on his own initiative or that of a UN political organ. This was the case in the Guyana–Venezuela boundary mediation and the *Rainbow Warrior* case. Also, his assumption of a good offices role may sometimes be in response to a formal or informal request from a regional grouping, as in the Western Sahara and Yugoslav crises.

Aside from these explicit or implicit authorizations, the Secretary-General, in order to perform his good offices functions, must retain the confidence of the principal organs and the major countries and regional groupings which constitute the organization. Thus the Secretary-General is constantly involved in informal consultations with the Security Council and with individual states. As a result, his discretion as to how to proceed in a given case may, in fact, be narrower than it appears on paper. Once a political organ begins to exercise its powers in respect of a situation, the Secretary-General's inherent powers, while not repealed, may need to be exercised in compliance with the specified—and perhaps even the implied—limits, directions, and parameters established by the political organ. This is especially so when the political organ involved is the Security Council. We have observed an instance of this in the limits which the Secretary-General perceived as having been placed on his discretion during the Iraq–Kuwait crisis.

2. The margin of discretion

Good offices are informal, loosely structured, and, to a large extent, depend on the flexibility, sensitivity, and imaginativeness of the good officer. The successful good officer thus usually demands the authority to operate within a wide margin of discretion.

[153] GA Res. 42/1 of 16 Oct. 1987, para. 4; SC Res. 637 of 27 July 1989, para. 5.

It is fortunate that most resolutions authorizing the Secretary-General to engage in good offices have accorded him wide discretion as to how to conduct his operation.[154] Delicate manœuvring is required when a UN political organ has taken a stridently adversarial position against the activities of the very state with which the Secretary-General is asked to negotiate in a good offices capacity. Thus, in the cases of Afghanistan, Cambodia, the Falkland Islands, and Namibia, the Secretary-General, with great care, strove to demonstrate that he was not merely the instructed agent of a UN political organ but also possessed the margin of discretion to act as a credible intermediary.[155]

On the other hand, it is sometimes useful for the Secretary-General's margin not to be too wide. His authority to promote compromise is always constrained by the fundamental norms laid down by the UN Charter.[156] However, an even more narrowly authorized margin may sometimes be helpful in resisting unacceptable pressures from either side to a conflict he is mediating. In the Cyprus negotiations the Secretary-General, on several occasions, has had occasion to remind the Turkish–Cypriot authorities that the 'essence of his mandate' was called into question by their insistence on a unilateral right of secession, which would violate the parameters for a constitutional settlement set out in the Security Council resolution authorizing his mediation.[157]

The Secretary-General, to a surprising degree, has been able to achieve a delicate balance between the often conflicting requirements of working for a politically predetermined outcome on the one hand, and of preserving an appearance of a mediator's professional impartiality on the other. Since the end of the Cold War, and the emergence of unipolarity in the UN's power equation, however, the Secretary-General may be experiencing new difficulty in reconciling his role as 'humble servant'[158] of

---

[154] UN Press Release SG/SM/4124, 20 Apr. 1988, p. 8.
[155] See also Pérez de Cuéllar's 1986 lecture at Oxford University, above, pp. 131–4. [156] Ibid.
[157] Report SG S/21183 of 8 Mar. 1990, p. 12 (annexe II).
[158] UN Press Release SG/SM/4752, 18 May 1992, p. 7.

the political organs with his position as a credible intermediary. The constraints under which he operated during
the Kuwait crisis may be a case in point. The Security
Council, in its resolutions, demanded total and immediate
Iraqi withdrawal, leaving little room for mediation. This,
however, was not the principal problem, according to his
advisers. More constraining were the insistent promptings
of some Permanent Members of the Security Council,
particularly those pertaining to the timing of his approaches
to Iraq.

In the case of the Security Council resolutions demanding that Libya comply with the US, French and British
requests to extradite alleged terrorists, the Secretary-
General was even more narrowly constrained to the 'letter-
carrier' role. This does not coexist comfortably with an
assignment to act as a true mediator in the same set of
circumstances, although the Secretary-General has sometimes succeeded in balancing the two functions. Moreover,
the 'letter-carrier' function, when assigned to the Secretary-
General in one crisis, extracts a cost that is a permanent
charge against the capital of his office. It is important for
states to recognize that, in so far as his success in performing
any and all good offices functions is based on his appearance of impartiality,[159] such 'letter-carrier' assignments
are costly.

3. To delegate or not to delegate

The Secretary-General cannot be everywhere at once. He
heads a large bureaucracy (the Secretariat), must perform
ceremonial and public relations functions, act as an inspi-
rational leader of public opinion, and meet with world
leaders. He is expected to attend important public meetings of the principal organs and engage in discussions
about their proposed resolutions with the sponsors. He
heads numerous field operations and needs to be aware of
their activities as also of impending crises in far-flung parts
of the world. When he undertakes a good offices task, it
is inevitable that his role, at least in some instances, cannot

---

[159] See Pérez de Cuéllar's 1986 Oxford lecture, above, pp. 133–5.

be that of the omnipresent mediator: that this function must be delegated. This has become truer in the post-Cold War era, as the number of tasks has burgeoned. To delegate is sometimes advantageous: more often it is simply unavoidable.

On occasion, however, delegation is specifically excluded. In the Cyprus case, the Security Council entrusted the Secretary-General specifically and personally with the good offices mandate.[160] Thus, although there is a Special Representative of the Secretary-General in Cyprus, he himself has met frequently with each of the parties or has brought them together to negotiate in his personal presence. In the case of the *Rainbow Warrior*, too, the arbitral function was assigned to him in his personal capacity and therefore could not be delegated.

In most instances, fortunately, the Secretary-General has discretion to intervene in person or to delegate the good offices task. An imminent threat to the peace may leave him little choice but to assume the role of good officer in person, especially when fighting has not yet broken out and may be prevented by a dramatic, personal last-ditch intervention. The Secretary-General's efforts in respect of the conflicts over the Falkland Islands and Kuwait are possible examples. In other cases, however, concern to husband the effectiveness of his role has led the Secretary General to stay in the background, appointing a Representative drawn from his inner Secretariat circle or utilizing a highly-regarded outsider who brings his or her own prestige to the process.[161]

---

[160] SC Res. 367 of 12 Mar. 1975, para. 6.

[161] When the Secretary-General delegates, it is to Personal or Special Representatives, usually trusted members of his Secretariat. The designation 'Special Representative' is usually employed when the Secretary-General acts on the basis of a mandate from one of the political organs, 'Personal Representative' when he acts on his own authority. However, not infrequently outsiders are appointed, as, for example, former US Secretary of State Cyrus Vance, who represented the Secretary-General in the Yugoslav crisis and conducted fact-finding missions to Nagorno–Karabakh. (UN Press Release SG/SM/4722, 26 Mar. 1992; UN doc. S/23904 of 12 May 1992). Other examples include the Vice-Chancellor of the University of the West Indies, Alister McIntyre, who acts on the Secretary-General's behalf in the border dispute between Guyana and Venezuela; and the former Foreign Minister of Pakistan, Yaqub Khan, who mediates in the Western Sahara conflict.

Such delegation may happen even in situations where a serious breach of the peace has occurred, if, in the Secretary-General's opinion, a protracted commitment of time is required, rather than a dramatic short-term initiative. Examples include the disputes concerning Afghanistan, Iran–Iraq, Libya, Middle East, Yugoslavia, and also the negotiations for the release of the hostages in Lebanon. In these delegated good offices operations, the Secretary-General is involved in the background. Some missions, such as those with respect to Central America and Somalia, concern questions of such a complex nature that the need for delegation is immediately apparent. Also the protracted, complicated, seemingly endless Afghanistan negotiations could not be conducted by the Secretary-General without imperilling the discharge of his many other functions.

Between those cases clearly calling for the Secretary-General's direct conduct of good offices, and those in which only delegation is appropriate, are those instances where the Secretary-General delegates, yet occasionally intervenes personally in order to break a deadlock or accelerate progress. This has happened, in different degrees, in the cases of Cambodia, Central America, Namibia, and Western Sahara.

(d) Effectiveness

The secrecy of the process ensures that the effectiveness of each good offices mission is hard to assess. The Secretary-General does not always publish mission reports and, when he does, may omit relevant details.[162] Moreover, it is difficult to evaluate his contribution when, as is often the case, he is but one of several players. Hard-nosed realists, for instance, attribute the successful outcome of the El Salvador talks in part to the US Congress's credible threat to reduce aid drastically if the El Salvador government proved too obdurate. This would have undercut the military establishment of that country, a reported stumbling-block to compromise.[163] Even to the extent this view may

[162] No report has been submitted about the efforts to release the hostages in Lebanon.

[163] See Terry Lynn Karl, 'El Salvador's Negotiated Revolution', *Foreign Affairs*, 71 (Spring 1992), pp. 159–60.

be true, it does not significantly detract from the Secretary-General's role as a catalyst for compromise, a formulator of structures for their implementation, and a resource that enables the parties, when agreement has been reached, to present it to disaffected parts of their domestic constituencies as the product of an irresistible global consensus.

The Secretary-General can sometimes reinforce this catalytic effect if he makes public certain aspects or preliminary results of the ongoing process. Increasingly, he issues very detailed interim reports on progress in the negotiations while sometimes, when progress is too slow, putting blame on one or both of the parties.[164] Despite the risk that such public finger-pointing will antagonize a party, it has proven a useful device to bring pressure to bear on behalf of closure.

The question of effectiveness is of more than theoretical interest. Failure harms the office. More important, when the Secretary-General accepts a doomed good offices mission he may be being set up as a respectable cover for stasis or failure.[165] This may be what has happened in the cases of Cyprus and the Western Sahara. To protect his office, therefore, Secretary-General Boutros-Ghali may deliberately choose to show annoyance, as he has done with the open-ended UN approach to Cyprus and his role in it.[166] On the other hand, stasis, even UN-facilitated stasis, may be preferable to some alternatives. In the case of Cyprus, to abandon the UN interposition entirely would expose the weaker side to potential disaster.[167] Moreover, even in a deadlock, the Secretary-General's activity keeps an item on the UN's agenda and thus, as in the case of East Timor, vestigially preserves the principle involved, even when the political organs have ceased actively to pursue it. His activity emphasizes the legitimacy

---

[164] See e.g. Reports SG S/21183 of 8 Mar. 1990, p. 12 (Cyprus); S/23693 of 11 Mar. 1992, p. 17 (Somalia); S/23900 of 12 May 1992, p. 2 (Yugoslavia); and the detailed reports on the missions to Central America, Namibia, and Western Sahara mentioned above.

[165] Pérez de Cuéllar's 1986 Oxford lecture, above, pp. 132–5 *passim*.

[166] Report SG S/23780 of 3 Apr. 1992, p. 9 (Cyprus); UN Press Release SG/SM/4727/Rev. 1, 10 Apr. 1992, p. 5.

[167] Pérez de Cuéllar's 1986 Oxford lecture, above, p. 132.

issue and preserves options, keeping them open for the future.

(e) Recent Trends and the Future of the Good Offices Function

In the four years after April 1988, when the conclusion of the Geneva accords on Afghanistan marked the end of the Cold War, the Secretary-General was able to achieve some remarkable successes in the exercise of his good offices function. Nevertheless, there is some reason to believe that his role's expansion may not continue, or that it may evolve into something qualitatively different, or that it may turn to a quite different set of issues, in the post-Cold War UN context. As we have indicated, the capacity of the Security Council to perform its political functions effectively has narrowed the former role of the Secretary-General as an honest broker between forces locked into intractable enmity. The Council, now more readily able to take decisions, tends to ask the Secretary-General to go to Tripoli and to Baghdad not to exercise an independent political role but more to help execute its own plan of action. Members of the Security Council should be aware of some potential costs such missions impose on the Secretary's good offices function. When he is perceived as a letter carrier doing the bidding of powerful states, that undermines his credibility as a true mediator.

A day may come when the Security Council will again be deadlocked and unable to act decisively. That is reason enough for all states to be careful not to undermine the potential of the good offices function by demeaning it with assignments incompatible with its integrity. Conceivably, the letter-carrier role in some instances could better be entrusted to the President of the Security Council when that organ is the letter's author. As the Secretary-General observed in 1992:

While the mediator's effectiveness is enhanced by strong and evident support from the Council, the General Assembly and the relevant Member States acting in their national capacity, the good offices of the Secretary-General may at times be employed most effectively when conducted independently of the deliberative bodies.[168]

The likelihood of a need for future recourse to the Secretary-General's independent good offices function, despite the Security Council's new-found capacity to address crises, is strongly suggested by the increase in conflict between rival political or tribal secessionist elements within states like Afghanistan, Cambodia, Yugoslavia, Somalia, parts of the former Soviet Union, and Central America. If this peace-threatening tendency continues, it is far from clear that the Security Council, with several of its Permanent Members themselves troubled by secessionist movements, will wish to use its powers under Chapters VI and VII of the Charter to intervene. The Council's failure to invoke Chapter VII for intervention on behalf of the Kurds in Iraq and its slowness to become embroiled in the political and security dimensions of the Yugoslav crisis suggests that it may be precisely in these sorts of domestically generated threats to international peace that the Secretary-General, with his greater flexibility, might fill a void and fruitfully bring his good offices to bear. The Secretary-General's comprehensive, yet low-key approach to the civil war in El Salvador—arranging a cease-fire, developing modalities for mutually disarming the combatants, supervising human rights, and negotiating constitutional guarantees—may be an augury of the future, when the good offices role becomes the organization's instrument not only of peace-making but primarily of peace-building.[169] This need may increase, too, if the present unipolarity of the UN political balance of power were to yield once again to a more traditional bipolarity or multipolarity.

As calls for good offices, peacekeeping, election-monitoring, and humanitarian assistance increase, the Secretary-General is likely to accelerate his search for

---

[168] Boutros Boutros-Ghali, *An Agenda for Peace*, June 1992, para. 37. (Below, Appendix A.)

[169] This shift of emphasis to 'peace-building' was explicated by the Secretary-General in the David Abshire Lecture, given on 13 May 1992 at the Dirksen Senate Office Building, Washington DC. UN Press Release SG/SM/4748, 13 May 1992.

suitable institutional partners to help shoulder the burden. The most promising candidates are the regional groupings, particularly in crises of primarily internal origin.[170] Throughout the civil war in Liberia, for instance, the Secretary-General deferred to ECOWAS, 'a subregional body', which, he declared, was 'dealing with the problem'.[171] In Somalia, the UN has worked in tandem with the League of Arab States and the Islamic Conference. In the Paris Conference on Cambodia, the UN was aided by the Association of South-East Asian Nations. In El Salvador, 'The Friends of the Secretary-General' were a useful grouping of states lending weight to the UN mediation.[172] At times, as was tried in the Croatian segment of the Yugoslav conflict, it is possible to conceive of a division of functions between the regional organization (brokering a political solution)[173] and the Secretary-General (arranging a cease-fire and its enforcement).

However, there are likely to be conflicts, particularly those involving secessionism and civil war, where the regional organization may be unsuitable as a partner in the good offices function because the states in the region may be suspected of having involvements or agendas of their own which tend to favour one or another of the disputants.[174] Especially in such circumstances, the independent role of the Secretary-General continues, is likely to increase, and ought to be reinforced.

[170] UN Press Release SG/SM/4752, 18 May 1992, p. 5; SG/SM/4748, 13 May 1992, pp. 5–7; SG/SM/4727/Rev. 1, 10 Apr. 1992, pp. 6–7; SC Res. 749 of 7 Apr. 1992, para. 6; SC Res. 746 of 17 Mar. 1992, para. 9.
[171] UN Press Release SG/T/1661, 7 June 1991.
[172] Boutros-Ghali, *Agenda for Peace*, para. 62.
[173] UN Press Release SG/SM/4748, 13 May 1992, p. 6.
[174] See e.g. Report SG S/23900 of 12 May 1992, p. 4 (concerning Bosnia–Herzegovina).

UN Peacekeeping
and Election-Monitoring

SALLY MORPHET

UNITED Nations peacekeeping on a large scale (in terms of numbers of peacekeepers) began when the UN Emergency Force (UNEF I) was set up by the General Assembly in the aftermath of the Suez Crisis in 1956. Peacekeeping had not been envisaged in the UN Charter, but it was in no way incompatible with its aims. Nor was peacekeeping a new phenomenon. The most relevant previous example is the 3,000-strong League of Nations International Force set up at the end of 1934 to ensure that the Saar plebiscite (to decide whether the Saar should join France or Germany) was conducted appropriately. Bowett suggests that 'the secret of its success lay in the fact that the force represented a "neutral" or truly international force which was able to remain aloof from the political issues of the plebiscite and thus obtain the respect and confidence of the population'.[1]

Since the UN was set up in 1945, it has created twenty-nine peacekeeping bodies, sixteen of them since 1987.[2] By January 1992 an estimated 528,000 military, police, and civilian personnel had served in them, and they had

---

The opinions expressed are the author's own and should not be taken as an expression of official government policy.

[1] D. W. Bowett, *UN Forces: A Legal Study of United Nations Practice* (London, 1964), p. 11. This chapter also gives details of a number of other peacekeeping precedents.

[2] For a list of twenty-nine UN peacekeeping operations with details including main authorizing resolutions, see Appendix E below. (This total includes UNOSOM II, the UN force established in Somalia in 1993 which departs in important respects from the traditional mandate of peacekeeping forces).

already cost an aggregate of $US 8.3 billion.[3] Peace-keeping has been characterized as 'international help which is sometimes sent to an immediate problem area when disputing states wish, at least for the time being, to live in peace. Accordingly, it is an activity of a secondary kind, in the sense that it is dependent, in respect of both its origin and success, on the wishes and policies of others'.[4] The then UN Under-Secretary-General for Peacekeeping Operations, Marrack Goulding, defined it as 'United Nations field operations in which international personnel, civilian and/or military, are deployed with the consent of the parties and under UN command to help control and resolve actual or potential international conflicts or internal conflicts which have a clear international dimension'.[5] Both definitions suggest that peacekeeping is dependent on the political will of the parties involved. By contrast, the term 'peace-enforcement' has often been used to describe the external imposition of solutions even in the absence of the parties' consent. The political process of attempting to address and resolve the underlying causes of conflict is commonly described (including in *An Agenda for Peace*) as 'peace-making'. In reality these categories overlap, and distinctions between them have become increasingly fuzzy.

A number of major questions in connection with UN peacekeeping operations arise: Why has UN peacekeeping developed so remarkably? In what ways have past peace-keeping bodies been successful? What is the significance of the UN system for peacekeeping? How have the political dynamics between the First (West), Second (East), and Third Worlds (South) affected UN peacekeeping? What has been the relationship between UN peacekeeping, peace-making, and peace-enforcement? Is current UN

[3] Boutros Boutros-Ghali, *An Agenda for Peace*, June 1992, para. 47. (Below, Appendix A.)

[4] Alan James, *Peacekeeping in International Politics* (London, 1990), p. 1. A further definition is given by Brian Uquhart in 'International Peace and Security: Thoughts on the Twentieth Anniversary of Dag Hammarskjöld's Death', *Foreign Affairs*, 60, no. 1 (Fall 1981), p. 6 n.

[5] *The Singapore Symposium: The Changing Role of the United Nations in Conflict Resolution and Peacekeeping 13–15 March 1991* (UN DPI, New York, Sept. 1991), p. 25.

peacekeeping different from past UN peacekeeping? Can its tasks be extended to include election-monitoring without changing its basic structure? Can its costs be met without bankrupting the UN? In what kinds of conflict can peacekeeping be used effectively? Various of these questions will be discussed in a historical overview of the development of UN peacekeeping; and a broad appraisal of the nature, strengths, and weaknesses of UN peacekeeping and election-monitoring will be undertaken in the final section.

(a) The First Phase: 1948–1966

Between 1948 and 1966 the UN set up ten peacekeeping bodies (four large-scale peacekeeping forces and six smaller observer missions). This section looks more closely at their achievements; the politics behind their inauguration; their connection with peace-making; and the nature of the conflict with which they became involved.

1. The Middle East

The problems posed for the international community of states by the complex and intractable nexus of problems associated with the Israel/Palestine dispute, and states' differing attitudes towards it, gave rise both to the first UN observer mission and to the first UN peacekeeping force, as well as to a number of subsequent peacekeeping bodies. Two other Middle Eastern peacekeeping bodies were set up in the period 1948–66—the first to calm the situation in Lebanon, and the second to help defuse the dispute between Egypt and Saudi Arabia in the Yemen civil war.

(i) *UNTSO*. The long-standing problem of division and guerrilla warfare between the Jewish and Arab communities in Palestine was turned over to the newly created UN by Britain, the mandatory power, in 1947. This led to an attempt at peace-making through the passing of a General Assembly resolution in November 1947 recommending partition into two states. This was supported by a coalition of Western, Eastern, and Latin American countries and opposed by a number of Third World countries. This division of opinion made it unlikely that peace-making would succeed. The subsequent war in 1948 led the Security Council (the Soviet Union abstaining) to set up a Truce Commission to which military observers were subsequently added (through a further Security Council resolution voted upon paragraph by paragraph), initially to supervise the truce. The resulting UN Truce Supervision Organization (UNTSO) is often regarded as the earliest UN observer mission. True, it had been preceded in 1947 by General Assembly authorization of observers in the Balkans, and Security Council authorization of a Consular Commission to help manage decolonization in Indonesia: however, these are usually not included in the category of UN observer missions since the observers supplied remained under national command.

The difficulties of peace-making as regards Israel/ Palestine are reflected in the fact that UNTSO is still operating. Since 1948, it has been charged by the Security Council with a variety of extra tasks including supervision of the 1949 armistice agreements; observation of the cease-fire in the Suez Canal area and the Golan Heights after 1967; and the provision of observers in Beirut after 1982. It has normally responded intelligently and flexibly, besides contributing to the development of the UN peacekeeping process by providing core personnel for numerous subsequent peacekeeping operations (e.g. UNGOMAP in Afghanistan and Pakistan). Its continuing relevance and political importance is demonstrated by the fact that French and US military personnel have served in it since its inception: they were joined by Soviet and Chinese colleagues in, respectively, 1973 and 1990.

(ii) *UNEF I.* The UN Emergency Force was the first major peacekeeping force to be set up by the UN. The situation in the Middle East in 1956 called for creative diplomacy: an enforcement force on the Korean model (i.e. based on the use of Chapter VII of the UN Charter[6])

---

[6] Chap. VII of the Charter, which has been increasingly used since the late 1980s, deals with 'action with respect to threats to the peace, breaches of the peace, and acts of aggression'. Once the Security Council has, under Chap. VII, determined the existence of any of the above, it has the choice of either making recommendations for action, or deciding what mandatory measures should be taken under Art. 41 (permitting sanctions) and/or Art. 42 (permitting military measures).

was impractical because of the involvement of two Permanent Members of the Security Council with veto powers. The 1949 armistice agreement between Egypt and Israel had broken down with the attack on Egyptian territory by Britain, France, and Israel in October 1956. This attack was launched despite the fact that the Security Council had just agreed requirements for the settlement of the Suez question following Egyptian nationalization of the Suez Canal Company in July. The USA immediately called for a meeting of the Security Council to vote on a draft resolution calling for Israeli withdrawal behind the armistice lines. This, and a similar resolution sponsored by the Soviet Union, were vetoed by France and Britain. The question was then transferred to an emergency special session of the General Assembly at the behest of Yugoslavia (an influential Third World leader) using the Uniting for Peace procedure.[7] The General Assembly then adopted a resolution calling for a cease-fire and withdrawal of all forces behind the armistice lines.[8]

On 3 November, at Canadian instigation, the General Assembly discussed a draft resolution asking the UN Secretary-General to submit a plan for setting up, with the consent of the states concerned, an emergency international UN force. Western and Third World support ensured its adoption on 4 November, by fifty-seven votes for, none against, and nineteen abstentions (including Britain, Egypt, France, Israel, the Soviet Union, and Eastern European states). A similar vote on 5 November established UNEF I 'to secure and supervise the cessation of hostilities', using UNTSO personnel to hasten its inception. A subsequent resolution approved guide-lines for the operation of the force drafted by the UN Secretary-General Dag Hammarskjöld. These included a recognition of the independence of the commander; the non-use of forces from the five

---

[7] This is a procedure for transferring discussion of a problem to the General Assembly if the Security Council is unable to take decisions on the problem because of the use of vetoes. For details see the chapter by Michael Howard above, pp. 66–7.

[8] GA Res. 997(ES-1) of 2 Nov. 1956. Britain, France, and Israel were among the countries which voted against it.

Permanent Members of the Security Council;[9] the need
for consent of the host state; and the requirement that the
force, though using military personnel, should *not* use
military force except in self-defence or to defend its
positions. Hammarskjöld also noted that the question of
financing required further study. The first peacekeepers
arrived in Egypt in November (they were never allowed
into Israel) and the force reached its authorized strength
of 6,000 in February 1957—the month in which a seminal
Status of Forces Agreement was agreed with Egypt.[10]

The force had overseen the establishment of a cease-fire
and the withdrawal of the British and French forces by the
end of 1956, and the withdrawal of Israeli forces by the
end of March 1957. Between April 1957 and May 1967,
in progressively reduced numbers (3,400 in May 1967), it
was deployed along the armistice demarcation line, helping to maintain stability between the two countries. In all
these areas, it can be judged a success, but little peace-
making went along with it, and it was to end in controversy
at the outbreak of war in 1967.

(iii) *UNOGIL.* The UN Observation Group in Lebanon
was authorized in June 1958 by the Security Council (with
a Soviet abstention) to ensure there was no illegal infiltration of personnel or arms across Lebanese borders after
the main regional body, the Arab League, had failed to
resolve increasing tensions between Christians and Muslims.
These had been exacerbated by fears concerning President
Nasser's intentions following the merger between Egypt
and Syria in February 1958. The overthrow of the mon-
archy in Iraq in July increased East–West suspicion, despite

[9] This is no longer in operation since all five Permanent Members contributed
military personnel to UNIKOM in 1991. The following peacekeeping bodies
used military personnel from Permanent Members before 1991: UNTSO (all
except the UK); UNMOGIP (USA); UNFICYP (UK); UNIFIL (France); and
UNTAG (UK). For more information, including details of voluntary contributions by Permanent Members, see UN, *The Blue Helmets: A Review of UN
Peacekeeping* (2nd edn., New York, 1990), pp. 419–49.

[10] Text in Rosalyn Higgins, *United Nations Peacekeeping 1946–1967: Documents
and Commentary*, vol. 1: *The Middle East* (Oxford, 1969), pp. 372–82. This set the
pattern for all future agreements of this type. The four volumes of documents
and commentary by Rosalyn Higgins are an indispensable aid to the study of
peacekeeping.

the presence of UNOGIL observers, and led to the USA sending substantial forces to Lebanon at the request of its government. Later that month the Soviet Union vetoed two Security Council resolutions suggesting a renewed role for UNOGIL. In August the General Assembly defused the tension by unanimously passing an Arab League-sponsored resolution implicitly suggesting that US troops should be replaced by UNOGIL—an example of the sometimes close relations between regional organizations and peacekeeping.[11] This face-saving device led to the withdrawal of US troops by the end of October 1958, followed by that of UNOGIL in December.

(iv) *UNYOM*. The UN Yemen Observation Mission, planned through the good offices of the UN Secretary-General, was designed to resolve problems arising from a civil war which had broken out in 1962 between royalists and republicans in the Yemen in which Egypt, Saudi Arabia, Britain (then still involved with the South Arabian Federation), and the superpowers had conflicting interests. In June 1963 the Security Council (with a Soviet abstention) authorized UNYOM to establish monitors on the Saudi-Yemen border to check observance of the terms of the Saudi–Egyptian disengagement agreement. Egypt (which had troops in Yemen) and Saudi Arabia had agreed to defray operational costs for two months. UNYOM operated between July 1963 and September 1964. It then withdrew (though Egyptian troops remained) as Saudi Arabia announced that it would no longer defray any expenses. Peacekeeping did not help resolve the problem primarily because the parties were not fully committed to disengagement.[12] However this episode, like others, points to the possibility of a creative role in dispute settlement by the UN Secretary-General, who maintained

---

[11] Regional organizations have also made important contributions to peacemaking. The Arab League was, for instance, able to defuse tension between Iraq and the newly independent Kuwait in 1961 while the Security Council was paralysed by Soviet vetoes.

[12] Henry Wiseman, 'United Nations Peacekeeping: An Historical Overview', in Henry Wiseman (ed.), *Peacekeeping: Appraisals and Proposals* (New York, 1983), p. 40.

a Personal Representative to deal with this question after
UNYOM had withdrawn.[13]

2. Africa

Africa's involvement with peacekeeping during the period
1948–66 was limited to the Congo. The UN operation
there in 1960–4 was the most controversial of all UN
peacekeeping operations and has often been cited as an
example of the legal, humanitarian, and political pitfalls
of peacekeeping, especially when it moves to a peace
enforcement role. The Congo operation nearly destroyed
the UN through the financial and constitutional crisis that
it created.

The original success of UNEF I made it likely that many
of those involved, particularly the UN Secretary-General,
would immediately think of a peacekeeping force when it
could be seen that problems were likely to arise in the
decolonization process in Africa with the accelerated withdrawal of Belgium from the Congo. Consequently UN–
Congo contacts were in train before independence, which
was on 30 June 1960. The situation deteriorated immediately after independence as a mutiny brought about
Belgian military intervention without the Congo government's consent. The Congo government thereupon went
to the Security Council which, in mid-July (after the
province of Katanga had announced its secession), adopted
a resolution (Britain and France abstaining[14]) calling
on the Belgian government to withdraw its troops and
authorizing the UN Secretary-General to provide, in consultation with the Congo government, such military assistance as might be necessary. The advance party of the
Opération des Nations Unies au Congo (ONUC), which
had, according to Brian Urquhart, been given a vain and

[13] See the chapter by Thomas Franck and Georg Nolte above.
[14] Rosalyn Higgins, *United Nations Peacekeeping 1946–1967: Documents and
Commentary*, vol 3: *Africa* (Oxford, 1980), pp. 16–17, notes that Britain abstained
because it considered the Belgian troops should only withdraw when they were
replaced by UN detachments. She also notes that the USA was concerned with
the same issue but read the resolution in a different way. This illustrates the
ambiguity (sometimes deliberate) which is often a hallmark of UN resolutions.
It can be both creative and the reverse.

arrogant commander,[15] arrived a few days later to monitor the withdrawal of Belgian forces and help restore law and order.

After the dismissal of the Prime Minister, Lumumba, by the President in early September 1960 the country lapsed into civil war (exacerbated by East–West rivalry). Following the first Soviet veto on a draft resolution on the Congo on 17 September the complex question was transferred to the General Assembly: this set up a peace-making Conciliation Commission. Those controlling ONUC, meanwhile, tried, without taking sides or using force except in self-defence, to prevent and control the conflict.[16] The problems were immense: in December Hammarskjöld gave specific consideration to the withdrawal of ONUC from the Congo.[17]

In February 1961, after the murder of Lumumba, the Security Council adopted a controversial resolution (France and the Soviet Union abstaining) authorizing ONUC to use force as a last resort to prevent civil war: some argue that this moved the basis of the operation from peace-keeping to peace-enforcement.[18] This authorization was implemented in April following agreement with the President, to prevent civil war and *inter alia* to deal with the problem of mercenaries backed by differing external forces. This led to attacks on UN troops: the situation was compounded by the apparently accidental death, in September, of Dag Hammarskjöld in an air crash on his way to meet the secessionist leader of Katanga. It was at this point that ONUC started killing people, thus becoming a part of the conflict it was 'supposed to be controlling, and therefore a part of the problem'.[19] Peace-enforcement proved problematical. In November 1961 the Security

---

[15] Brian Urquhart, *A Life in Peace and War* (London, 1987), p. 148.

[16] The literature on the complex problems thrown up by the Congo operation is huge. Worth consulting, apart from Higgins and Urquhart, are Georges Abi-Saab's useful book on legal aspects, *The United Nations Operation in the Congo 1960–1964* (Oxford, 1978); and Conor Cruise O'Brien, *To Katanga and Back: A UN Case-History* (London, 1962).

[17] Abi-Saab, *UN Operation in the Congo*, p. 95.

[18] See discussion ibid., pp. 99–110.

[19] Urquhart, *A Life in Peace and War*, p. 179

Council also authorized ONUC (Britain and France abstaining) to use force to deport foreign personnel and mercenaries. With many difficulties the secession of Katanga was brought to an end in January 1963, and ONUC finally withdrew in June 1964.

The operation was successful in fulfilling its mandate, in particular by contributing to the maintenance of Congo's territorial integrity, and averting Soviet intervention and superpower conflict. However it also led to widespread distrust of the possible ramifications of peacekeeping (because it had moved to a peace-enforcement role) both in the Third World, certain of whose representatives were concerned that weak states might become pawns of a peacekeeping body, and in the Soviet Union. The Permanent Members of the Security Council determined that no UN Secretary-General should ever become as dominant as Hammarskjöld: they attempted to establish that the Security Council was recognized as the only UN body which could set up peacekeeping operations, and that these should be set up for a fixed period, thus ensuring they could veto their continuation. Tough lessons for the 1990s emerge from this operation: 'The Congo reminds us that the UN will be capable of mounting effective peacekeeping missions in contested areas only in so far as the powers continue to cooperate, and warns us of the perils of assigning UN troops and negotiators complex tasks that are not supported by concrete agreements between the powers.'[20]

3. Asia

In the period up to 1966 more peacekeeping bodies (both UN and non-UN) were set up in Asia than anywhere else. They dealt with problems posed by decolonization and the dispute over the status of Jammu and Kashmir. The early 1947 Consular Commission set up to help manage Indonesian decolonization embodied many peacekeeping characteristics, though as its military observers were not

[20] Roland Paris, *United Nations Peacekeeping after the Cold War* (RUSI & Brassey's Defence Yearbook, 1991), p. 276.

under UN command, it will not be discussed here. Similarly the UN force in Korea (1950–3) will not be considered: as the first force established under Chapter VII of the Charter, it was a peace-enforcing not a peacekeeping body.[21]

(i) *Peacekeeping outside the UN system.* The UN has not been a suitable or effective vehicle for peacekeeping activity in all situations. The main peacekeeping and monitoring bodies set up outside the UN system during this period were the three International Commissions for Supervision and Control for respectively Cambodia, Laos, and Vietnam to implement the 1954 Geneva agreements marking French withdrawal from Indo-China. The commissions (staffed by Canada, India, and Poland) were not UN bodies, but in their early years played a role comparable to that played elsewhere by the UN.[22] The UN was not an appropriate body to deal with Indo-China in part because one of the major players, the People's Republic of China, did not represent China at the UN until 1971.

(ii) *UNMOGIP.* In January 1948 the Security Council (with an abstention from the Soviet Union) set up a small mission, the UN Commission for India and Pakistan (UNCIP), to investigate the problem of the status of Jammu and Kashmir, where hostilities had broken out following India's and Pakistan's independence. Jammu and Kashmir had been due to accede to India although its population was mainly Muslim. Three months later the Security Council, in a further peace-making attempt, placed its good offices at the disposal of each government to facilitate the holding of a plebiscite, and recommended that UNCIP should appoint military observers to supervise the cease-fire. The UN Military Observer Group in India and Pakistan (UNMOGIP) arrived in 1949 to supervise the cease-fire line and remains to this day. Although UNMOGIP has made a reasonable contribution to peacekeeping and played a useful role during the conflicts

[21] Some have included the UN force in Korea under the heading of peacekeeping. See Rosalyn Higgins, *United Nations Peacekeeping 1946–1967: Documents and Commentary*, vol. 2: *Asia* (Oxford, 1970), pp. 153–312.
[22] James, *Peacekeeping in International Politics*, p. 206.

between India and Pakistan in 1965–6 and 1971–2, few peace-makers have tried to resolve the dangerous and complex communal problems of Jammu and Kashmir, which are inextricably linked with India–Pakistan relations.[23] The requisite political will does not exist.

(iii) *UNSF.* The status of the territory of West New Guinea (West Irian) remained unresolved despite Indonesian independence in 1949. The Dutch maintained that the Papuans should be allowed to decide their own future: the Indonesians asserted that West Irian was part of Indonesia. In 1961 the UN Secretary-General began to use his good offices to try to resolve the problem. In September 1962 the General Assembly, in a resolution voted for by all the Permanent Members except the French, took note of a Netherlands–Indonesian agreement providing for the administration of West New Guinea to be transferred from The Netherlands to a UN Temporary Executive Authority (UNTEA). This was to be headed by a UN Administrator until May 1963, when the territory would be transferred to Indonesia. It also stipulated that the UN Secretary-General would provide a UN Security Force (UNSF) to assist UNTEA. This was the first time the UN had taken on full administrative control of a territory. In October the UNSF began to supervise the withdrawal of Indonesian and Dutch troops as well as acting as a police arm of UNTEA. Full administrative control was passed to Indonesia on 1 May 1963. The UNSF had been able to act as a face-saving device for The Netherlands and as 'an enormously useful tool'.[24]

(iv) *UNIPOM.* In August 1965 military incidents between India and Pakistan, once again over Kashmir, were followed by hostilities between the two states. This resulted in a Security Council resolution in September calling for a cease-fire and cooperation with UNMOGIP. Later the same month the Security Council, in a resolution voted for

[23] For more information see *The Blue Helmets*, 2nd edn., pp. 157–64.
[24] James, *Peacekeeping in International Politics*, p. 195. James also discusses the subsequent flawed exercise by the territory's population in 1969 of their right to self-determination. See also Michla Pomerance, *Self-Determination in Law and Practice: The New Doctrine in the United Nations* (The Hague, 1982), pp. 32–5.

by all the Permanent Members, called for observers to monitor the cease-fire line outside Kashmir, and established the UN India–Pakistan Observation Mission (UNIPOM). This played a useful calming role: it was withdrawn following a peace-making meeting in January 1966, under Soviet chairmanship, between the Prime Minister of India and the President of Pakistan.

4. Europe and Latin America

In Europe and Latin America there were few UN peace-keeping activities in the period 1948–66. The UN became involved in inter-state conflict in the Balkans after World War II, and in inter-state and communal conflict in Cyprus after Cyprus had achieved independence in 1960. In Latin America, its sole intervention in the period came after US troops were sent to protect US nationals following the overthrow of a junta in the Dominican Republic.

(i) *UNSCOB*. The UN Special Committee on the Balkans was established by the General Assembly by a resolution (voted against by the Eastern bloc and abstained on by many Third World states) in October 1947 to observe the compliance by Greece, Albania, Bulgaria, and Yugoslavia with, and assist them in implementing, recommendations designed to resolve disputes (relating to frontier, refugee and minority problems). It was replaced by a small number of military observers from the General Assembly's Peace Observation Commission in 1952. Mainly because it was unable to function except in Greece, it was not effective.[25] Since its troops were not under UN command, it is not classified as a UN peacekeeping force though it has obvious similarities. The matters under dispute are disturbingly similar to those that are being encountered some forty years later by UNPROFOR.

(ii) *UNFICYP*. The UN Peacekeeping Force in Cyprus was created in 1964 to deal with communal violence between the Greek and Turkish communities which had resulted from the breakdown of the constitutional arrangements agreed at independence in 1960. After the collapse

[25] Wiseman (ed.), *Peacekeeping: Appraisals and Proposals*, p. 25.

of an attempt to use forces of the guarantor powers, the British government initially sought to use NATO peace-keeping, but this, despite US pressure, remained unaccept-able to President Makarios and the Soviet Union. Britain therefore raised the problem in the Security Council in February 1964. The subsequent unanimous resolution recommended the setting up of a peacekeeping force with the consent of the Cyprus government 'to use its best efforts to prevent a recurrence of fighting and, as necessary, to contribute to the maintenance of law and order and a return to normal conditions'. Set up with similar guide-lines to UNEF I (though including civilian police and, unlike UNEF I, troops from one Permanent Member— Britain), UNFICYP still remains in existence. Its strength of 6,411 in June 1964 was gradually reduced in the early 1970s to just above 3,000. During this period 'it made a very significant contribution to the maintenance of peace'.[26] Peace-making was not feasible. UNFICYP's adapted role following Turkish military intervention after the Greek Cypriot coup against Makarios in July 1974 is discussed in the next section.

(iii) *DOMREP*. In the Americas before the blossoming of UN peacekeeping in 1989–92 there had been only one UN observer mission. Following the overthrow of a junta in the Dominican Republic in 1965, the USA, in an action reminiscent of Lebanon in 1958, announced that it was sending troops to protect its nationals. It also informed the Security Council that it had called for a meeting of the Organization of American States (OAS), which subsequently set up an Inter-American Peace Force (IAPF) to help restore normal conditions in the Republic. The Soviet Union had by then already brought the matter to the Security Council. At the instigation of certain non-aligned members, the Council eventually adopted a unanimous resolution in May 1965 calling for a cease-fire and inviting the UN Secretary-General to send a Representative to report on the situation. This Mission of the Representative of the Secretary-General in the Dominican Republic

---

[26] James, *Peacekeeping in International Politics*, p. 229.

(DOMREP), comprising the Special Representative, a Military Adviser, and two military observers, went to the Republic and stayed until withdrawn in October 1966 after the June 1966 elections, which were followed by the departure of the IAPF.

In his 1964–5 Annual Report the UN Secretary-General noted that his Representative had had a moderating effect on a difficult situation and that this had been the first time that a UN mission had operated in the same area and dealt with the same matters as a regional organization. He indicated, presciently, that this episode should stimulate thought concerning the character of regional organizations and the nature of their functions and obligations in relation to the responsibilities of the UN and the Charter.

5. *Peacekeeping finance and the crisis of 1960–1965*

The costs of peacekeeping forces have often caused the UN serious problems. Observer missions (whose maximum strength has usually been 600 or less) have been less controversial because they have been less costly. During the period 1948–66 all the UN observer missions plus UNSCOB, except UNYOM and UNSF, were financed from the UN regular budget. UNSF (set up in 1962) and UNYOM (set up in 1963), at the height of the UN financial crisis over the Congo, were, partially on this account, primarily financed by the states most involved.[27]

By contrast, the large-scale peacekeeping forces set up in the period 1948–66, with the exception of UNFICYP—which because it was set up during the financial crisis over the Congo, was financed on a voluntary basis—all posed serious financial problems. The first peacekeeping force, UNEF I, set the pattern for future peacekeeping finance. The General Assembly, which controls UN finances, agreed provisionally with the UN Secretary-General's proposals in

---

[27] The finances of UNYOM are discussed in Higgins, *UN Peacekeeping*, vol. 1, pp. 645–52. The main costs were met by the parties concerned but the UN Secretary-General made clear that he could use certain, limited, discretionary powers provided under GA Res. 1862 (XVII) if necessary. The finances of UNIPOM, the first UN peacekeeping body to be set up after the settlement of the Congo financial crisis, are discussed in Higgins, *UN Peacekeeping*, vol. 2, pp. 455–8.

early November 1956 that the cost of the force, except for equipment and salaries paid by the contributing states (a proposal subsequently substantially modified), should be borne by the UN, and that it should be financed by assessments (apportioned according to the regular budget) to be paid to a special account (and voluntary payments).[28] The problems that were raised by this unprecedented action continue to be one Achilles' heel of UN peacekeeping. Do states have an obligation to pay these assessed contributions? Such problems become particularly pressing when states consider that the political rationale for a peacekeeping force does *not* represent the interest of the international community as a whole and/or that they have other, to them more pressing, financial obligations.

The constitutional crisis that developed over this issue came to a head over Congo peacekeeping finances.[29] In December 1960 the General Assembly, recognizing 'that the expenses involved in the United Nations operations in the Congo for 1960 constitute "expenses of the Organization" within the meaning of Article 17, paragraph 2, of the Charter . . . and that the assessment thereof against Member States creates binding legal obligations on such States to pay their assessed shares', decided to establish an *ad hoc* account for UN expenses in the Congo apportioned on the basis of the regular scale of assessments.[30] Both Britain and the USA endorsed the majority view, and they were supported in this by an advisory opinion of the ICJ in 1962. However, the Soviet Union, France, and other dissenting countries refused to pay their assessments, arguing that the power of the General Assembly under Article 17 'to consider and approve' the budget referred only to the regular administrative budget and not to 'extraordinary peacekeeping costs raised under separate

[28] An account of the financing of UNEF is given in Higgins, *UN Peacekeeping*, vol. 1, pp. 415–56. Details of the question of the costs of equipment and salaries are given on pp. 417–20.
[29] See the chapter on finances in Higgins, *UN Peacekeeping*, vol. 3, pp. 274–303.
[30] The vote was forty-six for, seventeen against (the Eastern bloc and certain Arab states), twenty-four abstaining (including France).

accounts. The Soviet Union had also refused to pay for UNEF I as it did not recognize the competence of the General Assembly to establish peacekeeping forces. The position of France as regards payments for UNEF I was complex.[31] By 1961 it no longer considered it had any obligation to pay for these, though it continued to pay voluntarily.

The refusal of the Soviet Union and others to pay for UNEF I and ONUC caused a rapid deterioration in the financial position of the UN. The implication of the ICJ's advisory opinion was that states failing to pay for ONUC and UNEF I might be penalized by virtue of Article 19 of the Charter, which states that UN members with two years' arrears of contributions forfeit their right to vote in the General Assembly. By 1 January 1964 the Soviet Union and a number of other countries had become liable to lose their vote. The crisis only began to be resolved by a compromise reached in February 1965 when the General Assembly authorized its President to set up a Special Committee on Peacekeeping Operations (which still remains in existence) to undertake a 'comprehensive review of the whole question of peacekeeping operations in all their aspects, including ways of overcoming the present financial difficulties of the Organization'.

A temporary political solution, which like so many temporary solutions still underpins current thinking and actions on the subject, was finally reached in the summer of 1965 after the US government had made clear that, although it considered Article 19 was applicable, it recognized that the majority of the Assembly was against application of the Article. On 1 September, therefore, the USA joined other member states in accepting the Special Committee's recommendations that the applicability of Article 19 should not be raised in relation to ONUC and UNEF I; in agreeing that the General Assembly should carry on its work normally; and in suggesting that the financial

---

[31] A detailed discussion of the attitude of France to peacekeeping financing is given in Robert S. Wood, *France and the World Community* (Leiden, 1973), pp. 165–80.

difficulties of the UN should be solved through voluntary contributions by member states, with highly developed states making substantial contributions. An Irish proposal, building on a resolution of 1963,[32] and suggesting that future peacekeeping costs should be borne by members on the scale of 5 per cent among economically less developed member states, 25 per cent among economically developed states, and 70 per cent for Permanent Members provided they had voted in favour of the operation, subsequently became the subject of intense debate. Although not accepted in 1965, these ideas (except those concerning a positive vote by Permanent Members) have formed the basis for the financing of nearly all subsequent peacekeeping bodies beginning with UNEF II in 1973.

UNFICYP was financed from voluntary contributions as laid down in paragraph 6 of Security Council resolution 186, which recommended that all costs in the first three months should be met, 'in a manner to be agreed upon by them, by the Governments providing the contingents and by the Government of Cyprus'. Although certain other voluntary contributions have also been forthcoming, the continual deficits have meant difficulties for successive UN-Secretaries-General in paying bills presented by third parties and by troop-contributing governments for reimbursement of their extra and extraordinary costs.[33]

6. *The foundations of UN peacekeeping*

Despite the fact that the first phase of UN peacekeeping had raised financial and constitutional problems that many considered nearly destroyed the UN, by the mid-1960s the foundations of UN peacekeeping operations, including ways of tackling financing, had been laid. Many saw the multi-faceted contribution that these bodies (because they represented the international community as a whole) could make to the management or resolution of international disputes. Tacit agreement had been reached on a

[32] GA Res. 1874(S–IV) of 27 June 1963.
[33] See Rosalyn Higgins, *United Nations Peacekeeping 1946–1979: Documents and Commentary*, vol. 4: *Europe* (Oxford, 1981), pp. 286–301.

number of guiding principles: the important role of the UN Secretary-General and of UN command—albeit one that the Permanent Members had to keep an eye on; the necessity for agreement, both at the UN and on the ground, of the political parameters of the operation, including the need for consent of the host states, and also, in some cases, of the other main parties involved; the fact that those engaged in peacekeeping had to maintain neutrality and impartiality (as peacekeepers *not* peace-enforcers) so that they could contribute to the management of the problem rather than risk becoming part of it; the fact that the military should not use force except in self-defence or to defend their positions;[34] and the importance of creative flexibility (e.g. through use of police and administrators) in response to the varying situations that faced them on the ground.

How effective were these operations on a political level? Those dealing with short-term face-saving for major powers (UNOGIL, UNEF I during its first months, and DOMREP) and reasonably straightforward decolonization (UNSF) seem to have been more effective, at least where political circumstances were favourable, than longer-term bodies which got out of their depth (ONUC), or those dealing primarily with communal disputes (UNTSO, UNMOGIP, and UNFICYP). This is primarily because peacekeeping depends on the will of the parties involved: when this is not there (as in UNYOM) the body concerned can only help manage the existing status quo (a useful task in its own right[35]) rather than aid peace-making: peacekeeping cannot resolve underlying problems.

There was also a growing determination among the

---

[34] Marrack Goulding, in his illuminating and wide-ranging 1993 Cyril Foster Lecture at Oxford, points out that since 1973 'self-defence has been deemed to include situations in which peace-keepers were being prevented by armed persons from fulfilling their mandate'. Goulding, 'The Evolution of United Nations Peace-Keeping', *International Affairs*, 69, no. 3 (July 1993), p. 455.

[35] A good short description of the qualities needed by a peacekeeper is in chap. 2 of Michael Harbottle, *What is Proper Soldiering?* (Centre for International Peacebuilding, Chipping Norton, 1991). The most useful practical guide to peacekeeping is provided by the *Peacekeeper's Handbook* (International Peace Academy, New York, 1984).

Permanent Members to ensure that the Security Council, *not* the General Assembly, should authorize peacekeeping bodies.[36] The last peacekeeping force to be authorized by the General Assembly was the UNSF in 1962. Interestingly Britain, the Soviet Union, and the USA all voted for it: France, more consistent, abstained (as the Soviet Union should have done) in view of its concern that peacekeeping was a subject that should be dealt with by the Security Council.

More Soviet–US convergence on peacekeeping could be seen in the 1960s in a UN which was becoming more dominated by Third World concerns. In the 1950s the Soviet Union had abstained on (while the USA had voted for) the setting up of UNEF I and UNOGIL. In the 1960s the two superpowers voted together for the setting up of five of the six peacekeeping bodies which were established— ONUC (1960); UNSF (1962); UNFICYP (1964); UNIPOM (1965); and DOMREP (1965): the only exception was UNYOM (1963), on which the Soviet Union abstained on grounds of uncertainty about its duration and potential problems over its financing.[37] One reason for the more forthcoming Soviet attitude to peacekeeping in the 1960s may well have been the fact that the only financial cost to the Soviet Union (given its refusal to pay for ONUC) was for two small observer forces, UNIPOM and DOMREP, which were both financed from the UN regular budget. Another was that the Soviet Union, in certain cases (e.g. UNIPOM), wanted to exert some influence on the dispute and to accommodate Third World concerns.

(b) The Second Phase: 1967–1984

This phase began with a controversial event which has influenced views on UN peacekeeping ever since: the withdrawal of UNEF I from Egypt in May 1967, followed immediately by the Arab–Israel war. The refocusing on

---

[36] The votes of the representatives of the Taiwan regime were almost always identical to those of the USA.

[37] See Higgins, *UN Peacekeeping*, vol. 3, p. 621.

the Palestinian cause combined with the deterioration of Syrian–Israeli relations in early 1967 had led to President Nasser's request for the withdrawal of UNEF I in May. The debate over whether the UN Secretary-General, U Thant, was right to take the decision to withdraw, or whether the matter should have been taken to the General Assembly (and the Security Council), still continues.[38] U Thant's Advisory Committee was divided: Canada, Brazil, and Norway were against immediate action, India and Pakistan for. India and Yugoslavia insisted that their troops must be withdrawn. It was highly unlikely, as Brian Urquhart points out, that a majority of states in the General Assembly would have been prepared to convene an emergency special session to discuss this question, since they would have agreed that Egypt had a legal right to ask for UNEF withdrawal.[39] Recourse to the Security Council would have exposed divisions, including divisions between the superpowers. UN peacekeeping was at an impasse due to its reliance on the consent of the disputing parties.[40] However, it would almost certainly have been wiser for U Thant, who became a useful scapegoat for others, to have made even more effort to engage both the General Assembly and the Security Council during this tense period. After Egyptian closure of the Gulf of Aqaba, war broke out, and Israel occupied Sinai, the Syrian Golan Heights, and the territory ruled by Jordan west of the Jordan river. The withdrawal of UNEF I left UNFICYP as the only extant UN force.

1. A more positive approach in the Middle East 1968–1973

During the period 1968–73 Third World countries and the European Community were the main peace-making

[38] See the chapters by Nabil A. Elaraby on 'United Nations Peacekeeping: The Egyptian Experience', and by Michael Comay on 'United Nations Peacekeeping: The Israeli Experience', in Wiseman (ed.), *Peacekeeping: Appraisals and Proposals*, pp. 65–117; Major-General Indar Jit Rikhye, *The Sinai Blunder* (London, 1980); Higgins, *UN Peacekeeping*, vol. 3, pp. 260–78; Urquhart, *A Life in Peace and War*, pp. 209–16; James, *Peacekeeping in International Politics*, p. 223.

[39] Urquhart, *A Life in Peace and War*, p. 212.

[40] For a somewhat different view see Thomas M. Franck, *Nation against Nation: What Happened to the UN Dream and What the US Can Do about it* (Oxford, 1985), pp. 87–94.

initiators in the tense and complicated Arab–Israel dispute. By 1973 they were agreed on trying to secure the implementation of the 1967 Security Council resolution 242 with an additional reference to the fact that a just solution could be achieved only on the basis of respect for the rights and legitimate aspirations of the Palestinians (242 had only referred to refugees). In July 1973 the Egyptians put forward a draft Security Council resolution on these lines: it was voted for by all the Security Council except China (which did not participate) and the USA (which cast its fifth-ever veto). The October 1973 war followed. In the aftermath the Soviet Union voted with Britain, France, and the USA for two Security Council resolutions setting up UNEF II (which was to have a maximum strength of about 7,000 to supervise the cease-fire), and, unprecedentedly, began to pay its dues to the special account set up to finance it. It also, again unprecedentedly, joined the USA and France in sending observers to UNTSO: meanwhile Poland joined UNEF II, becoming the first eastern European state to join a UN peacekeeping body.

Once again the Israel/Palestine problem had brought about an innovation in previous peacekeeping practice. The Soviet Union seems to have considered that there was a chance that peace-making on its terms was possible: its subsequent realization that this might not be correct was influenced by the failure of the December 1973 Geneva peace conference. Despite this it was prepared to join the same three Permanent Members in voting in May 1974 for UNDOF, the UN Disengagement Observer Force (financed in the same way as UNEF II), to keep the peace between Israeli and Syrian forces on the Golan Heights in accordance with the 1974 Israeli–Syrian disengagement agreement.

These votes also marked the début on to the peacekeeping stage of the People's Republic of China, which had replaced Taiwan as the representative of China on the Security Council in 1971. It chose, until 1981, not to participate in resolutions authorizing peacekeeping bodies.

2. *Peacekeeping and peace-making in Cyprus and the Middle East 1974–1982*

After the middle of 1974 peacekeeping forces in Cyprus and the Middle East encountered difficulties, and no new forces were established under UN auspices except in Lebanon. In Cyprus the UN presence failed to prevent the degeneration of the situation, culminating in the Greek Cypriot coup by Nikos Sampson against President Makarios in July 1974. This triggered Turkish military intervention in the northern part of the island. UNFICYP took action to assume control over the airport and subsequently to act in the new buffer zone across the island. On 1 August the Soviet Union abstained on the Security Council resolution giving the UN Secretary-General authorization to redefine certain UNFICYP functions to deal with the new realities.[41] Many consider UNFICYP's continuing presence since this time has allowed the dispute to ossify.[42] Brian Urquhart has characterized subsequent peace-making negotiations over Cyprus 'as the most frustrating negotiations in my experience'.[43]

The deep and continuing conflict between Israel, the Palestinians, and Israel's Arab neighbours after the 1973 war demonstrated the complexity of the relations between peacekeeping and efforts at a political settlement. Such efforts sometimes caused acrimony, and did not always assist peacekeeping under UN auspices. Thus in October 1976 the Soviet Union continued to try to achieve a peace-making role by proposing that the Geneva peace conference should be reconvened. The USA and Israel were the only countries to vote against the subsequent General Assembly resolution on these lines.[44] The Soviet Union followed this by announcing at the end of the year that it would only pay half of its assessed expenses for UNEF II and UNDOF for 1975–76.

The administration of President Carter which came into

---

[41] See Higgins, *UN Peacekeeping*, vol. 4, pp. 370–2.
[42] See the chapter by Thomas Franck and Georg Nolte above, p. 156.
[43] Urquhart, *A Life in Peace and War*, p. 259.
[44] GA Res. 31/62 of 9 Dec. 1976.

office in early 1977 made UN peace-making and peace-keeping a more central part of its policy than its predecessor, especially with respect to the conflict in the Middle East. In October 1977, a joint US–Soviet statement was issued on the problems that needed to be resolved over Israel and Palestine in the framework of a comprehensive settlement of the Middle East problem.

These possibilities were short-lived. They were combated by the new Israeli Likud government which, in many ways, distrusted and ignored the UN, since it considered the PLO a terrorist organization, not a potential negotiating partner, and voted against the 1974 General Assembly resolution on the right of the Palestinians to self-determination.[45] Despite this it maintained its UN membership and some relationship with UNTSO, UNEF II, and UNDOF. UN peacekeeping therefore remained possible: UN peace-making was not. Following President Sadat's visit to Jerusalem in November 1977 the Arab world split and the USA embraced a more particular peace-making process which, in the first instance, excluded the UN and the Soviet Union.

The US-sponsored Camp David peace treaty between Egypt and Israel of March 1979, however, provided for the use of UN peacekeeping bodies to implement its security arrangements. It soon became clear that any attempt to agree this in the Security Council would be blocked by a Soviet veto: UNEF II was therefore wound up in July 1979, having fulfilled its mandate. In 1982, following implementation of the Camp David treaty's provisions for Israeli withdrawal from Sinai, a non-UN body took on a peacekeeping and observation role there: this is discussed further below.

3. The establishment and effectiveness of UNIFIL 1978–

The civil war in the Lebanon, which broke out in 1975, had not been resolved through the establishment, in 1976, of the Arab League's Arab Deterrent Force, mainly controlled by Syria. This war was compounded by the presence

---

[45] GA Res. 3236 (XXIX) of 22 Nov. 1974.

of PLO militias and long-standing Israeli involvement with certain Lebanese militias in southern Lebanon. Following a PLO commando raid near Tel Aviv, Israeli forces invaded Lebanon in March 1978 and occupied the whole of the southern region up to the Litani river. The Security Council responded by adopting a US draft resolution calling for Israeli withdrawal from Lebanon and the establishment of a UN Interim Force in Lebanon (UNIFIL) 'for the purpose of confirming the withdrawal of Israeli forces, restoring international peace and security and assisting the Government of Lebanon in ensuring the return of its effective authority in the area'. The Soviet Union abstained, 'having been begged by the Arabs not to sabotage the resolution'.[46] China once again did not participate.

UNIFIL's mandate, noted Brian Urquhart, 'looked good on paper, but had remarkably little to do with the cruel realities' of the presence of the PLO in southern Lebanon and the Israeli determination to occupy part of this by proxy.[47] Despite UNIFIL's size (nearly 6,000 at its height) it has not yet been able to fulfil its mandate. However it has had influence. One thoughtful observer has noted: 'the relative stability of the area . . . is in large part a measure of UNIFIL's success.' She also notes that 'in a wide range of ways the residents of the south have become directly or indirectly dependent on the Force for their protection, political influence and economic livelihood'.[48]

4. Peacekeeping outside the UN system

With the advent of President Reagan in early 1981, the US government's concern over what it saw as Third World dominance of much of the UN (the 1975 General Assembly association of Zionism and racism had had particular influence), and its inability to use the UN to monitor the Camp David accords because of the Soviet threat to use a

---

[46] Urquhart, *A Life in Peace and War*, p. 290.   [47] Ibid. p. 289.

[48] Marianne Heiberg, 'Peacekeepers and Local Populations: Some Comments on UNIFIL', in Indar Jit Rikhye and Kjell Skjelsbaek (eds), *The United Nations and Peacekeeping: Results, Limitations and Prospects* (London, 1990), pp. 166 and 155.

veto if such a proposal came to the Security Council, led it to establish monitoring machinery outside the UN. The Multinational Force and Observers (MFO), a body established outside the UN framework, began to function in Egyptian Sinai in 1982 following completion of an agreed total Israeli withdrawal from Sinai.[49]

The implementation of the 1979 Egypt–Israel agreement did not bring general peace to the Middle East. In June 1982 Israel invaded Lebanon (despite UNIFIL) in order to destroy the PLO presence there and, it hoped, to establish a regime favourable to its interests. The USA vetoed a draft Security Council resolution asking the Secretary-General to establish military observers in Lebanon. Instead a Western Multinational Force was set up in August to supervise the withdrawal of the PLO from Beirut. MNF 1 was then withdrawn only to be reconstituted, with the addition of a British contingent, as MNF 2, after the massacres of Palestinians at the Sabra and Chatila refugee camps in September 1982.

The resignation of the Israeli Prime Minister in August 1983 was followed by the withdrawal of Israeli forces from Beirut and the Shouf mountains: this led to renewed violence and the killing of both French and US personnel in MNF 2. The USA responded by taking what might be called peace-enforcement action (bombardment and air strikes against 'anti-government' positions). MNF 2 thus became part of the conflict.[50] In October it was attacked by a suicide bombing mission: 241 American and fifty-eight French soldiers were killed. MNF 2 had fallen into the Congo trap and acted without impartiality and as a peace-enforcer (with no UN mandate) and not a peace-keeper: it was withdrawn in 1984 despite the fact that the Soviet Union had vetoed a Security Council resolution which would have set up a UN force in Beirut to take over its role. There remained some fifty observers from UNTSO, which had been authorized by a unanimous Security Council resolution in August 1982 to monitor the situation in and around Beirut.

[49] For more information on this see James, *Peacekeeping in International Politics*, pp. 122–30. [50] Urquhart, *A Life in Peace and War*, pp. 357–60.

5. Peacekeeping and finance within the UN system 1967–1984

The intense conflict in the 1960s over UN peacekeeping financing was finally resolved in late 1973 when all concerned considered it necessary to set up a peacekeeping force after the second Arab–Israel war. The General Assembly decided in December that the costs would be borne by all its members (divided into four groups) through a special account set up outside the regular budget and apportioned as follows: Group A, Permanent Members (five), 63.15 per cent; Group B, economically developed member states (then numbering twenty-three) not Permanent Members, 34.78 per cent; Group C, economically less-developed member states (then eighty-two), 2.02 per cent; Group D least economically developed member states (then twenty-five), 0.05 per cent. These formulas, similar to those discussed in the mid-1960s, have, adapted to changing circumstances, continued in operation ever since.[51]

In the period 1967–84, and particularly after 1973, UN peacekeeping continued to be taken seriously by many states. A British initiative supported by the USA in September 1977 contained a proposal for the setting up of a UN peacekeeping force in Zimbabwe for the transition period:[52] ultimately however the election in 1980 was monitored by a Commonwealth force and observers. A year later Western and non-aligned countries voted for a Security Council resolution which, by twelve votes for, with Soviet and Czechoslovak abstentions and Chinese non-participation, agreed to establish the UN Transition Assistance Group (UNTAG) to assist the UN Secretary-General's Special Representative to ensure early independence of Namibia through free elections under UN supervision and control. This agreement finally bore fruit in 1989, as will be seen below.

Certain regional groups also remained concerned about

---

[51] GA Res. 3101 (XXVIII) of 11 Dec. 1973. See also Susan R. Mills, 'The Financing of UN Peacekeeping Operations: The Need for a Sound Financial Basis', in Rikhye and Skjelsbaek (eds.), *The UN and Peacekeeping*, pp. 91–110.

[52] See *Rhodesia: Proposals for a Settlement*, Cmnd. 6919 (HMSO, London, 1976).

the potential of peacekeeping. In late 1978 the European Community, and others, sponsored a General Assembly resolution which called for support for peackeeping operations; urged early completion of the guide-lines; invited interested states to consider training personnel for peacekeeping operations, and to provide information relating to possible stand-by capacities.[53] The Eastern countries voted against the resolution because they considered it belittled the decisive role of the Security Council in peacekeeping matters.

The financial problems of UN peacekeeping remained serious. The People's Republic of China, after taking its place in the UN in 1971, took the decision not to pay its assessed dues: this was compounded by the Soviet Union's decision at the end of 1976 to pay only half its assessed expenses for UNEF II and UNDOF. Ultimately however, China was constrained by the parameters of Article 19. In 1981, a year before it would have lost its vote in the General Assembly under this Charter Article, the General Assembly agreed a solution reminiscent of that formerly reached in the context of UNEF I and ONUC. Most countries, with the exception of the Eastern bloc, voted for a resolution asking the UN Secretary-General to put the past dues owed for peacekeeping by China into a special account; decided that the applicability of Article 19 in respect of these should not be raised; and welcomed China's decision to contribute its assessed expenses to UNDOF and UNIFIL from January 1982.[54] The imperative of finance also dictated the adoption, by consensus, of a Security Council resolution in April 1982 calling for voluntary funding to support the Pan-African Peacekeeping regional force which had been set up by the OAU in 1981 to help deal with the numerous problems relating to Chad.[55]

In 1983 the General Assembly, again through an alliance

---

[53] GA Res. 33/114 of 18 Dec. 1978.

[54] GA Res. 36/116A of 10 Dec. 1981.

[55] For useful material on peacekeeping and Africa see Nathan Pelcovits, 'Peacekeeping: The African Experience', in Wiseman (ed.), *Peacekeeping: Appraisals and Proposals*, pp. 256–97.

between Third World and Western countries, passed the first substantive resolution on peacekeeping since that of 1978. This urged the Special Committee on Peacekeeping Operations to complete its work on agreed guide-lines and devote further attention to the practical implementation of peacekeeping operations. Expressing its conviction that peacekeeping was an 'essential function' of the UN and stressing the 'collective responsibility' of member states to share equitably the financial burden of peacekeeping operations established by the Security Council, the resolution expressed concern about the difficult financial situation facing UN peacekeeping bodies.[56]

(c) The Third Phase: 1985 Onwards

One trigger for the changing role of the Soviet Union in the UN in the mid-1980s may well have been the need for the Soviet government to make up its mind about peace-keeping dues and whether it was prepared to lose its vote in the General Assembly because of its withholding from UNDOF and UNIFIL. The Soviet government eventually announced in April 1986 that it would begin paying its current assessed contributions to UNIFIL. In the same month Gorbachev (then General Secretary of the CPSU) was given a demonstration of the usefulness of multilateral approaches to Soviet problems by the response of the International Atomic Energy Authority (IAEA) to the Chernobyl disaster.

In late 1986 the Soviet Union was therefore ready, with China and the other Permanent Members of the Security Council, to discuss, at the instigation of the British Ambassador at the UN, whether the UN could provide more help to end the long-running war between Iraq and Iran. The permanent five eventually achieved agreement between themselves and the other Security Council members on resolution 598 of 20 July 1987: this contained a Chapter VII determination and laid down a number of elements, which, taken together, had to be fulfilled to

---

[56] GA Res. 38/81 of 15 Dec. 1983.

bring about an ending of the war. These included authorizing a UN observer team to monitor the eventual ceasefire and withdrawal. The almost unprecedented use of Chapter VII in a resolution related to peacekeeping was significant. The boundaries between peacekeeping and peace-enforcement were becoming slightly more blurred.

The Soviet change of policy on the UN was announced on 17 September 1987 through an article by Gorbachev published simultaneously in *Pravda* and *Izvestia*. This noted that the world was becoming increasingly interrelated and interdependent: there was therefore a need for a mechanism which was capable of discussing common problems. The Permanent Members could become guarantors of regional security. More use should be made of UN peacekeeping bodies, and of the UN Secretary-General's potential peace-making role. In early 1988 the Soviet government announced that it would begin to pay arrearages on its assessed contributions for peacekeeping operations.

Meanwhile the US Congress, under the impact of a growing US budget deficit, the Kassebaum Amendment, and a perception that UNIFIL was not successful, decided, in 1986, to reduce appropriations for US assessed contributions to UNIFIL. Subsequently Congress delayed by ten months (until March 1989) approval for funds to finance the US contribution to the Iran–Iraq observer force (UNIIMOG) and the anticipated operations for Angola and Namibia. The US administration then began to persuade Congress of the usefulness of peacekeeping, and partially succeeded in getting it to slow down the rate of withholding and to find ways of paying for old and new peacekeeping bodies.[57] Like China and the Soviet Union (now Russia), it is aware of the constraint of losing its vote in the General Assembly if more than two years behind in its arrears.

[57] See also one Congressional Research Service Report and two Issue Briefs: Marjorie Ann Browne, *United Nations Peacekeeping: Historical Overview and Current Issues* (1990) and its update of 27 Nov. 1991; and Vita Bite, *UN System Funding: Congressional Issues*, updated 20 Nov. 1991.

1. Afghanistan and Pakistan: UNGOMAP 1988–1990

The thawing of the Cold War, and the new cooperation among the permanent five, helped pave the way for the setting up of two UN observer missions in 1988. The first, the UN Mission in Afghanistan and Pakistan (UNGOMAP), was originally set up in May after an exchange of letters between the Secretary-General and the Security Council: these were confirmed in October by a unanimous Security Council Resolution. Its mandate was to assist the UN Secretary-General in the use of his good offices in the Afghan settlement of April 1988. It came to an end in 1990 having helped save the face of the Soviet Union in withdrawing the Soviet army. Unlike other operations set up during this period, it was financed from the regular budget because it had originally been conceived as an operation solely relating to the UN Secretary-General's good offices.

2. Iran and Iraq: UNIIMOG 1988–1991

The second UN observer mission, the UN Iran–Iraq Military Observer Group (UNIIMOG), stemmed from resolution 598. It was set up by the Security Council in August 1988 (again unanimously) to monitor the cease-fire which was about to come into operation. Like all subsequent UN peacekeeping bodies (with the exception of aspects of UNPROFOR in Bosnia) it was financed by assessments to a special account.[58] It was wound up at the end of February 1991 as the 1991 Gulf war came to a close, having fulfilled its purpose.

3. Persistent peacekeepers: UNTSO, UNMOGIP, UNFICYP, UNDOF, and UNIFIL

The five UN peacekeeping bodies and the one non-UN peacekeeping body set up before 1985 which still remain in operation should not be forgotten. The fact that four (UNTSO, UNDOF, UNIFIL, and the non-UN MFO) are

---

[58] For details of the way apportionments are made see 'Composition of the Existing Groups of Member States for the Apportionment of the Costs of Peace-Keeping Operations Financed through Assessed Contributions: Report of the Secretary-General', UN doc. A/47/484 of 29 Sept. 1992. See also below, p. 536.

closely involved in the nexus of problems stemming from
the Israel/Palestine dispute is indicative. They have not, so
far, been affected by the peace-making efforts embodied
in the US-sponsored talks which began in Madrid in
October 1991, and with which the UN is now more closely
associated. The mandates of UNDOF and UNIFIL continue to be renewed by the Security Council at six-monthly
intervals. Meanwhile UNMOGIP remains as a witness to
the intractable dispute over Jammu and Kashmir.

The frustrating peace-making negotiations over Cyprus
continue under UN auspices. By December 1992 the UN
Secretary-General noted that UNFICYP's viability was in
question: financing the force was becoming problematic
because of its dependence on voluntary funding, with
troop-contributing governments reducing their contributions to the force.[59] A draft resolution intended to change
the basis of funding to the ordinary system of peacekeeping assessments was vetoed by Russia on 11 May 1993.
Intensive negotiations followed, culminating in a Security
Council resolution on 27 May under which UNFICYP was
to be extensively restructured, and funded from late 1993
by standard peacekeeping assessments. This compromise
did not, however, assuage the concerns of many states
about the effectiveness of UNFICYP and about the priorities of the UN in agreeing to fund this while not establishing
forces in other strife-torn areas.

4. Southern Africa: UNAVEM I and II, UNTAG, ONUMOZ, and UNOMUR, 1988–

The changing situation in southern Africa, some active US
diplomacy in Angola and South Africa over Namibia, and
the ending of the Cold War all led to increased UN
involvement in the region, including in the important
matter of election-monitoring.[60] On Angola, one result
was a unanimous Security Council resolution in December
1988 on the establishment of an observer mission, the UN

[59] 'Report of the Secretary-General on the United Nations Operation in
Cyprus', UN doc. S/24917 of 1 Dec. 1992, para. 44.

[60] The Security Council even authorized the deployment of UN observers in
South Africa in Aug. 1992 in coordination with the structures set up under the
National Peace Accord. These may well become involved in election-monitoring.

Angola Verification Mission (UNAVEM I), to monitor the withdrawal of Cuban troops. This was achieved by May 1991. The Security Council then unanimously authorized a further peacekeeping body, UNAVEM II, which was to monitor the implementation of the May 1991 peace accords between the Angolan government and UNITA, including the election which was eventually held in September 1992. This election (like the 1990 Nicaraguan election monitored by ONUVEN—see below) showed how important it is for those representing the UN to ensure that the parties concerned accept the election result if the election has been free and fair. In this case the results were not accepted by UNITA, and violence ensued. In October 1992 the Security Council unanimously passed a resolution supporting its Special Representative's view that the elections 'were generally free and fair' and urging dialogue between the parties. Despite further Security Council resolutions the situation did not improve. Some have argued that UNAVEM II was under-financed and that the preparations for the election were insufficient: the similar Mozambique operation (see below) is substantially larger.

Once the Cuban troop withdrawal from Angola was under way the Security Council was able to begin to take action on Namibia—and, in particular, to implement the 1978 Security Council resolution which had envisaged the setting up of the UN Transition Assistance Group (UNTAG) to supervise Namibian independence. UNTAG was set up by a unanimous resolution in February 1989. The transition process began disastrously with clashes between SWAPO and the South African police. However UNTAG, headed by a civilian, eventually monitored the withdrawal of South African Defence Forces troops and others from Namibia; confined SWAPO troops to their Angolan and Zambian bases; helped, through its civilian component, to create the conditions for free and fair elections, held on 1 November 1989; and generally supervised Namibia's transition to independence, achieved in March 1990. UNTAG's achievement in managing the electoral process, including repatriation, was extremely significant. It simultaneously profited from the UN's long tradition of monitoring elections in dependent and trust territories, and pointed to the subsequent tentative steps that have been taken by the UN to monitor elections in independent countries. UNTAG was able to leave independent Namibia in March 1990, and has rightly been described as 'a great success'.[61]

As to the war in Mozambique, a peace accord was finally achieved between the Mozambique government and the Resistencia Nacional Moçambicana (RENAMO) in October 1992. This was swiftly followed by a unanimous Security Council resolution which approved the dispatch to Mozambique of a team of UN military observers. The UN Operation in Mozambique (ONUMOZ) was established by a unanimous Security Council resolution in December.

Following strife in Rwanda, a small UN Observer Mission on the Uganda–Rwanda border (UNOMUR) was set up in June 1993.

5. Latin America: ONUVEN, CIAV, ONUCA, ONUVEH, and ONUSAL 1989–

The post-Cold War climate, combined with Central American concern to tackle regional problems, could be seen in the unanimous Security Council resolution of July 1989 *inter alia* commending the 1987 Esquipulas Agreement, and noting (*not* authorizing[62]) the UN Secretary-General's agreement with Nicaragua to deploy a UN Observer Group for the Verification of Elections in Nicaragua (ONUVEN). This peace-making process had been activated by four (later five) Central American foreign ministers (the Contadora Group) whose efforts, antedating the end of the Cold War, had been endorsed by the Security Council as far back as 1983.[63] They played a vital role given the fact that the Sandinista government in Nicaragua distrusted the Organization of American States, which it saw as too much under the influence of the USA.

[61] Marrack Goulding in *Singapore Symposium*, p. 35.

[62] The constitutional point is significant: ONUVEN was *not* set up by the Security Council. Many countries were concerned to ensure that election-monitoring on its own was not considered to be under the jurisdiction of the Security Council as peacekeeping has been since 1963.

[63] Alvaro de Soto gives an absorbing account of this process in the *Singapore Symposium*, pp. 42–9.

ONUVEN (which was endorsed by the General Assembly) was the first UN electoral observer mission ever to monitor elections in an *independent country*. The UN Secretariat had previously often refused this role because a number of its members considered that such activity could not be held to have an international dimension, and could therefore be construed as intervening in the domestic affairs of states, thus conflicting with Article 2 (7) of the Charter.[64] The UN's role in monitoring this election, held in February 1990, was crucial. Those organizing the operation were able to ensure that they received an early accurate reading of the final result. The Secretary-General's Permanent Representative, helped by the Secretary-General of the OAS and former US President Jimmy Carter, thus had time to use their influence to get the President of Nicaragua, 'who had to assimilate the blow of an unexpected defeat', to accept the results of the elections.[65]

The International Support and Verification Commission (CIAV), representing the Secretaries-General of the UN and OAS, was set up in September 1989 to assist in the implementation of a joint plan for voluntary demobilization, repatriation, and relocation of members of the Nicaraguan resistance and others in the region. In November, the Security Council unanimously set up the UN Observer Group in Central America (ONUCA) with a mandate to observe and verify regional peace-making agreements. After a number of changes of mandate (which included disarming irregular forces and destroying weapons) ONUCA was finally terminated by the Security Council in January 1992. One innovation made in the context of ONUCA was the deployment of naval patrols to achieve certain of its objectives. Alvaro de Soto, the Personal Representative of the Secretary-General for the Central American Peace Process, suggests that innovations in the role of the UN in Central America include 'the new electoral component, the democratization component, the fact that we are dealing with internal problems with a certain international dimension, and where there is a

---

[64] de Soto, in *Singapore Symposium*, pp. 45–6.   [65] de Soto, ibid., p. 46.

certain clamour for the United Nations to be involved, to waive the normal requirements of Article 2, paragraph 7, of the Charter'.[66] This, in effect, meant that some countries now agreed to a less restrictive interpretation on the question of intervention in the domestic affairs of states.

The trend towards using the UN to monitor elections in independent countries was strengthened following the debate in the summer of 1990 on the question of election-monitoring in Haiti. The UN Observer Group for the Verification of Elections in Haiti (ONUVEH) was established by the General Assembly *not* the Security Council, even though it included some military personnel. The origins of ONUVEH's mandate are important: many in the General Assembly were not prepared to accept that the Security Council should assume responsibility for election-monitoring in independent countries, although they did accept that it could authorize election-monitoring in the context of peacekeeping. ONUVEH duly monitored the December elections. In September 1991 the elected government of Haiti was overthrown in a military coup. Prolonged negotiations involving the OAS, the UN, the USA, and the Haitian parties followed. In April 1993 the General Assembly established a joint UN–OAS mission to Haiti aimed at the restoration of President Aristide. In June the Security Council imposed trade sanctions.

In El Salvador, where there had been a long civil war, the peacekeeping process was further advanced by the unanimous Security Council resolution in May 1991 setting up the UN Observer Mission in El Salvador (ONUSAL). It was charged with monitoring agreements between the government and the opposition FMLN, including one relating to human rights[67]—an unprecedented UN peace-

[66] de Soto, in *Singapore Symposium*, pp. 48–9. A useful account of past 'Peace-keeping within the Inter-American System' is given in a chapter by Edgardo Paz-Barnica in Wiseman (ed.), *Peacekeeping: Appraisals and Proposals*, pp. 237–55.

[67] An interesting assessment of ONUSAL suggesting that it has mistakenly viewed its human rights and peace missions as contradictory can be found in *El Salvador Peace and Human Rights: Successes and Shortcomings of the United Nations Observer Missions in El Salvador (ONUSAL)* (Americas Watch, New York, Sept. 1992). It concludes 'On balance, . . . ONUSAL and the United Nations have made extraordinary contributions to peace in El Salvador. Their success has been intimately linked to the desire of both sides in the conflict to find a negotiated, rather than a military settlement.'

keeping role—and with reducing armed forces, training a new police force, and offering help over land transfers. This has added to the debate on intervention in matters within the domestic jurisdiction of states. ONUSAL became operational in July 1991. The armed conflict between El Salvador and the FMLN, which through the peace process became a legalized political party, was formally brought to an end on 15 December 1992. ONUSAL's supervision roles were extended to observing the 1994 elections.

6. *Iraq–Kuwait: UNIKOM and the UN guards 1991–*

The invasion and annexation of Kuwait by Iraq in August 1990 was eventually followed by the authorizing of an enforcement force against Iraq under Chapter VII of the Charter. This was the first time that this had happened since the authorization of the Unified Command in Korea in 1950. The US-led coalition forces which subsequently expelled Iraq from Kuwait were not themselves constituted under Chapter VII. Following the cessation of hostilities at the end of February 1991, the Security Council requested the UN Secretary-General, on 3 April, to plan for the immediate deployment of an observer mission to monitor the demilitarized zone between Iraq and Kuwait: the report was agreed unanimously in a further Chapter VII resolution on 9 April. The UN Iraq–Kuwait Observation Mission (UNIKOM), which was the first UN mission to include personnel from all the Permanent Members, began to monitor the zone a few days later. A Chapter VII resolution providing for the strengthening of this force was adopted in February 1993.

The Security Council unprecedentedly tackled the humanitarian problem arising from the repression of the Iraqi civilian population, particularly the Kurds, by insisting in resolution 688 (*not* seen as a Chapter VII resolution although it 'condemned the repression of the Iraqi civilian population . . . the consequences of which threaten international peace and security in the region') of 5 April 1991 'that Iraq allow immediate access by international humanitarian organizations to all those in need of assistance in all parts of Iraq and to make available all necessary facilities for their operations' and requested the Secretary-General 'to pursue his humanitarian efforts in Iraq'. The tensions provoked by this (already noticeable in the debate on election-monitoring) were laid bare in the vote: three non-aligned (Cuba, Yemen, and Zimbabwe) voted against, and India (also non-aligned) and China abstained. The USA, Britain, and France then proceeded to deploy troops to establish 'safe havens' inside Iraq: some have argued that this went beyond the provisions of Security Council resolution 688. UN officials subsequently went to Iraq and agreed a memorandum of understanding on 18 April with the government, which together with an annexe of 25 May provided for the deployment of a 500-strong UN guard contingent in northern Iraq. Its numbers were reduced in 1992 and 1993.[68]

The UN guards are *not* regarded within the UN as a peacekeeping body since they deal only with humanitarian issues and are *not* authorized by a Security Council resolution. Their use (as distinct from national contingents) was an interesting precedent, but not one likely to be followed on any large scale. Nevertheless, the events in northern Iraq had a strong impact on subsequent thinking (particularly regarding Somalia and former Yugoslavia) on the question of the extent to which the consent of the parties concerned is needed for the presence of such international bodies, and their precise character and purpose.

7. *Africa: Liberia, Western Sahara, Somalia and Eritrea 1990–*

During August 1990 the Economic Community of West African States (ECOWAS) pressed by Ghana and Nigeria took the decision, with some support from the OAU, to establish a regional peacekeeping body ECOMOG (Economic Community Monitoring Group) in Liberia,

---

[68] The texts of these agreements are given in UN doc. S/22663 of 31 May 1991. A letter from the Foreign Minister of Iraq to the UN Secretary-General opposing the setting up of centres in northern Iraq for displaced Iraqi citizens in Turkey by US and other foreign forces is given in UN doc. S/22513 of 22 Apr. 1991. For a useful discussion of this episode see Lawrence Freedman and David Boren, '"Safe Havens" for Kurds in Post-War Iraq', in Nigel Rodley (ed.), *To Loose the Bands of Wickedness: International Intervention in Defence of Human Rights* (London, 1992), pp. 43–92.

which had been in the throes of a bitter civil war since December 1989. This non-UN force achieved control of the capital Monrovia at the beginning of 1991 and has engaged more in peace-enforcement than peacekeeping activities. Senegalese initiatives led to agreement on a peace-making framework through the Yamoussoukro IV Accord in October 1991. The situation deteriorated in mid-1992 with the killing of six Senegalese soldiers: in October ECOWAS asked the Security Council to impose sanctions through a blockade of all points of entry into Liberia. The Security Council unanimously imposed an arms embargo under Chapter VII on 19 November, and in March 1993 unanimously declared its readiness to consider appropriate measures in support of ECOWAS.

Meanwhile a new attempt was being made to resolve the long-standing dispute between Morocco and its rival (the Polisario Front) over the status of the Western Sahara, from which Spain had withdrawn in 1976 having agreed that two-thirds should go to Morocco and one-third to Mauritania. Mauritania subsequently renounced its claim. Peace-making was subsequently attempted by both the OAU and the UN Secretary-General. Their joint mission of good offices led to an agreement in principle between the two parties in 1988. The UN Secretary-General's plan to implement this through a UN Mission for the Referendum in Western Sahara (MINURSO) to monitor the cease-fire and supervise a referendum for self-determination was agreed by a unanimous Security Council resolution in June 1990, and the Mission was established by a further unanimous Security Council resolution in April 1991: it became operational in September 1991. MINURSO continues to monitor the cease-fire but it has not yet, despite the efforts of the UN Secretary-General's Representative, been able to hold the referendum because of disagreements over the criteria for eligibility to vote.[69] In March 1993 the Security Council unanimously invited the Secretary-General and his Special Representative to intensify their efforts with the parties to resolve issues

[69] See 'The Situation Concerning Western Sahara: Report by the Secretary-General', UN doc. S/24464 of 20 Aug. 1992.

relating to the interpretation and application of the criteria for voter eligibility, and to make preparations for the referendum to be held by the end of the current year.

The civil war situation in Somalia, and the immense humanitarian issues it provoked, provided a challenge to the new UN Secretary-General, as an African, once he came into office in January 1992. The Security Council, in a unanimous Chapter VII resolution imposed an arms embargo the same month. This was followed, in April, by unanimous agreement in principle to establish a UN Operation in Somalia (UNOSOM), to monitor the cease-fire in Mogadishu, and to protect humanitarian relief supplies. UNOSOM began limited operations in July after many consultations between Somali factions and the UN Secretary-General's Special Representative, Mohamed Sahnoun. In a subsequent report, the Secretary-General argued that the UN efforts needed to be enlarged to provide a more comprehensive approach to deal with all aspects of the problem—namely the humanitarian relief and recovery programme; the cessation of hostilities and security; and the peace process and national reconciliation.[70] The Security Council passed a unanimous resolution in August authorizing an increase in its strength to 4,219. Sahnoun's resignation in October, however, exposed serious weaknesses in the UN's operation in Somalia.

On 3 December 1992 the Security Council unanimously approved a resolution, under Chapter VII, which gave a green light to the setting up of a peace-enforcement force in Somalia. Security Council resolution 794 both endorsed the Secretary-General's recommendation that action under Chapter VII of the Charter should be taken 'in order to establish a secure environment for humanitarian relief operations in Somalia as soon as possible' and welcomed the offer by a member state (the USA) concerning the establishment of such an operation. The multi-national US-led Unified Task Force (UNITAF) operated in Somalia from 9 December 1992 to 4 May 1993. On that

---

[70] 'Report of the Secretary-General on the Situation in Somalia', UN doc. S/24343 of 22 July 1992.

date, following a unanimous Security Council resolution passed on 26 March, UNITAF handed over responsibilities to UNOSOM II, a Chapter VII force whose size and mandate were expanded from those of the original UNOSOM, which had remained in Somalia throughout. UNITAF and UNOSOM II were the first peace-enforcement forces to be set up in the context of the perceived failure of an existing peacekeeping force. The only relevant historical analogy remains the Congo over thirty years earlier.

In Eritrea in April 1993, at the end of a long war for independence from Ethiopia, a UN Observer Mission to Verify the Referendum in Eritrea (UNOVER) confirmed that the referendum, in which an overwhelming majority voted for independence, was free and fair.

8. Cambodia: UNAMIC and UNTAC 1991–

The conflict in Cambodia, exacerbated by Sino–Soviet differences, had long been the focus of UN diplomatic efforts. After visiting the region in 1985 the UN Secretary-General saw possibilities for a comprehensive settlement. Attempts to make peace were renewed at the Paris Conference on Cambodia, convened by France and Indonesia in August 1989, and carried on by the five Permanent Members in 1990.[71] In August 1990 the Cambodian parties—including the Party of Democratic Kampuchea (PDK), representing the Khmer Rouge—agreed to accept the framework of a comprehensive settlement including the mandate of the UN Transitional Authority in Cambodia (UNTAC). The Security Council endorsed this unanimously in September 1990, and, by a further unanimous resolution in mid-October 1991, authorized a UN Advance Mission in Cambodia (UNAMIC) to be deployed once the final agreements had been signed, as they were in Paris on 23 October. The Mission began to function in November 1991 by discussing with the UN High Commissioner for Refugees repatriation routes, reception centres and resettlement areas: it subsequently established mine-awareness

---

[71] More information on this, in particular the long-standing involvement of ASEAN, can be found in Rafeeudin Ahmed, 'The United Nations Peace Plan for Cambodia', *Singapore Symposium*, pp. 65–8.

and clearance programmes, and was later merged into UNTAC.

UNTAC was finally set up by a unanimous Security Council resolution in February 1992: this constituted the first vote to set up a peacekeeping body by Russia, which had taken the place of the disintegrated Soviet Union in January. It also became the first UN force to include Japanese, following the controversial change of Japanese laws on sending troops abroad. UNTAC's complex mandate covers seven components: human rights, electoral, military, civil administration, police, repatriation, and rehabilitation. Thus UNTAC is very different from peacekeeping bodies as traditionally conceived: from the start it amounted to an administrative authority exercising key functions of government: there are, however, analogies with UNSF in West New Guinea three decades earlier.

During the summer of 1992 political concern focused on the intentions of the PDK, which was not carrying out the commitments into which it had entered. In October 1992 the Security Council passed a unanimous resolution welcoming the achievements of UNTAC in terms of extensive military deployment, promulgation of the electoral law and voter registration, registration of political parties, safe repatriation of over 150,000 refugees, progress in rehabilitation, and campaigns for respect for human rights. However it also *inter alia* deplored the fact that PDK had not yet complied with its obligations. A further unanimous resolution at the end of November confirmed that the election for a constituent assembly in Cambodia should be held not later than May 1993. Once again it urged the PDK to 'join fully' in implementing the Paris Agreements and urged (though, significantly, not under Chapter VII) that petroleum products should not be supplied to areas occupied by any Cambodian party not complying with their military provisions. The elections were held in May 1993, with a remarkably high turn-out, and were endorsed by the Security Council as free and fair. The result, a victory for the royalist party, was followed by protracted negotiations with the recalcitrant incumbent government over a possible coalition.

9. *Yugoslavia: UNPROFOR 1992–*

The breakup of Yugoslavia was signalled by the declarations of independence of two of its constituent parts (Slovenia and Croatia) in June 1991 followed by the intervention of troops from Yugoslavia into Slovenia. The CSCE Committee of Senior Officials agreed on 4 July that the EC should organize a mission to Yugoslavia: this was endorsed at an EC foreign ministers' meeting at The Hague the next day. EC monitors were first sent to the area later that month after the EC had reached agreement, at Brioni, with representatives from Croatia, Slovenia, and Yugoslavia. The continuing deterioration of the situation prompted UN involvement, despite potential Congo analogies. The UN role began with a unanimous Chapter VII Security Council resolution on 25 September 1991, imposing an arms embargo. A UN Protection Force (UNPROFOR) was subsequently set up through a unanimous, non-explicit Chapter VII Security Council resolution in February 1992. Deployed in March 1992, its purpose was to help defuse Croat–Serb tensions by supervising the withdrawal of the Yugoslav People's Army from Croatia together with the demilitarization of UN-protected areas where communal problems remain particularly complex.

The spread of the fighting to the Republic of Bosnia and Herzegovina which, like the Republics of Croatia and Slovenia, became a member of the UN in May 1992, marked the failure of the UN strategy of locating UNPROFOR headquarters in Sarajevo as a means of discouraging possible conflict in Bosnia. At the end of May the Security Council in resolution 757 (with abstentions from China and Zimbabwe) imposed Chapter VII economic sanctions against the Federal Republic of Yugoslavia (i.e. Serbia and Montenegro) in an effort to end the conflict in Bosnia, and, as noted in a further resolution in June, to create the 'necessary conditions for unimpeded delivery of humanitarian supplies to Sarajevo and other destinations in Bosnia and Herzegovina, including the establishment of a security zone encompassing Sarajevo and its airport'. However the situation continued to deteriorate. On 13

August the Security Council passed two further Chapter VII resolutions. The first (resolution 770), with abstentions from China, India and Zimbabwe, demanded that 'unimpeded and continuous access to all camps, prisons and detention centres' be granted to the ICRC and other relevant humanitarian organizations, and that 'all parties and others concerned take the necessary measures to ensure the safety of United Nations and other personnel engaged in the delivery of humanitarian assistance'. The second (resolution 771) unanimously demanded that all concerned desist from all breaches of international humanitarian law and threatened further action in the event of non-compliance.

Following the London Conference at the end of August 1992, the Security Council (with abstentions from China, India, and Zimbabwe) authorized the enlargement of UNPROFOR's mandate and strength in Bosnia. Resolution 776 also noted in a preambular paragraph that a number of states had agreed to provide military personnel to facilitate the delivery of humanitarian assistance 'without cost' to the UN. This was the first, albeit brief, departure from the method of funding UN peacekeeping bodies by assessed contributions from all UN members, employed (UNGOMAP excepted) since the mid-1960s.[72] The Federal Republic of Yugoslavia was subsequently suspended from participation in the General Assembly (although not from the whole of the UN) as both the Security Council and the Assembly passed resolutions stating that it could not automatically continue the membership of the former Socialist Federal Republic. In October the Council (unanimously, except for a Chinese abstention) set up a ban on unauthorized flights in the airspace of Bosnia, which was extended and strengthened in March 1993. A further resolution in November 1992 (with abstentions from China and Zimbabwe) under Chapter VII

[72] See also 'Report of the Secretary-General on the Situation in Bosnia and Herzegovina', UN doc. S/24540 of 10 Sept. 1992, para. 17. On 1 Apr. 1993 the financing of UNPROFOR changed back to the normal pattern. UNFICYP was established in 1964 with voluntary funding and continued to operate on that basis, until shifted to standard peacekeeping assessments in 1993.

prohibited the transshipment of crude oil, petroleum products, etc. through Serbia. In 1993, against a background of bitter fighting, sieges and 'ethnic cleansing', the Security Council passed further resolutions on former Yugoslavia, several of which involved an element of enforcement under Chapter VII: member states were authorized to take 'all necessary measures' to ensure compliance with the ban on flights over Bosnia; several threatened towns in Bosnia, including Srebrenica and Zepa, were declared to be safe areas which should be free from any armed attack; and more stringent economic sanctions were imposed on Serbia, Montenegro, and Serb areas of Bosnia and Croatia. UNPROFOR was strengthened and its mandate extended.

As regards the former Yugoslav Republic of Macedonia, on 11 December 1992 the Security Council authorized a presence of UNPROFOR: the first example of preventive deployment (sometimes called a tripwire) of UN peace-keepers. Macedonia had not then been admitted to UN membership because of the dispute with Greece concerning its name, but it was admitted in April 1993. In June the UN added a contingent of US troops.

(d) Conclusion

The momentum which has been given to the setting up of peacekeeping bodies in the post-Cold War era has engendered much discussion especially on the changing meaning of the term 'peacekeeping' and the related question of the need for consent of the parties. The influential *Agenda for Peace* has defined peacekeeping as 'the deployment of a United Nations presence in the field, *hitherto* [my italics] with the consent of all the parties concerned, normally involving United Nations military and/or police personnel and frequently civilians as well. Peacekeeping is a technique that expands the possibilities for both the prevention of conflict and the making of peace.'[73] The suggestion that the consent of the parties could be dispensed with in the context of peacekeeping (particularly

---

[73] Boutros-Ghali, *Agenda for Peace*, para. 20.

given the example of humanitarian intervention in Iraq after Kuwait had been liberated and the setting up of the UNITAF and UNOSOM II in Somalia) has disturbed a number of UN members, as has the suggestion that peace-enforcement can be subsumed under peace-making.[74]

Discussion about peacekeeping has not been helped by the misleading use of the word 'peacekeeping' for regional bodies such as the Indian 'peacekeeping' force in Sri Lanka (1987–90), ECOMOG in Liberia, and certain Russian interventions in new ex-Soviet states, whose rationale has primarily been peace-enforcement *not* peacekeeping.

The strengths and weaknesses of UN peacekeeping, and its changing character, may be illuminated by considering the following questions.

(i) *Why has UN peacekeeping developed so remarkably?*[75] Besides any immediate calming effect, UN peacekeeping activities have, often with reasonable success, served a twofold purpose. The first is that of helping manage situations which cannot yet be resolved, because either the international community, or those closely involved in the problem, or both, are not yet able to agree on a feasible and just solution. This seems to have been the case in Cyprus, Kashmir and Israel/Palestine. The second is that of helping out in situations of transition, where agreement has been reached. Here experienced and impartial peace-keepers can often be of use in enabling the desired solution to be achieved in practice. In the former case, where there has been no fundamental agreement, peace-keeping is more likely to become part of the problem inasmuch as it can provide an excuse not to tackle actual peace-making. In carrying out their mandates, peace-keepers and diplomats have benefited (albeit to varying degrees) from the legitimacy and impartiality that the UN can provide, and from the commitment of the international community to UN peacekeeping as the most likely way to

[74] Ibid., paras. 42–5.

[75] See also Henry Wiseman, 'Peacekeeping in the International Political Context; Historical Analysis and Future Directions', in Rikhye and Skjelsbaek (eds.), *The UN and Peacekeeping*, pp. 32–51.

help manage/defuse/contain problematic disputes until peace-making becomes possible.

(ii) *In what way have past peacekeeping bodies been successful?*[76] Certain peacekeeping bodies, whether under UN or other auspices, have succeeded, partially or wholly, in helping manage transition to an agreed political solution of the problem. Their effectiveness depends not only on their endeavours but also on the political support they receive. In Africa even ONUC helped to contribute to the stabilization of the new state of Congo (now Zaïre). The Commonwealth observation of the former Rhodesia elections was successful. The conditions were probably not ripe for the OAU force in Chad. UNAVEM I and UNTAG were particularly helpful in enabling Cuban troops to withdraw from Angola and in setting up the state of Namibia. In Asia both UNSF and UNIPOM were able to fulfil their mandates, as was UNGOMAP. In Latin America DOMREP was able to dampen down problems between the superpowers in a situation where the UN had to cope with a regional force dominated by one of them. ONUCA also seems to have succeeded. In the Middle East UNEF I was path-finding and UNEF II essential for management of an extremely dangerous situation. UNOGIL's face-saving qualities were notable. UNYOM could not underwrite change given the lack of political will. UNIIMOG and MFN 1 worked, while MFN 2 (partly because it did not have the legitimacy provided by the UN) became part of the problem. Of the long-standing peacekeeping bodies, UNTSO, MFO, and UNMOGIP have proved useful peacekeeping tools, as has UNDOF. There is less consensus about the achievement of either UNFICYP after 1974 or UNIFIL.

(iii) *What is the significance of the UN system for peacekeeping?* The functions of managing or resolving disputes have, since World War II, been most easily achieved through the UN in the context of Charter principles. The UN Secretary-General (with members of the UN Secretariat) has played a crucial role in using his good offices (e.g. in the context

---

[76] See also discussion on this by Brown, *UN Peacekeeping*, pp. 19–21.

of UNYOM and UNSF), offering impartiality,[77] ideas (e.g. the guide-lines for UNEF I), reports, and basic organization for UN peacekeeping bodies.

The involvement of both the General Assembly and the Security Council—each in its own way representative of the international community of states—has often been creative. Both had historically to find solutions acceptable to at least two of the three major groups of countries often called the First, Second, and Third Worlds. The General Assembly has to agree the overall financing of peace-keeping if it is to be paid for through the regular budget or assessed contributions. It found (through the diplomacy of its members) a flexible, temporary solution to the overall funding problem both in 1965 and (in the context of Chinese dues) in 1981. It was flexible enough to accept peacekeeping bodies set up with voluntary funding during the Congo crisis. It also set up the Special Committee on Peacekeeping Operations in 1965: this, with a number of other bodies and interested states (including the troop contributors,[78] particularly the Nordics), has helped develop ideas on peacekeeping. The Assembly set up UNEF I·in the context of Security Council vetoes, and the UNSF, as well as various election-monitoring bodies, including ONUVEH and UNOVER. The General Assembly is likely to continue to ensure that it remains the authorizing body for monitoring elections which are not an integral part of a peacekeeping body.

The Security Council has also played a creative role. It was able to set up peacekeeping bodies during the Cold War sometimes relying on Western and Third World votes: Soviet reservations were normally expressed through abstention on resolutions rather than through vetoes. However the Soviet Union did veto draft resolutions in the context of UNOGIL, and made clear that it would do so

[77] For useful material on the question of impartiality and peacekeeping, and its difference from neutrality, see the discussion in Rikhye and Skjelsbaek (eds), *The UN and Peacekeeping*, p. 3.

[78] The training activities for peacekeeping currently provided by twenty-one states are set out in 'Comprehensive Review of the Whole Question of Peace-keeping Operations in All Their Aspects: Report of the Secretary-General', UN doc. A/47/597 of 28 Oct. 1992.

if attempts were made to extend the mandate of UNEF II. On the other hand it voted for setting up five of the six peacekeeping bodies established by the UN during the 1960s, as well as for two out of three in the 1970s. The People's Republic of China, after it took over the China seat in 1971, chose to avoid participation in peacekeeping votes rather than use its veto; then in 1981 it took the decision to begin contributing to peacekeeping: it would otherwise have risked losing its vote in the General Assembly. The record of Western powers is also note-worthy: the first vetoes in a peacekeeping context were cast by France and the United Kingdom over Suez in 1956, and the USA vetoed an attempt to use observers from UNTSO during the 1982 Israeli invasion of the Lebanon. Since 1987 the Permanent and other Security Council Members have voted unanimously for the original resolu-tion setting up each of the sixteen new peacekeeping bodies.

Before 1987 nearly all peacekeeping bodies set up by the Security Council had (implicitly) been set up under Chapter VI of the Charter, which covers peaceful settle-ment of disputes, and *not* under Chapter VII. There were two exceptions: the first-ever Chapter VII resolution was passed in the context of a call for a Palestine cease-fire (resolution 54 of July 1948); and, of course, the mandate of ONUC was changed so that it moved from a peace-keeping to a peace-enforcement mould.

Since 1987 a notable feature of Security Council practice has been the frequent use of Chapter VII in resolutions associated with peacekeeping: resolution 598 in 1987 in the context of the Iran–Iraq war *inter alia* requesting the UN Secretary-General to send observers to supervise a cease-fire; resolution 689 in 1991 on Iraq–Kuwait setting up UNIKOM; resolution 713 in 1991 imposing an arms embargo against the former Yugoslavia; and the non-explicit resolution 743 in 1992 setting up UNPROFOR. By the end of May 1993 this had been followed by twelve explicit Chapter VII resolutions on Yugoslavia, including two on economic sanctions and one on enforcement of the no-fly zone. In addition, arms embargoes under Chapter

VII were imposed against Liberia and Somalia in 1992. These developments, and the precedent set by the establishment of the peace-enforcement forces in Somalia in December 1992 and May 1993, could make one of the main distinctions between peacekeeping and peace-enforcement operations (consent of the parties) less clear than it has been hitherto.

(iv) *How have the political dynamics between the West, East, and Third World affected peacekeeping?* There have been a number of international crises—including Hungary (1956), Vietnam (late 1950s to early 1970s), Czechoslovakia (1968), and Afghanistan (1980–5)—in which peacekeeping played no part. It was obvious from the beginning, either through the use of vetoes (e.g. that of the Soviet Union over Afghanistan), or because each superpower was so involved, that there was no possibility of using peacekeeping in such cases. Indeed, UN peacekeeping has only been employed in a minority of wars and crises during the whole UN period. What remains surprising is the number of times that the Security Council (and sometimes the General Assembly) has been able to set up peacekeeping bodies.

The USA has on occasion found peacekeeping a useful face-saver (UNOGIL and DOMREP). It has also found it sufficiently worthwhile to set up its own peacekeeping forces such as the MNF and MFO. It is arguable that the Soviet Union became more supportive of peacekeeping operations between 1960 and 1986 because Third World countries accepted that peacekeeping bodies could be helpful to them in certain circumstances. It therefore tended to abstain or vote for them rather than use its veto. This seems to be the second main reason for the Chinese decision to start contributing financially to UN peacekeeping in 1981, the first being the threat to its right to vote in the General Assembly.

The shift in political attitudes which enabled the working together of the Permanent Members on the Security Council was given its first public expression at the UN through the unanimous passing of the Chapter VII resolution on an Iran–Iraq settlement in July 1987. This new unanimity—based, in part, on a more positive Soviet attitude to peacekeeping and a growing determination of regional actors to confront regional problems (e.g. in Central America and Cambodia)—underlies the proliferation of new peacekeeping bodies. The numbers reflect the fact that certain ossified problems (e.g. Afghanistan—UNGOMAP; Namibia and Angola—UNAVEM I and II and UNTAG; and Central America—ONUCA and ONUSAL) became more susceptible of resolution in a changed international climate. Other peacekeeping bodies such as UNIIMOG, UNIKOM, and ONUMOZ were set up to deal with specific problems arising, respectively, from the end of the Iran–Iraq war, the withdrawal of Iraq from Kuwait, and the peace agreement among the Mozambique parties. The possibility of sorting out the long-standing problems of the Western Sahara and Cambodia led to the setting up of MINURSO, and UNAMIC and UNTAC. The disintegration of both Yugoslavia and the Soviet Union in 1991–2 (Russia took over the Soviet seat in the Security Council in January 1992) has already provided additional post-Cold War problems, and led directly to the setting up of UNPROFOR originally for Croatia but now also operating in Bosnia and the former Yugoslav Republic of Macedonia. UNOSOM I and II (as well as the Unified Task Force) were set up to deal with humanitarian issues in the context of the Somali civil war. Although the Permanent Members were able to agree on many of these actions, differences between them became increasingly pronounced over former Yugoslavia. Serious doubts remain about the general advisability or even viability of peace-enforcement.

Southern countries are now the most apprehensive group. They appreciate straightforward peacekeeping operations (like UNTSO, UNDOF, and UNIFIL) because, within their parameters, the principle of host government consent is well established and the rules on the use of force by peacekeepers (only in self-defence and to defend their positions) are well understood. But some are worried (see below) about the potential interlinking between peace-keeping and peace-enforcement, and the increasing financial burdens imposed by the proliferation of peacekeeping bodies. Many are concerned that 'humanitarian' Security Council resolutions, like those on access of international humanitarian organizations to parts of Iraq, and on intervention in Somalia, could be used against them. The African states, in particular, would prefer to deal with conflicts on a regional basis, but have lacked the resources to address problems on the magnitude of the civil wars in Somalia, Sudan and Mozambique, and have had difficulty in maintaining the political and financial support necessary effectively to resolve conflict in Liberia. The non-aligned movement has tried to deal with these concerns by, *inter alia*, coming closer to China, a Permanent Member with veto powers, whose application to become an observer in the movement was accepted in May 1992. At their Jakarta Summit in September 1992, they reacted to their fears of marginalization by emphasizing, in the Jakarta Declaration, the observation in *Agenda for Peace* that 'democracy within the family of nations would require the fullest consultation, participation and engagement of all States, large and small, in the work of the Organization'.

(v) *What has been the relationship between UN peacekeeping, peace-making, and peace-enforcement?* UN peacekeeping and peace-making are much more likely to reinforce each other in a situation in which both the international community and the protagonists wish to resolve the conflict and have agreed on the means to do so. Almost all of the fifteen UN peacekeeping operations that have now been wound up have, arguably, made some contribution to the peace-making process, because in most cases these conditions were present. There is more controversy over the role of certain long-standing peacekeeping forces, UNFICYP and UNIFIL in particular. UNFICYP is considered to have played a role in permitting the ossification of the Cyprus problem after 1974 to the detriment of peace-making efforts. UNIFIL's mandate is thought to be flawed. Peacekeeping can work against peace-making. However, long-stay peacekeeping forces remain useful in so far as they contribute to the stabilization of the conflict at a time when its resolution remains impossible. Thus UNDOF, with a precise mandate, is generally thought to be of positive use in contributing to the relaxation of Syrian–Israeli tension on the Golan Heights. UNTSO has made a similar contribution since the 1940s. Although UNDOF and UNTSO are exceptions, it does appear that the neutrality and impartiality of UN peacekeeping bodies can be more easily compromised in a long-stay situation. Corruption (e.g. smuggling) can also become a problem.

As to the connection between peacekeeping and peace-enforcement, ONUC was given new mandates from the Security Council in order to change from a peacekeeping to a peace-enforcement operation. UNIKOM was set up in the wake of the UN's second peace-enforcement operation. The distinction between peacekeeping and peace-enforcement is becoming further blurred by the increased use of 'humanitarian' issues as a reason for the use of Chapter VII resolutions. It was widely feared that a change from peacekeeping to peace-enforcement in the context of Bosnia could, as happened in the case of ONUC, undermine the political acceptance of the original peacekeeping force at both the international and local levels. This could tarnish the UN's image as an impartial peacekeeper in future conflicts. Deployment of peace-enforcement forces while peacekeepers remain in the same area could result in peacekeepers becoming a target for one or more of the parties concerned.

(vi) *Is current UN peacekeeping different from past UN peacekeeping?* Though some argue that current peace-keeping possibilities have been transformed by the end of the Cold War, the record shows that the foundations had been laid by the mid-1960s, and that even in its first 'generation' UN peacekeeping was complex and varied. Nevertheless there are certain differences, apart from the fact that peacekeeping now has a wider geographical spread and an increased range of states contributing personnel. More emphasis is certainly being given to the regional contribution to peacekeeping: this is both because the UN itself is overstretched, and because bodies like the European Community, the CSCE and, even more recently, NATO and WEU, have—like the OAS, OAU, Arab League, OIC, ASEAN, and associated regional bodies—begun to experience the realities of peacekeeping. Some of the problems this may bring (i.e. the potential conflict between regional and UN bodies) were earlier aired on a small scale in the context of DOMREP.

There is also an increased hybridization of peacekeeping in terms of the elements—including humanitarian and human rights components in some cases—which now make up the peacekeeping process. The most extreme example of this trend remains UNTAC with its seven, complicated distinct components. The UNTEA/UNSF and UNTAG operations also had hybrid characteristics. The borders between external/internal issues and peacekeeping/peace-making are now becoming ever murkier, as *Agenda for Peace* demonstrated. As the UN Secretary-General has pointed out, UN peacekeeping bodies are increasingly being established 'in situations where the success of the operation depends on the cooperation of non-governmental entities or irregular groups'.[79] New ideas and practical experimentation are being advocated. Some raise highly contentious UN constitutional points that are already becoming a focus of North–South division. A more general difference relates to the unreal expectations of peacekeeping that have been given credence in the Western media and elsewhere. Peacekeeping is not a magic wand: it can only succeed in conditions where the parties wish to cooperate.[80] It needs to be related to peace-making attempts to find lasting solutions to the underlying causes of the conflict. This lesson has also been learnt in the past.

(vii) *Can its tasks be extended to include election-monitoring without changing its basic structure?* Peacekeeping operations were first extended to election-monitoring with the creation of UNSF in 1962. Namibia in 1989–90 was a successful operation. However, in Angola the 1992 elections were followed by renewed civil war; and the UN continued to face difficult situations in Cambodia, Mozambique, and

[79] See 'Report of the Secretary-General on the Work of the Organization', UN doc. A/47/1 of 11 Sept. 1992, p. 35.
[80] This was reiterated by Marrack Goulding, the Under-Secretary-General for Peacekeeping Operations, in an article in *The Times* (London), 1 Oct. 1992.

Western Sahara. Peacekeeping and election-monitoring are often best conducted in tandem, although these techniques on their own are frequently insufficient to reconcile deeply divided societies. No one, at present, is challenging the view that the Security Council alone can authorize peacekeeping operations and that these can include provisions for election-monitoring.

However this question also needs to be looked at in the context of the long-running controversy (manifest for example in September 1989 when there was a dispute on the subject of the entitlement of the Security Council to discuss questions concerning narcotics trafficking) about the respective powers of the Security Council and the General Assembly. Many Southern countries are concerned to ensure that the General Assembly, *not* the Security Council, should authorize election-monitoring operations in independent countries (even if they include a few military observers). This explains the controversy surrounding the setting up of ONUVEN and ONUVEH.[81] Future election-monitoring operations are likely to be authorized by the General Assembly.

The UN has a long history of involvement with election-monitoring, though not in independent countries: this had already been usefully drawn upon in the provision of technical assistance for plebiscites in a number of countries.[82] Election monitors need to be particularly adept at ensuring the acceptance of election results by those who have not done as well as they hoped. This has been demonstrated in the context of the elections in Nicaragua in 1990 and Angola in 1992.

(viii) *Can its costs be met without bankrupting the UN?* The prognosis is not good. In 1992 the UN owed $US 800 million to troop-contributing countries, while approved peacekeeping operations were estimated to cost close to

---

[81] See section (c)(5) above.

[82] 'Report of the Secretary-General on the Work of the Organization' (1992), p. 26, pointed out that in 1992 the UN provided technical assistance for elections in Albania, Angola, Congo, El Salvador, Ethiopia, Guinea, Guyana, Liberia, Madagascar, Mali, Rwanda, and Togo besides assisting in preparations for the planned referendums in Eritrea and Western Sahara.

$3 billion a year.[83] The UN Secretary-General pointed out in September 1992 that unpaid contributions towards peacekeeping totalled $844.4 million. He recommended the establishment of a revolving peacekeeping reserve fund (a $150 million fund was in fact established by the General Assembly at the end of 1992); the appropriation of one-third of the estimated cost of operations by the General Assembly once a peacekeeping body had been authorized by the Security Council; and authority to place contracts without competitive bidding.[84] Member states have not, primarily for political reasons, been prompt payers of their dues, though they remain constrained by the prospect of losing their vote in the General Assembly. The financial problems raised by the Congo operation, and the way these nearly destroyed the UN, remain only too relevant. However, as Brian Urquhart has pointed out, there are double standards at work. 'The cost of two days of Desert Storm, at about a billion dollars a day, would have easily covered all the UN's expenses, including peacekeeping and emergency operations for a whole year.'[85] One potentially significant development was the decision of certain states, at the London Conference on Yugoslavia in August 1992, to make available military personnel to UNPROFOR, without cost to the UN, to facilitate the delivery of humanitarian aid. However, this experiment was not successful. In March 1993 the Security Council unanimously agreed that from 1 April the whole of UNPROFOR should be financed from assessed contributions.

(ix) *In what kinds of conflict can peacekeeping be used effectively?* Peacekeeping has proved to be a useful diplomatic and practical tool in certain conflicts since World War II. UN peacekeeping has in some cases been effective because the UN Secretary-General, Security Council, and General Assembly in their different ways represent the views of the community as a whole, particularly if they,

---

[83] *Agenda for Peace*, para. 47.

[84] 'Report of the Secretary-General on the Work of the Organization', (1992), p. 12.

[85] Brian Urquhart, 'A Double Standard', *New York Review of Books*, 9 Apr. 1992, p. 42. See also Urquhart's chapter above, p. 93.

together with the parties on the ground, can agree on the way the conflict should be handled within the parameters laid out in the UN Charter. However, there are some more sombre lessons from past experience: huge difficulties afflict peacekeeping bodies dealing with communal conflict (UNTSO, UNMOGIP, and UNFICYP, and now UNPROFOR) where the underlying political and societal divisions run very deep. Peacekeeping bodies obviously work better with precise, achievable mandates; and with such mandates they have been of considerable value in a variety of types of conflict. They can best be looked at as useful tools in dispute and conflict settlement. Their ultimate effectiveness or ineffectiveness stems partly from the type of conflict, but also from whether there is political agreement among those involved about the way it should be resolved. The reality is that peacekeeping can ultimately work only in favourable political conditions. Attempts to use it in unsuitable conditions carry a high price and produce little return, except perhaps for an element of face-saving for other states. There is also the danger that such attempts may be followed by pressure to turn the operation into one of peace-enforcement—an escalation which may be risky and counter-productive.

8

The UN and Human Rights: At the End of the Beginning

TOM J. FARER and FELICE GAER

(a) Human Rights in the Pre-Charter Era

UNTIL World War II, most legal scholars and governments affirmed the general proposition, albeit not in so many words, that international law did not impede the natural right of each equal sovereign to be monstrous to his or her subjects.[1] Summary execution, torture, arbitrary arrest, and detention: these were legally significant events beyond national frontiers only if the victims of such official eccentricities were citizens of another state. In that case international law treated them as the bearers not of personal rights but of rights belonging to their government and ultimately to the state for which it spoke. In effect, for the purposes of inter-state relations, the individual was nothing more than a symbol and a capital asset.

---

[1] Richard Bilder, 'An Overview of Human Rights Law', in Hurst Hannum (ed.), *Guide to International Human Rights Practice* (Philadelphia, 1984), pp. 4–5. See also Hersch Lauterpacht, 'General Rules of the Law of Peace', in Elihu Lauterpacht (ed.), *International Law: Collected Papers of Hersch Lauterpacht*, vol. 1 (Cambridge, 1970): 'The predominant theory is clear and emphatic. International Law is a law of States only and exclusively. Individuals are only the objects of international law' (p. 279). But he goes on to demonstrate that, over the course of the twentieth century, the predominant theory has become riddled with exceptions to such a degree as to require a far more qualified and nuanced statement of it. 'It may now be submitted, by way of summary, that these examples show that there is nothing in the existing international system [i.e. post-World War II] which makes it impossible for individiuals to be directly subjects of international duties [and correspondingly rights] imposed upon them as such . . . Secondly, reasons have been given why even in those cases in which States are formally made subjects of international duties, the actual centre of legal and moral responsibility is in the individual and not in the metaphysical personality of the State. Decisive reasons of progress in international law and morality seem to favour that construction' (p. 285). See also pp. 141–9.

Assaults on his person carried out or acquiesced in by representatives of another state were deemed assaults on the dignity and material interests of his state, requiring compensation.[2]

Guardians of the spiritual realm were episodically less permissive. Virtually from the start of that bloody enterprise known as the Spanish Empire in the New World, some priests struggled to moderate the awful cupidity and grotesque caprice of the *conquistadores*, their secular associates in Spain's civilizing mission.[3] In addition, Christian missionaries worked to alert decent opinion in Europe, such as it was, to the genocidal features of the trade in African slaves,[4] and thereafter to such abominations as the Belgian King Leopold's personal empire in the Congo.[5]

Even Europe's colonial powers thought, or at least found it convenient to appear to think, that the Congo's indigenous population required some guarantee of minimally decent treatment. And so, while negotiating the orderly division of Africa at the Congress of Berlin in 1884–5, they announced, and Leopold nominally accepted, arguably as a condition of his suzerainty over the Congo, an obligation to look after the well-being of its inhabitants.[6] Since the

[2] See L. Oppenheim, *International Law: A Treatise*, vol. 1 (7th edn., ed. H. Lauterpacht, London, 1948), pp. 304–6, 310; on reparations see pp. 318–19.

[3] See e.g. Roger Merriman, *The Rise of the Spanish Empire*, vol. 2 (New York, 1962), pp. 656–63.

[4] See e.g. D. B. Davis, *Slavery and Human Progress* (New Haven, Conn., 1984), pp. 304–5. See also Paul Lovejoy, *Transformations in Slavery* (Cambridge, 1983), pp. 253–4: '[The missionaries] were firmly opposed to the slave trade and enslavement; indeed, the missions were intimately associated with the abolition of the trans-Atlantic slave trade.' But, he adds, 'on the other hand, they generally concluded that [in Africa] conversion to Christianity should precede the abolition of slavery. Slave holders, for example, were allowed to become Christians, slavery was to be tolerated temporarily, so that the Christian church could be established. Only when Christians were a majority of the population would it be safe to abolish slavery.' The struggle for abolition, particularly when it assumed the form of pressure by Great Britain on other states and the stopping and boarding of vessels on the high seas, was, of course, an augury of movement in the architectonic plates of moral and legal sentiment.

[5] See generally Neal Ascherson, *The King Incorporated* (London, 1963). See also E. C. Stowell, *Intervention in International Law* (Washington DC, 1921), pp. 163–79.

[6] Lauterpacht, *International Law*, vol. 2 (1975), p. 103. To be precise, pursuant to Art. 6 of the Berlin Act, all the powers exercising rights in the Congo Basin undertook to care for the moral and material conditions of the natives. Similar provision in the Act concluding the Brussels Conference of 1890 was thought, Lauterpacht says, to require 'positive measures for the improvement of the natives' lot'.

Congress provided no enforcement mechanism, relying rather on the good faith of the ineffable Leopold, the people of the Congo did not quickly hear of or experience the good news.[7] Nevertheless, the very recognition of limits on a fellow sovereign's discretion in the disposition of his human assets was significant.

The effort to inhibit Leopold was one among a number of events in the latter part of the nineteenth century and the first part of the twentieth expressing an epochal shift in moral sentiment which would ultimately find expression in law. Heralds of this shift had appeared a good deal earlier to trumpet its arrival. While historians will always dispute when the first faint notes could be distinguished, the American and French revolutionists, by invoking on their own behalf universal and inalienable rights, unmistakably declared the new age. The often vacillating but finally decisive Anglo-French intervention in the Greek war of independence from Ottoman rule (1821–30),[8] justified in part by the allegedly peculiar cruelty of the Ottoman administration, reinforced the evangelical message of the French Revolution that, in the spirit of human solidarity, one state might choose to liberate the people of another from manifest oppression.

During the remainder of the nineteenth century, the Ottoman Empire continued to serve as a magnet for essays in 'humanitarian intervention' by great powers: the Russians, on behalf of Orthodox Christians, and the French, on behalf of Catholics.[9] There were also protests by Western powers against outbreaks of anti-Semitism in Russia. In addition to evidencing the power of transnational solidarities, these interventions demonstrated the possible incompatibility of such claims with harmony in the relations of states. The way in which World War I broke out from an assassination in Sarajevo tragically underscored the

[7] Massacre, mutilation, and forced labour continued at least through the first decade of the twentieth century. Ascherson, *The King Incorporated*, pp. 241–60.

[8] See generally Douglas Dakin, *The Greek Struggle for Independence 1821–33* (London, 1973).

[9] See generally Stanford and Ezel Shaw, *History of the Ottoman Empire and Modern Turkey*, vol. 2 (Cambridge, 1977).

potentially destructive impact on inter-state relations of claims for liberation and justice asserted by peoples against the political structures containing them. At the same time, however, because the Allies sought to marshal support by characterizing their exertions as a struggle to defend and promote freedom,[10] one consequence of the war was to enhance the perceived legitimacy of individual and group claims against the state.

The process of unpacking the individual from the state went on with the inclusion in the post-war settlement of provisions purporting to guarantee fair treatment for minorities, principally in the infant countries carved out of the Austro-Hungarian Empire's corpse. Subsequent experience suggested both the importance of such guarantees and the diffidence of guarantors on those many occasions when compassion did not coincide with more traditional state interests.

The minority provisions in the post-war treaties[11] created a special regime for the protection of a limited cluster of interests of carefully circumscribed peoples. In this respect they were not unique, having been preceded by the capitulations[12] coerced from the Ottoman Sultan, the Chinese Emperor, and other non-European dignitaries by Western governments determined to insulate their citizens, primarily traders, from local jurisdiction. But the capitulations were simply a discriminatory expansion of each state's acknowledged right to fair treatment for its own subjects when they were abroad, a right equally operative in relations among the great powers.

Even in making the treatment of the subjects of one sovereign a matter of legitimate concern to other sovereigns, the minority-protection clauses did not open entirely new ground. Under duress, the Sublime Porte had conceded

---

[10] 'We shall fight for the things which we have always carried nearest to our hearts, for democracy, for the right of those who submit to authority to have a voice in their own governments.' Woodrow Wilson, speech to Congress, 2 Apr. 1917, quoted in Frederick Calhoun, *Power and Principle: Armed Intervention in Wilsonian Foreign Policy* (Kent, Oh., 1986).

[11] See Lauterpacht, *International Law*, vol. 2, pp. 49, 147, and 506.

[12] Lord Kinross, *The Ottoman Centuries* (London, 1977), pp. 427 and 479; see also Shaw and Shaw, *History of the Ottoman Empire*, pp. 131, 300, and 367.

rights of protection over the Empire's Orthodox and Catholic populations to the Russians and the French respectively.[13]

In the final stages of World War II, the victorious allies decided to prosecute Nazi leaders not only for waging aggressive war and massacring people in occupied territories, but also for the slaughter of German citizens. In pressing this last matter, under the heading of 'crimes against humanity',[14] they were opening new territory. German nationals did not enjoy the protection of any special treaty regime. So if they had unconditional rights subject to violation by the Third Reich, these had to be rights under customary international law or under general principles of law to be found in every civilized society. Thus the judgment of the International Military Tribunal at Nuremberg, and the General Assembly Declaration affirming the legitimacy of the principles supporting that judgment,[15] implied a core of obligations applicable to all sovereigns concerning the treatment of their citizens. In this way the realm of human rights became available for general occupation.

In the ensuing decades, through both formal agreements and declarations evidencing the consensus necessary for customary law,[16] states have bound themselves not to torture or summarily execute or enslave their citizens;[17] not to convict them without due process of law; not to dissolve their trade unions; not to discriminate among them on the basis of race or religion; and not to do various other things which are the authors of despair. Many nations, going beyond declarations of self-restraint, have rallied with varying degrees of commitment behind the claim that the state has an affirmative obligation to protect its citizens from economic, social, and cultural impoverishment.

[13] See Kinross, *The Ottoman Centuries*, and Shaw and Shaw, *History of the Ottoman Empire*.   [14] Lauterpacht, *International Law*, vol. 1, pp. 470–1.
[15] GA Res. 95(I) of 11 Dec. 1946.
[16] See generally Anthony D'Amato, *The Concept of Custom in International Law* (Ithaca, NY, 1971).
[17] Some of these matters, including slavery, had been the subject of agreements well before the UN era. Note e.g. the 1926 Slavery Convention and 1930 ILO Convention Concerning Forced or Compulsory Labour.

(b) Building a Normative Framework

1. The UN Charter

At its inception, the United Nations seemed destined to be the engine of human rights. Article 1(3) of the Charter announces the UN's purposes to include 'promoting and encouraging respect for human rights and . . . fundamental freedoms for all without distinction as to race, sex, language, or religion'. Article 13 mandates the General Assembly to 'initiate studies and make recommendations for the purpose of . . . assisting in the realization of human rights'. Article 56, combined with Article 55, pledges all UN members 'to take joint and separate action in cooperation with the Organization for the achievement of . . . universal respect for, and observance of, human rights'. Article 68 requires the Economic and Social Council to 'set up commissions . . . for the promotion of human rights'.[18]

To be sure, these provisions did not spring from a fierce, collective will to shatter the wall of national sovereignty wherever it sheltered some variety of oppression. John P. Humphrey, the first Director of the Division of Human Rights at the UN, reports that, but for the efforts of a few deeply committed delegates, and the representatives of some forty-two private organizations brought in as consultants by the United States, human rights would have received 'only a passing reference'.[19] While in the end they obviously did much better than that, their subordination in the organization's hierarchy of purposes is evident, above all in the Charter's authorization of UN enforcement action only in case of 'any threat to the peace, breach of the peace, or act of aggression',[20] language clearly intended to evoke images of inter-state conflict.

Not only did the founders thereby appear to deny human rights the prospect of collective armed intervention on their behalf—an impression heightened by the

[18] See also the direct reference to human rights in the UN Charter Preamble and in Art. 62(2), 68, and 76(c).
[19] John P. Humphrey, 'The UN Charter and the Universal Declaration of Human Rights', in Evan Luard (ed.), *The International Protection of Human Rights* (New York, 1967), p. 39.   [20] Chap. VII, Art. 39–51.

Charter's broad prohibition[21] of forceful action by states except in self-defence—but in addition they incorporated language which could be construed as ruling out every sort of collective action against violations of human rights. Article 2(7) says: 'Nothing contained in the present Charter shall authorize the United Nations to intervene in matters which are essentially within the domestic jurisdiction of any state or shall require the Members to submit such matters to settlement under the present Charter.' That prohibition is, however, inapplicable where the Security Council decides a situation is a threat to international peace and security and takes action pursuant to its enforcement powers under Chapter VII of the Charter. But, with the exception of two notorious instances of racial discrimination—Rhodesia and South Africa—decades would pass before the Council would view massive violations of human rights as peace threatening. Hence Article 2(7) offered comfortable shelter for rogue regimes in the early postwar decades.

Events surrounding the adoption of the Charter and the UN's early life suggest that there was widespread ambivalence, if not towards human rights *per se*, then certainly to the prospect of their enforcement through the UN. The Soviet bloc quickly established the position to which it would thereafter cling, namely that UN activity should be confined to promulgating rights; enforcement, on the other hand, was a matter of purely domestic concern.[22] But it was hardly alone in wishing to keep the UN out of the enforcement business. The colonial powers were hardly more enthusiastic at the prospect of UN 'meddling' in their respective preserves.[23]

---

[21] Art. 2(4): 'All Members shall refrain in their international relations from the threat or use of force against the territorial integrity or political independence of any state, or in any other manner inconsistent with the Purposes of the United Nations.' Art. 51: 'Nothing in the present Charter shall impair the inherent right of individual or collective self-defence if an armed attack occurs against a Member of the United Nations.'

[22] Farrokh Jhabvala, 'The Soviet Bloc's View of the Implementation of Human Rights Accords', *Human Rights Quarterly*, 7 (1985), p. 466.

[23] 'General Romulo of the Philippines urged the Commission to conduct itself like a court of appeal, guaranteeing immunity to plaintiffs from any nation. Mrs Roosevelt reasoned that the Commission had power to make recommendations

It is, therefore, not surprising that a joint initiative by Panama and Chile to include in the Charter articles guaranteeing specific human rights, and also a Panamanian proposal for a separate Bill of Rights, were rejected as too controversial.[24] Nor is it grounds for astonishment that at its very first session the Commission on Human Rights determined that 'it had no power to take any action in regard to any complaints concerning human rights'.[25] Its immediate superior in the UN hierarchy, the Economic and Social Council, not only confirmed the Commission's marvellous self-restraint, but rubbed salt in the self-inflicted wound by deciding that Commission members should not even review the original text of specific complaints by individuals lest, one supposes, the horrors recounted therein should inspire second thoughts about the virtues of moral blindness.[26]

2. The international bill of rights

While some auguries for the future of the normative fledgeling were ominous, others promised achievement. Aside from their considerable prominence in the Charter itself, human rights got an early boost from President Harry S Truman when he addressed the closing session of the founding conference. 'We have good reason', he told the delegates, 'to expect the framing of an international bill of rights ... that ... will be as much a part of international life as our own Bill of Rights is a part of our Constitution' (which, he might have added, also began life

---

to ECOSOC, but not to conduct an inquiry. Australia, the United Kingdom, and the USSR opposed Commission review of individual petitions.' Howard Tolley, jun., 'The Concealed Crack in the Citadel: The United Nations Commission on Human Rights' Response to Confidential Communications', *Human Rights Quarterly*, 6 (1984), p. 422. The UK also proposed successfully that the right of petition, including petition to the UN, be removed from the final draft of the 1948 Universal Declaration of Human Rights. Ibid., p. 423.

[24] Peter Meyer, 'The International Bill: A Brief History', in Paul Williams (ed.), *The International Bill of Human Rights* (Glen Ellen, 1981), p. xxiv.

[25] Report of the first session, E/259 (1947), paras. 21 and 22.

[26] ECOSOC Res. 75(V) of 5 Aug. 1947. In a consolidated resolution in communications concerning human rights which the Council adopted in 1959, it reiterated its approval. Res. 728 F(XXVIII) of 30 July 1959.

without one).[27] As if inspired by the American President's vision, the Economic and Social Council (ECOSOC), having in early 1946 carried out its mandate to establish a Commission on Human Rights, made the drafting of an international bill of rights the Commission's first priority.

Led by Eleanor Roosevelt in her role as chairperson, the Commission went to work at a speed remarkable in comparison to the gait it would assume in later years when controversial issues of human rights begged for resolution. That the drafting task was destined for controversy quickly became apparent. As one could have predicted from the jousting over the Charter, the central point of conflict was whether, or to what extent, international concern for human rights should be allowed to breach the wall of national sovereignty. No state seemed more determined to keep the wall intact than the organization's most powerful enthusiast for transnational liberation movements, the USSR. When the first drafting stage culminated in the presentation to the General Assembly of the Universal Declaration of Human Rights, the Soviet delegate declared it defective primarily because 'a number of articles completely ignore the sovereign rights of democratic governments. . . . [T]he question of national sovereignty', he maintained, 'is a matter of the greatest importance.'[28]

Delegates also tended to polarize over the relative emphasis between individual rights and community interests. If the proposed Bill 'did not stipulate the existence of the individual and his need for protection in his struggle against the State', declared the distinguished philosopher Charles Malik, representing Lebanon, 'the Commission would never achieve its intended purpose'.[29] The Yugoslav representative insisted that, on the contrary, the 'new conditions of modern times [make the] common interest . . . more important than the individual interest'.[30]

In late 1947, facing the danger of impasse over political and ideological differences, the Commission on Human

[27] Cited in A. H. Robertson, *Human Rights in the World* (Manchester, 1972), p. 25.

[28] *GAOR*, 3rd session, part I, plenary meetings, 10 Dec. 1948, pp. 923–4.

[29] UN *Weekly Bulletin*, 25 Feb. 1947, pp. 170–1.   [30] Ibid.

Rights agreed to divide the Bill of Rights into three parts: a declaration of principles which the General Assembly could adopt; a Covenant rhetorically tied to the Declaration under which ratifying states would become subject to explicit legal obligations; and a separate agreement detailing enforcement machinery. As Peter Meyer notes in his 'Brief History' of the International Bill of Rights, the eight-person drafting committee appointed by the Commission rapidly completed a draft of the Declaration. Thereafter it 'wound its way through the full Commission, the Economic and Social Council ... and eighty-one meetings and 168 proposed amendments of the General Assembly's Third Committee [before ending up] in almost the same form as that first proposed by the committee.'[31]

Rejecting a Soviet proposal to postpone consideration until the following year,[32] on 10 December 1948 the General Assembly adopted the Universal Declaration by a vote of forty-eight to none, with eight abstentions: South Africa, the Soviet Union, the Ukraine, Byelorussia, Czechoslovakia, Poland, Yugoslavia, and Saudi Arabia.[33] When the vote was announced, Eleanor Roosevelt expressed the hope that the Declaration would be 'the Magna Carta of all mankind'.[34]

Since, under the Charter, most General Assembly action has a non-binding character, initially most scholars took the view that the Declaration expressed moral values rather than legally binding norms. However, in part because it had passed without a negative vote, in larger part because many of its provisions subsequently found their way into formal international agreements or were incorporated in national constitutions, it has acquired a legal aura, the appearance of stating, if not having by its existence created, binding norms of state behaviour.[35]

The Declaration, as Meyer notes, was only the first step

---

[31] Meyer, 'The International Bill', p. xxx.   [32] GAOR, n. 28 above, p. 929.
[33] GA Res. 217 (III)A of 10 Dec. 1948.
[34] Cited in Robertson, Human Rights in the World, p. 27.
[35] Egon Schwelb and Philip Alston, 'The Principal Institutions and Other Bodies Founded under the Charter', in Karel Vasak (ed.), The International Dimensions of Human Rights, vol. 1 (Westport, Conn., and Paris, 1982), p. 245.

of the International Bill—a quickstep compared with the eighteen-year trudge which followed.[36] Only through a further decoupling of the originally envisioned elements of the Bill were the disputants finally able to resolve their often rancorous differences. The old polarities—human rights versus national sovereignty, individual liberty versus communal needs—continued to discourage consensus. The former was concretized by the issue of international enforcement. The latter led to dispute primarily over two questions. One was whether economic, social, and cultural interests should be accorded the status of rights on a par with the traditional liberal values of free speech, religion, press, association, and so on. Despite Franklin Delano Roosevelt's inclusion in 1941 of 'freedom from want' among the 'four freedoms' for whose attainment the USA would face the risk of war, the Western allies as a group were inclined to answer 'no'. The Eastern bloc, increasingly supplemented by newly independent states from the Third World, said 'yes'. The question of whether the covenant should include a right to property created a similar grouping of antagonists.

The drafters finally broke free from their impasse by agreeing as follows. First, there would be two covenants, one dealing with political and civil rights, the other with economic, social, and cultural rights. Both these covenants were eventually concluded in 1966, and entered into force in 1976. Second, in so far as implementing machinery was concerned, states could ratify either or both conventions, without thereby assuming any more onerous obligation than provision of a periodic report.

The 1966 International Covenant on Civil and Political Rights requires states to submit reports 'on the measures they have adopted which give effect to the rights recognized [therein] and on the progress made in the enjoyment of those rights'. These reports are to be transmitted through the Secretary-General to an elected eighteen-person committee of experts authorized to study and thereafter transmit reports to the states parties and ECOSOC

---

[36] Meyer, 'The International Bill', p. xxxi.

together with 'such general comments as it may consider appropriate' (Article 40).

Reports under the 1966 International Covenant on Economic, Social and Cultural Rights cover 'the measures ... adopted and the progress made in achieving the observance of the rights recognized [therein]' (Article 16). These reports must be submitted to ECOSOC 'for consideration in accordance with the provisions of the ... Covenant', and it in turn transmits them to the Human Rights Commission 'for study and general recommendation' (Article 19).

Parties ratifying the Civil and Political Covenant have the option under Article 41 of recognizing the jurisdiction of the Covenant's Human Rights Committee to hear complaints from other states that have also accepted this procedure. The Committee may hold hearings and promote friendly settlement. What it apparently cannot do is form an independent judgement about the merits of the complaint.

That power is reserved for cases, if any, arising under the so-called (first) 'Optional Protocol' to the Civil and Political Covenant. States adhering to it recognize the Committee's authority to hear petitions from individuals alleging violations of their rights under the Covenant. After considering the petition 'in the light of all written evidence made available to it by the individual and by the State Party concerned ... The Committee shall forward its views to [them]' (Article 5). And then? The Protocol says only that 'The Committee shall include in its annual report ... a summary of its activities under the ... Protocol' (Article 6).

These weak and for the most part optional instruments of compliance mollified the opposition of those numerous governments hostile to external assessment of their domestic behaviour. Also, the form in which substantive norms are stated is anxiety-easing for such governments, since states are given a considerable margin of discretion. Many of the rights guaranteed in the Civil and Political Covenant, for instance, are subject to suspension 'in time of public emergency which threatens the life of the nation', albeit only 'to the extent strictly required by the exigencies of the situation' (Article 4). The rights to life and protection from torture are not derogable; but governments can, among other things, detain citizens for substantial periods of time on the basis of evidence normally insufficient for arrest and without expeditious charge and trial.[37]

A margin of state discretion is, moreover, incorporated in the very statement of certain rights. In the Civil and Political Covenant, for instance, the right to freedom of expression 'may . . . be subject to certain restrictions . . . provided by law and . . . necessary . . . for the protection of national security or of public order (*ordre public*), or of public health or morals' (Article 19). Article 20 actually requires the prohibition of 'any propaganda for war'. And Article 21, while recognizing the right of peaceful assembly, makes it subject to restrictions 'which are necessary in a democratic society in the interests of national security or public safety, public order, the protection of public health or morals or the protection of the rights and freedoms of others'.

Some flexibility in the interpretation and enforcement of most rights is, of course, essential, if for no reason other than to assure their availability to all groups in society and to maintain that degree of public order without which no right is secure. Everyone cannot exercise the right of assembly in the same place at the same time. If the government cannot referee, private power will be imperious and freedom correspondingly reduced. Governments must, therefore, have a margin of discretion: but if the exercise of that discretion is essentially unmonitored, a limited discretion readily deteriorates into licence.

The economic, social, and cultural realms are even less susceptible to categorical directives. Governments have a legitimate interest, for instance, in promoting a common culture which will help to harmonize the relations between diverse social groups. That interest must be balanced

---

[37] See generally Jaime Oraa, *Human Rights in States of Emergency in International Law* (Oxford, 1992); Subrata Roy Chowdhury, *Rule of Law in a State of Emergency: The Paris Minimum Standards of Human Rights Norms in a State of Emergency* (London, 1989).

against the equally appealing claim for freedom to maintain cultural identity within the framework of a multicultural state. Governments must also balance an interest in minimizing poverty for the current generation against the claims of the next for a higher standard of living; the latter requires among other things some postponement of consumption in favour of investment. Decisions concerning the language of public business and instruction, the organization of the economy, the allocation of wealth, the forms of taxation, and the model of economic and social development have (traditionally, at least) been thought of as falling exclusively within the range of national discretion.

It was only in 1966, after twenty years of struggle, that the two covenants and the separate protocol were finally put to the vote in the General Assembly.[38] The Covenant on Civil and Political Rights received 106 votes in favour, none against; its sibling Covenant on Economic, Social and Cultural Rights received 105 votes with none against. Despite the fact that a state's favourable vote did not commit it to subsequent ratification, the Optional Protocol managed to attract only sixty-six affirmative votes; there were two negatives and thirty-eight abstentions. Another ten years passed before the respective covenants received the thirty-five, and the protocol the ten, ratifications required for their entry into force.

(c) The Human Rights Machinery: Form

While enthusiasts for the International Bill of Rights were suffering through its prolonged gestation, the UN member states, rather than invoking that process as an excuse for avoiding initiatives certain to attract the same conflicts of interest and ideology as those delaying the Bill's delivery, moved forward (gingerly, to be sure) under the authority of the Charter and the banner of the Universal Declaration.

---

[38] International Covenant on Economic, Social and Cultural Rights, adopted by GA Res. 2200 (XXI) of 16 Dec. 1966, *GAOR*, 21st session, supplement no. 16(A/6316), pp. 49–52; International Covenant on Civil and Political Rights, ibid., pp. 52–8; Optional Protocol to the International Covenant on Civil and Political Rights, ibid., pp. 59–60.

The UN's relevant activities over the years fall into three distinct categories: defining and clarifying the rights of individuals (standard setting); studying particular human rights, or human rights in particular places, and recommending measures for their fuller realization (subdivided by some writers into 'promotional' and 'protective' functions); and providing assistance directly to victims of human rights delinquencies (the humanitarian function).

1. Humanitarian assistance

This is the activity which, in our time, has had without doubt the most tangible and far-ranging impact on human rights; yet it is the least controversial. Indeed, it often skips the minds of people when they talk about human rights activities of the United Nations (or disparage the absence thereof). The two most indisputably effective and important instruments of direct assistance have been the UN International Children's Emergency Fund (UNICEF)[39] and the UN High Commissioner for Refugees (UNHCR). Unlike many other economic and technical assistance organizations such as the World Bank (International Bank for Reconstruction and Development), UNICEF has concentrated its resources first on enabling the most desperate and vulnerable sectors of Third World populations to survive, and then on helping them to acquire the skills necessary for self-maintenance.

In addition, since the adoption in 1989 of the Convention on the Rights of the Child (CRC)—which covers, on the one hand, a wide range of economic and social rights and, on the other, civil and political rights—UNICEF has played a leading role in promoting adherence to the Convention and providing expert guidance to the new supervisory Committee on the Rights of the Child.

The office of the UNHCR has been less successful in avoiding controversy because its mission, protecting those who flee their native lands for fear of persecution,

[39] Founded as the UN International Children's Emergency Fund by UN GA Res. 57 (I) of 11 Dec. 1946, it became a permanent UN agency, and was renamed the UN Children's Fund, while keeping the same UNICEF acronym, by GA Res. 802 (VIII) of 6 Oct. 1953.

necessarily embroils it in the hot spots of international politics. The very act of extending protection to individuals is often a harsh commentary on the behaviour of the public authorities in the country from which they have fled. The High Commissioner may also find herself treated as a nuisance if not an outright adversary by the host government, as the refugees may complicate its relations with their home country. They may, moreover, cause difficulties locally by attempting to enter domestic labour markets or squatting on undeveloped land. Although the High Commissioner's original mandate contemplated a short-term protective mission for rather limited numbers of people pending negotiation of conditions for their safe return to the country of origin, the vast numbers actually displaced by civil war and persecution and the often indefinite prolongation of exile have required the High Commissioner and her colleagues to marshal resources for maintaining and in some cases integrating their clients into new lands. In a number of cases, the UNHCR has also provided assistance to internally displaced persons, that is, persons forced, usually by the pressures of civil armed conflict, to move within a country.

Today UNHCR's mandate also includes monitoring the fate of refugees voluntarily repatriated to their country of origin. This extended protective function has been exercised in such testing environments as Vietnam and Haiti. As if all these missions were not sufficiently challenging, the UNHCR has in addition been directed by the General Assembly to assist in identifying potential cases of mass exodus to the end of avoiding their occurrence.[40]

Unlike the function of defending individuals against the human rights delinquencies of their own governments, humanitarian assistance has not until recently directly challenged the traditional jurisdictional monopoly of governments over the lives of their own nationals on national territory. But the televised humanitarian disaster

---

[40] For an overview of the UN system's arrangements and capacity for providing humanitarian assistance, including the activities of UNHCR and UNICEF, see UN doc. A/46/568 (17 Oct. 1991), annexe I. With respect to the UNHCR see esp. pp. 10–12.

of the Iraqi Kurds, fleeing massacre at the hands of Baghdad after the Gulf war only to die of hunger and exposure in the country's northern mountains, seems finally to have forced reconsideration of the view that a government's request is necessary to trigger delivery of relief by the international community.

Of course, in the case of the Kurds, relief was finally delivered under the protective umbrella of Security Council resolutions and coalition airpower rather than a mandate from Baghdad. But the response of UN agencies was slow and disorganized, suggesting the need not only for greater centralization of authority, but also for an intense alertness, a readiness to act in response to human need rather than the appeal of the target state's government, an appeal that might never be forthcoming.

In the wake of the Kurdish disaster, Canada, the Nordic states, and a cluster of European Community members called for strengthening the international community's right to humanitarian intervention and the UN's capacity to deliver emergency aid promptly. They launched an initiative to establish an Emergency Relief Coordinator which quickly developed into a struggle between the 'North' and a large bloc of developing countries declaring their fear that 'the right to intervene' for humanitarian purposes would become an excuse for meddling in their internal affairs. Intense negotiations at the 46th General Assembly (1991) none the less led to the establishment of the proposed post.

To secure developing country support for the position, the North had to accept a body of guiding principles which included reference to the requirement of an appeal from the affected country. Speaking for the Group of 77, Ghana's delegate assured his colleagues in the Assembly that the final document detailing the principles 'rejected any form of humanitarian intervention' and that the new post represented no more than a step toward greater efficiency in the delivery of aid.[41] However, the pressure

---

[41] See GA Res. A/46/182 in UN Press Release GA/8307, 21 Jan. 1992, pp. 78–83, and UN Press Release GA/8304, 19 Dec. 1991, pp. 19–20.

on Serbia in 1992–3 to permit emergency assistance to Bosnia-Herzegovina, and the operations in Somalia by UN-authorized troops and by the UN itself, seem to reflect a growing willingness to demand rather than to await appeals from target states.

2. Standard-setting, promotion, and protection

A diagram of United Nations activities in the human rights field (see pp. 258–9) reveals a lush institutional ensemble. No management expert responsive to a single master would ever have endorsed this complex arrangement of bodies with often overlapping mandates. But arrangements that at first appear ripe for rationalization are at least partially an extemporized and creative response to obstacles erected by opponents of human rights activity generally or in particular instances. Advocates of a human rights mission for the UN have had to circumvent shifting strong points of opposition that could not be taken by a frontal assault.

The current system is composed mainly of commissions and one sub-commission, committees both regular and special, working groups, and special rapporteurs. The following brief summary should provide a basis for assessing the organization's present and potential efficacy in the human rights field.

The General Assembly (GA) reigns, of course, at the apex of the institutional pyramid, with plenary authority to create subsidiaries for any purpose enumerated or implied in the Charter (used, for example, to establish the Office of the High Commissioner for Refugees in 1951 and the successive committees on apartheid beginning with the Special Committee of 1962), and free to act either through those subsidiaries or directly on any human rights issue that engages the concern of its members.

While scholars and activists tend to focus on UN organs specializing in human rights, the GA remains a central actor in the human rights drama at the UN.[42] It supervises

---

[42] For a detailed discussion of the GA's role in the human rights field, see 'The General Assembly into the 1990s', by Australian diplomat John Quinn, in Philip Alston (ed.), *The United Nations and Human Rights: A Critical Appraisal* (Oxford, 1992).

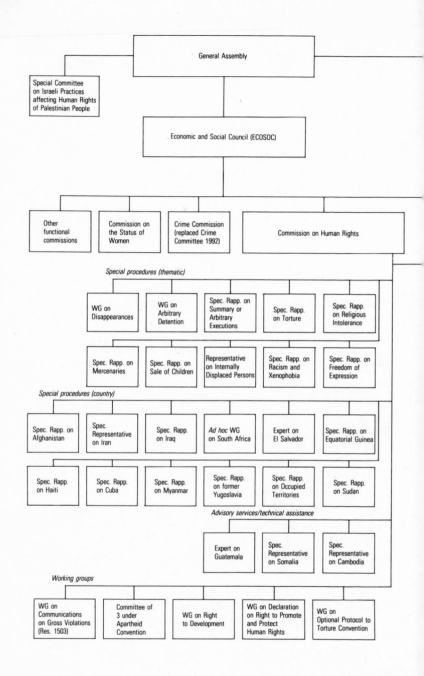

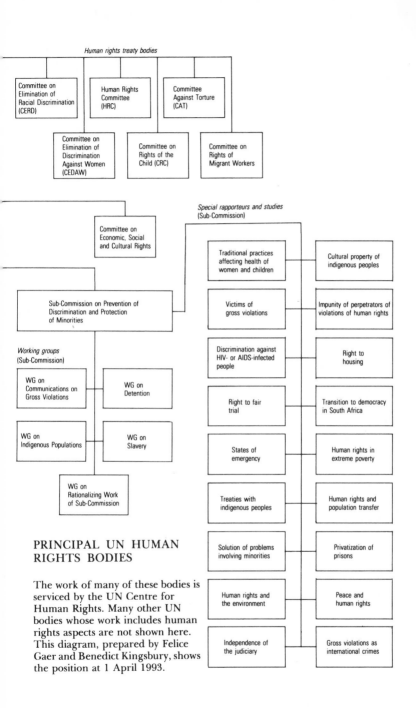

Human rights treaty bodies

Committee on Elimination of Racial Discrimination (CERD)

Human Rights Committee (HRC)

Committee Against Torture (CAT)

Committee on Elimination of Discrimination Against Women (CEDAW)

Committee on Rights of the Child (CRC)

Committee on Rights of Migrant Workers

Committee on Economic, Social and Cultural Rights

Special rapporteurs and studies (Sub-Commission)

Sub-Commission on Prevention of Discrimination and Protection of Minorities

Working groups (Sub-Commission)

WG on Communications on Gross Violations

WG on Detention

WG on Indigenous Populations

WG on Slavery

WG on Rationalizing Work of Sub-Commission

Traditional practices affecting health of women and children

Cultural property of indigenous peoples

Victims of gross violations

Impunity of perpetrators of violations of human rights

Discrimination against HIV- or AIDS-infected people

Right to housing

Right to fair trial

Transition to democracy in South Africa

States of emergency

Human rights in extreme poverty

Treaties with indigenous peoples

Human rights and population transfer

Solution of problems involving minorities

Privatization of prisons

Human rights and the environment

Peace and human rights

Independence of the judiciary

Gross violations as international crimes

PRINCIPAL UN HUMAN RIGHTS BODIES

The work of many of these bodies is serviced by the UN Centre for Human Rights. Many other UN bodies whose work includes human rights aspects are not shown here. This diagram, prepared by Felice Gaer and Benedict Kingsbury, shows the position at 1 April 1993.

all programmes in the field and ultimately determines what standards are adopted, what issues are addressed, and what proportion and kind of administrative and budgetary resources will be devoted to the UN's human rights machinery. Subject to the ultimate authority of the GA, the Economic and Social Council (ECOSOC) nominally directs and monitors the work of the organization's most active organ in the human rights field, that is, the Commission on Human Rights.

Articles 62–6 of the Charter authorize the Council to 'make recommendations for the purpose of promoting respect for, and observance of, human rights and fundamental freedoms for all', to 'prepare draft conventions for submission to the General Assembly', to call international conferences, to coordinate the activities of the specialized agencies, to obtain reports both from them and from member states 'on the steps taken to give effect to its own recommendations and to recommendations on matters falling within its competence made by the General Assembly', and to perform 'such other functions as may be assigned to it by the General Assembly'. The Council is a quintessentially political body, its fifty-four members, elected by the Assembly on the basis of so-called 'equitable geographical distribution', being formal representatives of UN member states.

Equally political in its form as in its functions is the Commission on Human Rights established by ECOSOC in 1946 to serve as the organization's principal *locus* for human rights activity.[43] Politicization of the Commission seems to have been a second thought, albeit one which came ever so quickly after the first. At its first session in 1946, ECOSOC appointed in their individual capacity nine members to serve as the nucleus of a larger body. The 'Nuclear Commission', as it was called, quickly issued a report recommending that 'all members of the Commission on Human Rights should serve as non-governmental

[43] ECOSOC Res. 5 (I), first session, Feb. 1946 (establishing the Nuclear Commission); and Res. 9 (II), second session, June 1946 (laying down the basic structure and guide-lines in light of, but not consistent with, key elements in the Nuclear Commission's Report).

representatives'. Meeting later in 1946, the Council rejected this proposal, deciding instead that the Commission should consist of one representative from each of eighteen members of the UN selected by the Council.[44]

The Commission has since grown to fifty-three state representatives elected, as has become customary in most parts of the UN, pursuant to precise understandings about the appropriate representation of every self-identified regional bloc. Following a determined effort by developing countries to gain control of the Commission by enlarging it, Africa now has fifteen of the fifty-three places, Asia has twelve, Latin America and the Caribbean eleven, eastern Europe five, and western Europe 'and others' (the USA, Canada, New Zealand, and Australia) have ten.[45]

In the performance of its several functions, to be discussed below, the Commission employs working groups and special rapporteurs. Some have standard-setting or investigative mandates with respect to what are called 'thematic issues', such as enforced or involuntary disappearances, arbitrary detention, and religious intolerance. Others are tasked to review human rights conditions in

[44] Schwelb and Alston ('The Principal Institutions', pp. 243–4) comment: 'To those who wanted the Commission to consist of persons serving as individuals and not as representatives of governments, a small concession was made by providing that "with a view to securing a balanced representation in the various fields covered by the Commission, the Secretary-General shall consult with the governments so selected before the representatives are finally nominated by these governments and confirmed by the Council." In the 34 years following the enactment of this provision no case of the Secretary-General objecting to the qualification of a representative, or of the Council refusing to confirm him, has become known.' (The Nuclear Commission's report was UN doc. E/38/Rev. 1.)

[45] ECOSOC Res. 1990/48 of 25 May 1990. The same resolution also provided for the establishment of the Commission's first mechanism for calling 'emergency sessions', and recommended that mandates of the Commission's thematic mechanisms (special rapporteurs and working groups) can be extended for three-year terms. The first emergency session was in fact held 13–14 August 1992 and addressed the situation in the former Yugoslavia. It resulted in the appointment of a Special Rapporteur, former Polish Prime Minister Tadeusz Mazowiecki, whose mandate is to receive information continuously and send reports to the Commission and the Secretary-General. The Commission resolution asked the Secretary-General to make the reports available to the Security Council. See CHR Res. 1992/S-1/1 (14 Aug. 1992) and ECOSOC Dec. 1992/305 (18 Aug. 1992). By June 1993 Mr Mazowiecki had undertaken five trips to the former Yugoslavia (reports A/47/418-S/24616; A/47/635-S/24766; A/47/666-S/24809; E/CN.4/1993/50; and S/25792).

particular countries. The thematic and country-specific activities, designated 'special procedures' by the Commission, are a relatively recent innovation, and have given the Commission a capacity for rapid and concrete action that would have been virtually unimaginable twenty years ago.

An additional flock of working groups and rapporteurs indirectly service the Commission through its principal subsidiary, the Sub-Commission on the Prevention of Discrimination and the Protection of Minorities ('the Sub-Commission').[46] In theory the twenty-six members of the Sub-Commission are elected as independent experts. However, in part because they must be nominated and re-nominated by states (in practice almost invariably their own state), many are no less instruments of their respective governments than their counterparts on the parent body. But at least until very recently, enough members have actually satisfied the formal requisites of independence and expertise to make this child considerably more adventurous than its parent.[47] At the end of its 1992

[46] For further information about the Sub-Commission's annual session, see official reports of the Sub-Commission (E/CN.4/1989/3, E/CN.4/1990/2, E/CN.4/1991/2, E/CN.4/1992/2, and E/CN.4/1993/2 covering the sessions 1988–92). Descriptive accounts of the decisions and negotiations leading to Sub-Commission actions can be found, for example, in the following: Martin Macpherson and Aku Gordon, 'United Nations Sub-Commission on Prevention of Discrimination and Protection of Minorities, Fortieth Session, Peoples for Human Rights', *IMADR Yearbook*, 1 (1988), pp. 83–105; K. Brennan, R. Brody, and D. Weissbrodt, 'The 40th Session of the UN Sub-Commission on Prevention of Discrimination and Protection of Minorities'. *Human Rights Quarterly*, 11 (1989), pp. 295–324; R. M. Maher and D. Weissbrodt, 'The 41st Session of the UN Sub-Commission on the Prevention of Discrimination and Protection of Minorities', *Human Rights Quarterly*, 12 (1990), pp. 290–327; R. Brody, M. Convery, and D. Weissbrodt, 'The 42nd Session of the Sub-Commission on Prevention of Discrimination and Protection of Minorities', *Human Rights Quarterly*, 13 (1991), pp. 260–90.

[47] On the earlier performance of the Sub-Commission, see e.g. Tom Gardeniers, Hurst Hannum, and Janice Kruger, 'The UN Sub-Commission on Prevention of Discrimination and Protection of Minorities: Recent Developments', *Human Rights Quarterly*, 4 (1982), pp. 353–70; and Peter Haver, 'The United Nations Sub-Commission on the Prevention of Discrimination and the Protection of Minorities', *Columbia Journal of Transnational Law*, 21 (1982), pp. 103–34. More recently, the Commission set forth (in CHR Res. 1991/56) guidelines for the work of the Sub-Commission. CHR Res. 1991/81 of 6 Mar. 1991 and ECOSOC Res. 1991/32 of 31 May 1991 address ways to strengthen the independence of the expert members of the Sub-Commission. The latter

session it had working groups on communications concerning consistent patterns of gross violation of human rights (where the screening of '1503' communications, discussed below, begins), on contemporary forms of slavery, on indigenous populations, and on other subjects. It also had present or former members at work on some eighteen special studies or reports addressing not only various issues related to minorities, but also such topics as discrimination against persons infected with HIV virus, states of emergency, impunity for violators of human rights, harmful traditional health practices affecting women, the right to adequate housing, and human rights and the environment.[48]

The Commission and the Sub-Commission are established as subsidiary bodies of UN Charter organs, as is the Committee responsible for monitoring of the Covenant on Economic, Social and Cultural Rights (CESCR). Other human rights bodies that function under the UN umbrella are the product of five UN human rights treaties, each of which establishes an independent committee charged with monitoring compliance. The treaties are: the Covenant on Civil and Political Rights (CCPR); the International Convention on the Elimination of All Forms of Racial Discrimination (CERD); the Convention Against Torture and Other Cruel, Inhuman

resolutions permit the Sub-Commission to utilize a secret ballot when considering votes on situations involving violations of human rights in particular countries. This action was triggered by increased recognition that the independent experts on the Commission were being subjected to government pressures—and often instructions—about their voting on country-specific resolutions. In authorizing a new inter-sessional working group on the rationalization of the work and agenda of the Sub-Commission, the Commission asked it to consider further measures to strengthen the independence of experts, as well as steps to assure that there are genuine in-depth discussions of the studies by the Sub-Commission's members, and to develop a procedure to evaluate and monitor implementation of recommendations made in the Sub-Commission's studies. See CHR Res. 1992/66 of 4 Mar. 1992. A highly critical assessment of the Sub-Commission has been set forth by Morris Abram, a member in the 1960s who served as US Ambassador to the UN Office in Geneva 1989–92: 'Human Rights and the United Nations: Past as Prologue', *Harvard Human Rights Journal*, 4 (1991), pp. 69–83.

[48] Report of the Sub-Commission on Prevention of Discrimination and Protection of Minorities on its Forty-Fourth Session, Geneva, 1992, UN doc. E/CN.4/1993/2, pp. 173–7. Some of these were new studies approved by the Commission in 1993.

or Degrading Treatment or Punishment (CAT); the Convention on the Rights of the Child (CRC); and the Convention on the Elimination of All Forms of Discrimination Against Women (CEDAW).[49]

These committees examine reports submitted pursuant to the treaties' requirements by parties thereto and are authorized to make general comments or recommendations. They themselves report annually to the General Assembly. Although theoretically independent of the UN's political organs (with the exception of the Economic and Social Rights Committee, which is established by and remains a subsidiary body of ECOSOC), the committees depend on the UN for logistical support and the treaties integrate the Secretary-General into both the country reporting procedures and the committees' electoral processes.

The committees have different reporting cycles and procedures; since their mandates overlap, they are capable of adopting conflicting definitions of enumerated rights; they are not obliged to share information or experiences.[50] In an effort to mitigate the potential for duplication and normative chaos immanent in the committee structure, the chairs of the committees have begun to meet biennially.[51] This extemporized response to the structural problem has not dimmed calls for rationalization of the system and for avoiding its further growth by requiring all future human rights treaties sponsored by the UN to be drafted as optional protocols to existing ones.

[49] A sixth treaty, the International Convention on the Protection of the Rights of All Migrant Workers and Members of their Families, was adopted in 1990 (GA Res. 45/158 of 18 Dec. 1990). When it enters into force, a new treaty supervisory committee will be established to monitor state compliance.

[50] The GA and the Commission have begun to examine short- and long-term issues stemming from this cumbersome treaty monitoring system: see UN doc. A/44/668 of 8 Nov. 1989, 'Effective Implementation of International Instruments on Human Rights, including Reporting Under International Instruments on Human Rights', Study on 'Long-term approaches to enhancing the effective operation of bodies established under United Nations human rights instruments', by Philip Alston; updated in A/CONF.157/PC/62/Add. 11 (1993).

[51] At four meetings of the chairs of the treaty committees to date, many issues of coordination and effectiveness of the treaty committees have been discussed, and suggestions proposed. Some of the proposals have reinvigorated and focused the work of the committees, for example, establishing rapporteurs for country reports, and encouraging concluding statements after such reports are reviewed. Reports of the meetings are contained in UN docs. A/39/484 (1984), A/44/98 (1988), A/45/636 (1990), A/47/628 (1992).

The committees established under the CCPR, CERD, and CAT have authority to review petitions from citizens of states that have adhered to optional protocols allowing individual complaints. By far the lion's share of cases filed under these protocols has come to the Human Rights Committee of the CCPR, a committee distinguished by the professional calibre of its work. It has produced the only substantial body of formal, carefully reasoned decisions on human rights complaints.

Article 28 of the CCPR calls for an eighteen-member committee composed of nationals of states parties to the Covenant elected by the parties from a list of nominees presented by them to the Secretary-General. The Committee's role is limited, so far as many states are concerned, to considering reports which the parties are required to submit concerning the measures they have taken to give effect to the rights enumerated in the Covenant. The same Committee has the power to hear complaints between states that have accepted Committee jurisdiction over such cases (Article 41 of the Covenant). As of June 1993 none had been received. In addition, under the first Optional Protocol of the Covenant, the Committee hears complaints by individuals against states that are party to it; just under 500 were registered by the Committee between 1977, when it began to function, and the end of 1991.[52] By February 1993 sixty-seven of the 114 states parties had ratified or acceded to the Optional Protocol.

Two decades ago, a sketch of UN institutions concerned with human rights which did not include the Special Committee on the Situation with Regard to the Implementation of the Declaration on the Granting of Independence to Colonial Countries and Peoples (the 'Committee of Twenty-four') would have seemed conspicuously incomplete, if for no other reason than that its name could, more easily than that of any other organ, form the substance of a mantra. Having been established essentially as a prod to decolonization by encouraging and defending indigenous

---

[52] Statement by E. Houshmand before the Third Committee of the GA, 12 Nov. 1991, p. 12.

political entrepreneurs and publicizing whatever it deemed to be foot-dragging on the part of the colonial power, its writ finds few places to run now that the list of colonial territories has shrunk to a few microscopic atolls and rocks. But even as it sinks toward desuetude, it leaves behind two not trivial legacies. One is a precedent for vigorous investigation and exposure in detail of official acts violating international norms. The second is the procedure, adopted in 1970 by the Commission on Human Rights, for the consideration of individual communications relating to gross violations of human rights. The Special Committee played a catalytic role in the process leading to adoption of this procedure.[53]

Unlike the Special Committee, the Commission on the Status of Women (CSW) has a future as well as a past. Established originally as a subsidiary of the Human Rights Commission, it was granted full Commission status by ECOSOC during the Council's second session in 1946.[54] Its initial mandate was (1) to prepare recommendations and reports to ECOSOC on promoting women's rights in political, economic, civil, social, and educational fields and (2) to make recommendations on urgent problems requiring immediate attention in the field of women's rights with the object of implementing the principle that men and women shall have equal rights, and to develop proposals to give effect to such recommendations.[55] In 1987 ECOSOC expanded the mandate to include (3) promoting the objectives of equality, development, and peace, (4) monitoring the implementation of measures for the advancement of women, and (5) reviewing and appraising progress made at the national, subregional, regional, sectoral, and global levels.[56]

The Commission has, through reports and conferences,

---

[53] Tolley, 'The Concealed Crack', pp. 424–9.

[54] See ECOSOC Res. 5(I) and 11(II), both in 1946.

[55] For a summary of its work, and UN action in the women's rights field in general, see Andrew Byrnes, 'Women, Feminism, and International Human Rights Law', *Australian Yearbook of International Law*, 12 (1992), pp. 205–40.

[56] ECOSOC Res. 1987/22 of 26 May 1987. See UN Doc. A/46/578, para. 58 on the revitalization of ECOSOC programmes.

drawn attention to the distinctive obstacles women face in attempting to enjoy the human rights theoretically guaranteed to all without distinction, and articulated detailed standards for guiding and measuring the efforts of states to reduce those obstacles. Among its achievements are the Declaration on the Elimination of All Forms of Discrimination against Women, adopted by the General Assembly in 1967, and the associated Convention approved by the Assembly in 1979.[57]

The CSW's little-used confidential communications procedure has recently elicited criticism from the non-governmental community because it serves only as a source for identifying general trends and patterns of women's rights violations to the end of guiding overall CSW policy recommendations. It is in no sense a mechanism for addressing individual cases or exposing general patterns of human rights delinquency in particular countries.[58] It thus falls far short of the procedures of effective human rights treaty bodies. NGOs have focused more on the Commission on Human Rights, pressing that body to integrate gender perspectives into all special procedures.[59]

The Commission on Human Rights, the Sub-Commission, the treaty bodies, and other activities are serviced by the UN Centre for Human Rights, which provides administrative support and some impetus for the organization's human rights machinery. Despite mushrooming need for its services, the Centre operates with a staff that has scarcely grown in twenty years. It receives 0.7 per cent of the UN budget. The 1993 Vienna Conference urged an increase.

Aside from those bodies formally dedicated to human rights activities, many (in an important sense all) UN organs and activities affect or have the potential to affect human rights. A 1989 so-called 'in-depth evaluation of UN

---

[57] GA Res. 2263 (XXII) of 7 Nov. 1967, and GA Res. 34/180 of 18 Dec. 1979.
[58] See Donna J. Sullivan, 'The Implementation of Women's Rights: The Effectiveness of Existing Procedures', in International League for Human Rights, *In Brief: Human Rights at the UN* (New York, 1990).
[59] See Byrnes and Gaer, in *In Brief*, 51 (New York, 1992).

human rights programmes' organized by the UN Secretariat identified 'at least eight . . . which contain elements [related to human rights]'. They included programmes on food and agriculture, human settlements, development, and science and technology, which were seen as being related to such economic and social rights as the rights to food, to adequate housing, and the general right to development.[60]

In noting a strong interrelationship between UN development programmes and the advancement of human rights, the internal evaluation entered contested terrain. One of the striking features of UN life, manifest at the 1993 World Conference in Vienna, is the fierce resistance of most Third World governments to the integration of human rights criteria into the UN's development work.

Provoked by the evaluation's recommendation that the Centre for Human Rights advise on UN Development Programme (UNDP) country projects involving human rights, they laboured successfully to block endorsement of the entire evaluation. Similarly, in 1991, when the UNDP's Human Development Report included a Human Freedom Index, Third World governments sought a formal directive forbidding mention of the subject in any future reports. Despite refinement in the Index's methodology (including a name change to the 'Political Freedom Index') and promises to consult with countries before evaluating them, the Group of 77, through its Pakistani president, rejected inclusion of such an index or ranking in any future studies. Evident among the Group's principal concerns was the prospect that the index—in other words a country's human rights performance—would some day be used to condition aid.[61]

Other than the Human Rights Centre itself, the UN organ with the most direct connection to the promotion of human rights is the Vienna-based Programme in Social Development and Humanitarian Affairs. Among the key instruments adopted or initiated by the Programme's

[60] UN doc. E/AC.51/1989/2, pp. 48–9.
[61] See UNDP, *Human Development Report 1991* (New York and Oxford, 1991), pp. 18–21, 98; and 'Regional Consultations on the Human Development Report', UN doc. UNDP/1992/13 of 22 Jan. 1992.

quinquennial Crime Congresses have been the Standard Minimum Rules for the Treatment of Prisoners, the Code of Conduct for Law Enforcement Officials, Basic Principles on the Independence of the Judiciary, and the Declaration of Basic Principles of Justice for Victims of Crime and the Abuse of Power.[62]

(d) The Human Rights Machinery: Praxis

It is a commonplace of scholarship to discern three phases in UN human rights activities during which the main focus was, in turn, standard-setting (conventions and declarations); promotion (advisory services, broad studies, and an incipient reporting system); and protection (establishment of procedures for assessing information received from private persons and groups concerning possible gross violations and reporting thereon to the general membership, fact-finding in certain cases where member states allege grave violations, and efforts to mitigate or terminate violations in particular cases). 'Since 1977', according to two scholars who seem to endorse this temporal ordering of UN activity, 'a fourth stage has ... emerged, which emphasizes the structural and economic aspects of human rights issues.'[63]

Like all scholarly efforts to order the confused scrum of life, these phases correspond only roughly to actual events within the UN system. For instance, the fact that the so-called fourth stage (also referred to commonly as the recognition of 'third generation rights') manifests itself to a large extent in proposed declarations and similar efforts at norm generation[64] nicely illustrates the overlapping, indeed cumulative, character of these phases.

[62] For an overview of the work of the Programme's Crime Committee and its relationship to UN human rights programmes, see Roger S. Clark, 'Human Rights and the UN Committee on Crime Prevention and Control', *Annals of the American Academy of Arts and Sciences*, 506 (1989), pp. 68–84.

[63] Schwelb and Alston, 'The Principal Institutions', pp. 250–1.

[64] For a biting and persuasive critique of efforts to transform every sort of interest, but particularly those frequently included in lists of 'third generation rights', into a human right, see Philip Alston, 'Conjuring up New Human Rights: A Proposal for Quality Control', *American Journal of International Law*, 78 (1984),

The phases themselves are not the expression of an ineluctable logic of sequence. One can argue, for instance, that standards spelt out in the first phase had in fact already been set even before the main human rights conventions were drawn up. Implicit in the Nuremberg indictments in 1945 was the proposition that, at least with respect to the right to life and freedom from torture, there already were clear norms. As for other rights essential to even the slimmest conception of human dignity, surely they were stated with sufficient clarity in the 1948 Universal Declaration to allow their immediate use for assessing the behaviour of member states.

One can also argue that the long years of the second phase, of advisory services and broad studies, were far from an essential precondition of the third phase, concerned with protection. Violations of those rights (like the right to life) the centrality of which is universally admitted— as evidenced, for example, by provisions in the principal

p. 607. He argues, therein, that the General Assembly's role as the authoritative definer of human rights is in serious danger of being undermined. The problem, as he sees it, is as follows: 'First, the General Assembly has, on several occasions in recent years, proclaimed new rights (i.e., rights which do not find explicit recognition in the Universal Declaration of Human Rights or the two International Human Rights Covenants) without explicitly acknowledging its intention of doing so and without insisting that the claims in question should satisfy any particular criteria before qualifying as human rights. Second, there has been a growing tendency on the part of a range of United Nations and other international bodies, including in particular the UN Commission on Human Rights, to proceed to the proclamation of new human rights without reference to the Assembly. Third, the ease with which such innovation has been accomplished in these bodies has in turn encouraged or provoked the nomination of additional candidates, ranging from the right to tourism to the right to disarmament, at such a rate that the integrity of the entire process of recognizing human rights is threatened.' Alston has been consistent and consistently persuasive in his scepticism. In an article published two years earlier he wrote: 'In many respects the concept of third generation rights smacks rather too strongly of a tactical endeavour to bring together, under the rubric of human rights, many of the most pressing concerns on the international agenda and to construct an artificial international consensus in favour of human rights by appealing to the "favourite" concerns of each of the main geopolitical blocs . . . In sum, the concept of third generation solidarity rights would seem to contribute more obfuscation than clarification in an area which can ill afford to be made less accessible to the masses than it already is.' 'A Third Generation of Solidarity Rights: Progressive Development or Obfuscation of International Human Rights Law?', *Netherlands International Law Review*, 29 (1982), p. 322.

covenants and conventions making them non-derogable—
have long been readily identifiable in any and every
context. Governments have not been in doubt about the
content of their obligations. The UN's protective activity,
such as it has been, came last and late because a large
proportion of governments, while not insisting on a plenary
discretion in the choice of means for their various ends,
were reluctant to subject themselves to the risk of exposure. Viewed only as an institution engaged in standard-
setting, the UN looks impressive. By very large majorities,
and now commonly without vote or by unanimity, the
General Assembly has approved declarations and conventions broadly elaborating the core rights of human dignity.
Its subordinate body, ECOSOC, has also set significant
standards. It has, for instance, gone beyond condemning
slavery to identifying and prohibiting slavery-like practices
such as debt bondage, trafficking in women, and sale of
children.[65] And in spelling out the rights of women, the
General Assembly itself has cut right across the grain of
custom in more than a few member states. When,
however, one views its efforts to protect the actual exercise
of enumerated rights, something less engaging meets the
eye.

1. The problematics of protection

To appreciate the UN's present capacity for protective
activity, one needs to examine the actions and omissions of
the Commission on Human Rights and the Sub-Commission
and their interactions with ECOSOC and the General
Assembly over the course of almost half a century, and to
look as well at the work of the Human Rights Committee
operating under the terms of the Covenant on Civil and
Political Rights. Attributing any capacity at all to the UN

[65] Supplementary Convention on the Abolition of Slavery, the Slave Trade,
and Institutions and Practices Similar to Slavery, adopted by Conference of
Plenipotentiaries convened by ECOSOC Res. 608, 21 UN ESCOR supp. no. 1
at p. 7, UN doc. E/2889 (1956), and done at Geneva on 7 Sept. 1956; entered
into force 30 Apr. 1957. For a balanced and hence somewhat mordant review
of UN activity with respect to the problem of slavery, see Kathryn Zoglin,
'United Nations Action against Slavery: A Critical Evaluation', *Human Rights
Quarterly*, 8 (1986), pp. 306–39.

or for that matter to other institutions both public and private engaged in protective activity requires a certain leap of faith in the efficacy of one weapon: exposure by a credible fact-finder.

The organs of the United Nations concerned with human rights, above all the Commission on Human Rights together with its institutional superior ECOSOC, have not, until recently, evinced much enthusiasm for the protective mission. Nor for much of their life were they vulnerable to the charge of impartiality. In light of the resounding affirmation of rights in the Universal Declaration, the Commission's timid beginnings seem especially repulsive. As early as January 1947, when the members of the Commission on Human Rights gathered for their first regular session, the UN had already received a large number of letters containing allegations of human rights violations.[66] In effect, the Commission was being petitioned for assistance in obtaining the redress of grievances against member states.

As noted above, it responded to this initial opportunity to define some protective role by concluding that it had none.[67] In the words of the report of that first session summarizing the Commission's reaction to individual communications: 'The Commission recognizes that it has no power to take any action in regard to any complaints concerning human rights.'[68] In what seemed an effort to avoid even inadvertent pressure on governments accused of human rights violations, it also decided that communications containing such allegations would not be circulated to the individual members even on a confidential basis. Rather they would receive, but only in private meetings, a confidential list containing only a brief, presumably sanitized indication of the substance of these dangerous if not positively offensive epistles.

To one of the legal paladins of that day, the Cambridge don Hersch Lauterpacht, the Human Rights Commission's crippling act of self-denial was wholly unjustified,[69] a view

[66] Schwelb and Alston, 'The Principal Institutions', p. 270.
[67] See above, nn. 25 and 26.   [68] E/259 (1947), paras 21 and 22.
[69] H. Lauterpacht, *International Law and Human Rights* (New York, 1950, repr. 1968), pp. 223–62.

the Economic and Social Council was unable to share. At the first opportunity it explicitly endorsed the Commission's position[70] while coincidentally rejecting a request from the Commission on the Status of Women for a clear mandate to make recommendations to the Council on urgent problems requiring immediate attention in defence of women's rights.[71]

For more than twenty years thereafter the UN Commission on Human Rights remained an instrument of non-protection lounging under the protective wing of ECOSOC. As proof of its existence, it summoned the energy to draft soaring standards and issue occasional reports of a comfortably general character. Yet, despite its fierce commitment to inoffensiveness, the Commission could not always manage to match ECOSOC's reticence. In 1950 it requested establishment of a system of annual human rights reports by member states. The Council responded by returning the proposal for further study.[72] And there it might have remained had not the United States taken up the matter in 1953, apparently as a counterweight to its concurrent declaration that it would not become a party to any general human rights treaty.[73] United States' support produced a prodding resolution addressed by the General Assembly to ECOSOC.[74] The latter body, moving with all its deliberate speed, managed in only three years to adopt an operative resolution.[75] This left the very making of a report to the discretion of states, so the reporting process was not calculated to upset any of the world's chancelleries.

It was not until 1967, the twentieth anniversary of the doctrine of impotence, that the Human Rights Commission and ECOSOC collaborated both to annul it and to concede the legitimacy and value of communications from the unofficial world of victims and their non-governmental

[70] See above, n. 26.   [71] ECOSOC Res. 76(V) of 5 Aug. 1947.
[72] ECOSOC Res. 303 E(XI) (1950).
[73] Statement by Secretary of State John Foster Dulles before the US Senate Judiciary Committee, 6 Apr. 1953, reproduced in 'Review of the United Nations Charter, A Collection of Documents, 83rd Congress, 2nd session', Senate doc. no. 87, 1954, pp. 295–6.   [74] GA Res. 739 (VIII) of 28 Nov. 1953.
[75] ECOSOC Res. 624 B (XXII) (1956).

champions.[76] The doctrine's fortifications collapsed under the weight of African voting power, which by the mid-1960s was becoming a decisive factor at the UN. In balancing their own vulnerability to charges of delinquency against their goal of ending colonial and racist rule in southern Africa, the African states came down in favour of risking the former to advance the latter.

The beginning of the end of the doctrine of impotence was signalled in 1965 when the Committee of Twenty-Four summoned ECOSOC's attention to information concerning violation of human rights in southern Africa submitted by petitioners to the Committee. As if awakened thereby from a long dream of sleep, ECOSOC responded immediately by inviting the Commission on Human Rights to consider as a matter of importance and urgency the question of the violation of human rights, including policies of racial discrimination and segregation and of apartheid in all countries, with particular reference to colonial and other dependent countries and territories, and to submit its recommendations on measures to halt those violations.[77] The extension of such scrutiny to include 'all countries' came at the initiative of the Western members of ECOSOC in the face of efforts by the resolution's sponsors—the USSR, Algeria, Cameroon, and Tanzania—to restrict the focus entirely to colonial and dependent territories.[78]

In their valuable survey of human rights institutions under the Charter, Schwelb and Alston summarize the successive actions of the General Assembly, ECOSOC, the Human Rights Commission, and the Sub-Commission on Discrimination and Minorities. During the period 1966–71 these bodies fashioned the machinery for human rights protection which has continued to operate without fundamental change.[79] The principal components of its normative framework are Commission resolution 8 (XXIII) of

[76] See generally Richard Lillich, *International Human Rights: Problems of Law, Policy, and Practice* (2nd edn., Boston, 1991), pp. 381–92.

[77] ECOSOC Res. 1102 (XL) (1966).

[78] See Tolley, 'The Concealed Crack', p. 426, for further discussion of this initiative and the way in which East–West rivalry affected the development of the new initiative.

[79] Schwelb and Alston, 'The Principal Institutions', pp. 272–3.

1967 and ECOSOC resolutions 1235 of 1967 and 1503 of 1970. In resolution 8 the Commission added an agenda item on the 'Question of Violations' and, in a marked expansion of Sub-Commission jurisdiction beyond the problems of minorities, directed it to bring to the attention of the Commission 'any situation which it has reasonable cause to believe reveals a consistent pattern of violations . . . [and] to prepare . . . a report containing information on violations of human rights and fundamental freedoms from all available sources'. Under its resolution the Commission could choose to initiate 'a thorough study' of the described situations which it said were exemplified by apartheid in South Africa and racial discrimination in Southern Rhodesia.

In resolution 1235, adopted on 6 June 1967, ECOSOC welcomed the Commission's decision, and declared the Commission's and the Sub-Commission's right 'to examine information relevant to gross violations of fundamental rights and fundamental freedoms' contained in the individual communications which, under ECOSOC's successive edicts, had been screened from Commission review since 1947.

These steps left in their wake uncertainty about the way in which communications would be handled and employed; and about the willingness of the Sub-Commission, Commission, and ECOSOC actually to study, much less publicize, human rights violations occurring outside southern Africa. Sensitivity on the latter point surfaced during the debate preceding the adoption of resolution 1235, expressed in the form of objections (from representatives of the United Kingdom, the Philippines, and Tanzania) to the very idea of studies being made without the target state's consent,[80] and in the successful amendment pressed by the Soviet Union and Afro-Asian states making racial discrimination the primary point of concern.[81] Continued sensitivity about publicizing the contents of private communications became apparent when some governments objected to use

[80] UN docs. E/AC.7/SR.567, E/AC.7/SR.569 (1967)
[81] Tolley, 'The Concealed Crack', p. 428.

by Sub-Commission experts of such communications as evidence in reports under resolution 1235 describing human rights violations by named states.[82]

While efforts by the Eastern bloc and most Afro-Asian states to impose a narrow focus as a matter of principle continued to be defeated by small margins, in practice the Human Rights Commission advanced only with studied caution beyond southern Africa and the territories occupied by Israel during the 1967 Middle East war. Moreover, the procedures finally adopted for handling private communications eased the concerns animating advocates of the narrow focus. Authorized by ECOSOC resolution 1503 (XLVIII) of 1970 ('Procedure for dealing with communications relating to violations of human rights and fundamental freedoms'), and elaborated by the Sub-Commission on Discrimination and Minorities in 1971, they operate in the following manner.[83]

Personnel of the UN Centre for Human Rights (formerly the Human Rights Division) prepare summaries of the hundreds of thousands of communications received annually alleging violations of human rights, and forward them to a five-member Working Group of the Sub-Commission on Discrimination and Minorities. The Working Group convenes for two weeks each summer, just prior to the annual four-week meeting of the Sub-Commission, and decides whether communications concerning a particular government, considered in light of that government's response, if any, 'appear to reveal a consistent pattern of gross and reliably attested violations of human rights and fundamental freedoms'. All communications satisfying that criterion, in the opinion of a majority of the Working Group (which must have the usual geographic balance), are placed on the Sub-Commission's agenda. The Working Group's meetings are closed and its decisions confidential.

Since neither the Secretariat nor the Working Group inform correspondents that their letters or petitions are

[82] Ibid., p. 429.
[83] There is a concise description ibid., at pp. 429–53. Lillich, *International Human Rights*, pp. 388–441, provides a well-documented and annotated case-study (Greece under military rule) of the organization's 1503 procedures.

being considered, the petitioners, if they are to supplement their original communication at all, must do so blindly—that is, without any knowledge either of the Working Group's initial reaction or of the contents of a government's response. The Working Group could, but apparently does not, alleviate this difficulty—indeed, one could argue, this fundamental unfairness in its procedures—by exercising its discretion to seek additional information. Yet resolution 1503 explicitly authorizes the Sub-Commission to take into account not only the communications brought before it by the Working Group and the replies of governments but also 'other relevant information'. Exclusion of correspondents and petitioners continues through all stages of the 1503 procedure.

Cases forwarded by the Sub-Commission (which often acts as if it enjoyed an uninhibited discretion to regulate the traffic[84]) must then pass successfully through the Commission's own five-member Working Group before arriving at last on the Commission's agenda. The Commission (deliberating in private) is empowered under resolution 1503 to respond in a variety of ways. It may, in effect, dismiss the case (technically it terminates consideration) either by finding that a consistent pattern of gross violations has not been established or, apparently, for any other reason it deems satisfactory. Or it may keep the case on its agenda for further consideration at a later session (a minimum delay of one year). Or it may decide to initiate a 'thorough study' of the situation, with or without the consent of the concerned government. Or, with the consent of the relevant government, it may investigate the situation through the medium of an *ad hoc* committee of 'independent persons whose competence and impartiality is beyond question'.

As an alternative, however, the Human Rights Commission could break out of the constraints of the resolution 1503 procedure. Drawing on its authority under resolution

[84] Most notoriously in 1972, when it decided to send the Greece, Iran, and Portugal cases back to its Working Group, ostensibly to provide the governments with yet additional time to respond. Since that inauspicious beginning, the Sub-Commission has been considerably less inhibited.

1235, it can appoint an *ad hoc* working group or a special rapporteur to study the situation, prepare a report and draft recommendations which the Commission can then debate publicly, adopt, and forward to ECOSOC.[85] Governments facing indictments have made strenuous efforts to bar public debate (and, *a fortiori*, action) concerning situations being considered under 1503—efforts which have, unfortunately, succeeded in some cases.[86]

[85] For an overview of the interaction between 1235 and 1503 procedures, see Tolley, 'The Concealed Crack', pp. 449–53. One example of the movement from confidential to public procedures is the case of Afghanistan. Monitoring under 1503 was discontinued in 1984 when the Commission appointed a Special Rapporteur to prepare a report. Paraguay has been subject to both procedures simultaneously; each one focused, however, on a different aspect of the situation in that country: alleged massacre and enslavement of Indian tribes was the subject of a 1503 procedure while a public resolution under 1235 addressed the country's prolonged state of siege. In 1982 Iran's treatment of the Bahais was the subject of both a public resolution and a confidential referral. Sub-Commission Res. 1982/25, UN doc. E/CN.4/1983/4.

[86] Tolley concludes acerbically that '[t]o the extent that an oppressive government feigns cooperation with the Commission's confidential scrutiny, it can escape public inquiry and political shame under the Resolution 1235 procedure'. He cites, as a case in point, the Commission's failure to place on its agenda the situation in Argentina during the era of the disappeared ('The Concealed Crack', p. 457). In contrast, the Argentine regime's contemporaneous effort to avert an Inter-American Commission on Human Rights report by a show of formal cooperation (e.g. rapid response to enquiries about disappeared persons; but in almost every case the substance of the response was a denial that the person had been detained by the security forces) was not successful. The most detailed account of the lengths to which Argentina went to avoid consideration under 1503, and then, later, to encourage it precisely in order to keep the discussion confidential, can be found in Iain Guest's piercing study *Behind the Disappearances: Argentina's Dirty War against Human Rights and the United Nations* (Philadelphia, 1990), esp. pp. 115–21 and 135–45. At the request of the successor government of Raul Alfonsin, the UN has made public the files from its 1503 procedure for Argentina. ECOSOC decision 1985/156 of 30 May 1985. See UN docs. E/CN.4/1985/Argentina, vols. i–vi. In 1977 a majority of the Commission invoked the confidential procedures while blocking a public inquiry into the situation in Idi Amin's Uganda. See statement of Mr Kooijmans of The Netherlands in UN doc. E/CN.4/1985/SR.45. Commission practice with respect to presentations by non-governmental organizations has been erratic. See Menno Kamminga and Nigel Rodley, 'Direct Intervention at the UN: NGO Participation in the Commission on Human Rights and its Sub-Commission', in Hannum, *Guide to International Human Rights Practice*, pp. 195–6: 'In 1978, an informal agreement was reached among members of the Commission that no public reference to situations which had already been considered behind closed doors under the 1503 procedure should be allowed. Several NGO representatives were interrupted during their oral statements and asked to identify the countries to which they were referring. If it was a country that had already been

2. 'Action' under resolutions 1235 and 1503

At the time of its adoption, resolution 1503 was widely seen by scholars and activists as a step beyond resolution 1235 in the development of protective machinery. This perception probably stemmed from the fact that, while initiatives under 1235 lie entirely in the hands of member states and hence are inevitably governed by political criteria, 1503 gave the power of initiative for the first time to individuals and non-governmental organizations. Under it, they could trigger action, even if only the action of confronting unpleasant facts of international life. To many, this seemed an enormously valuable precedent, a breach in the citadel of the mutual protection society, one that could be progressively enlarged. Perhaps in the long run it will turn out that the optimists were right. But to this point, 1235 has shown greater promise. What can nevertheless be said for resolution 1503 proceedings is that at least they have ceased to be a bottomless receptacle for petitions of the desperate.

UN action during the first years of the process was enough to depress Dr Pangloss. The case of Greece under military rule, 1967–74, was an early and well-documented fiasco.[87] A complaint was initiated by an extremely detailed and well-documented communication submitted by various private human rights organizations. Over a two-year period it was tossed forward and backward and forward again by the Sub-Commission and its Working Group, then dropped altogether by the former when the Greek military regime released a large number of detainees without altering at all the system of arbitrary detention and torture which had originally gobbled them up.

considered under the 1503 procedure, the NGO was prohibited from continuing its statement. The agreement applied only to that session, however, and in 1980 the Commission resorted to its earlier practice of scheduling the public discussion of country situations before the 1503 procedure, thus avoiding the problem.' They go on to point out that in 1981 the chair ruled, in effect, that NGO reference to particular countries was all right so long as a statement did not refer to decisions made or materials submitted under the confidential procedures.

[87] See Lillich, *International Human Rights*, pp. 388–441.

Idi Amin's Uganda was another case to pass vagrantly through the maze established by 1503. Communications concerning this regime of mass murder did reach the Human Rights Commission, apparently having been referred there by the Commission Working Group and the Sub-Commission in 1974 and again in 1976 and 1977.[88] Not until 1978, on the eve of Amin's flight following defeat by the Tanzanian armed forces aided by Ugandan insurgents, did the Commission take any action at all. That action assumed the form of a request to the Secretary-General to appoint a Special Representative to Uganda under the confidential procedure.

Like others who would later be dispatched pursuant to 1503, the representative was given the vague mandate to make 'direct contacts' with the government and to report back. Inconsequential as this mission was regarding the situation in Uganda, it did serve as the seminal precedent for the extension of technical assistance ('advisory services') to governments trying with at least some show of sincerity to effect the transition back from a government of terror to one conducted by more-or-less legitimate means.[89] A second positive result of the Ugandan fizzle, according to Amnesty International's UN observer at the time, was 'to [shake] up the system so much that it led to a number of developments which had not been politically possible or had not been thought of before'.[90]

Although, as already suggested, the Sub-Commission on Discrimination and Minorities can hardly be accused of carrying out its tasks with reckless zeal, since 1973 it has forwarded for Human Rights Commission consideration

---

[88] Tolley 'The Concealed Crack', p. 442.

[89] Although this area was expanded in the late 1980s, one close observer of the UN human rights machinery has argued that the UN Centre for Human Rights 'lacked the skills, authority, and most importantly the professional resources necessary [to provide this kind of assistance adequately]'. Margo Picken, 'A Review of the UN Advisory and Technical Assistance Programs in Human Rights', in Radda Barnen and the International Commission of Jurists, Swedish Section, *UN Assistance for Human Rights* (Sept. 1988), p. 31.

[90] Ibid., p. 119.

a substantial number of cases.[91] They have included regimes aligned with both the USA and the former USSR, as well as some more-or-less unaligned in global politics. Two experts in the non-governmental community, Frank Newman and David Weissbrodt, estimate a referral rate from the Sub-Commission Working Group of eight to ten cases a year.[92] From 1978, when the Commission began naming countries that had been the subject of 'decisions' (without at first indicating the nature of the decision) to 1992, some forty-six countries[93] had been the subject of some Commission decision (including being dropped from the agenda). Latin American countries took up the lion's share of 1503 decisions during the 1970s and early 1980s. But by the beginning of the 1990s, African and Asian countries were beginning to predominate.[94]

While the names have changed, inaction under 1503 remains all too common. Since adoption of the 1503 procedure, the Commission has neither exercised its power to undertake a thorough study nor sought the consent of a delinquent state for the creation of an investigating committee.[95]

[91] Tolley 'The Concealed Crack', p. 446, lists twenty-eight governments subject to Commission decisions under resolution 1503 from 1978 to 1984. They were as follows: seven in *Africa*: Benin, Central African Republic, Equatorial Guinea, Ethiopia, Malawi, Mozambique, Uganda; nine in *Asia*: Afghanistan, Burma, Indonesia, Iran, Japan, Republic of Korea, Malaysia, Pakistan, Philippines; nine in *Latin America*: Argentina, Bolivia, Chile, El Salvador, Guatemala, Haiti, Paraguay, Uruguay, Venezuela; two in *eastern Europe*: Albania, German Democratic Republic; one in *western Europe and other*: Turkey. By 1992 eleven more had been subject to confidential decisions, including Chad, Somalia, Sudan, Zaïre, Brunei Darussalam, and Myanmar (Burma), which were continued for at least one year, and Iraq, Syria, Gabon, Grenada, and Honduras, none of which was actually taken up for continuing consideration. See UN Commission on Human Rights reports, UN docs. E/CN.41984/14, 22, E/CN.4/1986/22, E/CN.4/1987/18, E/CN.4/1988/12, E/CN.4/1989/20, E/CN.4/1990/22, E/CN.4/1991/22, and E/CN.4/1992/84.

[92] F. Newman and D. Weissbrodt, *International Human Rights* (Cincinnati, 1991), p. 119.

[93] Confidential interview with Felice Gaer, Jan. 1992.

[94] See UN doc. E/1991/22, p. 268. Zaïre has agreed to receive UN theme special rapporteurs to conduct fact-finding inquiries independent of the 1503 procedure. See further E/CN.4/1992/84, p. 298.

[95] The closest it has come is in the case of Equatorial Guinea, another of the great abbatoirs of our time. For depressing accounts see Thomas Franck, *Nation against Nation* (Oxford, 1985), pp. 234–5; and Marc Bossuyt, 'The Development of Special Procedures of the United Nations Commission on Human Rights', *Human Rights Law Journal*, 6 (1985), p. 179.

Although the two specific provisions of 1503 authorizing systematic inquiry have really not been utilized, the Commission has improvised informal mechanisms of interaction with target governments that contain at least a potentially inquisitorial element, albeit one that has been employed with extreme delicacy. The principal mechanisms are written questions and the dispatch of one or more Commission representatives (normally a member or 'independent expert') to 'establish direct contacts' and then report back.[96] Even in the grossest cases, such as Myanmar (Burma) and Haiti, this has not resulted in the production of public conclusions and recommendations under the 1503 procedure itself. However, by 1992 both had been moved to the 1235 public procedure and assigned special rapporteurs. The same happened to Zaïre in 1993.

The 1503 procedure, once the subject of great hopes, has simply not lived up to them. While its painfully slow and secret processes can in theory be a means of gradually increasing pressure on offending governments, in practice they seem to have served more often as a screen behind which gross violators dance a long, slow, diplomatic minuet without ceasing to torture and kill. We see no reason to disagree with Newman and Weissbrodt's conclusion that '[if] the objective is to obtain prompt publicity or public action for serious human rights violations, the 1503 procedure is inappropriate'.[97]

While the Commission has done little to vitalize the 1503 procedure, it has not abjured a protective function. As already suggested, it has acted, either expressly or implicitly, pursuant to the grant of authority under resolution 1235 and/or *ad hoc* requests for action from the General Assembly or ECOSOC. The brutal overthrow of the democratically elected government of Salvador Allende in Chile in 1973 stimulated the first serious rights-protecting initiative of the Commission—and, indeed, of the UN system as a whole—which was not related to conditions in colonial territories, Israeli-occupied territories, and South Africa.

[96] See Newman and Weissbrodt, *International Human Rights*, p. 120.
[97] Ibid., p. 123.

Thomas Franck, in his useful and provocative study of the UN, *Nation against Nation*, describes the system's response:

On March 1, 1974, the Commission . . . [authorized] its chairman to address a cable to the Chilean military authorities expressing the members' concern for the protection of the lives of political prisoners and calling for strict observance of the principles of the United Nations Charter and the International Covenants on Human Rights. ECOSOC, by consensus, quickly seconded that demand. Next, the Sub-Commission . . . called for a 'study' of Chilean human rights violations, and the General Assembly—charging the Chilean junta with 'gross and massive violations,' including 'the practice of torture' and operating 'concentration camps'—demanded the immediate release of all political prisoners and safe conduct out of the country for those who desired it.

In the spring of 1975 the Human Rights Commission set up a working group of five members to inquire into these charges. Although the working group was refused admission to Chile, it was able to report to the 1975 Assembly, which, in turn, expressed '*its profound distress* at the constant flagrant violations of human rights, including the institutionalized practice of torture, cruel, inhuman or degrading treatment or punishment, arbitrary arrest, detention and exile.' . . . The vote on this resolution was 95 to 11, with 23 abstentions. The United States, Canada, and all of Western Europe voted for its adoption.[98]

Since the establishment of the Chile Working Group, UN human rights investigations of particular countries have been carried out by other *ad hoc* working groups, by special rapporteurs of the Commission, or by experts appointed by the UN Secretary-General (called 'Special Representatives'). In March 1993 the subjects of such 1235 procedures included Afghanistan (since 1984), Cuba (since 1991), Haiti (since 1992, having been considered previously by an 'Expert' under the Advisory Services rubric), Iran (since 1984), Iraq (since 1991), Myanmar (since 1992), South Africa (since 1967), the former Yugoslavia (since the first-ever emergency session of the Commission in 1992), Sudan (since 1993), and Occupied Territories (since 1993). Experts with essentially the same investigative

---

[98] Franck, *Nation against Nation*, pp. 238–9.

and reporting responsibilities as the Rapporteurs and Special Representatives were appointed in 1992 for El Salvador (succeeding a Special Rapporteur operating since 1981), and Equatorial Guinea (which had an Expert appointed under the 'Advisory Services' rubric for over a decade). Special Representatives were appointed for Cambodia and Somalia in 1993 under 'Advisory Services'.

The confused reader should note that the precise title and agenda item under which a country-investigator is appointed to carry out the work has become a source of considerable politicking within the Commission, and several countries have been 'promoted' or 'demoted' from year to year to less or more onerous formulas. A rough hierarchy has been emerging, with 'Special Rapporteur' (of the Commission, appointed by its chair) at the top, followed by 'Special Representative' of the Secretary-General (who appoints the person), and by 'Independent Expert' (appointed by the Commission or Secretary-General, depending on the resolution), who may operate either under the resolution 1235 'Gross violations' agenda topic where country situations are normally considered, or under 'Advisory Services'. The latter is nominally at the request of the government involved, and presumed to be a less confrontational form of attention to a country deemed less deserving of the opprobrium of being designated under the 'violations' rubric; in practice, however, the Experts under Advisory Services have often been assigned the same fact-finding and reporting functions as those appointed under resolution 1235.[99]

[99] Three countries under continuing study (as of Jan. 1993) have seen Commission scrutiny shift: (1) Equatorial Guinea (Special Rapporteur, 1979–80; Expert under the 'Advisory Services' agenda item, 1980–92; Expert under the 1235 'Violations . . .' agenda item, beginning 1992); (2) Guatemala (Special Rapporteur under 1235 'Violations' item, 1983–6; Special Representative under 1235, 1986–7; Expert under 'Advisory Services', 1987–92 and continuing); and (3) Haiti (Expert, 1987–91, under different agenda items; Special Rapporteur, beginning 1992). Five other countries were subjected previously to special procedures under 1235 in which individuals were appointed to examine and report on conditions: Bolivia (Special Envoy, 1981–4); Chile (*Ad Hoc* Working Group, 1973–8; Expert on Disappeared, 1977; Special Rapporteurs, 1979–91); occupied Kuwait (Special Rapporteur, 1992); Poland (Special Representative, 1982–4); Romania (Special Rapporteur, 1989–92). Additionally, the Commission

In practice these *ad hoc* arrangements have in varying degrees satisfied many of the conditions suggested earlier for effective enforcement institutions. They are normally staffed by independent experts who undertake detailed studies, where possible including on-site investigations, and who present reports publicly to their parent bodies and sometimes to the UN General Assembly as well. Often the country rapporteurs intercede with governments by transmitting appeals and inquiries regarding individual cases, sometimes on an urgent basis. The rapporteurs normally present findings and recommendations, and the Commission often adopts some or all of them.

Since the substantive criteria for determining when a country mechanism should be established have not been formalized and the mechanism itself has about it an air of the *ad hoc* in comparison to the over-elaborate procedures that often delay when they do not paralyse UN activities, and since at any given moment not every delinquent is

mandated the Secretary-General to provide it with reports on Nicaragua (1979) and Albania (1990–), although no special representative or expert was appointed to investigate conditions in either case. Commission resolutions which were critical, or at least concerned, about human rights conditions, but which did not establish ongoing special investigations, also addressed Democratic Kampuchea, Malawi, and (in 1993) Indonesia concerning East Timor. Apparently taking its cue from the presidential statements at the Security Council, the Commission has begun to adopt country-specific 'statements' read out by its chairman, negotiated in private but not requiring formal action. These statements—e.g. concerning Burma (1989), Lithuania and Latvia (1991), and Sri Lanka and East Timor (1992)—represent a consensus, but do not normally involve any 'special procedure' or investigator to follow up on the situation, nor do they appear among the resolutions or decisions of the Commission. Instead, the statements have been carefully hidden in the descriptive or procedural sections of the Commission's annual reports.

Since 1968, when the General Assembly established it, there has been scrutiny by the Special Committee to Investigate Israeli Practices affecting the Human Rights of the Population of the Occupied Territories. It reports directly to the Assembly and its three members are states, which designate government representatives. It thus differs from the Commission's country-specific procedures staffed by experts appointed under 1235 to serve in their personal capacity. For further details on the mandates, reports, and documents related to these procedures, see Felice D. Gaer, *United Nations 'Special Procedures' to Implement International Human Rights Guarantees: A Guide* (International League for Human Rights, New York, 1992); and Philip Alston, 'The Commission on Human Rights', in P. Alston (ed.), *The United Nations and Human Rights: A Critical Appraisal* (Oxford, 1992), pp. 159–64. See also United Nations, *United Nations Action in the Field of Human Rights* (UN, Geneva, 1988), pp. 264–82.

included, target states have tended to claim they have been chosen for political reasons. In light of the difficulty of identifying a target state that has not earned the distinction, one need not worry excessively about these claims. A legitimate source of concern, on the other hand, is the insufficiency of staff support and funds to support extended on-site visits.

More unsatisfactory still is the seemingly unprincipled variability in the mandates given working groups and rapporteurs. While some have been asked to conduct a thorough study (e.g., Afghanistan, El Salvador, Iraq), others (e.g. Iran, Cuba) have been asked only to establish direct contacts with the government. Permission to visit is then treated as a major accomplishment and may come to overshadow the ongoing condition of human rights. This can happen, however, even when the mandate appears to include an authorization for inquiry and report. Lacking rigorous mandates and clear precedents, eager for permission to enter and thereby to establish direct contact, certain rapporteurs have converted themselves into something more like mediators between the government and the international community and have correspondingly tempered their findings.[100]

3. Thematic working groups and rapporteurs

Because political pressure is exerted annually on the country-specific mechanisms and because of continuing claims that the selection of targets is not even-handed, support has been growing for thematic inquiries,[101] that

[100] See e.g. The Watch Committees, *Four Failures: A Report on the U.N. Special Rapporteurs on Human Rights in Chile, Guatemala, Iran and Poland* (New York, 1986); National Council for Resistance, *Human Rights Betrayed* (Paris, 1990); and International League for Human Rights, *In Brief: Iran—The First Human Rights Mission* (New York, June 1990).

[101] For more extended discussions of the mechanism, see M. T. Kamminga, 'The Thematic Procedures of the UN Commission on Human Rights', *Netherlands International Law Review*, 34 (1987), pp. 299–323; Nigel S. Rodley, 'United Nations Action Procedures against "Disappearances", Summary or Arbitrary Executions, and Torture', *Human Rights Quarterly*, 8 (1986), pp. 700–30; and David Weissbrodt, 'The Three "Theme" Special Rapporteurs of the UN Commission on Human Rights', *American Journal of International Law*, 80 (1986), pp. 685–99.

is, global inquiries into such phenomena as summary execution, officially organized disappearances, and arbitrary detention. These mechanisms were first used as a means for evading opposition to a focus on the extermination campaign carried out by the military government of Argentina in the period 1976 to 1979.[102] Since establishing the Working Group on Disappearances in 1980,[103] the Commission has authorized nine other so-called 'theme mechanisms': the themes are Summary and Arbitrary Executions (1982); Torture (1985); Religious Intolerance (1986); Mercenaries (1987); Sale of Children (1990), Arbitrary Detention (1991), Internally Displaced Persons (1992), Racism and Xenophobia (1993), and Freedom of Expression (1993). Most may, like the country-specific mechanism, intervene in individual cases for the purpose of taking 'effective action'; the exceptions to date are the Rapporteurs on Mercenaries and the Sale of Children, and the Representative on Internally Displaced Persons.

It seems fair to say that the theme mechanisms have fundamentally altered what the UN can and to some significant degree does accomplish in aiding victims of human rights violations. Each year the thousands of new appeals that arrive from all parts of the world actually find a concerned party able and in general willing to inquire into the condition of alleged victims and to do so with expedition in cases where there remains a chance of averting or mitigating the violation of their rights.

The persons participating in these mechanisms are experts, selected as such, and have in general seemed insulated from the sort of political pressure that cripples effective and impartial inquiry. They utilize information from all relevant sources, including non-governmental organizations. And, with rare exceptions, they place their activities, including details of their inquiries and the names of alleged victims, on the public record. Finally, any

---

[102] See generally Guest, *Behind the Disappearances*.

[103] For a detailed account of the activities of the Working Group, see J. Daniel Livermore and B. G. Ramcharan, '"Enforced or Involuntary Disappearances": An Evaluation of a Decade of United Nations Action', *Canadian Human Rights Yearbook, 1989–90*, pp. 217–30.

well-informed and impartial observer must conclude that in general the working groups and rapporteurs have used their mandates for all they were worth, including the making of recommendations that push beyond traditional thinking and practice at the UN.

All the above is good news. There is more to the story. Other than in the case of the Disappearances Working Group, the mechanisms do not result in systematic follow-up on cases after the initial inquiry. Even if additional information is received, it is not consistently communicated to the public. Persons outside the mechanisms or at least outside the overall human rights machinery usually do not receive information about what happens after a government responds to an inquiry. They never learn what, if anything, the rapporteur or group does or thinks can be done about unanswered or insufficiently answered inquiries.

Moreover, the reports generated by the thematic mechanisms are rarely discussed at the Commission on Human Rights in any systematic way. At best, they may come up in the course of general debate on an agenda item or in the discussion on 'gross violations'. The Commission does not discuss the accounts of on-site observations and often the visits are not even noted by name in the annual resolution welcoming the reports in the most general terms. Since exposure is the principal instrument at the disposal of the UN for the defence of human rights, the lack of open and sustained discussion and pointed resolutions limits the potential efficacy of the special procedures.

(e) The Future of UN Action in the Human Rights Field

The United Nations is now a participant, however ambivalent, in the defence of human rights. That is indisputable. Equally indisputable has been its highly uneven attitude toward enforcement and its reluctance outside the context of decolonization to recommend or appeal for sanctions purely on human rights grounds. Nor until the end of the Cold War were the great bulk of General Assembly or

Security Council Members inclined to concede a connection between gross violations of human rights and threats to the peace, the condition of UN enforcement action under Chapter VII of the Charter.

Now the sanguinary force of events in the Balkans and the Gulf, and the awful scenarios they conjure, have begun to shift the perceptions of governing élites, particularly in the West's most powerful states. In condemning 'the repression of the Iraqi civilian population', declaring that the consequences of that repression 'threaten international peace and security', demanding that Iraq 'immediately end this repression', insisting that Iraq 'allow immediate access by international humanitarian organizations to all those in need of assistance', and appealing 'to all Member States and to all humanitarian organizations to contribute to these humanitarian relief efforts', the Security Council seemed in its now famous resolution 688 of 5 April 1991 to be setting off in a direction that not long before appeared barred by immovable political forces.

Shortly thereafter, the precedent's implications broadened when US, British, and French troops, acting under the umbrella of resolution 688, established a safe haven for the Kurdish peoples in northern Iraq. That was quickly followed by agreements[104] between the regime in Baghdad and the United Nations allowing the latter to establish UN 'Humanitarian Centres' complete with UN guards in both the northern and southern parts of the country, an agreement negotiated against the background threat of indefinite continuation of humanitarian relief under the umbrella of coalition military force.

By itself, the Iraq case might be dismissed as *sui generis*, a kind of humanitarian intervention so entwined with a classic collective security operation as to be indistinguishable from it. But then in 1992 came the operations arising out of the disintegration of Yugoslavia, operations combining, on the one hand, peacekeeping and humanitarian aid, conditioned on consent of the relevant state parties, and, on the other, sanctions against Serbia, the *de facto*

---

[104] UN doc. S/22663 of 31 May 1991.

opponent of humanitarian aid. Here, too, one might try and mince the apparent precedent for collective humanitarian intervention by treating the dissolution of Yugoslavia into multiple independent states as an accomplished fact and thus converting the slaughter of Sarajevo into a breach of the peace. But the effort to do so cannot be wholly persuasive, because inter-ethnic and self-determination struggles among hostile regions of existing states, struggles marked by incremental and discriminating acts of recognition from the larger international community, are a likely paradigm of the dawning era. We can reasonably anticipate more Yugoslavias and therefore more calls for collective humanitarian initiatives backed, where necessary, by coercion. Likewise peacekeeping and even peace enforcement forces are increasingly tools of human rights protection.

The extent to which real democracy becomes widely established, and the success or otherwise of efforts to develop effective guarantees for minority interests,[105] will affect the incidence of inter-ethnic and separatist conflicts. In the wake of the Cold War the UN has finally become an agent for democratization and minority protection.[106]

With respect to the promotion of democracy, building on its oversight of decolonization plebiscites, the UN has recently become active as a monitor of electoral processes, a role expanded by a 1991 General Assembly resolution[107] into the provision of electoral aid. Indeed, UN ballot-monitoring in Namibia, Nicaragua, El Salvador, Angola, Haiti, Eritrea, Cambodia, Western Sahara, and Mozambique presages a much wider role as a participant in the administration of complex social and political transitions required for the settlement of chronic armed conflicts. As in the

[105] For an astute anticipation of today's minorities problems, see Inis L. Claude, Jr., *National Minorities: An International Problem* (Cambridge, Mass., 1955).

[106] The first and to this date only attempt by the UN at a comprehensive study of minority rights is Francesco Capotorti's 'Study on the Rights of Persons Belonging to Ethnic, Religious, and Linguistic Minorities' (reprint of UN doc. E/CN.4/Sub.2/384 and Adds. 1 to 7, June 1977).

[107] UN GA Res. 46/137, 17 Dec. 1991. See also UN doc. A/46/609 and Adds. 1 and 2, 1991, a report of the Secretary-General examining the UN's experience in election-monitoring together with comments from various member states on the advisability of an election-monitoring programme.

case of El Salvador, this role may include not only protecting people from renewed human rights abuse, but also providing the population with an account of past violations so that the new constitutional order can be construed on the basis of an authoritative—albeit often terrible—history.

Within its human rights organs, the United Nations has at last turned seriously to the question of minority rights. To be sure, the topic is not a stranger to the institution's agenda. Early in its life, and consistent with its named mission, the Sub-Commission on the Prevention of Discrimination and the Protection of Minorities set about trying to define 'minority' and to identify measures that the General Assembly could recommend to states for their protection. In the words of a Special Rapporteur appointed in the 1970s, the 'only positive accomplishment of the work accomplished between 1947 and 1954 was . . . the preparation of the draft text of Article 27 of the [Political] Covenant'.[108] In the latter year, having failed to achieve a consensus definition, the Sub-Commission abandoned the topic as such in favour of concentration on actions to promote non-discrimination.[109]

Article 27 of the Covenant declares: 'In those States in which ethnic, religious, or linguistic minorities exist, persons belonging to such minorities shall not be denied the right, in community with the other members of their group, to enjoy their own culture, to profess and practice their own religion or to use their own language.' That language could be read to impose obligations on governments to conduct public business in all the languages native to the cultural groups within the state's frontiers and to fund a multi-cultural education system. By concentrating on issues of non-discrimination, however, the Sub-Commission seemed to reject this reading in favour of the view that a minority's rights are best perceived as merely the sum of the rights of the individuals comprising

[108] Capotorti, 'Study on the Rights of . . . Minorities', p. 28.
[109] For an account of the historical evolution of the Sub-Commission's view of its task, see Nathan Lerner, 'From Protection of Minorities to Group Rights', *Israel Yearbook on Human Rights*, 18 (1988), pp. 101–20.

it, rights essentially indistinguishable from those enjoyed by the majority. All persons enjoy, for example, the right to freedom of religion and of association, plus the right not to be discriminated against on the basis of race, ethnicity, and other ascriptive traits.

The virtual exclusion of minority rights from the UN agenda amounted to standing the approach of the League of Nations on its head. For the League, while serving nominally as the guardian of the minority-rights provisions in various post-World War I treaties affecting the nations of eastern Europe, assumed no role in the protection of individual rights, a concept whose time had not yet come. Opposition to recognition of minority rights in the UN rested on several stated grounds: that they might again, as during the 1930s, serve as a pretext for foreign intervention; that they encouraged separatist tendencies threatening the territorial integrity of existing states; that the diversity of the condition of minorities precluded the evolution and even-handed application of universal standards; and that they could generate special measures of protection that would constitute reverse discrimination against majority interests.[110]

If not the rational force of these claims, then the political weight of those making them was sufficient to sidetrack the issue from 1954 until 1972, when the Sub-Commission commissioned Francesco Capotorti of Italy to undertake a study of the subject. A year after its completion in 1977, the Commission activated a Working Group to study a draft declaration on minority rights offered by none other than the Yugoslavian delegation. The Working Group proceeded at an extremely studied pace until, following the devolution of central authority in the Soviet Union and auguries of war in Yugoslavia, the General Assembly called for completion of a Commission-endorsed Declaration. Properly galvanized, the Commission completed its work rapidly, and the Declaration was adopted by the General Assembly in 1992.[111]

[110] These arguments, Capotorti notes in his report, 'are basically the same as those raised for many years in respect of international protection of human rights in general' ('Study on the Rights of . . . Minorities', p. iv).

[111] The General Assembly adopted the Declaration in Res. A/47/135 of 18 Dec. 1992.

Close analysis of the Declaration would carry us beyond the compass of this chapter.[112] Suffice it to say that the Declaration is notably vague in comparison to, for instance, the standards of fair treatment incorporated in the 1990 Copenhagen document of the Conference on Security and Cooperation in Europe (CSCE). The UN Declaration seemingly adheres to the view that minorities as collective entities have no rights independent of the individuals comprising them. It contains no enforcement mechanism, not even a reporting system.

The Declaration is no more than a beginning, a concession that the issues implicated in the phenomenon of intensely experienced sub-national communal identities cannot be evaded. It is increasingly clear that international peace and security requires the international community to take proactive measures including providing a forum where aggrieved communities can seek third party assistance in peaceful settlement and/or redress of grievances.

(f) Conclusion

The trajectory of political and social development within and among nations will determine the form and vigour of future UN-sponsored activity. Predicting that trajectory is work more for the seer than for the analyst. One thing can be said with confidence: human rights will remain a field strewn with political land mines.

How could it be otherwise? As Stanley Hoffmann noted shortly after the inauguration of Jimmy Carter: 'The issue of human rights, by definition, breeds confrontation. Raising the issue touches on the very foundations of a regime, on its sources and exercise of power, on its links to its citizens or subjects. It is a dangerous issue.'[113] But

---

[112] For an extended treatment see Patrick Thornberry, *The UN Declaration on the Rights of Persons Belonging to National or Ethnic, Religious and Linguistic Minorities* (London: Minority Rights Group, 1993). Cf. 'Report of the Working Group on the Rights of Persons Belonging to National, Ethnic, Religious, and Linguistic Minorities', UN doc. E/CN.4.1992/48, annexe 1.
[113] 'The Hell of Good Intentions', *Foreign Policy*, 29 (1977–8), p. 8.

the history of the years since World War II suggests that, absent a nuclear holocaust, it will remain an unavoidable one.

It will remain so despite the not infrequent claims of certain political leaders that many of the civil and political rights enumerated in the Universal Declaration and the other sacred texts, rather than reflecting universally relevant demands and interests, are provincial products of the West's singular historical experience and the liberal ideology stemming therefrom.[114]

Let us assume that the assumptions and values of liberalism have contributed enormously, perhaps were preconditions to, the idea of human rights, and have determined much of its content. And let us concede that liberalism is a product of Western origin. For that matter, so are socialism and nationalism and they certainly have found good markets throughout the world. The appetite for various Western ideologies may have spread in part because victory lends prestige to the ideas as well as to the bayonets of the victors, in part because an impulse to expand and exert influence has animated all Western institutions, including those organized to transmit culture and belief as well as those of a military, political, and economic character.

But surely cultural products spread for much the same reason as material ones—because they serve the consumer's needs. Nationalism helped to mobilize indigenous resistance to colonial rule and to stabilize the post-independence ethnic and tribal mix. Socialism, or at least its harsh communist deviation, helped for many years to justify concentration of power in the new political élites and to explain economic failure when it occurred. Liberalism had its problems for non-Western consumers, yet also a certain utility, initially as a means for eroding the moral basis of Western hegemony. Now, in the post-imperial era, for the burgeoning middle classes of the Third World it has the

---

[114] See e.g. the statement of Chinese Premier Li Peng to the first-ever heads-of-state meeting of the Security Council on 31 Jan. 1992. UN doc. S/PV.3046, pp. 92–3.

same appeal it had originally for their Western counter-parts who had invoked its name and its reasons as they fought to break loose from the suffocating grip of absolute monarchies and narrow aristocracies. The idea of human rights—today, in fact, a not always comfortable coalition of liberal and socialist values—may have been born in the West, but it has made its venue global.

The key question of whether human rights are universally applicable, or are conditioned by local, religious, or cultural differences, was confronted before and during the June 1993 World Conference on Human Rights in Vienna. The three intergovernmental regional preparatory meetings, held in Tunis, San José, and Bangkok, had emphasized the unacceptability of using human rights issues as a form of political pressure on states regarding their domestic actions. The Asian regional meeting in Bangkok had taken a notably hard line in favour of regional 'particularities'. By contrast, the Vienna Declaration and Programme of Action of June 1993 affirmed that universality is beyond question—a position strongly supported by the many NGOs from around the world. The Declaration cited the duty of all states to promote and protect human rights, and said that the lack of development can never be used as an excuse for noncompliance with human rights. However, it did admit elements of compromise, including a formulation which, echoing Bangkok, noted that 'the significance of national and regional particularities and various historical, cultural and religious backgrounds must be borne in mind'.

The 1993 Vienna Conference also adopted a Plan of Action, focusing significantly on implementation and institutional reform. The conference stressed the need to strengthen human rights protection mechanisms; and, after its most contentious debate, and notwithstanding Secretary-General Boutros Ghali's publicly expressed misgivings about such an innovation, it revived and endorsed the long-dormant proposal for the creation of the post of High Commissioner for Human Rights. The conference also advocated improved coordination of

human rights activities throughout the UN system, closer
links between peacekeeping and human rights, establishment of a special rapporteur on violence against women,
human rights field officers, and the long-overdue
provision of greater resources for the UN Centre for
Human Rights.

Out of the ruins of World War II came the Word, the
Universal Declaration. Since then, the word has acquired
a little flesh. Within its means, means so conspicuously
limited by the fact that material sanctions and incentives
remain at the discretionary disposition of powerful states,
the United Nations Organization has helped. Historical
perspective eases the pull of cynicism. Having won a
revolution in the name of man's inalienable rights, the
Founding Fathers of the United States incorporated slavery
into the new nation's constitutional foundations. Seventy-
six years passed before formal emancipation. And another
century passed before African-Americans in the United
States could enjoy the full rights of citizenship.

Finally it can honestly be claimed that the United
Nations Organization has reached the end of the beginning of serious efforts to protect the rights of the globe's
peoples. The distance it has travelled since its first timid
steps in the field offers one ground for optimism about its
future course. Another is the effort so many governments
have made to restrain the organization's forward progress
and to evade its primitive machinery of enforcement. By
their acts they have acknowledged the influence the idea
of human rights has acquired over the minds of their
subjects. Hypocrisy continues to offer credible evidence of
the possibility of virtue.

9

The UN and the Problem of
Economic Development

KENNETH DADZIE

THE first part of this chapter is a brief survey of the four main phases, and essential features, of the UN's involvement with economic development. The second part sets forth some personal reflections on the issues and challenges of the future.

One of the Purposes of the United Nations as set forth in its Charter is to achieve international cooperation in solving international problems of an economic and social character, and to be a centre for harmonizing the actions of nations in the attainment of this common end.[1] For this purpose the UN is required to promote higher standards of living, full employment, and conditions of economic and social progress, backed by a pledge by all member states to take joint and separate action in cooperation with the organization for the fulfilment of these objectives.[2] These propositions suggest that in 1945 the concept of interdependence was in the forefront of the thinking of the Charter's framers. They fully accepted that every country had an obligation to work towards the well-being of its people not only, of course, for its own sake, but also for the sake of the world community at large. The role of the UN was to promote international cooperation, and harmonize national actions favouring world economic growth and development.

By conventional measures, such as growth of per capita national income, and improvement in various other social and economic indicators, an unprecedented degree of

---

[1] UN Charter, Art. 1.   [2] Ibid., Arts. 55 and 56.

development has taken place since the UN's founding. Much of that development has been very uneven across and within countries and, of course, it was often not a direct product of UN-related activities. At the same time, poverty, disease, hunger, inadequate housing, unemployment, and other deprivations now exist on a much vaster absolute scale, and continue to grow.

(a) Four Phases of UN Involvement in Development

1. The first phase: 1945–1963

Four broad phases may be distinguished in the evolution of the UN's involvement with economic development since 1945. The first stretches from 1945 to 1963. One striking development at an early stage was the recognition by member states of the need for a measure of accountability to the international community in the economic and social domain. This development culminated in a report published in 1949 on national and international measures for full employment,[3] which led to a decision setting in motion a process of monitoring the progress of the world economy and the extent to which countries were meeting their employment commitments. The report also addressed the reduction of unemployment in the underdeveloped world, as it was then called, but only as an aspect of the broader question of world economic growth.

In this post-war colonial period systematic thinking on economic development was still in its infancy. The intellectual landmark of the period was a report prepared in 1950 by a group of five experts, which set the stage for UN development activity.[4] Curiously the report made no attempt to discuss the meaning of economic development, presumably because this was considered self-evident. Its main message was that underdeveloped countries should

---

[3] UN, *National and International Measures for Full Employment* (New York, 1949).

[4] *Measures for the Economic Development of Under-developed Countries* (UN, New York, 1951).

promote 'progressive attitudes and organizations', 'receptiveness to progressive technology', increased domestic capital formation, and reduced population growth. Thus development was essentially, indeed almost exclusively, a matter for 'measures requiring domestic action'. The report did, however, represent a departure from what was called 'colonial economics', in that it addressed the issue of society- and institution-building under the broad rubric of the preconditions for economic development, in which were included the removal of relevant structural impediments through, for instance, land reform. The report pointed to the administrative and legal actions, both in the public and private sectors, that were necessary for 'economic progress'. It also recognized a somewhat expanded role for government in the promotion of economic development, going beyond the simple provision of physical infrastructure, social services, and adminstration.

These ideas bear a noticeable resemblance, in their essentials, to those advanced by Professor Arthur Lewis, who was actually a member of the expert group, in his book *The Theory of Economic Growth*, published a few years later.[5] (Interestingly, domestic measures and policies were to resurface in the 1980s, in some circles, as the new hallmark of development wisdom.) Measures by developed countries in support of development were limited to a show of self-restraint in refraining from subsidizing certain products competing with the exports of underdeveloped countries. International action was restricted to increasing World Bank lending, and organizing technical assistance through an international development authority.

The impact on UN development activity was to be seen in the spread of 'development planning', the techniques and priorities of which were spelled out in the expert group's report; in the sectoralizing of international assistance, and the related evolution of technical assistance programmes; and in the targeting of development resource transfers from developed countries. The UN First Development Decade, which was actually proclaimed in 1962, was

[5] W. Arthur Lewis, *The Theory of Economic Growth* (London, 1955).

in effect an operationalized version of basic ideas contained in the original expert group's report.

This first phase of the UN's involvement with economic development was also characterized by the absence of a collective presence on the part of the developing countries; by the implicit assertion of a wholly convergent process of world development; and by the assumption of an essentially benign external policy environment, and hence of the irrelevance of negotiated policy reform addressing the structures and arrangements underpinning international economic relations.

2. The second phase: 1963–1982

The second phase in the evolution of the UN's involvement with economic development extends from 1963 to about 1982. The impulses for new orientations in this period were many. They included the decolonization process, the radical transformation this effected in the UN's membership, and the interest of many of the newly independent nations in socialist doctrines. As the period progressed a clearer perception emerged of the reality that political independence did not itself bring economic growth and development. These countries began to articulate the need for a framework of international economic relations that would be more conducive to the realization of their development aspirations. This perception, triggered by the more blatant abuses by transnational enterprises and reinforced by these countries' awareness of their potential power as a source of supply and as a market for the industrialized world, contributed to the evolution of a new outlook on relations between the developed and developing countries.

By the mid-1960s the UN was ripe for a major revision of its development philosophy. This time the intellectual underpinning was provided by the developing world itself, in the form of the doctrines of Raúl Prebisch and his collaborators at the Economic Commission for Latin America. Although these ideas were being shaped from the latter part of the 1940s onward,[6] they did not emerge in the form of specific propositions for North–South, or, as it was then called, centre–periphery, relationships until the first UN Conference on Trade and Development (UNCTAD) was held in 1964, with Prebisch as its Secretary-General.[7]

The notions that informed the new approach to development theory and practice were radically different from those of the 1950s and of the First Development Decade. The new approach asserted the existence of a process of inequalizing exchange between the North and South, as the latter's terms of trade of primary commodities exports for manufactured imports persistently deteriorated, as economic surplus was transferred from the South to the North through transnational enterprises, as mercantilist policies restricted access to technology, and as international capital limited structural change and constrained the potential for growth. A distinguishing feature of the new theories was that they ruled out the possibility of self-correcting forces operating spontaneously to restore equilibrium in the world economy. Persistent divergence between North and South was seen as the natural order. If these tendencies were to be corrected, deliberate policy actions would have to be taken, and thus international policy negotiations would become a special and continuing responsibility of the UN. There was accordingly a concentration on improving the international economic environment to promote development across a broad front. This was an attempt to rectify the gaps and short-comings of the post-war system (encompassing IMF, IBRD, and GATT), which had given insufficient weight to the development issue. In this sense, the original, virtually exclusive, preoccupation with 'measures requiring domestic action' as the critical determinant of development was

[6] UN, Economic Commission for Latin America, *The Economic Development of Latin America and its Principal Problems* (UN, Dept. of Economic Affairs, New York, 1950); and Hans Singer, 'The Distribution of Gains between Investing and Borrowing Countries', *American Economic Review*, 40, no. 2 (May 1950), p. 473.

[7] *Towards a New Trade Policy for Development: Report by the Secretary-General of UNCTAD* (UN, New York, 1964).

relegated to a less important place in the UN approach to economic development.

During this period therefore the focus of attention in the UN, and especially in UNCTAD, turned to the negotiation of international policies and principles, organized on the basis of four country groupings—the Group of 77 (developing countries), the developed market-economy countries, the socialist countries of eastern Europe, and China. The main areas of negotiation were commodity prices, trade in manufactures, the international monetary system, the transfer of technology, transnational corporations, restrictive business practices, international shipping, and, at a more general level, the economic rights and duties of states. Many of these negotiations led to agreements, codes, and resolutions, some with greater legal significance than others.[8] Underlying these processes was a belief that market forces alone could not be relied upon to promote development, even if the policies of developing countries were optimal. Governmental intervention in cases of market failure was therefore necessary to support the development effort, and national strategies in developed and developing countries alike would have to be adjusted to one another with a view to a consistent set of international economic policies supportive of the development of the Third World.

At the same time, it must be said, a different path was being pursued by the International Monetary Fund and the World Bank where, increasingly, access to their resources was being made conditional on the adoption of domestic measures and policies recommended by them. During this period too there was an impressive growth in technical and financial assistance to the various sectors of economic activity in developing countries, intended to enhance these

[8] Examples include International Commodity Agreements, the Agreement establishing the Common Fund for Commodities, the Code of Conduct on Liner Conferences, the Set of Principles and Rules on Restrictive Business Practices, the Generalized System of Preferences, the resolution on debt relief for the least-developed countries, and the Charter on Economic Rights and Duties of States. Negotiations on proposals for Codes of Conduct on the Transfer of Technology, and on Transnational Corporations, ran into intractable difficulties which have yet to be resolved.

countries' domestic capabilities. In the field of technical cooperation there was a considerable expansion in the range and volume of activity by the UN Development Programme (UNDP), which was formed in 1965 by a merger of the UN Expanded Programme of Technical Assistance and the UN Special Fund. This expansion was itself to give rise to continuing questions about the UNDP's priorities, coherence, and cost-effectiveness.

The action taken by OPEC in 1973 was seen by developing countries as a successful, even if painful, example of the assertion of endogenous control over national resources and as an inspiration to refashion the international economic system in the interests of efficiency and equity. This naturally gave a strong new impetus to the 'policy negotiation' approach to international economic cooperation for development. It lent credence to the possibility of fundamental change, and to the aspiration that a world of ecónomic equity and justice, as envisaged by the developing countries, might actually be created. The 1974 Declaration on the Establishment of a New Internatioal Economic Order (NIEO) and its accompanying Programme of Action embodied this new message of strength and purpose.[9] The impulses for change deriving from this sense of commodity power were so strong that the period from 1973 might well be considered a distinct sub-phase, or even a new phase altogether. Essentially, they underscored the developing countries' conviction that change was needed in the structure and operation of the international economic system, and that such change could be effected through a process of global negotiation, in a context of the developing countries' strengthened bargaining power, and of the concrete realities of global interdependence. It is worth noting, for example, that the NIEO was ostensibly proclaimed to reassert and strengthen the 'spirit, purposes and principles of the Charter of the United Nations'.

Despite the language and the ambitiousness of the programme of international economic reform, as well as the more explicitly confrontational approach of the post-

---

[9] GA Res. 3201 (S-VI) of 1 May 1974.

1973 period, many of the measures envisaged for their realization dated back several years. However, in practical terms the new consciousness of and stress on 'permanent sovereignty over natural resources' gained in influence, while the notion of interdependence emerged more explicitly and with greater clarity as a rationale for international economic *management*. These approaches, together with the basic ideas associated with the founding of and developments in UNCTAD, merged with the older development currents of the 1950s to influence the shape and content of the International Development Strategy as proclaimed for the second and third UN Development Decades (which began respectively in 1971 and 1981).[10]

3. The third phase: the decade of the 1980s

The third phase dates from the early 1980s. The new strength and hopes inspired by the NIEO were to be relatively short-lived. By about 1982 the servicing of the massive petrodollar borrowing of developing countries ran into severe difficulty as recession in the North, brought about by anti-inflationary monetary and fiscal policies, curtailed the export earnings of developing countries.[11] Besides this, a number of other influences had a modifying effect on the UN's development philosophy. There was much disappointment over the failure to negotiate or implement important aspects of the international agenda— international commodity agreements, the Common Fund for Commodities, the Code of Conduct for the Transfer of Technology, and the NIEO. The weakening of commodity power generally, including that of OPEC, diminished the Third World's bargaining power. The revival of the arms race, and continuing East–West tensions, put the North–South dialogue lower on the agenda of international concerns.

The period witnessed a return, primarily at the insistence of the developed market-economy countries, to a preoccupation with national measures and policies of

---

[10] GA Res. 2626 (XXV) of 24 Oct. 1970, and 35/56 of 5 Dec. 1980.
[11] UNCTAD, *Trade and Development Report, 1986* (Geneva, 1986).

developing countries, similar to that of the 1950s. In major Western economies, the ascendancy of neo-classical economics with its faith in market forces, together with the trend towards deregulation and privatization, went hand in hand with a reduced interest and investment in forms of international management. These tendencies signalled a diminished concern with negotiated international policies for the promotion of international economic cooperation for development. They also pointed to a greater role for the private enterprise sector in the promotion of international cooperation and development.

Not surprisingly the period saw a weakening of the development consensus underlying the UN's work in this field.[12] Fundamental differences became apparent in economic philosophies, and in perceptions of the capabilities of governments in national and international policy-making. The role of governments and of intergovernmental institutions on the one hand, and of private market forces on the other, became the subject of renewed controversy. Disagreement surfaced about the interplay of domestic policies and the external environment, and of the public and private sectors of economic activity. Indeed, governments came to hold divergent views even on how agreed common interests are best pursued in an international and multilateral context; such was the case, for example, on issues of global economic management, trade policies in the context of increasing protectionism, international monetary reform, the evolving international debt strategy, and resource flows to the developing world.

Yet there was no attempt to abrogate the goals and objectives of the International Development Strategy for the Third Development Decade.[13] On the contrary, member states registered their concern about the substantial deterioration of the situation of many developing countries, particularly in Africa, together with the disquieting

[12] Ibid., annexe 1.
[13] See the Agreed Conclusions section of 'Report of the Committee on the Review and Appraisal of the Implementation of the International Development Strategy for the Third UN Development Decade', UN doc. A/40/48 (New York, 1985).

dimensions that the problem of indebtedness had assumed for a large number of them.

Meanwhile, increased interdependence within and among different groups of countries through trade and production went hand in hand with, and was reinforced by, closer financial linkages. These, in turn, enhanced the influence of international finance over trade. Propelled by new developments in information and communications technologies, domestic financial markets increasingly became part of and subordinate to international markets; and the markets for different assets themselves became more intermeshed. The role of private international markets in the net flow of financial resources, particularly between developed and developing countries, assumed vast proportions. The international financial system as a whole became more sensitive to changes in the ability of developing countries to service their debts. Consequently, as countries became more exposed to international financial influences, the impact of fluctuations in world monetary and financial conditions on their output, employment, and price levels became more pronounced.

4. The fourth phase: from the turn of the decade

In the early 1990s the world community may be moving into a new, more mature phase of international economic cooperation for development. The shifts that have been under way for some years in approaches to economic and social organization, and in perceptions of development policy, accelerated around the beginning of the decade. Much of the new momentum derived from the dramatic developments that took place in the central and eastern European countries, including the Soviet Union, leading to the introduction of democratic forms of government in place of existing regimes and the supersession of central planning systems by moves towards market-based economies. The challenges posed by the shifts just mentioned are described in the second part of this chapter, but they have laid bare many of the ingredients for a fresh development consensus.[14]

---

[14] GA Res. S-18/3 of 1 May 1990 entitled 'Declaration on International Economic Cooperation, in particular the Revitalization of Economic Growth and

The retreat from multilateralism has come to a halt, prompted possibly by calculations of long-run self-interest on the part of major industrial countries—manifested, for instance, at the 1992 Conference on Environment and Development—and partly by considerations of common interest and mutual benefit. Development itself is increasingly seen as a people-centred and equitable process whose ultimate goal must be the improvement of the human condition. Political arrangements are regarded as viable and important for the development process to the extent that they are based on consent, and the observance of human rights is widely accepted as a source of creativity, innovation, and initiative. A convergence of views has occurred on the necessity of supportive frameworks of broad economic policy, both national and international.

Reliance on market forces and competitiveness, and the fostering of entrepreneurial initiative, have become common features of the pursuit of economic efficiency. Approaches to sustainable growth are no longer confined to such criteria as the avoidance of high inflation, large payments imbalances, and sharp cyclical swings: they now encompass the improvement of medium-term growth potential through, for instance, policies that improve the functioning of markets, enlarge human capital, enhance labour mobility, promote openness to international trade, encourage competitiveness, and incorporate respect for the environment. The sharp rise in the level of concern for the health of the global environment and for the long-term security of the planet's ecology base has underscored the need to manage natural resources wisely and to evolve production and consumption patterns in ways consistent with the protection of the environment. Moreover, countries accept that high priority must be accorded to such aspects of the development process as the eradication of poverty and hunger, human resource and institutional development, and improved population policies, as well as the protection of the environment.

Development of the Developing Countries'; and 'A New Partnership for Development: The Cartagena Commitment' in 'Report of UNCTAD on its Eighth Session (February 1992)', UN doc. TD/364 of 6 July 1992, pp. 6–60.

The proposition that, while the external economic environment is critical for small and open economies, developing countries have the primary responsibility for their own development remains unquestioned: there is no substitute for sustained national policies aimed at liberating and mobilizing the latent energies and impulses for development within developing countries, at promoting efficiency in the allocation and use of resources, and at taking advantage of the opportunities for trade, investment, and technological progress provided by the changing global environment. Indeed, it is these policies that have determined and will continue to determine how changes in external variables affect the pace of development.

Another factor now widely seen as inseparable from the success of development efforts is the quality of public management. The concept of good governance—or, less controversially, good management—has many dimensions, and it is ultimately defined by a wide variety of historical, cultural, social, and political considerations. As currently understood it encompasses governmental action to establish appropriate frameworks and rules of the game for the effective and proper functioning of markets, and a healthy climate for economic activity.[15] This purpose entails the provision of physical and social infrastructure, the pursuit of sound macroeconomic policies, the creation of a conducive policy environment, and the development of human resources required to support economic activity, as well as policies that promote efficiency in the use and allocation of resources. It also requires clear legal and regulatory frameworks, transparent processes for rule-setting and decision-making, and efficient institutions for the management of resources.

Good management should furthermore stimulate entrepreneurship and productivity growth; help to expand employment opportunities; and promote, or where necessary undertake, functions which cannot be adequately

---

[15] *Accelerating the Development Process: Report by the Secretary-General of UNCTAD to the Eighth Session of the Conference*, part 2, chap. 1, 'Market Forces, Public Policy and Good Management'; and 'Report of UNCTAD on its Eighth Session (1992)', n. 14 above.

initiated or performed by the private sector. It calls, in addition, for the use of economic and regulatory instruments when markets left to themselves are unable to deal with the phenomenon of externalities and public goods, or to integrate environmental costs adequately into economic activities. Questions of income distribution also need to be addressed, including economic and social safety nets, and assistance to disadvantaged groups to gain access to market opportunities. Likewise, public intervention may be required to foster competition, particularly where concentrations of market power create excessive rents. Finally, strengthened systems of dispute settlement and conflict resolution, with an appropriate role for courts of law and guarantees for their independence, are essential.

As already indicated, the international aspects of good management are also important. Most governments acknowledge, in varying degrees, that the efforts of developing countries in particular to improve their domestic economic policy framework will not have the desired outcome without a supportive international economic environment. Such an environment is seen as depending critically on greater dynamism in the global economy, and on the loosening of such constrictions on development as external indebtedness, inadequate development finance, high trade barriers, depressed commodity prices, and adverse terms of trade. The industrialized countries, it must be said, accept the importance of appropriate national macroeconomic and structural policies aimed at non-inflationary growth and structural adjustment and at avoiding undesired exchange-rate fluctuations and financial market disturbances. What would be even more helpful is a strong commitment to narrowing their imbalances in a manner that would benefit other countries, to stepping up their efforts to invigorate world economic growth, and bringing about a supportive and predictable international economic environment for development.

UN bodies have played a key role in the shaping of these common attitudes. They have also sought to encapsulate the guide-lines stemming from them into such major texts as the resolution adopted at the 18th Special Session of the General Assembly in May 1990;[16] the International Development Strategy for the Fourth Development Decade, adopted in December 1990;[17] the Cartagena Commitment adopted by UNCTAD VIII in February 1992;[18] and, from a different vantage point, in the final outcome of the 1992 Rio Conference on the Environment and Development.[19]

In the short time that has passed since these texts were adopted, the results have been mixed. Perceptions of certain problems, particularly poverty eradication and environmental protection, have sharpened, and greater recognition of the paths to be followed has emerged. But the recession in the developing market economies, and the persistence of an unsupportive economic environment, not to speak of the 1991 Persian Gulf war and the dissolution of the Soviet Union, have weakened some of the basic premises of the guide-lines these documents embody. The gap between international commitments made, and action taken by some of the key actors, has been large.

Effectively mobilized, the common attitudes just mentioned could evolve into a conviction that world economic stability and growth depend on higher levels of international cooperation for the management of interdependence. Interdependence could become a consistent vehicle of growth and development, bringing benefits for all in a positive sum game, on two conditions. One is that national policies, particularly those of the economically powerful, are formulated in a mutually reinforcing fashion to favour constructive adjustment and adaptation in the world economy. The other is that cooperative efforts are pursued to improve the systems, structures, and arrangements that have thus far underpinned international economic relations, particularly as regards trade, money, and finance.

Whether the necessary political determination among

[16] GA Res. S-18/3 of 1 May 1990.

[17] GA Res. 45/199 of 21 December 1990, annexe, 'International Development Strategy for the Fourth UN Development Decade'.

[18] 'Report of UNCTAD on its Eighth Session (1992)', n. 14 above.

[19] For the Rio Declaration and other documents adopted at the United Nations Conference on Environment and Development, see *International Legal Materials*, 31 (1992), pp. 814–87. See also Patricia Birnie's chapter below.

countries can be mustered to build on these perceptions so as to reactivate growth and development in the world economy is another matter. The vast enterprise that it entails requires countries both rich and poor to promote a new partnership for development based on the recognition of sovereign equality, mutual interests, and shared responsibilities. Its success depends crucially, of course, on the concerted efforts of the UN together with the family of organizations that has been built up around it.

If the UN is effectively to address the challenges that these unprecedented changes pose for development, its capacity to deal with their various facets in an integrated manner—and within a coherent conceptual framework—will have to be enhanced. It is to be hoped that the current wave of reform in the UN, which follows closely upon far-reaching institutional reforms undertaken in UNCTAD, will make a stronger contribution to this objective.

(b) Issues and Challenges of the Future

1. Changes in the global political and economic context

Changes, many unforeseen, in the global political and economic environment have opened up prospects for constructing a world order founded on peace, cooperation, and the betterment of the human condition. The means of overcoming many of the obstacles to the development process have come within reach. But the prospects are fraught with a multitude of serious problems and risks, national and international responses to which will determine progress towards a healthy, secure, and equitable world economy. The marked easing of tension among the major powers promises to lend substance to the age-old vision of beating swords into ploughshares. In industrial countries, the disarmament process would help release resources for easing global economic strains and for supporting the development process. Developing countries too should be better able to redeploy much of the resources currently devoted to military expenditures to raising domestic living standards. Moreover, the broad tide of political and economic reform and respect for human rights in many parts of the world has gathered pace. These developments have fuelled expectations that governments will now act with resolve to broaden access to opportunities at both the national and international levels for all peoples to attain economic and social well-being.

At the same time, many uncertainties remain. Political instability and tension persist in a number of regions. Fierce new assertions of nationalism, social strife, and the use of violence to subvert democratic processes threaten peace and security in several countries. Economic imbalances continue to be a source of unpredictability. There is also concern that, in the absence of carefully designed stimulative fiscal policies, excessive reliance on monetary policies might delay and even prevent economic recovery in the industrial world.

The impact on East–West relations of the momentous changes in central and eastern Europe has raised questions in the developing world about its place in the emerging configuration of political and economic power. One of the immediate repercussions of these changes was of course the drastic reduction or abandonment by the countries in that region of official development assistance to the developing countries, particularly those perceived as following socialist paths to economic and social development. More than that, the changes have given rise to two important issues with far-reaching implications. The first is how to integrate the countries of central and eastern Europe into the international financial system without undue stress on the system itself, especially in the light of current concerns about the adequacy of institutional capacity to general finance for investment. The second is how to meet their large and growing capital needs without diverting development resources, particularly official flows, from developing countries. For all these and other reasons there is serious disquiet that single-minded support for the reform processes in central and eastern Europe, including the republics of the former Soviet Union, might, despite the longer-term benefits they would eventually bring to the world economy, blunt the impetus to multilateral action on poverty and underdevelopment in the developing world.

Many of the structural changes that have taken place in the world economy since the early 1980s have their origin in technological progress. As already noted, technological innovation facilitated the emergence, triggered by the deregulation trends of the 1970s, of a huge global market for funds and financial instruments. Largely because of advances in information technologies, the 1980s witnessed another wave of international linkage, dominated by flows of investment and technology and by increased international corporate and research networking. This globalization process, as the phenomenon came to be described, made innovation, together with flexibility in the location of production, distribution, and service facilities, even more crucial for profitability. One result is that a growing share of international trade now takes place within corporations or among related firms. Another is that corporate decisions on sourcing, production, and marketing are increasingly taken within a global frame of reference. The interplay between trade, investment, technology, and services as well as their financial underpinning has accordingly increased in density, giving additional impulse to the growth of interdependence.

These new factors have eroded the capacity of governments to determine the course of economic events, and have in particular tightened the constraints on the scope for autonomous policy-making in developing countries. They have also heightened the vulnerability of small economies that are open enough to come under considerable influence from abroad but are not sufficiently large for their own policies to make a significant impact on others.

The past few years have also seen a resurgence of interest in integration arrangements centring on common markets, customs unions, or free trade areas. Groupings aimed at enhancing economic cooperation among developing countries are being strengthened. Large economic spaces involving major trading partners have emerged, which could contribute to trade liberalization and, through their growth effects, impart new dynamism to the multi-lateral trading system. Yet, if managed without due regard to the principles, rules, and disciplines of the system, they could become inward-looking, shift the burden of adjust-ment to third parties, cause trade diversion and other problems for developing country exporters, and increase the potential for trade disputes and tensions.

Population growth and fertility, compounded by atten-dant changes in the age structure of populations, are increasingly critical issues for the sustainability of develop-ment. They are creating serious problems of savings mobilization and resource allocation, and have increased the pressures on employment creation, education, training, and social services in many developing countries. Inter-national migration too has become a matter of increasing concern in both originating and receiving countries. Not-withstanding current initiatives in both groups of countries, the central question in the long run remains whether the international community can mobilize the necessary political commitment to reduce the motivation to emigrate by speeding up sustainable development world-wide.

Yet another cluster of issues for the future arises from the interplay between environment and development which was the subject of the major UN conference held in June 1992.[20] In reaffirming the concept of sustainable develop-ment, the Conference stressed the mutual interests and responsibilities of all countries, and placed environment concerns firmly within the context of growth. It gave salience to such topics as patterns of economic activity that cause ecological damage, the persistence of poverty, the quality of development, and the adaptations of domestic and international economic management necessary for sustainable development. The challenge now facing the international community is to translate the consensus of the Rio Conference into reality by ensuring, among other things, that wealth does not continue to generate waste of natural resources, and that poverty is steadily eliminated as a source of their degradation. With this in mind,

[20] For documents of the Conference on Environment and Development held at Rio in 1992, see n. 19 above.

protecting the environment and fostering economic growth must go hand in hand.

Ensuring sustainable development will clearly require far-reaching changes in macro- and microeconomic policies in all countries. As well as a reassessment of hitherto accepted consumption patterns and life-styles in industrial countries and better management of natural resources in developing countries, it will require strong international cooperation to promote, among other things, the development of and access to environmentally sound technologies, substantial additional resource flows to developing countries, and the elimination of trade barriers. Further work and negotiations in UN bodies, involving the full participation of all countries, will no doubt be required. This is particularly important where solutions are indeterminate in formal economic theory, or where externalities need to be internalized and responsibilities assigned for the protection and management of the assets of nature. Indeed, sustainable development provides substantially greater scope for all countries, developed as well as developing, to pursue many of their vital interests in the context of the development dialogue. It thus offers opportunities unprecedented in recent years, even though fraught with difficulty, for strengthening international economic cooperation for development.

2. Criticisms of the UN's development performance

Well-publicized criticisms have recently been voiced of the UN's performance in regard to its development assistance mission. Most of these criticisms are not new, and they are probably no more or less severe than those raised in the national debates on economic and financial management in many countries. However, on the world scale that the UN represents, well-considered judgements are often constrained by the lack of exposure to the relevant facts or to legitimate differences of opinion. As a result, assessments are made, sometimes by professional experts and, from time to time, under the sponsorship of influential governments, on the basis of incorrect information (frequently of the more newsworthy type) or of incomplete evidence and analysis.

The recent revival of criticisms of the UN may well be more closely related to the marked shifts that have occurred in political and economic philosophy which have already been examined, and to a diminished political and financial commitment on the part of those governments to multilateral cooperation for economic development, than to substantial new deterioration in the capability and performance of the UN.

The traditional lines of criticism, especially in official circles in the developed countries, are clear enough. In 1985 they were outlined by Maurice Bertrand with great intellectual incisiveness.[21] According to these views, the UN, in seeking to execute the duty undertaken by its members to 'achieve international cooperation' for economic and social development, operates a system that is not well adapted to the execution of development assistance programmes. In specific terms, its individual sector programmes are viewed as conceptually disparate and out of harmony with the development *problématique*, fragmented, doctrinally incoherent, and operated by remote control. As such, they seem to lack analytical and functional integration and to be devoid of a sense of priority; they are prone to waste through duplication of effort and an unproductive division of responsibility. On top of these operational defects—perhaps to some extent a cause of them—is an unmanageable intergovernmental negotiating and decision-making apparatus; one, moreover, that lacks systemtic resource allocation procedures and effective accountability mechanisms. More recently, many such strictures have focused on the need to upgrade administrative and management practices within the UN Secretariat as a whole. They were, for instance, forcefully articulated in early 1993 in a report submitted to the Secretary-General by Dick Thornburgh, the outgoing Under-Secretary-General for Administration and Management, which attracted much press attention.[22]

---

[21] Maurice Bertrand, 'Some Reflections on Reform of the United Nations' (JIU Report 85/9), UN doc. A/40/988 of 6 Dec. 1985.

[22] 'Report to the Secretary-General of the United Nations', by Dick Thornburgh, dated 1 Mar. 1993, unpublished.

These are indeed very serious and substantial criticisms. It is not difficult to discover instances of most of these defects in the UN institutions devoted to economic development. To the extent that these and other defects exist and can be corrected with generally beneficial results, the reforms under way ought to be vigorously pursued. The importance of continuing vigilance and rigorous reform has in fact led to a focus in the current restructuring efforts within the UN at the intergovernmental level on the governance and coordination of development assistance activities, on financing arrangements, on linkages between the major operational agencies in this area, and on arrangements for coordination and collaborative programming of those activities at the country level.

At the level of the UN Secretariat, the far-reaching organizational reforms of New York-based entities in the economic and social fields that the UN Secretary-General put in place in February 1992—which had mixed reactions from some outside observers—are currently under review in the light of experience. More than that, the reform process is to be extended to other parts of the economic and social sectors of the organization. In pursuing this process, the UN Secretary-General has set forth the vision of an organization which views its economic and social objectives with the same sense of responsibility and urgency as its commitments in the political and security area; which takes full advantage of the central coordinating capacity available to it on economic, social, and humanitarian issues, and of the inter-sectoral capabilities at its disposal in the regional commissions and in the various UN programmes and organs; and in which economic and social research and policy analysis, operational activities, humanitarian assistance, and the promotion of human rights support and reinforce each other. The essence of his proposals in this regard—aimed at a more effective, revamped Secretariat, providing improved service to governments and to the intergovernmental machinery— was endorsed by the member states in April 1993. Member states generally recognized that the Secretary-General's restructuring measures could result in a more responsive and cost-effective Secretariat in which the work of its component units would have a sharper focus as well as clearer lines of responsibility, and where duplication and overlapping would be eliminated in favour of coherent action towards higher levels of organizational performance.

An additional illustration of the current focus on institutional reform was provided by UNCTAD VIII in February 1992. The decisions reached at the Conference, to which full effect has now been given, encompass a redefinition of the functions of UNCTAD, a restructuring of its intergovernmental machinery, a comprehensive reorganization of its substantive work, and an overhaul of its methods of work. The objective of these reforms is to enhance the capacity of UNCTAD to address the new challenges and opportunities that have arisen for international economic cooperation and development. They have been hailed as a model for institutional reform elsewhere in the UN. It may however be noted that the new methodology of work in particular has been criticized by some developing countries for appearing to downgrade the negotiating process from its central place in UNCTAD's work in favour of analysis, reflection, and progressive consensus-building.

Yet, productive as these reforms may be, it is open to question whether the defects at which they are aimed lie at the root of the dissatisfaction with the UN's role and performance in regard to development. In any event, the correction of essentially organizational and methodological flaws is not all that is required for a decisive, qualitative improvement in international cooperation for development. No less crucial are the quality of the international commitment to world development and the political dimensions of international economic policy. The focus has therefore to be widened beyond the UN.

3. Broadening the scope of analysis

The 'purposes and principles' inscribed in the UN Charter are self-imposed guide-lines set by states to direct their overall international conduct; they are not duties to be honoured merely in so far as countries participate in, and finance, certain common activities executed through the agency of the UN. If there is to be a balanced or even a comprehensible assessment of the UN's role and performance in regard to economic development, we must take a broader view of the issue. This view cannot be limited to the UN, but must encompass the whole complex of international economic organizations and economic relations among states.

In such a perspective, while the UN's efforts and resources are relatively small, its potential contribution to international policy assumes a much greater salience. In this perspective too, there may be a better appreciation of the exogenous limits to the effectiveness of the UN's efforts, and of the reasons why operational reforms of the UN, whilst valuable, cannot themselves put right what is wrong with international cooperation for development. Current critiques of the UN's role in economic development need to be complemented by reflections of a more fundamental nature on the foundations, practice, and future of a broader conception of international development cooperation.

Any such reflections would probably begin with some hesitation about the strength of the UN's commitment to development. Some have certainly doubted the credibility of this commitment.[23] Compared with the purposeful and direct language used in the UN Charter in regard to peace—'to save succeeding generations from the scourge of war', 'to maintain international peace and security and . . . to take effective collective measures for the prevention and removal of threats to the peace'—that used in respect of development has been viewed as fragile and ambiguous. The words are 'to employ international machinery for the promotion of the economic and social advancement of all peoples', and 'to achieve international co-operation in solving international problems of an economic . . . character'.[24]

In the years since 1945 a number of concepts have been invoked to underpin the UN's commitment to

[23] UN, Dept. of Public Information, *Is Universality in Jeopardy?* (UN, New York, 1987), a collection of papers prepared for a symposium commemorating the UN's fortieth anniversary.   [24] UN Charter, Preamble and Art. 1.

development—from self-help and fair opportunity in the 1950s to reason and generosity in the 1960s; from partnership and mutual interest in the 1970s to interdependence and collective security in the 1980s. Despite the many substantial advances registered, none of these notions has yet been succeeded in inspiring durable foundations for a dynamic and predictable system of international cooperation for development. Cooperation on this scale has not in the past been a spontaneous habit of a self-catalysing impulse. On the contrary, defection from organized, systemic cooperation often seemed an attractive option. There are thus, from the start, challenging, indeed critical, questions to be faced. Is there a credible, compelling rationale for global development cooperation? Are the hopeful signs identified earlier sufficient to generate the necessary momentum? Or do we now need more penetrating insights into the actual evolution of cooperative forms in human society as a basis for organizing more realistic models for facilitating social progress? Would such models of international cooperation be more or less anthropographical, integrated, planned, evolutionary . . .?

Such a formulation of the issue goes much beyond questions about the appropriate structure for North–South dialogue and negotiations. Economic issues do need a higher profile in UN affairs: greater coherence in the policies and activities of the various international economic institutions would certainly be beneficial, as would improvements to the negotiating machinery. Nevertheless, as indicated above, the case has not been made that organic restructuring and reforms of intergovernmental deliberative and negotiating procedures are a sufficient answer to more fundamental issues about the quality of the commitment of UN member states to world development and to shared management of the international economic system.

4. Dogmatism and single models of development

It seems unlikely that in the near future there could be in a world of over 180 extremely heterogeneous states a common, universal understanding of the meaning of development, or of the measures and policies by which the development objectives of states may be attained. Whilst, as indicated above, there are many areas of convergence, there remain considerable differences of outlook and method as between many developing countries and the donors of development assistance. These differences are frequently at the heart of questions about the role and performance of development cooperation. They have been reflected in frictions between developing countries on the one hand and the IMF and the World Bank on the other. The latter are still often viewed as dispensing more or less uniform prescriptions for a wide variety of economic ailments and circumstances, and thus as being insufficiently sensitive to the peculiar features and potential of each developing country, and to the goals that these countries have or would like to set for themselves. Access to the resources of these insitutions and, through their seal of approval, to the private capital market is usually conditional upon acceptance and monitored implementation of their recommendations. In many cases there are no alternatives open to developing countries, short of autarky.

Two basic concerns are common to most of the criticisms that are made in respect of this area of international cooperation for development. First, there is some uneasiness about the precision and dogmatism which characterize the prevailing underlying theory of development, based, as it is argued, virtually exclusively on the role of prices— the prices of product, capital, labour, and foreign exchange —and on the overriding importance of 'getting these prices right'. In response, a substantial volume of carefully researched criticism has accumulated over the years.[25] A second concern stems from doubts that a single model of development can be recommended as a universal norm in

---

[25] Useful summary material and further references may be found in *Towards a New Bretton Woods: Challenges for the World Financial and Trading System* (Commonwealth Secretariat, London, 1983); Edmar L. Bacha and Richard E. Feinberg, 'The World Bank and Structural Adjustment in Latin America', *World Development*, 14, no. 3 (1986), p. 333; Tony Killick, *Balance of Payments Adjustment and Developing Countries* (Working Paper no. 17, Overseas Development Institute, London, June 1985); and Robert Cassen (ed.), *Does Aid Work? Report to an Intergovernmental Task Force* (Oxford, 1986).

a world in which the circumstances, possibilities, socio-economic preferences, and political values of developing countries are so varied. States of East and South-East Asia are sometimes singled out as 'success stories'. Strong reservations have been raised about the standards employed in identifying and determining this 'success'. More than that, these portrayals of economic success, drawn solely and explicitly in terms of the dominance of private enterprise systems and openness to foreign investment and trade—outward orientation, as it is called—have been countered, even in respect of these countries, by more cautious and perhaps more revealing interpretations.[26]

There has long been a current of legitimate criticism of such approaches in countries that are major contributors to development assistance. One example is worth quoting:

In the end, market forces and policies matter; import substitution and export promotion occur simultaneously and in a more supportive relationship than is generally supposed. But, in the name of even-handedness, it is not a helpful circumstance to have our premier international financial institutions wedded to a single model of what constitutes a successful development policy or to a narrow definition of what constitutes an effective stabilization programme. It seriously undermines the role of the Fund and the Bank in the world economy by restricting their scope and their effectiveness. It politicizes them by having them represent . . . an ideology, when their role is to be responsive to a variety of types of governments and economic systems.[27]

The point developed in that testimony represents an extremely difficult challenge for the future. How can international resources for development be liberated from the confines of a predetermined political ideology and a fixed norm of economic development? By what means can the international financial institutions be made more open and responsive to the views of developing countries and alert to a more eclectic scholarship?

---

[26] John P. Lewis and Valeriana Kallab (eds.), *Development Strategies Reconsidered* (Overseas Development Council, Washington DC, 1986).

[27] Testimony of Colin I. Bradford, jun., Associate Director, Yale Center for International and Area Studies, before the US House of Representatives Sub-Committee on International Development Institutions and Finance, 25 July 1985.

5. The importance of the international economic policy environment

The prospects for development also depend on the external policy environment, as distinct from external development assistance. This environment is ultimately a good deal more important than resource transfers: to a large extent it determines the capacity of developing countries to earn their own resources for development. Development assistance can only be a supplement to domestic efforts. It is not surprising therefore that international economic policy should be an arena of conflict between developing and developed countries.

Thus any evaluation of the UN's role and effort in support of development would not be complete without attention being given to the external policy aspect. It is surprising that such disproportionate attention should be devoted to the efficiency of the administration of the relatively small share of development assistance (estimated at less than 10 per cent of the total) that UN bodies account for, to the exclusion (1) of the much greater share managed by the complex of international economic institutions other than the UN and by national governments; and (2) of international economic policy as one of the important determinants of development performance internationally.

The UN and its organs, including UNCTAD, have provided forums in which international economic policy as it affects the developing countries is debated, and reforms and innovations negotiated at the levels both of principle and of practice. These efforts have in the main been directed to securing a more liberal and fair international trading system for the exports of developing countries, more stable conditions for trade in primary commodities, and a more predictable and supportive international monetary and financial system. Concern with these aspects of international economic policy has become more urgent over the last few years, as higher and new protectionist barriers have been imposed; as real prices of some important commodities have sunk to the levels of 1890; as debt burdens, particularly of the poorer countries, have escalated at a time of much diminished capacity to service them; and as disorder has become an enduring feature of the international monetary system. While there have been considerable achievements in those forums over the past twenty-five or more years, the record, on the whole, has fallen short of the possibilities and expectations.

The critical issue has been the apparent reluctance of the great industrial powers to match their recognition of the reality of world economic interdependence with a preparedness to share with their developing country partners the management of the global economic commons that the world's trading, monetary, and financial systems represent. The basic facts on these matters are clear enough. Improvements within the UN are needed, often desperately, to the quality of research, to the analysis of developing countries' domestic policies, to the reform of working methods and work orientations, and to the logistics of negotiating procedures. But there remains much room for scepticism that, in the final analysis, these are the decisive impediments to the improvement of international economic policy. It is regrettable that many evaluations of the UN's involvement with international cooperation for development should, because of their limited focus on development assistance, fail to envision much scope for shared international economic management as an instrument of this wider cooperation.

The challenges of the future are no less daunting in regard to these international policy issues. By what means can the governments of the major industrial countries be induced to upgrade the existing level of consensus on such matters as the need for shared management of the international economic system, in their own longer-range interest? If this proves to be an impossible task, would the integration of the South in all its diversity into a hegemonic North be a politically feasible and durable proposition? Or will parallel North–South antagonistic systems emerge? Is the only approach open to the UN, as some feel, that of pursuing with tenacity any advances— however marginal—towards the distant goal of international society?

(c) Concluding Observations

This chapter has raised a number of basic, challenging questions concerning international cooperation for development. In doing so, it has tried to place the UN's involvement in the broader context of the purposes and principles subscribed to by governments independently of the organization they established. It has no special wisdom to offer on these questions and challenges, other than what is hinted at in their formulation.

There are other important related questions left unexamined. For example, what can be done to improve the capacity of developing countries themselves to formulate their own development objectives in the form of coherent long-range programmes? What mechanism, beyond those currently employed in the OECD Development Assistance Committee, should be put in place to induce greater complementarity and efficiency of effort, as well as enhanced flows of development assistance, among donor countries, bearing in mind that bilateral flows represent some 75 per cent of total official development assistance? What can be done to enlarge the contributions of the often overlooked autonomous agencies which together with the UN proper constitute the UN system?

Yet other questions, only hinted at here, call for thorough exploration. What must be the role of the UN in ensuring coherent and mutually reinforcing approaches in key economic policy areas? Policy inconsistencies are apt to surface between, for instance, the efforts of debtors to meet their debt service obligations, and the protectionist policies of some of the creditor countries; between aspects of structural adjustment programmes, and the sluggish growth of the world economy as a whole; between the development objectives set by the international community, and the stagnating flows of concessional (and, as regards some parts of the world, non-concessional) resources; between the recognition of the urgent need of developing countries for additional import capacity, and the inadequacy of financial resources commensurate with the generally accepted scale of the problem; and between the broad policy approaches being pursued towards political and economic problems respectively.

Though of the greatest importance to the ultimate success of the UN's task, these and other questions raised in this chapter tend to be regarded as somewhat removed from the detailed preoccupations of the day. Nevertheless, every opportunity must be seized to air and reflect on these concerns and to generate constructive insights with a view to improving our common understanding.

The UN and the Environment

PATRICIA BIRNIE

(a) Framework for UN's Development of Environmental Programmes

1. Absence of environmental dimension to UN's stated purposes

THE UN Charter makes no mention of environmental protection. It does not specifically refer in setting out its objects and principles to the aims of preventing pollution, conserving resources, or to the need for sustainable development. This is hardly surprising since, following the League of Nations' failure to prevent World War II, the perceived need was for the Charter to remedy those of the League's deficiencies that were thought to have contributed to that failure together with the violations of human rights that had occurred in the course of these events. Moreover there was no consciousness in 1945 of any need to protect the environment, except on an *ad hoc* basis outside the UN.

Though the Charter seeks primarily to prohibit the use of force against the territorial integrity of its member states, the founders realized that peace and security required establishment of conditions under which respect for treaty and other obligations of international law could be maintained as well as promotion of economic and social progress, referred to in terms of 'better standards of life in larger freedoms', which required establishment and use of new international machinery. When environmental issues finally reached the UN's agenda these broad purposes and the wide powers of the political and administrative organs established under the Charter were relied on to introduce an environmental dimension into the UN's programmes.

In 1945, however, environmental awareness, except

amongst a few non-governmental organizations, was low; apart from a few fishery commissions, a convention on whaling, and some agreements on migratory birds, all unrelated to the UN, few multilateral laws or action plans had been developed internationally.

This situation changed dramatically both within and outside the UN system following the convening in Stockholm by the UN General Assembly of the 1972 UN Conference on the Human Environment (UNCHE). This conference drew attention to the right of human beings to an environment of quality, and to the need to deal with a variety of emerging problems affecting this, such as prevention of pollution from all sources and conservation of living resources. Much progress has been made since then, for example in concluding large numbers of conventions, many under the auspices of the UN or one of its specialized agencies or programmes. The economic and technological disparities between the developed and developing world have become a matter of heightened concern—in part because they inhibit both global implementation of existing conventions, such as those on the ozone layer, climate change, and biodiversity, and conclusion of new ones on such contentious issues as deforestation. Development has come to be seen as a key issue in resolving those problems, but the economic costs for both North and South are formidable. The UN sought to focus the world's attention simultaneously on both environment and development by convening in Rio de Janeiro—significantly in a developing country—the 1992 UN Conference on Environment and Development (UNCED).

2. Developmental priorities

Why have environmental issues been so overlooked until recently, given the current sense of environmental crisis in the world?[1] As Caldwell pointed out, critical environmental issues are perceived differently in science and

---

[1] Even in the 1st edition of this book, published in 1988, by which date it had become widely recognized that environmental issues are in the front rank of those now dividing the world, no chapter was devoted to them and only one contributor—Judge Singh, in a brief discussion of protection of the 'global

public affairs, those categorized as such by the former do not always correspond to the perceptions and priorities prevailing in governments and international agencies and their constituencies.[2] Thus there are no universal criteria for categorizing the critical issues, and in the UN system development was the prime goal of the majority of states in the 1960s and 1970s as former colonies gained their independence. In 1962 the UN General Assembly adopted a resolution on Permanent Sovereignty over Natural Resources[3] declaring the right of peoples and nations to such sovereignty. It made no specific reference to the need to conserve these resources, or maintain the yield of living resources. Rather it required that the rights must be exercised in the interest of national development and well-being of those in the state concerned, though the latter requirement could, from the hindsight of an environmental perspective, be said to imply that some attention be paid to securing the long-term sustainability of such resources. Even after the 1972 UN Conference on the Human Environment (UNCHE), the General Assembly adopted in 1974 both a Declaration on Establishment of a New International Economic Order (NIEO) and a Charter of Economic Rights and Duties of States,[4] that stressed economic development and states' rights to choose the means and goals for its achievement. Though the latter resolution recognized that, in exploiting natural resources shared between countries, states must cooperate and inform and consult each other, the expressed purpose was to achieve optimum use of resources, albeit without causing damage to the legitimate interest of others. The latter phrase might include protection or conservation of these resources, but this was not spelt out.

The UN was from its foundation largely set on a course which separated economic development issues from

commons'—specifically referred to them. *United Nations, Divided World* (1st edn., Oxford, 1988), pp. 186–7. (Also below, pp. 414–15.)

[2] L. Caldwell, *International Environmental Policy* (2nd edn., Durham, NC, 1990), pp. 15–16.

[3] GA Res. 1803 (XVIII) of 14 Dec. 1962.

[4] GA Res. 3201 (XXIX) and 3202, both of 1 May 1974.

environmental issues, despite the fact that many forms of development erode the environmental resources on which they are based. A turning-point was the publication of the Report of the World Commission on Environment and Development (WCED) in 1987.[5] The WCED Report finally called for adoption of a new path, 'sustainable development', which it identified as becoming the goal of both developing and industrialized states.[6] Whereas environmental protection, unlike economic, political, and social issues, had not previously been seen as a mainstream issue so far as preserving international security—the UN's main objective—was concerned, it was thereafter presented as a crucial element in ensuring stability and securing mankind's survival. The WCED Report inspired the General Assembly to convene the 1992 UN Conference on Environment and Development (UNCED), aimed at synthesizing the environmental and developmental aspects of its and other relevant programmes. To understand the problems involved in achieving these objectives it is necessary to appreciate the reasons for and results of the generally pragmatic and sectoral approaches to environmental protection previously followed in the UN.

3. Organizational framework for the UN's environmental policy

The founders of the UN system perceived that an underlying reason for the failure of the League of Nations had been its lack of institutional means of addressing widespread economic and social problems. The League had had to rely on various internal committees: the only functional international organization established with a relation to it was the International Labour Organization, though various intergovernmental public unions existed outside it, and a few environmentally oriented non-governmental bodies, such as the Zoological Society and the International Council for Exploration of the Sea (ICES), had respectively addressed such issues as migratory birds and animals, including over-exploitation of whales. Various relevant

[5] *Our Common Future*, Report of the World Commission on Environment and Development (Oxford, 1987). [6] Ibid., pp. 2–4.

international conferences had been held and some international agreements concluded.[7]

Seizing the opportunity provided in 1945 to change this system, the drafters of the UN Charter expressed its aims in much wider terms than those of the League and included commitments 'to achieve international cooperation in solving international problems of an economic, social, cultural or humanitarian character and in promoting and encouraging respect for human rights and for fundamental freedoms for all'. They provided for the UN 'to be a centre for harmonizing the action of nations in the attainment of these common ends', and equipped it with a wider range of organs—a General Assembly, a Security Council, an Economic and Social Council (ECOSOC), a Trusteeship Council, a Secretariat, and an International Court of Justice. An International Law Commission was subsequently established under the Charter, charged with the codification and progressive development of international law.

The UN was also furnished with five regional economic commissions—for Africa (ECAF); Latin America (ECLA); Western Asia (ECWA); Asia and the Pacific (ESCAP); and Europe (ECE). Although their purpose was clearly to promote economic development these bodies have subsequently, within the broadly stated aims of the Charter, been able to develop programmes for environmental action. For example, ECAF is now involved in environmental assessment and management of use of natural resources, including, since the exposure in the 1980s of the dumping of toxic waste in Africa, pollution control and waste disposal. It is, however, the ECE that has been the most active, concluding and administering conventions on Long-Range Transboundary Air Pollution (LRTAP)[8] and on Environmental Impact Assessment,[9] as well as developing protocols to the LRTAP Convention and a long-term

[7] See Caldwell, *International Environmental Policy*, pp. 30–40, for examples.

[8] 1979 Convention on Long-Range Transboundary Air Pollution, Geneva, *International Legal Materials*, 18 (1979), p. 1442.

[9] Convention on Environmental Impact Assessment in a Transboundary Context, Espoo, Finland, *International Legal Materials*, 30 (1991), pp. 802–19.

Regional Strategy for Environmental Protection and Rational Use of Natural Resources in its member states up to the year 2000 and beyond, whch has involved it in extensive review of the status of wildlife protection laws and agreements in the region, as well as other resources.

The UN has over time also established numerous committees, commissions, councils, and autonomous units within its structure. The powers of its major decision-making bodies were expressed in wider terms and their decision-making procedures were more flexible than the League's—resolutions could be adopted even in the absence of unanimity—which has facilitated introduction of environmental units, strategies, and action plans. However, given the political division between North (developed states) and South (developing states) in the UN, these are generally expressed in broad 'goal-setting' terms: examples include the World Charter for Nature (WCN)[10] and the Global Perspective to the Year 2000 and Beyond[11] adopted by the General Assembly.

Particularly important was the linking of the UN to various specialized agencies, established autonomously by intergovernmental agreement, which have wide international responsibilities, as defined in their constitutive treaties, in economic, social, cultural, educational, health and related fields. Specialized agencies directly involved in issues related to environmental protection include the International Labour Organization (ILO), Food and Agriculture Organization (FAO), International Maritime Organization (IMO), United Nations Educational, Scientific, and Cultural Organization (UNESCO), World Health Organization (WHO), World Meteorological Organization (WMO), International Bank for Reconstruction and Development (IBRD or World Bank). The International Atomic Energy Agency (IAEA) is associated with the UN and involved in environmental policy, although it is not a specialized agency.

The terms of the relationship between the UN and the

---

[10] GA Res. 37/7 of 9 Nov. 1982, *International Legal Materials*, 22 (1983), p. 455.
[11] Text in *Environmental Policy and Law*, 18 (1988), pp. 37–8.

agencies vary according to the agency concerned since ECOSOC is empowered to enter into agreements with them which define those terms; it can also coordinate their activities through consultation with and recommendations to such agencies and through recommendations to UN bodies.[12] As ECOSOC can make or initiate studies and reports concerning economic, social, cultural, educational, health, and related matters and make recommendations thereon not only to the General Assembly or UN members but to the concerned specialized agencies[13] it could potentially play a major role in developing environmental policies throughout the whole UN system.

For some years ECOSOC's responsibility, under the Charter, for economic and social matters only indirectly led it to consider environmental issues, for example in various studies undertaken for the Third UN Law of the Sea Conference, as its functional commissions were more involved in developmental and human rights issues than environmental ones. Moreover, its role was largely taken over by the General Assembly, under whose authority it operates and whose policies were thus dominant. However, the UN's current reform initiative[14] aims to revitalize and restructure the UN in economic, social, and related fields. It is intended, amongst other things, to re-focus ECOSOC and promote an integrated approach to the UN's programmes: the complementarity of the work of the UN General Assembly and ECOSOC is being reviewed by the former, with a view to avoiding existing duplication, including in their decision-making, review, and monitoring roles. The reforms provide an opportunity for making these bodies more fitted to the tasks they will need to undertake in execution of UNCED's action programme, known as Agenda 21. It remains to be seen whether this opportunity will be fully taken, given the divisions between

[12] UN Charter, Art. 57.   [13] UN Charter, Art. 63.
[14] See in particular UN doc. A/Res/45/264 of 30 May 1991: 'Restructuring and Revitalization of the United Nations in the Economic, Social and Related Fields'.

North and South that were apparent at UNCED[15] and have long dominated debate in both the GA and ECOSOC. ECOSOC initiated the 1972 UNCHE and is especially well placed to promote the sustainable development policies laid down in Agenda 21 because of its power to make recommendations to specialized agencies.

ECOSOC elects the members of the Commission on Sustainable Development (CSD), created by the UN General Assembly in 1992, ensuring its involvement in the post-UNCED processes. The High Level Advisory Board, approved by UNGA in 1992 and convened by Secretary-General Boutros-Ghali, advises the Secretary-General on aspects of sustainable development. The Secretary-General has tried to build a unity of purpose for the economic, social, and environmental sectors of the organization as part of his restructuring of the Secretariat.[16] But there remains a need to strike a more rational distribution of responsibilities between UN Headquarters and the UN Centres in Geneva, Nairobi and Vienna, and among global, regional, and field structures. CSD itself should also bolster ECOSOC's efforts to promote coherence and coordination in these fields. However, some NGOs have criticized the link between CSD and ECOSOC, regarding the latter as a moribund institution. Much thus depends on the extent and success of the Secretary-General's reforms, and on the vigour and aspirations of CSD.

[15] These are clearly revealed in 'Environment and Development: Towards a Common Strategy of the South in the UNCED Negotiations and Beyond' (South Centre, Follow-Up Office of the South Commission, Geneva, 1991), which stresses the need for the South to pursue a restructuring of global economic relations that will allow it to obtain the resources for sufficiently *rapid* development to meet the needs and aspirations of its growing population, and that the South has adequate 'environmental space' for this purpose. (See pp. ii-iii and 3–9.)

[16] See e.g. *Environmental Policy and Law*, 22 (1992), pp. 302 and 304–6. There was an implicit recognition that the UN Headquarters staff needed more environmental expertise and awareness effectively to enhance the environment and development programmes of the UN system. In 1992–3 a Department for Policy Co-ordination and Sustainable Development was established, headed by Under-Secretary-General Desai.

4. Legal basis of the UN's Environmental Programme

No specific or clear basis for the adoption of environmental programmes or actions was provided in the UN Charter or in the constituent instruments of the individual specialized agencies. Nevertheless the powers of the UN and relevant agencies were expressed in sufficiently wide and comprehensive terms to permit them to deal with environmental issues should a broad interpretation be approved, since such issues have economic, social, and humanitarian aspects.

International law approves the doctrine of 'implied powers', i.e. the permanent organs of an organization have power to interpret the constituent instrument, including the powers of action that must necessarily be implied from the expressed powers and from its objects and purposes. It is also widely accepted that, if legally possible, an 'effective' interpretation should be adopted—one that gives effect to the objects and purposes.[17] The ICJ approved these doctrines in the *Reparations case*,[18] and the UN and its agencies have gradually acted upon this decision to bring environmental issues within their scope.

(b) Emergence of Environmental Issues at the International Level

After the establishment of the UN, most cooperative action on environmental matters continued to take place, as before, outside the UN, mainly through the convening of meetings by non-governmental bodies. An important event, however, was the setting up in 1948—outside the UN system but at a conference convened by UNESCO—of the International Union for the Conservation of Nature and Natural Resources (IUCN), now known as the World Conservation Union. Not only governments but individual departments and agencies of government and non-governmental organizations can become members of

[17] I. Brownlie, *Principles of Public International Law* (4th edn., Oxford, 1990), pp. 689–91.
[18] *Reparation for Injuries Suffered in the Service of the United Nations, ICJ Reports*, 1949, p. 174.

IUCN. This mix has enabled it to be more forward-looking and innovative in its approaches than exclusively intergovernmental agencies: private, public, and governmental concerns can be brought together to prepare more coherent environmental strategies, which can then be submitted through an interested government to the UN for approval as resolutions. The World Charter for Nature was adopted by these means, having been put forward by Zaïre. The IUCN has proved an effective lobbyist for bringing environmental issues to the attention of policy-makers at the international level, and published its own World Conservation Strategy in 1980 (updated in 1992).

Though the UN convened some conferences on environmental issues before UNCHE, their scope was limited. For example, the 1949 UN Scientific Conference on the Conservation and Utilization of Resources was limited by ECOSOC to exchanging experiences in resource use and conservation techniques, and even the 1968 UNESCO Conference of Experts on a Scientific Basis for Rational Use and Conservation of the Resources of the Biosphere (the Biosphere Conference), though a landmark in recognizing at the international level man's relationship to nature, addressed the problems only in so far as they were relevant to the life-support systems of plants and animals. None the less, it marked the first time the UN had addressed a wide range of issues in an ecological context. The conference's final report stressed the lack of comprehensive environmental management policies and the growth of public concern; man himself now had the capability and responsibility to determine or influence the future of his environment, and this was leading to the beginnings of national and international action to correct threatening developments. This would necessitate serious and bold departures from past policies. In 1970, an FAO Technical Conference drew attention to the possibly damaging effects of marine pollution and over-exploitation of the living resources of the sea. The concern at national and local levels generated by perceived environmental degradation was thus finally emerging at the international level and being voiced in the UN.[19]

(c) UN Conference on the Human Environment (UNCHE) 1972

1. Concerns leading to UNCHE.

(i) *Environmental concerns of developed states.* By 1972, the concerns of private citizens, as formulated by a variety of non-governmental environmental organizations (NGOs), led certain states—including Canada, Japan, Sweden, the UK, and, especially, the USA—not only to place environmental issues on their political agenda but to enact some influential national legislation: for example, the US 1969 Endangered Species Act and 1972 Marine Mammal Protection Act, and the Canadian 1970 Arctic Waters (Pollution Prevention) Act.[20] States sought to replicate these national approaches on an international basis, spurred on by the fact that many leading NGOs were now themselves beginning to develop international programmes as they perceived the major environmental issues to be resolvable only by action on the international plane. Both older NGOs, such as the US Sierra Club, and new NGOs established in the 1960s, such as World Wildlife Fund, Friends of the Earth, and Greenpeace, began to lobby governments and conferences on selected environmental issues such as whaling, pollution, and nuclear testing. However, not all governments agreed on the priorities to be accorded to the particular environmental problems; nor did they agree on the relative weight to be accorded to the developmental concerns on the one hand, and to the new environmental concerns on the other. It was thus

---

[19] A number of seminal books and articles had stimulated public awareness; including R. Carson, *Silent Spring* (Harmondsworth, 1962); D. Meadows *et al.*, *The Limits to Growth* (a report of the Club of Rome, London, 1972); B. Commoner, *The Closing Circle* (New York, 1971); R. Falk, *This Endangered Planet* (Toronto, 1971).

[20] See also the 1969 US National Environmental Policy Act, the 1971 UK Clean Air Act; the 1971 UK Prevention of Oil Pollution Act.

developed states which at this date were pressing most strongly for more emphasis on the environment.

(ii) *Developmental concerns of developing states*. The newly emerging ex-colonial states were anxious to develop, and viewed the environmental movement as a potential threat to this aspiration, even as a colonialist conspiracy to thwart development by imposing upon them extra costs and prohibitions that developed states had not faced in the nineteenth and early twentieth centuries in implementing their pollution-generating, resource-consuming industrial revolutions. The so-called 'socialist' countries supported these objections, attributing the environmental crisis to capitalism and colonialism.

(iii) *Recognition of environment–development relationship*. A catalytic event, facilitating the success of UNCHE, was the convening of a meeting at Founex, Switzerland, in 1971, to consider a study (instigated by the UNCHE Prepcom) on environment and development. The study group brought together representatives of international development agencies and governments, including economists, bankers, planners, social scientists, and ecologists. Its conclusion that 'the kind of environmental problems that are of importance in developing countries are those that can be overcome by the process of development itself'[21] reassured developing countries, which were wavering in their support for the conference. Twenty-five guide-lines were laid down aimed at protecting their interests. This articulation of the symbiosis of environment and development was thus from the beginning central to the UN's work in the environmental field. Although the relationship has been phrased in a variety of different ways in over two decades since UNCHE—ranging from references to 'sustainable utilization of resources', as in IUCN'S World Conservation Strategy (WCS), to 'sustainable development', as propounded by WCED—essentially the problem remains the same, that of achieving the balance and symbiosis between environmental protection and development.

[21] Development and Environment: Report and Working Papers of a Panel of Experts Convened by the Secretary-General of the UN Conferences on the Human Environment; held at Founex, Switzerland, 4–12 June 1971; pub. UNEP.

2. The convening of UNCHE 1972

This catalytic event was set under way when, in 1968, ECOSOC—responding to Sweden's proposal that a UN conference on the human environment should be convened and following the debates on the issues raised at the Biosphere Conference—adopted a resolution requesting the UN to convene such a conference and to put on the General Assembly's agenda 'The problem of the human environment'.[22] The UN agreed unanimously to this request and instigated the necessary preparatory work.

UNCHE's terms of reference were 'to provide a framework for comprehensive consideration within the United Nations of the problems of the human environment and also to identify those aspects of it that can only, or best be solved through international agreement'. Studies of the work currently undertaken on the environment and the problems facing developed and developing countries were instituted for submission to ECOSOC. Following these reports, the General Assembly established a Preparatory Commission (Prepcom) to lay the foundations for UNCHE, which Sweden was invited to host. The organizational aspects of the Conference were, however, entrusted to a small *ad hoc* secretariat, directed by Maurice Strong, a Canadian official, whose dynamism in this role and as Secretary-General of UNCHE itself contributed greatly to its success and confounded the large number of sceptics throughout the international community, who considered that the issues and the interests of states were too wide, divergent, and contentious to permit any progress on environmental protection.

Six subjects were placed on UNCHE's agenda: planning and management of human settlements for environmental quality; environmental aspects of natural resource management; identification and control of pollutants and nuisances of broad international significance; educational, informational, social, and cultural aspects of environmental issues; development and environment; international organizational implications of action proposals. The aim was to adopt a Declaration on the Human Environment.

[22] ECOSOC Res. 1346 (XLV) of 30 July 1968.

The very acts of convening the conference, preparing an agenda, and aiming for a wide-ranging declaration occasioned world-wide activity throughout the scientific and environmental community. Vast numbers of seminars, conferences, and debates took place: governments, required to produce background papers on their environmental programmes and positions, had to consider the environmental aspects of the work of all their departments. IUCN and ICSU (Internationl Council of Scientific Unions) were particularly active in endeavouring to influence the UNCHE agenda.

However, despite this awareness, environmental issues were, and generally still are, dealt with sectorally within the UN system. This is because by 1970 environmental concerns of one kind or another had appeared on the agendas of numerous existing UN specialized agencies (as well as outside bodies) as, in their view, part of their appropriate areas of concern. For example, atmospheric pollution was already within the ambit of WHO, WMO, ICAO, FAO, UNESCO, and IAEA; the marine environment was covered by IMO (then known as IMCO), FAO, UNESCO, WHO, and IAEA; land-use and conservation of natural resources by FAO and UNESCO; urban environmental problems by WHO, FAO and UNESCO; regulation of and standard-setting for selected pollutants by IMO, UNESCO (by its International Oceanographic Commission), WHO, and IAEA. Other UN bodies, including the regional economic commissions (especially ECE), were, as noted, involved in specialized aspects of the problems. There was, however, a lack of coordination of all these emerging activities: it was clear that a more directed environmental focus was required. One of UNCHE's aims was to provide this by establishing an appropriate institution for this purpose. The machinery established by UNCHE for promoting environmental issues served, however, in the decade after UNCHE, to increase the sectoral division between environment and development, with the UN Conference on Trade and Development (UNCTAD), the UN Industrial Development Organization (UNIDO), the UN Development Programme (UNDP), and the World

Bank addressing developmental concerns and promoting progress towards the New International Economic Order (NIEO) proclaimed by the General Assembly in 1974, whilst the UN Environment Programme (UNEP), established by the UN on the recommendation of the UNCHE, pursued environmental problems and objectives. As the majority of the membership in all the UN's specialized agencies and regional commissions (other than the World Bank and ECE) consists of developing states, development issues have remained the prime concern, and the World Bank itself until recently paid scant attention to the environmental effects of its development loans and their attached conditions.

3. The new institutional framework: UNEP and the Action Plan

In the event, 113 states participated in the UNCHE.[23] The USSR and other Eastern-bloc states did not participate because whilst West Germany (a member of WHO) was invited to attend, East Germany (still excluded from the UN) was not; but over time the USSR did come to participate fully in UNEP and its programmes.

The Conference established a UN environment programme consisting of four major elements: (i) an Action Plan—a policy-oriented document; (ii) an Environment Fund to be established by voluntary contributions from states; (iii) a new UN mechanism (UNEP) for administering and directing the programme; (iv) a Declaration of twenty-six principles on the Human Environment 'to inspire and guide the peoples of the world in the preservation and enhancement of the human environment', Principles 8–14 of which concern the interests of developing states in development.

(1) *The Action Plan.* This comprised 106 recommendations falling into three components. One component was establishment of a Global Assessment Programme, Earthwatch, which was to include a Global Environmental

---

[23] For details see Report of the UN Conference on the Human Environment, Stockholm, 5–16 June 1972 (United Nations, New York, 1973), UN doc. A/Conf. 48/14/Rev. 1.

Monitoring Service (GEMS) and an International Referral Service (now entitled the International Referral System for Sources of Environmental Information, better known as INFOTERRA). GEM's purposes were to gather information; to provide warning of environmental crises; to stimulate scientific research; to evaluate and review all this; and to link by computer nationally held information. The last two proved too grandiose an objective for UNEP, as established, and were reduced to the linking of sources from which information could be obtained through a Global Resource Information Database (GRID); even this has not yet been used as widely as expected. These resources, as well as an International Register of Potentially Toxic Chemicals (IRPTC), combine information from governments, intergovernmental and non-governmental organizations, and companies. Plans to establish a global data bank never materialized. The second component of the Action Plan concerned natural resource management—goal-setting, planning, consultation, conclusion of agreements. The third comprised supporting measures such as training, education, and provision of information.

(ii) *UNEP*. Of particular significance was the introduction of new machinery into the UN system: the secretariat (UNEP); the fifty-eight-state Governing Council; and the Environmental Co-ordination Board (since disbanded). UNEP was deliberately instituted as a *small* secretariat (it has grown from about 100 to 200 persons) to administer and promote the aims of the UN Environment Programme, because so many of the specialized agencies were already involved in various aspects of environmental protection. It was established by resolution of the General Assembly,[24] pursuant to a recommendation of UNCHE, not as a specialized agency or other form of independent UN body but as an autonomous unit within the broader framework of the UN Secretariat. It has no independent powers, still less any supranational authority, and thus cannot itself monitor or enforce environmental law, though it can make proposals in these fields, and its annual report on *The State*

[24] GA Res. 2997 (XXVII) of 15 Dec. 1972.

of the World's Environment is a form of monitoring exercise. It was located, under pressure from developing states, not in Geneva as had been expected, alongside many of the UN agencies with which it would have closely to work and whose activities it was expected to help coordinate, but in Nairobi. It was the first UN body to be located in a developing country. This gesture was intended to encourage the participation of developing states by assuaging their suspicions that an environmental Action Plan was part of a capitalist plot to inhibit their growth: but its location was hardly likely to facilitate its coordination role, which was soon shifted to the UN's own Administrative Committee on Co-ordination (ACC), within which it was difficult for UNEP to play a leading role. However, all three Executive Directors of UNEP since its inception, Maurice Strong (Canada), Mustafa Tolba (Egypt), and Elizabeth Dowdeswell (Canada), have adopted vigorous leading roles in environmental issues.

UNEP's scope was restricted not only by its size and location but also by the limitations of its method of funding, its uncertain legal status, and its ambiguous terms of reference, as laid down in the General Assembly Resolution establishing it. This required UNEP to act as 'a focal point' for environmental action and coordination within the UN system and 'to promote international co-operation in the field of the environment and to recommend, as appropriate, policies to this end; [and] to provide general policy guidance for the direction and co-ordination of environmental programmes within the United Nations System'. It was thus made clear that UNEP was not to undertake a managerial or leadership role, but was to serve as a catalyst in developing and coordinating an environmental focus in other organizations' programmes. Maurice Strong interpreted its role as 'to complexify', that is, 'to remind others of, and help them to take into account all the systems interactions and ramifications implied in their work'.[25] He noted that it was the lack of this cross-

---

[25] UNEP Governing Council, Introductory Statement by the Executive Director, UNEP/GC/31, 11 Feb. 1975, p. 10; and the Proposed Environment Programme: Note by the Executive Director, UNEP/GC/31, 11 Feb. 1975, p. 124.

sectoral, cross-disciplinary view that had led to many environmental problems.

The priority areas that became the target of UNEP's initial programme were: human settlements and habitats; the health of people and their environment; terrestrial ecosystems, their mangement and control; environment and development; oceans; energy; and natural disasters. This list has been revised and expanded over the years: energy and natural disasters no longer appear within the broad groupings of UNEP's current programme, which as well as the five other original topics now includes water, air, lands and desertification, the environment and armaments, and regional technical cooperation;[26] it has never specifically included development of international law, though law is relevant to all these topics. Although not given an express mandate to develop international environmental law, UNEP has found it increasingly necessary to promote legal developments. Mostly these have been in the form of standards, guide-lines, codes, and principles, frequently now referred to as 'soft law' because of the non-binding nature of the form and instruments in which they are initially expressed,[27] although some have taken the form of binding treaties.

The UNEP machinery includes a Governing Council (GC) of fifty-eight states (not required to be members of the UN), elected triennially by the General Assembly on the basis of equitable geographic distribution. The GC is responsible to the General Assembly and reports to it through ECOSOC. The GC, which has generally met annually, has wide-ranging tasks: promoting environmental cooperation and recommending appropriate policies; providing policy guidance for direction and coordination of environmental programmes in the UN system; reviewing the world environment situation; and promoting the

[26] See 'Institutional Profiles: UNEP', *Int. Envt'l. Affairs*, 26.221 (1989), pp. 65–7, at p. 66.

[27] T. Grouchalla-Wisierski, 'A Framework for Understanding "Soft Law"' *McGill Law Journal*, 30 (1984), p. 34; C. Chinkin, 'The Challenge of Soft Law: Development and Change in International Law', *International and Comparative Law Quarterly*, 38 (1989), p. 850.

contribution of relevant scientific and other professional communities to acquisition, assessment, and exchange of environmental knowledge and information and to the technical aspects of the formulation and implementation of environmental programmes in the UN system.[28]

(iii) *Controlling funding and UNEP's environmental activities.* The GC has acted as a watch-dog to ensure that UNEP does not exceed the role allotted to it by the General Assembly; in particular that it concentrates on supporting the programmes of others rather than introducing grand designs of its own. This has always remained a concern: during the later stages of the climate change debate, the UN General Assembly itself stepped into the leading role, establishing its own machinery (the Intergovernmental Negotiating Committee on climate change) to ensure that the interests of the international community in both environment and development were balanced in any resultant measures.

UNEP's role has been further restricted by the generally inadequate funds available to it. Although as part of the UN Secretariat much of its and the GC's administrative costs are borne by the UN budget, its implementation of the UNCHE Action Plan depends on monies drawn from the Environment Fund, which is based on pledging by UN members of voluntary contributions. These have always been inadequate for the huge tasks confronting UNEP, and frequently have not been paid up either on time or in full. Developed states, which are the main contributors, have been anxious to ensure that UNEP does not develop the role and powers to interfere with industrial development, encroach on the roles of existing sectoral organizations, or seek itself to become a specialized agency. Initially, $US 20 million was pledged to the Fund; by 1975 UNEP had approved projects costing $21,897,000. Its budget was severely cut in the 1980s following the UN policy of tight budgetary restraints, and some regular contributors, such as the UK, cut their contributions. However, following the growth of environmental crises and concerns in recent

[28] GA Res. 2997 of 15 Dec. 1972, s.I, para. 2.

years, a few states, including the UK, have increased their payments. Even so, in 1987–9 UNEP's two-year budget was only $25,846,000.[29] With recession in the North and debt crisis in the South, UNEP was not able to expand its activities greatly. However, in light of world-wide concern over problems such as the ozone layer, hazardous wastes, possible climate change, and preservation of biological diversity, in pursuit of all of which UNEP assumed a leading role, there were significant signs before and after UNCED that state policies towards UNEP were changing. There are proposals to increase its budget to $100 million. One of the options considered by the UNCED Prepcom was the strengthening of UNEP, perhaps even transforming it also into a specialized agency, but UNCED rejected this idea.

(iv) *Problems of coordination in the UN system.* The third component of the UNEP machinery, the Environmental Coordination Board (ECB), was intended to address the problems involved in one of UNEP's major tasks— coordination of environmental activities throughout the UN system, which involves monitoring and evaluating the programmes of the large number of specialized agencies and other UN bodies concerned and encouraging co-operation among them. It was intended that, under the chairmanship of UNEP's Executive Director, it would meet periodically and report annually to the GC, but ECB was soon discontinued and its role allocated to the UN's Administrative Committee on Co-ordination (ACC), established by ECOSOC in 1946. ACC convenes biennial meetings of the heads of the specialized agencies and related bodies (including UNEP) under the chairmanship of the UN Secretary-General. ACC decided in 1992 to establish an Inter-Agency Committee on Sustainable Development, comprising representatives of FAO, UNESCO, WHO, the World Bank, WMO, UNDP, UNEP, IMO, and IAEA. This Committee is open to interested ACC members, and is intended as the main source for advice to ACC in discharging its duties on sustainable development arising

[29] Proposed Budget for Programme and Programme Support Costs of the Environment Fund for the Biennium 1988–9, UNEP/GC/14/21, 2 Mar. 1987.

from UNCED. UNEP itself, however, now provides the secretariat for the UN's two principal coordinating committees for environmental and developmental matters, namely the Designated Officials for Environmental Matters (DOEM), under ACC, and the Committee of International Development Institutions on the Environment (CIDIE), on which are represented UNEP, the World Bank, UNDP, and eleven other intergovernmental financial institutions.[30] The World Bank is not a member of DOEM, though it has in recent years expanded its environmental activities.[31]

Although UNEP has taken various additional initiatives in arranging joint programmes and inter-agency meetings and consultations, bringing together, for example, the heads of secretariats concerned with marine pollution, and has itself been included in consultation meetings initiated by other organizations, its ability to fulfil its potential as a coordinator was widely called into question in the lead-up to UNCED. For example, the UN System-Wide Medium-Term Environment Programme (SWMTEP),[32] developed under UNEP auspices, describes the activities in the UN system that are relevant to many of the major issue areas covered in Agenda 21 but does not aim to be the mechanism for welding these into a coherent environmental programme across the board. Lack of effective coordination and thus much wasteful overlap in activities is perceived to be a major problem in the present UN system of environmental protection. Numerous proposals for reform have been made:[33] some were considered in the Preparatory Commission of UNCED and at the Rio Conference itself.

Despite the constraints imposed on UNEP by its organizational and financial framework and terms of reference, its first two Executive Directors seized the opportunities provided by ambiguities in the latter to expand UNEP's

---

[30] *The World Bank and the Environment; A Progress Report*, Fiscal 1991 (World Bank, Washington DC, 1991). [31] Ibid.

[32] The United Nations System-Wide Medium-Term Environment Programme 1990–1995, UNEP, Nairobi, 1988.

[33] See L. A. Kimball, *Forging International Agreements: Strengthening Inter-Governmental Institutions for Environment and Development* (World Resources Institute, Washington DC, 1992).

role. The General Assembly decreed, in establishing UNEP, that its Executive Director was, amongst other things, to provide, on the request of all parties concerned, advisory services for the promotion of international cooperation in the environmental field and perform such other tasks as may be entrusted to UNEP.[34]

4. Significance of 1972 Stockholm Declaration[35]

The Stockholm Declaration (a formalization used in the UN only when principles of special importance are being proclaimed) laid down twenty-six disparate principles, addressing developmental as well as environmental issues: two proclaimed rights; four related to conservation of resources; two to pollution; eight to development; nine to general topics; one called for acceptance of state responsibility for environmental damage. Its preamble refers to the need for international action on problems affecting 'the common realm', and its first Principle states 'the common conviction' that 'Man has a fundamental *right* to freedom, equality and adequate conditions of life in an environment of quality that permits a life of dignity and well-being, and he bears a solemn responsibility to protect and improve the environment for present and future generations' (emphasis added). Others require prevention of pollution and safeguarding of natural resources 'for future generations' and maintenance of their renewability. The Declaration introduced not only a basis for law-making on such matters, but also a basis for new theoretical approaches which subsequent UN and other conventions have increasingly espoused, at least in their preambles. These subsequent innovatory notions include inter-generational rights;[36] 'third-generation' environmental human rights; and a 'common heritage', 'common interest', or 'common concern' approach to developing

[34] GA Res. 2997 of 15 December 1972, at II(e) and (j) respectively.

[35] Report of the UNCHE, above n. 23, pp. 3–5; for evaluation see L. Sohn, 'The Stockholm Declaration on the Human Environment', *Harvard International Law Journal* (1973), pp. 423–515.

[36] E. Brown-Weiss, *In Fairness to Future Generations: International Law, Common Patrimony and Intergenerational Equity in Environmental Law* (Dobbs Ferry, NY, 1989).

regimes for protecting resources in areas beyond national jurisdiction or of common interest such as deep sea-bed minerals, Antarctica, and climate—areas often now referred to as 'common spaces' or 'global commons'. Conventions have since been concluded or extended to protect these areas—the 1982 UN Law of the Sea Convention, the Antarctic Treaty Environmental Protocol of 1991,[37] and the Climate Convention concluded at UNCED in 1992.[38] But progress has been slowed by the need for accommodation of development and environment interests inherent in Principle 21 of the Stockholm Declaration (reiterated in the 1992 Rio Declaration), which accepts that 'States have, in accordance with the Charter of the United Nations and the principles of international law, the sovereign right to exploit their own resources pursuant to their own environmental policies'. This right, however, is modified by the accompanying responsibility not to cause environmental damage to other states or international areas. The UN included this principle in Part XII of UNCLOS which relates to Protection and Preservation of the Marine Environment: Article 193 provides that 'States have the sovereign right to exploit their natural resources pursuant to their environmental policies' but adds the limitation that they must do so 'in accordance with their duty to protect and preserve the marine environment'. Most subsequent environmental developments in the UN have been based on similar compromises, in order to balance not only environmental and developmental concerns, but also states' sovereign rights and international community interests in ensuring protection of the environment. In the latter case the UN has, by introducing the new concept of 'common concern' or 'common interest' in preambles to conventions and in recommendatory resolutions, been able to adopt resolutions and develop conventions on a variety of topics which many states might otherwise consider as falling within their areas of sovereignty or sovereign rights: a particular example is the controversial resolution adopted

[37] *International Legal Materials*, 30 (1991), p. 1461.
[38] *International Legal Materials*, 31 (1992), p. 851.

in 1988 declaring that possible global climate change was 'the common concern of mankind'. Whilst not having the status of a binding principle of law, this resolution legitimized the placing of such issues on the UN agenda and thus their discussion by the General Assembly.[39]

5. UNEP's role in development of international environmental law

UNEP itself set to work in the immediate aftermath of UNCHE to fulfil its mandate to promote the principles in the Stockholm Declaration through a strategy of co-ordinated action and close collaboration amongst governments, IGOs, NGOs, UN bodies, and private societies of all kinds on a wide variety of environmental issues. This included conducting numerous studies, and providing technical assistance, for example assisting developing countries to draft environmental legislation, as well as beginning to develop international environmental law.

Its early programmes were clearly too ambitious in relation to its resources and were thus only partially fulfilled in its first decade. States attending its tenth anniversary meeting in Nairobi in June 1982 expressed concern at this low rate of achievement and called not only for intensification of effort but for inculcation of new perceptions, especially of transboundary problems. These states issued a declaration emphasizing the problems of developing countries, the need for more equitable distribution of technical and economic resources, and the importance of using environmentally sound techniques, stressing the need to prevent rather than repair damage.[40] UNEP itself took a more positive view of its own achievements by this date, especially in the field of developing international environmental law under its 1981 Montevideo Programme.

---

[39] GA Res. 43/53 of 6 Dec. 1988, adopted by consensus. F. L. Kirgis, 'Standing to Challenge Human Endeavors that Could Change the Climate', *American Journal of International Law*, 84 (1990), pp. 525–30, points out that, whilst not having the status of a legal principle or rule, the acceptance of such matters as a 'comon concern' allows them legitimately to be placed on the UN's agenda for discussion and recommendation.

[40] Nairobi Declaration on the State of the World Environment, UNEP/GC/ 10/INF 5, 19 May 1982, *International Legal Materials*, 21 (1982), p. 676.

The GC has over the years asked UNEP to prepare various conventions and guide-lines, using for the purpose *ad hoc* groups of legal and related experts. Such groups have produced ten sets of guide-lines, as well as conventions and protocols, on the ozone layer and transboundary movement of hazardous waste. They have also produced a series of eleven conventions and protocols protecting various regional seas, developed as part of UNEP's 'Regional Seas Programme',[41] which has been highly successful so far as installation of conventions is concerned, but not in their implementation.

UNEP's usual method of international environmental law-making has been to begin by getting scientists together to formulate scientific positions. This has been particularly successful in resolving conflicts of views, for example concerning the effect of CFCs and other gases on the ozone layer. UNEP then develops legal strategies and in the process builds up political support; an important role is allocated to negotiating 'soft-law' guide-lines, principles, and so on, rather than conventions, when the issue is fraught with scientific uncertainty or has serious economic implications, or both. In the support-building process many compromises have to be arrived at, especially in maintaining the 'sustainable development' policy elaborated in UNCED's Agenda 21. The legal instruments adopted often employ vague terms or constructive ambiguities—to disguise differences between states, especially North and South—and the more controversial issues are left initially to 'soft-law' processes. The final status of such instruments is often opaque. Thus though UNEP has now adopted a considerable number of guide-lines which have been endorsed by General Assembly resolutions, the General Assembly has been cautious in relation to their status. It only asked states to '*use* the 1978 UNEP Principles on Shared Natural Resources as guidelines and recommendations in formulating conventions' (emphasis added); the

---

[41] For a critique of these conventions and texts see P. Sand, *Marine Environment Law in the United Nations Environment Programme* (London and New York, 1988).

1980 Weather Modifications Provisions were 'for consideration in the formulation and implementation of programmes and activities relating to that field'; the 1982 Offshore Mining Conclusions were to be considered 'when formulating national legislation or undertaking negotiations for the conclusion of international agreements', and have since formed the basis of a Protocol to UNEP's Kuwait Regional Seas Convention, and of negotiations concerning a new Protocol to UNEP's Barcelona Convention on the Mediterranean. The 1983 Montreal Guidelines on Land-based Pollution, the most damaging form of marine pollution and the most difficult to control as its sources lie within state territory and fall therefore wholly within national jurisdiction, were to be 'taken into account' in the process of developing national legislation and appropriate agreements. It was hoped that they might form the basis of a convention as no global convention on this source exists, but preliminary discussions in the preparations for UNCED revealed too many divisions of opinion to secure the necessary agreement. The 1987 Cairo Guidelines on Waste Management were merely addressed to states 'with a view to assisting them in the process of developing *policies*' (emphasis added), but did provide the basis for rapid adoption through UNEP of the 1989 Basle Convention on the Control of Transboundary Movement of Hazardous Waste, when the need urgently arose, following public disclosure of the scandalous practice of some Western industrialists in dumping such waste in certain developing states in Africa and elsewhere. Because of the need to induce industrialized states to adhere to it, the Basle Convention controls but does not ban transboundary movement of hazardous wastes. Many African countries regard the Basle Convention as unacceptable, and ten African states signed the prohibitory Bamako Convention in 1991. The 1987 London Guidelines on Information Exchange on Traded Chemicals were presented to states 'to help them in the process of increasing chemical safety in all countries'. Procedural provisions in UNEP guide-lines on environmental impact assessment (EIA) have encouraged better and wider adoption of

EIA, and were utilized in the 1991 ECE Convention on Environmental Impact Assessment.

In a different category from the UNEP guide-lines, though it builds to some extent on the Principles on Shared Natural Resources, is the UN's World Charter for Nature (WCN), which uses peremptory language throughout. It was put forward in 1982 by Zaïre, which had been assisted in its preparation by IUCN and UNEP. It states that the principles set forth therein, which in fact are expressed in very general terms, '*shall* be reflected in the law and practice of each State, as well as at the international level' and that 'nature *shall* be respected and its essential processes *shall* not be impaired' (emphasis added). Although the aim of this language was clearly to render the Charter more authoritative, its promulgation as a General Assembly resolution means its status is recommendatory only and not mandatory. The attempt to give it the trappings of a binding commitment gave rise to controversy in the General Assembly and resulted in the USA voting against it.

Finally, UNEP has financed, staffed, and otherwise assisted commissions, secretariats, conferences of the parties, standing committees, etc. under many of the conventions in the conclusion of which it has participated, such as the 1980 Bonn Convention on Conservation of Migratory Species of Wild Animals, the 1989 Basle Convention on Transboundary Movement of Hazardous Waste, the 1985 Vienna Convention on Protection of the Ozone Layer, and the Regional Seas conventions.

(d) Impact of UNCHE Principles and UNEP on the UN System

1. UN environmental conferences

Although the Founex report's conclusions and the UNCHE had drawn attention to the need to address issues of development and environmental protection in tandem, the UN system did not respond in the aftermath of the UNCHE by integrating these aspects. It continued to follow a pragmatic and sectoral approach in relation to both the distinct programmes of each agency and to the series of strategic conferences that the UN convened in the decade following the UNCHE. It organized conferences on: Habitat in Vancouver in 1974; the World Population in Bucharest, the same year; World Food in Rome in 1974 in conjunction with FAO; International Women's Year in Mexico City in 1975; Desertification in Nairobi in 1977; Water in Mar del Plata in 1977; New and Renewable Sources of Energy in Nairobi in 1981; and stretching over nine years from 1973–82, UNCLOS. The two UN Special Sessions of the General Assembly on exploitation of raw materials and development, at which developing states sought new terms of social justice in use of the world's natural resources through an NIEO, were also held during this period, but significantly in isolation from and unrelated to the environmental conferences. As a result, though the law and policy of international development began to evolve alongside environmental law and policy, the paths were separate and tension between the two remained.

The achievements of this strategy of convening *ad hoc* uncoordinated conferences on environmental and development issues were difficult to measure since the conferences were often deeply divided on the issues concerned and thus failed to reach substantial conclusions—ending instead in very general declarations or resolutions of a policy-oriented, target-setting nature, or mere statements of intent. It was hoped, for example, that the 1974 population conference would set population norms, but this was strongly opposed by Argentina, Brazil, China, and the Vatican. Instead it adopted a Plan of Action, recognizing that an effective solution of the problem of expanding populations depended upon socio-economic transformation. Countries with birth rates 'detrimental to their national purposes' were invited to consider setting quantitative goals with a view to attaining them by 1985. This was recognized to require 'substantial' national effort supported by 'adequate' international assistance and 'appropriate' education. Similarly, NGOs hoped the Food Conference would increase food production in developing countries, improve food distribution, and provide a better system of world food security by creating a World Food Bank and buffer food and fertilizer stocks. Instead the conference adopted an International Undertaking on World Food Security calling for a coordinated system of nationally held reserves and a limited commitment to provide commodities and finance for food limited to a minimum of 10 million tons of cereals for three years.

No doubt the conferences did serve, as UNCHE had done, to raise the profile of these issues and created public awareness, largely because of the participation of NGOs and the national preparations involved in arriving at positions. Some institutional developments did result, including the establishment in 1977 of the Habitat Secretariat in Nairobi and the International Fund for Agricultural Development (IFAD) in Rome. Existing institutions such as the World Food Council (established in 1961), and the UN Population Commission (established in 1946), could, of course, also develop some of the proposals adopted at these conferences. But, apart from the 1973–82 UNCLOS, which was exceptional both in scope and in addressing practical issues concerning the law of the sea, the convening of vast but brief conferences on highly controversial subjects had not served to bring about positive results in the short term. It was thus not surprising that prior to the 1992 UNCED there was scepticism concerning the likelihood of its reaching agreement on the vast number of multifarious issues relating to sustainable development that were put before it.

2. *The roles of the sectoral specialized agencies*

As indicated in the introduction to this chapter, the specialized agencies were, except for ILO, established *ad hoc* in the decade following the institution of the UN, each set up by its own separate convention, laying down its particular mandate. Even before UNCHE, following such aims as improving world health (WHO) or food supplies (FAO) or regulating shipping (IMO), the agencies had begun to involve themselves, on a sectoral basis, in what are now regarded as environmental issues. After UNCHE, they increased their involvement in such matters and developed their own environmental programmes on a similar basis. In endeavouring to coordinate and influence *ex post facto* these well-established activities, UNEP has been faced with a difficult, if not impossible task, as also has the UN's ACC. To understand the problems, however, it is necessary to have some idea of the nature and range of the activities taking place, and some awareness of the fact that most of the original programmes were designed from a post-war, post-colonial development perspective by bodies whose membership soon included a majority of developing states, with pressing developmental needs. While most agencies have already introduced or strengthened environmental objectives, in the light of UCNED's Agenda 21 these agencies will have to achieve a better balance between environmental and developmental perspectives, to adopt a more cross-sectoral approach, and to persuade their developed country members to do more to assist developing countries, by provision of financial incentives, technology transfers, etc. It is thus impossible to categorize the agencies as either primarily environmental or primarily developmental in their roles, as each is increasingly having to assume both. However, that said, the financial institutions and arrangements (World Bank, IMF, GATT) have until recently had a more purely economic and developmental perspective than the others, as have UN programmes such as UNDP, UNCTAD, and UNIDO, although the UNDP as the main source of funding of technical assistance clearly can play an environmental role also. Given the number of agencies and the incremental growth of their environmental programmes since 1972, these can be referred to here only briefly.[42]

(i) *IMO* has responsibility for promoting the safety of ships and prevention of pollution. As problems have grown so has its involvement in all aspects of these issues. It has adopted over thirty major conventions and promulgated numerous statements and guide-lines covering such

[42] For a full account of relevant agencies see A. Kiss and D. Shelton, *International Environmental Law* (London, 1991), chap. III; P. Birnie and A. Boyle, *International Law and the Environment* (Oxford, 1992), pp. 53 ff.

matters as pollution from ships, liability and compensation for oil pollution damage, collision regulations, intervening in oil-pollution casualties, preparedness for dealing with oil pollution, and carriage of dangerous goods by sea. Often these have been concluded in response to major disasters such as the *Torrey Canyon*, *Amoco Cadiz* or *Exxon Valdez* strandings. IMO's implementation of its standards is being somewhat undermined by increasing resort, for economic reasons, to flags of convenience. It has recently appointed a Sustainable Development Officer.

(ii) *FAO* has an interest in conservation of natural resources, but this has been inhibited until recently by the need to promote the development of agriculture and fishing in its predominantly developing state membership. It has, however, participated in hydrographic basin management, plant and soil protection agreements, and in establishing various fisheries commissions. Its new awareness of the need to relate fisheries to environmental protection has led it also to designate an officer responsible for Sustainable Development, and in response to UNCED's demands for a new convention it convened a Technical Consultation on High Seas Fishing beginning in 1992.

(iii) *WHO* has produced numerous studies, guides, standards, etc. furthering health protection which have given it an interest in marine and air pollution and toxic chemicals; a European Charter on Environmental Health was adopted in 1989 under its auspices.

(iv) *WMO*'s role in weather prediction and monitoring has led it into environmental spheres such as negotiation of conventions on weather modification, climate change, the ozone layer, and long-range transboundary atmospheric pollution.

(v) *ILO* is also involved in standard-setting, and has concluded numerous conventions on the safety and health of workers, the rights of indigenous peoples, shipping labour standards, etc. It has convened important technical meetings, including for example its 1988 African Regional Conference which discussed hazardous waste disposal.

(vi) *UNESCO* has a particularly broad mandate involving it in research and co-operation in material and social sciences, public education, training, and technology transfer, which it could develop further in environmental fields. UNESCO is also involved in nature conservation through its 1972 Convention on the World Cultural and Natural Heritage, which allows for listing of outstanding natural areas. It is notable that though the USA and UK withdrew from UNESCO in the 1980s, they continue to support its International Oceanographic Commission (IOC) and participate in its various marine pollution programmes.

(vii) *IAEA*, though not strictly a specialized agency, contributes to UN environmental activities by recommending international safety standards for use of nuclear plants and materials. Its Safeguards Committee provides guide-lines for the agreements required under the 1968 Non-Proliferation Treaty, and for the agreements on notification of nuclear accidents and provision of technical assistance thereafter, concluded under its auspices after Chernobyl.

All these agencies co-operate as occasion requires on particular issues, such as IMO with ILO on a convention on minimum standards for seafarers; or IMO with UNEP on preparedness for oil spills; or WMO with the ECE and UNEP on climate change. But, for the reasons given earlier, this falls far short of what is required for co-ordinated programming for sustainable development.

3. The roles of the financial specialized agencies

Provision of financial assistance is a key aspect of sustainable development for developing countries, and the UN bodies involved in this are therefore of particular importance. Promoting development was initially the prime concern of agencies such as the World Bank, but environmental awareness has gradually increased in all the agencies established under the Bretton Woods system.

(i) *World Bank*: It has a staff of almost 6,000 compared to UNEP's 200 and IMO's 300; in 1991 it had at its disposal $23 billion. It can play a major role in influencing environmental protection in countries to which it makes loans, both in its choice of projects and in the conditions it attaches to funding. It is endeavouring to overcome the poor environmental reputation that it gained from financing such environmentally destructive projects as vast hydroelectric schemes and the felling of tropical rain forests to facilitate development projects. Examples include the Polonoroeste project in Brazil aimed at encouraging settlement in the forests of Rondonia, the Narmada Valley dams in India, and the assistance given to the transmigration project of Indonesia. NGOs were particularly critical of the lack of consultation with the local people involved and the lack of awareness of the human and environmental consequences of the projects.

Informed NGO criticism brought about major changes in the Bank's policies in the 1980s.[43] In 1987, the Bank set up a central environment department and environmental units in its four regional bureaux; more funds were allocated to purely environmental loans—$1.6 billion in 1991 compared to $400 million in all previous years taken together[44]—and to environmental studies, e.g. on cleaning up the Black Sea. Country environmental issue papers have also been started to ensure a coherent inter-sectoral approach. The Bank's example is being pursued by the Asian, African, and Inter-American Development Banks, although this will involve a huge burden in terms of resources, training, and reorganization. The European Bank for Reconstruction and Development is already implementing new policies based on its greater resources.

(ii) *GEF*: The World Bank's environment department is responsible for administering the Global Environmental Facility (GEF),[45] established following a recommendation in the Brundtland Report. This is an innovatory scheme established to help developing countries to contribute to

[43] As acknowledged by J. Warford and R. Ackerman, 'Environment and Development: Implementing the World Bank's New Policies' (Development Committee, Paper 17, IMF/World Bank, Washington DC, 1988). See also K. Piddington, 'The World Bank and the Environment', in A. Hurrell and B. Kingsbury (eds.), *The International Politics of the Environment* (Oxford, 1992).

[44] H. F. French, *After the Earth Summit: The Future of Global Environmental Governance* (Worldwatch Paper 107, Washington DC, 1992), p. 39; *The World Bank and the Environment: A Progress Report*, Fiscal 1991 (World Bank, Washington DC, 1991).

[45] Relevant documents in *International Legal Materials*, 30 (1991), pp. 1735–72.

solving global environmental problems in four areas: reducing global warming by supporting energy efficiency and new and renewable energy activities; protecting international waters by supporting contingency planning, pollution abatement, provision of reception facilities, the cleaning up and also conservation of unique bodies of water; preserving biological diversity by supporting efforts to preserve and prevent further depletion of existing ecosytems; and protecting the ozone layer by aiding developing countries to move from use and production of CFCs to substitutes and alternatives. The initial arrangement recommended to participants was for a Facility of SDR 1 billion, with participation on a voluntary basis. Responsibility for its implementation is shared with UNEP and the UNDP.[46] The funds are being contributed on various bases, including direct contributions, co-financing arrangements, and grant equivalents by twenty-one countries, fourteen of them developed,[47] to total amounts of SDR 783.66 m. Taking into account other possible contributions to the Interim Fund of the Montreal Protocol to the Ozone Convention,[48] the total administered through the GEF amounted by 1993 to the SDR 1 billion aimed at.

Although the GEF has been welcomed as at least a start to providing the financial assistance to support sustainable development that developing countries have demanded in all available forums, it has also been criticized for the limited number of projects involved and the voluntariness and small amount of the fund in relation to the tasks in hand. As an indication of scale, the UNCED Secretariat estimated that implementation of Agenda 21 by the South alone would require at least $600 billion, of which the external aid component was $125 billion.

(iii) *IMF*: The IMF was created to provide short-term balance of payments support in order to stabilize the world economic system. In recent years the IMF has required

---

[46] Ibid.

[47] Austria, Brazil, China, Denmark, Egypt, Finland, France, Germany, India, Indonesia, Italy, Japan, Mexico, The Netherlands, Norway, Pakistan, Spain, Sweden, Switzerland, Turkey, and the UK. Other states are expected to join these.   [48] *International Legal Materials*, 30 (1991), pp. 1773–7.

recipient countries to introduce stringent 'structural adjust-ment programmes' prescribed by it to restore their economy. This includes cutting expenditure, which can inhibit both the taking and enforcing of environmental measures. These requirements have been much criticized in the Third World and by development experts, who question their long-term benefit; moreover the need to promote exports can lead to destruction of natural resources and promotion of environmentally degrading industries, such as mining or other forms of ill-thought out industrialization.[49]

(iv) *GATT*: The General Agreement on Tariffs and Trade (GATT), with IMF and IBRD, was one of the three major elements of the Bretton Woods system. It is not, like the others, an institution, but a regulatory mechanism aimed at liberalizing trade by reducing tariffs and barriers. The post-war economic theory on which this system was based was oblivious of any environmental consequences. Its assumptions that the free market benefits social welfare and results in socially acceptable levels of consumption of natural resources have palpably been proved wrong but, as the system seems, at least in the short term, here to stay, given the economic failure of the alternative 'socialist' system, the problem now is how to use both market forces and regulatory mechanisms in optimal combination to achieve sustainable development.[50] However, the ruling óf a GATT dispute settlement panel in 1991 proposing that the use of trade sanctions even to achieve environ-mentally beneficial results in the global commons—in this case the USA's ban, imposed under a relevant US law, on import of Mexican tuna caught by seine nets that also capture and kill dolphins—is contrary to GATT rules[51] also highlighted the problematic interrelationship of inter-national trade and environment. The relationship between

[49] French, *After the Earth Summit*, p. 41.

[50] See D. Pearce, A. Markandya, and E. Barbier, *Blueprint for a Green Economy* (Earthscan, London, 1989); and D. Pearce (ed.), *Blueprint 2: Greening the World Economy* (Earthscan, London, 1991), for a market-oriented view. However, the ideas expressed therein remain controversial.

[51] GATT Panel Report on US Restrictions on Imports of Tuna, *International Legal Materials*, 30 (1991), pp. 1598–1623.

these has only recently begun to be accorded any significance by GATT. Thus the Brundtland Report, which recognized that trade practices would have to be reconciled with environmental aims if sustainable development is to be achieved, proposed the reform of GATT on this basis. This demand has been taken up by concerned governments and NGOs,[52] but given the difficulties experienced in negotiating the GATT Uruguay round it seems unlikely that GATT will give high priority to this reform in the short term.

(e) Impact of UNCHE Principles outside the UN System

1. Regulation under ad hoc *treaty regimes*

Numerous regional and *ad hoc* bodies have been established over the years following the first sealing and fishery commissions and arrangements for migratory birds.[53] Most of these still exist, though revised in the light of experience, or to accommodate the extension of coastal states' maritime jurisdiction approved in UNCLOS. Terrestrially based as well as marine species have in the last twenty years been protected by a widening range of treaties at global and regional level, several encouraged by IUCN. The most successful is the Convention on Trade in Endangered Species, which established an efficient secretariat (supported by UNEP) to oversee the implementation of the system of import and export permits for trade in such species. A key to its success has been the opportunity the permit system provides for NGOs to monitor its application and report failures to governments and the secretariat. All such treaties are administered by *ad hoc* secretariats or existing bodies. Much less successful has been the Bonn Convention on Conservation of Migratory Species of Wild Animals (another IUCN/UNEP treaty), which has not attracted sufficient parties to provide funds

---

[52] R. Stein and B. Johnson, *Banking on the Biosphere? Environmental Procedures and Practices of Nine Multilateral Development Agencies* (Lexington, Mass., 1979).

[53] For details of these see S. Lyster, *International Wildlife Law* (Cambridge, 1985).

for its tiny secretariat (originally funded by UNEP) to be active, and has been unable to gather the support necessary for it to conclude the Range State agreements vital to its success.[54]

Since UNCHE, regional and *ad hoc* commissions for prevention of pollution from all or from discrete sources have proliferated. Even before UNEP's Regional Seas Programme was launched in 1976, the 1972 Oslo Commission covering Ocean Dumping in the North Sea and North Atlantic had been established, followed in 1974 by the Paris Commission on Land-Based Sources of Pollution covering the same area, and the Helsinki Commission concerning various sources of pollution in the Baltic Sea. These conventions adopted the approach of fishery commissions and pioneered the establishment of pollution control commissions with powers, by voting, to administer and amend attached annexes of pollutants, which states parties were required, according to the relevant listing, either to prohibit or control. Such flexible techniques allow for revision as scientific knowledge advances and awareness grows; these instruments provided models for subsequent UN conventions such as those on the ozone layer and climate change.

Such arrangements have the advantage that they provide a forum for balancing states' interests and equities, and for evaluating environmental protection measures against developmental needs. The disadvantage is that generally only a limited number of issues are addressed, chosen by the states concerned, and progress on these is limited by national political considerations and priorities. As most of these bodies were established *ad hoc* they lack any coordinating mechanisms, though some regional bodies provide forums for an overview. Both the members of and areas covered by such bodies vary and frequently overlap but they also leave gaps. Major problems are now arising, for example, from the adoption of the EEZs approved by UNCLOS. EEZs have not generally achieved the expected

---

[54] Birnie and Boyle, *International Law and the Environment*, see chaps. 11–13 covering sustainable development of living resources.

improvement in enforcement, since over-exploitation by local vessels has often replaced the former excess of foreign vessels, and displaced foreign vessels are fishing high seas areas more intensively. Stocks straddling borders are especially susceptible to over-exploitation, as the recent dispute between Canada and the EEC has highlighted.

2. *Proliferation of environmental programmes under other institutions*

The North Sea area reflects the environmental organizational problems facing the UN as a whole since a large number of existing, as well as new, regional bodies developed environmental roles after UNCHE, e.g. the Council of Europe, OECD, NATO's CCMS (Committee on the Challenges of Modern Society), the Nordic Council, and the EC. The surrounding states have since 1984 held a series of International North Sea Conferences (INSC) at ministerial level to set goals and harmonize their policies. They influence the programmes of the relevant regional bodies which are required to execute the measures laid down in the INSC's final declarations. A breakthrough has occurred in that the participating states have now committed themselves to implement the 'precautionary principle', which they interpret as requiring states to act when it seems *likely* that adverse effects might result from their activities rather than waiting for proof that such effects are actually occurring. Of course, it remains to be determined at what point this likelihood arises, and controversy can still arise concerning this decision. The Declarations have also, *inter alia*, set target dates for phasing out incineration at sea and ocean dumping. At the third INSC in 1990, the problems of depletion of certain marine living resources began to be discussed for the first time and research was instituted. This regional acceptance of the precautionary principle, evidenced also in the 1992 revised Convention on the Baltic Sea, may hasten its slow progress at the global level.

Since UNCHE, almost all regions have addressed some if not all of their environmental problems and developed new institutions;[55] and existing regional organizations have all developed environmental programmes. For example, the Council of Europe (CE), OECD, the EC, OAS, OAU and ASEAN (Association of South-East Asian Nations) have established various bodies, but few regions, other than the South Pacific in its 1986 Noumea Convention, have adopted the holistic approach recommended by many ecologists and NGOs. An incremental approach has been preferred, based on *ad hoc* conventions for each source of pollution, or a framework convention to which protocols on particular sources can be added as growing scientific knowledge and pressure generates the necessary state will to tackle these.

Notable developments amongst the programmes of these regional bodies include the CE's 1980 Convention on Conservation of European Wildlife and Natural Habitats, OAS's 1940 Convention on Nature Protection and Wildlife Preservation in the Western Hemisphere, which it is updating; OAU's forward-looking, but dormant, 1968 African Convention on the Conservation of Nature and Natural Resources, which it is now trying to revise and revitalize; and ASEAN's 1985 Convention on Conservation of Nature and Natural Resources.

OECD, having established a Committee on the Environment in 1970, has adopted several recommendations and generated new principles, including the polluter pays principle (PPP), which are based on and make use of economic theory for purposes of environmental protection. With similar considerations in mind it has also addressed problems of assessing compensation for pollution damage. Its ideas have been influential. The EC, for example, has also adopted the PPP, which is widely followed, despite the fact that ultimately it imposes pollution damage costs on consumers as well as polluters. OECD has also pioneered such principles as 'prior informed consent', notification of emergencies, and non-discrimination in application of laws, and has set standards for chemicals and toxic and

---

[55] See Kiss and Shelton, *International Environmental Law*, pp. 73–93; Birnie and Boyle, *International Law and the Environment*, chap. 2.

hazardous waste, including radioactive substances, which have had considerable impact on international and other regional developments.

(f) UNCED: Success or Failure?

The Brundtland Report called upon the General Assembly to transform its conclusions into a UN Programme of Action on Sustainable Development, for a conference to be convened to review progress on this, and for follow-up arrangements to be instituted to 'set benchmarks and maintain human progress within the guidance of human needs and natural law'. The General Assembly decided to convene UNCED in 1992, and established a Preparatory Commission (Prepcom) to prepare for it. Before UNCED it was hoped that the Conference would conclude conventions on climate change and biological diversity, consider the possibility of a convention on forestry and the instruments that might appropriately be developed to control land-based pollution, produce an Earth Charter setting out the principles of conduct for environmental protection and sustainable development, and adopt a programme of action for the implementation of these principles. It was intended that this programme, known as Agenda 21 because it directed attention to action in the twenty-first as well as the twentieth century, was to set out the goals of sustainable development and the means of achieving them. It was realized that study of so-called 'cross-sectoral issues' would be vital, including transfer of technology, scientific and technological requirements, poverty, human settlements, the role of women, health, and education.

Two unusual features of UNCED were: first, its sponsorship not only by donor governments but also by major companies (e.g. ICI) and foundations (e.g. MacArthur and Rockefeller); and secondly, the fact that, unlike at UNCHE, NGOs were allowed to play a major role in its Prepcoms. The negotiating climate in these was often hostile, as major differences emerged on the basic questions of how much weight was to be given to development, as opposed to environment; whether the two can be separated; and the content of sustainable development. As in the debates in the UN and specialized agencies, the developing states characterized the environmental crisis as a long-term developmental one, and the developed states saw it as a more immediate technical problem. The former thus endeavoured to direct discussion, precisely as in the 1974 debates on the NIEO, to the underlying causes rather than the symptoms, and pressed the case for reform of the international economic system as a prerequisite for effective environmental action. Major differences thus arose along a North–South divide on issues relating to sovereignty over natural resources, sharing of economic costs, equity, funding, the role of multi-lateral institutions, transfer of technology, climate change, biological diversity, and deforestation. The Northern proposals on the last two, in particular, were seen as indicative of the continued imperialism of industrialized states—an invasion of sovereignty. The pressure for global action on climate change was seen in the South as an inequitable attempt to force developing states to share the costs and burdens of a problem created almost entirely by the industrialized states.

It has been suggested that only a new sense of solidarity among states, as prevailed in 1945 at the time of the founding of the UN, can bring about the reforms in the UN system that are required to make effective any programmes for development, let alone the complex processes involved in sustainable development.[56] Many had hoped that the threat to global security posed by the environmental crises would stimulate that sense. There was little evidence of this in the UNCED Prepcoms, or at the Rio Conference itself until the final days.

Given these difficulties, it is not surprising that the Rio Conference was not asked to adopt an Earth Charter or conventions on land-based pollution or deforestation. However, after intense pressure and extended negotiation, the Secretary-General of the Prepcom (Maurice Strong) succeeded in putting forward drafts of Agenda 21 and a

[56] D. Williams, *The Specialized Agencies and the United Nations: The System in Crisis* (London, 1987), pp. 238–9.

Declaration on Environment and Development, as well as Climate Change and Biological Diversity Conventions; and the chairman of the Conference itself (Tommy Koh) succeeded in persuading the delegates and the 103 heads of government who attended the 'Earth Summit' to adopt these, albeit in a watered-down form.[57]

Many goverments as well as NGOs, however, expressed regret that the climate treaty was weakened, that many crucial issues were removed from or diluted in Agenda 21, that the USA initially refused to sign the treaty on biological diversity in order to protect the interests of the US pharmaceutical industry, that Malaysia blocked consideration of a treaty on forests, and that only vague commitments were made by developed states on provision of financial resources and debt reduction. Despite these deficiencies, some spirit of solidarity (referred to as the 'Spirit of Rio') did prevail, and some new instruments and an agenda for future action emerged from the negotiations. A contributing factor was the unprecedented level of public participation in the negotiations in the lead-up to UNCED, and the vast number of NGO observers who were present in Rio to lobby government delegates. The instruments adopted at Rio were as follows:

(i) *The Rio Declaration on Environment and Development.* This is a set of twenty-seven principles, expressed in very general terms, finely balanced between the priorities of developed and developing states, governing individual behaviour in relation to sustainable development.

(ii) *Agenda 21*, a programme covering over 100 areas ranging from alleviation of poverty to strengthening national and international society's ability to protect the atmosphere, oceans and other waters, mountains, and areas vulnerable to desertification. Chapter 17 on the oceans, for example, provides an integrated strategy for managing the oceans, regional seas, and enclosed seas, and calls for a conference to resolve the problem of over-fishing of stocks that straddle the boundaries of

[57] Earth Summit Documents, *International Legal Materials*, 31 (1992), pp. 814–87. *Agenda 21* (New York: United Nations, 1992).

jurisdictional zones. Dropped from Agenda 21, however, were such contentious issues as population, resource consumption patterns, Third World debt, export of hazardous wastes, forests, the role of the military. These thus remain as priority areas for future negotiation and action. The agenda does provide a plan for action which recognizes for the first time the interconnections between economic, environmental, poverty, and development issues, and seriously endeavours to integrate environment and development.

It includes a financial chapter requiring developed countries to reach a target of 0.7 per cent of GNP for development assistance by the year 2000, or as soon as possible thereafter, and refers to provision of a further 'Earth Increment' to augment the funds of the International Development Association (the soft-loan arm of the World Bank) as well as reforms of the GEF to broaden its base and enhance its acceptability to developing states. Some governments (e.g. of Germany, Japan, Canada, the UK) and the EC immediately pledged various sums, estimated as amounting to between $6 and $7 billion a year. The cost of Agenda 21 was, however, estimated by UNCED to require $125 billion in assistance for developing countries alone, which would require developed states to double their present combined level of aid. Prospects for provision of the financial aid essential to implementation of much of Agenda 21 are, therefore, poor.

(iii) *Framework Convention on Climate Change.* The preamble to the convention, acknowledging the threat posed to the climate by carbon dioxide and other gases, says that developed countries bear the major responsibility and thus need to take immediate action to reduce these emissions. It also recognizes the concerns of the states vulnerable to sea-level rise. The climate should be protected and emissions should be limited to levels which do not endanger it and will allow natural recovery of systems already affected, but no targets are set for reduction. As the convention also calls for sustained economic growth and development, and requires that measures taken should not 'unjustifiably' inhibit free and open international trade, it has been criticized by NGO's and concerned governments. However, these compromises, especially the failure to set reduction targets, though weakening the convention, represented the *realpolitik* required to secure the support of, in particular, the USA. Financial assistance and technological transfer are recommended, but without specific provision.

The convention seems unlikely to lead to drastic action in the short term, although some governments and the EC did individually commit themselves to various targets and, as in the case of UNEP's regional seas programmes and the ozone convention, it is likely that the framework convention will eventually be supplemented by protocols fixing emission and other targets. However, 153 governments signed the convention, with the notable exception of Malaysia, and the vagueness of its terms means that it is likely soon to obtain the fifty ratifications necessary to bring it into force.

(iv) *Convention on Biological Diversity*. Although the provisions of the Convention are qualified throughout with such imprecise phrases as 'as far as possible and appropriate', it does require parties to take action in many key areas such as: developing national plans etc. for sustainable use of biodiversity; making inventories of its components and threats to these; developing and strengthening *in situ* mechanisms for conservation of biodiversity both within and outside protected areas and developing complementary *ex situ* mechanisms; restoring degraded ecosystems and endangered species; regulating the release of genetically modified organisms; preserving indigenous and local systems of management; and equitably sharing benefits with local communities. It remains unclear, however, precisely what action will ensue from such general provisions. Concern remained about a number of other weaknesses such as confused provisions on intellectual property rights, the use of the controversial GEF as the interim funding mechanism, and failure to address key underlying issues such as land reform, the exact role of local communities, and the debt factor. Attention must be directed to specification of interim measures for action on all these major points, perhaps involving the setting up by UNEP of an Intergovernmental Committee on the Convention.

(v) *The Commission on Sustainable Development (CSD).* In assessing the adequacy of the Commission for its task it is useful to compare it to other proposals considered by UNCED for new institutional responses. These will be examined, along with CSD, in the next section.

(g) The UN System after UNCED

1. Can the UN system assure sustainable development?[58]

As this chapter has sought to demonstrate, the historical background and original goals of the UN and its agencies have not generated a system that is well suited to synthesizing the environmental with the developmental problems, a fusion that UNCED has identified as the key issue in the achievement of sustainable development. The UN's original security-oriented purposes, the politicization of its organs along divides such as East–West and North–South, the stubborn sectoralism of the specialized agencies, the proliferation of programmes and autonomous units with different objectives, the large number of concerned bodies that exist outside the UN, have made coordination difficult, especially as this is the aspect in relation to which the UN's machinery is at its weakest—coordinating committees such as ACC, DOEM, and CIDIE have not been given sufficient authority to have a radical impact on the system of sectoralism so far.

(1) *The changes introduced by UNCED.* As the UN's SWMTEP points out, while the objectives of all the elements of the

[58] On this see French, *After the Earth Summit*; Kimball, *Forging International Agreements*; P. S. Thacher, *Global Security and Risk Management: Background to Institutional Options for Management of the Global Environment and Commons* (Geneva, World Federation of United Nations Associations, 1991); P. S. Thacher, 'The Role of the United Nations', in Hurrell and Kingsbury (eds), *The International Politics of the Environment* (Oxford, 1992); P. Sand, *Lessons Learned in Global Environmental Governance* (World Resources Institute, Washington DC, 1990); C. Tinker, *Making UNCED Work: Building the Legal and Institutional Framework for Sustainable Development at the Earth Summit and Beyond*, UNA-USA Occasional Paper No. 4, March, 1992; see also WCED Report, n. 5 above. For a critique of UNCED institutional arrangements see L. A. Kimball and W. C. Boyd, 'International Institutional Arrangements for Environment and Development: A Post-Rio Assessment' (unpublished paper, 1992), on the conclusions of which this section is largely based.

UN system are compatible and complementary, they are different.[59] Each organization has its own mandate, its own constituency of member states, and its own objectives. This makes planning and implementation of programmes a complex process, but because this forces interactions, it could also become a strength; a convergence of planning procedures is required and UNCED's Agenda 21 sets out the ways of achieving this. SWMTEP provided a coherent overall framework for environmental programmes, without rigid prescription for action. UNCED's Agenda 21 is cast in similarly broad and flexible terms but takes matters a stage further by encouraging the embodiment of environmental concerns in the activities of the development agencies and programmes generally and indicating the action required.

The UN system is not effective in assessing, reviewing, and monitoring either the effects of activities or compliance with prescribed measures. Effective scrutiny has been left to NGOs, which have performed the task efficiently in several areas, but their activities are necessarily issue-oriented: they cannot themselves carry out the required reforms to remedy the whole range of weaknesses in the system, especially the coordinative failures. It is governments that have to legislate and to ensure that their national programmes conform to the UN goals for sustainable development. It is here that NGOs (now often referred to as NGAs—non-governmental actors) can provide the necessary stimulus.

Will the institutional reforms initiated by UNCED be sufficient to set in motion the rethinking, redirection and review necessary to enable Agenda 21 targets to be met? The criteria agreed in 1972 by governments for the institutional aspects of the UNCHE Action Plan continue to apply: instituting a mechanism for agreeing on the action required; use of existing organizations; developing institutional networks with linkages and 'switchboard mechanisms' rather than a new supranational agency;

[59] *United Nations System-Wide Medium Term Environment Programme 1990–1995* (UNEP, Nairobi, 1988), p. 101.

providing for flexibility and evolution in the context of incomplete knowledge; avoiding overlap by coordination and rationalization; ensuring that any policy centres established to influence and coordinate activities do not have operational funtions that compete with cooperating organizations; strengthening regional capability; retaining the UN as the main centre for international cooperation but strengthening and reinforcing the whole UN system whilst taking account of the wide variations in environmental conditions among states.[60]

Debates prior to UNCED made clear that there was no political support for creation of a new supranational UN environment and development agency, or even endowing any one existing agency with a lead role. Options considered in the UNCED process included: (1) transforming UNEP into a Specialized Agency; (2) expanding UNDP's role; (3) establishing an intergovernmental Standing Committee on Environment and Development; (4) creating an Expert Panel on Environment and Development; (5) revising the composition of the Security Council.[61] In the aftermath of UNCED there was some movement on each of these issues.

(ii) *Role of UNEP.* Tranforming UNEP into a specialized agency attracted little support. Developed states rejected both the extra costs and political implications of such a change, and there was no enthusiasm for more bureaucratization of the UN. Proposals for moving UNEP from Nairobi to a more central UN location in Geneva or New York were not popular with African states.

There was, however, support for strengthening UNEP in its present role and location. UNCED opted for this, giving UNEP a clear mandate to promote cooperation on policy-making, monitoring, and assessment, and calling upon it specifically to develop international environmental law. It will be required also to promote such techniques as environmental impact assessment and environmental

---

[60] Thacher, *Global Security and Risk Management.*
[61] These proposals are elaborated upon in Kimball, *Forging International Agreements*; and French, *After the Earth Summit.*

auditing, to disseminate information and raise environmental consciousness, to promote regional and sub-regional cooperation, and so on. UNEP's role in coordinating the growing number of treaties was also encouraged, and the possibility of co-locating any new secretariats or intergovernmental bodies that may be established was mooted. The problem of funding this expanded role was not addressed, however, and UNEP has not been accorded any new powers or authority.

(iii) *Role of UNDP*. Agenda 21 designated UNDP as the lead organization for building capacity for sustainable development at local, national, and regional levels by, amongst other things, strengthening the role of its resident representatives in each country to coordinate UN technical cooperation efforts in the field. The aim is to encourage countries to identify their own needs and priorities for technical assistance, releasing the UN agencies to provide research, analysis, and technical advice as required. Agenda 21 called on every country to review its capacity-building requirements by 1994 and develop its own Agenda 21 action programme; with the UN Secretary-General to report by 1997 on means of strengthening the technical cooperation programmes in support. This 'bottom up' rather than 'top down' approach is another key component of UNCED's strategy. By stressing the need for states to evaluate their own situation as a prerequisite of technical assistance, and encouraging a much wider role for NGOs in creating awareness and monitoring compliance, Agenda 21 aims to overcome some of the difficulties created by the rigid adherence of many developing states to a narrowly defined concept of sovereignty.

(iv) *An Intergovernmental Standing Committee on Environment and Development*. It was suggested that the General Assembly and Security Council could establish such a committee with a membership that balanced North and South and included UNEP and UNDP Governing Council members, and observers from relevant bodies. According to its advocates, such a committee would oversee SWMTEP and monitor progress on priority issues in the specialized agencies. It would endeavour to influence the General

Assembly's agenda and redirect debates so that serious discussion of sustainable development could take place, and would prompt the raising in the Security Council of matters affecting environmental security. It could also relate to public and private sector funding bodies, pressing targets upon them.

It was envisaged that such a committee would be backed by a strengthened ACC, which might set up an Inter-Agency Board on Environment and Development—UNEP and UNDP heads could act as its vice-chairmen. The ACC's subsidiary inter-agency units could be regrouped around the Agenda 21 topics, and corresponding units set up within the UN under the chairmanship of the Secretary-General. The Board's membership would include representation of the UN agencies, especially the financial ones, with regional development banks and organizations in association. Its role could include appropriate policy research, including on funding targets. Various funding innovations (the Montreal Protocol to the Ozone Convention, the *ad hoc* Fund for the Wetlands Conventions, the World Heritage Fund, the GEF) could be used as models, with EC procedures providing a regional model. NGOs could be drawn upon for advice.

This was regarded at UNCED as the most attractive and politically feasible idea, and was adopted in a modified form. A Commission on Sustainable Development (CSD), reporting to ECOSOC, was established by the General Assembly at its forty-seventh session in 1992.[62] Its close relation to ECOSOC has caused criticism, since ECOSOC now has almost 200 bodies and subsidiaries thereof reporting to it: the Secretary-General is recommending a slimming-down of this substructure. CSD consists of representatives of fifty-three states elected by ECOSOC for a three-year term. NGO criticism of the exclusively inter-governmental membership of CSD was mollified to a limited extent by the setting up of a High Level Advisory Board (HLAB) of eminent experts on environment and development to advise the Secretary-General and through

---

[62] See GA Res. 47/191 of 22 Dec. 1992.

him CSD, ECOSOC, and the General Assembly. It includes a wide range of experts from all sectors of society, particularly NGOs and industry. CSD meets annually for two to three weeks (the first substantive session was in June 1993) and is supported by an identifiable secretariat which will also service a new Inter-Agency Committee on Sustainable Development which will co-ordinate the work of the different UN agencies. The General Assembly decided that its secretariat would 'be funded to the maximum extent possible by the UN's budget': despite a Swiss offer of substantial support for a Geneva secretariat, New York was chosen as the principal location. The General Assembly decreed that the CSD's task was to monitor the progress of implementation of Agenda 21 and the other instruments adopted by UNCED; to review the financial and other provisions; to enhance the dialogue between the UN, NGOs, and other outside bodies; and to consider information on sustainable development provided by governments, who will be expected to submit national reports and other communications. CSD has been instructed to adopt a 'multi-year thematic programme' of work, identifying what will be discussed and when. Issues will include: financial resources and transfer of technology; implementation of Agenda 21 at all levels 'in an integrated manner'; and the convening of a high-level meeting, including ministerial participation, to ponder an integrated overview of implementation of Agenda 21, consider energy policy issues, and try to generate the necessary political impetus for promoting the UNCED conventions and declarations.

It seems unlikely that the post-UNCED institutional innovations will prove much more in the short term than yet more cogs in the UN's slow-turning wheel. CSD will not have the direct relation to the General Assembly and Security Council that was envisaged by some, nor will it have the role in coordinating UN organs proposed in earlier versions of Agenda 21. Its role in reviewing the progress of Agenda 21 could nevertheless be influential in the same way that the UN Human Rights Commission, which it closely resembles, has impact, using material supplied by NGOs as well as by governments and organizations to promote implementation of environmental treaties, standards, and programmes.[63]

Governments can submit to CSD information on problems encountered in implementing Agenda 21, as under the ozone, climate change, and biodiversity treaties, including those arising from finance and technology deficiencies.

UNCED also acted upon the proposal that the ACC should be 'revitalized', under the direct leadership of the Secretary-General, as the inter-agency mechanism for programme review, coordination, and interrelationship with the multilateral financial institutions. It envisaged that a task force might facilitate this, but left it to the Secretary-General to decide the supporting arrangements for both the Standing Commission and ACC. A problem in any reorganization to accommodate Agenda 21 is that UNEP, UNDP, and UNCTAD remain as autonomous units, as do the specialized agencies. Further reform of the Secretariat to consolidate programmes relevant to sustainable development under the responsibility of one high-level UN official also seems essential.[/]

(v) *An Expert Panel on Environment and Development.* The idea behind this proposal was to make available to the UN the best advice from outside, as the best information is not always available within UN organizations. It was envisaged that such a body could review government progress reports and investigate any violations of the laws and standards set. Such a role would be likely to be attacked by many states as an invasion of sovereignty, as frequently happens in the Human Rights Commission (HRC). UNCED nevertheless accepted in principle the need for an expert advisory body, but left it to the UN Secretary-General to make recommendations leading to the appointment in 1993 of the High Level Advisory Board of eminent persons.

(vi) *Revising the composition of the Security Council.* Proposals for reform of the composition of the Security Council are

---

[63] On the Human Rights Commission, see the chapter by Farer and Gaer in this volume, esp. at pp. 260–2 and 271–88.

being pursued with some vigour.[64] Some argue that it is desirable to introduce a broader representation of environmental and developmental interests by providing seats for, for example, Brazil, India, Japan, Nigeria, and the EC, so that the Security Council might better deal with conflicts raising environmental issues that threaten peace and security. Like proposals for transforming the mandate of the moribund Trusteeship Council into a trusteeship council for the environment, reform of the Security Council would almost certainly involve major revision of the Charter, and would thus depend on long and complex negotiations in which explicit environmental and developmental issues would probably figure only slightly.

(vii) *Other proposals.* A wide range of other pre-UNCED proposals included: setting up a UN Centre for Development Analysis; enhancing the role of NGOs to improve monitoring of compliance; and establishing an Environmental Court and other environmentally oriented dispute settlement mechanisms to supplement the ICJ, as the ICJ itself has attracted few environmental cases. Of these proposals, only enhancement of the NGO role was pursued by UNCED.

It was always unlikely that a conference on the scale of UNCED, divided by such a variety of interests, would adopt strong measures or establish powerful new machinery. What UNCED produced was a set of tools for achieving these goals in the long term. Much depends, as always, on the will of states to use these effectively. Agenda 21 is likely to influence environmental and developmental cooperation and initiatives well into the next century.

This is the most important outcome of UNCED. As Mrs Brundtland said in commenting on UNCED's achievements: 'Progress in many fields, too little progress in most fields, and no progress at all in some fields . . . But the direction of where we are heading has been set.'[65] Moreover, the establishment by NGOs, including IUCN and

[64] See generally in this volume the editors' Introduction, pp. 39–43, and Peter Wilenski's chapter, pp. 441–4.

[65] As quoted by M. El-Ashry, 'Reflections on UNCED', *Rio Review* (Centre for Our Common Future, 1992), p. 11.

ICSU, of a parallel Earth Council in Costa Rica as a global focal point for information on public and private progress to sustainable development will help to ensure tht the CSD is kept active.

(viii) *Unfinished business.* A number of major issues remain unresolved. UNCED did not attempt to conclude conventions on desertification and deforestation or on land-based pollution, for example, nor was it able to develop, in any but the most general terms, proposals for dispute settlement, international enforcement mechanisms, or state responsibility for damage. Some of the underlying causes of many environmental problems included in the original list of 'cross-cutting' issues in Agenda 21 were debated by UNCED but still remain to be resolved. It seems unlikely that the Commission on Sustainable Development and other standing bodies will in the near future be able to generate the impetus necessary to find effective solutions to any of these issues.

(h) Strengths and Weaknesses of the Existing System of Institutions

No doubt it is still possible to mitigate environmental problems to a considerable extent without changing the underlying political and economic factors responsible for environmental degradation: 'discrete, reformist, institutionalised measures have been effective'[66] in several instances. Although international institutions have not been systematically integrated, their environmental efforts have complemented each other better than might have been expected; their achievements stem not from large bureaucratic operations or enforcement powers, but from their catalytic role in 'increasing governmental concern, enhancing the contractual environment and increasing national political and administrative capacity'.[67]

However, several questions have still to be addressed in evaluating the UN's role in environmental protection: does the institutional structure on to which the UNCED

---

[66] Ibid. [67] Ibid.

reforms have to graft work? If not why not? If it works only partially, what other improvements are required and what are the options? Are the solutions adopted by UNCED sufficient?

1. Institutional obstacles

Though clearly progress has been made, it remains insufficient to resolve the major problems. It has become increasingly apparent that environmental problems cannot be resolved in isolation from developmental ones. The UNCED process served to highlight this as perhaps the key substantive issue. At the institutional level, there are major failings in the UN's structure as a whole—the lack of coordination among the UN's own organs, programmes, committees, etc., among the specialized agencies, and between them and the UN—as well as the relative weakness of UNEP and UNDP relative to the specialized agencies.[68] The major problem arises from the historical fact that the specialized agencies were instituted as autonomous bodies and have almost all haphazardly take on environmental activities which they are reluctant to surrender. Although concerned agencies have adopted active programmes and made major contributions, they lack coherence. There is much overlapping, even duplication, following the desire of all concerned agencies after UNCHE to ensure that they reserved to themselves action on issues they thought appropriate to them. Thus WHO, IMO, UNESCO, UNEP, UN regional bodies, and FAO are all now interested in pollution control, along with a wide range of bodies outside the UN. The UN itself has had to achieve consensus in setting goals and broad strategies: thus these are framed in general terms. UNEP, established in a minimalist form, without powers to override the more powerful autonomous agencies, has to find ways to attract their cooperation, again often by resorting to generalities: thus SWMTEP is more descriptive than prescriptive. Development responsibilities are also divided between different units and programmes of the UN secretariat as well as

[68] See works cited in n. 58 above.

specialized agencies. The idea that UNEP, as constituted, could successfully coordinate environmental programmes, inside and outside the UN system, was early abandoned, and its Environmental Coordination Board disbanded without anything more effective being put in its place. It was generally concluded that in the absence of major reform the UN's Administrative Committee on Co-ordination (ACC) was not an adequate substitute given the scale and complexity of the problems.

2. A look to the future

As Kimball says, 'UNEP is at the heart of the international system's thrust to achieve sustainable development.'[69] However, achieving coherence in environmental standard-setting and implementation will require more than further coordination of UN organizations, codification, or further institution-building. All available international machinery needs to be activated and accelerated now without waiting for new institutions, since the existing structure is already too complex. There is also a need for constant review of the mechanisms and regimes now provided for in many conventions, inside and outside the UN system.[70]

To attract the participation of developing states in the UN's environmental programmes, more positive assistance in the form of financial, technical, and educational aid has to be provided both in and outside the UN system. The problems encountered in the climate change and bio-diversity negotiations, and the failure to adopt any convention on deforestation, emphasize the urgency of this need. Though the UNCED Prepcom undertook the most wide-ranging and thorough review ever conducted of the UN's environmental and developmental activities and the whole range of environmental and developmental agreements and institutions world-wide, UNCED failed to reach agreement on any one radical solution for reforming the UN system. Its review revealed the wide range of available machinery, and that there was little need for new additions.

---

[69] Kimball, *Forging International Agreements*, p. 7.
[70] Sand, *Lessons Learned in Global Environmental Governance*.

It also showed the need for rationalization and coordination: that the system could be made to work effectively but does not now do so. No doubt their involvement in the Prepcom, UNCED, and the preparation of Agenda 21 will itself have made the specialized agencies and other bodies more aware of the shortcomings in the system and of their role in it. But it is on better responses to the 'cross-cutting issues'—including finance, transfer of technology, scientific and technological requirements, human settlements, women, poverty, health, and education—that much long-term progress will depend.

(i) Conclusions

It is difficult to predict the form that future developments in the UN will take in this field once the UNCED reforms and Agenda 21 get under way. On the one hand, as Hurrell and Kingsbury have pointed out: 'It would be wrong to assume . . . that the universal rhetoric of ecological interdependence translates readily into effective international action,'[71] a point reinforced by the UNCED process. On the other, we can also look with some optimism at the remarkable impact that the Stockholm Conference, Declaration, Action Plan, and institutions have had on the international system as a whole, both inside and outside the UN, despite contemporaneous criticisms of their weakness and of UNCHE's 'failure'. Although 'sovereignty remains the legal cornerstone of the environmental order',[72] and governments thus stress the need for action at the national rather than international level, it is quite clear that new life was breathed into the UN system after UNCED and the post-UNCED reforms. Fundamental questions remain. One is whether the post-UNCED process will be sufficiently energizing to generate sustainable

[71] A. Hurrell and B. Kingsbury, 'The International Politics of the Environment: An Introduction', in *The International Politics of the Environment*, p. 47.

[72] M. A. Levy, P. M. Haas, and R. O. Keohane, 'Institutions for the Earth', *Environment*, 34, no. 4 (1992), pp. 12–17 and 29–36. See also P. M. Haas, M. A. Levy, and E. A. Parson, 'How Should We Judge UNCED's Success?', *Environment*, 34, no. 8 (1992), pp. 6–11 and 26–33.

development—or to overcome fundamental differences on what must be done. Another is whether the balancing of environment and development required by the Rio Declaration will in fact result in the subordination of environmental to developmental goals.[73]

---

[73] See M. Pallemaerts, 'International Law from Stockholm to Rio: Back to the Future?', *Review of European Community and International Environmental Law*, 1 (1992), pp. 254–65.

11

The UN and the Development of International Law

NAGENDRA SINGH

THIS survey of the UN's role in the development of international law will examine the contribution of the Charter, of various UN organs, and of the specialized agencies. It will then look at some examples of the new legal concepts which these contributions have pioneered. Finally, a brief conclusion will refer to some continuing gaps and ambiguities in contemporary international law, and to the important problem of implementation of the law.

International law is ordinarily defined as the body of legal rules which applies between sovereign states *inter se* and to other entities possessing international personality. A subject of international law, according to the advisory opinion of the International Court of Justice in the *Reparation for Injuries* case, is an entity 'capable of possessing international rights and duties, and . . . [which] has capacity to maintain its rights by bringing international claims'.[1]

The sources of international law are numerous, and include all those listed in Article 38 of the Statute of the International Court of Justice.[2] Not all sources and developments

---

[1] *ICJ Reports*, 1949, p. 179.

[2] Article 38(1) of the 1945 Statute of the International Court of Justice states:

The Court, whose function is to decide in accordance with international law such disputes as are submitted to it, shall apply:

  (a) international conventions, whether general or particular, establishing rules expressly recognized by the contesting states;
  (b) international custom, as evidence of a general practice accepted as law;
  (c) the general principles of law recognized by civilized nations;
  (d) subject to the provisions of Article 59, judicial decisions and the teachings of the most highly qualified publicists of the various nations, as subsidiary means for the determination of rules of law.

can be covered here. In this chapter I will concentrate on the threefold contribution of the UN.

First, apart from establishing a mechanism to promote new laws and to revise old ones, the UN Charter itself enunciates new principles of international law. This aspect requires examination at the very outset because some of these new principles, such as the principle of decolonization and that of self-determination, have significantly transformed the international community.

Second, a number of UN bodies with the specific task of developing international law have contributed much over five decades to the progressive development of international law. These UN bodies include the General Assembly, many resolutions of which have a progressive forward thrust; the International Law Commission, which has worked on the codification and progressive development of international law; and the International Court of Justice.

Third, the numerous specialized agencies of the UN have been active in developing different spheres of international law. These specialized agencies include the International Civil Aviation Organization (ICAO); the International Maritime Organization (IMO); the International Telecommunication Union (ITU); and the International Labour Organization (ILO).

Each of these three is discussed in turn below.

(a) The UN Charter: New Principles of International Law

1. The League Covenant and UN Charter compared

The League of Nations Covenant (1919) opens with these words:

The High Contracting Parties,
In order to promote international cooperation and to achieve international peace and security by the acceptance of obligations not to resort to war . . .

However, there was no assumption that non-resort to war was an established rule: it was simply the object of a possible voluntary commitment. Thus the French text speaks merely of 'certain' obligations not to resort to war.

The Covenant contained several provisions concerning collective security in the face of aggression, and concerning disarmament. However, there is one phrase in Article 12 that speaks volumes. Referring to the arbitration or judicial decision of disputes, it provides that the members of the League 'agree in no case to resort to war until three months after the award by the arbitrators or the report by the Council'. Such a weak restraint would be unthinkable in any international agreement today. Contrast Article 2, paragraph 4, of the UN Charter:

All members shall refrain in their international relations from the threat or use of force against the territorial integrity or political independence of any state, or in any other manner inconsistent with the Purposes of the United Nations.

The League Covenant went on to speak of international relations founded upon justice and honour, but I do not observe any reference to honour in the UN Charter. Yet what is wrong with honour? Is it not an admirable concern? Well, its exclusion from the Charter is not in fact such a backward step as might appear. For it was 'honour' which the militaristic powers had most regularly invoked to justify war in the days when that word still retained its aura of glory.

Furthermore, the preamble of the Covenant enjoins 'scrupulous respect for all treaty obligations in the dealings of organized peoples with one another'. What did this mean? Who were then the *disorganized* peoples with whom the High Contracting Parties might conclude treaties which it was pardonable to disrespect? Doubtless some anarchistic tribal groupings who were there only to be hoodwinked. One recalls the noted nineteenth century author of a code of international law who allowed the use of machine-guns but condemned 'savages' for such unfair practices as the dipping of their arrowheads in poison.[3] The Covenant, in other words, still contained

---

[3] Johann C. Bluntschli, *Das moderne Völkerrecht der civilisierten Staaten* (Nördlingen, 1878), p. 314. To be fair, it must be added that this author inveighed against genocide and emphasized the humane 'education' of the 'uncivilized'.

remnants of a class system among peoples, attended by legal disqualifications for the lower classes.

In apparent contrast, the UN Charter contains many provisions devoted to the emergence of subject peoples from colonialism to independence and full membership of the international community. But the seeds had been sown in the 'sacred trust' provisions of the Covenant which underlay the mandates system, and which the Charter transformed into the trusteeship regime.

The reference in the Statute of the International Court of Justice, which is annexed to the UN Charter and forms part of it, to 'the general principles of law recognized by civilized nations' has also been attacked for being discriminatory. This text dates back in fact to the early 1920s, for the Statute of the Court is virtually the same as that of its predecessor, the Permanent Court of International Justice. But I am not so sure that this particular expression is inept. Should we not rather draw the converse conclusion, namely that only nations which recognize general principles of law may be regarded as civilized?

Finally, the preamble to the Covenant of the League of Nations speaks of 'the firm establishment of the understandings of international law as the actual rule of conduct among Governments'. Now this is a very curious word, a very hesitant word: 'understandings'. It is as if the parties cannot bring themselves quite to admit the existence of norms, let alone rules of international law. Yet the French text uses a far stronger word: 'prescriptions'. The French text also implies, as the English does not, that *all* the prescriptions of international law are now or henceforth recognized as actually governing the conduct of states. These are significant differences. They show that the Covenant was situated on the brink of a transition from cautious approval of international law to its whole-hearted acceptance. Why the English text is on one side of the brink and the French on the other is a matter I must leave to the specialists of *travaux préparatoires*. But these differences show the immensity of the transformation that has been completed since. They point to the contribution of the UN both to the development of international law and to the

firming up of the concept of international law as a regulatory force and not as a mere collection of indications of
inter-state understandings.

What in fact happened in 1945 with the foundation of
the United Nations was the culmination of a process that
had been going on for some 300 years but, in the last 100,
had gathered momentum in response to ever more fright-
ful wars. This process, in a nutshell, was the transformation of the law of nations into international law. One might
almost say that it was also the transformation of the law of
war into the law of peace.

For what had been the law of nations? The term itself
was simply a translation of the Latin *jus gentium*, an
extremely broad expression of which the possible connota-
tions range from 'the code of conduct of patrician families'
to 'the rights of peoples'. The one thing it does not suggest
is the modern state. In practice, the law of nations, two or
three hundred years ago, had not advanced very far from
simply constituting the rules governing the relations of
princes: diplomatic practice, in short. Since the main
criterion of those relations was whether the princes were
at war with each other or at peace, the law of nations was
conceived as a diptych—one panel bearing the table of the
rules of war, the other displaying the rules of peace. Those
general rules were not written down in instruments bearing the princes' signatures, but were left to be made
explicit by scholars such as Gentili, Grotius, and Vattel,
who by recording and systematizing practice in a sober
and not utopian manner earned respect and began in
essence the modern work of codifying custom.

Meanwhile the nations continued in the main to subsist
side by side in a relationship either of armed benevolence
or of outright hostility, and the customary law of nations
was in practice reduced to the observance of the different
etiquettes which either situation required. It had a split
personality, and as a result much intellectual effort went
into defining the conditions and rules of belligerency and
neutrality, when in fact the outlawing of war was the only
worthy goal.

Gradually, however, the realization emerged that only

one panel of the diptych was worthy of development as law in the sense of a perennial expression of what was right and just. To be sure, if there had to be a war, it was best that it should not be totally lawless, for to abandon all rules would be to withdraw protection from the helpless and condone the infliction of needless suffering. The war-rules panel of the now outmoded diptych had therefore to be preserved in some form, and this has eventually been achieved in international humanitarian law, otherwise called the law of war, a corner of international law which throws an essential bridge between human rights and the conduct of states during hostilities. Apart from humanitarian obligations, proportionate self-defence is the only aspect of warfare which still constitutes a universally accepted component of international legality. The question of the right of legitimate national liberation movements to use force in their struggles, and of third states to assist them, continues to be controversial.

The prohibition of war is all to the good—or almost all to the good. Nobody, least of all myself, would question the outlawing of aggressive war. But by placing aggressors beyond the pale, we have also risked putting them beyond our grasp. This is a real dilemma. Only the untrammelled operation of the Red Cross and Red Crescent can ensure that the implementation of the 1949 Geneva Conventions and related agreements is monitored. It is fortunate that those magnificent organizations were created in time to alleviate so much of the sufferings of war that this century has known. But there are disquieting signs. New efforts will have to be made to ensure that international standards can be enforced even within situations of international illegality.

2. New principles in the UN Charter

The Charter introduces a new chapter in the development of international law, not only by crystallizing the still evolving and emerging rules, but also by enunciating new principles. At least in theory, these new principles of the Charter promote international peace, although they may lack the sanction and vigour necessary for their enforcement

or due observance. It is sometimes said that the League of
Nations had fostered the spirit of peace more effectively
than does the UN. This observation would appear to be
somewhat superficial. After World War I there was a great
enthusiasm for promoting peace and the rule of law. This
spirit was symbolized by two multilateral treaties of 1928:
the General Act for Pacific Settlement of International
Disputes, and the General Treaty for the Renunciation of
War (the Kellogg–Briand Pact). There was an inclination
among nations to respect the law and to avoid conflicts
which could cause great destruction of both life and
property. The same feeling did manifest itself after World
War II, but perhaps not with the same intensity. In any
case, my impression is that the lessons of the two world
wars are gradually being forgotten, and that resort to
force is becoming increasingly frequent in international
relations. This may be the result of structural weaknesses
in the UN, or of its defective functioning. But no fault lies
with the enunciation of the new principles embodied in
the Charter itself. Any survey of the development of
international law must therefore give a prominent place
to these principles of the Charter which, I believe, continue to indicate the path to peace. Some of them are listed
below.

(i) The principle of non-use of force in international
relations, and the consequent illegality of right of conquest
as a mode of acquiring territory, has its origin in Articles
2(3) and 2(4) of the Charter. This has reversed the
centuries-old recognition of the right of conquest as a
means of acquiring territory.

(ii) The principles of the independence and the sovereign
equality of states, and the concept of decolonization, are
equally significant. They have led to a restructuring of
the international community by more than doubling the
number of its members.

(iii) The principle of equal rights and self-determination
of peoples is stressed in Article 1(2) of the Charter. Article
55 further elaborates it by asserting that it would be a
function of the UN to foster respect for 'the principle
of equal rights and self-determination of peoples'. This

principle has been linked to that of decolonization to establish the right to independence and sovereignty of the erstwhile colonies and dependencies.

(iv) The principles of non-interference in the domestic or internal affairs of states is spelt out in Article 2(7) of the Charter, which reads as follows:

Nothing contained in the present Charter shall authorize the United Nations to intervene in matters which are essentially within the domestic jurisdiction of any state or shall require the Members to submit such matters to settlement under the present Charter.

(v) The principle of non-discrimination is codified in Article 1(3), Article 13(b), and Article 55(c) of the Charter. In all these articles the Charter enjoins the promotion of universal respect for human rights and fundamental freedoms without distinction as to race, sex, language, or religion.

(vi) The principle of interdependence and international cooperation is enunciated in Article 13(b). This Article requires the General Assembly to make recommendations for '(a) Promoting international cooperation in the political field and encouraging the progressive development of international law and its codification; (b) promoting international cooperation in the economic, social, cultural, educational, and health fields, and assisting in the realization of human rights and fundamental freedoms for all without distinction as to race, sex, language, or religion.'

(vii) The principle of good neighbourliness and friendly relations is recited in several different parts of the Charter, including Article 1(2), Article 55, and Article 74. The General Assembly has further developed this and other principles in its 1970 Declaration on Principles of International Law concerning Friendly Relations and Cooperation among States in accordance with the Charter of the United Nations.

(viii) The Charter espouses principles of human rights in various articles. Article 1(3) states that the purposes of the UN include 'promoting and encouraging respect for human rights', and Article 13(1) talks of 'assisting in the realization of human rights'. Article 55 (c) pledges the UN to promote 'universal respect for, and observance of, human rights', and Article 62(2) empowers ECOSOC to make recommendations to this end. Under Article 76(c) an objective of the trusteeship system was 'to encourage respect for human rights'.

(ix) The principle of obligatory registration of treaties is enunciated in Article 102 (1), which also provides for the Secretariat to publish all registered treaties. Unregistered treaties may not be invoked before any UN body. This system is helpful in listing and publishing the treaties which the members of the UN have to respect. Unfortunately publication of the *United Nations Treaty Series* is at present lagging several years behind, due to the failure of the UN budgetary organs to allocate sufficient funds to it. It is to be hoped that this important work will soon take higher priority.

Although many of these principles predate the UN Charter, they now enjoy a precise formulation and a distinct legal status by being incorporated in a multilateral treaty of exceptional standing. This represents a significant development in the field of international law which is clearly attributable to the UN.

(b) UN Organs for the Development of International Law

UN bodies with the specific task of developing international law include:

1. the UN General Assembly and its committees;
2. conferences convened by the UN;
3. the International Law Commission;
4. the International Court of Justice.

These are examined in turn below:

1. The UN General Assembly and its committees

The General Assembly influences the development of international law in many ways. First, it adopts general legal conventions, or convenes *ad hoc* global international conferences, almost the size of the General Assembly's Committee of the Whole, to give birth to new international conventions. Second, the General Assembly has been busy formulating resolutions by consensus, without vote, or by a majority vote. Third, it considers the reports of such organs as the International Law Commission, as well as working through committees, such as the Sixth Committee and the Committee on Outer Space, to tackle problems of inter-state relations and in the process to develop international law. An attempt will now be made to summarize some of these activities of the General Assembly.

(i) *The Genocide Convention.* A very early instance of the UN's involvement in the development of international law is to be seen in the 1948 Genocide Convention, adopted during the third session of the General Assembly.[4] The revulsion and horror inspired by the Nazi holocaust was of course the catalyst for this instrument. The Genocide Convention is a prime example of the swiftness with which international law can leap forward in modern circumstances, given the kind of forum which only the UN and its kindred agencies can provide. The scene for the elaboration and adoption of this convention was set by a request by Cuba, India, and Panama to include an item on genocide in the agenda of the General Assembly's first session, in 1946. This session adopted a unanimous resolution affirming genocide to be a crime under international law.

The Convention on the Prevention and Punishment of the Crime of Genocide was adopted on 9 December 1948, after a mere two years of preparatory work. Such alacrity would have been inconceivable without the UN.

The final text of this Convention is markedly different from the initial draft prepared by the legal section of the

---

[4] The very word 'genocide' was still a neologism—or at least had enjoyed general currency only for the briefest of periods. All too unhappily, the phenomenon itself was far from new. Discussion of the international criminality of genocide prompted the Assembly to request the new International Law Commission to study the possibility of establishing a criminal chamber of the International Court of Justice—an idea which was to prove technically too difficult of attainment.

UN Secretariat.[5] The initial draft had presented a far wider definition of genocide than eventually prevailed. Massacre was not its sole theme, for it had subsumed under 'genocide' such acts as destroying the specific characteristics of groups by the desecration of their shrines, the confiscation of their property, the deprivation of their means of livelihood, the prohibition of their language, the destruction of their books; in a word, the annihilation of their culture. In the final text, genocide is confined to killing, maiming, deliberate starvation, sterilization, and the forcible dispersal of the children of a group.

Of course, the one word 'genocide' could not have borne the full load of the original draft, and possibly the international civil servants, in the first flush of enthusiasm, had exceeded their responsibilities and trespassed on the field of legal development. It was very significant that the text (albeit in its revised form) was adopted by the fifty or so independent states of 1948, some of whom could not yet be exonerated of the charge of repressing ethnic groups by the pursuit of colonial policies. We see in that zealous Secretariat draft not only the definite link between the liberation of Europe and the liberation of Africa and Asia, a link which those who saw to the draft's later abridgement must have been quick to disapprove, but also—astoundingly—the implied requirement of a complete programme for the protection of human rights, family values, religious beliefs, the rights to work, to art, and to cultural heritage.

The Genocide Convention is in a somewhat Janus-like position. Although widely seen as a progressive development of international law, it also had an element of codification of existing law. Even before the Convention, no one except possibly the warped-minded perpetrators of the hideous acts it defines seriously believed in the lawfulness of such acts. In a way, the Convention simply stated accepted principles of law and thus could be regarded as a codification, especially as it was concluded so quickly that nobody could claim that the law had actually developed between its initial proposal and its adoption.

---

[5] 'Draft Convention on the Crime of Genocide', UN doc. E/447 (1947).

Nevertheless, the Convention was a seminal development. Many of the ethnic or cultural groups who had been victims of genocide had actually been citizens of the perpetrating states. Yet action directed against a state's own citizens was now declared an offence against *international* law! This early initiative of the General Assembly thus placed a fateful gloss upon the principle of non-intervention in domestic affairs, a key safeguard which, as noted above, had been written into the Charter as Article 2(7).

(ii) *Other human rights conventions.* Later human rights instruments influenced by the Genocide Convention precedent include the 1966 International Convention on the Elimination of All Forms of Racial Discrimination, the 1973 International Convention on the Suppression and Punishment of the Crime of Apartheid, and the 1979 Convention on the Elimination of All Forms of Discrimination Against Women.

In my view, these and similar treaties (including the two 1966 international human rights covenants) show that the efforts of the representatives of states gathered together in the legal councils of the UN have not all been selfishly directed to building an invulnerable carapace around the national leviathan, but have made a serious contribution to piercing through the leviathan's tough hide in order to soothe and succour the victims in his maw.

These conventions, like several hundred other treaties, include a clause conferring jurisdiction upon the International Court of Justice in the event of a dispute as to their application or interpretation.[6] One of that Court's earliest tasks was to give its opinion on the effects of reservations made to the Genocide Convention.[7]

---

[6] The number of treaties with compromissory clauses providing specifically for disputes arising under them to be referred to the International Court of Justice has risen from five in 1946 to at least 242 in 1980. It may now be as many as 400.

[7] *Reservations to the Genocide Convention, ICJ Reports*, 1951, p. 15. The Court's decision of principle in this case, making the compatability of any reservation with the object and purpose of the convention a test of the validity of the reservation, was eventually reflected in the 1969 Vienna Convention on the Law of Treaties, Arts. 19–23.

(iii) *General Assembly resolutions.* Many resolutions of the General Assembly have contributed significantly to the development of international law. When a General Assembly resolution on a basic tenet of law is not merely passed by a majority but is unanimous, it represents not just the *opinio juris* of many individual states but the *opinio juris communis*: the common opinion of states as to the law, which joins hands with custom and practice to become a rule from which no state may depart without positive proof of its having withheld consent.

There has always been much confusion and heated argument about the binding character of such General Assembly resolutions as general international law. It is often argued that the Assembly can legislate *vis-à-vis* the members of the UN in their capacity as such. But whether it can lay down norms of law, or whether its resolutions purporting to determine legal situations can or cannot be challenged by its members, are questions fiercely debated. Owing to the dominance of the Group of 77 in the General Assembly and the continuing limits to the influence of this group in the Security Council, the normative importance of General Assembly resolutions is naturally emphasized by this group of states. Many of these states argue that General Assembly resolutions have the character of international legislation, but other groups of states have not accepted this view.[8]

To blunt the edge of the problem it is often said that some of its resolutions are 'normative', which is a way of avoiding the statement that they are law-making. However, the important question is not whether they would stand up to legal challenge, but whether they actually *are* challenged. If they are not, the application of the simple— or simple-seeming—doctrine of acquiescence will in the course of time create at least a rebuttable presumption that

---

[8] On this question, see generally J. Castaneda, *Legal Effects of United Nations Resolutions* (New York, 1969); R. P. Anand, 'Sovereign Equality of States in International Law', in the Hague Academy of the International Law's *Recueil des Cours*, 197 (1986), pp. 9–228; and B. Sloane, 'General Assembly Resolutions Revisited (Forty Years After)', *British Year Book of International Law*, 58 (1987), pp. 39–150.

what those resolutions proclaim is law as between the member states. And since the membership of the UN verges on the universal, and since no non-member state seems to hold a particularly eccentric view of international law, we can properly assume—remembering yet again that international law is the emanation of states—that the general norms of conduct proclaimed by UN resolutions, if adopted in full plenary unanimously or by an over-whelming majority, do become part and parcel of general international law. However, not all resolutions of the General Assembly can be so classified.

The General Assembly passes a wide assortment of resolutions every year. They include decisions as well as declarations. Their sum total each year could be in the vicinity of 300, but they are not all law-making. For example, the General Assembly's resolution adopting the Declaration on the Right of Peoples to Peace merely approves a text which is annexed to the resolution and requests the Secretary-General 'to ensure the widest dissemination of the Declaration to States, intergovernmental and non-governmental organizations'.[9] This declaration thus received UN approval and has a recommendatory force, but cannot be said to be legally binding. Again, the General Assembly passes resolutions on certain specific events or incidents which involve a member state of the UN. For example, the General Assembly passed a resolution on 15 November 1984 on 'The situation in Afghanistan and its implications for international peace and security'.[10] This resolution recognized the right of the Afghan people to determine their own form of government, and called for the immediate withdrawal of the foreign troops from Afghanistan. It requested the Secretary-General to keep member states informed of progress towards the implementation of the resolution and decided to include that

---

[9] GA Res. 39/11 of 12 Nov. 1984, *GAOR*, 39th session, supplement no. 51 (UN doc. A/39/51).

[10] GA Res. 39/13 of 15 Nov. 1984, *GAOR*, 39th session, supplement no. 51 (UN doc. A/39/51). Similar resolutions were passed every year from the entry of USSR troops into Afghanistan in Dec. 1979 until the negotiations under UN auspices for withdrawal of these troops were well advanced.

item in the agenda of its next session. Such resolutions concerning specific cases have their own impact in the political field. They are certainly not law-making but they do apply the law to the facts of a particular case and draw their own conclusion. This is really the working of the General Assembly in the discharge of its obligations to maintain international peace. Such resolutions do not make law as such.

Certain resolutions of the General Assembly have been specifically declared to be law-making by the International Court of Justice. Such findings by the International Court of Justice are important in authoritatively recognizing these resolutions as legally binding. The resolutions in this category include:

• General Assembly resolution 1514 (XV), the 'Declaration on the Granting of Independence to Colonial Countries and Peoples', was cited by the Court with approval in the *Namibia* advisory opinion in 1971.[11] This observation represents an important stage in the development of international law in regard to non-self-governing territories. Again, in the *Western Sahara* advisory opinion in 1975 the Court referred to the resolution in enunciating the principle of self-determination as a right of peoples.[12]

• General Assembly resolution 1541 (XV), 'Principles which Should Guide Members in Determining Whether or Not an Obligation Exists to Transmit the Information Called for under Article 73 of the Charter', was also cited in the *Western Sahara* advisory opinion.[13]

• General Assembly resolution 2131 (XX) entitled 'Declaration on the Inadmissibility of Intervention in the Domestic Affairs of States and the Protection of their Independence and Sovereignty' was quoted with approval by the Court in the *Nicaragua* v. *USA (Merits)* case. The Court observed:

The principle has since been reflected in numerous declarations adopted by international organizations and conferences in which the United States and Nicaragua have participated, e.g.

---

[11] *ICJ Reports*, 1971, p. 31.   [12] *ICJ Reports*, 1975, pp. 31–2.
[13] Ibid., pp. 32–3.

General Assembly resolution 2131 (XX), the Declaration on the Inadmissibility of Intervention in the Domestic Affairs of States and the Protection of their Independence and Sovereignty. It is true that the United States, while it voted in favour of General Assembly resolution 2131 (XX), also declared at the time of its adoption in the First Committee that it considered the declaration in that resolution to be 'only a statement of political intention and not a formulation of law' (Official Records of the General Assembly, Twentieth Session, First Committee, A/C.1/SR.1423, p. 436). However, the essentials of resolution 2131 (XX) are repeated in the Declaration approved by resolution 2625 (XXV), which set out principles which the General Assembly declared to be 'basic principles' of international law, and on the adoption of which no analogous statement was made by the United States representative.[14]

The Court thus took into consideration the question of consent by states to General Assembly resolutions.

• General Assembly resolution 2625 (XXV), the 'Declaration of Principles of International Law concerning Friendly Relations and Co-operation among States in accordance with the Charter of the United Nations' was endorsed in the advisory opinion on *Western Sahara*.[15] Furthermore, in *Nicaragua* v. *USA* the Court observed apropos the same resolution: 'The adoption by States of this text affords an indication of their *opinio juris* as to customary international law on the question.'[16]

• General Assembly resolution 3314 (XXIX), the 'Definition of Aggression', has been accepted by the Court as one that could be 'taken to reflect customary international law'.[17]

It must be emphasized that reference here is to resolutions enshrining general norms of conduct, not to positive rules of specific application. There is thus no contradiction between the view that the requirements of treaty law compel caution in general use of a convention until its universality is formally provable, and the view that these requirements can be softened in testing resolutions for their normative effect. To be committed to a principle

---

[14] *ICJ Reports*, 1986, p. 107
[16] *ICJ Reports*, 1986, pp. 100–1.

[15] *ICJ Reports*, 1975, p. 33.
[17] Ibid., p. 103.

under a resolution is not quite the same as to be bound by a rule under a convention, even if the element of voluntary consent is present in each case.

Among the most important UN General Assembly resolutions are those approving key declarations and treaties, including the 1948 Universal Declaration of Human Rights; the two 1966 Covenants, on Civil and Political Rights, and on Economic, Social, and Cultural Rights; the 1974 Charter of Economic Rights and Duties of States; and the 1970 Declaration on Principles of International Law concerning Friendly Relations and Co-operation Among States.

Such resolutions and declarations as these are truly normative, in the sense of laying down norms and standards of international or even domestic conduct. As solemn proclamations of principle freely adopted, they amount to undertakings entered into by the principal subjects of international law, that is to say, the community of states. They form, in my view, contracts partaking of treaty law although they do not possess the formality of treaties. Formality is, however, a declining requirement for the validity of international commitments, as the jurisprudence of the International Court of Justice (to be surveyed below) has on more than one occasion made plain.

(iv) *General Assembly committees.* The General Assembly functions through Main Committees which are assigned specific roles. For example, the Sixth Committee is the legal committee comprising the legal advisers of the member states. It examines the report of the International Law Commission and makes concrete recommendations on legal problems or trends which concern the international community. The General Assembly also establishes special committees to examine specific legal matters. This is a regular procedural feature which helps to develop the law on the subject. For example, a special committee worked for many years on the question of defining aggression. Other special committees include the Committee on the Peaceful Uses of Outer Space, the Special Committee against Apartheid, and the Special Committee on Decolonization.

Several human rights conventions establish committees with supervisory or quasi-judicial powers. These committees all report to the General Assembly. In this category are the Committee on the Elimination of Racial Discrimination, established by the 1965 Convention on the Elimination of All Forms of Racial Discrimination; and the Human Rights Committee established by the 1966 International Covenant on Civil and Political Rights.

2. *Conferences convened by the UN*

(i) *Vienna conventions on diplomatic relations and on treaties.* Another example of the negotiation of important multi-lateral conventions by *ad hoc* conferences is furnished by the Vienna diplomatic conference of 1960, which laid the groundwork for the 1961 Vienna Convention on Diplomatic Relations and the 1963 Vienna Convention on Consular Relations. The 1969 Vienna Convention on the Law of Treaties was similarly adopted by an *ad hoc* conference convened at the instance of the UN. Each of these conferences had the benefit of draft texts prepared by the International Law Commission at the instance of the UN General Assembly.

In the case of the law of treaties it was realized that, with the tremendous proliferation of international agreements, it was for the good of the entire world community that certain choices should be made, and henceforth adhered to, as between different doctrines of treaty interpretation. It was understandable that, with wide variations in domestic theories of contract, there should on the one hand have been those who favoured adherence to the plain meaning of treaties, and on the other hand those who felt it permissible to look behind the text to the intentions of the parties as revealed in the preparatory work. There were those who would only permit the placing of a literal construction on a treaty provision, while others wanted the spirit of a treaty to prevail. There were different schools of thought as to whether and how treaties could die a natural death, and as to whether their object and purpose could alter with changing circumstances. In a polyglot world, these doctrinal quarrels were dangerous sources of tension, but by imposing uniform rules of interpretation, freely agreed upon by the world community, the Vienna

Convention (which came into force in 1980) has laid them largely to rest. The late and deeply missed Sir Humphrey Waldock was in no small degree responsible for this great work and, dare I say, for swinging its general emphasis towards the common-sense—by which I mean common law—intepretation of agreements. This was a sensible as well as an amazing achievement, because, when faced with a welter of texts in several official languages, it is obvious that only a flexible, though methodical, approach could produce consistent results in treaty interpretation.

(ii) *Law of the sea conventions.* Codification of the law of the sea has been the object of three major UN conferences. The first, in 1958, led to the adoption of four conventions which are still in force. The second conference, in 1960, was unable to reach agreement on several divisive issues. Many of these issues were resolved by the monumental Third United Nations Conference on the Law of the Sea (1973–82). This conference adopted the comprehensive 1982 UN Convention on the Law of the Sea. The Convention will not enter into force until after sixty states have ratified or acceded to it.

3. The International Law Commission

Article 13 of the UN Charter provides: 'The General Assembly shall initiate studies and make recommendations for the purpose of . . . encouraging the progressive development of international law and its codification.' Responding to this requirement, the General Assembly established the International Law Commission by a resolution adopted on 21 November 1947.

Considering that international law is an emanation of states, whose opinion as to what the law is—*opinio juris*—is fundamental not only to its concretization but to its acceptance, it would not prima facie be entirely unreasonable if the members of the Commission were government appointees. But the majority view did not support this suggestion. Bearing in mind the scholarly nature of the work and the demands of objectivity, detachment, and continuity, it was decided to define its members simply as 'persons of recognized competence in international law'.

The candidates can, however, be nominated by governments, and to ensure fair and balanced representation no two members can hold the same nationality. The official representatives of states play a formal role only when a conference is held to consider a draft code or convention prepared by the Commission.

Many initial drafts prepared by the Commission were eventually turned into multilateral conventions by special conferences convened by the UN, including the four 1958 conventions on the law of the sea, the 1961 and 1963 conventions on diplomatic and consular relations, the 1969 convention on special missions, the 1969 convention codifying the law of treaties, and the 1970 convention on the succession of states in respect of treaties.

The Commission has worked to develop new texts on, *inter alia*, the international responsibility of states, the status of the diplomatic courier and pouch, the relations between states and international organizations, the liability of states for transboundary damage (including pollution), and the law of international rivers. It has also prepared a declaration on the rights and duties of states; a draft code of crimes against the peace and security of mankind; model rules of arbitral procedure; and articles on most favoured nation clauses.

The basic nature of a treaty is to be binding on the parties—but only on the parties. A convention may therefore proclaim, as it were, until it is blue in the face that it is laying down universal rules for the conduct of states in a particular domain, but it will never be self-fulfilling. Only as more and more states accede to its provisions will it have a chance of making good its claim to universality of application as treaty law. I emphasize, as treaty law, because there are numerous recent examples of courts, tribunals, and the legal officers of governments looking even to draft conventions, or conventions yet to come into force, for serious indications of the trend, if not the current state, of international law.

In pursuance of the General Assembly's Charter obligation to encourage the *codification* of international law, a Codification Division was set up in the Legal Department of the UN—a division which incidentally provides the International Law Commission with an excellent secretariat. But no division was set up corresponding to the other, associated obligation of the Assembly under Article 13, namely to encourage the *progressive development* of international law. This was no accidental omission. It illustrates the fact that, as in any national system, while it is a proper task for civil servants to assist in the recording and classification of existing law, i.e. codification, the development of the law is not a matter for civil servants—even international civil servants. In national systems, it is, in different measure, according to varying traditions, a matter for legislatures and the jurisprudence of courts. Naturally, private scholarship is always at liberty to help the process along, to point to new paths, to criticize, and encourage. But not the civil servants.

In the international community, the development of the law is a matter for states. They can act obliquely through their conduct, modifying practice and establishing custom, or intervene directly through the sponsorship or support of innovatory proposals. But this they need to do in a forum, whether within the standing organs of international organizations or agencies, or in the *ad hoc* multilateral conferences set up for specific subject areas. The great merit of the International Law Commission is to act as a bridge or two-way valve between the private scholars, who receive through their participation in the Commission's work an enhanced authority and status as international consultants, and the Sixth (Legal) Committee of the UN General Assembly, where the representatives of states who understand the Commission's work meet to sift its proposals and take over the most approval-worthy as a basis for progressive development. That is how Article 13(1)(a) of the Charter, which revealingly associates such work in one seamless phrase with the promotion of 'international co-operation in the political field', is implemented in practice. This sub-paragraph has proved one of the most fruitful of the entire UN Charter.

4. *The International Court of Justice*

The International Court of Justice is open to all states members of the UN, and other states (such as Nauru and

Switzerland) are also parties to the ICJ Statute. The jurisdiction of the ICJ depends on the consent of the states concerned. Such consent may take the form of a special agreement (or, occasionally, implied consent) to submit a particular dispute to the ICJ, or it may be a more general consent through a jurisdictional clause in a treaty, or a declaration accepting the compulsory jurisdiction of the Court. By July 1991, fifty-three states had made such declarations, some 400 treaties containing ICJ jurisdictional clauses were in force, and eleven cases had been submitted to the ICJ by special agreement.

The ICJ may also give advisory opinions on legal questions to the General Assembly and twenty-one other UN organs and international agencies competent to request them. Such opinions are not generally binding, but nevertheless several of the twenty opinions delivered by the ICJ from 1948 to 1991 have had considerable legal significance.

The case-law of the International Court of Justice is an important aspect of the UN's contribution to the development of international law. The modest number of its judgments and advisory opinions—these are listed in full in Appendix F to this volume—gives no inkling of the importance of its case-law, as this permeates into the international legal community not only through its decisions as such but through the wider implications of its methodology and reasoning. A few examples may be cited.

The dicta of the Court can be very general, and may flower greatly in the minds of legal advisers. It is impossible, for example, since the Court's *Barcelona Traction* judgment (1970) to maintain, before an international court, that risk capital placed abroad has any general right to diplomatic protection. The same judgment distinguished between obligations owed by states towards specific interests and their obligations toward the international community at large. The Court also observed:

In view of the importance of the rights involved, all States can be held to have a legal interest in their protection; they are obligations *erga omnes* . . . Such obligations derive, for example, in contemporary international law, from the outlawing of acts of aggression, and of genocide, as also from the principles and rules concerning the basic rights of the human person, including protection from slavery and racial discrimination.[18]

The implication is that any member of the world community is in principle entitled to call states to account for breaches of those obligations.

In the *Western Sahara* advisory opinion (1975), the Court struck a final blow against the notions of the 1885 Congress of Berlin which underlay the scramble for Africa, by finding that the concept of inhabited territory being *res nullius*—or territory belonging to no one, hence capable of being seized—no longer had any place in international law.[19] An earlier contribution to decolonization was the Court's *Namibia* opinion of 1971, which upheld the General Assembly's termination of South Africa's mandate to rule Namibia.[20]

In 1974 the Court might have had the opportunity to deal with the very thorny issue of responsibility for transboundary radioactive pollution, when Australia and New Zealand brought their *Nuclear Tests* cases against France.[21] But the French President declared before the cases were heard that France would cease atmospheric nuclear testing. The Court found this made the cases moot, and so judged. Its judgment nevertheless made a conspicuous contribution to the progressive development of international law, for never before had it so plainly been held that the high representative of a state could bind it with a public oral statement *erga omnes*. The Court has indeed consistently looked beyond formalities to the real substance and effect of statements made in the context of international relations. As it observed in the *Nuclear Tests* cases:

The unilateral statements of the French authorities were made outside the Court, publicly and *erga omnes*, even though the first of them was communicated to the Government of Australia. As was observed above, to have legal effect, there was no need for

[18] *ICJ Reports*, 1970, p. 32. The Court went a step further when it observed later in the same case (p. 47) that 'with regard more particularly to human rights . . . it should be noted that these also include protection against denial of justice'.
[19] *ICJ Reports*, 1975, p. 30.   [20] *ICJ Reports*, 1971, p. 16.
[21] *ICJ Reports*, 1974, p. 257.

these statements to be addressed to a particular State, nor was acceptance by any other State required. The general nature and characteristics of these statements are decisive for the evaluation of the legal implications, and it is to the interpretation of the statements that the Court must now proceed. The Court is entitled to presume, at the outset, that these statements were not made *in vacuo*, but in relation to the tests which constitute the very object of the present proceedings, although France has not appeared in the case.[22]

The successful resolution of the border dispute between Burkina Faso and Mali in the 1986 *Frontier Dispute* case illustrates the utility of judicial decision as a means of settlement in territorial disputes. The case was submitted to a Chamber of the ICJ pursuant to a special agreement concluded by the parties in 1983. In December 1985, while written submissions were being prepared, hostilities broke out in the disputed area. A cease-fire was agreed, and the Chamber by an Order of 10 January 1986 directed the continued observance of the cease-fire, the withdrawal of troops within twenty days, and the avoidance of actions tending to aggravate the dispute or prejudice its eventual resolution. The case proceeded, and in its judgment of 22 December 1986 the Chamber determined the overall course of the frontier line. The Presidents of Burkina Faso and Mali publicly welcomed the judgment and indicated their intention to comply with it.[23]

Several judgments of the Court have influenced the development of the law of the sea, and have been reflected in the work of conferences called by the United Nations to deal with this vital subject.

The Court's decision in the *Fisheries* case (1951) between the United Kingdom and Norway put an end to a long-standing controversy which had aroused considerable interest in maritime states. The Court held that the method

---

[22] *ICJ Reports*, 1974, p. 269.

[23] *Frontier Dispute*: Provisional Measures Order of 10 Jan. 1986, *ICJ Reports*, 1986, p. 3; judgment of 22 Dec. 1986, ibid., p. 554. The statements by Captain Thomas Sankara and General Moussa Traoré are annexed to ICJ Press Communiqué No. 87/1 of 16 Jan. 1987.

adopted in a Norwegian decree of 1935 for calculating the baselines from which to measure the territorial sea was not contrary to international law. It laid down three criteria in this connection:

• that the baselines should not appreciably depart from the general direction of the coast;

• that the sea areas lying within these lines should be sufficiently closely linked to the land domain to be subject to the regime of internal waters; and

• that consideration should be given to the economic interests peculiar to the region in question, the reality and importance of which are clearly evidenced by a long usage.[24]

The Court rejected the view that, in international law, bays with an entrance more than ten miles wide could not, unless they were of the nature of so-called 'historic' bays, be regarded as internal waters.

In the *North Sea Continental Shelf* cases (1969), Denmark, The Netherlands, and the Federal Republic of Germany asked the Court to decide what principles of international law were applicable to the delimitation of that continental shelf. The Court rejected the contention that the delimitation in question had to be carried out in accordance with the principle of equidistance as defined in the 1958 Geneva Convention on the Continental Shelf. The Court took account of the fact that the Federal Republic of Germany had not ratified that Convention, and held that the equidistance principle was not inherent in the basic concept of continental shelf rights, that this principle was not a rule of customary international law. The Court promulgated the customary international law principles then applicable to delimitation of the continental shelf, enabling the parties to reach agreement on division of the contested shelf area.[25] This agreement was essential for drilling for oil and gas to proceed in these areas.

The Court has further elaborated the law on delimitation of the continental shelf in the *Tunisia/Libya* case (1982)

---

[24] *ICJ Reports*, 1951, p. 116.   [25] *ICJ Reports*, 1969, p. 3.

and the *Libya/Malta* case (1985). Similar issues were also considered by a Chamber of the ICJ in determining a single maritime boundary, applicable to the continental shelf and to the superjacent waters, between Canada and the United States in the *Gulf of Maine* case (1984). This series of maritime boundary cases has greatly enriched an increasingly important area of law, and has assisted other states seeking to delimit such boundaries through negotiation or arbitration.[26] In these three cases the Court took account of the 'new accepted trends' which appeared in the Third UN Conference on the Law of the Sea (1973–82) and in the resulting 1982 UN Convention on the Law of the Sea. Although that convention is not yet in force, the Court viewed certain of its provisions as evidence of new customary international law. Thus the Court held that claims to Exclusive Economic Zones of up to 200 miles are now permissible, and noted the significance for maritime boundary delimitations of the automatic entitlement to a 200-mile continental shelf.

In the *Fisheries Jurisdiction* case (*United Kingdom* v. *Iceland*, 1974) the International Court of Justice contributed to the firm establishment in law of the idea that mankind needs to conserve the living resources of the sea and must respect these resources. The Court observed:

It is one of the advances in maritime international law, resulting from the intensification of fishing, that the former *laissez-faire* treatment of the living resources of the sea in the high seas has been replaced by a recognition of a duty to have due regard to the rights of other States and the needs of conservation for the benefit of all. Consequently, both Parties have the obligation to keep under review the fishery resources in the disputed waters and to examine together, in the light of scientific and other available information, the measures required for the conservation and development, and equitable exploitation, of these resources, taking into account any international agreement in

---

[26] *Continental Shelf (Tunisia/Libyan Arab Jamahiriya)*, judgment, *ICJ Reports*, 1982, p. 18; *Continental Shelf (Libyan Arab Jamahiriya/Malta)*, judgment, *ICJ Reports*, 1985, p. 13; *Delimitation of the Maritime Boundary in the Gulf of Maine Area*, judgment, *ICJ Reports*, 1984, p. 246. See also *Maritime Delimitation in the Area between Greenland and Jan Mayen (Denmark* v. *Norway)*, judgment, *ICJ Reports*, 1993.

force between them, such as the North-East Atlantic Fisheries Convention of 24 January 1959, as well as such other agreements as may be reached in the matter in the course of further negotiation.[27]

The Court also held that the concept of preferential rights in fisheries limits is not static:

This is not to say that the preferential rights of a coastal State in a special situation are a static concept, in the sense that the degree of the coastal State's preference is to be considered as fixed for ever at some given moment. On the contrary, the preferential rights are a function of the exceptional dependence of such a coastal State on the fisheries in adjacent waters and may, therefore, vary as the extent of that dependence changes.[28]

The Court's judgment in the *Fisheries Jurisdiction* case contributes to the development of the law of the sea by recognizing the concept of the preferential rights of a coastal state in the fisheries of the adjacent waters, particularly if that state is in a special situation with its population dependent on those fisheries. Moreover, the Court proceeds further to recognize that the law pertaining to fisheries must accept the primacy of the requirement of conservation based on scientific data. The exercise of preferential rights of the coastal state, as well as the historic rights of other states dependent on the same fishing grounds, have all to be subject to the overriding consideration of proper conservation of the fishery resources for the benefit of all concerned. The Court held:

In the fresh negotiations which are to take place on the basis of the present Judgment, the Parties will have the benefit of the above appraisal of their respective rights, and of certain guidelines defining their scope. The task before them will be to conduct their negotiations on the basis that each must in good faith pay reasonable regard to the legal rights of the other in the waters around Iceland outside the 12-mile limit, thus bringing about an equitable apportionment of the fishing resources based on the facts of the particular situation, and having regard to the interests of other States which have established fishing

[27] *ICJ Reports*, 1974, p. 31.   [28] Ibid., p. 30.

rights in the area. It is not a matter of finding simply an equitable solution, but an equitable solution derived from the applicable law.[29]

(c) The Role of the UN Specialized Agencies

Any assessment of the efforts of the UN in the development of international law must give a prominent place to the contribution of the specialized agencies. Some of the agencies of the UN system have revolutionized international law in their own domain and even established a full legal regime with its own sanctions to enforce obedience to the laws generated in that particular field. This observation applies particularly to the International Maritime Organization (IMO), the International Telecommunication Union (ITU), the International Labour Organization (ILO), the International Civil Aviation Organization (ICAO), and other organizations in technical spheres. But important legal instruments have also been adopted by UNESCO, the World Health Organization (WHO), the Office of the United Nations High Commissioner for Refugees (UNHCR), and other bodies. Some of this work merits particular attention here.

1. Universalism of domestic standards through inter-state regulation

We may take for example the world-wide regulation promoted by the ILO. Its conventions and recommendations cover such matters as hours of work, manning, and wages for factory and other workers. Each state has its own laws to regulate the hours of work or wages of the labour so employed, but the ILO has set uniform minimum standards to which most states have adhered.

2. Automatic ratification of amendments

Problems occur where urgently required amendments to existing conventions are negotiated, but do not come into force for some or all states owing to slowness of ratification

[29] Ibid., p. 33.

processes. In the maritime field, the IMO has made path-breaking progress towards overcoming such problems. Certain conventions concluded or administered by the IMO now compel state parties to accept in a limited way the principle of automatic acceptance of amendments after the lapse of a certain period of time. Thus, for example, Article XV(2) of the 1972 Convention on the Prevention of Marine Pollution by Dumping of Wastes and Other Matter provides that amendments of a scientific and technically specialized nature, if approved by a two-thirds majority of those present and voting at a meeting called in accordance with the provisions of the Convention, 'shall enter into force for each Contracting Party immediately on notification of its acceptance to the Organization and 100 days after approval by the meeting for all other parties except for those which before the end of 100 days make a declaration that they are not able to accept the amendment at that time'. This formulation does away with the need for a prescribed number of ratifications prior to entry into force of the amendments, and throws the burden on the dissenting minority to assert itself if it wishes to prevent the amendment from coming into force.

The 1974 Safety of Life at Sea (SOLAS) Convention also provides for automatic adoption of certain types of amendments six months after acceptance by two-thirds of the contracting states. Amendments adopted by the Maritime Safety Committee come into force two years after being communicated to the contracting states, unless rejected either by one-third of them, or by contracting states responsible for half of the world's gross tonnage of merchant shipping.

Similarly, the 1973 International Convention for the Prevention of Pollution from Ships (the MARPOL Convention) adopts in its Article 16(2)(d), (e), and (f) the method of accepting an amendment to an appendix by fixing a period of time 'not less than 10 months' after the lapse of which the amendment would come into force 'unless within that period an objection was communicated to the Organization by not less than one-third of the parties whose combined fleets constitute not less than 50 per cent of the gross tonnage of the world merchant fleets'.

This is in sharp contrast to the classical concept of sovereignty of states in international law, according to which a two-thirds majority could not, as a matter of right, bind the one-third minority since the consent of each state was essential to create binding obligations.

3. Effective enforcement in particular fields

Most of the main maritime conventions, including the 1974 SOLAS Convention and the 1966 International Convention on Load Lines, are enforced by the port authorities of the countries visited by ships for trade and commerce. There are no protests from the foreign-flag ships that are penalized by the port authorities for having violated the Plimsoll mark by overloading.

What is still more significant is that even the 'non-convention' ships, that is ships flying the flag of countries that have not ratified the maritime conventions, have to obey the law of the conventions because most port states have ratified these conventions. The non-convention ships thus have no option but to comply with the conventions, because they cannot avoid visiting the ports of convention states. This ensures virtually universal obedience to the convention laws.

(d) Legal Innovation under UN Auspices

The contributions of the UN, surveyed in the preceding parts of this chapter, have assisted the development and promotion of several new international legal concepts. Many of these spring from the UN's global character, which promotes a global approach to problems. Hence, for example, the genuine universalism of much contemporary international law, enabling the law to avoid more regional or parochial lines of development which would have been a disaster; hence also the concept of human rights as rights of the entire human kind, both individually and collectively, irrespective of national boundaries, and without discrimination as to race, religion, or sex. Two of the new concepts with a strong universalist character merit further consideration here: the concept of 'global commons' (or common heritage of mankind), and proposals for a 'New International Economic Order'.

1. 'Global commons' and environmental protection

The territorial jurisdiction of the state—whether on land, sea or air—is by and large well established. But technology is opening up areas beyond the traditional terrestrial jurisdiction of states. These areas, often described as 'international commons' or 'extraterritorial spaces', are increasingly the subject of international legal regulation. The *high seas*, as an international highway for the passage of merchant ships, was the first recognized common space legally beyond the territorial sovereignty of any state. A legal regime for the sea-bed beyond the limits of national jurisdiction was formulated in the 1982 Law of the Sea Convention. However, the Convention has yet to come into force, and this regime has not attracted universal support.

There are other extraterritorial spaces, such as outer space or the atmosphere, which are neither fully nor effectively covered by an up-to-date legal system. Environmentalists are attempting to secure the protection, care, and conservation of the *atmosphere* as a 'common heritage of mankind', while *outer space* is regulated by specific rules rather than a codified general regime. *Antarctica* is regulated by a limited group of states under the 1959 Antarctic Treaty: the General Assembly began to take an interest in Antarctica in the early 1980s.

Mankind's principal use of another common resource, the earth's *electromagnetic environment*, is in the field of communications. An international organization, the International Telecommunication Union (ITU), has been created to facilitate international cooperation in this whole field. In a world so dependent on telecommunications, there is an overwhelming practical need for the performance of such tasks as allocation of radio frequencies and establishment of common technical standards. Much functional legal cooperation is achieved by the ITU and other bodies.

The concept of global commons carries with it common sharing, with common benefits and common costs. If it is a key characteristic of the concept of global commons that they cannot be appropriated by a single state, it follows that there must not only be common sharing in the name of humanity as a whole, but also respect for the needs of future generations.

2. The 'New International Economic Order'

The classical principles and standards of international treaty practice—such as national treatment, preferential treatment, fair treatment, reciprocity, and the international minimum standard—continue to develop and form part of many international economic treaties and organizations. Owing to their applicability to states with different economic systems, they reconcile the need for international cooperation with the diversity of national economic and legal systems. On the other hand, the various levels of private and public national and international economic law are slowly being integrated into a comprehensive 'international economic law' with mutually interacting and complementary structures and developments, such as the distinct tendency in both national and international economic law to supplement the classical principles of freedom and formal equality by new principles of substantive equality and solidarity.

The main contribution to the concept of the New International Economic Order was the 1974 General Assembly resolution on the Charter of Economic Rights and Duties of States.[30] This was adopted by a vote of 120 in favour, six against, and ten abstentions. Further developments in state practice, spurred in part by the work of the UN and its agencies, have aided the legal development of many aspects of the NIEO, although other aspects depend on further negotiations in the political sphere.

[30] GA Res. 3281 (XXIX) of 12 Dec. 1974, *GAOR*, 29th session, supplement no. 31 (UN doc. A/9631). On the NIEO see also Kenneth Dadzie's chapter above, pp. 303–4.

(e) Conclusions: Problems of Contemporary International Law

Although international law has developed markedly since 1945, both within and without the auspices of the UN, several fundamental problems remain unsolved. These relate especially to conflicts between international law principles, to gaps within the current body of international law, to regrettably frequent divergences between principles and practice, and to problems of implementation and enforcement. These are complex matters which cannot be treated extensively here. What follows will simply touch lightly on some areas of difficulty, without attempting to do so in a formal legal way, still less to propose solutions.

1. Conflict between principles

The content of international law is very much influenced by the practice and interests of states. International law rules are often formed as a compromise between different interests, whether economic, military, social, or other interests. General principles are agreed and applied, but in difficult or unusual cases it is not uncommon for them to appear to conflict. In many cases such apparent conflict can be resolved by detailed examination of all the legally relevant material germane to the case in hand. At the political level, however, there are often disputes as to which principle is applicable. There may be, for instance, tension between the principle of human rights and that of non-intervention, or between the principle of self-determination of peoples and that of the territorial integrity of states, or between the principle of freedom of the high seas and that of the common heritage of mankind.

A different dichotomy has occasionally been perceived between regionalism and universalism in international law. To a large extent this tension is illusory. Regional mechanisms for implementing and enforcing law can be very successful, as is evident for instance in the human rights field. The Court and Commission established under the European Convention on Human Rights are good examples which increasingly have parallels in other regions. Regional institutions may also use law to regulate local arrangements for navigation, carriage of goods, customs, fisheries, and a myriad of other matters. Such institutions do not affect the universality of general international law, which continues to apply in all regions. The fragmentation of universal international law into different bodies of law applying in different regions, without unifying principles or institutions, would be a disastrous regression: fortunately, there is little sign of this happening, and the trend is towards the further strengthening of general international law.

2. Gaps and ambiguities in international law

The progressive development of international law is a continuing process, and there remain a number of areas in which agreement on more detailed legal regimes is still needed. In some cases this is because international opinion is only just becoming seriously interested in particular problems. Rigorous international regulation of environmental pollution has begun in many areas, but, for instance, the possible problems of climate change are only just beginning to be addressed by effective legal measures. Similarly, international law does not yet have an explicit means of taking into account the interests of future generations in their environment. Another area of increasing international activity concerns the protection of the rights of indigenous peoples: the UN Working Group on Indigenous Populations is busy formulating appropriate international standards in response to growing recognition of the importance of this issue. A third problem of mounting contemporary urgency is the problem of mass exodus of persons, whether spurred by war, natural disaster, tyranny, or economic deprivation. The existing international law on refugee status was not devised to deal with mass exodus, but it has not yet proved possible to adopt a comprehensive new legal regime in this difficult but vital area.

Other alleged gaps in international law relate to subjects which may not, or not yet, be so well suited to international legal regulation. Thus contemporary international law does not explicitly address the existence of so-called 'spheres of influence', of the sort associated (rightly or wrongly) with the 1945 Yalta Agreement, although the anti-imperialist principles of decolonization, non-intervention, and sovereign equality are formally opposed to spheres of influence. Similarly, general international law has relatively little impact on national immigration policies, although immigration matters are dealt with in many bilateral and other treaties. Views also differ on the international legality of certain forms of military activity, including the circumstances in which military interventions of various kinds may or may not be reconcilable with fundamental principles of international law.

3. Discrepancies between principles and practice

The practice of states and of international bodies conforms to international law in the vast majority of cases. Discrepancies may nevertheless appear on occasion. In some instances this is because international treaty standards are set at very high levels of attainment, and perfect universal compliance cannot be achieved instantly. Thus the growing body of human rights treaties does not instantly bring an end to all violations of human rights, much as the criminal law does not easily put an end to organized crime. Similarly, war has remained a feature of international life, despite the fundamental prohibitions on resort to aggressive war and the provisions for peaceful settlement of disputes contained in the UN Charter.

If humanity is to make progress, aspirational standards must often be set above the lowest common denominator—although not so far above as to flaw their efficacy. International legal standards will often be inconvenient to the short-term ends of a particular government. What is essential is that the international rule of law be effectively implemented and enforced.

4. Implementation and enforcement

The effectiveness of the law depends in part on the effectiveness of sanctions and recourses suitable for the protection of the victims of its violation. Without sanctions and without recourses, a legal regulation, as perfect as it may seem with regard to its content, risks remaining just empty words. Sanctions and recourses have developed considerably in the period since 1945, as indicated by the survey in this chapter. Further progress must still be made; the work of the International Law Commission in codifying the principles of state responsibility, when complete, will make an important contribution in this sphere.

More important than new formal procedures, however, is the task of increasing among states the habit of compliance with law. This cannot be left entirely to the states themselves. It is the responsibility of international organizations, of non-governmental organizations, of the news media, of individuals, and of international public opinion to castigate those who violate international law and to ensure better observance of it. The UN has an important role in coordinating these efforts as well as in facilitating the further development of international law. I am confident that future generations will be equal to this task.

The Historical Development of Efforts to Reform the UN

MAURICE BERTRAND

THE notion of 'UN reform' has several meanings, and use of the term has varied according to the mood of public opinion concerning the world organization. These meanings are:

1. Tinkering with the structure of the Secretariat, i.e. changing the organization-chart, eliminating the 'dead wood', reducing the number of posts, particularly the number of top posts.

2. Defining priorities, i.e. suppressing obsolete programmes, in order to concentrate resources on the most important ones. The idea of a better coordination of the UN system can be associated with this usage.

3. Reorganizing the intergovernmental machinery, in order to render it more efficient or more representative of the international community. A very important distinction has to be made between:

   (a) Reorganization without reforming the Charter, e.g. 'revitalizing ECOSOC' by modifying its agenda or its relations with the General Assembly, increasing or reducing the membership of various committees, creating new committees or merging existing ones, streamlining the whole intergovernmental machinery.

   (b) Restructuring the main organs—i.e. the Security Council, ECOSOC, the General Assembly—which implies Charter reform. Reforming UNCTAD (which does not imply Charter revision) can be included in this category, because of the taboos concerning the existence of this organization.

Those who believe that the efficiency of the UN is a question of management give to the words 'UN reform' the meanings nos. (1), (2), and (3*a*). This has long been, and still is, the American and more generally the Northern (including East and West) understanding of the problem. The representatives of developing countries, while sharing parts of the Northern understanding, insist generally on enlarging the membership of committees, including ECOSOC and the Security Council. They have succeeded twice in changing the Charter: by enlarging the membership of the Security Council from eleven to fifteen; and that of ECOSOC from eighteen to twenty-seven, and then to fifty-four.[1] Finally, some people use the meaning (3*b*) when recommending a partial or complete restructuring of the Charter, for example reducing the membership of ECOSOC, merging ECOSOC and UNCTAD, creating an 'Economic Security Council', changing the relationship between the UN and its specialized agencies, or enlarging the number of Permanent Members of the Security Council. Germany and Japan began to advocate this last idea with vigour from about 1992.

For a correct understanding of the historical development of efforts to reform the UN, a few preliminary remarks are necessary. One of the most important changes in UN activities is a result of the invention of peacekeeping forces (blue helmets) in the field of security, on the initiative of Lester Pearson and Dag Hammarskjöld in 1956. This has been, without touching the Charter, a fundamental reform of the UN. Nevertheless the word reform has never been used in this connection.

Implementing fully the provisions of the Charter has also never been considered as a reform. For example, Article 43 provides for 'special agreements' on assignment of military forces to the Security Council; and Article 47 assigns major responsibilities to the Military Staff Committee. Any implementation of these articles, as proposed by Secretary-General Boutros-Ghali, would represent an

---

[1] Amendments to Arts. 23, 27, and 61 were adopted on 17 Dec. 1963. A further amendment to Art. 61 was adopted on 20 Dec. 1971. See Appendix B to the present volume.

important reform of the UN as it has operated since 1945. Yet such proposals have been described as 'revitalization' rather than 'reform'.

We are now witnessing a slow but fundamental change in the conception of UN reform. Since the origin of the UN (and even since the founding of the League of Nations), understanding of the reform of the world organization has been (with rare exceptions) a mixture of meanings (1), (2), and (3a). Since 1985 the meaning (3b), i.e. the notion that the UN should undergo a far more important restructuring, and that the Charter could be changed, has been gaining ground.

(a) The Traditional Conception of UN Reform

The major world organizations have since their inception been periodically submitted to examination. Studies, reform projects, and restructuring operations are permanent items on their agendas.

1. The League of Nations

In the League of Nations, established in 1919, the need continually to adapt the structure of the political international organization was recognized from the outset. The last study bearing on reform of the League of Nations became famous, probably due to the date at which its conclusions were published. The group of experts chaired by the Australian Stanley Bruce finalized its report in 1939. It recommended the creation of a central committee for economic and social questions, with the mission to direct and control the 'technical activities' previously addressed by the Council and the Assembly of the League. It envisaged participation of states which were not members of the League, and decision-making by majority. This audacious reform project—which six years later suggested to the fathers of the UN Charter the idea of the Economic and Social Council—was the outcome of reflections which had continued throughout the League's life: the Brussels Conference of September–October 1920; the preparation for the establishment of the Economic and Financial

Committee by the Under-Secretary-General Jean Monnet;[2] the Geneva Economic Conference of 1927; and the work of the Committee of Twenty-Eight in 1936.

2. The UN's first forty years

As for the United Nations, it would be overly fastidious to enumerate all the intergovernmental committees and groups of experts which have examined such issues as methods of work, financial difficulties, personnel policy, salaries, budgets, plans, economic and social programmes, decentralization, coordination, structure of the Secretariat, functioning of the intergovernmental machinery, and evaluation of results.

Initiatives of this type for reform of the UN fall into two distinct periods. In the first, which lasted until the mid-1960s, initiatives for reflection and change mainly came from the Secretary-General, who proposed that the General Assembly create committees to help him in his task: for example the Group of Three Experts appointed by Trygve Lie in 1954, the Salaries Survey Committee of 1957, and the Group of Eight Experts approved by the General Assembly in 1960 to help Dag Hammarskjöld to define the Secretariat's structure. This Group of Eight, chaired by Guillaume Georges Picot, considered and rejected Khrushchev's proposal for a 'troika' of three Secretaries-General.[3]

The second period began some years after Hammarskjöld's death. Henceforth the initiative was taken by member states, and the process of reflection and reform

---

[2] Jean Monnet (1888–1979) was one of the main initiators of the European Economic Community. After leaving the League of Nations in 1923, he was in private business until 1938. In 1939 he was chairman of the Franco-British Economic Coordination Committee, and later served as a member of the French Committee of National Liberation in Algiers. From 1947 to 1952 he was Commissioner of the first French Development Plan. He originated the Schuman Plan (1950), and was first president of the High Authority of the European Coal and Steel Community. In 1956 he became chairman of the Action Committee for the United States of Europe, which helped to prepare the Treaty of Rome of 1957.

[3] 'Review of the Activities and Organization of the Secretariat: Report of the Committee of Experts Created by Resolution 1446 (XIV)', UN doc. A/4776 of 14 June 1961. Khrushchev had made his 'troika' proposal at the General Assembly in 1960.

became a permanent function. From that time onward the number of committees and surveys on reform increased exponentially. In 1966, as a consequence of the financial crisis which resulted from the refusal by the USSR and France to pay their share of the expenses of ONUC in the Congo, a report of the Committee of Fourteen proposed measures concerning planning, programming, monitoring, evaluation, budgetary presentation, economic and social programmes, and so on.[4] In 1969 a study on the capacity of the UN development system, concentrating on UNDP, was completed.[5] In 1975 the report of a Group of (twenty-five) Experts on the Structure of the United Nations System recommended the creation of the post of Director-General for Development, and the extension of the role of the Committee for Programme and Coordination (CPC).[6] Finally, throughout the whole period, numerous other studies by various special committees dealt with the financial situation and other administrative problems.[7]

In 1968 the Joint Inspection Unit (JIU) embarked on its never-ending task of considering how to improve the functioning of all the agencies of the UN system.[8] In its

[4] 'Second Report of the Ad hoc Committee of Experts to Examine the Finances of the United Nations and the Specialized Agencies' (Committee established by resolution 2049 (XX) of 13 Dec. 1965), UN doc. A/6343 of 19 July 1966.

[5] A Study of the Capacity of the United Nations Development System, vols. 1 and 2 (UN, Geneva, 1969), sales no. E.70.1.10. The main author of the study was Sir Robert Jackson.

[6] 'A New United Nations Structure for Global Economic Cooperation: Report of the Group of Experts on the Structure of the UN System', UN doc. E/AC.62/9 (New York, 1975).

[7] Among others: 'Report of the Committee on the Reorganization of the Secretariat' (Committee of Seven), Nov. 1968; 'Report of the Special Committee on the Financial Situation of the UN' (Committee of Fifteen), 1972; 'Report of the Working Group on the UN Programme and Budget Machinery', 1975; 'Report of the Negotiating Committee on the Financial Emergency of the UN' (Committee of Fifty-Four), 1976; 'Report of the Ad hoc Committee on the Restructuring of the Economic and Social Sectors of the UN System' (Committee of the Whole), Dec. 1977; 'Report of the Committee of Governmental Experts to Evaluate the Present Structure of the Secretariat in the Administrative, Finance and Personnel Areas' (Committee of Seventeen), Nov. 1982. For details of these reports see the relevant volumes of the Yearbook of the United Nations.

[8] The Joint Inspection Unit was established on an experimental basis by GA resolutions 2150 (XXI) of 4 Nov. 1966, 2360 (XXII) of 19 Nov. 1967, 2735 (XXV) of 17 Dec. 1970, and 2924 B (XXVII) of 24 Nov. 1972. It was established on a permanent basis, from 1 Jan. 1978, by GA Res. 31/192 of 22 Dec. 1976,

first twenty years the JIU published well over 200 reports, dealing with administrative, financial, and structural aspects of the activities of these organizations. The JIU has secured implementation of a number of recommendations for reform, particularly in the recruitment of personnel, the adoption of medium-term plans and programme budgets, and improvement of methods of monitoring and evaluation.

By the mid-1980s the lessons to be drawn from this experience were clear: discussion of reform had been largely driven by the UN's financial difficulties, the cyclical worsening of which is a permanent feature of the life of the organization. Reform proposals had always been vigorously resisted by the Secretariat. Some measures aiming at modernization had been attempted:[9] but any limited results of these efforts had rapidly been eroded. It had never really been possible to revitalize the organization, which—buffeted by successive crises and efforts at reform— had become more and more marginalized.

the annexe of which contains the Statute of the Unit. The JIU is composed of eleven Inspectors, who have the status of officials of the UN but are not staff members. The Inspectors 'have the broadest powers of investigation in all matters having a bearing on the efficiency of the services and the proper use of funds'; 'they make on-the-spot inquiries and investigations . . . as and when they themselves may decide, in any of the services of the organizations' of the UN system; they 'may propose reforms or make recommendations they deem necessary to the competent organs of the organizations'; they 'draw up, over their own signature, reports for which they are responsible and in which they state their findings and propose solutions to the problems they have noted . . . Upon receipt of reports, the executive head or heads concerned shall take immediate action to distribute them, with or without their comments, to the States members of their respective organizations.'

[9] For example, the development of a sophisticated system of planning, programming, budgeting, and evaluation, the adoption of precise regulations and rules on this topic, and the establishment of competitive examinations for recruitment of junior professionals. In each case, despite unanimous approval by member states, implementation was greatly hindered by resistance from the Secretariat. On programming cf. JIU report 79/5 (UN doc. A/34/84) of 26 Mar. 1979, on 'Medium-term Planning in the United Nations'; and UN doc. A/36/171 'The Setting of Priorities and Identification of Obsolete Activities in the United Nations'. On personnel matters, see the first, second, and third reports of the JIU on the implementation of the personnel policy reforms approved by the General Assembly in 1974 (UN doc. A/31/264; JIU report 78/4; and UN doc. A/35/318); and the JIU report on 'Competitive Examinations in the United Nations' (JIU report 84/11 of Aug. 1984).

LIVERPOOL
JOHN MOORES UNIVERSITY
TRUEMAN STREET LIBRARY
TEL. 051 231 4022/4023

(b) Diagnoses and Proposals in the 1980s

In the mid-1980s the UN entered a period of acute crises, in significant part the result of an anti-UN mood in the US Congress. This mood led in particular to the Congress's approval of the Kassebaum Amendment in 1985, which, combined with other US legislation adopted that year, threatened severe financial difficulties for the UN.[10] During this period of crises, the proposals for reform were not very different from those put forward in the past. It would be hard to present the creation in 1986 by the General Assembly of a new group of experts, the Group of Eighteen, as an exceptional phenomenon. Its report, presented the same year, contained numerous recommendations that were simply repetitions of past proposals on intergovernmental organs, personnel policy, coordination methods of inspection, planning, programming, and evaluation.[11]

[10] The Kassebaum Amendment, adopted by the US Senate in August 1985, was intended to force a 20% cut in the US contribution to the UN budget, unless a system of weighted voting for financial decision-making was introduced. This would have entailed a reduction in the US contribution to the UN budget from 25% down to 20%. The Sundquist Amendment of October 1985 was intended to deny the US contribution to the salaries of Soviet bloc UN staff members, in protest against their having to relinquish part of their pay cheques to their own governments. Another piece of legislation bearing on the level of the US contribution to the UN was the Gramm-Rudman Act (the Balanced Budget and Emergency Deficit Control Act) of Dec. 1985 which provided for reduced federal deficits over the following five years, with the intention of achieving a balanced budget in 1991. This Act provided that, if deficits were expected to be higher than those specified, starting in the 1986 fiscal year, funds were to be cut from most federal programmes, including those concerning payments to the UN regular budget and to forty-three other international organizations.

The combination of these measures led to a reduction of approximately 50% in the US contribution to the UN in 1986. The large-scale withholdings of assessed payments by the US over several years precipitated the UN financial crisis. Already by the end of 1985, eighteen member states, including four of the five Permanent Members of the Security Council, had combined withholdings of about $US 120 m.; overall, unpaid dues for 1985 and earlier years had reached a grand total of $225 m. The UN regular budget was then approximately $800 m. per year. The only flexibility was provided by the UN's working capital fund of $100 m., and this was quickly exhausted. The UN has no borrowing power, if not expressly authorized by the General Assembly. On withholdings, see also Zoller, *American Journal of International Law*, 81 (1987), p. 610. Since 1986 the USA has softened its policy in principle, and authorized some payments of part of its contribution: see below, n. 13.

[11] 'Report of the Group of High-Level Intergovernmental Experts to Review the Efficiency of the Administrative and Financial Functioning of the UN', UN doc. A/41/49 (1986).

Nevertheless, a relatively new tone was identifiable in the consensus report of the Group of Eighteen. Several abusive practices and problems of mismanagement affecting the Secretariat were confronted directly for the first time, including the harmful proliferation of the posts of Under-Secretary-General and Assistant Secretary-General; the inadequacy of qualifications of staff, particularly in these top posts; and the complex, fragmented, and top-heavy structure of the Secretariat. The report represented a sincere effort to reverse past tendencies in recommending reducing the number of Under-Secretary-General and Assistant Secretary-General posts by 25 per cent over a period of three years, and in acknowledging the necessity of pursuing in-depth studies of the structure of the intergovernmental machinery, a subject until now shielded from critical investigation.

An important sign of a sincere desire for change was the particular attention paid by the Group of Eighteen to reform of the intergovernmental mechanisms which prepare the decisions on budgets, even if the Group was not able to reach a consensus on this subject. Many experts advocated the creation of a Committee of Programme and Budget, with a limited membership, a geographical distribution ensuring that the 'major contributors' would have reasonable representation, consensus decision-making, and a mandate to advise the General Assembly on the content of the UN's programme and the size of the budget. Despite the fact that such a proposal had often been made in the past and would have been the logical conclusion of the adoption in 1974 of medium-term planning and programme budgeting, even the 1986 reforms did not put it fully into effect.[12]

---

[12] By its resolution 41/213 of 19 Dec. 1986, the General Assembly finally approved, with a number of reservations, the recommendations of the Group of Eighteen concerning the structure of the Secretariat, reduction of staff, personnel policy, inspection, coordination, etc. On the budgetary process, the General Assembly decided to request the Secretary-General to prepare an outline of the programme budget one year in advance, and to give the existing Committee for Programme and Coordination the mandate to consider this outline. The CPC was to 'continue its existing practice of reaching decisions by consensus', and to transmit its conclusions and recommendations to the General

The Group of Eighteen's report, and the ensuing debates in the General Assembly, reflected the then current diagnosis of the UN's crisis. This diagnosis had three main components:

1. The prime cause of the crisis was thought to be the general 'crisis of multilateralism', in other words the 'lack of political will' of member states.

2. There was a lack of effective management, a problem which could be rectified mainly by 'reinforcing the power' of the Secretary-General.

3. The UN suffered from some structural deficiencies, mostly in the Secretariat and in some subsidiary intergovernmental organs dealing with programme and budget, which could be greatly ameliorated by the creation of a special committee to deal with these problems.

Such a diagnosis led naturally to the conclusion that some minor changes and improved management could solve the UN's crisis, but that a change in the political climate was needed before a real revitalization of the UN could be achieved.

(c) New Approaches since the Late 1980s

Since the crisis of the mid-1980s, the conception of UN reform has begun to change. But this evolution has not yet been fully achieved, and it is premature to predict its final result. It is only possible to analyse the reasons for this change and the various types of new approaches.

First, of course, the UN environment, that is, the international landscape, has been transformed. Beginning with the Gorbachev era, changes such as the success of the 1986 CSCE negotiations in Stockholm on the development of confidence-building measures, the conclusion of arms

Assembly. The General Assembly would continue to decide on the programme-budget in conformity with Arts. 17 and 18 of the Charter. In response, the US administration indicated that it would recommend to Congress that it be more positive in its financial support of the UN. Overall, the passage of GA Res. 41/213 did not represent real progress in the direction of better mutual understanding of the role of the UN; it did not alleviate the financial and political crisis.

reduction agreements (the 1987 Treaty on Intermediate Nuclear Forces, the 1990 Treaty on Conventional Armed Forces in Europe, and the 1991 and 1993 Strategic Arms Reduction treaties), the destruction of the Berlin wall, the reunification of Germany, the changes of regimes in eastern Europe, the collapse of communism in the USSR, and the emergence of the Commonwealth of Independent States have put the UN in a totally different situation.

The main direct consequences for the world organization were the complete change of attitude of the USSR and then Russia toward the UN, the agreements between the USA and the USSR to put an end to numerous local and regional conflicts, and the decision to request the UN to help in various ways to this end. Consequently peacekeeping operations have been developed, notably in Yugoslavia and Cambodia, and the five Permanent Members of the Security Council have found themselves able to agree on numerous problems. This permitted, in particular, the authorization by the Security Council of the use of force in the 1991 Gulf war, and in Somalia in 1992.

The public mood *vis-à-vis* the UN has followed these trends. The UN has suddenly become popular in the West, and the prestige of the Security Council and of the UN Secretary-General has greatly increased. However, this new fashion has not extended to finding a durable solution to the financial crisis.[13] Nevertheless, ideas for reform are still numerous, and it is possible to discern various contradictory trends.

The *management* approach is still alive. There is persistent pressure from the USA and even from the majority of member states, at least in the North, for the UN to

[13] On 31 Dec. 1991 the members who had not paid their dues owed to the regular budget and peacekeeping operations a combined amount of $US 900 m.: $439.3 m. to the regular budget and $463.5 m. to the peacekeeping budget. The US was the greatest debtor, being responsible for $407.3 m., of which $266.4 m. was to the regular budget. By 31 Dec. 1992 the overall figure for unpaid dues had increased to $1,265 m.: $500 m. to the regular budget (equal to 42% of the regular budget for 1992), and $765 m. to the peacekeeping budget. The US debt to the regular budget (largely comprising dues unpaid before 1990) had been reduced to $240 m., and was being paid off progressively. Eighty-seven other states were in arrears to the regular budget.

continue to streamline the Secretariat and to reduce the budget. Secretary-General Boutros-Ghali decided, within two months of taking office, to suppress some fourteen posts of Assistant Secretary-General and of Under-Secretary-General in the Secretariat. These measures concerned only the economic and social departments, not the administrative ones, but were nevertheless welcomed by the main member states. Further measures were foreshadowed.

Proposals for reform concerning the main organs, i.e. implying Charter reform, have developed significantly since 1985. They are following three different trends.

(i) *Economic and social reform.* The first trend reflects concern with the economic and social part of the UN: mainly with the Economic and Social Council (ECOSOC), which has for decades been in a state of permanent crisis. To give ECOSOC some credibility and authority, it has been proposed either to reduce the number of its members, or to enlarge it to include all member states; to suppress at the same time the Second and Third Committees of the General Assembly (which fulfil practically the same functions); and to create an 'Economic Security Council' of a very limited membership. This Economic Security Council would include the richest and the most populated member states, the other ones being represented on a regional basis. This type of proposal was made in 1985 by a JIU report;[14] in 1987 by the UNA-USA's 'Panel of 22' in a report entitled *A Successor Vision*;[15] and in 1992 by UNDP in the Third Human Development Report, which contained even more drastic proposals.[16]

[14] 'Some Reflections on Reform of the United Nations' by Maurice Bertrand, esp. paras. 65–70 on 'Nature of the Activities of the System and the Notion of a World Consensus' (JIU report 85/9), UN doc. A/40/988 of 6 Dec. 1985.

[15] UNA-USA, *A Successor Vision: The United Nations of Tomorrow* (New York, 1987).

[16] This UNDP report, in its chapter V entitled 'A New Vision for Global Human Development', lists reform proposals made (1) in 1989 by the World Institute for Development Economic Research, part of the UN University, for the establishment of a World Economic Council; (2) in 1991 by the Nordic UN Project for a 'high-level International Development Council'; (3) in 1991 by the Group of Fifteen comprising the largest developing countries, at its summit meeting in Caracas.

The report says (p. 82): 'Economic and social issues are supposed to be

(ii) *Reform of Security Council membership.* The idea here is to make this organ more representative. Two main conceptions exist. The first (an old claim of the developing countries) is to end the veto privilege of the Permanent Members and to increase the total membership; the second is to permit other member states to enter the list. This latter conception is supported by Germany and Japan; and countries such as India, Brazil, and Nigeria are also possible candidates.

(iii) *Enhancing effective power of the Security Council.* The third approach to structural reform also addresses security matters, but in a different way. It would put at the disposal of the Security Council a military force, and revitalize the machinery foreseen by Chapter VII, with its system of identification of aggressors by the Security Council (Articles 39 and 40), economic and military sanctions (Articles 41 and 42), the provision of military contingents by member states according to special agreements (Article 43), and the establishment and exercise of responsibility by the Military Staff Committee (Article 47).

The implementation of this full system of collective security as envisaged in 1945 was in large measure recommended by Secretary-General Boutros-Ghali in 1992 in *An Agenda for Peace.* The report adds candidly: 'Forces under Article 43 may perhaps never be sufficiently large or well enough equipped to deal with a threat from a major army equipped with sophisticated weapons. They would be useful, however, in meeting any threat posed by a military force of a lesser order.'[17] It is also proposed to complement

---

coordinated by the Economic and Social Council. In practice they are not. ECOSOC's fifty-four member structure is too large and unwieldy, and the most powerful industrial countries have regarded this and other UN fora as unmanageable and unprofessional. Effective economic management would require a much smaller and more tightly organized forum, a Development Security Council.' The proposal is for a Council of twenty-two members, eleven permanent and eleven on the basis of rotational election. Other proposals are the creation of a global central bank, for international taxation with a system of progressive income tax, an international trade organization, and a transitional strategy with reforms of the IMF, the World Bank, and GATT.

[17] Boutros Boutros-Ghali, *An Agenda for Peace*, June 1992, para. 43. (Below, Appendix A.)

these military arrangements by 'peace-enforcement units', more heavily armed than peacekeeping units, that could be called upon to restore and maintain cease-fires, when such agreements are violated.

Thus Secretary-General Boutros-Ghali argues that the UN should have at its disposal a full range of military forces of various types. The hypothesis is the same as those of 1919 and 1945: that a definitive consensus exists among the great powers, enabling them to constitute a military alliance able to impose their conception of international order on the whole planet. The passage quoted above, concerning the improbability of the international force controlled by the Security Council being able to oppose a 'major army', shows clearly which political philosophy inspires the whole scheme. The objective is to repress small aggressors; it is not envisaged that one of the great powers could be opposed to the others. If accepted, this version of full implementation of the Chapter VII of the Charter would represent a complete change in the character of the UN.

(d) The Prospects for Real UN Reform

The renewal of interest in improving the UN's efficiency through fundamental structural reforms may seem encouraging. The fact that the taboo against touching the Charter is apparently fading could be considered as especially positive. But the prospects that a comprehensive conception of UN reform will gain acceptance in the near future remain slight.

The various existing proposals are inspired by different visions of the future and of the role of a world organization. There is no consensus of any kind among specialists, diplomats, governments; and public opinion does not seem to be much concerned. This absence of consensus has different consequences in the economic/social and in the security fields.

1. Economic and social issues

In economic and social matters there is still a split between North and South. The diplomats of developing countries continue to press for the enlargement of all committees in the UN and for the development of the economic and social programme. The countries of the North are not much interested in most of the UN's economic and social activities and prefer to rely upon the IMF and the World Bank. The so-called North–South dialogue has stopped. The situation could seem paradoxical since acknowledgement of interdependence has now become a commonplace. Since the first oil crisis in 1973, governments and public opinion have learned to recognize that there is no way to establish independent national strategies in the economic and social fields, or to ignore the strategies, methods, and principles accepted by the rest of the world. Third World debt, international migrations, nuclear accidents, ozone layer depletion, climate change, the spread of international terrorism, drugs, exchange-rate variations, and the activities of transnational corporations have permanently demonstrated that countries are no longer protected by their borders.

Even more important, the good fortune of any country can no longer be built exclusively on the misfortune of others, and the need for economic solidarity has become more significant than the advantages of competition. The prosperity of the USA is indispensable for the prosperity of Europe and Japan, and the reverse is also true. No major creditor-country, international bank, or large corporation can accept the bankruptcy of a major debtor. The principles on which international economic relations were based are in a process of radical modification. The priority that a government is ready to accord to obtaining the establishment of, and respect for, common rules—for arms control, or for the equilibrium of external trade—is now often higher than the one it attaches to monopolizing its own resources to ensure its security or its prosperity.

The direct consequence of these new principles is the need for reliable political institutions at the international and global level. Such institutions have to provide for medium-term commitments to implement common economic policies, for example those agreed in the decisions of the Western summits. The collective decisions of such institutions tend to be more credible than the resolutions of the UN General Assembly.

In other words, as the phenomenon of interdependence gains greater acceptance, there is more need for a solid world political framework. Such a framework does not exist at present. It is in the process of being established, but outside the UN. The rapid development of international intergovernmental organizations, which began in the middle of the nineteenth century, has spawned many institutions outside the UN. Despite their theoretical membership in the UN system, the financial world organizations—the International Monetary Fund, the World Bank, and GATT—have in fact operated as independent entities, in which a country's ministries of Finance, Economy, and Trade are represented without being really connected with its Ministry of Foreign Affairs. For the major powers, the growing emphasis, particularly in western Europe and North America, on economic cooperation and progressive integration at the regional and even the intercontinental level has reduced considerably interest in the UN as a forum for discussing economic matters. Finally, particularly since 1970, regular summits have been instituted between the major Western powers—the United States, Canada, Europe, and Japan—to address the harmonization of their monetary and economic strategies. The experimental meeting at Cancún (Mexico) in 1981, which involved fourteen developing countries and eight industrialized states, indicated a possible future model for such consultations.

Clear trends which can be identified in these new political institutions include representation at the highest level;[18] and the limitation of membership to the most important countries—which means the exclusion of small countries and (despite the fleeting exception of Cancún) of the Third World.

[18] The main levels of representation one can distinguish are: prime minister and heads of state (as in the Western and European summits, etc.); ministers (as in the Council of the European Community); ambassadors (as in the Security Council); and diplomats below the rank of ambassador (as in the majority of the UN committees, ECOSOC, the Trade and Development Board, and the Main Committees of the General Assembly).

In these circumstances it does not appear that the UN as presently structured is likely to play a major role in the economic and social fields; nor does it appear that the UN will soon be reformed in order to contribute more effectively in these fields.

2. *International security*

In the field of security, the situation is different because there has been since 1987 an illusion of consensus. The agreement of the five Permanent Members on authorizing the 1991 Gulf war, on trying to end regional conflicts, and on supporting a larger use of peacekeeping activities created the idea that the Cold War had been the only reason for the absence of consensus, and that a real system of collective security was now possible.

The philosophy underlying the approach of *An Agenda for Peace* is based on the following hypotheses:

• the existing consensus among the Permanent Members of the Security Council on the conception of international relations, which seemed to exist during the 1990–1 Gulf crisis, will exist for a long period;

• this consensus will be strong enough to overcome any reluctance on the part of the great powers to send their armed forces to a war to impose peace, anywhere in the world, even if their national interests are not directly threatened;

• the great majority of small and middle powers will support in all circumstances the policy defined by the great powers and their conception of international order.

Such a philosophy, which seems to forget the lessons of history, is more apparent than real. The Secretary-General's proposals to create an international army have not received very much support in the Security Council. Everyone knows that a system of collective security is conceived for inter-state conflicts and is not able to deal well with internal ones. The traditional kind of disputes between states are not frequent today, and will not be so. The present security threats are those occurring largely within a single country or former country, as shown by too many examples: Afghanistan, Angola, Azerbaijan, Cambodia,

El Salvador, Ethiopia, Liberia, Mozambique, Nicaragua, Somalia, and Yugoslavia; or they involve non-state actors such as terrorists and ethnic groups.

The idea of 'peace-enforcement units' that was a tentative response to these problems has not generated much enthusiasm because of the risks such a creation would entail. It is more likely that this philosophy, which remains verbal without any general commitment to its implementation, is designed to allow the great powers, or the hegemonic one, to use the UN when necessary for supporting their national interests or their conception of international order. This is in line with the repressive conception of security which is developing in the countries of the North with respect to the troubles that could occur in the South, as demonstrated by the setting up of various long-distance intervention forces by NATO and some great powers.

In these circumstances, prospects for a real reform of the UN in the security field are hardly any better than in the economic and social fields. The debate on the possible enlargement of the Security Council will contribute to deeper reflection on the type of world organization which is needed at the beginning of the third millennium. But it will take time.

The Structure of the UN in the Post-Cold War Period

PETER WILENSKI

THROUGH the worst years of the Cold War the UN was no more than a bit player in international peace and security issues: at its worst a propaganda forum, at its best playing a supporting role in the provision of peacekeeping forces once regional hostilities had ceased. It did have some achievements during this period—such as its contribution to decolonization and to the development of international law on human rights and other issues—but it did not play the role that its founders had anticipated. With the end of the Cold War, the outbreak of numerous regional conflicts, and the simultaneous rise of a new international agenda of issues outside the security area, the UN's position has almost overnight been transformed. It suddenly finds itself overburdened by the many new tasks which governments have given to it and the high expectations which the peoples of the world have for it.

This chapter will begin with a brief summary of the major functions the UN is now expected to perform. It will then look at the structures of the UN, will ask whether they are adequate for the new tasks, will examine some of the proposals that have been made to improve these structures, and will finally look at the difficulties that those who seek even relatively modest reform at the UN must overcome.

(a) Major Functions of the UN

The structures of the UN cannot be examined in isolation from the functions which the UN is expected to carry out.

As a management dictum goes, 'form follows function'. Of course the functions of the UN are always changing and always the subject of fundamental disagreement among members. If structural reform is delayed until there is final and unanimous agreement on function, then it will never take place. There appears however to be some consensus developing as to the broad objectives which the UN must now address. For the purpose of this chapter these priority functions are discussed briefly below under five headings, so that present and proposed structures can be measured against what is expected of them.

1. The establishment of a system of collective security

Although there is growing recognition of the importance of non-military threats to security, the primary aim of the UN remains the maintenance of peace by deterring aggression. This requires a credible *system* which will convince potential aggressors that if they go ahead with their intentions they will face punitive action by the UN— ranging from sanctions to armed force. Ideally, also, a system of deterrence should (and is beginning to) extend to dealing, not only with aggression, but also with states which refuse to abide by the normal standards of international behaviour, e.g. promoters of international terrorism. While the 1990–1 Gulf war was in most respects a special case, and doubts must continue as to the consistency with which sanctions will be applied by the Council, UN action against Iraq had undoubtedly added to the credibility of UN deterrence in general. Thus the basics are there, but for the system as a whole to be effective it needs further structural change. It requires an increase in the preventive diplomacy or peace-making capacity of the UN so that the organization can help to resolve disputes while aggression is being deterred. It requires mechanisms which will increase the likelihood that *in extremis* member states will make their armed forces available for collective action. It also requires structures through which reductions in armaments and in particular the prevention of the spread of weapons of mass destruction can be negotiated: if aggressors are heavily armed, especially with weapons of mass destruction, they are less likely to find the threat of collective action against them credible.

2. Prevention or settlement of regional conflicts

Many conflicts today are not ones to which the theory of collective security applies. They do not arise from the clear-cut aggression typical of the 1930s which motivated the writers of the Charter, but from the spread of local conflicts, usually of an ethnic nature, with long-standing root causes and with no party having a monopoly of right on its side. These are the conflicts which the UN is increasingly called upon to prevent or settle. For the UN to deal with them effectively it needs (again) a greatly expanded capacity for preventive diplomacy, a greatly improved Secretariat support structure, a better system for launching and maintaining peacekeeping operations, and, increasingly important, a guaranteed financial base to pay for the operations.

3. The promotion of economic development

In the promotion of economic development, the elimination of poverty, and the removal of underlying economic problems which may lead to conflict, the UN has not undergone the same revival in function as it has in the peace and security area. Nevertheless development remains the first priority of the majority of its member states. While the failure to deal with these issues is largely one of political will, new negotiating structures may facilitate a revitalized approach to the issue.

4. The new international agenda

Quite apart from its new security role following the end of the Cold War, the UN is facing a new international agenda of important socio-economic problems in relation to which countries are so interdependent that no country can solve them on its own. Examples are the global environment, AIDS, drugs, and the mass movements of populations. These are, for the most part, issues which were placed on the international agenda some years after the UN Charter was written. The question is whether the structures in the Charter are sufficient to meet these new tasks or to what extent new structures may be needed.

5. *The spread of human rights, democracy, and the rule of law*

The UN is taking an increasingly assertive stance towards the protection of human rights in member states—both in the increasing use of existing structures and in the incorporation of this element into the mandate of peacekeeping operations, e.g. in El Salvador and Cambodia. The controversial boundary between international prerogatives to protect human rights and claims of domestic sovereignty is steadily shifting into previously sovereign territory, and UN structures are slowly adapting to this expanding international role.

These are the present and unparalleled challenges for the world body. The structures of the UN may have been adequate for the more limited role that it played during the Cold War; its inadequacies have been exposed by the enormous new demands now placed on it. To catalogue some of the ills: the composition of the Security Council reflects the realities of power at the end of World War II rather than those of the 1990s; peacekeeping operations are a craft industry ill-adapted to massive new demands; the General Assembly is tedious and repetitive in its resolutions and has lost much of its effectiveness as a moral and political beacon for humankind; the UN intergovernmental structures in the economic field yield decisions without impact on economic reality; the Secretariat, despite improvements after the appointment of Dr Boutros-Ghali, has been poorly managed and structured for its new tasks and has been unable, in many areas, to provide the necessary independent intellectual leadership.

Up to now, the UN has mostly managed to meet the challenge, but with increasing difficulty. The new political and policy issues which need to be solved (such as the role of peacekeeping forces when cease-fire arrangements break down, and the selective use of force) are beyond the scope of this chapter. What follows is an examination of the major structures in order to measure them against the demands which will be placed upon them and to consider what improvements could be made.

(b) The Security Council

As the UN body responsible for international security issues and the only UN body whose decisions are binding on member states, the Security Council—with the end of the Cold War and new-found agreement among previously hostile major powers—is at last in a number of conflicts working as intended. It is wielding considerable power and is clearly the single most important organ of the UN. However, its revival has highlighted the gap between the Council and the member states not represented on it (as well as the gap between the Permanent and temporary Members of the Council) and has generated demands that the composition of the Council should no longer be dominated by the victors of World War II but should more accurately reflect the modern world. Any change however will not come easily or quickly as, under the Charter, it requires the assent of each of the five current Permanent Members (P5).

1. Reforming the composition of the Security Council

While the Council was relatively ineffective, there were few serious attempts to alter its composition, apart from the successful moves in 1963–5 to increase the non-permanent membership from six to its current ten. In 1979, India proposed that the Non-permanent Members be expanded from ten to fourteen, with the four extra to come as follows: two from the African Group (making a total of five), and one each from the Asian and Latin American Groups (bringing each up to three). All the P5 except China were opposed to any expansion, and the issue was never thoroughly debated by the General Assembly: within a few years it had lost all momentum, although the item remained on the Assembly's agenda.

Discussion of possible changes to the Council now focuses on the central questions of permanent membership and veto power. While there are few formal proposals, the

countries most generally mooted for permanent membership of the Council are: Japan, Germany, India, Indonesia,
Brazil, Mexico, Nigeria, and Egypt.

Japan is the one candidate which figures on nearly all
lists: its economic power is undisputed and it is the second
largest contributor to the UN's budget. While Japan's
claims are probably the most widely recognized, a simple
P5 plus 1 scenario is unlikely, as the wider UN membership would probably not countenance any expansion which
did not take account of the aspirations of other emerging
powers.

Germany's preoccupation with domestic issues arising
from its unification in 1990, and the long-standing caution
lest Germany appear overly assertive in the sensitive
sphere of international peace and security, meant that its
leaders, while expressing an interest in a permanent seat,
kept a low profile on the expansion issue. As Germany
increasingly asserts itself in Europe, it is likely to become
more vigorous in pursuing a reconsideration of its role in
the multilateral system.

An informal proposal by the then Italian Foreign
Minister, to replace France and the UK with Japan and
the European Community (P5 minus 2 plus 2), has the
virtue of keeping the Council the same size, but is for the
time being unrealizable: the EC faces formidable difficulties in the coordination of foreign policy, and France and
the UK fervently defend their P5 status as a symbol of
their role in world affairs. This proposal, too, does not
address the aspirations of the Third World. Thus, when
reform finally occurs, it may have to be wide-ranging. One
possibility, proposed by Brazil, is that of an additional
category of Permanent Members without veto powers.[1]

Perhaps the greatest practical risk in enlarging the
Security Council is that decision-making would be more
difficult. The behind-the-scenes negotiation of the texts of
resolutions would become even more complex and tedious.
P5 cooperation, while at times frustrating to the rest of the
membership, has brought great benefit in the resolution

[1] UN doc. A/44/PV.4 of 25 Sept. 1989, p. 17.

of regional conflict. There is considerable resistance to tampering with the Council just at the time it is showing it can work. It must remain able to respond quickly to threats to international security. Delays in decision-making would carry with them the risk not merely that responses would be too late, but also that the major powers would become less willing to devote the time and effort needed to work through the Council, and would be readier to act unilaterally or in like-minded coalitions.

The challenge is thus to ensure that any change to the Council's structure both accurately reflects current global power relationships and is implemented in such a way as to minimize any reduction in the speed and efficiency of the decision-making process. The forces against change ensure that this is a challenge which will not be taken up until well into the 1990s when the Council's membership is likely to be so at odds with geopolitical and geoeconomic realities that the legitimacy of the Council's decisions is undermined.

In the mean time, only very minor procedural reforms (e.g. regular procedures for informing the rest of the UN membership of the calling of Council meetings and of the progress of informal consultations) are likely to be accepted. Such reforms may close slightly the gap between the Council and the rest of the membership. The most important gap is, however, more political than procedural. While member states at the end of the Cold War have been prepared to accept the leadership of the P5 in general and of the USA in particular, there has been increasing concern at the lack of consultation with non-P5 states, especially the Third World membership. Even within the Council, consultation with non-P5 members has sometimes been characterized as *pro forma* or desultory. This has given rise to the ironic use of the term 'temporary ten' to highlight the difference in standing and influence of the two categories of members.

The Security Council depends for its effectiveness on the commitment of the member states (e.g. in the application of sanctions), so it is essential that it maintain genuine joint decision-making if its moral legitimacy is to be retained. *The Economist* warned in 1992: 'If the United

Nations is the world's voice, its Security Council must be seen to be more than a western clique.'[2] It is this problem to which the Secretary-General was referring when he argued in *An Agenda for Peace* that 'agreement among the permanent members must have the deeper support of the other members of the Council, and the membership more widely, if the Council's decisions are to be effective and endure'.[3] Thus the obligation lies with the P5, and particularly the USA, to maintain sensitive and effective consultation with the rest of the membership in reaching Council decisions.

2. Article 43 agreements and the Military Staff Committee

The Council has not made the originally-intended use of the power in Article 42 to undertake military action, but has several times authorized member states to undertake military intervention themselves. This has left the Council with a very limited role in the oversight of the conduct of such intervention, and has led to numerous suggestions that structures provided for in the Charter which would allow the Security Council actually to conduct military operations should be brought into existence. During the Cold War such suggestions were clearly of no practical significance since it was impossible to envisage that the conflicting super-powers would cooperate in such a way. However the Secretary-General has again called for the negotiation of the special agreements foreseen in Article 43 whereby member states undertake to make armed forces, assistance, and facilities available on a permanent basis to the Security Council for use in enforcement action under Article 42. The Secretary-General said that, while such forces would be inadequate to meet a threat from a major army, they would be useful in deterring military action by a force of a lesser order 'since a potential aggressor would know that the Council had at its disposal a means of response'.[4] The Military Staff Committee would thus have for the first time

---

[2] *The Economist* (London), 29 Aug. 1992, p. 10.
[3] Boutros Boutros-Ghali, *An Agenda for Peace*, June 1992, para. 78. (Below, Appendix A.)   [4] Ibid., para. 43.

a useful role in advising the Council on the use of such force.

The Secretary-General is undoubtedly correct in arguing that the use of this machinery would add to the effectiveness of the UN, but most observers would agree that member states are unlikely to accept the proposal. National governments, not least that of the USA, are extremely reluctant to make an advance commitment of their military personnel to participate, possibly with high casualties, in areas not of their own but of the UN's choosing, and not under their own command but under the command of an international bureaucracy. As the Secretary-General—and, indeed, the member states— opposes the use of the Military Staff Committee in purely peacekeeping operations (where the Council has always delegated authority directly to the Secretary-General), it is unlikely that UN structures relating to the conduct of military action will be established or revitalized in the near term, however desirable that may be in enabling an early response to the increasing number of calls for UN action. The global collective security system seems likely therefore to remain essentially *ad hoc*, dependent on the cumbersome political processes of the Security Council, and leaving the Secretary-General, like the Pope, with no divisions.

(c) The General Assembly

The General Assembly is the major deliberative body of the UN. It is a political forum which can discuss virtually any issue. Its resolutions are not binding on its member states, but can help to set new norms of international behaviour, can establish new treaties to which states can later adhere, or can imbue declarations with considerable moral force.

1. Structural and operational issues

The Assembly is also sometimes said to be a world parliament where the voices of the world's people may be heard. However, the General Assembly of course consists of representatives of governments and not of peoples; it is an inter-*governmental* body, the heir to the League of Nations and before that a long series of *ad hoc* inter-governmental conferences.

Some proposals for its restructuring are based on the view that to the extent that representatives are not democratically based, the authority of the Assembly's role is diminished and that 'We the peoples of the United Nations' (to use the words of the Charter) should be better heard. Other types of bodies have been advocated to which people could more directly send representatives, or in which perhaps parliamentarians might have a greater voice. While there may be a place for another international organ of that sort, none of these proposals circumvents the difficulty that, if countries are non-democratic, they are also unlikely to agree to genuine elections to international bodies. Nor is Charter change of this sort politically feasible.

Furthermore, such proposals misunderstand the nature of the General Assembly: there is a real need for an intergovernmental body such as the Assembly, since it is only governments which have the authority to make their commitments stick. Nor is there much difference (with perhaps the important exception of certain resolutions dealing with human rights) in the voting patterns in the Assembly of democratic and non-democratic states with similar national interests. Thus it would seem that the constitutional basis of the General Assembly is the right one, and that attention should be focused on achieving more on that basis. The best hope for increased democratic legitimacy is through the spread of genuine democratic institutions in member states.

At the same time there is a need, despite the unease of governments on this issue, to give a greater voice within the UN to non-governmental organizations: to build up connections with them and, when relevant, with others such as transnational corporations. This is being pursued to a degree in relation to the environment, but is a major issue that requires a more systematic approach.

The Assembly has had its ups and downs as a political

forum. Whichever group has been in the minority has denounced resolutions passed by the majority as politically irresponsible vehicles for propaganda and point-scoring. Whatever the truth of any particular claim, it is certainly correct that the Assembly has at times been a forum in which political differences have been exacerbated rather than reconciled.

This has not been the dominant mood in the post-Cold War period. There is now usually a genuine search for consensus, and the Assembly has some recent achievements to its credit. Thus, to take a few of many examples, the forty-fourth General Assembly (1989–90) adopted the following: the Convention on the Rights of the Child; the Second Optional Protocol to the Covenant on Civil and Political Rights (on the Abolition of the Death Penalty); a Declaration on Apartheid which for the first time provided a consensual basis for international agreement for the abolition of that system; and a resolution which effectively ensured the cessation of large-scale driftnet fishing by 1992. Each of these established new international norms; collectively these and other comparable initiatives represent substantial confirmation that the General Assembly's role in such standard-setting is acceptable to the international community.

It is true that the agenda of the General Assembly is overcrowded and allows insufficient time to debate many of the items. This creates a special problem for small states which lack sufficient delegates to follow the whole agenda. At the same time, however, states very jealously guard their rights to place whatever is of concern to them on the Assembly's agenda.

Recent proposals to improve the workings of the Assembly, even though extremely modest, have made no headway. The one main structural change proposed—amalgamation of the Fourth Committee (which deals with the shrinking agenda of decolonization issues) with the Special Political Committee—met heavy resistance. For the most part, the Special Political Committee's agenda is an unglamorous collection of left-overs, missing a central theme. Some governments—more especially their delegates in New York—are concerned that decolonization, one of the proudest achievements of the UN, not be relegated to that status.

What might genuinely improve the effectiveness of the Assembly is more long-term planning of its agenda so that each session could deal substantively with one or two major issues on which a properly prepared declaration or convention could be adopted. This would contribute to the progressive building-up of the Assembly's norm-setting role, reduce the need for special sessions, and give a greater focus to the annual deliberations. It would require a planning committee of the whole into which both member states and the Secretariat (and perhaps NGOs) might make an input on substantive proposals.

2. Arms control and disarmament

Two special bodies established by the Assembly and reporting to it deal with disarmament issues. The Disarmament Commission was established in 1978 as a deliberative body of the Assembly. It has universal membership and is enjoined to make its recommendations by consensus. The second institution, the thirty-nine-member Conference on Disarmament, was reconstituted from its predecessor structure in 1979 as a negotiating body. It too moves by consensus and at a very slow pace, and for most of its existence has had little concrete to show for the efforts of the delegates: principally because of the superpowers' preference during the 1980s for private bilateral negotiations. With the end of superpower rivalry, multilateral issues, such as the prevention of the spread of weapons of mass destruction, became central, and the CD had its major success in the negotiation of a text of a Chemical Weapons Convention which was adopted by the 1992 General Assembly. None the less procedures remain cumbersome and lacking in urgency. The Security Council Summit Declaration on 31 January 1992 also staked a claim to the disarmament area for the first time. Thus UN structures to develop treaties in these vital areas are increasingly seen to be inadequate, but little thought has been given to their replacement.

(d) The Secretariat

While the intergovernmental organs of the UN receive the greatest attention, it is in the Secretariat that the greatest returns from effort at structural change can be attained. This is for two reasons. First, Secretariat reform, while very difficult, can proceed without Charter change and, often, without the need for Assembly resolutions. Many changes lie within the prerogative of the Secretary-General, and can be made without months of tedious intergovernmental negotiation, especially where they do not have major budgetary implications. Secondly, it so happens that many of the key areas where change is needed and can make an immediate and significant impact on UN activities are in the province of the Secretariat. Thus the UN urgently needs: a better base of information, analysis, and policy development to underpin the deliberations of its intergovernmental bodies; a greatly increased capacity for preventive diplomacy and peace-making; and a far more effective support structure for peacekeeping operations. All these responsibilities depend heavily on the Secretariat, and are discussed below.

While the efficiency and effectiveness of the Secretariat require urgent improvement, and criticisms of it often contain much truth, they do not usually take sufficient account of the absolute need for the Secretariat, if it is to be both trusted and effective, to include nationals of all the various cultures and political tendencies of the UN member states. The consequent problems of welding different national and management cultures into an effective operation require far greater skills and sensitivity than are needed to run a national bureaucracy in a single state. Thus it is difficult to make simple comparisons between the Secretariat and national bureaucracies. In any event, the Secretariat should not be measured against some idealized standard that national bureaucracies do not themselves attain.

Furthermore, it is insufficiently remarked that the Secretariat has been as much a victim of the Cold War as have the other institutions of the UN. First, the Permanent

Members have been reluctant to support for the Secretary-General's job candidates whom they perceived as being too independent-minded and forceful. Sometimes, none the less, decisive individuals ready to make hard decisions, such as Hammarskjöld and Boutros-Ghali, have been appointed; but some other Secretaries-General have introduced or tolerated management and patronage practices which have had severe and damaging long-term effects. Secondly, the refusal on political grounds of member states to pay assessed contributions has meant that UN management has had to proceed for much of the time in a state of financial crisis.[5] Thirdly, the placement into high-level Secretariat positions, by some of the most powerful member states, of individuals who did not accept the principles of the international civil service but whose primary loyalty was to their own countries made it impossible for the Secretary-General to establish a senior management team in which he could confide and which could set priorities and provide leadership for the entire organization. For the same reason the Secretary-General often found it difficult to delegate real authority.

Furthermore, in an organization where in many areas little effective work could be done because of disagreement among the members, it was difficult to resist the claims of countries outside the P5 also to place their nationals in senior jobs, so senior positions multiplied till the organization-chart totally lacked logic or cohesion. At the end of 1991, over thirty officials had direct reporting responsibilities to the Secretary-General. Duplication, lack of cohesion, and wasteful competition within the Secretariat were inevitable. At the same time the example of patronage and poor management at the top had its effect on the lower levels. A proper system of promotion on the basis of merit, career development, mobility, and equal employment opportunity was never developed, and staff morale

[5] As at 30 June 1992 US arrears in payments due under the regular budget were $US 256.4 m., with $298.6 m. of the 1992 assessment also still unpaid. Comparable figures for Russia were $45.4 m. and $92.6 m. See 'Status of Contributions', UN doc. ST/ADM/SER.B/384 of 6 July 1992, pp. 7 and 8. On arrears, see also above, p. 13 and p. 429 n.

was poor. In these circumstances it is not surprising that much of the key work was done by a small group of talented individuals handpicked by the Secretary-General, and that the lack of communication between the 'thirty-eighth floor' (where the Secretary-General's office and cabinet are located) and the rest of the Secretariat was often the subject of outside criticism.

1. Reforms undertaken

The state of disorganization and inefficiency within the Secretariat had in the 1980s led to financial pressure from the USA, which, against bitter resistance, resulted in a 14 per cent cut-back in the number of staff.[6] However, by 1990 the mood amongst member states on all sides at the UN had changed: pressure developed not for more staff cuts but for genuine reform of the Secretariat so that it could effectively implement its tasks. The arrival of a new Secretary-General at the beginning of 1992 was seen as the ideal opportunity for reform to be introduced. Those member states seeking reform met as an informal group, which pressed for two central elements of change. The first was a rationalization of the Secretariat structure so as to group the major activities of the Secretariat on a functional basis into a small number of departments (preferably four), under Deputies to whom the Secretary-General could delegate real authority. This was seen as critical in improving the Secretary-General's control of the organization, allowing him to focus on priority tasks, streamlining and focusing decision-making, reducing duplication, enhancing the activities in the same sector, and facilitating a focus on results to be achieved.

The second element was the introduction of a more equitable and transparent method of selection of senior officers, so as to appoint the most outstanding applicants from all regions. In the past, certain countries, particularly the P5, had held a virtual monopoly on particular jobs, nominating a successor as the incumbent retired. Vacancies had rarely been publicly notified, and often the availability

---

[6] See the chapter by Maurice Bertrand, above, pp. 426–7.

of a job was not announced until a decision had been made on who was to fill it. The reform group wanted a system under which vacancies were to be made widely known so that qualified individuals could apply. They asked that the Secretary-General have the freedom to choose the best possible candidates from as wide a geographical base as possible, and that the practice whereby a person was chosen solely on the grounds that he or she was a nominee of a particular government should be abolished. These principles—and others such as improving the representation and status of women in the higher echelons of the Secretariat—were incorporated in a General Assembly resolution adopted in 1992.[7] It was also clear that these changes at the top needed to be underpinned by the introduction throughout the Secretariat of modern management and budgetary approaches and modern personnel methods.

The new Secretary-General, as early as his first two months in office, made a purposeful start on implementing reform. He rationalized the activities of the New York Secretariat into six departments (political affairs, peace-keeping operations, economic and social development, humanitarian affairs, administration and management, and legal affairs) and significantly reduced the number of senior staff. Unfortunately from the point of view of the reformers, at the top level of the ten Under-Secretaries-General (a number seen as too high) he appointed no women but maintained the practice of giving five jobs to nationals of each of the P5, thus increasing their stranglehold at the most senior level, and undermining the drive for transparency in the selection process for senior appointments. Nevertheless the Secretary-General had taken a bolder step in the consolidation and streamlining of Secretariat activities than had ever been taken before. Furthermore he promised that this was the first phase of reform. His senior appointments initially were for one year only, and further reforms in the Secretariat structure were planned at the end of his first year.

[7] GA Res. 46/467 of 20 Dec. 1991.

2. Areas of needed reform

With a much better framework in place it ought to be possible for the Secretary-General to initiate further structural reform in the Secretariat. Much has been foreshadowed in his various reports. We have noted above three key areas where further reform is needed, namely the provision of intellectual leadership, the expansion of preventive diplomacy, and the proper conduct of peacekeeping operations. Each is briefly discussed below.

(i) *Intellectual leadership.* In relation to the first, Urquhart and Childers say: 'Intellectual leadership and the generation and following-up of new ideas are an urgent necessity . . . Developing an active consensus about the world agenda and the UN system's part in it should become a central task for the Secretary-General and his or her colleagues in the UN system.'[8]

However, the intellectual leadership role of the Secretariat has never been allowed fully to develop. In many international organizations, intergovernmental discussions proceed on the basis of well-prepared staff papers outlining the facts, analysing the issues, and presenting the options. Member states have never permitted the Secretariat fully to play this role, nor to have this degree of independence or influence. During the Cold War both superpowers were very suspicious of any independent analysis by the Secretariat; and their example led other delegations also to lobby, often successfully, to suppress any draft document which they saw as not being in their interest. Secretaries-General, cautious both by nature and in their desire not to offend major states, reinforced this tendency: thus a general mood of caution—even timidity—pervaded the Secretariat in relation to policy issues. True, excellent work was done in preparing broad background analysis, particularly in the social and economic areas; and in some parts of the system—such as UNCTAD—the Secretariat was prepared to play a more activist role. But at New York

[8] Brian Urquhart and Erskine Childers, *A World in Need of Leadership: Tomorrow's United Nations*, issue of *Development Dialogue* (Uppsala), 1–2 (1990), p. 13.

Headquarters the documents prepared for meetings have tended to be bland, turgid, and voluminous.

This cautious approach to policy has meant that the Security Council has often met to discuss major world problems without any documentation at all. Representatives of countries with large foreign ministries have had their own briefs (from their own country's perspective of the facts) but the representatives of small countries sometimes had little more to go on than what they would pick up in the corridors and from the press. Only the larger members could put the work into devising solutions (again from their own national standpoints). Sometimes the Secretary-General has been called upon for a report, and some of these have been helpful—but often they have gone little beyond a bland recitation of the issues.

Similarly the negotiations in the General Assembly and its committees are usually based on the national positions that each country brings to the issue. Resolutions often represent the lowest common denominator. Member states will of course always be guided by their national interests, but more imaginative solutions, possibly equally acceptable to all, which might have emerged from high-quality Secretariat analyses are, under the present system, left unconsidered and unrealized because they did not happen to emerge from the negotiating process.

One should not exaggerate the passivity of the Secretariat: it does, for example, often have a major influence when at a time of deadlock the chair is asked to prepare a draft, and sometimes intrudes its own proposals into debate via sympathetic delegations. Nor can one expect it to produce the sort of analyses on really sensitive political issues which would lead to debilitating attacks on the Secretariat itself by the membership. But short of this there is a far larger role for it to play in preparing documentation that could help member states to negotiate creative solutions to the problems before them. This appears to have been recognized by the Secretary-General when, in introducing his note on the restructuring of the Secretariat, he referred to the need for Secretariat assistance to place a premium not only on 'integrity', 'impartiality', and 'efficiency', but also on 'creativity'.[9]

(ii) *Preventive diplomacy and peace-making*. The second key area of structural change required in the Secretariat is an expansion of its capacity for 'preventive diplomacy' (defined as 'action to prevent disputes from arising between parties, to prevent existing disputes from escalating into conflicts and to limit the spread of the latter when they occur'); and 'peace-making' (defined as 'action to bring hostile parties to agreement, essentially through . . . peaceful means').[10] During the Cold War the UN was seldom called upon to undertake preventive diplomacy as the organization was seen as ineffective: thus the structures supporting this activity remain rudimentary and *ad hoc*. In *An Agenda for Peace* Secretary-General Boutros-Ghali outlined a number of inventive and far-reaching approaches to these activities, but to be successful they require structural support within the Secretariat itself. The Secretariat must now have the capacity to gather, receive, and analyse information, to prepare recommendations on possible action, and to support action which the Secretary-General or the Security Council may mandate.

All this is the normal role of a foreign ministry, but there is no need for the Secretariat to establish a structure parallel to those of foreign ministries. What is required is a more systematic approach to information-gathering, not only of the facts but of the grievances, concerns, and interests of the parties to a dispute. 'Fact-finding' missions should be routine rather than initiated by a crisis, so that a mission is not seen to internationalize a dispute, and UN representatives can gain the early confidence of the parties. The most important gap to be filled is in the *analysis* of information and its provision to the Secretary-General (or through him to the Security Council) in such a form that the need for action can be weighed and the forms of such action considered. These activities will require a small

---

[9] Boutros Boutros-Ghali, 'Review of the Efficiency of the Administrative and Financial Functioning of the United Nations: Restructuring of the Secretariat of the Organization—Note by the Secretary-General', UN doc. A/46/882 of 21 Feb. 1992, p. 1.   [10] Boutros-Ghali, *Agenda for Peace*, para. 20.

nucleus of foreign affairs specialists and policy analysts, possibly organized on a geographical basis, within the Department of Political Affairs. Action to mediate in disputes may still be undertaken by the Secretary-General, or at his behest by an Under-Secretary-General or a Special Representative, but it should be underpinned by a core of officers with knowledge of the particular area, the confidence of the parties, and experience in conflict resolution. An evaluation mechanism should be developed within the Secretariat systematically to collect, analyse, and retain experience gained from such activities and which would prove useful in other similar situations. In other words, preventive diplomacy should be conducted not as an *ad hoc* response by persons drawn from other routine tasks, as has happened so often in the past, but on the basis of a professional support system.

3. Structural support for peacekeeping

As the Secretary-General notes, the number of peace-keeping operations has expanded sharply (thirteen set up in 1945–87, and thirteen more 1987–mid-1992), and these operations have become increasingly diverse, extending to supervision of elections and even to national administration. Furthermore the Secretary-General contemplates still further elements that such operations could embrace, under the rubric of 'peace-building'.[11] Clearly the present Secretariat structure cannot support this expansion of activity.

A study in 1992 succinctly identified the present structural problems relating to the organization of peacekeeping:

Peacekeeping is still administered and funded as though it were a rare emergency activity rather than a normal one that sometimes deals with emergencies. The UN's overworked apparatus for planning and implementing peacekeeping operations is small, scattered and cannot long continue to meet the rising global demand.[12]

[11] Ibid., paras. 55–9.
[12] W. J. Durch and B. M. Blechman, *Keeping the Peace: The United Nations in the Emerging World Order* (Henry L. Stimson Centre, Washington DC, 1992), p. iii.

The most pressing problems are a lack of forward planning capacity, financial and administrative obstacles to the launch of an operation, fragmentation of authority in its conduct, and failure of member states to pay their assessed dues.

The problems of planning and control of operations could be ameliorated if all the elements of the Secretariat currently involved in peacekeeping (including parts of the Field Operations Division currently in the Department of Administration and Management) were brought together in an enlarged professional unit under one Under-Secretary-General. The post of Military Adviser could be changed to Assistant Secretary-General for Planning and Operations. Particularly in the early stages of new operations and at other periods of peak demand, there needs to be an increase in staff—though this could be provided in part by secondment, to a Secretariat core, of personnel from member states.

Solutions to the problems of getting a new operation off the ground—and thus avoiding the risk that an agreement might break down before the blue helmets arrive—have been widely canvassed and many were enumerated again in *An Agenda for Peace*: a revolving peacekeeping reserve fund or an expansion of the Working Capital Fund so that there is no need to wait for members' contributions on each occasion; agreement that one-third of the estimated costs of each new peacekeeping operation be appropriated by the Assembly as soon as the Council decides to establish it; an increase in the Secretary-General's commitment authority so that purchasing can begin immediately; a pre-positioned stock of basic peacekeeping equipment; stand-by arrangements with member states for the provision of trained personnel.[13] More radical proposals include annual regular assessments for peacekeeping (as opposed to assessments for each peacekeeping operation) to be paid into a Peacekeeping Fund in order that peacekeeping be accepted as a normal and routine part of UN activities rather than an exceptional one. Until now member states

---

[13] *Agenda for Peace*, paras. 51–3 and 70–3.

have resisted even the most modest of these proposals, largely on financial grounds. However, funding processes were accelerated for the first time during the establishment of UNTAC in Cambodia in 1991–2, and the increased number and prominence of peacekeeping operations is causing a reassessment of opinion among some member states. Even with all these improvements it is unlikely that the Secretariat could mount operations in all the different situations where there are demands for a UN presence. Administrative capacity will be a constraint on the number of operations that can be conducted at any one time— which will place increased responsibility on policy-makers to develop criteria for UN intervention (and withdrawal) from conflict situations.

4. UN finances

A discussion of the Secretariat must include reference to the general financial problems of the UN. These date back to the 1970s and have been caused by the late payment by member states—in particular the USA—of assessed contributions, and by mounting arrears. The rapidly expanding mandate of the organization has compounded the problem. Early in his term, Secretary-General Boutros-Ghali endorsed various proposals made by his predecessor to meet the crises as well as adding his own. The fact is however that the financial problems are not really soluble through structural reform (the concern of this chapter): indeed to the extent that devices such as special funds or borrowings tide the UN through particular periods of difficulty, they only encourage recalcitrant states to delay their dues still further. In the end there are only two realistic alternatives: either the payment of dues, or a drastic reduction in the aspirations of member states for UN action. This is in no way to understate the gravity of the problem—it may well become the most important obstacle to the UN playing an expanded role, especially in peacekeeping and peace-making. As the Secretary-General notes: 'A chasm has developed between the tasks entrusted to this Organization and the financial means provided to it.'[14]

---

[14] Ibid., para. 69. See also the Ford Foundation report, above p. 13 n.

(e) Economic and Social Structures

The UN has long recognized the fundamental importance of promoting economic development, eliminating poverty and social distress, and enhancing respect for human rights. These are the issues of greatest concern to most of the peoples of the world, and to most of the member countries of the UN. They are important ends in their own right, and their attainment would remove some of the root causes of international conflict. Thus in many respects the political, economic, and social missions of the UN are inseparable: yet while the political structures of the UN have undergone a well-publicized revival, the economic and social structures have lagged behind.

1. *Reasons for ineffectiveness*

The strengths of the UN's economic and social activities have always been more apparent at the field level than at the policy-making centre in New York. Even UN agencies which have not been acclaimed for their administrative efficiency, such as the Food and Agriculture Organization, have generally enjoyed a good reputation for delivery of appropriate technical assistance programmes.

However, the central economic policy-making organs have been largely ineffective. Resolutions on economic issues adopted by these organs have gone largely unread and ignored. They have been hammered out in debate by serious and dedicated middle-ranking officials of foreign ministries in ECOSOC and the Second Committee of the General Assembly—officials with absolutely no influence over the economic policies of their countries. In so far as the texts have been scrutinized in capitals it is to ensure that they included nothing new that might be contrary to existing policy. They have not been read by the economic ministers of either developing or industrialized countries, who had more practical matters with which to concern themselves.

This irrelevance is partly the fault of the UN's founders, who, while recognizing the economic and social causes of much international conflict, did not clearly think out the role of the various UN bodies in international economic issues. The Charter is muddled in the way it sets out their various responsibilities. The failure is also partly the fault of the member states. The industrialized countries have preferred to discuss the key international economic issues in other forums: in particular the Bretton Woods institutions, where voting entitlements reflect economic strength. The developing countries were for a long time more concerned with the declaratory impact of resolutions passed by large majorities than with trying to find issues on which the General Assembly or UNCTAD could have a practical effect. The tedious and repetitive debates in multiple forums, and the wordy and unread resolutions that all this created, were in no one's interest. But the majority of developing countries not unreasonably showed little interest in (and indeed often obstructed) the reform of structures or procedures for as long as the major industrialized countries were totally unwilling to engage in serious consideration of issues of substance.

2. Proposals for reform

Various proposals were made at different times for the revival of these organs, the most ambitious being for a new organ paralleling the Security Council—an Economic Council including the G7 countries, the major developing countries, and others on a rotational basis.[15] But such structural reform was unlikely so long as the major countries did not want to use the UN as an economic forum. However, there are some signs in the 1990s that the economic and social structures have begun to emerge from their worst years. This progress has been based on two developments: one intellectual and one more practical.

The intellectual development was a recognition that resolutions passed even by large majorities in the economic forums were having no effect in the real world, and that a different use had to be made of these structures. It was a recognition that in the economic field,

---

[15] See the chapter by Maurice Bertrand in this volume; and UNA-USA, *A Successor Vision: The United Nations of Tomorrow* (New York, 1987).

lacking genuine control over both events and actors, the United Nations should seek to achieve intellectual influence. The United Nations should exert leadership through ideas, vision and initiative. This cannot be accomplished by resolutions that are not read by policy makers in national Governments. It can be achieved by discussion, dialogue and exchange that involves these policy makers as well as others.[16]

This approach has led to agreement on considerable change in the workings of ECOSOC and UNCTAD. In ECOSOC, principal among the changes negotiated in 1991 was a reduction in meetings, a more focused agenda, and the creation of the so-called High-Level segment. In the first of these High-Level discussions, held in 1992, the participation of ministers ensured a far greater degree of governmental attention to the economic issues being debated.

At the same time UNCTAD, in which North–South conflict had become institutionalized, decided at Cartagena in February 1992 to reform itself.[17] The existing consultative bodies and negotiating groups were suspended and replaced by a number of new groups working on key issues in the international economic and development agenda. The aim was to promote policy dialogue between the developed and developing countries without the development of 'bloc' views and to produce policy approaches which will influence both the international financial institutions and national policy-makers.

3. Environment and sustainable development

While these changes represent a significant attitudinal shift and carry some prospect of greater future relevance of UN structures in the economic area, it cannot be claimed that they have as yet much enhanced the effectiveness of these structures. A more significant impact comes from the introduction into these structures of the practical issue of the environment and sustainable development.

---

[16] John P. Renninger, 'Improving the United Nations System', *Journal of Development Planning* (UNITAR, New York), 17 (1987), p. 101.

[17] See the chapter by Kenneth Dadzie, above, esp. p. 318.

This holds the prospect of real discussion and negotiation: for the first time, in the economic area, the developing countries have some substantial bargaining chips. The industrialized countries are urging the developing countries to follow a growth path which will cause less damage to the global environment (and the environment in the industrialized countries) than the present one—i.e. a growth path different from that which was pursued by the industrialized countries themselves and which is continuing to cause such environmental damage. In order to do this the developing countries need economic assistance—and thus the prerequisites are there for effective bargaining on sustainable development options, energy usage, transfer of technology on concessional terms, and so forth.

The principal vehicle for this discussion will be the Commission on Sustainable Development, the establishment of which was one of the outcomes of the 1992 UN Conference on Environment and Development (UNCED). The Commission is a subsidiary of ECOSOC. Its role is to ensure the effective follow-up of the conference, in particular to 'examine the progress of implementation of Agenda 21 at the national, regional and international levels'.[18] Agenda 21 is the action plan established by UNCED; it touches on almost all the economic and social issues dealt with by the UN system. While its overall objective is the integration of environment and development, its action programmes also pursue environment and development goals independently from each other. The Commission is thus expected to be a major focus within the UN for discussion of economic and social issues.

One of the other roles the economic and social organs of the UN are expected to perform is the supervision of the operational activities of bodies such as the Development Programme (UNDP) and the UN Children's Fund (UNICEF), and the coordination of the specialized agencies. These supervisory functions are also poorly performed, and proposals for reform abound. One—known as the

---

[18] UN doc. A/CONF.151/26 (vol. iii), 14 Aug. 1992, p. 90; and GA Res. 47/191 of 22 Dec. 1992, on post-UNCED institutional arrangements.

Nordic Project—suggests the creation of a UN International Development Council in which overall policy guides can be evolved.[19] Secretary-General Boutros-Ghali has also presented a number of alternatives including the creation of a development cooperation board. Improved coordination is also being pursued by better use of the Administrative Committee on Coordination.

While the issue is likely to continue to be debated, improved coordination of the agencies is an elusive and ill-defined goal. It is not at all clear what coordination means in practice, other than in specific programme areas. Nor is it at all clear how agencies with their separate budgets, separate constitutions, and separate governing boards can really be coordinated. Finally it is highly unlikely that governments, whose different representatives on the different governing bodies cannot agree, will be able to agree at the centre on directives to the agencies.

Where coordination is important is at the field level, and fortunately this is where effort is now being directed. Governments should not have to deal with different UN agencies each pursuing its own goal in order to carry out a particular project. The Secretary-General has announced his support for a 'unified UN presence at the country level'.[20] Better coordination is more likely to come through better project delivery than through the creation of new policy organs.

Indeed there are some new structures being developed to ensure the actual delivery of technical and humanitarian assistance. One example is the establishment after the 1991 General Assembly of the Department of Humanitarian Affairs to coordinate and accelerate the work of the various UN central and specialized agencies which respond to a humanitarian crisis. Another is the combination, following the 1990 General Assembly, of the three pre-existing UN drug bodies into the UN Drug Control Programme.

[19] Nordic UN Project, *The United Nations in Development: Reform Issues in the Economic and Social Fields: A Nordic Perspective: Final Report* (Stockholm, 1991).

[20] Boutros-Ghali, 'Enhancing International Cooperation for Development: The Role of the United Nations System—Report of the Secretary-General', UN doc. E/1992/82/Add. 1 of 26 June 1992, p. 8.

Thus in sum the UN is gradually rationalizing and modernizing the delivery systems for its economic and social programmes to meet the crises and continued problems of the post-Cold War period. This goes on gradually, largely independent of the policy debate in ECOSOC and other policy organs. These continue to make little impact on real world policy-making, but new structures, new processes, and the link between environment and development may gradually bring them back into a position of greater policy significance in the economic debates of the 1990s.

4. Human rights

Progress in the field of human rights is one of the UN's stories of relative success, and an instance of the manner in which the UN achieves its goals not by the overnight creation or abolition of structures but by incremental change and the slow adaptation and growth of existing bodies. There has been, since World War II, an increasing acceptance by governments that they are accountable internationally for their human rights records, and the General Assembly has adopted a number of major international treaties protecting particular rights. The principal body concerned in UN activities is the Commission on Human Rights (CHR) (a subsidiary of ECOSOC, established in 1946) plus its subsidiary, the Sub-Commission on Prevention of Discrimination and Protection of Minorities. Each of the main human rights treaties also has its own expert committee. In the 1960s the CHR adopted the mechanism of country rapporteurs to report on particular situations of human rights abuse, and has extended this since 1980 to the appointment of working groups and of individuals as thematic rapporteurs (e.g. on torture, summary or arbitrary execution, religious intolerance).[21]

At the end of the Cold War, with changes in the attitude of the former Eastern bloc, UN human rights activity has expanded rapidly in line with the change in perceptions

[21] See the chapter by Tom Farer and Felice Gaer, above, and in particular the diagram on pp. 258–9.

about the appropriate balance between domestic sovereignty and international prerogatives to protect rights. The UN role in calling attention to rights violations is widely accepted, and the debate has moved on to whether the international community has a right to intervene to provide humanitarian assistance—even perhaps without the explicit consent of the country involved. In the words of Javier Pérez de Cuéllar in 1991: 'We are clearly witnessing what is an irresistible shift in public attitudes towards the belief that defence of the oppressed in the name of morality should prevail over frontiers and legal documents.'[22]

While this represents a considerable shift in philosophy it seems that it can be accommodated largely within existing structures. Existing mechanisms such as peace-keeping operations are being adapted to include new purposes. Thus the mandate for the UN force which helped bring about the end of war in El Salvador (ONUSAL) specifically included human rights issues, as did the mandate for UNTAC in Cambodia.[23] The CHR itself has developed a procedure whereby it can be convened rapidly in times of human rights emergency. A focal point has been established within the Secretariat in New York at a senior level to coordinate the UN's response to requests for electoral assistance. Thus change is incremental and evolutionary—both in terms of practice and in terms of the structural support for such practice. It seems that in this area the UN can best adapt to the next decade without radical structural change.

(f) Prospects for Reform

This chapter has pointed to the slow evolution, and the further changes needed, in the UN's structures for it to

---

[22] 'Secretary-General's Address at University of Bordeaux', UN Press Release SG/SM/4560, 24 Apr. 1991.

[23] For ONUSAL, see the July 1990 San José Agreement (UN doc. A/44/971-S/21541 of 16 Aug. 1990), and SC Res. 693 of 20 May 1991. For UNTAC, see annexe 1, section E of the October 1991 Paris Agreement on a Comprehensive Political Settlement of the Cambodia Conflict, UN doc. A/46/608-S/23177 of 30 Oct. 1991, p. 27; and see also SC Res. 718 of 31 Oct. 1991; SC Res. 745 of 28 Feb. 1992.

achieve its potential. Reform at the UN is extraordinarily difficult. Any organization of course has great difficulty in reforming itself from within. Those working within it do not see, or are all too ready to make allowances for, its inefficiencies, and they fear that change will affect their bases of power. They always see the dangers of change more clearly than the defects of the status quo: they resist change for what they see as the best of reasons. This is no different in the UN whether one looks at the officials in the Secretariat or at the governmental delegates who make a career serving in its commissions or committees.

Effective reform of *national* government organizations occurs only if there is a special combination of factors: a sense of crisis, an external reformer or reform team, and above all the strong political backing of a powerful figure, usually a minister or the prime minister or president. Political will is the key ingredient for any radical reform.

These conditions for the attainment of change occur rarely enough in national government, but the model cannot be applied at all to intergovernmental organizations. No single individual or country has the power to impose reforms. (The threat of US non-payment of dues in the 1980s resulted in cut-backs in staff and expenditure but in little genuine reform.) Reform in intergovernmental bodies thus requires a coalition of political interests to gain the necessary majorities. But countries have varying interests—some may be opposed to the very idea of an effective intergovernmental institution in a field in which they are powerful—and thus, such coalitions are likely to arise only on a very narrow range of subjects and for limited times. Many governments have little invested in desired outcomes and are thus quite happy to adhere indefinitely to parochial positions, even at the expense of organizational effectiveness.

Furthermore, national governments are not likely to give high-level political attention to an international organization for very long. On most issues, they are usually guided by their experts, who in turn are likely to have a vested interest in limited movement from the status quo.

At the UN, there is a further factor. Any reform which

requires amendment of the Charter not only needs a two-thirds majority of the member states but must be ratified by each of the P5. Even where no Charter amendment is required, a number of the institutions and negotiating groups tend to work on the basis of consensus. This is often a formula for agreement only on the lowest possible common denominator of change, and extends a near veto on change to the most obstructive member states.

For these reasons, radical reform of the UN is unlikely even if the majority of member states could agree what sort of radical reform was desirable. Numerous committees and commissions (official and unofficial) over the past twenty years have seen the more broad-ranging of their recommendations come to nothing.[24] Incremental or step-by-step reform is far more likely as the path ahead.

However, the prospects for change are better than ever before. The five Permanent Members of the Security Council are for the first time in agreement on a range of issues, and the tone of the North-South confrontation has also become more muted. Many of the structures of the UN have shown themselves to be reasonably flexible and adaptable for new purposes, and there is a greatly heightened awareness that in the face of enormous challenges still greater flexibility is needed. The Secretariat requires major reform, but the Secretary-General appears ready to build on the considerable start he has made. Financing remains a major problem, but there is greater pressure on governments to support the UN, and the Clinton administration may be readier to meet US obligations. Thus the path is open in the 1990s for much larger steps than at any time in the UN's history: a series of incremental changes through the 1990s may well see, by the year 2000, an organization much better structured for its greatly expanded role.

[24] In particular see: UN, 'Report of the *Ad hoc* Committee on the Restructuring of the Economic and Social Sectors of the United Nations System', UN doc. A/32/34 (13 Jan. 1978); UN, 'Report of the Group of High-Level Intergovernmental Experts to Review the Efficiency of the Administrative and Financial Functioning of the UN', UN doc. A/41/49 (15 Aug. 1986); UN, 'Report of the Special Commission of the Economic and Social Council on the In-Depth Study of the United Nations Intergovernmental Structure and Functions in the Economic and Social Fields', UN doc. E/CSN.1/L (1 June 1988).

Appendix A

An Agenda for Peace

Introductory Note by Boutros Boutros-Ghali

The origins of *An Agenda for Peace* lie in the first-ever meeting of the Security Council at the level of heads of state and government, held as I began my term of office, in January 1992.

The Report, which I published in June 1992, makes a number of proposals and suggestions, addressed to member states, for enhancing the capacity of the organization to respond to the challenges of the post-Cold War world. They encompass peace-making, peacekeeping, and preventive diplomacy. In addition, they address the new and related concept of post-conflict peace-building—the identification and reinforcement of structures which support and solidify peace.

The response of member states to *An Agenda for Peace* has been overwhelmingly positive. There are understandable differences of emphasis, but there is no opposition in principle to the proposition that the United Nations should acquire an enhanced capacity for preventive diplomacy, peace-making and peacekeeping. In the General Assembly debate in the autumn of 1992 member states were virtually unanimous in accepting that the United Nations would be the key instrument of the international community in establishing and maintaining a new framework for international relations.

A variety of suggestions and proposals has already been put forward by member states. These include proposals for active preventive diplomacy and the establishment of a global monitoring network, including the development of planning, crisis-management, and intelligence-analysis

This Introductory Note was added by Boutros Boutros-Ghali for this volume.

capacities within the Secretariat. There is a widespread consensus that regional organizations must take on an enhanced role in preventive diplomacy and crisis prevention, working closely with the United Nations.

The Security Council is conducting its own review of the Report, and has been considering how the Secretariat should be strengthened to cope with the much greater responsibilities the United Nations is being asked to undertake in the field of peacekeeping; one proposal involves the reinforcement of the Secretariat in the military field, possibly through a permanent United Nations military staff. The Security Council has also invited member states to state what armed forces they are prepared to put at the disposal of the United Nations.

The concept of post-conflict peace-building—reaching beyond the immediate issues of conflict resolution and peacekeeping to the construction of institutions that can establish the essential conditions for lasting peace—is new to the United Nations. Some of my proposals—for example for cooperative projects in previously disputed territories—are addressed to the United Nations system as well as to member states. There is an increasing recognition of the importance of political participation, through free and fair elections, in sustaining the institutions which emerge from the peace-making process. The building and enhancement of the capacity of democratic institutions is increasingly being seen as one of the operational functions of the United Nations in the development field.

The task which we have embarked upon involves no less than the refashioning of the instruments bequeathed to us by the Charter of the United Nations, to help construct a new system of international relations. The task of reconstruction of a system whose efficient functioning was stymied in the past by the bipolar competition will be long, arduous, and complex. But I am optimistic that, with patience, commitment, and determination, we will succeed. The years leading to 1995, the fiftieth anniversary, will determine the future of the organization.

An Agenda for Peace

Preventive Diplomacy, Peacemaking and Peace-keeping

*Report of the Secretary-General pursuant to the statement
adopted by the Summit Meeting of the Security Council on
31 January 1992*

INTRODUCTION

1.   In its statement of 31 January 1992, adopted at the conclusion of the first meeting held by the Security Council at the level of Heads of State and Government, I was invited to prepare, for circulation to the Members of the United Nations by 1 July 1992, an 'analysis and recommendations on ways of strengthening and making more efficient within the framework and provisions of the Charter the capacity of the United Nations for preventive diplomacy, for peacemaking and for peace-keeping.'[1]

2.   The United Nations is a gathering of sovereign States and what it can do depends on the common ground that they create between them. The adversarial decades of the cold war made the original promise of the Organization impossible to fulfil. The January 1992 Summit therefore represented an unprecedented recommitment, at the highest political level, to the Purposes and Principles of the Charter.

3.   In these past months a conviction has grown, among nations large and small, that an opportunity has been regained to achieve the great objectives of the Charter—a United Nations capable of maintaining international peace and security, of securing justice and human rights and of promoting, in the words of the Charter, 'social progress and better standards of life in larger freedom'. This opportunity must not be squandered. The Organization must never again be crippled as it was in the era that has now passed.

4.   I welcome the invitation of the Security Council, early in my tenure as Secretary-General, to prepare this report. It draws upon ideas and proposals transmitted to me by Governments, regional agencies, non-governmental organizations, and institutions and individuals from many countries. I am grateful for these, even as I emphasize that the responsibility for this report is my own.

---

[1] See S/23500, statement by the President of the Council, section entitled 'Peacemaking and peace-keeping'.

5. The sources of conflict and war are pervasive and deep. To reach them will require our utmost effort to enhance respect for human rights and fundamental freedoms, to promote sustainable economic and social development for wider prosperity, to alleviate distress and to curtail the existence and use of massively destructive weapons. The United Nations Conference on Environment and Development, the largest summit ever held, has just met at Rio de Janeiro. Next year will see the second World Conference on Human Rights. In 1994 Population and Development will be addressed. In 1995 the World Conference on Women will take place, and a World Summit for Social Development has been proposed. Throughout my term as Secretary-General I shall be addressing all these great issues. I bear them all in mind as, in the present report, I turn to the problems that the Council has specifically requested I consider: preventive diplomacy, peacemaking and peace-keeping—to which I have added a closely related concept, post-conflict peace-building.

6. The manifest desire of the membership to work together is a new source of strength in our common endeavour. Success is far from certain, however. While my report deals with ways to improve the Organization's capacity to pursue and preserve peace, it is crucial for all Member States to bear in mind that the search for improved mechanisms and techniques will be of little significance unless this new spirit of commonality is propelled by the will to take the hard decisions demanded by this time of opportunity.

7. It is therefore with a sense of moment, and with gratitude, that I present this report to the Members of the United Nations.

I. THE CHANGING CONTEXT

8. In the course of the past few years the immense ideological barrier that for decades gave rise to distrust and hostility—and the terrible tools of destruction that were their inseparable companions—has collapsed. Even as the issues between States north and south grow more acute, and call for attention at the highest levels of government, the improvement in relations between States east and west affords new possibilities, some already realized, to meet successfully threats to common security.

9. Authoritarian regimes have given way to more democratic forces and responsive Governments. The form, scope and intensity of these processes differ from Latin America to Africa to Europe to Asia, but they are sufficiently similar to indicate a

global phenomenon. Parallel to these political changes, many States are seeking more open forms of economic policy, creating a world-wide sense of dynamism and movement.

10. To the hundreds of millions who gained their independence in the surge of decolonization following the creation of the United Nations, have been added millions more who have recently gained freedom. Once again new States are taking their seats in the General Assembly. Their arrival reconfirms the importance and indispensability of the sovereign State as the fundamental entity of the international community.

11. We have entered a time of global transition marked by uniquely contradictory trends. Regional and continental associations of States are evolving ways to deepen cooperation and ease some of the contentious characteristics of sovereign and nationalistic rivalries. National boundaries are blurred by advanced communications and global commerce, and by the decisions of States to yield some sovereign prerogatives to larger, common political associations. At the same time, however, fierce new assertions of nationalism and sovereignty spring up, and the cohesion of States is threatened by brutal ethnic, religious, social, cultural or linguistic strife. Social peace is challenged on the one hand by new assertions of discrimination and exclusion and, on the other, by acts of terrorism seeking to undermine evolution and change through democratic means.

12. The concept of peace is easy to grasp; that of international security is more complex, for a pattern of contradictions has arisen here as well. As major nuclear Powers have begun to negotiate arms reduction agreements, the proliferation of weapons of mass destruction threatens to increase and conventional arms continue to be amassed in many parts of the world. As racism becomes recognized for the destructive force it is and as apartheid is being dismantled, new racial tensions are rising and finding expression in violence. Technological advances are altering the nature and the expectation of life all over the globe. The revolution in communications has united the world in awareness, in aspiration and in greater solidarity against injustice. But progress also brings new risks for stability: ecological damage, disruption of family and community life, greater intrusion into the lives and rights of individuals.

13. This new dimension of insecurity must not be allowed to obscure the continuing and devastating problems of unchecked population growth, crushing debt burdens, barriers to trade,

drugs and the growing disparity between rich and poor. Poverty, disease, famine, oppression and despair abound, joining to produce 17 million refugees, 20 million displaced persons and massive migrations of peoples within and beyond national borders. These are both sources and consequences of conflict that require the ceaseless attention and the highest priority in the efforts of the United Nations. A porous ozone shield could pose a greater threat to an exposed population than a hostile army. Drought and disease can decimate no less mercilessly than the weapons of war. So at this moment of renewed opportunity, the efforts of the Organization to build peace, stability and security must encompass matters beyond military threats in order to break the fetters of strife and warfare that have characterized the past. But armed conflicts today, as they have throughout history, continue to bring fear and horror to humanity, requiring our urgent involvement to try to prevent, contain and bring them to an end.

14. Since the creation of the United Nations in 1945, over 100 major conflicts around the world have left some 20 million dead. The United Nations was rendered powerless to deal with many of these crises because of the vetoes—279 of them—cast in the Security Council, which were a vivid expression of the divisions of that period.

15. With the end of the cold war there have been no such vetoes since 31 May 1990, and demands on the United Nations have surged. Its security arm, once disabled by circumstances it was not created or equipped to control, has emerged as a central instrument for the prevention and resolution of conflicts and for the preservation of peace. Our aims must be:

• To seek to identify at the earliest possible stage situations that could produce conflict, and to try through diplomacy to remove the sources of danger before violence results;

• Where conflict erupts, to engage in peacemaking aimed at resolving the issues that have led to conflict;

• Through peace-keeping, to work to preserve peace, however fragile, where fighting has been halted and to assist in implementing agreements achieved by the peacemakers;

• To stand ready to assist in peace-building in its differing contexts: rebuilding the institutions and infrastructures of nations torn by civil war and strife; and building bonds of peaceful mutual benefit among nations formerly at war;

• And in the largest sense, to address the deepest causes of conflict: economic despair, social injustice and political oppression.

It is possible to discern an increasingly common moral perception that spans the world's nations and peoples, and which is finding expression in international laws, many owing their genesis to the work of this Organization.

16.   This wider mission for the world Organization will demand the concerted attention and effort of individual States, of regional and non-governmental organizations and of all of the United Nations system, with each of the principal organs functioning in the balance and harmony that the Charter requires. The Security Council has been assigned by all Member States the primary responsibility for the maintenance of international peace and security under the Charter. In its broadest sense this responsibility must be shared by the General Assembly and by all the functional elements of the world Organization. Each has a special and indispensable role to play in an integrated approach to human security. The Secretary-General's contribution rests on the pattern of trust and cooperation established between him and the deliberative organs of the United Nations.

17.   The foundation-stone of this work is and must remain the State. Respect for its fundamental sovereignty and integrity are crucial to any common international progress. The time of absolute and exclusive sovereignty, however, has passed; its theory was never matched by reality. It is the task of leaders of States today to understand this and to find a balance between the needs of good internal governance and the requirements of an ever more interdependent world. Commerce, communications and environmental matters transcend administrative borders; but inside those borders is where individuals carry out the first order of their economic, political and social lives. The United Nations has not closed its door. Yet if every ethnic, religious or linguistic group claimed statehood, there would be no limit to fragmentation, and peace, security and economic well-being for all would become ever more difficult to achieve.

18.   One requirement for solutions to these problems lies in commitment to human rights with a special sensitivity to those of minorities, whether ethnic, religious, social or linguistic. The League of Nations provided a machinery for the international protection of minorities. The General Assembly soon will have before it a declaration on the rights of minorities. That instrument, together with the increasingly effective machinery of the United Nations dealing with human rights, should enhance the situation of minorities as well as the stability of States.

19. Globalism and nationalism need not be viewed as opposing trends, doomed to spur each other on to extremes of reaction. The healthy globalization of contemporary life requires in the first instance solid identities and fundamental freedoms. The sovereignty, territorial integrity and independence of States within the established international system, and the principle of self-determination for peoples, both of great value and importance, must not be permitted to work against each other in the period ahead. Respect for democratic principles at all levels of social existence is crucial: in communities, within States and within the community of States. Our constant duty should be to maintain the integrity of each while finding a balanced design for all.

II. DEFINITIONS

20. The terms preventive diplomacy, peacemaking and peacekeeping are integrally related and as used in this report are defined as follows:

Preventive diplomacy is action to prevent disputes from arising between parties, to prevent existing disputes from escalating into conflicts and to limit the spread of the latter when they occur.

Peacemaking is action to bring hostile parties to agreement, essentially through such peaceful means as those foreseen in Chapter VI of the Charter of the United Nations.

Peace-keeping is the deployment of a United Nations presence in the field, hitherto with the consent of all the parties concerned, normally involving United Nations military and/or police personnel and frequently civilians as well. Peace-keeping is a technique that expands the possibilities for both the prevention of conflict and the making of peace.

21. The present report in addition will address the critically related concept of post-conflict *peace-building*—action to identify and support structures which will tend to strengthen and solidify peace in order to avoid a relapse into conflict. Preventive diplomacy seeks to resolve disputes before violence breaks out; peacemaking and peace-keeping are required to halt conflicts and preserve peace once it is attained. If successful, they strengthen the opportunity for post-conflict peace-building, which can prevent the recurrence of violence among nations and peoples.

22. These four areas for action, taken together, and carried out with the backing of all Members, offer a coherent contribution towards securing peace in the spirit of the Charter. The United Nations has extensive experience not only in these fields, but in the wider realm of work for peace in which these four fields are set. Initiatives on decolonization, on the environment and sustainable development, on population, on the eradication of disease, on disarmament and on the growth of international law—these and many others have contributed immeasurably to the foundations for a peaceful world. The world has often been rent by conflict and plagued by massive human suffering and deprivation. Yet it would have been far more so without the continuing efforts of the United Nations. This wide experience must be taken into account in assessing the potential of the United Nations in maintaining international security not only in its traditional sense, but in the new dimensions presented by the era ahead.

III. PREVENTIVE DIPLOMACY

23. The most desirable and efficient employment of diplomacy is to ease tensions before they result in conflict—or, if conflict breaks out, to act swiftly to contain it and resolve its underlying causes. Preventive diplomacy may be performed by the Secretary-General personally or through senior staff or specialized agencies and programmes, by the Security Council or the General Assembly, and by regional organizations in cooperation with the United Nations. Preventive diplomacy requires measures to create confidence; it needs early warning based on information gathering and informal or formal fact-finding; it may also involve preventive deployment and, in some situations, demilitarized zones.

Measures to build confidence

24. Mutual confidence and good faith are essential to reducing the likelihood of conflict between States. Many such measures are available to Governments that have the will to employ them. Systematic exchange of military missions, formation of regional or subregional risk reduction centres, arrangements for the free flow of information, including the monitoring of regional arms agreements, are examples. I ask all regional organizations to consider what further confidence-building measures might be applied in their areas and to inform the United Nations of the

results. I will undertake periodic consultations on confidence-building measures with parties to potential, current or past disputes and with regional organizations, offering such advisory assistance as the Secretariat can provide.

Fact-finding

25. Preventive steps must be based upon timely and accurate knowledge of the facts. Beyond this, an understanding of developments and global trends, based on sound analysis, is required. And the willingness to take appropriate preventive action is essential. Given the economic and social roots of many potential conflicts, the information needed by the United Nations now must encompass economic and social trends as well as political developments that may lead to dangerous tensions.

(*a*) An increased resort to fact-finding is needed, in accordance with the Charter, initiated either by the Secretary-General, to enable him to meet his responsibilities under the Charter, including Article 99, or by the Security Council or the General Assembly. Various forms may be employed selectively as the situation requires. A request by a State for the sending of a United Nations fact-finding mission to its territory should be considered without undue delay.

(*b*) Contacts with the Governments of Member States can provide the Secretary-General with detailed information on issues of concern. I ask that all Member States be ready to provide the information needed for effective preventive diplomacy. I will supplement my own contacts by regularly sending senior officials on missions for consultations in capitals or other locations. Such contacts are essential to gain insight into a situation and to assess its potential ramifications.

(*c*) Formal fact-finding can be mandated by the Security Council or by the General Assembly, either of which may elect to send a mission under its immediate authority or may invite the Secretary-General to take the necessary steps, including the designation of a special envoy. In addition to collecting information on which a decision for further action can be taken, such a mission can in some instances help to defuse a dispute by its presence, indicating to the parties that the Organization, and in particular the Security Council, is actively seized of the matter as a present or potential threat to international security.

(*d*) In exceptional circumstances the Council may meet away from Headquarters as the Charter provides, in order not only to inform itself directly, but also to bring the authority of the Organization to bear on a given situation.

Early warning

26.   In recent years the United Nations system has been developing a valuable network of early warning systems concerning environmental threats, the risk of nuclear accident, natural disasters, mass movements of populations, the threat of famine and the spread of disease. There is a need, however, to strengthen arrangements in such a manner that information from these sources can be synthesized with political indicators to assess whether a threat to peace exists and to analyse what action might be taken by the United Nations to alleviate it. This is a process that will continue to require the close cooperation of the various specialized agencies and functional offices of the United Nations. The analyses and recommendations for preventive action that emerge will be made available by me, as appropriate, to the Security Council and other United Nations organs. I recommend in addition that the Security Council invite a reinvigorated and restructured Economic and Social Council to provide reports, in accordance with Article 65 of the Charter, on those economic and social developments that may, unless mitigated, threaten international peace and security.

27.   Regional arrangements and organizations have an important role in early warning. I ask regional organizations that have not yet sought observer status at the United Nations to do so and to be linked, through appropriate arrangements, with the security mechanisms of this Organization.

Preventive deployment

28.   United Nations operations in areas of crisis have generally been established after conflict has occurred. The time has come to plan for circumstances warranting preventive deployment, which could take place in a variety of instances and ways. For example, in conditions of national crisis there could be preventive deployment at the request of the Government or all parties concerned, or with their consent; in inter-State disputes such deployment could take place when two countries feel that a United Nations presence on both sides of their border can discourage hostilities; furthermore, preventive deployment could take place when a country feels threatened and requests the deployment of an appropriate United Nations presence along its side of the border alone. In each situation, the mandate and

composition of the United Nations presence would need to be carefully devised and be clear to all.

29. In conditions of crisis within a country, when the Government requests or all parties consent, preventive deployment could help in a number of ways to alleviate suffering and to limit or control violence. Humanitarian assistance, impartially provided, could be of critical importance; assistance in maintaining security, whether through military, police or civilian personnel, could save lives and develop conditions of safety in which negotiations can be held; the United Nations could also help in conciliation efforts if this should be the wish of the parties. In certain circumstances, the United Nations may well need to draw upon the specialized skills and resources of various parts of the United Nations system; such operations may also on occasion require the participation of non-governmental organizations.

30. In these situations of internal crisis the United Nations will need to respect the sovereignty of the State; to do otherwise would not be in accordance with the understanding of member States in accepting the principles of the Charter. The Organization must remain mindful of the carefully negotiated balance of the guiding principles annexed to General Assembly resolution 46/182 of 19 December 1991. Those guidelines stressed, *inter alia*, that humanitarian assistance must be provided in accordance with the principles of humanity, neutrality and impartiality; that the sovereignty, territorial integrity and national unity of States must be fully respected in accordance with the Charter of the United Nations; and that, in this context, humanitarian assistance should be provided with the consent of the affected country and, in principle, on the basis of an appeal by that country. The guidelines also stressed the responsibility of States to take care of the victims of emergencies occurring on their territory and the need for access to those requiring humanitarian assistance. In the light of these guidelines, a Government's request for United Nations involvement, or consent to it, would not be an infringement of that State's sovereignty or be contrary to Article 2, paragraph 7, of the Charter which refers to matters essentially within the domestic jurisdiction of any State.

31. In inter-State disputes, when both parties agree, I recommend that if the Security Council concludes that the likelihood of hostilities between neighbouring countries could be removed by the preventive deployment of a United Nations presence on the territory of each State, such action should be taken. The nature

of the tasks to be performed would determine the composition of the United Nations presence.

32. In cases where one nation fears a cross-border attack, if the Security Council concludes that a United Nations presence on one side of the border, with the consent only of the requesting country, would serve to deter conflict, I recommend that preventive deployment take place. Here again, the specific nature of the situation would determine the mandate and the personnel required to fulfil it.

Demilitarized zones

33. In the past, demilitarized zones have been established by agreement of the parties at the conclusion of a conflict. In addition to the deployment of United Nations personnel in such zones as part of peace-keeping operations, consideration should now be given to the usefulness of such zones as a form of preventive deployment, on both sides of a border, with the agreement of the two parties, as a means of separating potential belligerents, or on one side of the line, at the request of one party, for the purpose of removing any pretext for attack. Demilitarized zones would serve as symbols of the international community's concern that conflict be prevented.

IV. PEACEMAKING

34. Between the tasks of seeking to prevent conflict and keeping the peace lies the responsibility to try to bring hostile parties to agreement by peaceful means. Chapter VI of the Charter sets forth a comprehensive list of such means for the resolution of conflict. These have been amplified in various declarations adopted by the General Assembly, including the Manila Declaration of 1982 on the Peaceful Settlement of International Disputes[2] and the 1988 Declaration on the Prevention and Removal of Disputes and Situations Which May Threaten International Peace and Security and on the Role of the United Nations in this Field.[3] They have also been the subject of various resolutions of the General Assembly, including resolution 44/21 of 15 November 1989 on enhancing international peace, security and international cooperation in all its aspects in accordance with the Charter of the United Nations.

---

[2] General Assembly resolution 37/10, annex.
[3] General Assembly resolution 43/51, annex.

The United Nations has had wide experience in the application of these peaceful means. If conflicts have gone unresolved, it is not because techniques for peaceful settlement were unknown or inadequate. The fault lies first in the lack of political will of parties to seek a solution to their differences through such means as are suggested in Chapter VI of the Charter, and second, in the lack of leverage at the disposal of a third party if this is the procedure chosen. The indifference of the international community to a problem, or the marginalization of it, can also thwart the possibilities of solution. We must look primarily to these areas if we hope to enhance the capacity of the Organization for achieving peaceful settlements.

35. The present determination in the Security Council to resolve international disputes in the manner foreseen in the Charter has opened the way for a more active Council role. With greater unity has come leverage and persuasive power to lead hostile parties towards negotiations. I urge the Council to take full advantage of the provisions of the Charter under which it may recommend appropriate procedures or methods for dispute settlement and, if all the parties to a dispute so request, make recommendations to the parties for a pacific settlement of the dispute.

36. The General Assembly, like the Security Council and the Secretary-General, also has an important role assigned to it under the Charter for the maintenance of international peace and security. As a universal forum, its capacity to consider and recommend appropriate action must be recognized. To that end it is essential to promote its utilization by all Member States so as to bring greater influence to bear in pre-empting or containing situations which are likely to threaten international peace and security.

37. Mediation and negotiation can be undertaken by an individual designated by the Security Council, by the General Assembly or by the Secretary-General. There is a long history of the utilization by the United Nations of distinguished statesmen to facilitate the processes of peace. They can bring a personal prestige that, in addition to their experience, can encourage the parties to enter serious negotiations. There is a wide willingness to serve in this capacity, from which I shall continue to benefit as the need arises. Frequently it is the Secretary-General himself who undertakes the task. While the mediator's effectiveness is enhanced by strong and evident

support from the Council, the General Assembly and the relevant Member States acting in their national capacity, the good offices of the Secretary-General may at times be employed most effectively when conducted independently of the deliberative bodies. Close and continuous consultation between the Secretary-General and the Security Council is, however, essential to ensure full awareness of how the Council's influence can best be applied and to develop a common strategy for the peaceful settlement of specific disputes.

The World Court

38.   The docket of the International Court of Justice has grown fuller but it remains an under-used resource for the peaceful adjudication of disputes. Greater reliance on the Court would be an important contribution to United Nations peacemaking. In this connection, I call attention to the power of the Security Council under Articles 36 and 37 of the Charter to recommend to Member States the submission of a dispute to the International Court of Justice, arbitration or other dispute-settlement mechanisms. I recommend that the Secretary-General be authorized, pursuant to Article 96, paragraph 2, of the Charter, to take advantage of the advisory competence of the Court and that other United Nations organs that already enjoy such authorization turn to the Court more frequently for advisory opinions.

39.   I recommend the following steps to reinforce the role of the International Court of Justice:

(*a*)   All Member States should accept the general jurisdiction of the International Court under Article 36 of its Statute, without any reservation, before the end of the United Nations Decade of International Law in the year 2000. In instances where domestic structures prevent this, States should agree bilaterally or multilaterally to a comprehensive list of matters they are willing to submit to the Court and should withdraw their reservations to its jurisdiction in the dispute settlement clauses of multilateral treaties;

(*b*)   When submission of a dispute to the full Court is not practical, the Chambers jurisdiction should be used;

(*c*)   States should support the Trust Fund established to assist countries unable to afford the cost involved in bringing a dispute to the Court, and such countries should take full advantage of the Fund in order to resolve their disputes.

Amelioration through assistance

40.   Peacemaking is at times facilitated by international action to ameliorate circumstances that have contributed to the dispute or conflict. If, for instance, assistance to displaced persons within a society is essential to a solution, then the United Nations should be able to draw upon the resources of all agencies and programmes concerned. At present, there is no adequate mechanism in the United Nations through which the Security Council, the General Assembly or the Secretary-General can mobilize the resources needed for such positive leverage and engage the collective efforts of the United Nations system for the peaceful resolution of a conflict. I have raised this concept in the Administrative Committee on Coordination, which brings together the executive heads of United Nations agencies and programmes; we are exploring methods by which the inter-agency system can improve its contribution to the peaceful resolution of disputes.

Sanctions and special economic problems

41.   In circumstances when peacemaking requires the imposition of sanctions under Article 41 of the Charter, it is important that States confronted with special economic problems not only have the right to consult the Security Council regarding such problems, as Article 50 provides, but also have a realistic possibility of having their difficulties addressed. I recommend that the Security Council devise a set of measures involving the financial institutions and other components of the United Nations system that can be put in place to insulate States from such difficulties. Such measures would be a matter of equity and a means of encouraging States to cooperate with decisions of the Council.

Use of military force

42.   It is the essence of the concept of collective security as contained in the Charter that if peaceful means fail, the measures provided in Chapter VII should be used, on the decision of the Security Council, to maintain or restore international peace and security in the face of a 'threat to the peace, breach of the peace, or act of aggression'. The Security Council has not so far made use of the most coercive of these measures—the action by military force foreseen in Article 42. In the situation between Iraq and Kuwait, the Council chose to authorize Member States to take measures on its behalf. The Charter, however, provides a detailed approach which now merits the attention of all Member States.

43.   Under Article 42 of the Charter, the Security Council has the authority to take military action to maintain or restore international peace and security. While such action should only be taken when all peaceful means have failed, the option of taking it is essential to the credibility of the United Nations as a guarantor of international security. This will require bringing into being, through negotiations, the special agreements foreseen in Article 43 of the Charter, whereby Member States undertake to make armed forces, assistance and facilities available to the Security Council for the purposes stated in Article 42, not only on an ad hoc basis but on a permanent basis. Under the political circumstances that now exist for the first time since the Charter was adopted, the long-standing obstacles to the conclusion of such special agreements should no longer prevail. The ready availability of armed forces on call could serve, in itself, as a means of deterring breaches of the peace since a potential aggressor would know that the Council had at its disposal a means of response. Forces under Article 43 may perhaps never be sufficiently large or well enough equipped to deal with a threat from a major army equipped with sophisticated weapons. They would be useful, however, in meeting any threat posed by a military force of a lesser order. I recommend that the Security Council initiate negotiations in accordance with Article 43, supported by the Military Staff Committee, which may be augmented if necessary by others in accordance with Article 47, paragraph 2, of the Charter. It is my view that the role of the Military Staff Committee should be seen in the context of Chapter VII, and not that of the planning or conduct of peace-keeping operations.

Peace-enforcement units

44.   The mission of forces under Article 43 would be to respond to outright aggression, imminent or actual. Such forces are not likely to be available for some time to come. Cease-fires have often been agreed to but not complied with, and the United Nations has sometimes been called upon to send forces to restore and maintain the cease-fire. This task can on occasion exceed the mission of peace-keeping forces and the expectations of peace-keeping force contributors. I recommend that the Council consider the utilization of peace-enforcement units in clearly defined circumstances and with their terms of reference specified in advance. Such units from Member States would be available on call and would consist of troops that have volunteered

for such service. They would have to be more heavily armed than peace-keeping forces and would need to undergo extensive preparatory training within their national forces. Deployment and operation of such forces would be under the authorization of the Security Council and would, as in the case of peace-keeping forces, be under the command of the Secretary-General. I consider such peace-enforcement units to be warranted as a provisional measure under Article 40 of the Charter. Such peace-enforcement units should not be confused with the forces that may eventually be constituted under Article 43 to deal with acts of aggression or with the military personnel which Governments may agree to keep on stand-by for possible contribution to peace-keeping operations.

45. Just as diplomacy will continue across the span of all the activities dealt with in the present report, so there may not be a dividing line between peacemaking and peace-keeping. Peacemaking is often a prelude to peace-keeping—just as the deployment of a United Nations presence in the field may expand possibilities for the prevention of conflict, facilitate the work of peacemaking and in many cases serve as a prerequisite for peace-building.

V. PEACE-KEEPING

46. Peace-keeping can rightly be called the invention of the United Nations. It has brought a degree of stability to numerous areas of tension around the world.

Increasing demands

47. Thirteen peace-keeping operations were established between the years 1945 and 1987; 13 others since then. An estimated 528,000 military, police and civilian personnel had served under the flag of the United Nations until January 1992. Over 800 of them from 43 countries have died in the service of the Organization. The costs of these operations have aggregated some $8.3 billion till 1992. The unpaid arrears towards them stand at over $800 million, which represent a debt owed by the Organization to the troop-contributing countries. Peace-keeping operations approved at present are estimated to cost close to $3 billion in the current 12-month period, while patterns of payment are unacceptably slow. Against this, global defence expenditures at the end of the last decade had approached $1 trillion a year, or $2 million per minute.

48. The contrast between the costs of United Nations peace-keeping and the costs of the alternative, war—between the demands of the Organization and the means provided to meet them—would be farcical were the consequences not so damaging to global stability and to the credibility of the Organization. At a time when nations and peoples increasingly are looking to the United Nations for assistance in keeping the peace—and holding it responsible when this cannot be so—fundamental decisions must be taken to enhance the capacity of the Organization in this innovative and productive exercise of its function. I am conscious that the present volume and unpredictability of peace-keeping assessments poses real problems for some Member States. For this reason, I strongly support proposals in some Member States for their peace-keeping contributions to be financed from defence, rather than foreign affairs, budgets and I recommend such action to others. I urge the General Assembly to encourage this approach.

49. The demands on the United Nations for peace-keeping, and peace-building, operations will in the coming years continue to challenge the capacity, the political and financial will and the creativity of the Secretariat and Member States. Like the Security Council, I welcome the increase and broadening of the tasks of peace-keeping operations.

New departures in peace-keeping

50. The nature of peace-keeping operations has evolved rapidly in recent years. The established principles and practices of peace-keeping have responded flexibly to new demands of recent years, and the basic conditions for success remain unchanged: a clear and practicable mandate; the cooperation of the parties in implementing that mandate; the continuing support of the Security Council; the readiness of Member States to contribute the military, police and civilian personnel, including specialists, required; effective United Nations command at Headquarters and in the field; and adequate financial and logistic support. As the international climate has changed and peace-keeping operations are increasingly fielded to help implement settlements that have been negotiated by peacemakers, a new array of demands and problems has emerged regarding logistics, equipment, personnel and finance, all of which could be corrected if Member States so wished and were ready to make the necessary resources available.

Personnel

51.   Member States are keen to participate in peace-keeping operations. Military observers and infantry are invariably available in the required numbers, but logistic units present a greater problem, as few armies can afford to spare such units for an extended period. Member States were requested in 1990 to state what military personnel they were in principle prepared to make available; few replied. I reiterate the request to all Member States to reply frankly and promptly. Stand-by arrangements should be confirmed, as appropriate, through exchanges of letters between the Secretariat and Member States concerning the kind and number of skilled personnel they will be prepared to offer the United Nations as the needs of new operations arise.

52.   Increasingly, peace-keeping requires that civilian political officers, human rights monitors, electoral officials, refugee and humanitarian aid specialists and police play as central a role as the military. Police personnel have proved increasingly difficult to obtain in the numbers required. I recommend that arrangements be reviewed and improved for training peace-keeping personnel—civilian, police, or military—using the varied capabilities of Member State Governments, of non-governmental organizations and the facilities of the Secretariat. As efforts go forward to include additional States as contributors, some States with considerable potential should focus on language training for police contingents which may serve with the Organization. As for the United Nations itself, special personnel procedures, including incentives, should be instituted to permit the rapid transfer of Secretariat staff members to service with peace-keeping operations. The strength and capability of military staff serving in the Secretariat should be augmented to meet new and heavier requirements.

Logistics

53.   Not all Governments can provide their battalions with the equipment they need for service abroad. While some equipment is provided by troop-contributing countries, a great deal has to come from the United Nations, including equipment to fill gaps in under-equipped national units. The United Nations has no standing stock of such equipment. Orders must be placed with manufacturers, which creates a number of difficulties. A pre-positioned stock of basic peace-keeping equipment should be established, so that at least some vehicles, communications equipment, generators, etc., would be immediately available at

the start of an operation. Alternatively, Governments should commit themselves to keeping certain equipment, specified by the Secretary-General, on stand-by for immediate sale, loan or donation to the United Nations when required.

54. Member States in a position to do so should make air- and sea-lift capacity available to the United Nations free of cost or at lower than commercial rates, as was the practice until recently.

VI. POST-CONFLICT PEACE-BUILDING

55. Peacemaking and peace-keeping operations, to be truly successful, must come to include comprehensive efforts to identify and support structures which will tend to consolidate peace and advance a sense of confidence and well-being among people. Through agreements ending civil strife, these may include disarming the previously warring parties and the restoration of order, the custody and possible destruction of weapons, repatriating refugees, advisory and training support for security personnel, monitoring elections, advancing efforts to protect human rights, reforming or strengthening governmental institutions and promoting formal and informal processes of political participation.

56. In the aftermath of international war, post-conflict peace-building may take the form of concrete cooperative projects which link two or more countries in a mutually beneficial undertaking that can not only contribute to economic and social development but also enhance the confidence that is so fundamental to peace. I have in mind, for example, projects that bring States together to develop agriculture, improve transportation or utilize resources such as water or electricity that they need to share, or joint programmes through which barriers between nations are brought down by means of freer travel, cultural exchanges and mutually beneficial youth and educational projects. Reducing hostile perceptions through educational exchanges and curriculum reform may be essential to forestall a re-emergence of cultural and national tensions which could spark renewed hostilities.

57. In surveying the range of efforts for peace, the concept of peace-building as the construction of a new environment should be viewed as the counterpart of preventive diplomacy, which seeks to avoid the breakdown of peaceful conditions. When conflict breaks out, mutually reinforcing efforts at peacemaking

and peace-keeping come into play. Once these have achieved their objectives, only sustained, cooperative work to deal with underlying economic, social, cultural and humanitarian problems can place an achieved peace on a durable foundation. Preventive diplomacy is to avoid a crisis; post-conflict peacebuilding is to prevent a recurrence.

58. Increasingly it is evident that peace-building after civil or international strife must address the serious problem of land mines, many tens of millions of which remain scattered in present or former combat zones. De-mining should be emphasized in the terms of reference of peace-keeping operations and is crucially important in the restoration of activity when peacebuilding is under way: agriculture cannot be revived without de-mining and the restoration of transport may require the laying of hard surface roads to prevent re-mining. In such instances, the link becomes evident between peace-keeping and peacebuilding. Just as demilitarized zones may serve the cause of preventive diplomacy and preventive deployment to avoid conflict, so may demilitarization assist in keeping the peace or in post-conflict peace-building, as a measure for heightening the sense of security and encouraging the parties to turn their energies to the work of peaceful restoration of their societies.

59. There is a new requirement for technical assistance which the United Nations has an obligation to develop and provide when requested: support for the transformation of deficient national structures and capabilities, and for the strengthening of new democratic institutions. The authority of the United Nations system to act in this field would rest on the consensus that social peace is as important as strategic or political peace. There is an obvious connection between democratic practices— such as the rule of law and transparency in decision-making— and the achievement of true peace and security in any new and stable political order. These elements of good governance need to be promoted at all levels of international and national political communities.

VII. COOPERATION WITH REGIONAL ARRANGEMENTS AND ORGANIZATIONS

60. The Covenant of the League of Nations, in its Article 21, noted the validity of regional understandings for securing the maintenance of peace. The Charter devotes Chapter VIII to regional arrangements or agencies for dealing with such matters

relating to the maintenance of international peace and security as are appropriate for regional action and consistent with the Purposes and Principles of the United Nations. The cold war impaired the proper use of Chapter VIII and indeed, in that era, regional arrangements worked on occasion against resolving disputes in the manner foreseen in the Charter.

61. The Charter deliberately provides no precise definition of regional arrangements and agencies, thus allowing useful flexibility for undertakings by a group of States to deal with a matter appropriate for regional action which also could contribute to the maintenance of international peace and security. Such associations or entities could include treaty-based organizations, whether created before or after the founding of the United Nations, regional organizations for mutual security and defence, organizations for general regional development or for cooperation on a particular economic topic or function, and groups created to deal with a specific political, economic or social issue of current concern.

62. In this regard, the United Nations has recently encouraged a rich variety of complementary efforts. Just as no two regions of situations are the same, so the design of cooperative work and its division of labour must adapt to the realities of each case with flexibility and creativity. In Africa, three different regional groups—the Organization of African Unity, the League of Arab States and the Organization of the Islamic Conference—joined efforts with the United Nations regarding Somalia. In the Asian context, the Association of South-East Asian Nations and individual States from several regions were brought together with the parties to the Cambodian conflict at an international conference in Paris, to work with the United Nations. For El Salvador, a unique arrangement—'The Friends of the Secretary-General'—contributed to agreements reached through the mediation of the Secretary-General. The end of the war in Nicaragua involved a highly complex effort which was initiated by leaders of the region and conducted by individual States, groups of States and the Organization of American States. Efforts undertaken by the European Community and its member States, with the support of States participating in the Conference on Security and Cooperation in Europe, have been of central importance in dealing with the crisis in the Balkans and neighbouring areas.

63. In the past, regional arrangements often were created because of the absence of a universal system for collective

security; thus their activities could on occasion work at cross-purposes with the sense of solidarity required for the effectiveness of the world Organization. But in this new era of opportunity, regional arrangements or agencies can render great service if their activities are undertaken in a manner consistent with the Purposes and Principles of the Charter, and if their relationship with the United Nations, and particularly the Security Council, is governed by Chapter VIII.

64. It is not the purpose of the present report to set forth any formal pattern of relationship between regional organizations and the United Nations, or to call for any specific division of labour. What is clear, however, is that regional arrangements or agencies in many cases possess a potential that should be utilized in serving the functions covered in this report: preventive diplomacy, peace-keeping, peacemaking and post-conflict peace-building. Under the Charter, the Security Council has and will continue to have primary responsibility for maintaining international peace and security, but regional action as a matter of decentralization, delegation and cooperation with United Nations efforts could not only lighten the burden of the Council but also contribute to a deeper sense of participation, consensus and democratization in international affairs.

65. Regional arrangements and agencies have not in recent decades been considered in this light, even when originally designed in part for a role in maintaining or restoring peace within their regions of the world. Today a new sense exists that they have contributions to make. Consultations between the United Nations and regional arrangements or agencies could do much to build international consensus on the nature of a problem and the measures required to address it. Regional organizations participating in complementary efforts with the United Nations in joint undertakings would encourage States outside the region to act supportively. And should the Security Council choose specifically to authorize a regional arrangement or organization to take the lead in addressing a crisis within its region, it could serve to lend the weight of the United Nations to the validity of the regional effort. Carried forward in the spirit of the Charter, and as envisioned in Chapter VIII, the approach outlined here could strengthen a general sense that democratization is being encouraged at all levels in the task of maintaining international peace and security, it being essential to continue to recognize that the primary responsibility will continue to reside in the Security Council.

VIII. SAFETY OF PERSONNEL

66. When United Nations personnel are deployed in conditions of strife, whether for preventive diplomacy, peacemaking, peace-keeping, peace-building or humanitarian purposes, the need arises to ensure their safety. There has been an unconscionable increase in the number of fatalities. Following the conclusion of a cease-fire and in order to prevent further outbreaks of violence, United Nations guards were called upon to assist in volatile conditions in Iraq. Their presence afforded a measure of security to United Nations personnel and supplies and, in addition, introduced an element of reassurance and stability that helped to prevent renewed conflict. Depending upon the nature of the situation, different configurations and compositions of security deployments will need to be considered. As the variety and scale of threat widens, innovative measures will be required to deal with the dangers facing United Nations personnel.

67. Experience has demonstrated that the presence of a United Nations operation has not always been sufficient to deter hostile action. Duty in areas of danger can never be risk-free; United Nations personnel must expect to go in harm's way at times. The courage, commitment and idealism shown by United Nations personnel should be respected by the entire international community. These men and women deserve to be properly recognized and rewarded for the perilous tasks they undertake. Their interests and those of their families must be given due regard and protected.

68. Given the pressing need to afford adequate protection to United Nations personnel engaged in life-endangering circumstances, I recommend that the Security Council, unless it elects immediately to withdraw the United Nations presence in order to preserve the credibility of the Organization, gravely consider what action should be taken towards those who put United Nations personnel in danger. Before deployment takes place, the Council should keep open the option of considering in advance collective measures, possibly including those under Chapter VII when a threat to international peace and security is also involved, to come into effect should the purpose of the United Nations operation systematically be frustrated and hostilities occur.

IX. FINANCING

69. A chasm has developed between the tasks entrusted to this Organization and the financial means provided to it. The truth

of the matter is that our vision cannot really extend to the prospect opening before us as long as our financing remains myopic. There are two main areas of concern: the ability of the Organization to function over the longer term; and immediate requirements to respond to a crisis.

70. To remedy the financial situation of the United Nations in all its aspects, my distinguished predecessor repeatedly drew the attention of Member States to the increasingly impossible situation that has arisen and, during the forty-sixth session of the General Assembly, made a number of proposals. Those proposals which remain before the Assembly, and with which I am in broad agreement, are the following:

Proposal one. This suggested the adoption of a set of measures to deal with the cash flow problems caused by the exceptionally high level of unpaid contributions as well as with the problem of inadequate working capital reserves:

(*a*) Charging interest on the amounts of assessed contributions that are not paid on time;

(*b*) Suspending certain financial regulations of the United Nations to permit the retention of budgetary surpluses;

(*c*) Increasing the Working Capital Fund to a level of $250 million and endorsing the principle that the level of the Fund should be approximately 25 per cent of the annual assessment under the regular budget;

(*d*) Establishment of a temporary Peace-keeping Reserve Fund, at a level of $50 million, to meet initial expenses of peace-keeping operations pending receipt of assessed contributions;

(*e*) Authorization to the Secretary-General to borrow commercially, should other sources of cash be inadequate.

Proposal two. This suggested the creation of a Humanitarian Revolving Fund in the order of $50 million, to be used in emergency humanitarian situations. The proposal has since been implemented.

Proposal three. This suggested the establishment of a United Nations Peace Endowment Fund, with an initial target of $1 billion. The Fund would be created by a combination of assessed and voluntary contributions, with the latter being sought from Governments, the private sector as well as individuals. Once the Fund reached its target level, the proceeds from the investment of its principal would be used to finance the initial costs of authorized peace-keeping operations, other conflict resolution measures and related activities.

71. In addition to these proposals, others have been added in recent months in the course of public discussion. These ideas include: a levy on arms sales that could be related to maintaining an Arms Register by the United Nations; a levy on international air travel, which is dependent on the maintenance of peace; authorization for the United Nations to borrow from the World Bank and the International Monetary Fund—for peace and development are interdependent; general tax exemption for contributions made to the United Nations by foundations, businesses and individuals; and changes in the formula for calculating the scale of assessments for peace-keeping operations.

72. As such ideas are debated, a stark fact remains; the financial foundations of the Organization daily grow weaker, debilitating its political will and practical capacity to undertake new and essential activities. This state of affairs must not continue. Whatever decisions are taken on financing the Organization, there is one inescapable necessity: Member States must pay their assessed contributions in full and on time. Failure to do so puts them in breach of their obligations under the Charter.

73. In these circumstances and on the assumption that Member States will be ready to finance operations for peace in a manner commensurate with their present, and welcome, readiness to establish them, I recommend the following:

(a) Immediate establishment of a revolving peace-keeping reserve fund of $50 million;

(b) Agreement that one third of the estimated cost of each new peace-keeping operation be appropriated by the General Assembly as soon as the Security Council decides to establish the operation; this would give the Secretary-General the necessary commitment authority and assure an adequate cash flow; the balance of the costs would be appropriated after the General Assembly approved the operation's budget;

(c) Acknowledgement by Member States that, under exceptional circumstances, political and operational considerations may make it necessary for the Secretary-General to employ his authority to place contracts without competitive bidding.

74. Member States wish the Organization to be managed with the utmost efficiency and care. I am in full accord. I have taken important steps to streamline the Secretariat in order to avoid duplication and overlap while increasing its productivity. Additional changes and improvements will take place. As regards

the United Nations system more widely, I continue to review the situation in consultation with my colleagues in the Administrative Committee on Coordination. The question of assuring financial security to the Organization over the long term is of such importance and complexity that public awareness and support must be heightened. I have therefore asked a select group of qualified persons of high international repute to examine this entire subject and to report to me. I intend to present their advice, together with my comments, for the consideration of the General Assembly, in full recognition of the special responsibility that the Assembly has, under the Charter, for financial and budgetary matters.

X. AN AGENDA FOR PEACE

75.   The nations and peoples of the United Nations are fortunate in a way that those of the League of Nations were not. We have been given a second chance to create the world of our Charter that they were denied. With the cold war ended we have drawn back from the brink of a confrontation that threatened the world and, too often, paralysed our Organization.

76.   Even as we celebrate our restored possibilities, there is a need to ensure that the lessons of the past four decades are learned and that the errors, or variations of them, are not repeated. For there may not be a third opportunity for our planet which, now for different reasons, remains endangered.

77.   The tasks ahead must engage the energy and attention of all components of the United Nations system—the General Assembly and other principal organs, the agencies and programmes. Each has, in a balanced scheme of things, a role and a responsibility.

78.   Never again must the Security Council lose the collegiality that is essential to its proper functioning, an attribute that it has gained after such trial. A genuine sense of consensus deriving from shared interests must govern its work, not the threat of the veto or the power of any group of nations. And it follows that agreement among the permanent members must have the deeper support of the other members of the Council, and the membership more widely, if the Council's decisions are to be effective and endure.

79.   The Summit Meeting of the Security Council of 31 January 1992 provided a unique forum for exchanging views and

strengthening cooperation. I recommend that the Heads of State and Government of the members of the Council meet in alternate years, just before the general debate commences in the General Assembly. Such sessions would permit exchanges on the challenges and dangers of the moment and stimulate ideas on how the United Nations may best serve to steer change into peaceful courses. I propose in addition that the Security Council continue to meet at the Foreign Minister level, as it has effectively done in recent years, whenever the situation warrants such meetings.

80.   Power brings special responsibilities, and temptations. The powerful must resist the dual but opposite calls of unilateralism and isolationism if the United Nations is to succeed. For just as unilateralism at the global or regional level can shake the confidence of others, so can isolationism, whether it results from political choice or constitutional circumstance, enfeeble the global undertaking. Peace at home and the urgency of rebuilding and strengthening our individual societies necessitates peace abroad and cooperation among nations. The endeavours of the United Nations will require the fullest engagement of all of its Members, large and small, if the present renewed opportunity is to be seized.

81.   Democracy within nations requires respect for human rights and fundamental freedoms, as set forth in the Charter. It requires as well a deeper understanding and respect for the rights of minorities and respect for the needs of the more vulnerable groups of society, especially women and children. This is not only a political matter. The social stability needed for productive growth is nurtured by conditions in which people can readily express their will. For this, strong domestic institutions of participation are essential. Promoting such institutions means promoting the empowerment of the unorganized, the poor, the marginalized. To this end, the focus of the United Nations should be on the 'field', the locations where economic, social and political decisions take effect. In furtherance of this I am taking steps to rationalize and in certain cases integrate the various programmes and agencies of the United Nations within specific countries. The senior United Nations official in each country should be prepared to serve, when needed, and with the consent of the host authorities, as my Representative on matters of particular concern.

82.   Democracy within the family of nations means the application of its principles within the world Organization itself. This

requires the fullest consultation, participation and engagement of all States, large and small, in the work of the Organization. All organs of the United Nations must be accorded, and play, their full and proper role so that the trust of all nations and peoples will be retained and deserved. The principles of the Charter must be applied consistently, not selectively, for if the perception should be of the latter, trust will wane and with it the moral authority which is the greatest and most unique quality of that instrument. Democracy at all levels is essential to attain peace for a new era of prosperity and justice.

83. Trust also requires a sense of confidence that the world Organization will react swiftly, surely and impartially and that it will not be debilitated by political opportunism or by administrative or financial inadequacy. This presupposes a strong, efficient and independent international civil service whose integrity is beyond question and an assured financial basis that lifts the Organization, once and for all, out of its present mendicancy.

84. Just as it is vital that each of the organs of the United Nations employ its capabilities in the balanced and harmonious fashion envisioned in the Charter, peace in the largest sense cannot be accomplished by the United Nations system or by Governments alone. Non-governmental organizations, academic institutions, parliamentarians, business and professional communities, the media and the public at large must all be involved. This will strengthen the world Organization's ability to reflect the concerns and interests of its widest constituency, and those who become more involved can carry the word of United Nations initiatives and build a deeper understanding of its work.

85. Reform is a continuing process, and improvement can have no limit. Yet there is an expectation, which I wish to see fulfilled, that the present phase in the renewal of this Organization should be complete by 1995, its fiftieth anniversary. The pace set must therefore be increased if the United Nations is to keep ahead of the acceleration of history that characterizes this age. We must be guided not by precedents alone, however wise these may be, but by the needs of the future and by the shape and content that we wish to give it.

86. I am committed to broad dialogue between the Member States and the Secretary-General. And I am committed to fostering a full and open interplay between all institutions and elements of the Organization so that the Charter's objectives

may not only be better served, but that this Organization may emerge as greater than the sum of its parts. The United Nations was created with a great and courageous vision. Now is the time, for its nations and peoples, and the men and women who serve it, to seize the moment for the sake of the future.

Appendix B

Charter of the United Nations

The UN Charter was signed on 26 June 1945 by the representatives of fifty states in San Francisco, at the conclusion of the United Nations Conference on International Organization. It came into force on 24 October 1945.

Four articles of the Charter have been amended: 23, 27, 61, and 109. In each case this has been to take account of the increased membership of the UN. All the amendments appear in italics in the text below. The footnotes, which have been added by the editors of this book, show what the previous versions were, and when each amendment came into force.

The Statute of the International Court of Justice was adopted at the same time as the UN Charter but is not included here.

Charter of the United Nations*

WE THE PEOPLES
OF THE UNITED NATIONS
DETERMINED

to save succeeding generations from the scourge of war, which twice in our lifetime has brought untold sorrow to mankind, and

to reaffirm faith in fundamental human rights, in the dignity and worth of the human person, in the equal rights of men and women and of nations large and small, and

to establish conditions under which justice and respect for the obligations arising from treaties and other sources of international law can be maintained, and

to promote social progress and better standards of life in larger freedom,

---

* *Source: Yearbook of the United Nations 1991.* (Dordrecht, 1992). There have been no further amendments since this version was published.

AND FOR THESE ENDS

to practice tolerance and live together in peace with one another as good neighbours, and

to unite our strength to maintain international peace and security, and

to ensure, by the acceptance of principles and the institution of methods, that armed force shall not be used, save in the common interest, and

to employ international machinery for the promotion of the economic and social advancement of all peoples,

· HAVE RESOLVED TO
COMBINE OUR EFFORTS TO
ACCOMPLISH THESE AIMS

Accordingly, our respective Governments, through representatives assembled in the city of San Francisco, who have exhibited their full powers found to be in good and due form, have agreed to the present Charter of the United Nations and do hereby establish an international organization to be known as the United Nations.

Chapter I
Purposes and Principles

ARTICLE 1

The Purposes of the United Nations are:

1. To maintain international peace and security, and to that end: to take effective collective measures for the prevention and removal of threats to the peace, and for the suppression of acts of aggression or other breaches of the peace, and to bring about by peaceful means, and in conformity with the principles of justice and international law, adjustment or settlement of international disputes or situations which might lead to a breach of the peace;

2. To develop friendly relations among nations based on respect for the principle of equal rights and self-determination of peoples, and to take other appropriate measures to strengthen universal peace;

3. To achieve international co-operation in solving international problems of an economic, social, cultural, or humanitarian character, and in promoting and encouraging respect for human rights and for fundamental freedoms for all without distinction as to race, sex, language, or religion; and

4. To be a centre for harmonizing the actions of nations in the attainment of these common ends.

ARTICLE 2

The Organization and its Members, in pursuit of the Purposes stated in Article 1, shall act in accordance with the following Principles.

1. The Organization is based on the principle of the sovereign equality of all its Members.

2. All Members, in order to ensure to all of them the rights and benefits resulting from membership, shall fulfil in good faith the obligations assumed by them in accordance with the present Charter.

3. All Members shall settle their international disputes by peaceful means in such a manner that international peace and security, and justice, are not endangered.

4. All Members shall refrain in their international relations from the threat or use of force against the territorial integrity or political independence of any state, or in any other manner inconsistent with the Purposes of the United Nations.

5. All Members shall give the United Nations every assistance in any action it takes in accordance with the present Charter, and shall refrain from giving assistance to any state against which the United Nations is taking preventive or enforcement action.

6. The Organization shall ensure that states which are not Members of the United Nations act in accordance with these Principles so far as may be necessary for the maintenance of international peace and security.

7. Nothing contained in the present Charter shall authorize the United Nations to intervene in matters which are essentially within the domestic jurisdiction of any state or shall require the Members to submit such matters to settlement under the present Charter; but this principle shall not prejudice the application of enforcement measures under Chapter VII.

Chapter II
Membership

ARTICLE 3

The original Members of the United Nations shall be the states which, having participated in the United Nations Conference on International Organization at San Francisco, or having previously signed the Declaration by United Nations of 1 January 1942, sign the present Charter and ratify it in accordance with Article 110.

ARTICLE 4

1. Membership in the United Nations is open to all other peace-loving states which accept the obligations contained in the present Charter and, in the judgment of the Organization, are able and willing to carry out these obligations.

2. The admission of any such state to membership in the United Nations will be effected by a decision of the General Assembly upon the recommendation of the Security Council.

ARTICLE 5

A Member of the United Nations against which preventive or enforcement action has been taken by the Security Council may be suspended from the exercise of the rights and privileges of membership by the General Assembly upon the recommendation of the Security Council. The exercise of these rights and privileges may be restored by the Security Council.

ARTICLE 6

A Member of the United Nations which has persistently violated the Principles contained in the present Charter may be expelled from the Organization by the General Assembly upon the recommendation of the Security Council.

Chapter III
Organs

ARTICLE 7

1. There are established as the principal organs of the United Nations: a General Assembly, a Security Council, an Economic and Social Council, a Trusteeship Council, an International Court of Justice, and a Secretariat.

2. Such subsidiary organs as may be found necessary may be established in accordance with the present Charter.

ARTICLE 8

The United Nations shall place no restrictions on the eligibility of men and women to participate in any capacity and under conditions of equality in its principal and subsidiary organs.

Chapter IV
The General Assembly

Composition

ARTICLE 9

1. The General Assembly shall consist of all the Members of the United Nations.

2. Each Member shall have not more than five representatives in the General Assembly.

Functions and powers

ARTICLE 10

The General Assembly may discuss any questions or any matters within the scope of the present Charter or relating to the powers and functions of any organs provided for in the present Charter, and, except as provided in Article 12, may make recommendations to the Members of the United Nations or to the Security Council or to both on any such questions or matters.

ARTICLE 11

1. The General Assembly may consider the general principles of co-operation in the maintenance of international peace and security, including the principles governing disarmament and the regulation of armaments, and may make recommendations with regard to such principles to the Members or to the Security Council or to both.

2. The General Assembly may discuss any questions relating to the maintenance of international peace and security brought before it by any Member of the United Nations, or by the Security Council, or by a state which is not a Member of the United Nations in accordance with Article 35, paragraph 2, and, except as provided in Article 12, may make recommendations with regard to any such questions to the state or states concerned or to the Security Council or to both. Any such question on which action is necessary shall be referred to the Security Council by the General Assembly either before or after discussion.

3. The General Assembly may call the attention of the Security Council to situations which are likely to endanger international peace and security.

4. The powers of the General Assembly set forth in this Article shall not limit the general scope of Article 10.

ARTICLE 12

1. While the Security Council is exercising in respect of any dispute or situation the functions assigned to it in the present Charter, the General Assembly shall not make any recommendation with regard to that dispute or situation unless the Security Council so requests.

2. The Secretary-General, with the consent of the Security Council, shall notify the General Assembly at each session of any matters relative to the maintenance of international peace and security which are being dealt with by the Security Council and shall similarly notify the General Assembly, or the Members of the United Nations if the General Assembly is not in session, immediately the Security Council ceases to deal with such matters.

ARTICLE 13

1. The General Assembly shall initiate studies and make recommendations for the purpose of:

(a) promoting international co-operation in the political field and encouraging the progressive development of international law and its codification;

(b) promoting international co-operation in the economic, social, cultural, educational, and health fields, and assisting in the realization of human rights and fundamental freedoms for all without distinction as to race, sex, language, or religion.

2. The further responsibilities, functions and powers of the General Assembly with respect to matters mentioned in paragraph 1(b) above are set forth in Chapters IX and X.

ARTICLE 14

Subject to the provisions of Article 12, the General Assembly may recommend measures for the peaceful adjustment of any situation, regardless of origin, which it deems likely to impair the general welfare or friendly relations among nations, including situations resulting from a violation of the provisions of the present Charter setting forth the Purposes and Principles of the United Nations.

ARTICLE 15

1. The General Assembly shall receive and consider annual and special reports from the Security Council; these reports shall include an account of the measures that the Security

Council has decided upon or taken to maintain international peace and security.

2. The General Assembly shall receive and consider reports from the other organs of the United Nations.

ARTICLE 16

The General Assembly shall perform such functions with respect to the international trusteeship system as are assigned to it under Chapters XII and XIII, including the approval of the trusteeship agreements for areas not designated as strategic.

ARTICLE 17

1. The General Assembly shall consider and approve the budget of the Organization.

2. The expenses of the Organization shall be borne by the Members as apportioned by the General Assembly.

3. The General Assembly shall consider and approve any financial and budgetary arrangements with specialized agencies referred to in Article 57 and shall examine the administrative budgets of such specialized agencies with a view to making recommendations to the agencies concerned.

Voting

ARTICLE 18

1. Each member of the General Assembly shall have one vote.

2. Decisions of the General Assembly on important questions shall be made by a two-thirds majority of the members present and voting. These questions shall include: recommendations with respect to the maintenance of international peace and security, the election of the non-permanent members of the Security Council, the election of the members of the Economic and Social Council, the election of members of the Trusteeship Council in accordance with paragraph 1(c) of Article 86, the admission of new Members to the United Nations, the suspension of the rights and privileges of membership, the expulsion of Members, questions relating to the operation of the trusteeship system, and budgetary questions.

3. Decisions on other questions, including the determination of additional categories of questions to be decided by a two-thirds majority, shall be made by a majority of the members present and voting.

ARTICLE 19

A Member of the United Nations which is in arrears in the payment of its financial contributions to the Organization shall have no vote in the General Assembly if the amount of its arrears equals or exceeds the amount of the contributions due from it for the preceding two full years. The General Assembly may, nevertheless, permit such a Member to vote if it is satisfied that the failure to pay is due to conditions beyond the control of the Member.

Procedure

ARTICLE 20

The General Assembly shall meet in regular annual sessions and in such special sessions as occasion may require. Special sessions shall be convoked by the Secretary-General at the request of the Security Council or of a majority of the Members of the United Nations.

ARTICLE 21

The General Assembly shall adopt its own rules of procedure. It shall elect its President for each session.

ARTICLE 22

The General Assembly may establish such subsidiary organs as it deems necessary for the performance of its functions.

Chapter V
The Security Council

Composition

ARTICLE 23[1]

1. The Security council shall consist of *fifteen* Members of the United Nations. The Republic of China, France, the Union of Soviet Socialist Republics, the United Kingdom of Great Britain and Northern Ireland, and the United States of America shall

---

[1] Article 23(1) originally specified that the Security Council shall consist of *eleven* members, of whom *six* shall be elected by the General Assembly. Article 23(2), second sentence, originally read: 'In the first election of non-permanent members, however, three shall be chosen for a term of one year.' The current version came into force on 31 Aug. 1965.

be permanent members of the Security Council. The General Assembly shall elect *ten* other Members of the United Nations to be non-permanent members of the Security Council, due regard being specially paid, in the first instance to the contribution of Members of the United Nations to the maintenance of international peace and security and to the other purposes of the Organization, and also to equitable geographical distribution.

2. The non-permanent members of the Security Council shall be elected for a term of two years. *In the first election of the non-permanent members after the increase of the membership of the Security Council from eleven to fifteen, two of the four additional members shall be chosen for a term of one year.* A retiring member shall not be eligible for immediate re-election.

3. Each member of the Security Council shall have one representative.

Functions and powers

ARTICLE 24

1. In order to ensure prompt and effective action by the United Nations, its Members confer on the Security Council primary responsibility for the maintenance of international peace and security, and agree that in carrying out its duties under this responsibility the Security Council acts on their behalf.

2. In discharging these duties the Security Council shall act in accordance with the Purposes and Principles of the United Nations. The specific powers granted to the Security Council for the discharge of these duties are laid down in Chapters VI, VII, VIII, and XII.

3. The Security Council shall submit annual and, when necessary, special reports to the General Assembly for its consideration.

ARTICLE 25

The Members of the United Nations agree to accept and carry out the decisions of the Security Council in accordance with the present Charter.

ARTICLE 26

In order to promote the establishment and maintenance of international peace and security with the least diversion for armaments of the world's human and economic resources, the Security Council shall be responsible for formulating, with the assistance of the Military Staff Committee referred to in Article 47, plans to be submitted to the Members of the United Nations for the establishment of a system for the regulation of armaments.

Voting

ARTICLE 27[2]

1. Each member of the Security Council shall have one vote.

2. Decisions of the Security Council on procedural matters shall be made by an affirmative vote of *nine* members.

3. Decisions of the Security Council on all other matters shall be made by an affirmative vote of *nine* members including the concurring votes of the permanent members; provided that, in decisions under Chapter VI, and under paragraph 3 of Article 52, a party to a dispute shall abstain from voting.

Procedure

ARTICLE 28

1. The Security Council shall be so organized as to be able to function continuously. Each member of the Security Council shall for this purpose be represented at all times at the seat of the Organization.

2. The Security Council shall hold periodic meetings at which each of its members may, if it so desires, be represented by a member of the government or by some other specially designated representative.

3. The Security Council may hold meetings at such places other than the seat of the Organization as in its judgment will best facilitate its work.

ARTICLE 29

The Security Council may establish such subsidiary organs as it deems necessary for the performance of its functions.

ARTICLE 30

The Security Council shall adopt its own rules of procedure, including the method of selecting its President.

---

[2] Article 27(2) and (3) originally specified affirmative votes of *seven* members. The current version came into force on 31 Aug. 1965.

ARTICLE 31

Any Member of the United Nations which is not a member of the Security Council may participate, without vote, in the discussion of any question brought before the Security Council whenever the latter considers that the interests of that Member are specially affected.

ARTICLE 32

Any Member of the United Nations which is not a member of the Security Council or any state which is not a Member of the United Nations, if it is a party to a dispute under consideration by the Security Council, shall be invited to participate, without vote, in the discussion relating to the dispute. The Security Council shall lay down such conditions as it deems just for the participation of a state which is not a Member of the United Nations.

Chapter VI
Pacific Settlement of Disputes

ARTICLE 33

1. The parties to any dispute, the continuance of which is likely to endanger the maintenance of international peace and security, shall, first of all, seek a solution by negotiation, enquiry, mediation, conciliation, arbitration, judicial settlement, resort to regional agencies or arrangements, or other peaceful means of their own choice.

2. The Security Council shall, when it deems necessary, call upon the parties to settle their dispute by such means.

ARTICLE 34

The Security Council may investigate any dispute or any situation which might lead to international friction or give rise to a dispute, in order to determine whether the continuance of the dispute or situation is likely to endanger the maintenance of international peace and security.

ARTICLE 35

1. Any Member of the United Nations may bring any dispute, or any situation of the nature referred to in Article 34, to the attention of the Security Council or of the General Assembly.

2. A state which is not a Member of the United Nations may bring to the attention of the Security Council or of the General Assembly any dispute to which it is a party if it accepts in advance, for the purposes of the dispute, the obligations of pacific settlement provided in the present Charter.

3. The proceedings of the General Assembly in respect of matters brought to its attention under this Article will be subject to the provisions of Articles 11 and 12.

ARTICLE 36

1. The Security Council may, at any stage of a dispute of the nature referred to in Article 33 or of a situation of like nature, recommend appropriate procedures or methods of adjustment.

2. The Security Council should take into consideration any procedures for the settlement of the dispute which have already been adopted by the parties.

3. In making recommendations under this Article the Security Council should also take into consideration that legal disputes should as a general rule be referred by the parties to the International Court of Justice in accordance with the provisions of the Statute of the Court.

ARTICLE 37

1. Should the parties to a dispute of the nature referred to in Article 33 fail to settle it by the means indicated in that Article, they shall refer it to the Security Council.

2. If the Security Council deems that the continuance of the dispute is in fact likely to endanger the maintenance of international peace and security, it shall decide whether to take action under Article 36 or to recommend such terms of settlement as it may consider appropriate.

ARTICLE 38

Without prejudice to the provisions of Articles 33 to 37, the Security Council may, if all the parties to any dispute so request, make recommendations to the parties with a view to a pacific settlement of the dispute.

Chapter VII
Action with Respect to Threats to the Peace, Breaches of the Peace, and Acts of Aggression

ARTICLE 39

The Security Council shall determine the existence of any threat to the peace, breach of the peace, or act of aggression and shall make recommendations, or decide what measures shall be taken in accordance with Articles 41 and 42, to maintain or restore international peace and security.

ARTICLE 40

In order to prevent an aggravation of the situation, the Security Council may, before making the recommendations or deciding upon the measures provided for in Article 39, call upon the parties concerned to comply with such provisional measures as it deems necessary or desirable. Such provisional measures shall be without prejudice to the rights, claims, or position of the parties concerned. The Security Council shall duly take account of failure to comply with such provisional measures.

ARTICLE 41

The Security Council may decide what measures not involving the use of armed force are to be employed to give effect to its decisions, and it may call upon the Members of the United Nations to apply such measures. These may include complete or partial interruption of economic relations and of rail, sea, air, postal, telegraphic, radio, and other means of communication, and the severance of diplomatic relations.

ARTICLE 42

Should the Security Council consider that measures provided for in Article 41 would be inadequate or have proved to be inadequate, it may take such action by air, sea, or land forces as may be necessary to maintain or restore international peace and security. Such action may include demonstrations, blockade, and other operations by, air, sea, or land forces of Members of the United Nations.

ARTICLE 43

1. All Members of the United Nations, in order to contribute to the maintenance of international peace and security, undertake to make available to the Security Council, on its call and in accordance with a special agreement or agreements, armed forces, assistance, and facilities, including rights of passage, necessary for the purpose of maintaining international peace and security.

2. Such agreement or agreements shall govern the numbers and types of forces, their degree of readiness and general location, and the nature of the facilities and assistance to be provided.

3. The agreement or agreements shall be negotiated as soon as possible on the initiative of the Security Council. They shall be concluded between the Security Council and Members or between the Security Council and groups of Members and shall be subject to ratification by the signatory states in accordance with their respective constitutional processes.

ARTICLE 44

When the Security Council has decided to use force it shall, before calling upon a Member not represented on it to provide armed forces in fulfilment of the obligations assumed under Article 43, invite that Member, if the Member so desires, to participate in the decisions of the Security Council concerning the employment of contingents of that Member's armed forces.

ARTICLE 45

In order to enable the United Nations to take urgent military measures, Members shall hold immediately available national air-force contingents for combined international enforcement action. The strength and degree of readiness of these contingents and plans for their combined action shall be determined, within the limits laid down in the special agreement or agreements referred to in Article 43, by the Security Council with the assistance of the Military Staff Committee.

ARTICLE 46

Plans for the application of armed force shall be made by the Security Council with the assistance of the Military Staff Committee.

ARTICLE 47

1. There shall be established a Military Staff Committee to advise and assist the Security Council on all questions relating to the Security Council's military requirements for the maintenance of international peace and security, the employment and command of forces placed at its disposal, the regulation of armaments, and possible disarmament.

2. The Military Staff Committee shall consist of the Chiefs of Staff of the permanent members of the Security Council or their representatives. Any Member of the United Nations not permanently represented on the Committee shall be invited by the Committee to be associated with it when the efficient discharge of the Committee's responsibilities requires the participation of that Member in its work.

3. The Military Staff Committee shall be responsible under the Security Council for the strategic direction of any armed forces placed at the disposal of the Security Council. Questions relating to the command of such forces shall be worked out subsequently.

4. The Military Staff Committee, with the authorization of the Security Council and after consultation with appropriate regional agencies, may establish regional sub-committees.

ARTICLE 48

1. The action required to carry out the decisions of the Security Council for the maintenance of international peace and security shall be taken by all the Members of the United Nations or by some of them, as the Security Council may determine.

2. Such decisions shall be carried out by the Members of the United Nations directly and through their action in the appropriate international agencies of which they are members.

ARTICLE 49

The Members of the United Nations shall join in affording mutual assistance in carrying out the measures decided upon by the Security Council.

ARTICLE 50

If preventive or enforcement measures against any state are taken by the Security Council, any other state, whether a Member of the United Nations or not, which finds itself confronted with special economic problems arising from the carrying out of those measures shall have the right to consult the Security Council with regard to a solution of those problems.

ARTICLE 51

Nothing in the present Charter shall impair the inherent right of individual or collective self-defence if an armed attack occurs against a Member of the United Nations, until the Security Council has taken measures necessary to maintain international peace and security. Measures taken by Members in the exercise of this right of self-defence shall be immediately reported to the Security Council and shall not in any way affect the authority and responsibility of the Security Council under the present Charter to take at any time such action as it deems necessary in order to maintain or restore international peace and security.

Chapter VIII
Regional Arrangements

ARTICLE 52

1. Nothing in the present Charter precludes the existence of regional arrangements or agencies for dealing with such matters relating to the maintenance of international peace and security as are appropriate for regional action, provided that such arrangements or agencies and their activities are consistent with the Purposes and Principles of the United Nations.

2. The Members of the United Nations entering into such arrangements or constituting such agencies shall make every effort to achieve pacific settlement of local disputes through such regional arrangements or by such regional agencies before referring them to the Security Council.

3. The Security Council shall encourage the development of pacific settlement of local disputes through such regional arrangements or by such regional agencies either on the initiative of the states concerned or by reference from the Security Council.

4. This Article in no way impairs the application of Articles 34 and 35.

ARTICLE 53

1. The Security Council shall, where appropriate, utilize such regional arrangements or agencies for enforcement action under its authority. But no enforcement action shall be taken under regional arrangements or by regional agencies without the authorization of the Security Council, with the exception of measures against any enemy state, as defined in paragraph 2 of this Article, provided for pursuant to Article 107 or in regional arrangements directed against renewal of aggressive policy on the part of any such state, until such time as the Organization may, on request of the Governments concerned, be charged with the responsibility for preventing further aggression by such a state.

2. The term enemy state as used in paragraph 1 of this Article applies to any state which during the Second World War has been an enemy of any signatory of the present Charter.

ARTICLE 54

The Security Council shall at all times be kept fully informed of activities undertaken or in contemplation under regional arrangements or by regional agencies for the maintenance of international peace and security.

Chapter IX
International Economic and Social Co-operation

ARTICLE 55

With a view to the creation of conditions of stability and well-being which are necessary for peaceful and friendly relations among nations based on respect for the principle of equal rights and self-determination of peoples, the United Nations shall promote:

(a) higher standards of living, full employment, and conditions of economic and social progress and development;

(b) solutions of international economic, social, health, and related problems; and international cultural and educational co-operation; and

(c) universal respect for, and observance of, human rights and fundamental freedoms for all without distinction as to race, sex, language, or religion.

ARTICLE 56

All Members pledge themselves to take joint and separate action in co-operation with the Organization for the achievement of the purposes set forth in Article 55.

ARTICLE 57

1. The various specialized agencies, established by intergovernmental agreement and having wide international responsibilities, as defined in their basic instruments, in economic, social, cultural, educational, health, and related fields, shall be brought into relationship with the United Nations in accordance with the provisions of Article 63.

2. Such agencies thus brought into relationship with the United Nations are hereinafter referred to as specialized agencies.

ARTICLE 58

The Organization shall make recommendations for the co-ordination of the policies and activities of the specialized agencies.

ARTICLE 59

The Organization shall, where appropriate, initiate negotiations among the states concerned for the creation of any new specialized agencies required for the accomplishment of the purposes set forth in Article 55.

ARTICLE 60

Responsibility for the discharge of the functions of the Organization set forth in this Chapter shall be vested in the General Assembly and, under the authority of the General Assembly, in the Economic and Social Council, which shall have for this purpose the powers set forth in Chapter X.

Chapter X
The Economic and Social Council

Composition

ARTICLE 61[3]

1. The Economic and Social Council shall consist of *fifty-four* Members of the United Nations elected by the General Assembly.

2. Subject to the provisions of paragraph 3, *eighteen* members of the Economic and Social Council shall be elected each year for a term of three years. A retiring member shall be eligible for immediate re-election.

3. *At the first election after the increase in the membership of the Economic and Social Council from twenty-seven to fifty-four members, in addition to the members elected in place of the nine members whose term of office expires at the end of that year, twenty-seven additional members shall be elected. Of these twenty-seven additional members, the term of office of nine members so elected shall expire at the end of one year, and of nine other members at the end of two years, in accordance with arrangements made by the General Assembly.*

[3]. Article 61 has been amended twice.

In the original version Article 61(1) specified that ECOSOC shall consist of *eighteen* members; 61(2) specified that *six* shall be elected each year; and 61(3) read as follows: 'At the first election, eighteen members of the Economic and Social Council shall be chosen. The term of office of six members so chosen shall expire at the end of one year, and of six other members at the end of two years, in accordance with arrangements made by the General Assembly.'

On 31 Aug. 1965 an amended version came into force, in which Article 61(1) specified that ECOSOC shall consist of *twenty-seven* members; 61(2) specified that *nine* shall be elected each year; and 61(3) read as follows: 'At the first election after the increase in the membership of the Economic and Social Council from eighteen to twenty-seven members, in addition to the members elected in place of the six members whose term of office expires at the end of that year, nine additional members shall be elected. Of these nine additional members, the term of office of three members so elected shall expire at the end of one year, and of three other members at the end of two years, in accordance with arrangements made by the General Assembly.'

The current version came into force on 24 Sept. 1973.

4. Each member of the Economic and Social Council shall have one representative.

Functions and Powers

ARTICLE 62

1. The Economic and Social Council may make or initiate studies and reports with respect to international economic, social, cultural, educational, health, and related matters and may make recommendations with respect to any such matters to the General Assembly, to the Members of the United Nations, and to the specialized agencies concerned.

2. It may make recommendations for the purpose of promoting respect for, and observance of, human rights and fundamental freedoms for all.

3. It may prepare draft conventions for submission to the General Assembly, with respect to matters falling within its competence.

4. It may call, in accordance with the rules prescribed by the United Nations, international conferences on matters falling within its competence.

ARTICLE 63

1. The Economic and Social Council may enter into agreements with any of the agencies referred to in Article 57, defining the terms on which the agency concerned shall be brought into relationship with the United Nations. Such agreements shall be subject to approval by the General Assembly.

2. It may co-ordinate the activities of the specialized agencies through consultation with and recommendations to such agencies and through recommendations to the General Assembly and to the Members of the United Nations.

ARTICLE 64

1. The Economic and Social Council may take appropriate steps to obtain regular reports from the specialized agencies. It may make arrangements with the Members of the United Nations and with the specialized agencies to obtain reports on the steps taken to give effect to its own recommendations and to recommendations on matters falling within its competence made by the General Assembly.

2. It may communicate its observations on these reports to the General Assembly.

ARTICLE 65

The Economic and Social Council may furnish information to the Security Council and shall assist the Security Council upon its request.

ARTICLE 66

1. The Economic and Social Council shall perform such functions as fall within its competence in connexion with the carrying out of the recommendations of the General Assembly.

2. It may, with the approval of the General Assembly, perform services at the request of Members of the United Nations and at the request of specialized agencies.

3. It shall perform such other functions as are specified elsewhere in the present Charter or as may be assigned to it by the General Assembly.

Voting

ARTICLE 67

1. Each member of the Economic and Social Council shall have one vote.

2. Decisions of the Economic and Social Council shall be made by a majority of the members present and voting.

Procedure

ARTICLE 68

The Economic and Social Council shall set up commissions in economic and social fields and for the promotion of human rights, and such other commissions as may be required for the performance of its functions.

ARTICLE 69

The Economic and Social Council shall invite any Member of the United Nations to participate, without vote, in its deliberations on any matter of particular concern to that Member.

ARTICLE 70

The Economic and Social Council may make arrangements for representatives of the specialized agencies to participate, without vote, in its deliberations and in those of the commissions established by it, and for its representatives to participate in the deliberations of the specialized agencies.

ARTICLE 71

The Economic and Social Council may make suitable arrangements for consultation with non-governmental organizations which are concerned with matters within its competence. Such arrangements may be made with international organizations and, where appropriate, with national organizations after consultation with the Member of the United Nations concerned.

ARTICLE 72

1. The Economic and Social Council shall adopt its own rules of procedure, including the method of selecting its President.

2. The Economic and Social Council shall meet as required in accordance with its rules, which shall include provision for the convening of meetings on the request of a majority of its members.

Chapter XI
Declaration regarding Non-self-governing Territories

ARTICLE 73

Members of the United Nations which have or assume responsibilities for the administration of territories whose peoples have not yet attained a full measure of self-government recognize the principle that the interests of the inhabitants of these territories are paramount, and accept as a sacred trust the obligation to promote to the utmost, within the system of international peace and security established by the present Charter, the well-being of the inhabitants of these territories, and, to this end:

(a) to ensure, with due respect for the culture of the peoples concerned, their political, economic, social, and educational advancement, their just treatment, and their protection against abuses;

(b) to develop self-government, to take due account of the political aspirations of the peoples, and to assist them in the progressive development of their free political institutions, according to the particular circumstances of each territory and its peoples and their varying stages of advancement;

(c) to further international peace and security;

(d) to promote constructive measures of development, to encourage research, and to co-operate with one another and, when and where appropriate, with specialized international bodies with a view to the practical achievement of the social, economic, and scientific purposes set forth in this Article; and

(e) to transmit regularly to the Secretary-General for information purposes, subject to such limitation as security and constitutional considerations may require, statistical and other information of a technical nature relating to economic, social, and educational conditions in the territories for which they are respectively responsible other than those territories to which Chapters XII and XIII apply.

ARTICLE 74

Members of the United Nations also agree that their policy in respect of the territories to which this Chapter applies, no less than in respect of their metropolitan areas, must be based on the general principle of good-neighbourliness, due account being taken of the interests and well-being of the rest of the world, in social, economic, and commercial matters.

Chapter XII
International Trusteeship System

ARTICLE 75

The United Nations shall establish under its authority an international trusteeship system for the administration and supervision of such territories as may be placed thereunder by subsequent individual agreements. These territories are hereinafter referred to as trust territories.

ARTICLE 76

The basic objectives of the trusteeship system, in accordance with the Purposes of the United Nations laid down in Article 1 of the present Charter, shall be:

(a) to further international peace and security;

(b) to promote the political, economic, social, and educational advancement of the inhabitants of the trust territories, and their progressive development towards self-government or independence as may be appropriate to the particular circumstances of each territory and its peoples and the freely expressed wishes of the peoples concerned, and as may be provided by the terms of each trusteeship agreement;

(c) to encourage respect for human rights and for fundamental freedoms for all without distinction as to race, sex, language, or religion, and to encourage recognition of the interdependence of the peoples of the world; and

(d) to ensure equal treatment in social, economic, and commercial matters for all Members of the United Nations and their nationals, and also equal treatment for the latter in the administration of justice, without prejudice to the attainment of the foregoing objectives and subject to the provisions of Article 80.

ARTICLE 77

1. The trusteeship system shall apply to such territories in the following categories as may be placed thereunder by means of trusteeship agreements:

(a) territories now held under mandate;

(b) territories which may be detached from enemy states as a result of the Second World War; and

(c) territories voluntarily placed under the system by states responsible for their administration.

2. It will be a matter for subsequent agreement as to which territories in the foregoing categories will be brought under the trusteeship system and upon what terms.

ARTICLE 78

The trusteeship system shall not apply to territories which have become Members of the United Nations, relationship among which shall be based on respect for the principle of sovereign equality.

ARTICLE 79

The terms of trusteeship for each territory to be placed under the trusteeship system, including any alteration or amendment, shall be agreed upon by the states directly concerned, including the mandatory power in the case of territories held under mandate by a Member of the United Nations, and shall be approved as provided for in Articles 83 and 85.

ARTICLE 80

1. Except as may be agreed upon in individual trusteeship agreements, made under Articles 77, 79, and 81, placing each territory under the trusteeship system, and until such agreements have been concluded, nothing in this Chapter shall be construed in or of itself to alter in any manner the rights whatsoever of any states or any peoples or the terms of existing

international instruments to which Members of the United Nations may respectively be parties.

2. Paragraph 1 of this Article shall not be interpreted as giving grounds for delay or postponement of the negotiation and conclusion of agreements for placing mandated and other territories under the trusteeship system as provided for in Article 77.

ARTICLE 81

The trusteeship agreement shall in each case include the terms under which the trust territory will be administered and designate the authority which will exercise the administration of the trust territory. Such authority, hereinafter called the administering authority, may be one or more states or the Organization itself.

ARTICLE 82

There may be designated, in any trusteeship agreement, a strategic area or areas which may include part or all of the trust territory to which the agreement applies, without prejudice to any special agreement or agreements made under Article 43.

ARTICLE 83

1. All functions of the United Nations relating to strategic areas, including the approval of the terms of the trusteeship agreements and of their alteration or amendments, shall be exercised by the Security Council.

2. The basic objectives set forth in Article 76 shall be applicable to the people of each strategic area.

3. The Security Council shall, subject to the provisions of the trusteeship agreements and without prejudice to security considerations, avail itself of the assistance of the Trusteeship Council to perform those functions of the United Nations under the trusteeship system relating to political, economic, social, and educational matters in the strategic areas.

ARTICLE 84

It shall be the duty of the administering authority to ensure that the trust territory shall play its part in the maintenance of international peace and security. To this end the administering authority may make use of volunteer forces, facilities, and assistance from the trust territory in carrying out the obligations towards the Security Council undertaken in this regard by the administering authority, as well as for local defence and the maintenance of law and order within the trust territory.

ARTICLE 85

1. The functions of the United Nations with regard to trusteeship agreements for all areas not designated as strategic, including the approval of the terms of the trusteeship agreements and of their alteration or amendment, shall be exercised by the General Assembly.

2. The Trusteeship Council, operating under the authority of the General Assembly, shall assist the General Assembly in carrying out these functions.

Chapter XIII
The Trusteeship Council

Composition

ARTICLE 86

1. The Trusteeship Council shall consist of the following Members of the United Nations:

- (*a*) those Members administering trust territories;
- (*b*) such of those Members mentioned by name in Article 23 as are not administering trust territories; and
- (*c*) as many other Members elected for three-year terms by the General Assembly as may be necessary to ensure that the total number of members of the Trusteeship Council is equally divided between those Members of the United Nations which administer trust territories and those which do not.

2. Each member of the Trusteeship Council shall designate one specially qualified person to represent it therein.

Functions and powers

ARTICLE 87

The General Assembly and, under its authority, the Trusteeship Council, in carrying out their functions, may:

- (*a*) consider reports submitted by the administering authority;
- (*b*) accept petitions and examine them in consultation with the administering authority;

(c) provide for periodic visits to the respective trust territories at times agreed upon with the administering authority; and

(d) take these and other actions in conformity with the terms of the trusteeship agreements.

ARTICLE 88

The Trusteeship Council shall formulate a questionnaire on the political, economic, social, and educational advancement of the inhabitants of each trust territory, and the administering authority for each trust territory within the competence of the General Assembly shall make an annual report to the General Assembly upon the basis of such questionnaire.

Voting

ARTICLE 89

1. Each member of the Trusteeship Council shall have one vote.

2. Decisions of the Trusteeship Council shall be made by a majority of the members present and voting.

Procedure

ARTICLE 90

1. The Trusteeship Council shall adopt its own rules of procedure, including the method of selecting its President.

2. The Trusteeship Council shall meet as required in accordance with its rules, which shall include provision for the convening of meetings on the request of a majority of its members.

ARTICLE 91

The Trusteeship Council shall, when appropriate, avail itself of the assistance of the Economic and Social Council and of the specialized agencies in regard to matters with which they are respectively concerned.

Chapter XIV
The International Court of Justice

ARTICLE 92

The International Court of Justice shall be the principal judicial organ of the United Nations. It shall function in accordance with the annexed Statute, which is based upon the Statute of the Permanent Court of International Justice and forms an integral part of the present Charter.

ARTICLE 93

1. All Members of the United Nations are *ipso facto* parties to the Statute of the International Court of Justice.

2. A state which is not a Member of the United Nations may become a party to the Statute of the International Court of Justice on conditions to be determined in each case by the General Assembly upon the recommendation of the Security Council.

ARTICLE 94

1. Each Member of the United Nations undertakes to comply with the decision of the International Court of Justice in any case to which it is party.

2. If any party to a case fails to perform the obligations incumbent upon it under a judgement rendered by the Court, the other party may have recourse to the Security Council, which may, if it deems necessary, make recommendations or decide upon measures to be taken to give effect to the judgment.

ARTICLE 95

Nothing in the present Charter shall prevent Members of the United Nations from entrusting the solution of their differences to other tribunals by virtue of agreements already in existence or which may be concluded in the future.

ARTICLE 96

1. The General Assembly or the Security Council may request the International Court of Justice to give an advisory opinion on any legal question.

2. Other organs of the United Nations and specialized agencies, which may at any time be so authorized by the General Assembly, may also request advisory opinions of the Court on legal questions arising within the scope of their activities.

Chapter XV
The Secretariat

ARTICLE 97

The Secretariat shall comprise a Secretary-General and such staff as the Organization may require. The Secretary-General shall be appointed by the General Assembly upon the recommendation of the Security Council. He shall be the chief administrative officer of the Organization.

ARTICLE 98

The Secretary-General shall act in that capacity in all meetings of the General Assembly, of the Security Council, of the Economic and Social Council, and of the Trusteeship Council, and shall perform such other functions as are entrusted to him by these organs. The Secretary-General shall make an annual report to the General Assembly on the work of the Organization.

ARTICLE 99

The Secretary-General may bring to the attention of the Security Council any matter which in his opinion may threaten the maintenance of international peace and security.

ARTICLE 100

1. In the performance of their duties the Secretary-General and the staff shall not seek or receive instructions from any government or from any other authority external to the Organization. They shall refrain from any action which might reflect on their position as international officials responsible only to the Organization.

2. Each Member of the United Nations undertakes to respect the exclusively international character of the responsibilities of the Secretary-General and the staff and not to seek to influence them in the discharge of their responsibilities.

ARTICLE 101

1. The staff shall be appointed by the Secretary-General under regulations established by the General Assembly.

2. Appropriate staffs shall be permanently assigned to the Economic and Social Council, the Trusteeship Council, and, as required, to other organs of the United Nations. These staffs shall form a part of the Secretariat.

3. The paramount consideration in the employment of the staff and in the determination of the conditions of service shall be the necessity of securing the highest standards of efficiency, competence, and integrity. Due regard shall be paid to the importance of recruiting the staff on as wide a geographical basis as possible.

Chapter XVI
Miscellaneous Provisions

ARTICLE 102

1. Every treaty and every international agreement entered into by any Member of the United Nations after the present Charter comes into force shall as soon as possible be registered with the Secretariat and published by it.

2. No party to any such treaty or international agreement which has not been registered in accordance with the provisions of paragraph 1 of this Article may invoke that treaty or agreement before any organ of the United Nations.

ARTICLE 103

In the event of a conflict between the obligations of the Members of the United Nations under the present Charter and their obligations under any other international agreement, their obligations under the present Charter shall prevail.

ARTICLE 104

The Organization shall enjoy in the territory of each of its Members such legal capacity as may be necessary for the exercise of its functions and the fulfilment of its purposes.

ARTICLE 105

1. The Organization shall enjoy in the territory of each of its Members such privileges and immunities as are necessary for the fulfilment of its purposes.

2. Representatives of the Members of the United Nations and officials of the Organization shall similarly enjoy such privileges and immunities as are necessary for the independent exercise of their functions in connexion with the Organization.

3. The General Assembly may make recommendations with a view to determining the details of the application of paragraphs 1 and 2 of this Article or may propose conventions to the Members of the United Nations for this purpose.

Chapter XVII
Transitional Security Arrangements

ARTICLE 106

Pending the coming into force of such special agreements referred to in Article 43 as in the opinion of the Security Council enable it to begin the exercise of its responsibilities under Article 42, the parties to the Four-Nation Declaration, signed at Moscow, 30 October 1943, and France, shall, in accordance with the provisions of paragraph 5 of that Declaration, consult with one another and as occasion requires with other Members of the United Nations with a view to such joint action on behalf of the Organization as may be necessary for the purpose of maintaining international peace and security.

ARTICLE 107

Nothing in the present Charter shall invalidate or preclude action, in relation to any state which during the Second World War has been an enemy of any signatory to the present Charter, taken or authorized as a result of that war by the Governments having responsibility for such action.

Chapter XVIII
Amendments

ARTICLE 108

Amendments to the present Charter shall come into force for all Members of the United Nations when they have been adopted by a vote of two thirds of the members of the General Assembly and ratified in accordance with their respective constitutional processes by two thirds of the Members of the United Nations, including all the permanent members of the Security Council.

ARTICLE 109[4]

1. A General Conference of the Members of the United Nations for the purpose of reviewing the present Charter may be held at a date and place to be fixed by a two-thirds vote of the members of the General Assembly and by a vote of any *nine* members of the Security Council. Each Member of the United Nations shall have one vote in the conference.

2. Any alteration of the present Charter recommended by a two thirds vote of the conference shall take effect when ratified in accordance with their respective constitutional processes by two-thirds of the Members of the United Nations including all the permanent members of the Security Council.

[4] Article 109(1) originally specified a vote of any *seven* members of the Security Council. The current version came into force on 12 June 1968.

3. If such a conference has not been held before the tenth annual session of the General Assembly following the coming into force of the present Charter, the proposal to call such a conference shall be placed on the agenda of that session of the General Assembly, and the conference shall be held if so decided by a majority vote of the members of the General Assembly and by a vote of any seven members of the Security Council.

Chapter XIX
Ratification and Signature

ARTICLE 110

1. The present Charter shall be ratified by the signatory states in accordance with their respective constitutional processes.

2. The ratifications shall be deposited with the Government of the United States of America, which shall notify all the signatory states of each deposit as well as the Secretary-General of the Organization when he has been appointed.

3. The present Charter shall come into force upon the deposit of ratifications by the Republic of China, France, the Union of Soviet Socialist Republics, the United Kingdom of Great Britain and Northern Ireland, and the United States of America, and by a majority of the other signatory states. A protocol of the ratifications deposited shall thereupon be drawn up by the Government of the United States of America which shall communicate copies thereof to all the signatory states.

4. The states signatory to the present Charter which ratify it after it has come into force will become original Members of the United Nations on the date of the deposit of their respective ratifications.

ARTICLE 111

The present Charter, of which the Chinese, French, Russian, English, and Spanish texts are equally authentic, shall remain deposited in the archives of the Government of the United States of America. Duly certified copies thereof shall be transmitted by that Government to the Governments of the other signatory states.

IN FAITH WHEREOF the representatives of the Governments of the United Nations have signed the present Charter.

DONE at the city of San Francisco the twenty-sixth day of June, one thousand nine hundred and forty-five.

Appendix C

Member States of the United Nations

The 184 states members of the UN are listed below, with the dates on which they became members, and the percentage contribution to the UN's regular budget assessed for each state by the UN General Assembly in 1993. (An asterisk denotes an original member, as per Article 110 of the Charter.)

Member	Date of admission	% assessed
Afghanistan	19 Nov. 1946	0.01
Albania	14 Dec. 1955	0.01
Algeria	8 Oct. 1962	0.16
Andorra[1]	28 July 1993	—
Angola	1 Dec. 1976	0.01
Antigua and Barbuda	11 Nov. 1981	0.01
*Argentina	24 Oct. 1945	0.57
Armenia	2 Mar. 1992	0.13
*Australia	1 Nov. 1945	1.51
Austria	14 Dec. 1955	0.75
Azerbaijan	2 Mar. 1992	0.22
Bahamas	18 Sept. 1973	0.02
Bahrain	21 Sept. 1971	0.03
Bangladesh	17 Sept. 1974	0.01
Barbardos	9 Dec. 1966	0.01
*Belarus[2]	24 Oct. 1945	0.48
*Belgium	27 Dec. 1945	1.06
Belize	25 Sept. 1981	0.01
Benin[3]	20 Sept. 1960	0.01
Bhutan	21 Sept. 1971	0.01
*Bolivia	14 Nov. 1945	0.01
Bosnia and Herzegovina	22 May 1992	0.04
Botswana	17 Oct. 1966	0.01
*Brazil	24 Oct. 1945	1.59
Brunei Darussalam	21 Sept. 1984	0.03
Bulgaria	14 Dec. 1955	0.13

Note: This information is based in part on material supplied by the UN Department of Public Information, and was current as of 31 July 1993.
[1] Contribution expected to be 0.01%.
[2] On 19 Sept. 1991 Byelorussia informed the UN that it had changed its name to Belarus.　　　　　　　　　　　　　　　　[3] Formerly Dahomey.

Member	Date of admission	% assessed
Burkina Faso[4]	20 Sept. 1960	0.01
Burundi	18 Sept. 1962	0.01
Cambodia[5]	14 Dec. 1955	0.01
Cameroon	20 Sept. 1960	0.01
*Canada	9 Nov. 1945	3.11
Cape Verde	16 Sept. 1975	0.01
Central African Republic	20 Sept. 1960	0.01
Chad	20 Sept. 1960	0.01
*Chile	24 Oct. 1945	0.08
*China[6]	24 Oct. 1945	0.77
*Colombia	5 Nov. 1945	0.13
Comoros	12 Nov. 1975	0.01
Congo	20 Sept. 1960	0.01
*Costa Rica	2 Nov. 1945	0.01
Côte d'Ivoire	20 Sept. 1960	0.02
Croatia	22 May 1992	0.13
*Cuba	24 Oct. 1945	0.09
Cyprus	20 Sept. 1960	0.02
Czech Republic[7]	19 Jan. 1993	—
Democratic People's Republic of Korea	17 Sept. 1991	0.05
*Denmark	24 Oct. 1945	0.65
Djibouti	20 Sept. 1977	0.01
Dominica	18 Dec. 1978	0.01
*Dominican Republic	24 Oct. 1945	0.02
*Ecuador	21 Dec. 1945	0.03
*Egypt[8]	24 Oct. 1945	0.07

[4] Formerly Upper Volta.

[5] In the late 1970s and the 1980s, Democratic Kampuchea.

[6] By Res. 2758 (XXVI) of 25 Oct. 1971, the General Assembly decided 'to restore all its rights to the People's Republic of China and to recognize the representatives of its Government as the only legitimate representatives of China to the United Nations, and to expel forthwith the representatives of Chiang Kai-shek from the place which they unlawfully occupy at the United Nations and in all the organizations related to it'.

[7] Czechoslovakia was an original member of the UN from 24 Oct. 1945. After the bifurcation of Czechoslovakia on 1 Jan. 1993, the Czech Republic and the Slovak Republic each applied for, and obtained, membership of the UN as new members. It is expected that the contribution assessed for Czechoslovakia (0.55%) will be divided between these two states.

[8] Egypt and Syria were original members of the UN from 24 Oct. 1945. Following a plebiscite on 21 Feb. 1958, the United Arab Republic was established by a union of Egypt and Syria and continued as a single member. On 13 Oct. 1961, Syria, having resumed its status as an independent state, resumed its separate membership in the United Nations. On 2 Sept. 1971 the United Arab Republic changed its name to the Arab Republic of Egypt.

Member	Date of admission	% assessed
*El Salvador	24 Oct. 1945	0.01
Equatorial Guinea	12 Nov. 1968	0.01
Eritrea[9]	28 May 1993	—
Estonia	17 Sept. 1991	0.07
*Ethiopia	13 Nov. 1945	0.01
Federated States of Micronesia	17 Sept. 1991	0.01
Fiji	13 Oct. 1970	0.01
Finland	14 Dec. 1955	0.57
*France	24 Oct. 1945	6.00
Gabon	20 Sept. 1960	0.02
Gambia	21 Sept. 1965	0.01
Georgia	31 July 1992	0.21
Germany[10]	18 Sept. 1973	8.93
Ghana	8 Mar. 1957	0.01
*Greece	25 Oct. 1945	0.35
Grenada	17 Sept. 1974	0.01
*Guatemala	21 Nov. 1945	0.02
Guinea	12 Dec. 1958	0.01
Guinea-Bissau	17 Sept. 1974	0.01
Guyana	20 Sept. 1966	0.01
*Haiti	24 Oct. 1945	0.01
*Honduras	17 Dec. 1945	0.01
Hungary	14 Dec. 1955	0.18
Iceland	19 Nov. 1946	0.03
*India	30 Oct. 1945	0.36
Indonesia[11]	28 Sept. 1950	0.16
*Iran	24 Oct. 1945	0.77
*Iraq	21 Dec. 1945	0.13
Ireland	14 Dec. 1955	0.18
Israel	11 May 1949	0.23
Italy	14 Dec. 1955	4.29
Jamaica	18 Sept. 1962	0.01

[9] Contribution expected to be 0.01%.

[10] The Federal Republic of Germany and the German Democratic Republic were admitted to membership in the UN on 18 Sept. 1973. Through the accession of the German Democratic Republic to the Federal Republic of Germany, effective from 3 Oct. 1990, the two German states united to form one sovereign state.

[11] By letter of 20 Jan. 1965 Indonesia announced its decision to withdraw from the UN 'at this stage and under the present circumstances'. By telegram of 19 Sept. 1966 it announced its decision 'to resume full cooperation with the United Nations and to resume participation in its activities'. On 28 Sept. 1966 the General Assembly took note of this decision and the President invited representatives of Indonesia to take seats in the Assembly.

Member	Date of admission	% assessed
Japan	18 Dec. 1956	12.45
Jordan	14 Dec. 1955	0.01
Kazakhstan	2 Mar. 1992	0.35
Kenya	16 Dec. 1963	0.01
Kuwait	14 May 1963	0.25
Kyrgyzstan	2 Mar. 1992	0.06
Lao People's Democratic Republic	14 Dec. 1955	0.01
Latvia	17 Sept. 1991	0.13
*Lebanon	24 Oct. 1945	0.01
Lesotho	17 Oct. 1966	0.01
*Liberia	2 Nov. 1945	0.01
Libya	14 Dec. 1955	0.24
Liechtenstein	18 Sept. 1990	0.01
Lithuania	17 Sept. 1991	0.15
*Luxembourg	24 Oct. 1945	0.06
Madagascar	20 Sept. 1960	0.01
Malawi	1 Dec. 1964	0.01
Malaysia[12]	17 Sept. 1957	0.12
Maldives	21 Sept. 1965	0.01
Mali	28 Sept. 1960	0.01
Malta	1 Dec. 1964	0.01
Marshall Islands	17 Sept. 1991	0.01
Mauritania	27 Oct. 1961	0.01
Mauritius	24 Apr. 1968	0.01
*Mexico	7 Nov. 1945	0.88
Moldova	2 Mar. 1992	0.15
Monaco[13]	28 May 1993	—
Mongolia	27 Oct. 1961	0.01
Morocco	12 Nov. 1956	0.03
Mozambique	16 Sept. 1975	0.01
Myanmar[14]	19 Apr. 1948	0.01
Namibia	23 Apr. 1990	0.01
Nepal	14 Dec. 1955	0.01
*Netherlands	10 Dec. 1945	1.50
*New Zealand	24 Oct. 1945	0.24
*Nicaragua	24 Oct. 1945	0.01
Niger	20 Sept. 1960	0.01

[12] The Federation of Malaya joined the UN on 17 Sept. 1957. On 16 Sept. 1963 its name was changed to Malaysia, following the admission to the new federation of Singapore, Sabah (North Borneo) and Sarawak. Singapore became an independent state on 9 Aug. 1965 and a UN member on 21 Sept. 1965.

[13] Contribution expected to be 0.01%.

[14] Formerly Burma.

Member	Date of admission		% assessed
Nigeria	7 Oct.	1960	0.20
*Norway	27 Nov.	1945	0.55
Oman	7 Oct.	1971	0.03
Pakistan	30 Sept.	1947	0.06
*Panama	13 Nov.	1945	0.02
Papua New Guinea	10 Oct.	1975	0.01
*Paraguay	24 Oct.	1945	0.02
*Peru	31 Oct.	1945	0.06
*Philippines	24 Oct.	1945	0.07
*Poland	24 Oct.	1945	0.47
Portugal	14 Dec.	1955	0.20
Qatar	21 Sept.	1971	0.05
Republic of Korea	17 Sept.	1991	0.69
Romania	14 Dec.	1955	0.17
*Russian Federation[15]	24 Oct.	1945	6.71
Rwanda	18 Sept.	1962	0.01
Saint Kitts and Nevis	23 Sept.	1983	0.01
Saint Lucia	18 Sept.	1979	0.01
Saint Vincent and the Grenadines	16 Sept.	1980	0.01
Samoa	15 Dec.	1976	0.01
San Marino	2 Mar.	1992	0.01
São Tomé and Príncipe	16 Sept.	1975	0.01
*Saudi Arabia	24 Oct.	1945	0.96
Senegal	28 Sept.	1960	0.01
Seychelles	21 Sept.	1976	0.01
Sierra Leone	27 Sept.	1961	0.01
Singapore	21 Sept.	1965	0.12
Slovak Republic[16]	19 Jan.	1993	—
Slovenia	22 May	1992	0.09
Solomon Islands	19 Sept.	1978	0.01
Somalia	20 Sept.	1960	0.01
*South Africa	7 Nov.	1945	0.41
Spain	14 Dec.	1955	1.98
Sri Lanka	14 Dec.	1955	0.01

[15] The Union of the Soviet Socialist Republics was an original Member of the UN from 24 Oct. 1945. In a letter dated 24 Dec. 1991 Boris Yeltsin, the President of the Russian Federation, informed the Secretary-General that the membership of the Soviet Union in the Security Council and all other UN organs was being continued by the Russian Federation with the support of the eleven member countries of the Commonwealth of Independent States. The USSR comprised fifteen republics: Russia; Belarus and Ukraine (both original members of the UN); and twelve other republics, each of which was admitted to membership of the UN in 1991 or 1992.   [16] See n. 7 above.

Member	Date of admission	% assessed
Sudan	12 Nov. 1956	0.01
Suriname[17]	4 Dec. 1975	0.01
Swaziland	24 Sept. 1968	0.01
Sweden	19 Nov. 1946	1.11
*Syria[18]	24 Oct. 1945	0.04
Tajikistan	2 Mar. 1992	0.05
Thailand	16 Dec. 1946	0.11
The former Yugoslav Republic of Macedonia[19]	8 Apr. 1993	—
Togo	20 Sept. 1960	0.01
Trinidad and Tobago	18 Sept. 1962	0.05
Tunisia	12 Nov. 1956	0.03
*Turkey	24 Oct. 1945	0.27
Turkmenistan	2 Mar. 1992	0.06
Uganda	25 Oct. 1962	0.01
*Ukraine	24 Oct. 1945	1.87
United Arab Emirates	9 Dec. 1971	0.21
*United Kingdom of Great Britain and Northern Ireland	24 Oct. 1945	5.02
United Republic of Tanzania[20]	14 Dec. 1961	0.01
*United States of America	24 Oct. 1945	25.00
*Uruguay	18 Dec. 1945	0.04
Uzbekistan	2 Mar. 1992	0.26
Vanuatu	15 Sept. 1981	0.01
*Venezuela	15 Nov. 1945	0.49
Viet Nam	20 Sept. 1977	0.01
Yemen[21]	30 Sept. 1947	0.01

[17] Formerly Surinam.

[18] See n. 8 above.

[19] Provisional name of the state for UN purposes: see SC Res. 817 of 7 Apr. 1993. Contribution not yet assessed. It is expected that the rate assessed will be deducted from that shown for Yugoslavia.

[20] Tanganyika was a member of the UN from 14 Dec. 1961 and Zanzibar was a member from 16 Dec. 1963. Following the ratification on 26 Apr. 1964 of Articles of Union between Tanganyika and Zanzibar, the United Republic of Tanganyika and Zanzibar continued as a single Member, changing its name to the United Republic of Tanzania on 1 Nov. 1964.

[21] Yemen was admitted to membership in the UN on 30 Sept. 1947 and Democratic Yemen (i.e. South Yemen) on 14 Dec. 1967. On 22 May 1990 the two countries merged and have since been represented as one member with the name 'Yemen'.

Member	Date of admission	% assessed
*Yugoslavia[22]	24 Oct. 1945	0.16
Zaïre	20 Sept. 1960	0.01
Zambia	1 Dec. 1964	0.01
Zimbabwe	25 Aug. 1980	0.01

[22] In accordance with a recommendation contained in SC Res. 777 (19 Sept. 1992) the General Assembly resolved (GA Res. 47/1, 22 Sept. 1992) that the Federal Republic of Yugoslavia (Serbia and Montenegro) could not continue automatically the membership of the former Socialist Federal Republic of Yugoslavia; that the Federal Republic of Yugoslavia (Serbia and Montenegro) should apply for membership; and that it should not participate in the work of the General Assembly. SC Res. 821 of 28 Apr. 1993 excluded the Federal Republic of Yugoslavia from participating in the work of ECOSOC for its summer session. Of the six constituent republics of the former Socialist Federal Republic of Yugoslavia, the following were admitted to membership of the UN in 1992 or 1993: Bosnia and Herzegovina; Croatia; the former Yugoslav Republic of Macedonia; Slovenia.

NOTE ON PEACEKEEPING ASSESSMENTS

Peacekeeping costs are apportioned on a somewhat different basis from the percentage figures for the regular budget as shown in the right-hand column above. Peacekeeping assessments are made under a formula agreed by the General Assembly (see GA Res. 46/233) under which states are divided into four groups. *Group D*: Some 55 least-developed states, almost all in Africa or Asia, are assessed for peacekeeping at 10% of their percentage rates for the regular budget: the rate for each of these states, being the minimum 0.01% for the regular budget, is 0.001% of total assessed peacekeeping costs. *Group C*: Some 100 less-developed states are assessed for peacekeeping at 20% of the rate at which they are assessed for regular budget: several of these states are relatively prosperous, and there has been pressure for them to graduate to Group B. *Group B*: Approximately 23 states, comprising most of the OECD states and a few east European and other states, are assessed for peacekeeping at the same percentage rate as for the regular budget. *Group A*: The five states in Group A are the permanent members of the Security Council: they are responsible for the shortfall resulting from the reductions allowed to Group D and Group C, and in practice are assessed at rates about one-fifth higher than their percentages of the regular budget (see p. 13 above).

Appendix D

Secretaries-General of the United Nations

1 February 1946–10 April 1953	Trygve Lie, b. 1896, d. 1968. Norwegian. (Tendered resignation on 10 November 1952.)
10 April 1953–17 September 1961	Dag Hammarskjöld, b. 1905, d. 17 September 1961 in Northern Rhodesia. Swedish.
3 November 1961–31 December 1971	U Thant, b. 1909, d. 1974. Burmese. (Was Acting Secretary-General until 1 January 1962.)
1 January 1972–31 December 1981	Kurt Waldheim, b. 1918. Austrian.
1 January 1982–31 December 1991	Javier Pérez de Cuéllar, b. 1920. Peruvian.
1 January 1992–	Boutros Boutros-Ghali, b. 1922. Egyptian.

Appendix E

List of UN Peacekeeping and Observer Forces

This is a quick-reference chronological list of UN peacekeeping and observer forces whose composition includes military or police units contributed for the purpose by member states. This list does not refer to smaller special missions, investigatory panels, election monitors where there was no peacekeeping element, or advisory groups. Information is given in the form: *Name of force (acronym), location, years of operation, a principal authorizing resolution. Maximum strength. Strength on 31 March 1993 (if applicable).*

For further information, see: United Nations, *The Blue Helmets: A Review of United Nations Peace-Keeping* (2nd edn., United Nations, New York, 1990); Rosalyn Higgins, *United Nations Peacekeeping*, 4 vols. (Oxford, 1969–81); United Nations, *Summary of Contributions to Peace-keeping Operations by Country* (mimeo, monthly).

(a) UN PEACEKEEPING AND OBSERVER FORCES

United Nations Truce Supervision Organization (UNTSO), several areas in the Middle East, 1948– , SC Res. 54 of 15 July 1948. Maximum strength: 572 (1948). Strength in March 1993: 239.

United Nations Military Observer Group in India and Pakistan (UNMOGIP), Jammu and Kashmir, 1949– , SC Res. 47 of 21 April 1948. Maximum strength: 102 (October 1965). Strength in March 1993: 38.

United Nations Emergency Force (UNEF I), Suez Canal, Sinai, Gaza, 1956–67, GA Res. 1000 (ES-I) of 5 November 1956 and GA Res. 1001 (ES-I) of 7 November 1956. Maximum strength: 6,073 (February 1957).

United Nations Observation Group in Lebanon (UNOGIL), Lebanon, 1958, SC Res. 128 of 11 June 1958. Maximum strength: 591 (November 1958).

United Nations Operation in the Congo (Opération des Nations Unies pour le Congo = ONUC), Republic of the Congo, 1960–4, SC Res. 143 of 14 July 1960. Maximum strength: 19,828 (July 1961).

United Nations Security Force in West New Guinea (UNSF), established to assist the *United Nations Temporary Executive Agency (UNTEA)*, West Irian, 1962–3, GA Res. 1752 (XVII) of 21 September 1962. Maximum strength: 1,576.

United Nations Yemen Observation Mission (UNYOM), Yemen, 1963–4, SC Res. 179 of 11 June 1963. Maximum strength: 189.

United Nations Peacekeeping Force in Cyprus (UNFICYP), Cyprus, 1964– , SC Res. 186 of 4 March 1964. Maximum strength: 6,411 (June 1964). Strength in March 1993: 1,531.

Mission of the Representative of the Secretary-General in the Dominican Republic (DOMREP), Dominican Republic, 1965–6, SC Res. 203 of 14 May 1965. Strength: 2.

United Nations India–Pakistan Observation Mission (UNIPOM), India–Pakistan border, 1965–6, SC Res. 211 of 20 September 1965. Maximum strength: 96 (October 1965).

United Nations Emergency Force II (UNEF II), Suez Canal, Sinai, 1973–9, SC Res. 340 of 25 October 1973. Maximum strength: 6,973 (February 1974).

United Nations Disengagement Observer Force (UNDOF), Golan Heights, 1974– , SC Res. 350 of 31 May 1974. Authorized strength: 1,450. Strength in March 1993: 1,121.

United Nations Interim Force in Lebanon (UNIFIL), southern Lebanon, 1978– , SC Res. 425 and 426 of 19 March 1978. Authorized strength: 7,000. Strength in March 1993: 5,216.

United Nations Good Offices Mission in Afghanistan and Pakistan (UNGOMAP), Afghanistan and Pakistan, April 1988–March 1990, SC Res. 622 of 31 October 1988. Maximum strength: 50 (May 1988).

United Nations Iran–Iraq Military Observer Group (UNIIMOG), Iran and Iraq, August 1988–February 1991, SC Res. 598 of 20 July 1987 and SC Res. 619 of 9 August 1988. Strength (June 1990): 399.

United Nations Angola Verification Mission (UNAVEM I), Angola, January 1989–June 1991, SC Res. 626 of 20 December 1988. Maximum strength: 70 (April–December 1989).

United Nations Transition Assistance Group (UNTAG), Namibia and Angola, April 1989–March 1990, SC Res. 435 of 29 September 1978 and SC Res. 632 of 16 February 1989. Maximum military strength: 4,493 (November 1989).

United Nations Observer Group in Central America (ONUCA), Costa Rica, El Salvador, Guatemala, Honduras, Nicaragua, December 1989–January 1992, SC Res. 644 of 7 November 1989. Maximum strength: 1,098 (May 1990).

United Nations Iraq–Kuwait Observation Mission (UNIKOM), Kuwait–Iraq DMZ, April 1991– , SC Res. 689 of 9 April 1991 and SC Res. 806 of 5 February 1993. Authorized strength: 500. Strength in March 1993: 71 troops, 247 military observers.

United Nations Angola Verification Mission II (UNAVEM II), Angola, June 1991– , SC Res. 696 of 30 May 1991. Maximum strength: 350 military observers, 126 police monitors, 400 electoral observers (September 1992). Strength in March 1993: 75 military observers, 30 police monitors.

United Nations Observer Mission in El Salvador (ONUSAL), El Salvador, July 1991– , SC Res. 693 of 20 May 1991 and SC Res. 729 of 14 January 1992. Authorized strength: 1,000 military and police, 146 international civilian staff (mainly human rights observers). Strength in March 1993: 286 civilian/ police monitors, 94 military observers, 7 troops.

United Nations Mission for the Referendum in Western Sahara (MINURSO), Western Sahara, September 1991– , SC Res. 658 of 27 June 1990. Authorized strength: 1,695 military observers and troops, 300 police, and up to 1,000 civilians. Strength in March 1993: 224 military observers, 110 troops.

United Nations Advance Mission in Cambodia (UNAMIC), Cambodia, October 1991–March 1992, SC Res. 717 of 16 October 1991. Strength: 380. Absorbed by UNTAC.

United Nations Protection Force (UNPROFOR), Bosnia and Herzegovina, Croatia, Federal Republic of Yugoslavia (Serbia and Montenegro), the former Yugoslav Republic of Macedonia, March 1992– , SC Res. 743 of 21 February 1992, SC Res. 761 of 29 June 1992, SC Res. 776 of 14 September 1992, SC Res. 795 of 11 December 1992, SC Res. 836 of 4 June 1993. Authorized strength: over 20,000. Strength in March 1993: 22,534 troops, 394 military observers, 621 civilians/police.

United Nations Transitional Authority in Cambodia (UNTAC), Cambodia, March 1992– , SC Res. 745 of 28 February 1992. Replaced and absorbed the United Nations Advance Mission in Cambodia (UNAMIC). Authorized strength: up to 20,000 (military; civilian police; electoral; civil administration; human rights; repatriation; rehabilitation). Strength in March 1993: 3,578 civilians/police, 15,023 troops, 488 military observers.

United Nations Operation in Somalia (UNOSOM I), Somalia, April 1992–April 1993, SC Res. 751 of 24 April 1992 and SC Res. 775 of 28 August 1992. Strength in March 1993: 893 troops. Absorbed by UNOSOM II.

United Nations Operation in Mozambique (ONUMOZ), Mozambique, December 1992– , SC Res. 797 of 16 December 1992. Authorized strength: 7,000–8,000. Strength in March 1993: 1,082 troops, 153 observers.

United Nations Operation in Somalia II (UNOSOM II), May 1993– , SC Res. 814 of 26 March 1993: Authorized strength: approx. 30,000.

United Nations Observer Mission Uganda–Rwanda (UNOMUR), Uganda–Rwanda border, August 1993– , SC Res. 846 of 22 June 1993. Authorized strength: 81 military observers.

(In addition, the Security Council, in Res. 849 of 9 July 1993, expressed its readiness to establish a force of 50 military observers in Georgia once it was notified that a cease-fire had been implemented and that conditions permitted their deployment. This proposed force was provisionally known as the *United Nations Observer Mission in Georgia—UNOMIG.*)

(b) A NOTE ON CERTAIN OTHER FORCES

Many other types of force have operated under UN auspices or in some relation with the UN.

Two earlier forces performed functions similar to those later fulfilled by UN observer forces, but are not included in the list of UN peacekeeping and observer forces mainly because contingents remained under national command. These were:

United Nations Observers in Indonesia (the Consular Commission), Indonesia, 1947–50, SC Res. S/525 (I) and (II) of 25 August 1947.

United Nations Special Committee on the Balkans (UNSCOB), Balkans, 1947–52, GA Res. 109 (II) of 21 October 1947.

The *United Nations Force in Korea*, Korea, 1950–3, is not generally regarded as a peacekeeping or observer force, especially as it was under national rather than UN command, was not based on the consent of the parties to the conflict, and was fully engaged in active combat operations. It was authorized by SC Res. 84 of 7 July 1950.

The *Allied Coalition* which operated against Iraq in 1990–1 is not generally regarded as a UN force. In Res. 678 of 29 November 1990 the Security Council authorized 'Member States co-operating with the Government of Kuwait ... to use all necessary means to uphold and implement resolution 660 (1990) and all subsequent relevant resolutions and to restore international peace and security in the area'. However, the force was not *established* by the Security Council, and was not under UN command.

The *Unified Task Force* (UNITAF) which operated in Somalia from December 1992 to May 1993 is not generally regarded as a UN force. In Res. 794 of 3 December 1992 the Security Council welcomed the offer of the United States to lead a multi-state force to establish a secure environment for humanitarian operations in Somalia, and authorized 'the Secretary-General and member States co-operating to implement the offer ... to use all necessary means to establish as soon as possible a secure environment for humanitarian relief operations in Somalia'. The force was under US command, although there was liaison with UNOSOM and with the UN. In April–May 1993 UNOSOM II took over responsibilities from UNITAF, absorbing some UNITAF personnel.

Appendix F

Judgments and Opinions of the International Court of Justice

In the period from its foundation in 1946 up to 31 December 1992 the International Court of Justice in The Hague dealt with (to final disposition) forty-one contentious cases between states, and also delivered twenty-one advisory opinions—making a total of sixty-two. These are listed below. Several of these involved more than one phase, and a number of the contentious cases involved more than two states parties.

The ICJ, which is a successor to the Permanent Court of International Justice (1922–46), was constituted by the Statute of the ICJ. This was adopted with the UN Charter by the San Francisco Conference on 26 June 1945. All UN member states are also parties to this Statute. The text of the Statute may be found in the *Yearbook of the United Nations* and in numerous other sources.

(a) Contentious Cases

1. CASES TERMINATED BY A JUDGMENT ON THE MERITS

	Reference to *ICJ Reports*
Corfu Channel	*1947–48*, p. 15
	1949, pp. 4, 244
Asylum (with *Haya de la Torre*)	*1950*, pp. 266, 395
	1951, p. 71
Fisheries	*1951*, p. 116
Rights of Nationals of the United States of America in Morocco	*1952*, p. 176
Ambatielos	*1952*, p. 28
	1953, p. 10
Minquiers and Ecrehos	*1953*, p. 47

2. CASES TERMINATED BY A JUDGMENT ON A PRELIMINARY OBJECTION OR OTHER INTERLOCUTORY POINT

3. CASES TERMINATED BY DISCONTINUANCE PRIOR TO A JUDGMENT ON THE MERITS

(b) Advisory Opinions

1. UPON REQUEST BY THE GENERAL ASSEMBLY OF THE UNITED NATIONS

2. UPON REQUEST BY THE SECURITY COUNCIL OF THE UNITED NATIONS

3. UPON REQUEST OF THE UNITED NATIONS COMMITTEE ON APPLICATIONS FOR REVIEW OF ADMINISTRATIVE TRIBUNAL JUDGMENTS

4. UPON REQUEST BY THE EXECUTIVE BOARD OF UNESCO

Reference to
ICJ Reports

5. UPON REQUEST BY THE ASSEMBLY OF IMCO

*Constitution of the Maritime Safety Committee of
the Inter-Governmental Maritime Consultative
Organization*   *1960*, p. 150

6. UPON REQUEST BY THE WORLD HEALTH ASSEMBLY

*Interpretation of the Agreement of 25 March 1951
between the WHO and Egypt*   *1980*, pp. 67, 73

7. UPON REQUEST BY THE UN ECONOMIC AND
SOCIAL COUNCIL

*Applicability of Article VI, Section 22, of the
Convention on the Privileges and Immunities of
the United Nations*   *1989*, pp. 9, 177

Appendix G

Select Further Reading

ABI-SAAB, GEORGES, *The United Nations Operation in the Congo 1960–1964*, Oxford University Press, Oxford, 1978.

ALSTON, PHILIP (ed.), *The United Nations and Human Rights: A Critical Appraisal*, Oxford University Press, Oxford, 1992.

ARCHER, CLIVE (ed.), *International Organizations*, 2nd edn., Routledge, London, 1992.

BAEHR, PETER and GORDENKER, LEON, *The United Nations in the 1990s*, St Martin's Press, New York, 1992.

BAILEY, SYDNEY, *The General Assembly of the United Nations*, rev. edn., Pall Mall Press, London, 1964.

—— *How Wars End: The United Nations and the Termination of Armed Conflict 1946–1964*, 2 vols., Oxford University Press, Oxford, 1982.

—— *The Procedure of the UN Security Council*, 2nd edn., Oxford University Press, Oxford, 1988.

—— *The United Nations: A Short Political Guide*, 2nd edn., Macmillan, Basingstoke, 1989.

BARDONNET, DANIEL (ed.), *The Adaptation of Structures and Methods at the United Nations*, Hague Academy of International Law Workshop, Martinus Nijhoff, Lancaster, 1986.

BEIGBEDER, YVES, *Management Problems in United Nations Organizations*, Frances Pinter, London, 1987.

BENNETT, A. LEROY, *International Organizations: Principles and Issues*, 5th edn., Prentice-Hall, Englewood Cliffs, NJ, 1991.

BERRIDGE, GEOFF, *Return to the UN: UN Diplomacy in Regional Conflicts*, Macmillan, London, 1991.

BERTRAND, MAURICE, *Refaire l'ONU: Un programme pour la paix*, Zoé, Geneva, 1986.

—— *The Third Generation World Organization*, Martinus Nijhoff, Dordrecht, 1989.

BOWETT, DEREK W., *United Nations Forces: A Legal Study of United Nations Practice*, Stevens, London, 1964.

BROMS, BENGT, *The United Nations*, Suomalainen Tiedeakatemia, Helsinki, 1990.

CASSESE, ANTONIO (ed.), *United Nations Peacekeeping: Legal Essays*, Sijthoff and Noordhoff, Alphen aan den Rijn, 1978.

—— (ed.), *UN Law/Fundamental Rights: Two Topics in International Law*, Sijthoff and Noordhoff, Alphen aan den Rijn, 1979.

—— (ed.), *The Current Legal Regulation of the Use of Force 40 Years after the UN Charter*, Martinus Nijhoff, Lancaster, 1986.

CASTANEDA, JORGE, *Legal Effects of United Nations Resolutions* (tr. Alba Amoia), Columbia University Press, New York, 1969.

CLAUDE, INIS, *Swords into Ploughshares: The Problems and Progress of International Organisation*, 4th edn., Random House, New York, 1971.

CORDIER, ANDREW, *et al.* (eds.), *Public Papers of the Secretaries-General of the United Nations*, 8 vols., Columbia University Press, New York, 1969–77.

COT, JEAN-PIERRE, and PELLET, ALAIN (eds.), *La Charte des Nations Unies*, 2nd edn., Economica, Paris, 1991.

DELL, SIDNEY SAMUEL, *The United Nations and International Business*, Duke University Press, Durham, NC, 1990.

DUGARD, JOHN, *Recognition and the United Nations*, Grotius Publications, Cambridge, 1987.

ELMANDJRA, MAHDI, *The United Nations System: An Analysis*, Faber, London, 1973.

FALK, RICHARD, KIM, SAMUEL and MENDLOVITZ, SAUL (eds.), *The United Nations and a Just World Order*, Westview Press, Boulder, Col., 1991.

FINGER, SEYMOUR M., and SALTZMAN, ARNOLD A., *Bending with the Winds: Kurt Waldheim and the United Nations*, Praeger, New York, 1990.

FINKELSTEIN, LAWRENCE (ed.), *Politics in the United Nations System*, Duke University Press, Durham, NC, 1988.

FORSYTHE, DAVID (ed.), *The United Nations in the World Political Economy: Essays in Honour of Leon Gordenker*, St Martin's Press, New York, 1989.

FRANCK, THOMAS M., *Nation against Nation: What Happened to the UN Dream and What the US Can Do about It*, Oxford University Press, New York, 1985.

GOODRICH, L. M., *The United Nations in a Changing World*, Columbia University Press, New York, 1974.

—— HAMBRO, E., and SIMONS, A. P., *Charter of the United Nations: Commentary and Documents*, 3rd edn., Columbia University Press, New York, 1969.

HAMMARSKJÖLD, DAG, *The Servant of Peace: A Selection of the Speeches and Statements of Dag Hammarskjöld* (ed. Wilder Foote), Bodley Head, London, 1962.

HANNUM, HURST (ed.), *Guide to International Human Rights Practice*, Macmillan, London, 1984.

HARROD, JEFFREY, and SCHRIJVER, NICO (eds.), *The UN under Attack*, Gower, Aldershot, 1988.

HAZZARD, SHIRLEY, *Defeat of an Ideal: A Study of the Self-Destruction of the United Nations*, Little, Brown & Co., Boston, 1973.

—— *Countenance of Truth: The United Nations and the Waldheim Case*, Viking, New York, 1990.

HIGGINS, ROSALYN, *The Development of International Law through the Political Organs of the United Nations*, Oxford University Press, London, 1963.

—— *United Nations Peacekeeping*, 4 vols., Oxford University Press, Oxford, 1969–81.

HILDEBRAND, ROBERT, *Dumbarton Oaks: The Origins of the United Nations and the Search for Postwar Security*, University of North Carolina Press, Chapel Hill, NC, 1990.

HILL, M., *The United Nations System: Coordinating its Economic and Social Work*, Cambridge University Press, Cambridge, 1979.

HOGGART, RICHARD, *An Idea and its Servants: UNESCO from within*, Chatto & Windus, London, 1978.

HUMPHREY, JOHN T. P., *No Distant Millennium: The International Law of Human Rights*, UNESCO, Paris, 1989.

IMBER, MARK, *The USA, ILO, UNESCO, and IAEA: Politicization and Withdrawal in the Specialized Agencies*, Macmillan, London, 1989.

INTERNATIONAL COURT OF JUSTICE, *The International Court of Justice*, 3rd edn., ICJ, The Hague, 1986.

JACKSON, RICHARD, *The Non-aligned, the UN and the Superpowers*, Praeger for the Council on Foreign Relations, Eastbourne, 1983.

JACKSON, ROBERT, *A Study of the Capacity of the United Nations Development System*, 2 vols., United Nations, New York, 1969.

JACOBSON, HAROLD KARAN, *The USSR and the UN's Economic and Social Activities*, University of Notre Dame Press, Notre Dame, Ind., 1963.

JAMES, ALAN, *Peacekeeping in International Politics*, Macmillan, London, 1990.

JENSEN, ERIK, and FISHER, THOMAS (eds.), *The United Kingdom, the United Nations*, Macmillan, London, 1990.

JORDAN, ROBERT S. (ed.), *International Administration: Its Evolution and Contemporary Applications*, Oxford University Press, New York, 1971.

—— (ed.), *Dag Hammarskjöld Revisited: The UN Secretary-General as a Force in World Politics*, Carolina Academic Press, Durham, NC, 1983.

KAPTEYN, P. J. G., *et al.* (eds.), *International Organization and Integration: Annotated Basic Documents and Descriptive Directory of International Organizations and Arrangements*, vol. 1A: *The United Nations Organization*, vol. 1B: *Organizations Related to the United Nations*, Martinus Nijhoff, The Hague, 1981 and 1982.

KARNS, MARGARET P., and MINGST, KAREN A. (eds.), *The United States and Multilateral Institutions: Patterns of Changing Instrumentality and Influence*, Routledge, London, 1992.

KAUFMAN, JOHAN, *United Nations Decision-Making*, Sijthoff & Noordhoff, Rockville, Mich., 1981.

—— and SCHRIJVER, NICO, *Changing Global Needs: Expanding Roles for the United Nations System*, Academic Council on the United Nations System, Hanover, NH, 1990.

KIRGIS, FREDERIC L., *International Organizations in their Legal Setting*, 2nd edn., West Publishing Co., St Paul, Minn., 1993.

LAWSON, EDWARD H., *Encyclopedia of Human Rights*, Taylor & Francis, London, 1991.

LEVITSKY, MELVYN, *UN Coordination for a Global Drug Strategy*, US Department of State, Washington DC, 1990.

LIE, TRYGVE, *In the Cause of Peace: Seven Years with the United Nations*, Macmillan, New York, 1954.

LIU, F. T., *United Nations Peacekeeping and the Non-use of Force*, L. Rienner, Boulder, Col., 1992.

LUARD, EVAN (ed.), *International Agencies: The Emerging Framework of Interdependence*, Macmillan, London, 1977.

—— *The United Nations: How It Works and What It Does*, Macmillan, London, 1979.

—— *A History of the United Nations*, vol. 1: *The Years of Western Domination, 1945–1955*, vol. 2: *The Age of Decolonization, 1955–1965*, Macmillan, London, 1982 and 1989.

LYOU, BYUNG-HWA, *Peace and Unification in Korea and International Law*, University of Maryland School of Law, Baltimore, 1986.

MCWHINNEY, EDWARD, *United Nations Law Making: Cultural and Ideological Relativism and International Law Making for an Era of Transition*, Holmes & Meier, London, 1984.

MERON, THEODOR, *The UN Secretariat: The Rules and the Practice*, D.C. Heath, Lexington, Mass., 1977.

—— (ed.), *Human Rights in International Law: Legal and Policy Issues*, Clarendon Press, Oxford, 1984.

—— *Human Rights Law-Making in the United Nations: A Critique of Instruments and Process*, Clarendon Press, Oxford, 1986.

MISRA, KASHI PRASAD, *The Role of the United Nations in the Indo–Pakistan Conflict of 1971*, Vikas, Delhi, 1973.

MOSKOWITZ, MOSES, *The Roots and Reaches of United Nations Actions and Decisions*, Sijthoff and Noordhoff, Alphen aan den Rijn, 1980.

MOYNIHAN, DANIEL PATRICK, *A Dangerous Place*, Secker & Warburg, London, 1979.

MÜLLER, JOACHIM, *The Reform of the United Nations*, 2 vols., Oceana, New York, 1992.

MURPHY, JOHN F., *The United Nations and the Control of International Violence: A Legal and Political Analysis*, Manchester University Press, Manchester, 1983.

NASSIF, RAMSES, *U Thant in New York, 1961–1971: A Portrait of the Third UN Secretary-General*, C. Hurst, London, 1988.

NICHOLAS, H. G., *The United Nations as a Political Institution*, 5th edn., Oxford University Press, Oxford, 1975.

NORDIC UN PROJECT, *The United Nations in Development: Reform Issues in the Economic and Social Fields: A Nordic Perspective: Final Report*, Nordic UN Project, distributed by Almqvist & Wiksell International, Stockholm, 1991.

—— *The United Nations: Issues and Options: Five Studies on the Role of the UN in the Economic and Social Studies Fields Commissioned by the Nordic UN Project*, distributed by Almqvist & Wiksell International, Stockholm, 1991.

O'BRIEN, CONOR CRUISE, *To Katanga and Back: A UN Case History*, Hutchinson, London, 1962.

—— and TOPOLSKI, FELIKS, *The United Nations: Sacred Drama*, Hutchinson, London, 1968.

OSMANCZYK, JAN EDMUND, *Encylopedia of the United Nations and International Agreements*, 2nd edn., Taylor & Francis, London, 1990.

PATIL, ANJALI V., *The UN Veto in World Affairs 1946–1990: A Complete Record and Case Histories of the Security Council's Veto*, Unifo, Sarasota, Fl., 1992.

PÉREZ DE CUÉLLAR, JAVIER, *Anarchy or Order: Annual Reports 1982–1991*, United Nations, New York, 1991.

PETERSON, M. J., *The General Assembly in World Politics*, Allen & Unwin, Boston, 1986.

PIETILA, HILKKA, *Making Women Matter: The Role of the United Nations*, Atlantic Highlands, London, 1990.

PITT, DAVID, and WEISS, THOMAS, *The Nature of United Nations Bureaucracies*, Croom Helm, London, 1986.

POGANY, ISTVAN, *The Security Council and the Arab–Israeli Conflict*, Gower, Aldershot, 1984.

RAMCHARAN, B. G., *The International Law and Practice of Early-Warning and Preventive Diplomacy: The Emerging Global Watch*, Martinus Nijhoff, Dordrecht, 1991.

RENNINGER, JOHN (ed.), *The Future Role of the United Nations in an Independent World*, Martinus Nijhoff, Dordrecht, 1989.

RIKHYE, INDAR JIT, *The Theory and Practice of Peacekeeping*, Hurst, London, 1984.

—— *United Nations Peacekeeping and the Congo Crisis*, C. Hurst, London, 1990.

—— and SKJELSBAEK, KJELL (eds.), *The United Nations and Peacekeeping: Results, Limitations and Prospects: The Lessons of 40 Years of Experience*, Macmillan/International Peace Academy, Basingstoke, 1990.

RODLEY, NIGEL (ed.), *To Loose the Bands of Wickedness: International Intervention in Defence of Human Rights*, Brassey's, London, 1992.

ROSENAU, JAMES N., *The United Nations in a Turbulent World*, L. Rienner, Boulder, Col., 1992.

ROVINE, ARTHUR, *The First Fifty Years: The Secretary-General in World Politics 1920–1970*, Sijthoff, Leiden, 1970.

ROYAL INSTITUTE OF INTERNATIONAL AFFAIRS, *United Nations Documents 1941–1945*, RIIA, London, 1946.

RUSSELL, RUTH, *The United Nations and United States Security Policy*, Brookings Institution, Washington DC, 1968.

—— and MUTHER, JEANETTE, *A History of the United Nations Charter: The Role of the United States 1940–1945*, Brookings Institution, Washington DC, 1958.

SCHIAVONE, GIUSEPPE, *International Organizations: A Dictionary and Directory*, 3rd edn., Macmillan, London, 1992.

SEYERSTED, FINN, *United Nations Forces in the Law of Peace and War*, Sijthoff, Leiden, 1966.

SHERRY, GEORGE, *The United Nations Reborn: Conflict Control in the Post-Cold War World*, Council on Foreign Relations, New York, 1990.

SIEKMANN, ROBERT, *Basic Documents on United Nations and Related Peace-Keeping Forces*, Martinus Nijhoff, Dordrecht, 1989.

SIMMA, BRUNO et al. (eds.), *Charta der Vereinten Nationen: Kommentar*, C. H. Beck'sche Verlagsbuchhandlung, Munich, 1991. (English translation, Oxford University Press, 1994.)

SOHN, LOUIS B. (ed.), *Cases on United Nations Law*, Foundation Press, Brooklyn, 1967.

STONE, JULIUS, *Conflict through Consensus: United Nations Approaches to Aggression*, Johns Hopkins University Press, London, 1977.

TAYLOR, PAUL, *International Organization in the Modern World: The Regional and the Global Process*, Pinter, London, 1993.

—— and GROOM, A. J. R. (eds.), *International Institutions at Work*, Pinter, London, 1988.

—— ——(eds.), *Global Issues in the United Nations' Framework*, Macmillan, Basingstoke, 1989.

THANT, U, *Toward World Peace: Addresses and Public Statements, 1957–1963*, Thomas Yoseloff, New York, 1964.

—— *Portfolio for Peace: Excerpts from the Writings and Speeches of U Thant, 1961–1968*, 2nd edn., United Nations, New York, 1970.

—— *View from the UN*, David & Charles, Newton Abbott, 1978.

TWITCHETT, KENNETH J. (ed.), *The Evolving United Nations: A Prospect for Peace?*, Europa, London, 1971.

UNITED NATIONS, *Yearbook of the United Nations*, New York, annually.

—— *Everyone's United Nations: A Handbook on the Work of the United Nations*, 10th edn., United Nations (sales no. E.85.I.24), New York, 1986.

—— *The United Nations and Disarmament: A Short History*, United Nations, New York, 1988.

—— *The Blue Helmets: A Review of United Nations Peace-Keeping*, 2nd edn., United Nations Department of Public Information, New York, 1990.

—— *Verification and the United Nations: The Role of the Organization in Multilateral Arms Limitation and Disarmament Agreements*, United Nations, New York, 1991.

UNITED NATIONS ASSOCIATION OF THE USA, *A Successor Vision: The United Nations of Tomorrow: Final Panel Report*, UNA–USA, New York, 1987.

UNITED NATIONS CONFERENCE ON INTERNATIONAL ORGANISATION (San Francisco, 1945), *Documents*, 22 vols., United Nations and Library of Congress, London, 1945–66.

URQUHART, BRIAN, *Hammarskjöld*, Alfred A. Knopf, New York, 1972.

—— *A Life in Peace and War*, Weidenfeld & Nicolson, London, 1987.

—— *Ralph Bunche: An American Life*, Norton, New York, 1993.

—— and CHILDERS, ERSKINE, *A World in Need of Leadership: Tomorrow's United Nations*, Dag Hammarskjöld Foundation, Uppsala, Sweden, 1990.

URQUHART, BRIAN, and CHILDERS, ERSKINE, *Towards a More Effective United Nations*, Dag Hammarskjöld Foundation, Uppsala, Sweden, 1992.

VINCENT, JACK, *Support Patterns at the United Nations*, University Press of America, Lanham, Md., 1991.

WAINHOUSE, D. W., et al., *International Peacekeeping at the Crossroads: National Support—Experience and Prospects*, Johns Hopkins University Press, Baltimore, 1973.

WALDHEIM, KURT, *Building the Future Order*, The Free Press, New York, 1980.

—— *The Challenge of Peace*, Weidenfeld & Nicolson, London, 1980.

—— *In the Eye of the Storm: The Memoirs of Kurt Waldheim*, Weidenfeld & Nicolson, London, 1985.

WEISS, THOMAS, *Multilateral Development Diplomacy in UNCTAD: The Lessons of Group Negotiations 1964–84*, Macmillan, London, 1986.

—— (ed.), *The United Nations in Conflict Management: American, Soviet and Third World Views*, International Peace Academy, New York, 1990.

WELLS, CLARE, *The UN, UNESCO and the Politics of Knowledge*, Macmillan, London, 1987.

WHITE, N. D., *The United Nations and the Maintenance of International Peace and Security*, Manchester University Press, Manchester, 1990.

WILLIAMS, DOUGLAS, *The Specialized Agencies and the United Nations: The System in Crisis*, C. Hurst & Co., London, 1987.

WISEMAN, HENRY (ed.), *Peacekeeping: Appraisals and Proposals*, Pergamon Press, New York, 1983.

YESELSON, ABRAHAM, and GAGLIONE, ANTHONY, *A Dangerous Place: The United Nations as a Weapon in World Politics*, Grossman, New York, 1974.

YODER, AMOS, *The Evolution of the United Nations System*, Crane Russak, New York, 1989.

Index

Index compiled by Frank Pert

STANFORD, CA
PROPERTY OF THE LIBRARY
FEDERAL RESERVE CENTER
BOARD OF GOVERNORS